WORDS OF DELIGHT

Words of Delight

A Literary Introduction to the Bible

Second Edition

Leland Ryken

B

Baker Academic

a division of Baker Publishing Group
Grand Rapids, Michigan

© 1992 by Leland Ryken

Published by Baker Academic
a division of Baker Publishing Group
P.O. Box 6287, Grand Rapids, MI 49516-6287
www.bakeracademic.com

Originally published as *Words of Delight* and *Words of Life*, © 1987 by Baker Book House

Printed in the United States of America

Library of Congress Cataloging-in-Publication Data

Ryken, Leland
    Words of delight : a literary introduction to the Bible / Leland Ryken — 2d ed.
        p.   cm.
    Includes bibliographical references and index.
    ISBN 10: 0-8010-7769-9
    ISBN 978-0-8010-7769-2
    1. Bible as literature. 2. Bible—Criticism, interpretation, etc. I. Title.
    BS535.R94   1992
    809'.93522—dc20   92–42603

Contents

Preface

This is a book of literary criticism on the Bible. Its format is simple: it combines theoretic comments about various literary aspects of the Bible, accompanied by explications of selected texts to illustrate the theory. My intention is that this combination of theory and illustration will provide my readers with a methodology that they can apply to other biblical texts as well.

This revised edition of *Words of Delight* incorporates into it a volume that was originally a separate book—*Words of Life: A Literary Introduction to the New Testament.* The literary approach that I develop in this combined volume parallels that in my book *How to Read the Bible as Literature* (Zondervan, 1984), but this book contains actual explications of texts lacking in the other book.

My footnotes constitute my list of sources that I think readers would most benefit from consulting. A glossary of literary terms appears at the end of the book.

Wheaton College
August 1992

Introduction
Reading the Bible as Literature

"There was a man who had two sons."

"The Lord is my shepherd."

"Behold, a great red dragon, with seven heads and ten horns."

If these excerpts were the only information that we had about the Bible, they would be enough to dispel a common misconception. Because the Bible is a book with religious authority, we tend to assume that it is a theology book. But if we look at how the Bible presents its material, it resembles a literary work more than anything else. It is filled with stories, poems, visions, and letters. The thing that it is emphatically *not* is what we so often picture it as being—a theological outline with proof texts attached.

To say that the Bible is a very literary book should not be controversial. The approaches of biblical scholars are becoming more literary with every passing year. An expository sermon on a biblical passage has more in common with a literary approach to the Bible than with traditional methods of biblical scholarship. The purpose of this introduction is to explore what it means to approach the Bible as literature.

What Kind of Book Is the Bible?

The Bible is unique. Part of its uniqueness is the combination of material that we find in it. Three types of writing predominate and are intermingled throughout the Bible. I will call them theological or moral exposition, history, and literature.

The Three Types of Writing in the Bible

By theological exposition I mean this type of material:

> But God, who is rich in mercy, out of the great love with which he loved us, even when we were dead through our trespasses, made us alive together with Christ (by grace you have been saved), and raised us up with him, and made us sit with him in the heavenly places in Christ Jesus. . . . For by grace you have been saved through faith. [Eph. 2:4–8]

The leading features of such writing are obvious. The governing purpose is to convey theological or moral information. Such writing is strongly conceptual, and the vocabulary tends toward abstraction with such words as *love, mercy, grace,* and *faith.* The basic strategy is to tell us about the subject, not (as in literature) to recreate an experience. It appeals to our intellectual grasp of propositional truth.

A second type of writing in the Bible is historical. It shares with theological writing the impulse to convey information. Here is a specimen:

> In the thirty-eighth year of Asa king of Judah, Ahab the son of Omri began to reign over Israel. . . . And Ahab the son of Omri did evil in the sight of the LORD more than all that were before him. . . . He erected an altar for Baal in the house of Baal, which he built in Samaria . . . . Ahab did more to provoke the LORD, the God of Israel, to anger than all the kings of Israel who were before him. [1 Kings 16:29–33]

Such writing is governed by the documentary impulse to record the facts of the matter. Like the previous selection, it is expository or informational writing. Writing like this aims to tell us what happened and does not share the preoccupation of literature to tell us what happens universally. Historical writing in the Bible does not tell *only* the facts of the matter, however. It obviously puts the historical facts into an interpretive moral and spiritual framework in which, for example, the writer does not hesitate to align himself against Ahab.

The third dominant type of writing in the Bible is literature. Here is an example:

> [1]Now the serpent was more subtle than any other wild creature that the LORD God had made. He said to the woman, "Did God say, 'You shall not eat

of any tree of the garden'?" ²And the woman said to the serpent, "We may eat of the fruit of the trees of the garden; ³but God said, 'You shall not eat of the fruit of the tree which is in the midst of the garden, neither shall you touch it, lest you die.' " ⁴But the serpent said to the woman, "You will not die. ⁵For God knows that when you eat of it your eyes will be opened, and you will be like God, knowing good and evil." ⁶So when the woman saw that the tree was good for food, and that it was a delight to the eyes, and that the tree was to be desired to make one wise, she took of its fruit and ate; and she also gave some to her husband, and he ate. ⁷Then the eyes of both were opened, and they knew that they were naked; and they sewed fig leaves together and made themselves aprons. [Gen. 3:1–7]

The passage appeals primarily to our imagination (our image-making and image-perceiving capacity). The governing purpose is to recreate the actual scene and event in sufficient detail that we can imaginatively experience them. The writer even quotes the very speeches of the characters, and nothing can be more actual and concrete than that.

The writer's chief aim in this passage is to tell a story, not to develop a theological argument. Whereas expository writing gives us the precept, literature incarnates the precept in an example—an example that does not simply illustrate the truth but is itself the meaning. A work of literature is incarnational—it embodies meaning. The customary literary terminology for talking about this is to say that the writer of literature shows rather than tells.

The story of the fall illustrates this distinction particularly well. The writer tells us that the serpent was subtle. The subsequent action shows us that subtlety. Several things are subtle about the serpent's opening question, "Did God say, 'You shall not eat of any tree of the garden'?" Even to state it as a question implies incredulity over a command by God that is made to appear unreasonable and arbitrary. The serpent also subtly amplifies the prohibition by speaking of how God has said that Adam and Eve cannot eat of *any* tree of the garden. The cleverness of the serpent is further demonstrated in verses 4 and 5, where he adopts a more aggressive stance by directly contradicting God, by giving Eve a motivation for eating the fruit, by cloaking his evil intention as benevolent concern for Eve, and by instilling in Eve the false belief that she can eat the forbidden fruit with impunity.

As we read the story of the fall, we sense that it tells us not only what happened on that fatal day, but also what happens in human experience generally. A literary passage like this is filled with recognizable human experiences. Here we relive such common experiences as temptation, sin, and guilt.

The Mixture of Theology, History, and Literature

These, then, are the three impulses that we find intertwined throughout the Bible. One of them usually dominates a given passage, but not necessarily to the exclusion of the others. The theological excerpt from Ephesians contains such metaphors as God's being *rich* and people's being *dead* in sin and our being made to *sit* with Christ. The historical account of King Ahab in the second excerpt offers a spiritual and moral assessment of him and thus implies a theological outlook. The story of the fall in the third excerpt is theologically important and obeys the historical impulse to record what happened.

Given this mixture of types in the Bible, it is obvious that the same passage can be approached from different perspectives and with different interpretive methods. In addition to thinking in terms of three types of writing, therefore, we also have to be aware that there are three interpretive approaches to the Bible. The theological approach is primarily concerned with the moral and theological ideas contained in a passage. The historical approach is preoccupied with the actual characters and events about which biblical authors write. A literary approach focuses on the features of texts that I will explore in more detail in the remainder of this introduction—the experiential concreteness of the text, the use of literary genres, the artistry with which the material is presented (with particular emphasis on unity), and literary resources of language.

Literature as a Genre

Genre is the literary term for a type or kind of writing. Story, for example, is a literary genre having identifiable characteristics. A literary approach to the Bible is based on an awareness that literature itself is a genre, and it is my purpose in the next several pages to identify its leading traits.

Imaging Reality

The most obvious feature of literature is that it images its subject matter. It prefers the concrete to the abstract. This is why it is often called *imaginative* literature: it appeals to our image-making and image-perceiving capacity. The result is that the subject of literature is not abstract information but human experience.

The tendency of literature to speak a language of images is most apparent in poetry:

> Lead thou me
> to the rock that is higher than I;

> for thou art my refuge,
>> a strong tower against the enemy.
> Let me dwell in thy tent for ever!
> Oh to be safe under the shelter of thy wings! [Ps. 61:2–4]

Storytellers follow the same impulse to present human experience rather than to tell about it. They do so with such techniques as description, dialogue, and the actions of characters.

In sum, we can tell that a text is literary by its tendency to incarnate ideas in the form of poetic images, stories of characters in action, and situations in which readers can imaginatively participate. We might say that literature appeals to our understanding through our imagination. Modern psychology has discovered that the human brain assimilates truth in two distinct ways. Rational or abstract thinking tends to engage the left side of the brain, while imagining or intuitive thinking tends to activate the right side of the brain. Truth is more than propositional, and the Bible implicitly acknowledges this by giving us truth partly in a literary medium.

The Bible gives us pictures of life and reality as well as ideas. Its truth sometimes consists of ideas and propositions, but in its literary parts truth often takes the form of *truthfulness to reality and human experience*. The Bible is true in this way whenever we can say about its portrayal of life, "This is the way life is." We assimilate such truth whenever we *recognize* and *experience* it as we read, regardless of whether we formulate the truth as a proposition. If we *recognize* and *feel* the horror of Cain's behavior in the story of Cain and Abel, we have grasped the truth of the story.

Traditional approaches to the Bible lean heavily toward the conceptual and doctrinal. This is largely the result of the modern assumption that a person's world view and conception of truth are intellectual or ideational only. Yet, as a noted theologian rightly says, "we are far more image-making and image-using creatures than we usually think ourselves to be and . . . are guided by images in our minds. . . . Man . . . is a being who grasps and shapes reality . . . with the aid of great images, metaphors, and analogies."[1] Whenever we pattern our behavior on models that we have observed, we are imaging reality. A literary approach takes the images of the Bible seriously as something that embodies and communicates truth.

Literary Genres

One of the commonest ways of defining literature is by its literary genres or types. Through the centuries, people have regarded some genres as being literary in nature. Story and poetry are the most notable categories.

---

1. H. Richard Niebuhr, *The Responsible Self* (New York: Harper and Row, 1963), pp. 151–52, 161.

Other genres, such as theological treatises and historical chronicles, have been regarded as expository (informational) in nature. Other forms of writing can be either literary or expository, depending on how the writer handles them. Letters, sermons, and orations, for example, can become literary if their authors use the techniques that I outline in this introduction.

The concept of literary genre is so important that this book is organized according to different genres. Each genre has its distinctive features and its own "rules" or principles of operation. As readers, we need to approach passages in the Bible with the right expectations. Our awareness of genre programs our encounter with a biblical text, telling us what to look for and how to interpret what we see.

Because the Bible is an anthology of separate works, it contains a mixture of genres, some of them literary and some nonliterary. The main *literary* genres in the Bible are narrative or story, poetry (especially lyric poetry), proverb, and visionary writing (including both prophecy and apocalypse). Literary genres that appear less often include satire, epic, tragedy, epithalamion (wedding poem), elegy (funeral poem), drama, and encomium (a work that praises a quality or character type). Historical writing often moves in the direction of literary narrative by virtue of its experiential concreteness or the principles of pattern and artistry that it exhibits. The letters of the New Testament frequently become literary because of their artistic and poetic style.

Artistry

Another criterion of literature is artistry. Literature is an art form, characterized by beauty, craftsmanship, and technique. With literature, we focus not only on what is said but also on how it is said.

Literary artistry includes both skill with words and patterned composition. The elements of artistic form that all the arts share include pattern or design, theme or central focus, organic unity (also called unity in variety), coherence, balance, contrast, symmetry, repetition or recurrence, and unified progression. Subsequent chapters in this book will ring the changes on these motifs.

The purposes of artistry are at least two: artistry intensifies the impact of an utterance and is pleasurable for its own sake. Both of these purposes are well illustrated by Jesus' discourse about anxiety in the Sermon on the Mount (Matt. 6:25–34), as the following outline in figure 1 suggests.

Figure 1 **The outline of Jesus' discourse on anxiety (Matt. 6:25–34)**

1. The thesis . . .	Therefore I tell you, do not be anxious
2. . . . applied to two areas of life.	about your life, what you shall eat or what you shall drink, nor about your body, what you shall put on.
3. A twofold rhetorical question, arising from the double topic.	Is not life more than food, and the body more than clothing?
4. Not worrying about food: an analogy from nature.	Look at the birds of the air: they neither sow nor reap nor gather into barns, and yet your heavenly Father feeds them. Are you not of more value than they?
5. A rhetorical question about the futility of worry.	And which of you by being anxious can add one cubit to his span of life?
6. Not worrying about clothing: an analogy from nature.	And why are you anxious about clothing? Consider the lilies of the field, how they grow; they neither toil nor spin; yet I tell you, even Solomon in all his glory was not arrayed like one of these.
7. A second analogy from nature.	But if God so clothes the grass of the field, which today is alive and tomorrow is thrown into the oven, will he not much more clothe you, O men of little faith?
8. Summary statement about the two topics covered.	Therefore do not be anxious, saying, "What shall we eat?" or "What shall we drink?" or "What shall we wear?"
9. Two further reasons for not worrying.	For the Gentiles seek all these things; and your heavenly Father knows that you need them all.
10. The antidote to worrying.	But seek first his kingdom and his righteousness, and all these things shall be yours as well.
11. A final warning against anxiety.	Therefore do not be anxious about tomorrow, for tomorrow will be anxious for itself.
12. A concluding aphorism.	Let the day's own trouble be sufficient for the day.

Resources of Language

Literature uses special resources of language such as metaphor, simile, pun, allusion, paradox, and irony. Word play is particularly important in the literature of the Bible, and not just in the poetic parts. Although these resources of language are not limited to literary writing, they appear in much greater concentration in literary writing.

In addition to these individual linguistic devices, literary texts frequently possess rhetorical patterns. An example is the parallelism of biblical poetry, in which two or more consecutive clauses are arranged in similar grammatical form. Any language pattern that strikes us as unusually patterned might qualify as an example of literary rhetoric: series of' questions or statements that follow a common pattern, rhetorical questions (which are asked for the sake of effect rather than to elicit information), question-and-answer constructions, imaginary dialogues, and the aphoristic conciseness of a proverb.

Literary language calls attention to itself. It strikes us as more carefully crafted or more concentrated than ordinary discourse. In one way or another, it tries to do more with language than straightforward expository prose does. By this criterion, too, the Bible is a literary book.

A Test Case: The Account of Peter's Denial of Jesus

The story of Peter's denial of Jesus (Luke 22:54–62) provides a good illustration of my generalizations about what makes a text literary. The story is as follows:

> [54]Then they seized [Jesus] and led him away, bringing him into the high priest's house. Peter followed at a distance; [55]and when they had kindled a fire in the middle of the courtyard and sat down together, Peter sat among them. [56]Then a maid, seeing him as he sat in the light and gazing at him, said, "This man also was with him." [57]But he denied it, saying, "Woman, I do not know him." [58]And a little later some one else saw him and said, "You also are one of them." But Peter said, "Man, I am not." [59]And after an interval of about an hour still another insisted, saying, "Certainly this man also was with him; for he is a Galilean." [60]But Peter said, "Man, I do not know what you are saying." And immediately, while he was still speaking, the cock crowed. [61]And the Lord turned and looked at Peter. And Peter remembered the word of the Lord, how he had said to him, "Before the cock crows today, you will deny me three times." [62]And he went out and wept bitterly.

The passage is thoroughly experiential. The writer makes sure that we see and hear what happened in the courtyard. In fact, the stage directions are written right into this drama in miniature: *a maid, seeing him in the light and gazing at him, said. . . .* There is equal vividness in the time sequence: *after an interval of about an hour,* and *immediately, while he was still speaking. . . .* Luke also quotes the actual dialogue of the participants in the action. There are so many appeals to our imagination that we recreate the denial in vivid detail.

Literature works by a process of indirection. A story like this gives us the example and asks us to find the idea or theme. The story, moreover, gives us a picture of denial instead of a propositional statement. In fact, it is hard to state the meaning of the story as a generalization. It is the picture that counts. The whole story is the meaning. We experience the reality of denial and feel how it happens in a person's life instead of theorizing about it.

The account obviously belongs to the literary genre of narrative or story. As such, it has three main ingredients—setting, characters, and plot or action. The setting comes alive in our imagination with its references to *a fire in the middle of the courtyard* and Peter's sitting *in the light*. The setting is historical rather than fictional, and it is an utterly realistic scene of spectators outside a courtroom. The characters, too, are not fictional but come to us straight from the annals of history. The protagonist (the person with whom we go through the event) is Peter. The other chief character is Jesus. The additional people are accessory figures, necessary to the action but for purposes of the story not important in themselves.

We might think that in writing this historical account of an event Luke would be indifferent to how he told the story, but in fact the story is full of artistry. The story has shapeliness and a sense of directed movement. Like most brief stories, it falls into three parts. Verses 54 and 55 set the scene and introduce Peter into it. Verses 56–61 then narrate the main action. Verse 62 dismisses Peter from the scene. The story thus has what Aristotle said every good story must have—a beginning, a middle, and an end.

The central part of the story falls into a pattern frequently found in stories and known as threefold repetition. The pattern that is repeated in this story is accusation followed by denial. In telling the story, the writer does what storytellers usually do: he portrays the central character in a situation that tests him. Here Peter's loyalty to Jesus is tested. Equally conventional is the element of plot conflict underlying the action (Peter versus three accusers and at the end Jesus).

The most customary way to end a story is to have the protagonist experience a moment of epiphany (insight or illumination). In this story, the crowing of the rooster and the look of Jesus bring Peter to a sudden realization of what he has done. As readers we reach the moment of illumination with Peter. The climax is all the more forceful for having been set up earlier in the account of what happened on the evening of Jesus' arrest when Peter had boasted that he would never abandon Jesus (Luke 22:31–34).

The special resource of language that permeates this passage is irony. Dramatic irony consists of discrepancy between what we as readers know and the ignorance of characters in the story. In this story, we are aware, as Peter is not, that he is unwittingly fulfilling Jesus' prediction that Peter would deny him. There is also the irony of Peter's denying what everyone around the fire knows to be true.

The story of Peter's denial illustrates several leading features of literature as a form of discourse. The subject of literature is human experience concretely presented. Its truthfulness is truthfulness to life as we know it.

Literature embodies human experience in distinct genres. It is also a product of human art and craft, and it uses certain resources of language in more concentrated fashion than ordinary prose does.

A Literary Approach to the Bible

We might think that if some parts of the Bible possess the qualities that I have ascribed to literature as a genre, the literary approach to the Bible will follow automatically. This is emphatically not true. It is one thing to recognize that parts of the Bible are literature. It is quite another actually to approach those texts in a literary manner.

I noted earlier that three impulses combine in the Bible—the theological, the historical, and the literary. Biblical texts can be approached in all three ways, though the best results occur when an approach is applied to the type of text to which it corresponds. Let me say in this regard that it is possible to judge how literary a given piece of commentary is partly by noting the type of texts that a commentator chooses for literary analysis. I have seen literary methods of analysis applied to texts that are primarily expository or historical with meager results.

Traditional biblical scholarship has combined theological and historical approaches. It has been preoccupied with questions of authorship and origin. It has tended to break a biblical text into fragments and has been alarmingly indifferent to preserving the unity of passages. Theological approaches have been preoccupied with reducing the Bible to abstractions and propositions. Historians have been preoccupied with questions of the accuracy of the Bible's references to events.

It is not my purpose here to question the validity of these approaches. It is important, however, to differentiate them from a literary approach. A literary approach substitutes an entirely different agenda of interests and set of presuppositions, as the following outline of concerns will suggest.

Meaning Through Form

A literary approach to the Bible is preoccupied with questions of literary form. It is concerned not only with what is said but also with how something is expressed. In fact, a literary approach refuses to separate meaning from form (broadly defined). After all, everything that is communicated in a piece of writing is communicated through the form in which it is embodied.

While this is true for all types of writing, it is particularly important in literary texts. Literature has its own forms and techniques, and its own way of expressing truth. Stories, for example, tell us about life through setting, character, and action. We cannot get the message of a story without first interacting with the settings, characters, and events that make up a story. Poems communicate their meaning through images and figures of speech. As a result, it is impossible to determine the meaning of a poem without analyzing figurative language. A literary approach is thus characterized by a focus on the form and characteristics of a passage as the key to what it says.

An important part of this concern for the form that embodies the content is the literary critic's attention to literary genres. Every piece of writing must be approached in terms of what it is and the conventions that it presupposes. Literary genres carry with them sets of expectations that should guide our encounter with a text and our interpretation of it. We can tell when a piece of commentary on the Bible is literary in nature partly by whether the writer focuses on genre.

Unity and Literary Wholes

Another hallmark of the literary approach to the Bible is its emphasis on the unity of books and passages. Literary critics look for literary wholes. A pioneer in the literary approach to the Bible rightly commented that "no principle of literary study is more important than that of grasping clearly a literary work as a single whole."[2] A literary approach to the Bible is thus characterized partly by attention to unifying patterns in biblical texts.

This presupposes a willingness to deal with the text as it stands in the Bible. By contrast, redaction criticism in our century has undertaken textual "excavations" in an attempt to determine the various strata in the development of a text from its original form to its final written form. Equally destructive of the unity of a passage is the more traditional verse-by-verse commentary that organizes the Bible into a theological outline with proof texts. A literary approach assumes unity in a text and devotes its energies to demonstrating that unity exists.

Reading with the Right Side of the Brain

I spoke earlier of how recent psychology has documented that we assimilate reality and information with our imagination as well as with our intellect. Literature and the other arts work largely by means of the imagination, that is, through images. This suggests another thing that differentiates a literary approach to the Bible.

A literary approach is sensitive to the imaginative nature of the Bible. It discusses the human experiences that are presented, not simply the ideas. It helps us to recreate the experiences and sensations in passages. It takes concrete images seriously and does not regard them simply as a vehicle for

2. Richard G. Moulton, *The Modern Reader's Bible* (New York: Macmillan, 1895), p. 1719.

something more important. It operates on the assumption that the stories and poems and visions of the Bible give us pictures of the world as part of an overall world view.

A literary approach to a biblical text assumes a certain self-contained quality to the text. The customary way to express this is to say that a story or poem creates a whole world of interrelated parts. A literary approach is not eager to refer as quickly as possible to a set of facts beyond the text. Realizing that the whole story or the whole poem is the meaning and that many of the effects of literature are indirect and subtle, a literary critic wishes to make the whole world of the text come alive in the reader's imagination before building bridges to our world beyond the text.

Universality

The Bible records unique historical events. But it is also a book of universal experience. The historical facts are the domain of the historical approach to the Bible. In contrast, the literary critic tends to emphasize what is universal in the experiences recorded in the Bible. One of the most consistent claims made for literature through the ages is that it captures the experiences that are true for all people in all times. A literary critic is convinced that a work of literature is as pertinent today as it was when it was written.

A literary approach is thus concerned to build bridges between a biblical text and the life of the reader. It identifies the recognizable human experiences that we find in the stories and poems of the Bible. Part of the universality that a literary approach finds in the Bible consists of archetypes, which I will discuss shortly.

One of the things that virtually all commentators do is compare a text to other similar texts. Biblical scholars and historians compare the Bible to other ancient texts that most people have never heard about. Literary critics are more inclined to compare biblical stories and poems to familiar works of English and American literature, or even to the techniques of television drama. This, too, is part of the familiarity that a literary approach can lend to the Bible.

The Enjoyment of Artistic Beauty

A literary approach also sees value in the artistry that is everywhere evident in the Bible. It sees the individual works in the Bible as achievements that evoke delight and admiration. It aims to enhance our enjoyment in reading the Bible not only because of what the Bible says, but also because of the perfection of technique with which it says it.

A literary approach shows us that the Bible is an interesting rather than a dull book. It confirms the theory of writing expressed by the writer of Ecclesiastes when he said that his aim had been to arrange his proverbs *with great care* and *to find pleasing words* (12:9–10). A literary approach relishes the storytelling ability of the Bible's storytellers and the skill with words and metaphors that its poets and prophets display.

That the Bible possesses artistic beauty and excellence is indisputable. A literary approach to the Bible regards this as one of its glories, not something to ignore or (as I have seen done) disparage.

Sensitivity to Language

A literary approach to the Bible shares the biblical scholar's respect for the very words in which the Bible is written. For one thing, much of the Bible uses figurative language to express its meaning. There is also an abundance of word play and irony. The language of the Bible frequently does more than words normally do, and a literary approach is interested in these linguistic nuances.

A Literary Approach to the Story of Ehud

To illustrate the literary approach, I have selected part of the story of Ehud's assassination of Eglon (Judg. 3:15–26):

> [15]But when the people of Israel cried to the LORD, the LORD raised up for them a deliverer, Ehud, the son of Gera, the Benjaminite, a left-handed man. The people of Israel sent tribute by him to Eglon the king of Moab. [16]And Ehud made for himself a sword with two edges, a cubit in length; and he girded it on his right thigh under his clothes. [17]And he presented the tribute to Eglon king of Moab. Now Eglon was a very fat man. [18]And when Ehud had finished presenting the tribute, he sent away the people that carried the tribute. [19]But he himself turned back at the sculptured stones near Gilgal, and said, "I have a secret message for you, O king." And he commanded, "Silence." And all his attendants went out from his presence. [20]And Ehud came to him, as he was sitting alone in his cool roof chamber. And Ehud said, "I have a message from God for you." And he arose from his seat. [21]And Ehud reached with his left hand, took the sword from his right thigh, and thrust it into his belly; [22]and the hilt also went in after the blade, and the fat closed over the blade, for he did not draw the sword out of his belly; and the dirt came out. [23]Then Ehud went out into the vestibule, and closed the doors of the roof chamber upon him, and locked them. [24]When he had gone, the servants came; and when they saw that the doors of the roof chamber were locked, they thought, "He is only relieving himself in the closet of the cool chamber." [25]And they waited till they were utterly at a loss; but when he still did not open the doors of the roof chamber, they took the key and opened them; and there lay their lord dead on the floor. [26]Ehud escaped while they delayed.

Here is the kind of biblical passage that only a literary approach can do justice to.

The genre of the story is realistic narrative. Several things make up the realism. One is the choice of violence as the subject matter. The vividness of the details also makes the story come alive to our senses, as we feel the sharpness of the homemade sword plunging into a fat belly and see the entrails start to seep out and listen to the king's servants whisper in embarrassment among themselves about how long the king is taking in the toilet.

The story is also a drama in miniature, complete with stage directions and dialogue. Obviously the storyteller's impulse is to "show" rather than "tell," to enact rather than summarize, to make us share an experience with the characters rather than give us only the facts of what happened.

The story is built around a unifying plot conflict, which exists on several levels. The holy war between good and evil is also an international conflict between Israel and Moab, as well as a single combat between Ehud and Eglon. Unity stems not only from this heightened conflict, but also from the way in which the story is built around a single heroic act. There is nothing extraneous to the central feat of killing an oppressive foreign king. The economy of detail is masterful: with just a few brushstrokes, the whole scene comes alive in our imaginations.

The organization of the story shows an artistic impulse toward narrative shapeliness. The story is built on the pyramid principle of rising action followed by falling action. We build up to the climax of the actual stabbing and then gradually move away from it.

Much of the voltage of the story stems from its literary technique of dramatic irony. For one thing, the left-handedness of Ehud is in effect a disguise, allowing Ehud to carry his sword on the unsuspected right side instead of the customary left side. As readers we know something that Eglon does not.

Once we are alerted to this situation, almost every detail in the story has an ironic significance: the obesity of Eglon, the "secret message" that Ehud wishes to give to the king, Eglon's dismissing his attendants and standing up ceremoniously to receive the sword thrust, the hesitation of the king's servants to intrude on the king while he is in the bathroom and the assassin's consequent escape. As these details accumulate, the writer in effect exchanges a grim wink with us at the expense of the doomed victim. If we realize that this story has the mocking tone of slave literature, the incident recorded with such irony has the quality of an elaborate practical joke, and there is plenty of latent humor in the account.

As a literary hero, Ehud has a lot in common with Homer's Odysseus. "Clever Odysseus," as Homer repeatedly calls him, wins through trickery and mental resourcefulness as much as through physical courage. The writer of Judges likewise emphasizes his hero's cunning. Ehud stealthily sharpens a two-edged sword and craftily conceals it. He has the resourcefulness to manage to be alone with the king and to lock the doors of the king's chamber after carrying out his clever scheme. His words, too, are sharp and double-edged, as he talks about a secret message from God that turns out to be a sword thrust in the belly.

Despite all its realism, the story also uses some of the resources of symbol and metaphor that we associate more with poetry. There is paradox in the epithets used for Ehud in verse 15: *the Benjaminite, a left-handed man.* The name *Benjamin* means "child of my right hand." This particular child of the right hand is left-handed. Pretty tricky, which is exactly what the story is about.

Or consider the statement in verse 17 that *Eglon was a very fat man.* How did he get to be so fat? By overeating, no doubt. Images of gluttony, luxury, and exploitation of the Israelites arise in our imaginations. Fat becomes a moral monstrosity as well as a physical monstrosity, as in our snide remarks about a complacent person's being a fat cat. One commentator suggests "fat calf" as a loose translation of Eglon's name.[3] This, in turn, introduces the idea of a "fatted calf" or sacrificial animal ready for slaughter, an association strengthened by the fact that the same root word is used in the story of Abraham's sacrifice in Genesis 15 and the story of Aaron's golden calf.

The sense of repulsion that we feel toward the oppressive foreign king of course reaches its climax with the description of the murder. We read in the text that *the dirt came out.* The New American Standard Bible translates the word as "refuse" [garbage]. Biblical scholars have speculated on exactly how gruesome and scatological the details are, but the consensus confirms that at the very least the intestine of Eglon was pierced and that he lay in the chamber with dung seeping out while his attendants feared to enter because they thought the king was "relieving himself."

My analysis has demonstrated that a literary text calls for a literary approach. I have therefore discussed the story in terms of its narrative genre, its unity and realism, and its distinctly literary strategies of irony and word play. It is no doubt a story of God's providence and of the ability of a God-fearing champion to perform a feat of strength in the power of God. But no abstraction does justice to the meanings conveyed by the story. Here the whole story is, indeed, the meaning.

Master Images and Archetypes

The Bible is a universal book. Even though its world often seems strange

---

3. Robert G. Boling, *Judges,* vol. 6 of the Anchor Bible (Garden City, N.Y.: Doubleday, 1975), p. 85. Robert Alter, *The Art of Biblical Narrative* (New York: Basic Books, 1981), agrees with this interpretation (p. 39).

and remote, it has an elemental feel that enables any reader to walk into it and be at home. The experiences portrayed in biblical literature are the ones that we all know—work, love, worship, birth, death, nature, family, state, evil, guilt, suffering, salvation. The very vocabulary of the Bible "is compact of the primal stuff of our common humanity—of its universal emotional, sensory experiences."[4]

A major aspect of the universality of the Bible is its use of recurring master images. Literary critics are accustomed to call these recurrent images and symbols *archetypes*. Archetypes recur throughout literature because they are also pervasive in life. These master images are the building blocks of the literary imagination—the forms to which the imagination gravitates when it organizes reality and human experience.

The archetypes of literature, moreover, fall into a dialectical pattern of opposites. The two categories of archetypes form a pattern of ideal and unideal experience, wish and nightmare, tragedy and comedy. Together they are a vision of the world that people want and do not want. The following lists of master images are not intended to be exhaustive, but they include some of the most important archetypes in the Bible.

The Archetypes of Ideal Experience

The supernatural world: God; angels, the heavenly society.

The world of nature: the spring and summer seasons; the sun, moon, and stars; light, sunrise, day; the wind that inspires or from which God speaks; calm after the storm.

Landscape: a garden, grove, or park; the mountaintop or hill; the fertile and secure valley; pastoral settings or farms; the safe pathway or straight road.

Plants: green grass; the rose; the vineyard; the tree of life; the lily; evergreen plants; herbs or plants of healing.

Water: a river or stream; a spring or fountain; showers of rain; dew; flowing water or tranquil pools; water used for cleansing.

Animals: a flock of sheep or herd of cattle; the lamb; a gentle bird, often a dove; any animal friendly to people; singing birds; animals noted for their strength, such as the lion or eagle; fish.

Sounds: musical harmony; singing; laughter.

Direction or motion: images of ascent, rising, height (especially the mountaintop or tower); images of motion (as opposed to stagnation).

---

4. John Livingston Lowes, "The Noblest Monument of English Prose," in *Literary Style of the Old Bible and the New*, ed. D. G. Kehl (Indianapolis: Bobbs-Merrill, 1970), p. 9.

Human relationships: the community, city, or tribe; images of communion, order, unity, friendship, love; the wedding or marriage; the feast, meal, or supper; the harmonious family; covenant, contract, or treaty; freedom.

Clothing: any stately garment symbolizing legitimate position or success; festal garments such as wedding clothes; fine clothing given as gifts of hospitality; white or light-colored clothing; clothing of adornment (such as jewels); protective covering such as a warrior's armor.

Food: staples such as bread, milk, and meat; luxuries such as wine and honey; the harvest of grain; food such as wine and bread used for sacramental purposes; the clean animals of Old Testament ceremonial laws.

The human body: images of health, strength, vitality, potency, fertility (including womb and seed); feats of strength and dexterity; images of sleep, rest, happy dreams; birth.

Buildings: the city; the palace or castle; the military stronghold; the tabernacle, temple, or church; the house or home; the capital city (symbol of the nation).

The inorganic world: images of jewels and precious stones, often glowing and fiery; fire and brilliant light; burning that purifies and refines; rocks of refuge.

The Archetypes of Unideal Experience

The supernatural world: Satan; demons or evil spirits; evil beasts and monsters (such as those in the Book of Revelation); idols.

The world of nature: the autumn and winter seasons; the storm; drought; sunset, darkness, night.

Landscape: the wilderness or wasteland; the dark forest; the dangerous valley; the underground cave or tomb; the dangerous or evil pathway.

Plants: the thorn or thistle; weeds; dead or dying plants; unproductive plants; the chaff of grain.

Water: the sea and all that it contains (sea beasts and water monsters); stagnant pools (including the Dead Sea and cisterns).

Animals: monsters or beasts of prey; the wolf (enemy of sheep), tiger, dragon, vulture, owl, or hawk; the cold and earthbound snake; any wild animal harmful to people; the goat; the unclean animals of Old Testament ceremonial law.

Sounds: discordant sounds, cacophony, weeping, wailing.

Direction or motion: images of descent, lowness, stagnation or immobility, suffocation, confinement, imprisonment.

Human relationships: tyranny or anarchy; isolation among people; images of slavery, bondage, or torture (the cross, stake, gallows, stocks); images of war, riot, feud, or family discord.

Clothing: ill-fitting garments (often symbolic of a position that is usurped); garments that symbolize mourning (such as sackcloth, rent garments, dark mourning garments); tattered, dirty, or coarse clothing; any clothing that suggests poverty or bondage; a conspicuous excess of clothing.

Food: hunger, starvation, cannibalism; poison; drunkenness.

The human body: images of disease, deformity, barrenness, injury, or mutilation; sleeplessness or nightmare, often related to guilt of conscience; death.

Buildings: the prison or dungeon; the wicked city of violence, sexual perversion, crime, or luxurious excess; the tower of imprisonment or wicked aspiration (the tower of Babel); pagan temples.

The inorganic world: landscape in its unworked form of deserts, rocks, and wilderness; dust or ashes; fire that destroys and tortures instead of purifying; rust and decay.

The Importance of Archetypes

Being sensitive to archetypes is one of the most fruitful literary approaches we can take to the Bible. These master images are an important part of the unity of the Bible. As we read the Bible, we are constantly aware of being in a world of archetypes. Although the Bible appears at first glance to be a heterogeneous collection of fragments, it turns out to be a composite whole and a unified world in our imaginations.

The archetypal content of the Bible also helps to make the Bible a universal book. In Northrop Frye's words, "Some symbols are images of things common to all men, and therefore have a communicable power which is potentially unlimited."[5] The archetypes of the Bible are one of the things that allow us to see our own experience in the Bible. We have all experienced thirst and heat and dangerous pathways. The Samson and Delilah story is perennial. We all lose our paradise.

5. Northrop Frye, *Anatomy of Criticism: Four Essays* (Princeton: Princeton University Press, 1957), p. 99. On the master images of the Bible, see also Frye, *The Great Code: The Bible and Literature* (New York: Harcourt Brace Jovanovich, 1981).

Finally, the prevalence of master images in the Bible alerts us to how thoroughly the Bible is a work of the literary imagination. It communicates truth in image as well as abstraction. We could absorb as much of the truth of the Bible by tracing a master image (rock or water or city or journey) through its pages as by tracing an idea.

The Literary Unity of the Bible

The Bible is a large and complex work. It need not be an intimidating book, however, if we can catch a glimpse of its overall unity.

A Literary Anthology

The Bible is a collection or anthology of individual works. In its external form it thus resembles an anthology of English or American literature. Knowing this, we will not be overwhelmed by the sheer variety of forms that we find in it. The very word *Bible* means "little books" and hints at what is a fact—that this book is a small library of Hebraic-Christian writing that was produced by numerous writers over a span of many centuries.

The fact that the Bible is an anthology results in a remarkable range of forms and styles. It has a style for every temperament. Comprehensiveness of subject matter is another trait. Every aspect of human experience is covered in some form within the pages of the Bible.

Since the Bible is both comprehensive and written by a variety of authors, it preserves the complexities and polarities of human experience to an unusual degree. The paradoxes of human life are held in tension in what can be called the most balanced book ever written. Divine sovereignty and human responsibility, justice and mercy, law and freedom, the person's simultaneous smallness and greatness, the claims of the individual and of society, the worth of both earth and heaven—these paradoxes are affirmed throughout the Bible and constitute the poles between which God and people operate.

Because the individual parts of the Bible are interdependent, no single work or passage can be regarded as a totally self-contained unit. The meaning of an individual work is deepened and modified by other works. The portrait of God, for example, is built up by a brushstroke here and a brushstroke there, with each story or poem contributing a small part to the total effect. Similarly, no single work is likely to give full scope to the biblical view of the person, just as one cannot deduce the biblical attitude toward romantic love by reading only the Song of Solomon. A related principle is that the literary parts of the Bible will often be clarified by reference to what is contained in the expository parts.

Although the Bible is a collection of diverse works, it must also be regarded as a unified whole. There is unity of national authorship, with only two books in the whole Bible (Luke and Acts) not having been written by Jews. There is unity of subject matter, consisting most broadly of God's dealings with people and the relationships of people to God and fellow humans. There is a unity of world view and general theological outlook from book to book. The unifying purpose of the Bible is to reveal God to people so they might know how to order their lives.

Finally, there is a unity of literary texture based on allusion. By this I mean that various biblical writers allude to earlier works in the same canon, or to the same historical events, or to the same religious beliefs and experiences, or to the same cultural context. The resulting unity of reference is immediately evident when we consult a modern Bible containing cross-references in the marginal notes. No other anthology of literature possesses the unified texture of allusions that biblical literature displays.

What I have said about the Bible as an anthology suggests that it is a religious book from start to finish. Consciousness of God pervades it. Human experience is constantly viewed in its religious dimension. The oft-quoted statement of C. S. Lewis is right: The Bible is "not merely a sacred book but a book so remorselessly and continuously sacred that it does not invite, it excludes or repels, the merely aesthetic approach."[6]

The Bible shows a constant tendency to move from the particular event to the spiritual meaning or reality behind the event. What in most literature would be considered a purely natural event—the birth of a baby, a shower of rain, the daily course of the sun—is regarded in the Bible as being rooted in a divine reality beyond the natural world. There is a continual interpenetration of the supernatural world into the earthly order. God is a constant actor in human affairs. No other literature in the world conveys such a strong sense of the ultimacy of life.

The supernatural orientation of the Bible often takes the form of what I call the theme of the two worlds. The underlying premise of biblical literature is that there are two planes of reality—the physical world perceived through the senses, and the supernatural world, invisible to ordinary human view. Both worlds are objectively real, but whereas one order can be demonstrated empirically, the spiritual order must usually be accepted on faith. The constant appeal made by biblical writers is for people to order their lives by the unseen spiritual realities, even though doing so usually contradicts earthly or human standards.

Any anthology can be organized around its central topics and themes, and these, too, help to unify the Bible in our minds and give it a unity of faith or belief. Dominating everything is the character of God and the nature of his acts. Also pervasive is the view of people—the question of

6. C. S. Lewis, *The Literary Impact of the Authorized Version* (Philadelphia: Fortress, 1963), p. 33.

what people are really like. The divine-human relationship is a constant preoccupation, as is the problem of human evil and suffering. The interplay of law and grace, or law and gospel, or human sinfulness and divine mercy, organizes most passages in the Bible. Finally, the pattern of promise and fulfillment is a major motif in the Bible, especially as a framework for interpreting the relationship between the Old Testament and the New Testament.

The Bible as a Story

In addition to having the kinds of unity that we expect from an anthology, the Bible possesses an overarching narrative unity. Taken as a whole, the Bible tells a story that has a beginning, a middle, and an end. The Bible is above all a series of events, with interspersed passages that explain the meaning of those events.

This story has a unifying plot conflict consisting of the great spiritual struggle between good and evil. Virtually every event that we read about in the Bible shows some movement, whether slight or momentous, toward God or away from him, toward good or evil. The world of the Bible is claimed by God and counterclaimed by the forces of evil. Human choice is inevitable as the Bible concentrates on people at the crossroads. Every story has a protagonist, and in the Bible that protagonist is God. He is the central actor whose presence unifies the story of universal history. Roland M. Frye comments,

> The characterization of God may indeed be said to be the central literary concern of the Bible, and it is pursued from beginning to end. . . . Not even the most seemingly insignificant action in the Bible can be understood apart from the emerging characterization of the deity. With this great protagonist and his designs, all other characters and events interact, as history becomes the great arena for God's characteristic and characterizing actions.[7]

In the Bible, history is God's biography. Biblical scholars have popularized the term *salvation history* to refer to the Bible's story of God's acts of providence, judgment, and redemption.

Corresponding to the narrative nature of the Bible is the fact that its arrangement is loosely chronological. We can therefore arrange its major units in an unfolding sequence. Further unity emerges if we link each chapter in this ongoing story with a literary form (or phase of revelation) that we particularly associate with it:

7. Roland M. Frye, *The Bible: Selections from the King James Version for Study as Literature* (Boston: Houghton Mifflin, 1965), p. xvi.

1. The beginning of human history: creation, fall, and covenant (Genesis, or the story of origins).
2. Exodus (law).
3. Israelite monarchy (wisdom literature).
4. Exile and return (prophecy).
5. The life of Christ and salvation (Gospel).
6. The beginnings of the Christian church (Acts and Epistle).
7. Consummation of history (Apocalypse).

As I have already suggested, historical narrative is the literary form that molds these phases into a single coherent whole.

The Bible is a paradoxical book. It is a combination of the familiar and the unfamiliar. As a whole, it is unique, but in its parts it contains much that is like other types of writing. It is a literary book, but the literature of the Bible is intermingled with theology and history. It is a heterogeneous collection of fragments, yet upon analysis it is an amazingly unified book.

Biblical Narrative

1

Introducing Biblical Narrative

*What You Should Know
About the Stories of the Bible*

One of the most universal human impulses can be summed up in a familiar four-word plea: Tell me a story. The Bible constantly satisfies that demand. Narrative is the dominant form of the Bible. Despite the multiplicity of literary genres found in the Bible, it is above all a book of stories.

If you doubt this, imagine yourself trying to describe the content of the Bible to someone who has never read the Bible. You would very quickly find yourself describing what happens in the Bible, and to "tell what happens" is to tell a story. It is no wonder that Henry R. Luce, founder of *Time* magazine, quipped, "*Time* didn't start this emphasis on stories about people; the Bible did."

The stories of the Bible are both like and unlike the stories with which we are generally familiar. The purpose of this chapter is to outline some common tendencies of biblical narrative.

Realism

One of the dominant literary characteristics of Bible stories is their thoroughgoing realism. Several things combine to create this quality.

For one thing, biblical storytellers are at pains to place their stories in space-time history. Most stories in the Bible begin something like this:

And Abram took Sarai his wife, and Lot his brother's son, and all their possessions which they had . . . gotten in Haran; and they set forth to go to the land of Canaan. When they had come to the land of Canaan, Abram passed through the land to the place at Shechem, to the oak of Moreh. At that time the Canaanites were in the land. [Gen. 12:5–6]

This matter-of-fact approach produces passages that read more like entries in a diary or biography or history book than an ordinary story.

The impulse of the storytellers in the Bible is to give a circumstantial and factual basis to their stories. The result is what literary scholars call realism. Literary realism shares with history and biography the quality of being empirical (rooted in observable reality).

We also associate realism with the tendency to be concrete, vivid, and specific. Despite the extreme brevity of most stories in the Bible, there are constant appeals to our imagination. The realism in the story of Ehud's assassination of Eglon is typical:

And Ehud reached with his left hand, took the sword from his right thigh, and thrust it into his belly; and the hilt also went in after the blade, and the fat closed over the blade, for he did not draw the sword out of his belly; and the dirt [dung] came out. Then Ehud went out into the vestibule, and closed the doors of the roof chamber upon him, and locked them. [Judg. 3:21–23]

A storyteller cannot get more realistic than this. We visualize everything from the movements of Ehud to the disappearing knife. Part of the realism of Bible stories is the refusal of writers to omit sordid actions in the name of niceness. The stories of the Bible are of the earth, earthy.

We also associate realism with the portrayal of unidealized human behavior. By this criterion, too, the Bible is a realistic book. It paints its characters as Cromwell wished to be painted—warts and all. What a biblical scholar said about the patriarchs of Genesis is true of most biblical characters: they are so deeply flawed that "they have almost more shadow than light."[1] Among fully developed characters in the Bible, only a handful

1. Franz Delitzsch, *A New Commentary on Genesis*, trans. Sophia Taylor, 2 vols. (Edinburgh: T. and T. Clark, 1894), 2:275.

are wholly idealized characters: Joseph (some would dispute even him), Ruth, Daniel, Jesus.

Another thing that links the stories of the Bible with literary realism is their focus on common experience and characters of average social standing. The stories of the Bible are full of minor characters and ordinary people who are named and treated as significant in the stories. This is in sharp contrast to ancient stories like the epics of Homer, where only aristocratic characters count for much and people of lesser standing are a nameless, faceless crew.

Individuality is important in the Bible. We find lists of names of people who carried the tabernacle (Num. 10), came back to the Promised Land (Ezra 2), rebuilt the walls of Jerusalem (Neh. 3), and who were priests, gatekeepers, and singers in Jerusalem under David, along with those who mixed spices and made the flat cakes for worship (1 Chron. 9). And this is to say nothing of that great favorite of biblical writers, the genealogy.

There is an equal attention to common, everyday events. In Genesis we learn such seemingly insignificant things as the fact that Abraham planted a tamarisk tree in Beersheba (21:33), Isaac had several disputes with neighbors over a well (26:17–22), Rebekah's nurse was buried under an oak below Bethel (35:8), and Joseph shaved and changed his clothes before going to see Pharaoh (41:14). My personal favorite among the mundane events recorded in the stories of the Bible is the startling information that Benaiah "slew a lion in a pit on a day when snow had fallen" (1 Chron. 11:22).

The Bible conveys an astonishing sense of reality. The one charge that I have never seen leveled against the stories of the Bible is that the characters are not real. Wherever we turn, we find ourselves and our acquaintances.

The realism of biblical narrative is also part of its religious meaning. As we read these stories, we quickly sense that they have no intention of relegating the religious side of life to some other, spiritual world. Here the workings of God reach down into earthly experience. In the words of Erich Auerbach, the Bible "engenders a new elevated style, which does not scorn everyday life and which is ready to absorb the sensorily realistic, even the ugly, the undignified, the physically base."[2]

Literary Romance

If the stories of the Bible have the literary traits of realism, they also possess the qualities of a type of story that is in many ways the exact

---

2. Erich Auerbach, *Mimesis: The Representation of Reality in Western Literature,* trans. Willard R. Trask (Princeton: Princeton University Press, 1953), p. 72.

opposite and that literary scholars call romance. This is the type of story that delights in the extraordinary and miraculous. Like romance stories, the stories of the Bible are full of mystery, the supernatural, and the heroic.

Romance stories are replete with adventure, battle, capture and rescue, surprise, the exotic and marvelous, poetic justice (good characters are rewarded and bad ones punished), and happy endings. Such stories tend to portray life as we desire it to be: the underdog wins, the villain gets his just punishment, the slave girl marries the king, the dead come back to life.

The Bible's resemblance to this type of story is obvious. Its stories are filled with adventure, marvelous events, battles of many kinds, danger, supernatural characters, villains who get what they deserve, witches, heroes and heroines, an occasional talking animal, dragons, dungeons, castles, giants, quests, shipwrecks, captures and rescues, kings and queens, romantic love, and a few boy heroes. Bible stories, moreover, tend to be happy-ending stories in which good characters win and bad ones lose.

The story of God's rescue of Elisha when he was surrounded by the Syrian army in the town of Dothan epitomizes the romance quality of the stories of the Bible:

> When the servant of the man of God rose early in the morning and went out, behold, an army with horses and chariots was round about the city. And the servant said, "Alas, my master! What shall we do?" He said, "Fear not, for those who are with us are more than those who are with them." . . . So the LORD opened the eyes of the young man, and he saw; and behold, the mountain was full of horses and chariots of fire round about Elisha. And when the Syrians came down against him, Elisha prayed to the LORD, and said, "Strike this people, I pray thee, with blindness." So he struck them with blindness. . . . [2 Kings 6:15–18]

Here we are at an opposite pole from everyday realism. We are in a world of supernatural marvels that transcends the world of physical, earthly reality.

The Bible as a whole ends with an abundance of literary conventions that are familiar to us through our reading of fairy tales: a lady in distress who is miraculously rescued (Rev. 12:13–16), a hero who kills a dragon (Rev. 19:11–20:3), a wicked witch who is finally defeated (Rev. 17–18), the marriage of the triumphant hero to his bride and the celebration of the wedding with a feast (Rev. 19:6–8), and the description of a palace glittering with jewels in which the hero and his bride live happily ever after (Rev. 21).

It is no wonder that the stories of the Bible appeal to children. Nor is it surprising that they merge in a child's imagination with romance stories.

I can recall an occasion when my daughter, then aged five, recommended that I select "the story of Gideon, and his knights, and their fiery swords."

Along with this literary appeal, the romance side of the Bible's stories embodies an important religious message. In the Bible, reality exists at two levels—the physical, earthly realm, and the unseen spiritual world. Both are equally real. The supernatural orientation, and especially the miraculous intervention of God in earthly events, constantly opens up doors into the spiritual world. If, as I said earlier, the realism of biblical narrative shows us God's reaching down into earthly reality, the romance element in biblical narrative shows us the complementary way in which earthly life opens up into a spiritual world. Religious experience in the stories of the Bible is more than earthly, though the realism of these stories shows at the same time that it is not less than earthly.

The Double Quality of Bible Stories

The stories of the Bible combine the two tendencies of narrative that have most appealed to the human race and that we tend to think of as opposites. These stories are both factually realistic and romantically marvelous. They bring together two impulses that the human race is always trying to join—reason and imagination, fact and mystery. The stories of the Bible nourish our need for both down-to-earth reality and the more-than-earthly. They appeal both to that part of us that is firmly planted on the earth and to that part of us that soars to the heavens.

The stories of the Bible call for both a naive and a sophisticated literary response. They are both adult stories and children's stories. On the one hand, they are folk stories—brief, realisitic, vivid, uncomplicated in plot line. They are stories that elicit intuitive responses from children. Looking back at my own childhood responses to them, I can tell that my responses to such things as dramatic irony or poetic justice or characterization were usually the right ones, even though I lacked the literary terminology to name them.

But the stories of the Bible also ask of us a sophisticated response. Part of this is the ability to deal with what today we would call adult themes—violence, sex, deceit, death, the subtleties of tension in personal relations, and the ambiguous mixture of good and evil in people's character and actions.

Bible stories often carry a surface meaning that no one can miss, combined with difficult issues that require complex interpretive skills to notice and unravel. Consider the story of Joseph:

> Joseph, being seventeen years old, was shepherding the flock with his brothers; . . . and Joseph brought an ill report of them to their father. Now Israel loved Joseph more than any other of his children, because he was the

son of his old age; and he made him a long robe with sleeves. But when his brothers saw that their father loved him more than all his brothers, they hated him. . . . [Gen. 37:2–4]

The surface level is one that children are perhaps the best at picking up: this is a story built around such universal domestic experiences as sibling rivalry, parental favoritism, and tattling. At the level of the human experience that is presented, the story packs an immediate punch.

But questions arise when we stare at the passage more closely, or when we pick up more experience of life. All the simple reader needs to know is that Jacob favored his son Joseph. But the narrator invites us to consider an added level of human dynamics and psychology when he includes the explanation that Jacob preferred Joseph "because he was the son of his old age."

For the reader who is busy emoting over the sibling rivalry that is portrayed here, the important thing is that the younger brother tattled on his older brothers. But the more thoughtful reader wants to know whether this is good or bad behavior on Joseph's part. These two readings will lead to opposite conclusions on the question. To young people with an ingrained reaction against tattling, Joseph is a goody-goody who deserves much of what he gets. But we reach another assessment if we take a bigger view of the moral principle involved. The obligation to testify of wrong is necessary to the health of any society, and it became an Old Testament civil law (Lev. 5:1). Joseph, moreover, dissociates himself from a (quite literal) brotherhood of evil, and he shows an allegiance in the hierarchy of authority upward to his father rather than to his brothers.

How serious is it when two readings contradict each other in this way? It naturally influences how readers interpret the specific, local details in a story, but it very rarely determines how they interpret the overall meaning of a biblical story. Regardless of whether we think the youthful Joseph was an unsympathetic spoiled brat or a young man with unusual moral conscience and courage, our final understanding of the providential theme in the story as a whole will be the same. The stories of the Bible often communicate as much as our own range and depth of human experience equip us to see in them. These stories, someone has noted, are hard to interpret correctly but also are nearly impossible to totally misread:

> By foolproof composition I mean that the Bible is difficult to read, easy to underread and overread and even misread, but virtually impossible to . . . counterread. . . . The essentials are made transparent to all comers: the story line, the world order, the value system. The old and new controversies among exegetes, spreading to every possible topic, must not blind us (as it usually does them) to the measure of agreement in this regard.[3]

3. Meier Sternberg, *The Poetics of Biblical Narrative: Ideological Literature and the Drama of Reading* (Bloomington: Indiana University Press, 1985), pp. 50–51.

There is another way in which the stories of the Bible invite a double response. They are so filled with vivid (often spectacular) action that they focus our attention on what happened. At this level they invite us to lose ourselves in the story and not be preoccupied with how the story is told. We might consider this an unliterary reading of the stories in the sense that it is unconscious of artistic matters. Such a reading is an intuitive, self-forgetful absorption in the action.

But the stories of the Bible are so carefully and subtly crafted that they also invite a more conscious analysis of their literary composition. They exhibit a perfection of literary technique that can scarcely be accidental and that definitely allows for sophisticated literary analysis. There should be no doubt that the storytellers of the Bible were interested in narrative technique. Their stories are not randomly composed. They are small masterpieces, and analysis is capable of showing this. Among other things, this opens up an additional avenue for enjoying the stories and one that most people find interesting.

A final element of doubleness that we should note is that as readers we fill a double role. We are both spectators and participants as we go through the action. As *participants* we identify with the characters as the action unfolds. We become *spectators* whenever we sense a distance between ourselves and the characters in the story. This is not to deny that we are imaginatively present in the world of the story. But we are conscious that the action is not happening to us. In this regard we should not minimize that the Bible is ancient literature and that much about the actions and customs in Bible stories is strange to us.

We are normally both participants and spectators as we read the stories of the Bible. The extent to which we are one or the other depends partly on our own background of experiences. In both cases, we must make an act of the imagination in leaving our own time and place and entering a world remote from our own. The act of identifying with characters in stories has been somewhat overemphasized in literary theory, so let me underscore that there is nothing deficient in our reading when we are spectators rather than participants in the action. The stories of the Bible are based on the premise that something is wrong with us if we do *not* distance ourselves from much of what is portrayed.

Brevity and Plain Style

The naive and sophisticated levels of biblical narrative can be related to another trait for which these stories are famous—their conciseness. Biblical storytellers show a remarkable preference for the brief unit. An individual story or episode thus seems accessible even to the person with modest literary background. Of course this very brevity places an even greater burden of interpretation on the reader, as we shall see.

In addition to the brevity of the units, we find a predominantly plain, unembellished style. The classic source on the subject is Auerbach's great essay in which he compares storytelling technique in Homer's *Odyssey* and the Genesis story of Abraham's willingness to sacrifice Isaac (Gen. 22).[4] Whereas Homer elaborates the details of his story, the storytellers of the Bible give only the essentials and leave much unstated. With the biblical style, writes Auerbach,

> [we find] the externalization of only so much of the phenomena as is necessary for the purpose of the narrative, all else left in obscurity; the decisive points of the narrative alone are emphasized, what lies between is nonexistent; thoughts and feeling remain unexpressed, are only suggested by the silence and the fragmentary speeches; the whole, permeated with the most unrelieved suspense and directed toward a single goal (and to that extent far more of a unity), remains mysterious and "fraught with background" (pp. 11–12).

The effect of this unembellished storytelling technique is that the stories "require subtle investigation and interpretation" (p. 15). With so few details included, we need to get maximum mileage out of everything that the storyteller has included in the text.

The story of the call of Abraham (Gen. 12:1–4) illustrates what Auerbach claims:

> Now the LORD said to Abram, "Go from your country and your kindred and your father's house to the land that I will show you. . . . " So Abram went, as the LORD had told him; and Lot went with him.

Where was Abraham when God called him? What went through his mind on that occasion? How did the rest of the household react to the news? Why did Abraham respond with such prompt obedience and set out on such an indefinite itinerary? We can only guess, for the narrator does not tell us. The overwhelming sense of spiritual destiny and mystery is present, but (unlike the modern novel) there is no preoccupation with human psychology. As one literary scholar notes, "one of the great merits of these stories of the Bible is that they have no psychology in them, no discussion of motivation."[5]

4. Auerbach's essay (often reprinted) is the opening chapter of *Mimesis*. Robert Alter, *The Art of Biblical Narrative* (New York: Basic Books, 1981), also discusses "the Bible's highly laconic mode of narration."

5. Mark Van Doren and Maurice Samuel, *In the Beginning, Love: Dialogues on the Bible*, ed. Edith Samuel, new ed. (New York: Day, 1973), p. 66.

Clarity and mystery mingle as we move through these stories. In the formula of one scholar, the storytellers of the Bible tell us the truth, but not the whole truth.[6] What they tell us is reliable, but they leave so much unsaid. For the most part they describe but do not explain what happened. The result, already noted, is that it is easy to grasp the basic action in a biblical story, but difficult to interpret all of its meaning and all of its human dynamics.

So far as characterization is concerned, the brevity means that we do not find extended delineation of personality, though we may be able to produce a composite portrait by combining the fragments. In our actual reading experience,

> the great figures move in somewhat remote fashion, their characters illuminated as it were from the side by flashes of magnanimity, pity, anger; heroism, deceit, covetousness; suffering and the frequent cry of despair. . . . [The Bible is a] series of variegated patterns, lights and colours, shifting in time like a modern mobile, coalescing to break apart into new forms. . . . There are miniature vignettes, dramas of individuals.[7]

The Four Modes of Narration

What I have said regarding the unembellished narrative style becomes reinforced when we consider the modes of narration in these stories. A story itself consists of the interaction of three basic ingredients—setting, characters, and plot or action. There are four ways (called modes of narration) by which storytellers can present these ingredients.[8]

In *direct narrative*, storytellers simply report events, telling us in their own voice what happened. In *dramatic narrative*, writers dramatize a scene as though it were in a play, quoting the speeches or dialogue of characters and noting the surrounding context. In *description*, writers describe the details of setting or character. *Commentary* consists of explanations by storytellers about details in the story, background information, or the overall meaning of the story.

Each of these modes serves a specific function. Direct narrative provides fluidity and keeps a story moving. Dramatized narrative and description both slow the movement and focus our attention on a dramatic "scene" (as though we were seeing it staged in a play). Commentary allows storytellers to clarify anything that they think the audience needs to know.

6. Sternberg, *Poetics of Biblical Narrative*, pp. 230–63 and passim.
7. T. R. Henn, *The Bible as Literature* (New York: Oxford University Press, 1970), p. 31.
8. My framework here is a modification of the one proposed by Jacob Licht, *Storytelling in the Bible* (Jerusalem: Magnes, 1978), pp. 24–50.

Here is how the four modes appear in the story of the exchanged birthright (Gen. 25:29–34):

> [*description of the setting for the event to follow*] Once when Jacob was boiling pottage, Esau came in from the field, and he was famished. [*dramatic narrative*] And Esau said to Jacob, "Let me eat some of that red pottage, for I am famished!" [*commentary*] (Therefore his name was called Edom.) [*dramatic narrative*] Jacob said, "First sell me your birthright." Esau said, "I am about to die; of what use is a birthright to me?" Jacob said, "Swear to me first." [*direct narrative*] So he swore to him, and sold his birthright to Jacob. Then Jacob gave Esau bread and pottage of lentils, and he ate and drank, and rose and went his way. [*commentary*] Thus Esau despised his birthright.

As this analysis demonstrates, paying attention to the modes of narration is a useful framework when laying out the structure of a story in detail.

Another helpful aspect of the framework is that it gives us a new appreciation for how skillfully the stories of the Bible have been composed. They have enough direct narrative to keep them moving, sufficient focus on dramatic scenes to make the action come alive on the "stage" of our imagination, and occasional commentary to set the record straight. In addition to this principle of variety, we find a balance between overviews and close-ups.

The issue of narrative modes also has implications for interpreting the stories of the Bible. These stories show an overwhelming preponderance of dramatic narrative.[9] Bible stories always have direct narration of events, but this usually serves the function of lead-in and follow-up to the dramatized scenes.

As for description and commentary, they are so rare that it is relatively difficult to find stories that include both. In both cases, their very brevity functions to activate a reader. Descriptions give us brief information (such as that Joseph was handsome and wore a special robe), but the effect is to spur us to imagine things, not to describe precisely what they were. At the level of commentary, even when it appears, it tends to interpret only a specific detail in the story or only one aspect of the story's meaning. It can hardly be said to complete the task of interpretation.

This means that the focus of narrative interpretation is almost always on the dramatic scenes. The biblical imagination is strongly dramatic. The incidence of direct quotation of dialogue and speeches is completely without parallel until we come to the modern novel. The sense of *encounter* is strong in these stories (as indeed it is throughout the Bible).

---

9. For more on this, see ibid., pp. 30–50.

Drama is also the most objective of the literary genres, inasmuch as the storyteller simply lets the characters present the action and leaves it up to the audience to come to the right conclusions. Once again we can see that the stories of the Bible call for interpretation.

The fact that biblical storytellers depend most heavily on dramatic narrative to communicate their message is also one of the best proofs that the Bible is a literary book. If all that mattered is that we know what happened, a bare outline of events would suffice. But when biblical storytellers begin to quote speeches and compose dramatic scenes, they make it clear that they want us to picture *how* something happened. The literary impulse is to "show" rather than "tell"—to recreate an experience so we can go through it with the characters to whom it happened.

This, in fact, is a criterion by which we can know whether a given story in the Bible is literary in nature. The stories in the Bible exist on a spectrum. At one end is the brief fragment in which we are told only the facts about what happened. Here the historical or documentary impulse governs. At the other end are stories in which the writer images the events in sufficient detail that we can recreate the experience in our imagination. The farther a biblical narrative moves toward the second end, the more accurately we can call it a literary narrative.

Interpreting the Meaning of Bible Stories

The fact that the literary narratives of the Bible consist mainly of dramatized scenes and a minimum of explanatory commentary by the storyteller means that we need to know how to interpret the meaning from the story itself. One of the most salient characteristics of these stories is their vivid consciousness of values—of what is right and wrong, valuable and worthless. They confirm to perfection a comment by the modern novelist Joyce Cary: "All writers have, and must have, to compose any kind of story, some picture of the world, and of what is right and wrong in that world."[10] Biblical storytellers give us such an ordered world.

How, then, do biblical storytellers guide our interpretation of their stories? They use devices of disclosure, many of them relatively subtle, to influence our patterns of response to characters and events. In the next chapter I will discuss such devices as highlighting, contrast, selectivity of material for inclusion and exclusion, and arrangement. Biblical storytellers also assume that we will interpret their stories within a context of what the Bible says about moral and spiritual issues in its didactic expository parts.

For the moment let me emphasize something else—the *affective* strat-

10. Joyce Cary, *Art and Reality: Ways of the Creative Process* (Garden City, N.Y.: Doubleday, 1961), p. 174.

egy of biblical storytelling. A literary critic has said about stories in general that "the writer expresses what he knows by affecting the reader; the reader knows what is expressed by being receptive to effects."[11] One scholar studied the means by which novelists embodied their moral perspective in their stories and concluded that the moral meaning of a story "depended heavily on how successful its creator was in controlling our sympathy and antipathy toward, approval and disapproval of, characters, thoughts, and actions at every stage."[12] The stories of the Bible presuppose these same principles.

In the story of Naboth's vineyard (1 Kings 21), for example, our interpretation of the story is tied directly to our patterns of sympathy for and aversion to the principal characters. In fact, the storyteller handles the account in such a way as to make us *feel* strongly as we read. He deliberately includes details that show us that Ahab is covetous, dominated by his wife, and childish in his strategy of pouting until Jezebel in motherlike fashion notices that something is wrong. Similarly, the writer portrays Jezebel in such a way as to arouse our revulsion. She emerges as ruthless, domineering, cruel, and dishonest.

We are just as surely moved to sympathize with Naboth. He is the person of integrity who remembers the religious stipulation that the land inherited from the original ancestors who entered the Promised Land should not be transferred to another family (v. 3). Furthermore, one of the perennial principles of narrative is that we sympathize with the helpless victim of evil.

Stories are affective by their very nature. They draw us into an encounter with characters and events and make response inevitable. In this sense interpreting the stories of the Bible is simpler than the discussions of scholars might sometimes lead us to think. These stories often require intellectual analysis, but in the meantime we had better not overlook the obvious: stories communicate their meaning partly by getting us to respond favorably and unfavorably to what happens in the story. We should therefore pay attention to our intuitive responses when we formulate what a biblical story means.

Pattern and Repetition

The terse stories of the Bible are carefully patterned, as subsequent chapters will demonstrate. The opening chapter of the story of Ruth, for

11. David Lodge, *Language of Fiction* (London: Routledge and Kegan Paul, 1966), p. 65.

12. Sheldon Sacks, *Fiction and the Shape of Belief: A Study of Henry Fielding, with Glances at Swift, Johnson and Richardson* (Berkeley: University of California Press, 1964), p. 249.

example, is carefully designed to present an ever-expanding vision of emptiness. A literary critic describes it thus:

> Not only is this a carefully developed series, but it is also highly ordered. It starts on the widest of levels (man and the earth), then narrows down to the social level (man in the family), then narrows down once again to the most personal level (Naomi, the individual woman, in her anguish).[13]

Much of the patterning in biblical narrative consists of repetition.[14] A common strategy, for example, is threefold repetition, in which a similar event happens three times in succession. Often a crucial change is introduced the third time. Jesus told parables, for example, about three stewards, three people who refused invitations to a wedding, and three people who encountered a wounded man on a road. Jesus underwent three temptations, Peter denied Jesus three times, and Jesus restored Peter in three phases. In the Gospel of John, Jesus attends three Passovers and three other feasts, has his messiahship attested by John the Baptist three times, is three times condemned before his crucifixion, speaks three times from the cross, and makes three appearances after his resurrection. Why the emphasis on three? It is simply a convention of storytelling.

In the Old Testament narrative, the pattern of three-plus-one is also notable. The youthful Samuel has three unanswered calls and then the oracle from God (1 Sam. 3:2–14). The story of Elijah's being taken to heaven unfolds in a pattern of three identical exchanges between Elijah and Elisha, followed by a fourth incident in which Elijah is actually taken (2 Kings 2:1–12). In the story of Samson and Delilah, Samson resists Delilah's temptations three times, and then divulges his secret (Judg. 16:4–21). In these and similar examples, the vocabulary is nearly identical from one phase to the next.

Enough has been said to establish my point: biblical narrative is replete with patterns of repetition that range from units as small as repeated words and images throughout a story to units as large as repeated episodes. As readers we can learn to detect such patterns.

13. D. F. Rauber, "The Book of Ruth," in *Literary Interpretations of Biblical Narratives,* ed. Kenneth R. R. Gros Louis (Nashville: Abingdon, 1974), p. 166. Rauber leads up to his analysis with the type of generalization that has become common in literary commentary on the Bible: "More and more I become convinced that the great key to the reading of Hebraic literature is sensitivity to pattern" (p. 165).

14. This has become a prominent topic in recent criticism. For specimen studies, see Alter, *Art of Biblical Narrative,* pp. 88–113, and Licht, *Storytelling in the Bible,* pp. 51–95.

Archetypes

The subject of repeated patterns leads naturally to a final topic, the presence of archetypes in biblical narrative. In the introduction I noted that the Bible as a whole is unified by master images and symbols that recur throughout its pages. These master images of course appear in the stories of the Bible. In addition to archetypal images, we should note the presence of archetypal plot motifs and character types. The latter can be treated summarily. As we read the stories of the Bible, we keep encountering character types whom we meet elsewhere in our literary experience, both within and beyond the Bible. In keeping with the tendency of archetypes to fall into a dialectical pattern of opposites, these character types tend to fall into two categories.

In the positive column we enounter such figures as the hero or heroine (in a variety of specific forms), the virtuous wife/husband/father/mother, the bride and groom, the innocent child, the benevolent king or ruler, the conscientious priest, the true prophet, and the wise man. In the negative column we find such types as the villain, the tempter or temptress, the prostitute, the witch, the taskmaster, tyrant, or oppressor (usually a foreign oppressor), the outcast or exile, the traitor, and the false religious leader, priest, or prophet.

These lists are not exhaustive, and they do not exist to be memorized. Their purpose is to alert us to the principle of archetypes: stories are built around characters whose traits or roles remind us of similar characters elsewhere in literature and life. Identifying character types is simply part of organizing our experience of a given story.

Archetypal Plot Motifs

In addition to archetypal characters, we find archetypal plot motifs. The big framework in this regard is what literary critics call the monomyth (the "one story" of literature as a whole). This composite story is made up of all the individual stories we will ever read and is shaped like a circle with four separate phases. As such, it corresponds to some familiar cycles of human experience. The cycle of the year, for example, consists of the sequence summer-fall-winter-spring.

We can picture the "one story" of literature as it is in figure 2. Romance portrays ideal experience—life as we wish it to be. Its opposite, anti-romance, pictures a world of bondage and misery. Tragedy narrates a downward fall from bliss to misery, while comedy narrates a rise from bondage to freedom. Together these phases make up the composite story of literature. It is easy to see that the two columns of archetypal images and character types belong to the upper and lower levels of the diagram.

We can plot any biblical story somewhere on this framework. Individual

Figure 2 **The "one story" of literature**

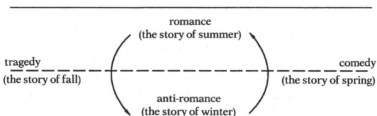

stories and episodes reenact one or more phases of this pattern, or perhaps the entire circle of action. The usefulness of the scheme is that it allows us to organize the overall pattern of every story we read.

The monomyth is the most general or universal narrative pattern in the Bible. It takes more specific forms as well, including these:

1. *The quest*, in which a hero struggles to reach a goal, undergoing obstacles and temporary defeat before achieving success.
2. *The death-rebirth motif*, in which a hero endures death or danger and returns to life or security.
3. *The initiation*, in which a character is thrust out of an existing, usually ideal, situation and undergoes a series of ordeals as he or she encounters various forms of evil or hardship for the first time.
4. *The journey*, in which characters encounter danger and experience growth as they move from one place to another.
5. *Tragedy*, or the more specific form of *the fall from innocence*, depicting a decline from bliss to woe.
6. *Comedy*, a U-shaped story that begins in prosperity, descends into tragedy, but rises to a happy ending as obstacles to success are overcome.
7. *Crime and punishment.*
8. *The temptation*, in which someone becomes the victim of an evil tempter or temptress.
9. *The rescue.*
10. *The suffering servant motif*, in which a character undergoes undeserved suffering for the benefit of others.
11. *The Cinderella or rags-to-riches motif*, in which a character overcomes the obstacles of ostracism and poverty.
12. *The movement from ignorance to epiphany* (insight, illumination).

This list, too, is not exhaustive. It simply represents the most common archetypal plot motifs. Its purpose is to help us organize what we encounter in stories by placing a given story into a familiar landscape.

Type Scenes

Biblical scholars today also speak of type scenes—repeated events or situations that recur throughout the Bible.[15] Most forms of communication, including stories, are built around understood conventions about what should be included and in what order items should appear. Some scholars imply that the presence of type scenes indicates that a work is fictional rather than factual, but this is an unwarranted presupposition.

Consider the typical brief interview on the television news. Its conventions include the following: an initial shot of the interviewer in front of a background that corresponds to the subject of the interview (the stands of a sports stadium or the wreckage of a disaster, for example); an exchange between interviewer and subject that follows a question-answer format; a return at the end to the interviewer, who looks into the camera and concludes the interview with some type of aphoristic summing up or interpretation of the topic just covered. Why would virtually every television news interview follow this format? It is simply the established convention of the genre.

When we come to the stories of the Bible, we find that they, too, fall into discernible type scenes. Some of these cut across various books of the Bible. Robert Alter lists as examples "the annunciation . . . of the birth of the hero to his barren mother; the encounter with the future betrothed at a well; the epiphany in a field; the initiatory trial; danger in the desert and the discovery of a well or other source of sustenance; the testament of the dying hero" (p. 51). The futile attempt to thwart or get around an oracle (prediction) that God has pronounced appears more than a dozen times.

Other type scenes are limited to individual stories or books of the Bible and seem to have a great deal to do with what the storyteller wished to accentuate. In the story of Abraham, for example, we repeatedly observe the following sequence: continuing anxiety over the unfulfillment of the promise of a son; discussion of this problem with either God or a human character; a proposed or attempted solution to the problem of producing a son who might fulfill the promise; frustration of this attempted solution. The type scene that dominates the epic of the Exodus is this sequence: crisis—complaint by the people—call to God by Moses—divine rescue/provision—revelation or rebuke by God.

Type scenes are equally prevalent in the stories of the New Testament. In the Gospels we find conventional elements, often in an expected order,

15. See especially Alter, *Art of Biblical Narrative*, pp. 47–62.

in healing stories, pronouncement stories, preaching stories, encounter stories, and Passion stories. In the Gospel of John, the type scene of the misunderstood statement occurs nine times and consists of three elements: Jesus makes a pronouncement, a bystander expresses a misunderstanding of the utterance, and Jesus proceeds to explain the meaning of the statement. In the Book of Acts, the following cycle of events is repeated: God raises up leaders who preach the gospel; they perform mighty works; crowds are drawn and many hearers are converted; opposition and persecution arise against the leaders; God intervenes to rescue them.

The subject of type scenes is a fitting conclusion to this chapter on storytelling technique in the Bible. The stories of the Bible are based on a whole set of narrative conventions. Some of these are somewhat distinctive to the stories of the Bible, while others are universal. We will enhance our understanding and enjoyment of Bible stories if we make the effort to familiarize ourselves with how stories work. We do not have to memorize lists of narrative "rules," but we do have to develop the right "antennae" by which to receive what these stories have to communicate. Doing so depends partly on an awareness of the techniques I have discussed in this chapter.

2

The Elements of Narrative
How Bible Stories Work

The stories of the Bible, like stories generally, are made up of three basic elements—setting, plot or action, and character. These three together make up the narrative world that we enter when we sit down to read a biblical story. The writer's goal in telling a story is to make us share an experience with the characters in the story. This means that a prime prerequisite for reading the stories of the Bible is the ability to empathize with the characters in the story. The stories of the Bible will succeed only to the extent to which we exercise our imaginations and allow ourselves to be transported from our own time and place into another time and place. Having been thus transported, we are both spectators and participants as the story unfolds.

The plot, characters, and setting of a story are the means by which the storyteller communicates something about reality. The American novelist Flannery O'Connor said something memorable when she said that a storyteller speaks *"with* character and action, not *about* character and action."[1] There is a discourse level to the stories of the Bible. The writers

1. Flannery O'Connor, *Mystery and Manners*, ed. Sally and Robert Fitzgerald (New York: Farrar, Straus and Giroux, 1957), p. 76.

tell their stories because they wish to say something significant about the meaning of life. The analysis of the means by which storytellers induce readers to move from the setting, action, and characters of a story to its meaning is variously called rhetorical criticism (analysis of the persuasive strategies of the storyteller) and point of view (analysis of the perspective from which the storyteller views the characters and action). Regardless of which term we use, studying the means by which storytellers signal how they wish readers to interpret the meaning of their stories is a necessary part of narrative interpretation.

In this chapter, I will devote separate sections to the three elements of narrative and to the process by which we move from story to theme or meaning. In both this chapter and the next one, all of my illustrations or applications will come from the Book of Genesis and accordingly represent a literary introduction to the first book of the Bible. Limitations of space have often led me to make generalizations that I have made no attempt to document exhaustively; in these instances, I leave it to my readers to complete what I begin.

Setting

I begin with the forgotten element in many people's analysis of stories. The setting of a story is much more complex, more interesting, and more important to the meaning of a story than is often realized. Settings serve a range of functions and fall into three types—physical, temporal, and cultural. Physical setting is the environment in which the characters move and the action occurs. Temporal setting is the time in which action takes place, either the time of day or year or the historical era. Cultural setting refers to the beliefs, attitudes, and customs that prevailed in the world of the story.

The most customary function of a setting is to serve as an appropriate container for the action and characters that are placed into it. A literary critic, Kenneth Burke, speaks of the *scene-agent ratio* and the *scene-act ratio*, meaning that there is ordinarily a consistency or correspondence between the scene and the other two elements. He writes,

> It is a principle of drama that the nature of acts and agents should be consistent with the nature of the scene. . . . The scene is a fit "container" for the act, expressing in fixed properties the same quality that the action expresses in terms of development. . . . There is implicit in the quality of a scene the quality of the action that is to take place within it. This would be another way of saying that the act will be consistent with the scene. . . . The scene-act ratio either calls for acts in keeping with scenes or scenes in keeping with acts—and similarly with the scene-agent ratio. . . . Both act and agent require scenes that "contain" them.[2]

2. Kenneth Burke, *A Grammar of Motives and A Rhetoric of Motives* (Cleveland: Meridian, 1962), pp. 3, 6–9, 15.

The rule of interpretation that follows from this is that we should look for a correspondence between the setting and the characters and actions that operate within it, realizing that there are occasional exceptions to the rule in which it is the clash between scene and agent or action that is important. We should ask simply, What is the relationship between this setting and the characters and events of the story?

The physical settings of stories serve secondary functions as well. In keeping with the impulse of literature to show rather than merely tell, settings appeal to a reader's imagination and make a story vivid. They sometimes build atmosphere. They frequently have symbolic overtones, without, of course, ceasing to be literal, physical settings. At the very least, settings often have a positive or negative moral or emotional meaning. In the stories of Genesis, for example, Sodom is a moral monstrosity, while Canaan is the land of promise.

In longer stories, settings can also become a leading element of structure and unity. Abraham's status as a wanderer is kept alive throughout his story by references to tents and the trees where Abraham camped. Jacob's story is punctuated with references to stones. Joseph's life is built around a sequence of places of imprisonment.

Knowing something about the *cultural* setting of a story is often necessary to prevent misreadings and to bring out aspects of the action that a modern reader would otherwise miss. To a modern reader, God's command to Abraham to sacrifice his son (Gen. 22) seems implausible. It does not even fit our categories. But the Genesis narrative makes it plain that someone whose cultural situation included contact with people who sacrificed their children as part of their religious duty knew what the command meant and promptly went about obeying it.

The functions of settings in stories are thus varied, but a simple rule of interpretation unifies them: *Pay close attention to every detail of setting that a storyteller puts into a story and observe how it contributes to the story.* I turn now to application of this priniciple to some passages from Genesis.

Elemental Nature

The world of the stories of Genesis (and of most biblical narrative) is both elemental and pastoral (rural or natural). Consider these specimen passages:

Cain said to Abel his brother, "Let us go out to the field." And when they were in the field, Cain rose up against his brother Abel, and killed him. [Gen. 4:8]

And Isaac sowed in that land, and reaped in the same year a hundred-fold. . . . And Isaac dug again the wells of water which had been dug in the days of Abraham his father. . . . [Gen. 26:12, 18]

"Now then, take your weapons, your quiver and your bow, and go out to the field, and hunt game for me." [Gen. 27:3]

In each case, the setting is unlocalized and elemental—so general and universal that any reader can link the setting with his or her own experience. We all have experiences of *field, land,* and *water*. The descriptive strategy in such passages is to provide the general outline and activate readers to fill in the details on the basis of their own memory and imagination.

The effect of such descriptions is double. One effect is concretion: we have a strong impression of the physical reality in which the action occurs. As we read biblical narrative, we remain rooted in the world of fields and crops and water. But along with this concretion is a certain reticence—a refusal to fill in the details and a corresponding invitation for readers to imagine the specifics of the scene.

We should note also that settings such as these reinforce the elemental or universal quality of the Bible. The Bible is a timeless book, always up to date. Howard Mumford Jones has this helpful comment:

> The themes of the Bible are simple and primary. Life is reduced to a few basic activities—fighting, farming, a strong sexual urge, and intermittent worship. . . . This elemental quality in the themes of the Bible is at once ground and occasion of a life and outlook quite as primary as and often more primitive than that in Homer or the Greek tragic poets. We confront basic virtues and primitive vices. . . . The world these persons inhabit is stripped and elemental—sea, desert, the stars, the wind, storm, sun, clouds and moon, seedtime and harvest, prosperity and adversity, famine and plenty. . . . Occupation has this elementary quality also.[3]

Indeterminate Settings

The tendency to give only the bare outline of a setting stands in the middle of the continuum that biblical storytellers use. Pressed further in one direction, the settings become even more indeterminate, in keeping with the supernatural nature of much of the action that occurs within them. Here are three examples:

> Now the LORD said to Abram, "Go from your country and your kindred and your father's house to the land that I will show you." [Gen. 12:1]

> After these things the word of the LORD came to Abram in a vision. . . . [Gen. 15:1]

3. Howard Mumford Jones, "The Bible from a Literary Point of View," in *Five Essays on the Bible* (New York: American Council of Learned Societies, 1960), pp. 52–53.

> After these things God tested Abraham, and said to him, "Abraham!" And he
> said, "Here am I." [Gen. 22:1]

Here we are not even given the minimal information about where the
characters are when the dialogue occurs. We have to imagine it all. We do,
of course, imagine or infer *something*, however sketchy. Erich Auerbach's
comment on the third of the quoted passages expresses it well:

> Where are the two speakers? We are not told. The reader, however, knows
> that they are not normally to be found together in one place on earth, that
> one of them, God, in order to speak to Abraham, must come from
> somewhere, must enter the earthly realm from some unknown heights or
> depths. . . . Moreover the two speakers are not on the same level: if we
> conceive of Abraham in the foreground, where it might be possible to picture
> him as prostrate or kneeling or bowing with outspread arms or gazing
> upward, God is not there too: Abraham's words and gestures are directed
> toward the depths of the picture or upward, but in any case the undeter-
> mined, dark place from which the voice comes to him is not in the
> foreground.[4]

The effect of these indeterminate settings is to imply a sense of mystery. In
these scenes God moves with mingled clarity and hiddenness. An overpowering sense of mystery pervades the whole.

I spoke earlier of the correspondence that normally exists between a
setting and the characters and actions that operate within it. In the quoted
passages, the action is a divine-human encounter. Such an action brings
together the earthly and the heavenly, the physical and the spiritual. The
technique of the indeterminate setting fits this action perfectly by combining the "voice" and palpable presence of God with an overwhelming sense
of his mystery and transcendence.

Geographic Settings

As noted, the generalized settings of field and tent can move in the
direction of greater indeterminacy. But the continuum also moves in the
other direction. The stories of Genesis (and indeed the Bible in general) are
filled with particularized geographic place names. Here are two specimens
that represent a major tendency in the stories of the Bible:

> When they had come to the land of Canaan, Abram passed through the land
> to the place at Shechem, to the oak of Moreh. . . . Thence he removed to the
> mountain on the east of Bethel, and pitched his tent, with Bethel on the west
> and Ai on the east. . . . [Gen. 12:5, 8]

4. Erich Auerbach, *Mimesis: The Representation of Reality in Western Literature*, trans.
Willard R. Trask (Princeton: Princeton University Press, 1953), pp. 8–9.

So Isaac departed from there, and encamped in the valley of Gerar and dwelt there. . . . From there he went up to Beersheba. [Gen. 26:17, 23]

Passages such as these read more like a diary or travel journal than something we would expect in a literary narrative. Certainly this matter-of-factness goes beyond the local color that storytellers sometimes put into their stories. From a literary viewpoint, such passages are extraneous and digressive. What are we to make of the situation?

These passages serve as a continuous reminder that in the stories of the Bible the literary impulse to recreate an experience is consistently combined with the documentary or historical impulse to record the facts of the matter. Throughout the Bible we find an intermixture of three types of writing (expository or theological, historical, and literary), and here we find another evidence of this unique blend.

But even if the main impulse behind such passages is historical or documentary, we can legitimately speak of literary effects. For one thing, the context into which something is placed always affects how we view it. In the present instance, the historical and geographical framework within which the stories of the Bible are placed signals the factual seriousness with which the writers expect us to regard their stories. People do not ascribe the same ontological status to factual and fictional events. If something really happened, it is in a different category from something that is merely imagined. The stories of the Bible do not give us the option of regarding the action as simply invented by the writer.

This was highlighted by a Bible translator's experience when he first read his translation of the Gospel of Matthew to a group of Binumeriens. He started with the genealogies with which Matthew begins, even though he feared that they might bore his audience. One of the burly men in the group responded by raising his hand and exclaiming, "Listen, all you people! *This* is what we wanted to know. This is *it*! Is the Bible the white man's myths or legends, or did it actually happen? Now we *know* it happened. What myth or legend carefully records family names down through history?"[5]

There are other literary effects as well. These interspersed geographic references give the action an epic scope. They also highlight the identity of the characters—as wanderers, for example, and as people with international experience and importance.

Setting as Atmosphere

In some stories, the physical setting contributes to the atmosphere of the story. As the scene-act ratio indicates, the physical environment cor-

5. *In Other Words*, April/May 1983, p. 1.

responds to the action that occurs within it. It provides an atmosphere in which the action seems inevitable.

The story of Joseph (Gen. 37) furnishes an illustration. This is a gripping story of sibling rivalry and hostility against a helpless victim. In this story of violence, the setting abets the crime of the brothers. It is a remote setting where crimes go unobserved. The landscape itself becomes Joseph's enemy, with its open pits into which people can be thrown and wild animals in whose blood a coat can be dipped to deceive a father. And the action occurs near the route traveled by trading caravans headed to Egypt. The very setting establishes an atmosphere of hostility. I might note in passing that one of the standard plot conflicts is people against their environment, and we find many examples in the stories of the Bible.

The same scene-act ratio can have the opposite effect of reinforcing positive action. The story of Abraham and Sarah's ideal hospitality (Gen. 18:1–8) is a good illustration. The setting for this beautiful story is what literary people call a pastoral setting. Pastoral is an image of the good life, conceived as rural simplicity and implying qualities of contentment, abundance, and satisfaction. In this pastoral interlude in the story of Abraham, we enter an idealized world of tent and trees, water and herds. The setting itself is an extension of the virtues that Abraham and Sarah display in the episode, and for which they are rewarded by God (one of the three angelic visitors).

This pastoral image of the good life is, of course, a foil that heightens the sordid degeneracy of the city of Sodom that appears in the very next chapter of Genesis. The latter story is a story of terror permeated by the greatest possible narrative tension. By contrast, the tone of the pastoral story of ideal hospitality is predominantly humorous, based on an elaborate incongruity in Abraham's behavior. In the presence of his guests, Abraham puts on a nonchalant air, using understatement as he offers *a little water* and *a morsel of bread* and then stands *by them under the tree while they [eat]*. Behind the scenes, however, Abraham is a frenzy of activity: *he hasten[s] into the tent to Sarah* to spread the word, he *[runs] to the herd*, and he *hasten[s] to prepare* the calf (note how the morsel of bread has become amplified). We cannot imagine such humor occurring in the sordid story set in Sodom.

So close is the correspondence between setting and action that the setting often figures prominently in the outcome of the action. In the episode of the substitute bride (Gen. 29:21–27), the cloak of night allows Laban to trick Jacob on the wedding night. Setting also gives the protagonist the advantage when Jacob bargains the birthright away from Esau (Gen. 25:27–34). The main action occurs in the tent, where Jacob is in his native element. Esau is the hunter of the fields, out of his depth in the kitchen. As we could predict, a pot of stew becomes a weapon in the hands of the family cook, and a person so governed by his physical appetite as Esau cannot possibly win in such a setting.

Setting as Symbol

Many of the settings in the stories of the Bible assume overtones of meaning beyond their physical qualities. We can appropriately speak of symbolic settings in these cases, provided we do not thereby minimize their literal, physical significance.

In the story of the separation of Abraham and Lot (Gen. 13), we read that "the land could not support both of them dwelling together" (v. 6). This struggle with the environment is more than the mainspring to the action, though it is certainly that. This is Canaan, the land of promise, yet it cannot even support the flocks of two members of the same family. The setting therefore becomes an implicit test of Abraham's faith.

The setting of the story of Abraham's "sacrifice" of Isaac (Gen. 22) has been much commented on. Throughout the story, setting is more spiritual that physical. We are told, for example, that Abraham "rose early in the morning" (v. 3), but this temporal setting is less literal than spiritual. It suggests both a psychological reality (Abraham spent a sleepless night) and a spiritual state of soul, prompt in its obedience to the command of God. The physical journey lasts three days, yet externally we are told nothing about it. In the words of Auerbach, "the journey is like a silent progress through the indeterminate" and positively demands a symbolic interpretation (p. 10). We quickly get the impression that the important thing is not the physical landscape but the spiritual landscape, and the physical journey actually marks the spiritual progress of Abraham toward an encounter with God. The mountain where the encounter occurs is less important as a physical phenomenon than as the place where earth meets heaven, that is, where the human encounters the divine.

There is also an incipient symbolism at work whenever a setting becomes an extension of a person's character. The prominence of stones in the story of Jacob illustrates this. Stones punctuate the action: Jacob puts a stone under his head at Bethel (Gen. 28:11), he sets up the stone as a commemorative marker after his vision of God (Gen. 28:18–22), he single-handedly moves the huge stone at the well that required shepherds to water their flocks only when they were all present (Gen. 29:10), he sets up a testimonial heap of stones when agreeing to a nonaggression pact with his father-in-law (Gen. 31:45–54), and he raises a pillar of stone at Bethel when he renews the covenant with God late in his life (Gen. 35:14). Robert Alter comments thus on the symbolic overtones of the motif: "Jacob is a man who sleeps on stones, speaks in stones, wrestles with stones, contending with the hard unyielding nature of things, whereas, in pointed contrast, his favored son will make his way in the world as a dealer in the truths intimated through the filmy insubstantiality of dreams."[6]

Cultural Setting

Physical settings are so palpably present that we cannot overlook them if we tried. The cultural setting is implied rather than stated, and as modern readers we need the help of archaeologists and historians to recover it. This assumed backdrop for the action can be crucial to our understanding of the action.

The story of the exchanged birthright (Gen. 25:29–34) is often described as Jacob's stealing of the birthright, but this is inaccurate. Ancient practice allowed for the transfer of a birthright through bartering. Jacob's cleverness in the matter is hinted when he makes Esau swear an oath before eating the stew (v. 33). This oath made the transfer legally binding. To regard this as a "stolen" birthright misrepresents almost everything about the transaction—Jacob's scheming mentality, Esau's inverted scale of values (as memorialized in our proverb about "selling one's birthright for a mess of pottage"), and the binding nature of the transaction.

The customs that are part of the cultural setting also explain what happens in such an episode as the decision of Abraham and Sarah to have a son by the maiden Hagar (Gen. 16:1–6). The relevant legal documents from the time show that Abraham and Sarah were not simply acting out of impulse but conforming to a prescribed custom of a barren wife's providing a concubine whose offspring would have the status of legal descendant.[7] The same documents indicate that if such a concubine tried to claim a position of equality with her mistress, she would be demoted to her former status of slave, though she could not be sold. This helps to explain why Sarah can legitimately press Abraham to do something when the pregnant Hagar shows contempt for Sarah, and why Sarah stops short of expelling Hagar.

Such cultural setting lies behind many of the stories of the Bible. The stories allude to customs and attitudes, but generally do not explain them. There is no easy way for a modern Western reader to recover these cultural settings. Doing so requires the effort of consulting scholarly (as distinct from devotional) commentaries, or books that specialize in detailing conditions in the Holy Land.[8]

Setting is an essential ingredient in most biblical stories. If we ignore

6. Robert Alter, *The Art of Biblical Narrative* (New York: Basic Books, 1981), p. 55.

7. See, for example, E. A. Speiser, *Genesis*, vol. 1 of the Anchor Bible (Garden City, N.Y.: Doubleday, 1964), pp. 119–21.

8. See, for example, Kenneth E. Bailey's two books on the parables of Jesus: *Poet and Peasant: A Literary-Cultural Approach to the Parables in Luke* and *Through Peasant Eyes: More Lucan Parables, Their Culture and Style* (Grand Rapids: Eerdmans, 1976, 1980).

setting, we will only impoverish our enjoyment and understanding of biblical narrative. The settings in these stories can be physical, temporal, or cultural, and they serve such distinct functions as making the story vivid to our imagination, reinforcing character and action, building an atmosphere, strengthening the structural unity of a story, and conveying symbolic meanings.

Plot and the Story of Abraham

In exploring the dynamics of plot, I will mingle theory with application to the story of Abraham as told in Genesis 11:27 through Genesis 25:10. In the process, I hope to give a methodology that can be applied to any story of the Bible, while at the same time giving a literary analysis of the story of Abraham.

The plot of a story is the arrangement of events.[9] Three time-honored principles on which a plot is constructed are unity, coherence, and emphasis. A plot is not simply a *succession* of events but a *sequence* of related events possessing a beginning, a middle, and an end. In other words, a plot gives us one or more *single* or *whole* actions.

This principle of narrative construction and wholeness is very different from what we find in a journalistic newspaper account of an event. The logic behind the news article is to give the most important information first and then accumulate pieces of information in an order of decreasing importance. The logic of a story is to progress from the beginning through a chain of events to the conclusion of the action. Paragraphs in a newspaper account of an event can be omitted or rearranged to fit the available space. By contrast, the order of events in a story is based on the principle of cause and effect in a way that precludes rearranging or omitting the individual units.

Plot Conflict and Suspense

The most customary pattern of organization in a plot is one or more conflicts, and it is really unwise not to attempt to formulate the unity of a story partly in these terms. The conflict can consist of physical conflict, character conflict, inner psychological conflict, or moral/spiritual conflict. A plot ordinarily consists of the progress of the conflict(s) toward a point of resolution. Occasionally (as I will note) some other principle provides the organization of the action, but it is a safe rule of interpretation always to look first for plot conflict(s).

The urge for conflict in a story is a manifestation of an even larger principle, that of *suspense* or *curiosity about outcome*. Stories succeed

9. Much of what I will say about plot can be traced back to Aristotle's *Poetics;* chapters 7–11 and 23 of this treatise have been rather definitive on the nature of plot, and they continue to be an excellent starting point on the subject.

only as they generate such curiosity. The novelist E. M. Forster has stated the matter thus: as story, a narrative "can only have one merit: that of making the audience want to know what happens next. And conversely it can only have one fault: that of making the audience not want to know what happens next."[10] I have found that an effective framework for organizing an analysis of an episode in a biblical story is to analyze exactly how the story engages my interest and arouses curiosity about outcome.

There are several ways in which the stories of the Bible make us interested spectators and/or participants in the action. The commonest strategy is to establish one or more plot conflicts that require a resolution. As a particular species under this principle, a staple of stories is to put characters into situations that test them or that simply pose a danger to them. Our interest can also be aroused by the presence of vivid characters about whose destiny we are made to care, with or without an element of plot conflict to reinforce that interest. The stories of the Bible are also filled with divine-human encounters. Some of these involve conflict, but others do not. In the latter case, we simply wonder how the meeting between a person and God will turn out. On still other occasions, an action is simply so striking or mysterious that we become interested in the outcome.

Suspense in the Story of Abraham

A brief look at selected episodes in the story of Abraham will illustrate the range of ways in which a story can generate suspense about outcome. The call of Abraham (Gen. 12:1-9) contains no element of plot conflict. God calls Abraham to leave his native land, and Abraham promptly obeys. Despite an absence of conflict, our interest in the action is assured. The command of God is a test of the hero, and we naturally wonder whether he will pass the test. A call requires a response, and the promises that God utters (vv. 2-3) make us wonder about their fulfillment. Once Abraham begins his quest for land and descendants, we are interested in his progress (or lack of progress) toward the goal of the quest.

The next episode is Abraham's encounter with the king of Egypt (Gen. 12:10-20). Here is a typical conflict story. Faced with the danger to his life and his inner fear about his vulnerability in a foreign land, Abraham assumes (without warrant, it turns out) that he is caught in a life-or-death struggle with Pharaoh. Within Abraham we infer a conflict between faith and expediency. Abraham resolves the conflict in the direction of expediency, and only God's intervention resolves the action in such a way as to preserve Abraham and Sarah's marriage.

10. E. M. Forster, *Aspects of the Novel* (1927; Harmondsworth: Penguin, 1962), p. 35. I recommend this book as an excellent repository of narrative theory, abundantly applicable to the stories of the Bible.

Many episodes in the story of Abraham are conversations, some of them involving no element of conflict. But a conversation implies an encounter, and this, in turn, generates our interest in how the encounter will conclude, especially if one of the characters in the dialogue is God. As a specimen, consider the conversation between God and Abraham when Abraham was ninety-nine years old and the fulfillment of the promise had been delayed for twenty-four years (Gen. 17). The main action is a dialogue or conversation. Despite the scarcity of external action, our interest is never in doubt. Even the opening is enough to arouse our interest: "When Abram was ninety-nine years old the LORD appeared to Abram, and said to him, 'I am God Almighty; walk before me, and be blameless.' " With such a sense of divine authority, we naturally wonder how the conversation will unfold. What will God say to Abraham this time? How will Abraham respond?

Equally important is the continuing suspense about how and when the quest for a son will be fulfilled, since this is the main topic of conversation. The sheer tension of Abraham's frustration reaches its focal point in his unrestrained laugh (v. 17), a laugh in which Abraham's pent-up feelings of incredulity, scorn, bitterness, and joy all converge. This is a good point at which to note, therefore, that in a long story like the story of Abraham, individual episodes are not wholly self-contained but derive part of their suspense from the ongoing story of Abraham's quest for a son. In fact, that quest generates much of the suspense along the way, and we soon begin to feel as though we are undertaking the long search with Abraham, sharing his responses to a twenty-five-year ordeal, making discoveries with him as he pursues one dead end after another until only a miracle can secure the promised son.

Sometimes as we read the stories of the Bible the sheer strangeness and mystery of what is happening are enough to engage our interest. The "cutting of the covenant" in Genesis 15 furnishes an example. In this episode, God and Abraham enact an ancient ritual. The ritual consisted of cutting animals in half as a way of confirming a contract or treaty. The parties to the agreement would walk between the divided carcasses, symbolically saying, "Let this be done to me if I break the covenant" (see Jer. 34:18–20). The whole atmosphere generated by the ritual is so solemn and mysterious that it guarantees our interest. Another way of saying this is that an element of strangeness in a story is quite capable of drawing us into it. Anything that does not fit arouses our curiosity. In the present instance, Abraham sleeps while God alone (in the form of a mysterious smoking pot and flaming torch) passes between the carcasses. Here, in fact, is the main point of this story: God in his sovereignty is the one who establishes his covenant with the human race.

To sum up, a good procedure for organizing the shape of a story is to analyze how the story generates our interest in its outcome. Most often we will find an element of plot conflict, but there are other ways in which the stories of the Bible draw us into their world.

Plot Unity

Well-constructed stories are unified actions. In more complex stories, there may be multiple actions (the story of Abraham provides an instance, as we shall see), but each one of these meets the criterion of a single coherent action. A main effort of literary analysis of a biblical story should be to formulate its unity. For the moment, my focus will be on the individual episodes in the overall story of Abraham; later I will discuss the special considerations that arise in connection with a longer story comprised of individual events.

The first step is to determine the precise boundaries of a given episode. Aristotle's formula is the most helpful guideline in this regard: an action is whole or complete if it consists of a beginning, a middle, and an end. In the call of Abraham (Gen. 12:1–9), for example, the beginning is obviously God's opening command to Abraham to "go from your country and your kindred and your father's house to the land that I will show you" (v. 1). This command requires a response, which is the main action of the episode (vv. 4–8). The concluding information that "Abram journeyed on, still going toward the Negeb" (v. 9) virtually announces, "So much for this episode; now on to the next one."

To some extent, we will set the boundaries of a biblical story in keeping with how minutely we wish to divide the story. It is always possible to divide a chapter very minutely or to stand back at a greater distance and divide it into bigger units. In general, our tendency should be to look for relatively large blocks. Not seeing the forest for the trees has been a constant problem in scholarly discussions of biblical stories.

Once we have determined the boundaries of a story, we can set about the task of determining the inner dynamics that constitute the unity of the action. I have already explored the central importance of plot conflict(s) as the unifying ingredient in a story and will not illustrate that point again; this is, however, the most important thing to keep in mind when formulating the unity of a story. A keen eye for archetypal plot motifs will often prove helpful, as will sensitivity to any other type of overall pattern or design.

Stories often focus on the motif of *choice.* We might say that narrative concentrates on the person at the crossroads. Thus the story of the separation of Abraham and Lot (Gen. 13) is unified by the great, life-influencing choices that the two principal characters make. Faced with the dilemma of Sarah's continuing barrenness, Abraham and Sarah choose to have a child by Hagar; the resulting story (Gen. 16) is built around (unified by) this choice and its consequences. Another way of formulating the unity of these two stories is the pattern of *problem and solution* (and of course the attempted solution might lead to a further cycle of problems).

Even more common is the *test motif.* Here characters find themselves in situations that test them. Sometimes the test that unifies a story is *physical,* as when Abraham defeats the forces that had carried Lot away captive (Gen. 14). Elsewhere the hero's *resourcefulness* is tested. Into this category we might put the stories of Abraham's ability (which he lacks) to mediate between Sarah and Hagar (Gen. 16:1–6), Abraham's delicate intercession on behalf of Sodom (Gen. 18:22–33), and the ability of Abraham's servant to find a suitable wife for Isaac in a foreign country (Gen. 24). A third type of test is the *mental* or psychological test that a character undergoes, as when Abraham repeatedly struggles with the frustration occasioned by the twenty-five-year delay in the fulfillment of the promise of a son.

The most profound type of testing in stories is the test of the hero's *moral or spiritual integrity.* The supreme example in the story of Abraham comes when God commands Abraham to sacrifice his son (Gen. 22), which in effect reenacts the death-birth archetype. But other episodes are also unified around the motif of moral and spiritual testing: the crisis of faith that Abraham twice faces when he finds himself in a foreign country (Gen. 12:10–20 and Gen. 20), and the test of Abraham and Sarah's hospitality, for which they are rewarded (Gen. 18:1–15).

If we were to move beyond the story of Abraham to other stories in Genesis, we would encounter further unifying motifs in individual episodes. There would be quests and journeys, stories of initiation and temptation and rescue, tragedy and the U-shaped pattern of comedy. Whatever the specifics, successful treatment of the plot of a story includes identifying what unifies the action and makes it a whole.

The Case of Long Narrative

From the individual episodes I turn to the case of the long story—the superstructure that includes the individual episodes. The overall story, too, is a unified action, and it is the task of the reader or expositor to identify it. The necessary preliminary step is to divide the overall story into its constituent parts. The customary term for these units is *episode,* and episodes are the building blocks from which the story is constructed. In a story like the story of Abraham, we have the additional complexity of a multiple plot—the presence of several intertwined strands of action.

To begin, the story of Abraham belongs to a category known as heroic narrative, to which I will devote a later chapter. In such stories, the unity of the story resides partly (though not wholly) in the unity of the hero. Even when such stories have a unity of action as well, the presence of the protagonist throughout the story imposes a unity on the story. As we move through the story of Abraham, we are continuously aware of the unifying presence of the hero. The story of Abraham is an ever-expanding definition of the hero, and as we progress through the story we can usually see that the portrait is a growing one in which something new is added with the successive episodes. When we consider Abraham as a unifying hero in his story, we continually notice two dimensions: Abraham is a religious hero and a domestic hero (as in Homer's *Odyssey*, home means land and possessions as well as family). We are never allowed to forget Abraham's relationship to God, and we are likewise always aware of his identity as head of a family.

Even more important than unity of character is unity of action. In a multiple plot like the story of Abraham, each thread of action is thus unified. The crucial principle is causal connection among the episodes. That is, we can see how one event leads to the next one. A plot is not a mere succession of events but a chain of events linked by cause and effect. Thus the mere chronology of the story of Abraham counts for less than various plot strands in which one thing builds upon another to produce a sustained chain of events.

The most obvious sustained plot in the story of Abraham is the quest. Beginning with God's call of Abraham (Gen. 12:1-3), virtually everything in the story relates in some way to the ongoing quest for a son and descendants, as well as for a promised land. The quest is partly physical, as Abraham journeys about searching for a place to call his own, and partly a process of trying to produce the promised son. Many of the conflicts in the story stem directly from these combined quests.

A second unifying action is the progressive revelation of the covenant. By a revelation of the covenant I mean speeches in which God promises to bless Abraham (and later the other patriarchs) and predicts what he will do for the world through him. These promises are couched in a discernible rhetorical pattern (chiefly a catalogue of predicted blessings), as illustrated by the first time that it appears in the story of Abraham:

> "I will make of you a great nation, and I will bless you and make your name great, so that you will be a blessing. I will bless those who bless you, and him who curses you I will curse; and by you all the families of the earth shall bless themselves [in you all the families of the earth shall be blessed]." [Gen. 12:2-3]

This is the language of the covenant, a language of blessing and promise. The covenant itself is a relationship between God and Abraham, a relationship involving promises on God's part and requiring obedience on the part of people.

Introduced at the very start of the story, the motif of God's covenant promises punctuates the action with predictable regularity. Considered as a plot, the important element in the pattern is that it is a progressive revelation. Every time the covenant promises are renewed by God, something is added. For example, when Abraham first arrives in the land of Canaan, God specifically promises *descendants* and *this land* (Gen. 12:7). After Abraham chooses Hebron as his dwelling place in deference to Lot, God amplifies the covenant promise by promising a line of descendants as numerous *as the dust of the earth* (Gen. 13:14–17).

Thereafter whole episodes are devoted to renewing the covenant, and in each case there is a progressive element at work. In Genesis 15 God informs Abraham that his own son will be his heir (v. 4) and that his descendants will be slaves in a foreign land for four hundred years, after which they will claim the land of Canaan as their own (vv. 13–21).

Genesis 17 is another whole chapter devoted to the progressive revelation of the covenant. New names appear for the first time in the story, a variation on the common storytelling strategy of character transformation. Because only a miracle by God can now produce the promised son, God calls himself by the new name of *God Almighty*, or "the Overpowerer" (literally *El Shaddai*). Abram ("exalted father") becomes *Abraham* ("father of a multitude"). Sarai's new name, *Sarah* ("princess"), means the same as her previous name, but in effect she is brought into the covenant promise directly for the first time. Even the promised son receives his name (*Isaac*, meaning "he laughs"), based on the ambiguous laugh of Abraham. Chapter 17 also introduces the covenant sign (circumcision).

Two final revelations of the covenant advance the motif still further. After Abraham and Sarah pass the test of their hospitality (Gen. 18:1–8), God rewards them with the specific news that the promise of a son will be fulfilled *in the spring*. The quest is nearing its goal. And then in the episode of the "sacrifice" of Isaac, after the quest for descendants is severely threatened, God renews the covenant a final time (Gen. 22:16–18).

Here, then, is another element of plot unity. The progressive revelation of the covenant is both a major part of the meaning of the story and a leading structural principle in the narrative.

A final unifying action in the story of Abraham is the conflict within Abraham between faith and expediency. On the one hand, he feels drawn to exercise faith in God's lavish promises and to obey God's commands. But on the other hand, he is repeatedly tempted to take matters into his own hands, to do what from a human perspective seems personally advantageous, to base his actions on the known rather than the unseen. The ethic of expediency worked well for another hero of ancient literature, Homer's Odysseus, but it repeatedly gets Abraham into difficulty.

Abraham's first action in the story—obeying God's startling command to leave his native land for an unnamed land of promise—is a great venture in faith. But it is followed immediately by a great venture in expediency, which takes the form of lying about Sarah's identity as his wife (Gen. 12:10–20). That Abraham deserves his traditional status as a hero of faith is obvious from his actions throughout the story, but this faith is set into tension with his lapses into expediency—when he decides to have offspring by Hagar (Gen. 16), when he lies to Abimelech about Sarah's identity (Gen. 20), when after the birth of Isaac he reaps the bitter harvest of his earlier act of expediency and responds with another act of expediency by sending Hagar and Ishmael away (Gen. 21:8–21).

The story of Abraham is thus a multiple plot, comprised of four main actions: the definition of the hero (the ongoing characterization of Abraham), the quest for land and descendants, the progressive revelation of the covenant, and the hero's conflict between faith and expediency. All four strands of plot converge and reach their climax in Genesis 22, the story of Abraham's willingness to sacrifice his son. Each of these motifs, if isolated by itself, is a single unified action. But of course the four plots are strongly intertwined in this complex story.

The success of any story depends on the reader's ability to keep the overriding framework in mind. Putting the unifying framework into the form of a chart often helps, as the diagram in table 1 suggests.

Table 1 **The framework of Genesis 12–25**

The passage in Genesis	Defining the hero	Progressive revelation of the covenant	The quest for a son and descendants	Conflict between faith and expediency	
				Faith	Expediency
12:1–9	•	•	•	•	
12:10–20	•				•
13	•	•	•	•	
14	•				
15	•	•	•	•	
16	•		•		•
17	•	•	•		•
18:1–15	•	•	•		
18:16–33	•				
19	•				
20	•				•
21:1–7	•		•		
21:8–21	•				•
21:22–34	•				
22	•	•	•	•	
23	•				
24	•		•		
25	•				

Several important conclusions can be drawn from this diagram, but I will mention just two. As we look back over the episodes that make up the plot, we can see the coherence of the story—the interrelatedness of the units that make up a given line of action. Narrative coherence normally consists of a cause-effect chain of events in which one thing produces the next, or in some way grows out of an earlier event. The impact of a story depends on the presence of such coherence.

The main lesson to be learned from the chart is that the unity of a story depends on our ability to see how individual episodes relate to the overriding framework(s). Individual episodes are not self-contained but exist in the context of the whole story. The principle involved here has been variously stated as the whole-part relationship, unity in variety, and theme-and-variation. With or without the use of a diagram, the best antidote to the fragmentation that is so common in discussions of biblical narrative is to relate episodes to the unifying plot motifs in a story. As Aristotle said regarding the individual episodes of a story, "We must see that they are relevant to the action."

Additional Plot Devices

The foregoing discussion of plot conflict, suspense (ways of generating interest about outcome), and unity has covered the basics of plot. But biblical storytellers use three additional devices so consistently that I should note them in passing.

Storytellers often introduce *foils* into their stories. A foil is literally something that sets off or heightens an element in the story. Usually this heightening consists of a contrast, but sometimes it is a parallel (so that we see the same thing twice, in different lights). A foil can be either a character or an event (or a plot line).

In the story of the separation of Abraham and Lot (Gen. 13), the materialism of Lot and the faith of Abraham are foils that heighten each other. The scene in which Abraham and Sarah entertain angelic visitors in an idealized pastoral setting (Gen. 18) is an elaborate foil to Lot's reception of two of those same visitors in the degenerate city of Sodom (Gen. 19). Abraham's trickiness in deceiving the king of Egypt about Sarah (Gen. 12:10–20) is a foil that is paralleled when the same trick is directed toward the king of Gerar (Gen. 20). The laugh of Sarah (Gen. 18:12) is both like and unlike the earlier laugh of Abraham (Gen. 17:17).

Dramatic irony occurs when the reader knows something that characters in the story do not.[11] The episode in which Lot chooses to pitch his tent toward Sodom is enveloped in irony because as readers we know that Lot's

11. An excellent source on irony and on Old Testament narrative generally is Edwin M. Good's *Irony in the Old Testament* (Philadelphia: Westminster, 1965).

choice will cost him all his earthly prosperity and domestic integrity. Irony lights up the episode in which Abraham and Sarah "entertained angels unawares" (the interpretation given to the episode in Hebrews 13:2); as readers we know who the angels are and that Abraham and Sarah's hospitality is being tested (as in analogues in other ancient literature), but Abraham and Sarah operate in ignorance of this information. Abraham intercedes in epic manner for the safety of Sodom (Gen. 18:22–33), but the ironic context is that the wickedness of the city is so great that no amount of bargaining will save it.

Storytellers are as addicted to *poetic justice* as they are to dramatic irony. Poetic justice (which in the Bible might more appropriately be called God's justice) occurs when good characters are rewarded and bad ones punished. Most stories end this way and thereby satisfy the reader's moral sense. Lot's greediness and worldly-mindedness are punished, while Abraham's faith in God is rewarded. Abraham's acts of expediency (previously noted) get him into trouble, while his acts of faith make him heroic.

By definition, stories narrate action. As a consequence, considerations of plot are bound to loom large in any analysis of a story. My analysis of plot conflict, suspense, and unity, as well as such plot devices as foils, dramatic irony, and poetic justice, has not constituted a complete analysis of the story of Abraham. But it is amazing how much is accounted for if we attend to the plot of a story. Plot is the organizing principle or backbone of a story. Without it, stories become a formless mass.

Character and the Story of Jacob

The question of whether plot or character is most important in producing a good story has generated debate throughout the centuries. Actually, these two ingredients set up a creative tension in a story. Some stories are more thoroughly plot stories, others more thoroughly character stories, but stories are finally an interaction between plot and character. Character produces action. Conversely, characters are known to us mainly through their actions, that is, through the plot.

Most literary critics and biblical expositors gravitate to plot as the basic framework for organizing a discussion of a story. I generally favor this procedure, but it requires more literary education to acquire the tools of plot analysis than it does to interact with the characters in a story. Events in a story are much more selective and highly structured than events in real life are, whereas characters in a story exist much as people in life do. I have often been favorably impressed by how thoroughly a student can handle a biblical story simply by concentrating on characterization.

In the discussion that follows, I will apply various considerations of characterization to the story of Jacob (Gen. 25:19 through Gen. 35). In the process, I hope to provide both a theoretic framework for characterization in all the stories of the Bible and a preliminary literary analysis of the story of one of the most colorful characters in the whole Bible.

Some Basic Terminology

I begin with a very brief excursion into the literary terms that pertain to characterization. It is really not possible to talk about the stories of the Bible without this basic vocabulary.

The central character in a story, whether sympathetic or unsympathetic, is the *protagonist*—the "first struggler" from whose viewpoint we go through the action. Characters arrayed against the protagonist go by the name *antagonist*. A *foil character* is a character that sets off or heightens another character, usually by being a contrast but occasionally by being a parallel. Jacob and Easu are obviously foils to each other throughout the story of Jacob.

It is natural to divide characters into the categories of *sympathetic* and *unsympathetic*, and of course many characters are in turn one and the other as a story unfolds. Whenever a character goes beyond being simply sympathetic to being the spokesperson or embodiment of the virtue or viewpoint that the storyteller espouses, that character can be called a *normative character* (embodying the standards, values, or norms that the story itself is offering for our approval). If a character is held up to satiric ridicule or rebuke, we can speak of a *satiric portrait*. A character who changes during the course of a story is a *developing character*, while one who remains the same is a *static character*.

Stories do not simply record the flow of events that happen to a person. They are much more selective and carefully structured than the events that happen to people in the course of a day. Part of this ordering is that in stories we are usually shown the *motivation* for a character's actions. To highlight human values, moreover, storytellers often build stories around *character transformation*.

How Writers Portray Character

We should briefly note the range of ways by which storytellers can choose to portray a character in a story. At the very least, this outline will help us to recognize when characterization is taking place. The simplest way in which storytellers present character is direct description or assessment. Here the writer tells us what a character is like. Consider this specimen:

> When the boys grew up, Esau was a skilful hunter, a man of the field, while Jacob was a quiet man, dwelling in tents. Isaac loved Esau, because he ate of his game; but Rebekah loved Jacob. [Gen. 25:27–28]

All we need to do is take the narrator's word for it. No act of interpretation is required of us. I should note emphatically, however, that this type of direct description and assessment of character by the storyteller is rare in the Bible. The usual way of portraying character is more indirect than this, requiring more interpretive activity on the part of the reader.

A second possibility is to portray character by showing how others respond to him or her. After Jacob has manipulated Esau into selling his birthright (Gen. 25:29–34) and has stolen the blessing (Gen. 27), Esau responds, "Is he not rightly named Jacob? For he has supplanted me these two times. He took away my birthright; and behold, now he has taken away my blessing" (Gen. 27:36). In this response from a brother, we see the character of Jacob highlighted: greedy, competitive, domineering, selfish, inconsiderate, unloving.

In addition to being characterized from the outside by either the narrator or other characters in the story, a character might be allowed to characterize himself or herself. An example occurs in Jacob's moving prayer uttered when he is at the end of his tether in fear over his approaching reunion with Esau:

> "O God of my father Abraham and God of my father Isaac, . . . I am not worthy of the least of all the steadfast love and all the faithfulness which thou hast shown to thy servant, for with only my staff I crossed this Jordan; and now I have become two companies." [Gen. 32:9–10]

Here, from Jacob's own mouth, is another accurate picture of the protagonist: God-fearing, son of a covenant line, unworthy of the success that God has bestowed on him, a person who started his adult life stripped of all his goods but now wealthy.

The commonest way by which biblical storytellers present their characters is not to have anyone tell us about them but simply to present them in action—either physical action, verbal action (speaking), or mental action (thinking). In the stories of the Bible, character is usually action. When Jacob performs an elaborate deception of his father (Gen. 27), we do not need anyone to tell us that he is a deceptive and fraudulent person; we have seen it with our own eyes. When Jacob single-handedly moves a stone from a well that usually required a whole group of shepherds to move (Gen. 29:10), his action establishes his enormous physical strength.

Viewed from the writer's perspective, then, there are four possible storytelling techniques by which to present character. One of three characters—the narrator, someone else in the story, or the person himself or herself—can describe and assess the character, or the character's own actions (whether external or mental) will embody one or more traits. The latter technique is the staple in biblical narrative.

How We Know What a Character Is Like

The foregoing section outlined the means by which storytellers can decide to portray a character. Regardless of how the writer chooses to "package" a character, that character is known to us in one or more of the following ways:

1. *Actions.* I would include a character's verbal actions (speech and language) here, since they are powerful actors in a story. Jacob's words and actions are characteristically either deceitful or calculating.
2. *Personal traits and abilities.* This is closely tied to the character's actions, but we can think of it as a separate category. It is the *interpretation* that we give to a character's actions. One of Jacob's traits is that he is the greatest lover among the patriarchs; one of the actions produced by this trait is that he worked seven years for Rachel, "and they seemed to him but a few days because of the love he had for her" (Gen. 29:20).
3. *Thoughts and feelings, including motivations and goals.* Performing actions and possessing certain abilities is only half of the picture; everything depends on the ends to which those actions and traits are directed. None of the patriarchs is as hard-working as Jacob. What drives this dynamo to work so relentlessly? Basically the drive to get ahead materially. Jacob is success-oriented.
4. *Relationships and roles.* Jacob is repeatedly known to us in terms of his relationship to God (a relationship in which God almost always takes the initiative) and his domestic roles (son, son-in-law, husband, father).
5. *Responses to events or people.* What characters do spontaneously in response to something that is placed before them tells us a great deal. When Jacob meets the pretty Rachel at the well, he kisses her and weeps aloud (Gen. 29:11), showing his strongly emotional temperament. His responses to promptings from God (e.g., at Bethel in Genesis 28:18–22, at the Brook Jabbok in Genesis 32:9–12, and in the return to Bethel in Genesis 35:1–15) show him in a much more favorable light than do his typical actions.
6. *Archetypal character types.* Sometimes we conceive a character's identity in terms of the additional category of a character type. Jacob is the archetypal trickster, in this instance a comic type that produces plenty of latent humor in the story.

This list strikes me as the most useful set of tools with which to go about getting to know a character in a story. I should guard against any appearance that this is a grocery list by which we have to measure every character that we encounter in the stories of the Bible. Good readers pay attention to these things intuitively. If the list seems burdensome, I would offer the following summary principle as an adequate way of dealing with characterization in a story: *View yourself as the observant traveling companion of the characters in a story (especially the protagonist) and simply get to know the characters as thoroughly as the details allow you to do.*

The Need to Interpret

I should guard against leaving the impression that getting to know a character is largely a descriptive process with little margin for error or variance. What I have nonchalantly called "getting to know a character" involves a continuous series of interpretive leaps and conclusions on the part of a reader.

For one thing, as readers we normally have to decide what a given detail in the story tells us about a character. When Jacob is reconciled with Esau (Gen. 33:1–11), we are told that he formed a careful procession with his children and wives, and "he himself went on before them, bowing himself to the ground seven times, until he came near his brother." It is up to the interpretive ability of the reader to see that the formal Jacob is comically overprepared (in contrast to the impulsive Esau, who "ran to meet him, and embraced him, and fell on his neck and kissed him"), and further that this is evidence of Jacob's calculating personality and guilty conscience.

In addition to drawing conclusions from specific details, a reader must be able to transform the particulars into an overall portrait of a person. When Jacob tricks Esau into selling his birthright for a mess of pottage, deceives his father into giving him the blessing, and concocts an elaborate plan to insure that Laban's flocks will produce spotted offspring (Gen. 30:37–42), it is obvious that Jacob belongs to the character type known as the trickster or con man. But the storyteller does not say this. It requires an act of interpretation from the reader.

Yet another type of interpretation that characterization requires is what I call choosing sides—determining whether a character is good or bad, sympathetic or unsympathetic, in a given trait or action. Of course there is always a possibility for variability of interpretation from one interpreter to another. Consider the incident in which Jacob awakens from his dream of the heavenly ladder at Bethel. Jacob vows, "If God will be with me, and will keep me in this way that I go, and will give me bread to eat and clothing to wear . . . of all that thou givest me I will give the tenth to thee" (Gen. 28:20–22). Is this yet another evidence of Jacob's scheming, mercenary, and bargaining mentality, rendered all the more repulsive by being directed toward God? Or is it evidence of a new capacity for spiritual response? As is usually true in biblical narrative, the writer narrates but does not explain what happens, and the reader is left to choose somewhat tentatively from alternate interpretations, realizing that usually the main meaning of the story is not affected by disagreements over interpretation of localized details.

I should note also that the unembellished style of biblical narrative, in which only the most important details are included and in which there is a minimum of authorial explanation, puts an even greater burden of interpretation on a reader. Alter is right to speak of "the Bible's highly laconic mode of narration" (p. 126). In biblical narrative, writes Auerbach, "the decisive points of the narrative alone are emphasized," and "therefore they require subtle investigation and interpretation" (pp. 11, 15). I should guard against the charge that this is a form of subjectivity introduced into the study of the Bible by the literary approach. Many biblical scholars have made unwarranted claims about how their methods establish objective controls on biblical interpretation. A survey of how biblical scholars interpret characterization in the stories of the Bible will reveal as much variability of interpretation as literary critics produce when they analyze characters in stories.

To illustrate all this theory about how characterization occurs in a story, I will conduct brief explications of selected episodes in the life of Jacob. I will limit my remarks to characterization, hoping to illustrate how much of the meaning of some biblical stories will emerge from an adequate analysis of characterization.

The Birth of the Hero (Gen. 25:19–26)

The characterization of the hero (Jacob) and his foil (Esau) in the story of their births foreshadows both the theme and the tone of the story that follows. An oracle from God predicts that *the one shall be stronger than the other, the elder shall serve the younger* (v. 23). Here is an interpretive framework for the entire story: within the story of salvation history, Jacob is the character of destiny, and there is a certain legitimacy about Jacob's supplanting Esau, though not in the way he goes about it.

The actual birth of the brothers in this episode foreshadows the comic tone of the story as a whole. The writer seizes upon what is laughable in the birth—the fact that the first came out red and hairy and that the second was grabbing the other's heel. In this comedy we can see something of the sheer humanity that is such a hallmark of the stories of Genesis. The story of the great patriarchs of Israel is filled not with grandeur but with the stuff of ordinary life.

Jacob's very first act in life captures his aggressive personality, and so does the name that the act earned him. We should note in passing that in the Bible people's names are something they either live up to or have to live down. The name *Jacob* means something like "grabby; he grabs by the heel; he supplants." The motif that unifies the story and that gets reenacted in every episode is the hero's living up to his basic identity (as Odysseus does in Homer's epic). The story of Jacob is the story of a hero who strives, who overcomes, who supplants.

One index to this emphasis is the concern in the story with Jacob's name. The motif begins in the story of his birth. It reappears when Jacob steals the blessing and Esau cries out, "Is he not rightly named Jacob? For he has supplanted me these two times." When Jacob wrestles with God and asks for a blessing, the angel asks, "What is your name?" (Gen. 32:27). Jacob gets a new name, but one that retains the idea of striving ("Israel," meaning "he who strives with God"). This emphasis on striving with people and God is the key to the hero's characterization. The portrait of Jacob that emerges from his story in Genesis is mainly a satiric portrait. Jacob is a deeply flawed character through most of his story.

The Selling of the Birthright (Gen. 25:27–34)

This story of sibling rivalry is based on an elaborate foil between two brothers. We are told at the outset that "Esau was a skilful hunter, a man of the field, while Jacob was a quiet man, dwelling in tents" (v. 27), and that each was favored by a different parent. The story is basically an outworking of this character situation of sibling rivalry and incompatibility. The story is told in such a way, moreover, as to render both brothers unsympathetic.

Jacob emerges from the episode as the clever schemer. He aggressively takes advantage of his brother's hunger by offering a bowl of stew in exchange for the birthright. He is devious, unfair, opportunistic, unscrupulous, unloving, materialistic (the birthright assured him of a double portion of the inheritance), willing to exploit a brother for his own advantage. His calculating mentality and business sense are evident in the fact that he makes Esau swear an oath, thereby making the exchange legally binding. It is a thoroughly negative portrait—an example of what anyone with a healthy moral sense would reject.

But lest we make the mistake of therefore sympathizing with Esau, the storyteller conducts the characterization of Esau in such a way as to make him even more unsympathetic in the story. Esau is an overgrown infant, whining that he is *about to die* simply because he is hungry. He is someone with an inverted sense of values, who lives only for the moment, is unable to postpone immediate gratification for a future benefit, and has no appreciation for the covenant promises that accompanied this particular birthright. The very vocabulary used by and about Esau demonstrates his lack of manners and vulgarity. English translations tone down Esau's speech in verse 30; an accurate rendering is, *Let me gulp down some of this red stuff.*[12] From this episode, the narrator tells us, Esau got his uncomplimentary nickname "Red" (v. 30). And in the final verse of the episode, the writer gives us "a staccato succession of five verbal forms *[ate, drank, rose, went, despised]* . . . calculated to point up Esau's lack of manners and judgment" (Speiser, p. 195).

The main meaning of the story emerges from what I have said about its characterization. There are two main themes, one moral in emphasis, the other spiritual. Esau's character focuses on the issue of values. The narrator's parting shot tells us that Esau *despised his birthright* (or as Speiser translates it, *misprized his birthright*), alerting us that Esau earned the Bible's later assessment of him as an *irreligious* or *profane* (KJV) person, insensitive to spiritual values. The proverb about selling one's birthright for a mess of pottage expresses it very well. The characterization of Jacob shifts the focus to a moral theme: by his unbrotherly behavior, Jacob shows what selfishness can do to family relations and one's own character.

The Stolen Blessing (Gen. 27)

The story of the stolen blessing is from a literary viewpoint one of the best stories ever told. It is filled with conflict, intrigue, suspense, dramatic irony (stemming from mistaken identity), and sudden discovery. But all of this richness of plot comes alive because of the characters involved.

The story is told like a play. The action falls into five acts or scenes, with two characters "on stage" in each act. As in a play, the impact of the story depends heavily on spectacle, and there is emphasis on dialogue and gesture, with the "stage directions" written right into the text. In keeping with all this drama, the writer presents the characters and events objectively, as if we were watching them on a stage, leaving us to draw our conclusions about the meaning.

Isaac and Esau are the victims of treachery in the episode, but this should not lead us to sympathize with them. Isaac is guilty of favoritism, and he prefers Esau for trivial and indulgent reasons (in fact, life seems to have narrowed down to Isaac's stomach in his old age). He ignores the earlier sale of the birthright and tries to thwart God's plan as announced by the oracle. Esau tries to violate the oath he swore when he sold the birthright and at the end of the event plots Jacob's murder.

Jacob once again lives up to his basic identity as the one who supplants. In this story of intrigue we are impressed by his ability to carry out a fraud based on mistaken identity. Once he enters Isaac's tent, Isaac's repeated questions show his incredulity and not only make it possible that Jacob will

12. Derek Kidner, *Genesis: An Introduction and Commentary* (Chicago: Inter-Varsity, 1967), p. 152. This work is a concise source of excellent literary commentary on Genesis.

get caught—they make it seem likely. Yet in all this suspense Jacob shows himself resourceful, crafty, dishonest, greedy—exactly what we have come to expect of this trickster. As for the mother who instigates the fraud, she is dishonest, guilty of parental favoritism, and domineering over her son (who, in fact, initially tries to get out of the scheme).

All four characters in this sordid family drama are portrayed unsympathetically. There is poetic justice, therefore, when they all end up losers at the conclusion of this emotion-packed event.

Jacob's Dream at Bethel (Gen. 28:10–22)

As narrated in Genesis, Jacob's life falls into three main parts that form a circle: early life in the parental home, a twenty-year exile in Haran, and a return to the land of the hero's origins. At the beginning of each phase, an encounter between God and Jacob foreshadows the next movement of the story. First there is the oracle that predicts that Jacob will supplant Esau. At Bethel God gives Jacob the promises of the covenant, even though Jacob does nothing to merit the prosperity that will be his. Later God wrestles with Jacob and gives him his covenant name, signaling the new and more sympathetic character that we find in the later stages of Jacob's life.

To sense what is happening in Jacob's life when he dreams of God at Bethel, we can profitably put the protagonist into the archetypal pattern of the young hero undertaking a secret or dangerous journey of initiation that will lead to his adulthood. Caught at a critical transition in his life, cut loose from the apron strings, Jacob is undergoing an identity crisis. We have gone on this journey of initiation many other times in our literary experience—with Joseph, Telemachus, Aeneas, Young Goodman Brown, and Huckleberry Finn, for example.

But it is not only the general pattern that is important in such stories. We also need to pay attention to what is unique in each reenactment of an archetype. In this story, an unworthy young man is brought into encounter with God by means of a miraculous vision in which angels ascend and descend. Here, in symbolic form, is something of which Jacob is hardly aware at this point in his human strivings—relationship with a covenant God who promises to bless *all the families of the earth* through him. Jacob's response upon awaking—*surely the LORD is in this place; and I did not know it*—shows, in however rudimentary fashion, a capacity for transcendental experience that we would not have guessed up to this point in the story.

Jacob and Laban (Gen. 29–31)

I will make no attempt to deal in detail with the story of Jacob's chaotic twenty years with his Uncle Laban. The sheer ambiguity of human character in its mixture of good and bad permeates the story. Jacob emerges from it all as a physically and psychologically strong but very worldly-minded person.

The technique of characterization that is particularly well illustrated here is that of the character foil. Jacob and Laban are mirrors of each other. They are both equally grasping, greedy, and competitive. Who would dare to buy a used camel from either one of them? They richly deserve each other, and when they get together the sparks fly. They are foils to each other in the sense that each highlights the bad qualities of the other. This satiric account is filled with the kind of humor that we have come to expect from stories that portray the archetypal trickster, a variation of the likeable or comic rogue.

Jacob's Wrestling with God (Gen. 32)

Jacob's story reaches its climax in the story of his epic wrestling match with a divine opponent. Here his character is transformed as he comes to an end of himself and into submission to God. The action occurs in the dark, in an atmosphere of danger and mystery that test character to the uttermost. There is something elemental about the character with whom we undergo the experience: he sent *everything that he had* across the stream, *and Jacob was left alone.* Jacob is thus reduced to essential humanity, like King Lear on the heath.

The whole earlier characterization of Jacob converges here. His immense strength is such that the wrestling continues *until the breaking of the day*, and yet the angelic wrestler *did not prevail against Jacob.* Jacob is still the one who grabs by the heel. When the angel commands that Jacob let him go, Jacob replies, *I will not let you go, unless you bless me.* Here, too, is Jacob's capacity to recognize supernatural reality when he finds it, as when he awoke from his dream at Bethel. God redirects and transforms but does not obliterate the hero's identity in the episode. His new name, *Israel*, retains the basic meaning of striving and overcoming, as indicated in the angel's statement:

> "Your name shall no more be called Jacob, but Israel, for you have striven with God and with men, and have prevailed."

The episode is the moment of epiphany toward which the story of Jacob moves. As the hero leaves the combat, *the sun rose upon him*, symbolic of a new beginning, and he goes *limping because of his thigh*, symbolic of the submission that he has reached before God.

Jacob had thought that his meeting with his brother the next day was his big problem. But when the reconciliation occurs (Gen. 33:1–11), it is anticlimatic. In this we can see a major strand in the characterization of

Jacob: through most of his life he was so preoccupied with life at the earthly level that he missed what was primary, his walk with God. It has been a satiric portrait, richly human and ending with a climactic encounter with God. The memorability of the story of Jacob rests largely in the colorful character of the hero, who generates conflict wherever he goes.

From Story to Meaning

Entering as fully as possible into the world of a biblical story is a necessary part of understanding the story. To get the point of a story, we need to participate in what happens to the characters. After all, the truthfulness of literature is partly a truthfulness to human experience. The stories of the Bible are not a collection of ideas. They consist of characters performing actions in lifelike settings. The prime literary rule of interpretation is *meaning through form*. Whatever a story communicates, it communicates through setting, character, and action. It is therefore necessary, not frivolous, to interact with a biblical story *as a story*.

But if this is a necessary part of understanding biblical narrative, it is not sufficient in itself. It is true that stories convey part of their truth simply by getting us to share an experience with the characters in the story. But any complete understanding of a story depends on our ability to formulate the intellectual truth of the story as well—not as a substitute for the imaged reality of the settings, characters, and events, but as an interpretive lens through which we see their significance. All of this is a way of saying that we need a methodology for getting from the story to the theme—from setting, character, and plot to an intellectual grasp of what the story is about and the perspective that the writer expects us to take toward that subject. To illustrate how we move from story to meaning, I have somewhat arbitrarily chosen the story about the separation of Abraham and Lot in Genesis 13.

The Story as a Story

The process begins with our interacting with the story as a story, that is, with the setting, characters, and plot. By being closely tied to the surface details of the story, this process tends toward description, but as suggested by my discussion earlier in this chapter, even in this phase of reading we are busy making interpretive leaps and drawing conclusions based on our description.

Setting precipitates the action of this story as the land itself is unable to support the combined herds of Abraham and Lot. Having generated the opening conflict, setting continues to be important in the story. In fact, choosing a setting is the main action of the story. The place that Lot chooses as his place to live is given a vivid physical identity. We read that

Lot "saw that the Jordan valley was well watered everywhere like the garden of the LORD, like the land of Egypt" (v. 10). At a physical level, this landscape is synonymous with material prosperity and wealth. But there is even more symbolism to the setting. Sodom has a strong moral identity in this story. It is a moral monstrosity, being associated with both sexual perversion and (on the basis of Ezekiel 16:49–50) the indifference of a materialistic society to the needs of the poor.

When we move from setting to character, we find our attention drawn equally to Lot and Abraham. We view them, as we usually do in biblical narrative, from the outside. The writer tells us what they do, but not why they do it. This is something we are left to infer from external action. As we observe Lot in action, we have no difficulty in inferring that he is selfish, greedy, materialistic, and willing to flirt with known evil. Abraham is a foil to all that: he is generous (allowing Lot to make the first choice and willing to take what is left), close to God, and content with God's promises for the future instead of immediate tangible advantage.

As for the plot of the story, it has an abundance of conflict—physical conflict in the form of people against their environment and family discord over money matters. Athough conflict thus initiates the action, the plot as a whole turns upon another staple of stories, choice. The main action is a great, life-changing choice that two characters make.

This brief analysis of the surface details in the story has laid the groundwork for interpreting what the story as a whole means. Let me say in passing that meanings emerge from literary *wholes*. We must, of course, describe and interpret the details accurately, but it is finally the whole story that embodies the theme(s). The meaning of a story does not consist primarily of making moralizing statements about the details as we move through a story.

Interpretive Presuppositions

In turning from analysis of setting, character, and plot to interpretations of what these mean, let me clarify the presuppositions that we will benefit from making at the outset. One of the interpretive assumptions that we make of stories is that storytellers intend to communicate meaning. Even in their choice of what stories to recount, storytellers gravitate toward stories in which (to use the French writer Baudelaire's words) "the deep significance of life reveals itself."[13] Surely this is the impression we get from the stories of the Bible. The primary rule of narrative interpretation is thus the rule of significance: we assume that the writer intends to say something significant about reality and human experience.

13. Quoted by J. Middleton Murry, *The Problem of Style* (London: Oxford University Press, 1922), p. 30.

A second presupposition is that the characters in a story (especially the protagonist) are intended to be representative or exemplary of people generally. In the words of O'Connor, "Any character . . . is supposed to carry a burden of meaning larger than himself" (p. 167). From at least as far back as Aristotle, this principle of universality has been one of the tests that people have used to determine whether something is literary in nature. A piece of literature is always up-to-date. If we can see our own experience in the characters and events of a story, it has captured something universal about life. History tells us what happened, while literature tells us what happens. The stories of the Bible, of course, do both, but it is important to realize that every good sermon or Bible study based on a biblical narrative is based on the literary principle that what happened to the characters in the story is somehow a model of the enduring human situation.

A third presupposition that I make of stories is that the characters (especially the protagonist) undertake an experiment in living. This experiment is tested during the course of the story. Its final success or failure is a comment on the adequacy or inadequacy of the morality or world view on which the experiment was based. Here is how two scholars have stated the matter: when we read a story, they claim, we are

> drawn into a confrontation with the protagonist. . . . We should consider the hero as one who makes an ultimate experiment—as one taking some line of action which in effect tests the kind of life he believes in. This way of reading considers the character . . . as one who pursues his experiment to its final stages and within a situation of ultimate meaning.[14]

What the Story Is About

We can profitably divide the task of interpreting a story into two steps. Keeping in mind that a storyteller both presents human experience and offers an interpretation of it, we should first identify what the story is about and then determine how the writer expects us to view that experience.

Repetition is often the best clue to what a story is about. Surely this is true of the story of Abraham as a whole, where, for example, his quest for a son, the progressive revelation of the covenant, and the conflict within Abraham between faith and expedience keep getting repeated. Within a single episode like Genesis 13, however, the very brevity of the account makes it unlikely that repetition will be the clue.

Instead, *highlighting* is our most reliable guide. The thing highlighted in this chapter is the choices that two characters make. The choice of Lot,

14. Richard Stevens and Thomas J. Musial, *Reading, Discussing, and Writing about the Great Books* (Boston: Houghton Mifflin, 1970), p. 24.

especially, is centrally placed in the middle paragraph (vv. 8–14) and therefore gets silhouetted with particular clarity. An opening paragraph (vv. 1–7) leads up to it, and a follow-up paragraph (vv. 14–18) casts a retrospective light on it. The follow-up paragraph, moreover, is a foil to the choice of Lot, and this is a specific form of highlighting. The choice of Lot stands out all the more clearly for its being contrasted to the choice of Abraham. I have already noted the nature of that contrast: Lot chooses on the basis of economic gain and is willing to live close to evil, while Abraham remains the archetypal wanderer, content with the promises of God in the absence of immediate tangible benefits.

What is the story about? It is about choosing a place to live, a lifestyle, a vocation, on two different foundations. It is a story about priorities.

From Topic to Theme

Once we have discovered what a biblical story is about (and it might be about more than one thing), we need to complete the task of interpretation by determining exactly what the storyteller says about and with that subject matter. What perspective are we invited to share with the storyteller as we look at the experience that is presented? The common literary term for this is *point of view*.

Storytellers can do two basic things to impose their interpretive point of view on the material. They can enter the story and comment on characters and events in their own voice. I call this *authorial assertion*. It happens at least once in the story of the separation of Abraham and Lot. Having said that Lot moved his tent as far as Sodom, the narrator tells us, "Now the men of Sodom were wicked, great sinners against the LORD" (v. 13).

Although such authorial commentary does occur in the stories of the Bible, the significant thing is how rarely it happens compared to what we find in stories outside the Bible. Sometimes the storytellers only move in the direction of authorial assertion. In the present story, the narrator does not tell us that Lot chose the Jordan valley because he was materialistic, but he makes it easy for us to draw that conclusion when he gives us this picture of what lies behind Lot's choice:

> And Lot lifted up his eyes, and saw that the Jordan valley was well watered everywhere like the garden of the LORD. [v. 10]

In our minds, Sodom is synonymous with sexual perversion, but the writer of Genesis wants us to see also the materialism of the place. We can catch a hint here of the later biblical portrait of Sodom as a city where people "had pride, surfeit of food, and prosperous ease, but did not aid the poor and needy. They were haughty . . . " (Ezek. 16:49–50).

A variation of the technique of a writer's commenting directly on the meaning of an event consists of placing the right or normative interpretation in the mouth of a character in the story. Sometimes as we read a story we encounter speeches by participants in the action that intuitively strike us as summing up what the story is saying. Whenever a character in a story thus interprets the meaning of the story, we can speak of a *normative spokesperson* in the story.

Within the Bible there is a special category of stories with normative characters, namely, stories in which God makes a stated or implied comment on the meaning of the action. The concluding paragraph of Genesis 13 (vv. 14–18) is in effect such an appearance by God. While God stops short of commending Abraham for having made the right choice in contrast to the choice of Lot, God's renewal of the covenant promise has the effect of placing divine sanction on Abraham's behavior in this episode. The pattern that we see here is common in ancient literature—the pattern of reward following a hero's passing a test.

In addition to putting the right interpretation of a story into the story itself, either in the form of direct authorial comment or a statement by a normative character, storytellers embody their point of view in their very *selectivity and arrangement* of details. There is, of course, always more than one way to tell a story. The story as it finally stands has been consciously assembled by the author for a calculated effect on the audience. In other words, storytellers control what we see and don't see, how we see it, and when we see it.

As for selectivity, we should operate on the premise that everything included in a story was included for a specific reason. O'Connor commented that a storyteller "makes his statements by selection, and if he is any good, he selects every word for a reason, every detail for a reason, every incident for a reason" (p. 75). We can also profitably reflect on how the story would be different if a given detail were omitted.

A particularly good illustration of this occurs in verse 10, where after telling us that the Jordan valley was a veritable paradise the writer adds a crucial piece of foreshadowing: *this was before the Lord destroyed Sodom and Gomorrah.* This is more than a piece of necessary explanation to the effect that the valley was different then than it is now. By thus alluding to the destruction of Sodom (a destruction that is narrated in one of the most vivid stories in the whole Bible), the writer unleashes in our consciousness moral revulsion against the moral monstrosity that Sodom represents. This effect is reinforced by the narrator's implied amazement at the sheer audacity of Lot in flirting with known evil: *Lot . . . moved his tent as far as Sodom* (v. 12).

In addition to selectivity, there is arrangement. The way in which a story ends is especially crucial in determining a reader's final impression. The effect of Genesis 13 is far different as it stands than it would be if the last paragraph were omitted. We end Genesis 13 with a sharp contrast in our minds and imaginations. On one side, we remember Lot lifting up his eyes to the well-watered Jordan valley and choosing to compromise his spiritual integrity on the basis of material advantage. On the other side, we hear God promising Abraham the whole land of Canaan, with Abraham implicitly being content with something as intangible as God's promise.

The rule of interpretation here is that we should look upon the conclusion of a story as an implied evaluation of the characters and events that the story has presented. The outcome of an action is an implied evaluation of it. At this point we need to place the episode of the separation of Abraham and Lot into the bigger narrative world of Genesis 12–25. It is one building block in a bigger edifice. The story of choice in Genesis 13 is the kind of crossroads experience that calls for a sequel. This is exactly what we get later in Genesis. Abraham's life blossoms into a life of spiritual and domestic blessing. In contrast, Lot's life degenerates into a sordid end (Genesis 19 tells the whole sickening story).

To sum up, storytellers use *devices of disclosure*, relatively subtle in nature, to influence how we interpret the meaning of stories. The writer of Genesis influences our *patterns of sympathy and aversion* toward characters and events in the story. Stories are affective in their strategy. They are a carefully designed system of influences on the audience. Responses can, of course, be ill-informed or simply wrong, but we cannot move from story to meaning without being sensitive to our own responses. The rule of interpretation that I have been urging is simply this: *Pay attention to the devices of disclosure by which a storyteller influences you to approve or disapprove of the characters, events, and settings of a story, and formulate what the story communicates about morality or values on the basis of this pattern.*

The Story as a Whole

Having isolated the elements of narrative and devoted separate sections to setting, plot, character, and theme, I find it necessary to close this chapter by heeding O'Connor's dictum that "the whole story is the meaning" (p. 73). In a well-told story, everything works together to produce the final effect. To illustrate the principle of composite narrative effect, I will conduct a brief explication of the story of Lot's rescue in Genesis 19.

The story is replete with conflict. Overiding the whole event is the moral conflict between God and the wicked city. Early in the action Lot struggles against the men of the city who surround his house. In the same incident we see the conflict within Lot between the obligations of a host to his guests and a father to his daughters. Later in the story Lot stands arguing with the angels about the escape route as the city is about to go up in flames, and the angels actually have to drag him, whimpering and protesting, from destruction.

The suspense of the story is intense and is the type that never loses its grip on us. Here is the type of action in which the suspense lives perpetually. No matter how well we know the story, it is told in such a way as to encourage us to wonder again whether Lot and his family will make it out of the city before it is destroyed.

Almost everything in the story, moreover, is heightened if we are aware that it is half of an elaborate foil with the preceding chapter of Genesis, where Abraham and Sarah entertain the same two angels in a relaxed pastoral setting. In contrast to the idealized rural world, here we have the wicked city. The angels visit Abraham to announce God's blessing, and they visit Lot to announce God's judgment. Instead of sitting down to a relaxing dinner, the angels this time have to deal with a terrifying mob. Abraham's family situation is about to reach its finest hour, while Lot's is about to end in the tragic loss of a sinful wife and incest between a drunken father and his daughters. Abraham's wife laughs in incredulity over God's blessing, while Lot's wife looks back in incredulity over God's judgment.

Characterization in the story is a triumph of understatement and indirection. The narrator engages in no moralizing over the characters. He lets their actions do the talking. To let us know what has become of Lot during the years in Sodom, the writer simply shows us the close link between Lot and Sodom. When the angels arrive in the evening (in contrast to the noontime visit to Abraham, incidentally), *Lot [is] sitting in the gate of Sodom* (v. 1), meaning that he was a member of the town council. In verse 7 Lot calls the townspeople *my brothers*. Later he lingers in the city until the angels finally *seized him . . . by the hand, . . . and set him outside the city* (v. 16). Once outside the city, Lot cannot envision life without at least a touch of Sodom in his life (vv. 18–20).

How can we reconcile this portrait of Lot with the picture in 2 Peter 2:6–10, where Lot is pictured as a righteous person, "greatly distressed by the licentiousness of the wicked" and "vexed in his righteous soul day after day with their lawless deeds"? Far from being incompatible with the Genesis story, this account highlights the tension of the story. We have here the spectacle of someone who cannot tear himself away from evil but who lives in it with a very bad conscience (see Kidner, p. 135). We might remember also that in the previous chapter Abraham interceded for "the righteous" of the city. This discrepancy between Lot's outward behavior and inner conviction produces the grim irony of the story—an ironic incongruity between what is and what ought to be, between behavior and conscience.

Life in Sodom has taken an even greater toll from Lot's wife and daughters. The daughters have become engaged to the only men available to them, and they end up committing incest with their father after having made him drunk. The characterization of Lot's wife was rendered memorable in the aphorism of Jesus, "Remember Lot's wife" (Luke 17:32). Jesus' cryptic comment is a tribute to the ability of literary images to embody truth. In the sheer spectacle of Lot's wife turned into a pillar of salt we can see a main principle of the whole story—inability to leave a sinful lifestyle behind, perhaps accompanied by incredulity about God's judgment.

From a literary point of view, the realism of the story is both striking and an important part of its meaning. In literary terminology, realism means writing that portrays life precisely as it is, without glossing its sordid side. In this story we encounter examples of homosexuality, drunkenness, and incest. The inclusion of such a story in the Bible alerts us that the Bible does not escape from real life. Its aim is thoroughly literary—to make us see life as it really is. In this story we are led to see immorality as it really is—repulsive, self-destructive, destructive of society, infectious, controlling anyone who lets it become a habit.

In addition to the literary realism, we should note the archetypes that are also an important part of the meaning. The plot motif that governs the action is the rescue, made all the more vivid by the reluctance of Lot and his family to be rescued.

The setting of the action is equally archetypal—the wicked city that is so prominent in literature generally and the Bible specifically. One function of stories is to help us organize our own experience by presenting for our contemplation powerful images that sum up important elements of life. In this story the image of the city becomes a symbol of people in community against God, and of the depths to which a person's sexual nature can descend. The impulse of the literary imagination is not to give us a discourse about sin but a picture of it.

A third master image of literature that appears here in memorable form is the image of cataclysmic destruction, associated in the Bible with God's judgment. The fire and brimstone that destroy Sodom and Gomorrah elicit our natural terror, just as the image of the city itself elicits our moral terror.

The story is the meaning. The intermixture of characters, events, realism, and archetypes add up to a picture of human fascination with evil and divine judgment against it. Put into the broader story of Genesis, here is the outcome of Lot's experiment in living. All of this is put into focus by Derek Kidner's comment about the story: "It is a superb study of the two aspects of judgment: the cataclysmic, as the cities disappear in brimstone and fire, and the gradual, as Lot and his family reach the last stages of disintegration" (p. 134). It is a story in which all of us participate. In that sense the Bible is a subversive book. It draws us into its stories in such a way that we see into the dark corners of our own souls. But of course the world of biblical narrative is a world of light as well as shadow. If there is destruction, there is also rescue. Biblical narrative is simultaneously an encounter with evil and an invitation to participate in a great rescue.

3

Artistry in Biblical Narrative

When I speak of artistry in this book, I am concerned with discourse (whether in prose or poetry) that calls attention to *how* the material is presented as distinct from *what* is said. In particular, I mean elements of pattern or design that call attention to themselves. Artistry is not simply literary excellence but excellence of a specific kind, namely, the ability to arrange material in ways that advertise the conscious craftsmanship of the writer.

This urge for pattern is what the modern Welsh poet Dylan Thomas had in mind when he said that he liked "to treat words as a craftsman does his wood or stone. . . , to hew, carve, mold, coil, polish, and plane them into patterns, sequences, sculptures. . . ."[1] The Bible possesses an abundance of this crafted quality. We have no way of knowing whether it is the result of the individual writer's self-conscious artistry, or inspiration, or the community's joint effort as it passed stories and poems along orally. All we really need to do is notice and enjoy such artistry. Its twin purposes are to add to the beauty of life and heighten the impact of an utterance.

1. Dylan Thomas, "Poetic Manifesto," in *The Poet's Work: Twenty-nine Masters of Twentieth-Century Poetry on the Origins and Practice of Their Art*, ed. Reginald Gibbons (Boston: Houghton Mifflin, 1979), pp. 185–86.

Artistry occurs in all the literary genres and in all the arts. The elements that comprise it include unity, central focus, pattern, variety in unity, progression, balance, contrast, symmetry, repetition, and recurrence or rhythm. In the present chapter I am concerned to show how these elements of artistic form pervade the stories of the Bible. They can be made from something as small as individual words arranged into patterns and as large as the episodes that make up a story. My explication of artistry in selected stories of Genesis illustrates what can be done with biblical narrative in general.

Genesis 1

Genesis 1 is the Bible's creation story. It is "matchless in its solemn and majestic simplicity."[2] The only active character in the story is God, whose mighty acts are the sole focus of our attention. The structural principle underlying the story is not plot conflict but the chronological catalogue of God's creative acts during the creation week. The absence of conflict in the story sets it apart from other ancient creation stories, which are stories of battle or strife. In the Babylonian creation story, for example, a female deity named Tiamat was cut in half by her son Marduk; half of Tiamat became heaven and half became earth. By contrast, the story of creation in Genesis 1 is the very epitome of harmony.

By means of its concentrated focus on the acts of God, the story conveys an overwhelming sense of God's transcendence. The very abruptness of the story's opening ("In the beginning God . . .") conveys this tone of authority. This divine hero needs no background explanation of who he is or how he came to be doing what he is doing, in contrast to other ancient creation stories. The latter are actually theogonies (stories about the origins of the gods) and therefore stress such background. Genesis 1 "has no notion of the birth of God and no biography of God. . . . To the Bible, God's existence is as self-evident as is life itself."[3]

The setting of the story reinforces its elemental simplicity. The physical setting is unlocalized and general. The dominant imagery is that of sky, water, and earth. The temporal setting, far in the distant past, at the margin of eternity and time, is equally indistinct.

This majestic simplicity is not unartistic, however. In fact, no story of the Bible is told with such self-conscious artistry as this one. The very style

2. Nahum M. Sarna, *Understanding Genesis: The Heritage of Biblical Israel* (1966; New York: Schocken, 1970), p. 10.

3. Ibid. C. S. Lewis argues that the Bible's way of beginning by answering the question, "Who made the world?" is itself unique, and that "creation, in any unambiguous sense, seems to be a surprisingly rare doctrine." See *Reflections on the Psalms* (New York: Harcourt, Brace and World, 1958), pp. 78–80.

of the story is a fit form for the content, which consists of God's great artistic act of creation. I should note in passing that it is precisely this artistic quality of the story that most obviously sets Genesis 1 apart from other ancient creation stories. In the parallel stories, it is hard even to follow what is happening.[4] By contrast, Genesis 1 contains such an abundance of artistry that it is difficult to discuss the story without using the terminology of visual art and music to describe the literary effects.

One element of artistic form that pervades the story is *recurrence*. The action of the story falls into six days of activity, each of which follows a similar pattern of events. The account of each day of creation begins with the common formula, *And God said, "Let. . . ."* A common refrain closes each day of creation: *And there was evening and there was morning. . . .* Other repeated phrases reinforce the effect: *Let there be . . .; God called . . .; and it was so; God saw that it was good.* Such repetition creates a ritualistic effect. In the words of Claus Westermann, "The first chapter of the Bible strikes one . . . like a mysterious song, like a festal celebration—one could almost say, like a heavenly liturgy. With a solemn, ponderous rhythm the same phrases keep reappearing throughout the entire chapter. It affects one as a litany."[5]

Along with this repetition there is elaborate *symmetry and design* in the story. It consists of the fixed pattern that underlies each day of creation. The pattern has five ingredients:

1. Announcement (*And God said . . .*).
2. Command (*Let there be*, or *let it be gathered*, or *let it bring forth*).
3. Report (*And it was so*, or, *And God made*).
4. Evaluation (*And God saw that it was good*).
5. Placement in a temporal framework (*And there was evening and there was morning, a [number stated] day*).

But this fixed pattern is played off against *variety*. Only one of the days of creation (the fourth) contains the five elements in sequence. Four of the other days repeat at least one of the ingredients, and the second day omits the evaluation. Only two days (the first and fifth) follow an identical pattern. The artistic principle at work is obviously *variety in unity*, or freedom within form.

Unified progression is yet another element of artistic form in the story. Each act of creation builds on something that has preceded. Thus the

---

4. For confirmation, see the creation stories collected by James B. Pritchard, ed., *Near Eastern Texts Relating to the Old Testament* (Princeton: Princeton University Press, 1950).

5. Claus Westermann, *The Genesis Accounts of Creation*, trans. Norman E. Wagner (Philadelphia: Fortress, 1964), p. 6.

creation of sky and sea precedes the creation of birds and sea creatures, and the creation of land occurs before the creation of land animals and man. The effect of reading Genesis 1 is like watching a painter paint a picture beginning with a blank area, then sketching a broad outline, and then filling in the details and colors. Someone has correctly stated that "the most striking feature of the Biblical record of creation is its progressiveness. Creation is described as a developing sequence."[6]

This progression moves in stately procession to the *climax*, which is also the finale—the creation of people. Several features of the account point to the uniqueness of the human creature. The paragraph devoted to the creation of people is by far the longest one in the chapter, and the five elements already noted are repeated until they explode into a total of fourteen units. The sheer abundance of details breaks the pattern that has been established. Instead of commanding *let there be*, God here communes with himself: *let us make man in our image* (v. 26). No other creature carries such a close resemblance to its creator. And to people alone God gives the command to *have dominion . . . over all the earth* (v. 26). Also climactic is the way in which the earlier statements that God saw that what he had created on a given day *was good* now rise to a crescendo in the comprehensive statement that *God saw everything that he had made, and behold, it was very good* (v. 31).

In a story where the various art forms keep coalescing and where various elements of artistic form combine, it is impossible to talk about the unified progression without also noting the elaborate element of *balance* that underlies the story. The basic pattern is three balanced pairs of days in which three settings are first created and then filled with appropriate creatures in the same sequence. Put into chart form, the balanced pattern looks like table 2.

Table 2 **The pattern of Genesis 1**

1	light	4	light bearers
2	sky and sea	5	birds and sea creatures
3	dry land and vegetation	6	land animals and man

Another balanced pattern that underlies the story is the simultaneous presence of images of order and images of energy. In this story the great opposites of human experience—rule and energy, order and impulse, restraint and abundance—complement each other.

On the one hand, the process of creation is described as an instantaneous act of God's word and as an ordering process. We might call it the

6. J. Barton Payne, *The Theology of the Older Testament* (Grand Rapids: Zondervan, 1962), p. 136.

technique of the creating word. God speaks and commands, and it comes to pass. The commands are breathtaking in their simplicity, as is the instantaneous obedience of the forces of nature: *And God said, "Let there be light"; and there was light* (v. 3). In this pattern, the verbs name acts of ordering, as God is said to have *separated, called,* and *set.*

But the technique of the creating word is balanced by passages that describe creation as an act of biological generation. The emphasis here is on living organisms producing other organisms in biological fashion. The imagery is physical rather than abstract, and the language stresses energy and vitality rather than rule and order. We read about *plants yielding seed* and *fruit trees bearing fruit in which is their seed,* about how *the earth put forth vegetation* and about how *the waters bring forth swarms of living creatures.* This motif reaches its climax in God's command to creatures to *be fruitful and multiply and fill the waters in the seas, and let birds multiply on the earth* (v. 22). Such images of overflowing generative energy complement the passages that describe creation as an ordering process brought about instantly by the word of God.

The Bible's creation story is not simply told with artistry; it is told with *conscious* artistry. There would have been other ways to tell the story than the highly patterned narrative that I have described. But the writer went out of his way to be artistic. Note, for example, the parallelism and verbatim repetition in verses 11 and 12:

> And God said, "Let the earth put forth vegetation, plants yielding seed, and fruit trees bearing fruit in which is their seed, each according to its kind, upon the earth." And it was so. The earth brought forth vegetation, plants yielding seed according to their own kinds, and trees bearing fruit in which is their seed, each according to its kind.

The story conveys a tremendous sense of *wholeness and completeness.* This is especially evident in verses that conclude the story, the first three verses of Genesis 2:

> Thus the heavens and the earth were finished, and all the host of them. And on the seventh day God finished his work which he had done. So God blessed the seventh day and hallowed it, because on it God rested from all his work which he had done in creation.

Here we find the first evidence in the Bible of the tendency to associate the idea of completeness with the number seven and the conception of a week. Here, too, is the note of rest after labor and celebration after the hero's performance of his mighty feat. Westermann is right to place the story of creation alongside the Old Testament psalms of praise that extol God as Creator (p. 5).

The Bible's story of creation begins with the evocative phrase *in the beginning.* It rises to a majestic display of God's creative power and artistry. And it ends on the note that *God finished his work which he had done* (Gen. 2:2). No other story in the Bible better embodies the paradox of majesty in simplicity.

Genesis 2

The artistry of Genesis 2 will emerge if we simply treat it as a companion story to Genesis 1. The impulse to compose pairs of art works (or simply to place art objects in pairs) is pervasive. The basic principle at work in such companion pieces is balance, and the dominant activity that an audience intuitively performs is to compare details in the two works. It so happens that many of the interpretive problems that some readers have seen in Genesis 1 and 2 will take care of themselves if we simply read Genesis 2 as a companion story to Genesis 1.

Genesis 2 is not a rival creation story that contradicts Genesis 1. It makes no attempt to cover the same territory. Genesis 1 is correctly entitled "The Creation of the World." Genesis 2 can appropriately be labeled "Life in Paradise." Once we realize that Genesis 2 is not a different version of the same events as were narrated in Genesis 1 but an entirely different story, the supposed discrepancies between the two accounts vanish.

Genesis 2 makes no attempt to recapitulate the creation of the cosmos. It is about a localized place known in the story as "the garden of Eden" and to the human race as paradise. The opening inscription of the story signals this by announcing that what follows will recount "the generations of the heavens and the earth when they were created" (Gen. 2:4). In other words, the second story will focus on the *offspring or descendants* of the heaven and earth whose creation was described in Genesis 1. The word *generations* does not denote origin but rather what followed, in this case the beginning of human history on earth. We might note in this regard that Genesis 2 presupposes the existence of the creation that we have seen assembled in Genesis 1, and that unlike the earlier creation story, it makes no attempt to give an account of those details, which are, after all, extraneous to the purpose of Genesis 2.

Viewed as a companion story to Genesis 1, Genesis 2 invites continuous comparison with the earlier account. Genesis 1 is unified by the catalogue of God's acts of cosmic creation; Genesis 2 is controlled by the catalogue of God's acts of provision for the human race. The setting in Genesis 1 is generalized, unlocalized, nonexistent in the usual sense. By contrast, Genesis 2 gives lavish attention to the physical setting, with verses 5–15 concerned almost exclusively with the paradisal setting. Whereas the scope of Genesis 1 is cosmic, summed up in the image of *the earth*, the whole focus of Genesis 2 is toward the localized, the specific, the enclosed, as summed up in the controlling image of *the garden.*

Genesis 1 speaks of the plants *upon the earth* (v. 11) and *beasts of the earth* (v. 24), while Genesis 2 focuses specifically on the *plant of the field* (v. 5) and the *beast of the field* (vv. 19–20). The latter terms refer specifically to plants and animals cultivated or controlled by people. Furthermore, the story of life in paradise omits the sea creatures, yet another evidence that the scope of Genesis 2 is limited to the garden that God had planted. We might also note that Genesis 2 speaks of God's having *planted a garden in Eden* (v. 8), not of his creating vegetation, as in Genesis 1.

Other aspects of Genesis 2 also balance and complement the earlier creation story. Whereas the first story is centered around a single protagonist, the second story features three characters (God, Adam, and Eve). The literary mode shifts from the simple catalogue of God's miraculous acts of creation to a combination of narration and dialogue. Dialogue, in turn, implies encounter and relationship. The role of God thus changes from the transcendent God who exists beyond the cosmos to the God who is immanent in his creation and to the covenant God who enters into relationship with people. The single focus of Genesis 1 on the role of God as creator now expands to include also God's roles as the one who provides for the human race, who communicates with people, who establishes the conditions of reality for humankind. Even the actions of God are more anthropomorphic (humanlike), as he *forms* man, *planted* a garden, *took the man and put him in the garden, brought* Eve to Adam, and so forth.

With this shifting characterization of God, it is not surprising that different names are used for God in these companion stories. The name for God in Genesis 1 is *Elohim*, that is, *the Mighty One*. This name occurs thirty-two times in the chapter, a strategy of repetition completely in keeping with the story's purpose to exalt the majesty of God.[7] The name used for God in Genesis 2 is *Yahweh Elohim*, or *the Lord God*. Whereas *Elohim* signifies deity in general, *Yahweh* is a more personal name and "carries the connotation of God's nearness, of His concern for man, and of His redemptive . . . revelation" (Payne, p. 148).

Instead of constituting a contradiction, the two pictures of God that emerge from Genesis 1 and 2 represent the complementary aspects of God's character that we see throughout the Bible. God is both transcendent and immanent. He stands outside of the created universe (Gen. 1), yet is continuously active in it (Gen. 2).

7. See Edward J. Young, *An Introduction to the Old Testament* (Grand Rapids: Eerdmans, 1964), pp. 48–49.

The foregoing analysis suggests that the main artistic principle at work in the first two chapters of the Bible is the companion principle in which the second story balances the first. This rhythm of the second unit completing the first is part of the "deep structure" of the biblical imagination. We are most familiar with it in the poetry of the Bible, where it takes the form of parallelism. But it is also present in biblical narrative.

With the story of cosmic creation standing as the background, then, the more narrowly focused story of Genesis 2 highlights the original life of innocence in paradise, the garden *in* Eden (v. 8). Permeating the whole story is one of the most evocative archetypes of the human consciousness, that of the earthly paradise. C. S. Lewis rightly speaks of this archetype as "a region of the mind which does exist and which should be visited often."[8] Even the descriptive technique of Genesis 2, where the imagery is generalized rather than specific, requires that readers fill in the details from their own memories and imaginations. To insure that we interpret the perfect garden as having a spiritual as well as physical identity, the writer describes paradise as both a place and a way of life.

The unifying narrative motif in Genesis 2 is God's provision for the human race. The story thus unfolds as an ever-expanding vision of what God provided for people: physical life (v. 7), an environment that was both functional and aesthetically beautiful (v. 9 speaks of God's planting "every tree that is pleasant to the sight and good for food"), work (v. 15), moral choice (v. 16), dominion over the earthly order (v. 20), human companionship and marriage (vv. 20–24), and, permeating it all, communion with God.

Genesis 3

The first two chapters of Genesis together form a unit. But as we read the third chapter, the story of the fall, we quickly sense that the first three chapters of Genesis also fit together, forming a triad of related actions. Genesis 1 narrates the creation of a perfect world, Genesis 2 adds a close-up of the original innocence of the human race in paradise, and chapter 3 brings it all to a tragic close by narrating how the perfection of the world and human innocence were lost.

The artistic design that dominates the story of the fall is primarily a series of *archetypal plot motifs* that converge in the story. These universal story patterns help to produce an action that is far more tightly organized than the events in our daily lives are. Such narrative structuring shows how the artistic ordering of literary narrative serves the function of heightening our insight into life.

8. C. S. Lewis, *The Allegory of Love: A Study in Medieval Tradition* (New York: Oxford University Press, 1936), p. 352.

To begin, the story of the fall in Genesis 3 is the prototypical *tragedy* of the Bible and of Western literature. Its stages are discernible and are the standard phases of a literary tragedy: an initial dilemma (whether to obey God or follow the advice of the serpent), a tragic choice (here an act of disobedience), catastrophe (loss of innocence), suffering (which here takes the form of a preview of life outside the garden and then expulsion from the garden), perception (which is both immediate, as Adam and Eve realize their guilt, and delayed, as God later pronounces judgment against them), and death (both spiritual separation from God and the promise of physical death).

The specific form that the tragedy takes is the archetypal *fall from innocence*. Genesis 2 describes the original state of innocence, Genesis 3:1–6 provides the transition from innocence to evil, and the remainder of Genesis 3 describes the effects of the fall in the lives of Adam and Eve and in the universe.

The *temptation motif* dominates the first six verses of Genesis 3. As in other temptation stories, our attention automatically focuses on three elements. One is the characterization of the tempter, whose leading trait is almost always subtlety, as is made clear in verse 1. The second ingredient is the process of persuasion by which the tempter manipulates the victim. Thirdly, we trace the back-and-forth process by which the victim initially resists the persuasive strategies of the tempter but then gradually succumbs to them.

Genesis 3 can also be viewed as a story of *crime and punishment*. Here, too, the action falls into a threefold pattern, one of the most universal elements of artistry in stories. It consists of our seeing the antecedents of the crime (the temptation in vv. 1–6), the occurrence of the crime (v. 6), and the consequences of the crime (vv. 7–24).

Once the crime has been committed, the story follows a pattern of *initiation*, in which characters encounter a new experience and situation for the first time. Beginning with verse 7, the story is an ever-expanding catalogue of such new experiences: shame and self-consciousness (v. 7), a guilty conscience and accompanying fear of being detected by God (vv. 8–10), spiritual conflict as a condition of living (v. 15), for woman the curse of pain in childbearing and subordination to man (v. 16), for man the curse of working for a livelihood in a hostile environment (vv. 17–19), and for both the prospect of life outside the garden (vv. 23–24).

In addition to the conventional narrative patterns that converge in the story and reinforce each other, Genesis 3 is constructed as a whole system of *contrasts and foils*. One thinks at once of such basic dichotomies as before and after the fall, the garden and the wilderness, God and Satan. Upon further reflection, we see a balance between sin and restoration, and between God's judgment and mercy. The latter takes three forms: the prediction that the seed of the woman will eventually conquer the seed of the serpent (v. 15), God's making garments to protect Adam and Eve (v. 21), and his expelling Adam and Eve from the garden, lest they eat of the tree of life and doom themselves to an endless physical life in a fallen world (vv. 22–23). Here we see the tendency of the whole Bible to balance a pessimistic awareness of the tragedy of life with an awareness of what is more than tragic in human failure.

The two human characters in the story are also foils to each other. Eve falls deceived by a gradual process and is misled by the serpent (see 1 Timothy 2:14 for commentary on the matter), whereas Adam falls instantly (v. 6). When accosted by God, Adam tries to evade responsibility for his sin by blaming both God and Eve (v. 12). By contrast, Eve is straightforward and honest in stating what happened and accepting her blame (v. 13). Eve's punishment is pain in childbearing and subordination in marriage (v. 16). Adam is assigned a "breadwinning" role and faces the curse of a struggle for livelihood (vv. 17–19).

Genesis 3 does not recount everything that happened in paradise on the fatal day. It is a tightly organized, highly artistic pattern that gives us a distillation of what was most important in the event. This is one of the functions of artistry in the stories of the Bible—to silhouette the essential meaning of events.

The Story of Joseph

The story of Joseph (Gen. 37, 39–46, 50) is built around an important character type of biblical literature, the suffering servant. Such a hero undergoes suffering, usually undeserved, that accomplishes great good for other people. Joseph is such an innocent sufferer who becomes a savior of people. His story is dominated by the theme of providence. Although events that happen to the hero seem at the time to be tragic, by the time the story is over they turn out to have been governed by God for a redemptive purpose. To highlight this providential theme, the writer has composed a story that is itself intricately designed and carefully planned.

Several elements provide overall unity for the story. The story follows the U-shaped movement of comic plots (plots with happy endings). Events descend into various types of catastrophe but then take an upward turn into a happy ending. The story is also structured around a sequence of roles that the protagonist fills as the action unfolds: family outcast, keeper of Potiphar's estate, prisoner, interpreter of dreams, and political administrator.

Further pattern is provided by three pairs of dreams that become realities: the sheaves and the sun, moon, and stars (Gen. 37), the two dreams of the prisoners (Gen. 40), and the two dreams of Pharaoh (Gen. 41). Dreams not only occur in pairs, thereby increasing the symmetry of the story. They also unify the story by foreshadowing the conclusion or climax. Already in the exposition (background action) of the story we can foresee its conclusion. As a result, a strong sense of providential destiny overshadows the entire life of Joseph. This foreshadowing is intensified when the two dreams of the prisoners become realities, since if these dreams became realities, so will Joseph's earlier dreams. The same effect emerges from the two fulfilled dreams of Pharaoh, which, like Joseph's, involve an unnatural inversion in which the weaker supplants the stronger.

Further pattern emerges from a sequence of four places of imprisonment that organizes the story. First there is the pit into which Joseph's brothers throw him. This is followed by servitude in Potiphar's house. Then Joseph is actually incarcerated in a prison. The final stages of the story focus on the land of Egypt itself, where the nation of Israel would soon be doomed to four hundred years of slavery. There is a principle of increasing threat underlying this sequence: to be temporarily thrown into a pit is less destructive than to be enslaved, which is less restrictive than being imprisoned. The eventual enslavement of the whole nation in Egypt is more drastic than the personal imprisonments of Joseph.

Despite this increasingly sinister series, however, there is something paradoxical about the places of imprisonment. They are places of preservation as well as of pain and suffering, places where the hero is saved as well as condemned. And the imprisonments themselves are less drastic than the alternative of death.

References to the garments of Joseph also form a unifying pattern in the story. In fact, they appear at transition points in the story and symbolize important phases of the action. At the very outset, the garment that Jacob gives to Joseph (Gen. 37:3) symbolizes the father's favoritism and foreshadows the story of sibling rivalry that occupies the rest of the story of the hero in his parental home. In the same chapter (v. 23), the disrobing of Joseph signals the hero's break from his home and family. In the scene of sexual temptation by Potiphar's wife, the wife's grabbing of Joseph's garment (Gen. 39:12–18) is part of Joseph's fall from favor on Potiphar's estate, foreshadowing his period as an outcast in prison.

When Joseph is summoned from prison to appear before Pharaoh, the writer goes out of his way to tell us that "when he had shaved himself and changed his clothes, he came in before Pharaoh" (Gen. 41:14). This is not an unexplained piece of information, nor the random detail designed to add to the everyday realism of the story. It forms part of an image pattern in which the clothing of Joseph indicates transition points in the story and foreshadows the next phase of the hero's career.

The final two references to clothes celebrate the triumphs in Joseph's life. Joseph is clothed in "garments of fine linen" when Pharaoh elevates him to a position of power (Gen. 41:42). And in the reunion scene with his brothers, Joseph "gave festal garments" to "each and all of them" (Gen. 45:22).

Part of the design of the story consists of the way in which events tend to fall into pairs. I have noted that dreams occur together as pairs. The robe that symbolizes Joseph's favored position with his father has as its counterpart the garments of fine linen that symbolize his favored position with Pharaoh. The brothers use the garment of Joseph to deceive their father, and the wife of Potiphar uses the garment of Joseph to deceive her husband. Joseph is twice robed as a sign of honor and twice disrobed in treachery. Joseph's pair of dreams in which his family unnaturally bows down to the youngest son has its counterpart in Pharaoh's pair of dreams in which the weaker unnaturally devours the stronger. Joseph correctly interprets two pairs of dreams. His brothers make two trips to Egypt for grain.

Most impressive of all is the type scene that dominates the story of Joseph and that occurs four times. The main phases of action in the story are Joseph in the parental home (Gen. 37), Joseph in Potiphar's house (Gen. 39:1–18), Joseph in prison (Gen. 39:19 through 41:36), and Joseph as Pharaoh's ruler (Gen. 41:37 through Gen. 47). In each of these phases, we can identify the following common ingredients: a head or ruler in a position of authority, the rise of Joseph to a position of dominance under that authority, people in a position of subservience under Joseph, a garment that symbolizes the moment of transition at the end of the phase, and a place that combines the qualities of imprisonment and preservation. This type scene shows at a glance the two main motifs of the story—the heroism of the protagonist and the providence of God that brings events to a redemptive conclusion.

The story illustrates particularly well the general tendency of biblical narrative to juxtapose hidden and apparent plots. The apparent plot is the foreground action—what appears to be immediately true for the characters involved in the story. In the story of Joseph, the apparent plot is a series of disasters. Viewed in terms of immediate impact, most of what happens to Joseph is tragic.

The hidden plot is the story that we as readers are aware of and that characters in the story come to perceive. It is not immediately evident as events unfold but is the background story toward which events gradually move. The hidden plot in the story of Joseph is the story of God's providence at work. It is a story, not of tragedy, but of redemption. At any point in the apparent plot, one could not predict a positive outcome to

Joseph's life. Joseph is first the outcast, then the slave, then the prisoner. In each case, the final triumph occurs *because of* (not in spite of) the apparently tragic events.

The hidden and apparent plots are well summarized in two passages near the end of the story. When Joseph reveals his identity to his brothers, they are understandably "dismayed at his presence" (Gen. 45:3). Joseph reassures them with the following interpretation of the events that had made up their mutual lives:

> "I am your brother, Joseph, whom you sold into Egypt. And now do not be distressed, or angry with yourselves, because you sold me here; for God sent me before you to preserve life. . . . So it was not you who sent me here, but God. . . ." [Gen. 45:4–8]

Here is the double plot of the story, which is simultaneously a story of human cruelty and divine redemption. The same double note is sounded when the brothers become fearful after the death of their father, Jacob. This time Joseph recapitulates the story of his life with the words,

> "As for you, you meant evil against me; but God meant it for good, to bring it about that many people should be kept alive. . . ." [Gen. 50:20]

Here is the paradox of the story, which is at once tragic and comic.

The story of Joseph is a masterful story of suspense, not in the sense of our not knowing how the story will turn out but in the sense of our not knowing how the predicted outcome will happen. The story opens with a preposterous narrative premise: Joseph, the youngest son, the despised brother, the outcast, will some day be ruler over his family. How can this promised conclusion possibly come true? The very name of the hero adds to our bewilderment. *Joseph* means "he adds." How can this be appropriate? The conclusion of the story is apparent in the opening: we know that Joseph will be elevated above his family. But *how* will it happen? If we were reading the story for the first time, we could not possibly see, as we move from episode to episode, how a given episode will contribute to the final situation. Even our knowledge about the final situation is incomplete: we know that Joseph's brothers will bow down to him, but we do not know how or where it will happen.

My discussion has focused on the overriding patterns in the story as a whole. When we look at the individual episodes, further patterns emerge: the ever-expanding vision of evil in the opening chapter of the story (Gen. 37), the archetypes of initiation and temptation in the story of Joseph's life in Potiphar's house (Gen. 39:1–20), the test motif and dramatic irony that dominate the story of Joseph's dealings with his brothers (Gen. 42–44), the convergence of such narrative patterns as poetic justice, climax, and recognition scenes late in the story.

One of the best tests of whether a story has been carefully constructed is whether it falls easily into a pattern that literary critics call the well-made plot. It consists of seven phases, and many of the stories of the Bible fall naturally into this pattern. Applied to the story of Joseph, the scheme yields the following pattern:

1. *Exposition* (background information): Joseph in his family environment.
2. *Inciting moment:* selling Joseph into Egypt.
3. *Rising action:* Joseph's fortunes in Egypt.
4. *Turning point* (the point at which we can see, at least in retrospect, how the plot will be resolved): the journey of Joseph's brothers to Egypt.
5. *Further complication:* Joseph's testing of his brothers.
6. *Climax:* Joseph's disclosure of his identity.
7. *Denouement* (tying up of loose ends): Jacob's moving to Egypt and the death of Joseph.

All that I have said about artistry in the story of Joseph confirms one scholar's rapturous judgment that "rarely in Western literature has form been woven into content, pattern sewn into meaning, structure forged into theme with greater subtlety or success."[9] In a story that demonstrates the presence of God's redemptive providence in the world, the very form of the story (an intricate system of patterned details) is part of its meaning.

This leads me to conclude this chapter by asking, What is important about the presence of artistic pattern and design in the stories of the Bible? For one thing, it is part of the craftsmanship and beauty that the Bible communicates, quite apart from its religious content. Its purpose is partly the aesthetic purpose of enjoyment and delight.

Artistic design also intensifies the impact of what a story says. A carefully designed story produces an effect that sprawling stories simply lack. The story of Joseph makes its point more effectively because we can see the progress of Joseph's life pictured in a sequence of garments and places of imprisonment, for example.

The high degree of pattern in the stories of the Bible points in the direction of self-conscious composition. A story always requires a series of

9. Donald A. Seybold, "Paradox and Symmetry in the Joseph Narrative," in *Literary Interpretations of Biblical Narratives*, ed. Kenneth R. R. Gros Louis (Nashville: Abingdon, 1974), p. 59. My discussion is indebted at every turn to this essay.

choices on the writer's part. There are many ways to narrate a given action. Storytellers make conscious choices when selecting and arranging details, and when deciding how to present them. The more pattern we see in a story, the more active the writer has been in composing the story according to a self-conscious plan.

Finally, identifying the pattern and design of a story is one of the major tasks of a reader or interpreter. Pattern of any type allows us to see the unity and organization of a story. It is a maxim of modern educational theory that details are simply inert facts unless they are placed into a unifying framework. An awareness of the patterns in a story is a necessary part of seeing how the details fit into a meaningful order.

4

Hero Stories

T he genre of hero stories (also called heroic narrative) is nearly synonymous with narrative itself. Loosely defined, hero stories are stories built around the life and exploits of the protagonist or hero (a term that I will use generically for masculine and feminine characters). Most stories follow this pattern. We should, however, define the concept of the hero more precisely than simply identifying it with a literary protagonist. A literary hero is a certain type of protagonist, as the following definition asserts:

> A traditional . . . hero must be more than merely the leading figure or protagonist of a literary work. The true hero expresses an accepted social and moral norm; his experience reenacts the important conflicts of the community which produces him; he is endowed with qualities that capture the popular imagination. It must also be remarked that the hero is able to act, and to act for good. Most important of all, the narrative of his experience suggests that life has both a significant pattern and an end.[1]

This is the framework that I propose to apply to selected biblical stories.

1. Walter Houghton and G. Robert Stange, eds., *Victorian Poetry and Poetics*, 2d ed. (Boston: Houghton Mifflin, 1968), p. xxiii.

Creating heroes is one of the most significant things that cultures do. In fact, choosing a hero is one of the most basic of all human activities. Heroes are always the product of the human imagination. Real life furnishes the materials out of which the imagination fashions heroes, but life does not furnish completely formed heroes. In creating heroes, the individual and cultural imagination selects, heightens, shapes, and interprets the materials that life provides. A hero is always a *distillation* of something from actual life. It focuses on a selected role, quality, or act of a person.

The heroes that we encounter in literature and the Bible represent one of the oldest and most universal impulses of the human race—the desire to embody accepted norms of thought, feeling, or action in a character whose destiny is typical or representative and in some sense exemplary. A hero is an idealized figure—a person whom people respect and admire. Heroes need not be wholly idealized, however, and in the Bible they rarely are.

We should, then, be on our guard against a particularly frivolous and persistent kind of misinterpretation—the attempt to make everything that a biblical hero does a norm to be emulated. The hero stories of the Bible give us positive examples of behavior to follow and negative examples to avoid. In either case, hero stories are in some sense example stories, though not in any simple or moralizing sense.

In addition to being idealized, a hero is representative. What happens to him or her is something with which all people can identify. In the heroes of the Bible, we see ourselves. Their stories tell not only what happened but also what happens. These people are not specimens in a historical museum; they are people from whom we can "build bridges" to our own experiences. Heroes carry a burden of meaning larger than themselves. In their qualities and lives the deep significance of life reveals itself.

Because heroes sum up what a whole culture wants to say, we can profitably view the image of the hero as a comment on the three great issues of life: *values* (what matters most and least), *morality* (what constitutes good and evil behavior), and *reality* (what really exists in life and the universe). Another helpful strategy for inferring the meaning of hero stories is to analyze their implied view of the person, of religion, and of society.

Heroes fall mainly into four categories. *Idealized heroes* are paragons of virtue whom we are asked to admire and emulate. *Tragic heroes* are not villains but essentially good people afflicted with a tragic flaw of character that leads them to make a great mistake. *Comic heroes* are also flawed characters, but their resilience in winning despite their mistakes leads us to sympathize with them. For want of a better term, I call the fourth category heroes of common humanity, or *realistic heroes*. They are essentially "one of us," possessing our strengths and weaknesses. Most biblical heroes fall into this category. As we move further along the continuum, we find characters so flawed or weak or unsuccessful that the term *hero* becomes a misnomer, and we should regard stories about such characters as satires and villain stories rather than hero stories.

Heroes serve several important functions, and these will help us in approaching the hero stories of the Bible. Heroes function as an inspiration. As a human race, we demand images of greatness. Heroes satisfy that demand. Heroes also codify a culture's and person's values and beliefs, and focus their consciousness. Heroes often serve the function of reconciling us to human failings and limitations.

The heroes that we read about in stories are known to us in five ways (identical with the ways in which any literary character exists): personal abilities, skills, qualities, and traits; actions; thoughts and feelings (including attitudes, motives, goals, and responses); relationships (including influence on other people); roles. The starting place is to *describe* a hero as precisely as possible in terms of these. On the basis of that description we can *interpret* what the storyteller is saying about life, especially about values, morality, and reality.

I should conclude by saying that hero stories are first of all *stories*. To understand and enjoy them, we need to remember all that I said about narrative generally in earlier chapters. The considerations that I have just discussed are things that we should add to our more general narrative analysis. Because hero stories focus so strongly on the protagonist, we cannot go far wrong if we simply concentrate on the hero. Even the plot conflict centers on the obstacles that the hero faces. The main meaning of a hero story will emerge if we pay attention to the hero's experiment in living and its outcome.

In summary, hero stories are about the struggles and triumphs of the human race. A hero is representative of a whole group and is a largely (though not necessarily wholly) idealized character. What happens to the hero is an implied comment about life and reality and is intended to furnish the reader with insight regarding how to live.

Most of the stories of the Bible are hero stories. The stories of Genesis discussed in the previous two chapters will profit from being analyzed as hero stories. To illustrate the dynamics of heroic narrative, I have turned to the stories of Daniel, Gideon, Ruth, and Esther. But this is a highly selective list. The Bible is quite literally an anthology of hero stories.

The Story of Daniel

The story of Daniel (Dan. 1–6) is so thoroughly governed by the principle of heroic narrative that it violates a basic rule of narrative, unity of action. The first six chapters of the Book of Daniel do not present a single sustained action. Each episode is self-contained, and Daniel himself does not even participate in two of the episodes. As we read these chapters, we participate in six separate ordeals spanning many years. The ordeals are, in order, the testing of the four Hebrew youths, Daniel's interpretation of Nebuchadnezzar's dream, the ordeal in the fiery furnace, Nebuchadnezzar's fall and restoration, Belshazzar's feast, and Daniel in the lions' den. The governing principle is to hold up models of heroism for our contemplation.

What principles of selection lie behind hero stories like this? The same principles that lie behind the selectivity that transforms a ball game into a few shots on the evening television news. Writers choose either the most crucial or decisive events in the hero's life, or the most typical or representative events. The first principle governs the hero stories in the Book of Daniel.

In addition to the model of heroism that appears in each episode of the Daniel story, three other motifs constitute a useful unifying framework (and we might note in passing that the principle of repetition is one means by which a storyteller signals what is most important in a story). All six ordeals involve a testing of the chief character and a rescue by God. This is the type scene that governs the story. Secondly, in a world where God's sovereign activity is a constant reality, every one of the episodes includes miraculous or supernatural activity by God. Finally, in three of the six episodes the heroic act involves some form of resistance to the surrounding (pagan) culture.

The conflicts in the story occur on both individual and national levels. On the individual level, Daniel (the chief hero) encounters a number of antagonists, including kings, a pagan lifestyle, the threat of losing Jewish identity, jealous colleagues, and hungry lions. But these personal conflicts occur in a broader context of international conflict between the Jewish nation, with a strong religious identity, and the Babylonians, who have an equally strong pagan orientation.

As we accompany Daniel on the ordeals that test him, the image of a wholly idealized hero quickly emerges. The first ordeal (Dan. 1) is a religious test of Daniel and his three young Hebrew friends. The whole crisis centers around the rich food and wine that the king served in the dormitory of the prize students of his realm. As is often true, externally small details mask larger spiritual issues.

The conflict is actually a clash between two lifestyles. Daniel's lifestyle is pastoral in its simplicity. His diet consists of "vegetables to eat and water to drink" (v. 12). The very presence of two sets of names for the youths (vv. 6–7) highlights the identity crisis in which the young men are trapped. At the king's feasts the food would undoubtedly have been dedicated to the gods, which explains why Daniel believed that to participate in the king's banquet would be to "defile himself" (v. 8). Faced with this test of his loyalty to God, Daniel initiates a test: let the Hebrew youths eat their pastoral diet and see how they fare (vv. 12–13).

The outcome of the test makes the story a favorite with children: "at the end of ten days it was seen that they were better in appearance and fatter in flesh than all the youths who ate the king's rich food" (v. 15). Here is poetic justice, the story of virtue rewarded.

The opening chapter of Daniel illustrates a common trait of heroic narrative—the search for superlatives. Hero stories exist partly to give us images of greatness. We therefore read about "youths without blemish, handsome and skilful in all wisdom, endowed with knowledge, under-standing, learning, and competent to serve in the king's palace," who were to learn "the letters and language of the Chaldeans" (v. 4). Again, "in every matter of wisdom and understanding concerning which the king inquired of them, he found them ten times better than all the magicians and enchanters that were in all his kingdom" (v. 20).

The search for superlatives spills over to the style of the story. Contrary to the style of most biblical narrative, the style of the story of Daniel is a high style. Characters speak in long, stately speeches. Decorous repetition of phrases and speeches abounds. The narrator and characters in the story heap synonym upon synonym until the style emerges as an epic style.

The second ordeal (Dan. 2) is a test of Daniel's ability to tell and interpret dreams. As in the testing of the four youths in the previous chapter, this ordeal moves toward exalting God's sovereign power. The statement of the Chaldeans that "there is not a man on earth who can meet the king's demand" (v. 10) serves as a foil to the greatness of God, who *can* meet the king's demand through Daniel. Faced with the crisis of interpret-ing the dream, Daniel turns naturally to prayer (vv. 17–18), which is followed by God's revelation in answer to the prayer (v. 19) and by Daniel's lyric poem praising God as the revealer of mysteries (vv. 19–23). The final element in the pattern is testimony, as Daniel testifies to the king regarding the power of God to reveal dreams (vv. 27–30).

Hero stories portray models of behavior. We can assume that the storyteller has included details that contribute to that controlling purpose. The sequence of events in which Daniel masters the problem posed by the king's unreasonable demand for others to tell him both the dream and its interpretation adds up to a heroic portrait of mental ability, prayer, dependence on God, thanksgiving, and testimony.

The ordeal of the fiery furnace (Dan. 3) combines all the leading motifs of the story—testing, courageous resistance to the surrounding culture, supernatural marvels by God, and miraculous rescue. The threat to Daniel's three friends again involves their loyalty to God and comes in the form of compulsory emperor worship. Here is one of many hero stories in the Bible that focus on the hero's moral dilemma. The three friends, like many another biblical hero, assume grandeur as they choose for God (vv. 16–18).

The background against which this heroic act stands silhouetted is the figure of Nebuchadnezzar, at least partly a comic figure and a case study in overreaction. We read that he "was full of fury, and the expression of his face was changed. . . . He ordered the furnace heated seven times more than it was wont to be heated" (v. 19). Along with the lions' den (three chapters later), the fiery furnace is one of the great images of terror in the hero stories of the Bible.

In the actions of Nebuchadnezzar we encounter something that pervades a lot of Old Testament narrative and is characteristic of slave literature. I refer to the mockery of the oppressive master nation, especially its king. Everything that the king does to punish the three friends turns against him. Faced with a miracle, his reflexive style leads him to the opposite extreme of commanding that anyone who "speaks anything against the God of Shadrach, Meshach, and Abednego shall be torn limb from limb, and their houses laid in ruins" (v. 29). Like other kings (such as Pharaoh and Ahasuerus) ridiculed in Old Testament slave narratives, Nebuchadnezzar obviously does not have himself under control, a motif elaborated in the next chapter's account of the decline and restoration of the king.

With chapter 5 the spotlight returns to Daniel, and again we find the leading ingredients of the story converging in a phantasmagoria of shocking events. It begins with King Belshazzar's desecrating the vessels of the Jewish temple for his drinking party. This is followed by the mystery and terror of a hand that comes out of thin air and writes in an unknown language on the wall of the palace banqueting hall. No wonder "the king's color changed, and his thoughts alarmed him; his limbs gave way, and his knees knocked together" (v. 6).

Into this chaotic scene of carousing and terror Daniel steps forward with his characteristic confidence and charisma. After all, he is the one in whom are found "an excellent spirit, knowledge, and understanding to interpret dreams, explain riddles, and solve problems" (v. 12). As is usually the case in the political world of this story, the dream turns out to have both a personal and a political significance: Belshazzar himself is "weighed in the balances and found wanting" (v. 27), and his kingdom is brought to an end (vv. 26, 28). The chaotic night at the palace concludes with a final bit of ironic reversal: the king clothes Daniel with purple and puts a chain of gold around his neck in proclamation that he should be third ruler in the kingdom (v. 29), but the next verses state laconically, "That very night Belshazzar the Chaldean king was slain. And Darius the Mede received the kingdom."

Daniel's position as one of three presidents in the kingdom of Darius (Dan. 6:1) is the final chapter in the life of a heroic statesman who was trusted by one king after another. The statement that "an excellent spirit was in him" (v. 3) is an apt summary of Daniel's superior abilities, which impressed everyone around him. Even more striking is his spiritual integrity, so pronounced that Daniel's jealous colleagues concede that "we shall not find any ground for complaint against this Daniel unless we find it in connection with the law of his God" (v. 5).

Once again the action revolves around a test and miraculous rescue. The test repeats the earlier episode of compulsory emperor worship, with the den of lions introducing the same element of terror as was earlier represented by the fiery furnace. The heroism of uncompromising faith in God is depicted in vivid descriptive detail:

> When Daniel knew that the document had been signed, he went to his house where he had windows in his upper chamber open toward Jerusalem; and he got down upon his knees three times a day and prayed and gave thanks before his God, as he had done previously. [v. 10]

Once again the foreign king is mocked, as the narrative makes it clear that Darius had been hoodwinked by his subordinates and spent a sleepless night while Daniel was locked in the lions' den (vv. 18–19).

As the foregoing survey of the separate ordeals has suggested, it is the emerging portrait of the hero that is important in hero stories. Daniel is one of only a handful of completely idealized heroes in the Bible. His heroism is seen especially in how he handles tests of his allegiance to God. His name turns out to be accurate, since it means "God is judge" or "God is my judge."

The definition of the hero that I offered at the beginning of this chapter serves as a good framework for summarizing the heroism of Daniel. The hero, says the definition, expresses "an accepted social and moral norm." Loyalty to God and nation is the norm that Daniel's life repeatedly expresses. According to the definition, the hero's experience "reenacts the important conflicts of the community which produces him." Daniel's life takes us right to the heart of what it means to be a member of a religious minority living in a pagan culture. His identity as a member of a religious subculture is continuously threatened and tested by the luxury and idolatry of his surrounding culture.

A hero "is endowed with qualities that capture the popular imagination," and again Daniel fits the definition. Daniel is a paragon of ability, courage, and integrity. He is valedictorian of his class, admired and befriended by one pagan king after another despite his strong religious convictions.

A hero "is able . . . to act for good." The story of Daniel is just such a story of success and virtue rewarded. In fact, every one of the ordeals ends with poetic justice, as evil characters are punished and Daniel and his friends are rewarded. Finally, a hero story "suggests that life has both a significant pattern and an end [goal]." The pattern of Daniel's life is a religious or spiritual pattern. Daniel is above all a religious hero. His life revolves around God. His religious intensity is what impresses the pagans around him, some of whom speak in uninitiated fashion about "the God of Daniel." Daniel is preeminently the man of God who does not allow his high position to lead him to compromise his faith. As we read the story, we are led to feel that God's blessing rests on such a life and that it is an adequate foundation for living.

The Story of Gideon

Two basic strategies dominate hero stories. The hero can either *achieve* or *display* heroism during the course of the story. In the former type, the *transformation* of the hero is the essential action. The latter type is the story of the *confirmation* of the hero.

The story of Daniel is the prototypical confirmation story in which everything that the hero does idealizes him. By contrast, the story of Gideon (Judg. 6–8) is par excellence the story of the *making* of a hero. The unifying narrative principle is God's transforming a person with a severe inferiority complex into a hero whose sheer mastery of situations takes our breath away. As the story unfolds, therefore, we have to keep adjusting our understanding of the hero's character.

Repetition is the best clue to what is important in a story. In the first half of the story of Gideon (Judg. 6:11–7:8), what keeps getting repeated is Gideon's feeling of inadequacy despite all the evidences of God's power to perform what he asks of Gideon. Midway through the story Gideon's faith in God's power and willingness to help overcomes his sense of inadequacy (7:9–18). In the second half of the story, we observe Gideon's mastery of his enemies and of every crisis that tests his resourcefulness, except for his failing at the very end of the story (8:27). I leave it to my readers to see how the individual episodes confirm the pattern I have outlined.

Because the idea of the hero is so pervasive in literature and in cultures, it is natural to compare images of the hero with each other. Anyone familiar with literature as a whole can scarcely avoid doing this when reading the hero stories of the Bible. What emerges is a simultaneous similarity and difference between the heroes of the Bible and those of other literature.

The best framework for understanding this pattern is something that recent literary criticism has called intertextuality. It results when we place one work of literature next to another one in such a way that the total meaning is not self-contained but depends on the action *between* the two texts (hence the idea of an intertext). The tension between much of what we find in the Bible (including its hero stories) and what we find elsewhere in literature is so pronounced that the biblical material emerges as a parody of extrabiblical literature. A parody is a literary work or motif that parallels another work, but with inverted effect. The new effect need not be humorous, even though this is the common understanding of parody.

The full meaning of the Gideon story emerges if we allow it to set up an intertext with other ancient hero stories. In its externals, the story has all the right ingredients for an epic story like the story of Achilles or Odysseus or Aeneas, or a romance story like the story of Arthur and his knights. In all these cases, the hero is a warrior. The crucial events occur on the battlefield. Delivering a nation from foreign oppression is the basic action. The hero's physical prowess, leadership abilities, and resourcefulness in overcoming enemies occupy center stage. The reward for such military endeavor is kingship.

But once we have noticed the similarities between the story of Gideon and other ancient military stories, further scrutiny shows how profoundly the conventional patterns have been broken. The conventions are foils that highlight the biblical concept of heroism. The usual military hero is a study in self-reliance. His chief assets are physical strength and courage. He fights at least partly to gain honor for himself, and this honor is won through prowess on the battlefield. The conventional hero utters boastful speeches, calls attention to his own abilities, and accepts kingship as his reward.

The story of Gideon belongs to a large class of hero stories in the Bible that break this pattern at many points. Instead of praising human strength, the story of Gideon depicts the small place that human effort plays in the victory over Midian. In fact, once God has bolstered Gideon's low self-esteem, he puts Gideon through a series of maneuvers designed to strip away any illusion that Gideon has won the battle through human means (Judg. 7:1–8). Only three hundred Israelite soldiers are allowed to undertake the battle, "lest Israel vaunt themselves against [God], saying, 'My own hand has delivered me' " (Judg. 7:2).

Whereas the conventional military hero of literature is of royal blood or even (as in the case of Aeneas, for example) is said to be the offspring of a god or goddess, Gideon describes himself as coming from the weakest clan in his tribe and as being the least in his family (Judg. 6:15). Without external claim to heroism, he has nothing but God's assistance to make him heroic. Whereas the conventional hero story celebrates the deliverance brought about by great and strong armies, the story of Gideon emphasizes the military inadequacy of the Israelite forces, thereby extolling the supernatural nature of the deliverance.

The conventional hero, relying on his own abilities, wins victory through heroic action and is rewarded with fame and a political kingdom. Gideon, by contrast, relies on God's help. When offered the kingship, he refuses it on the ground that God, the real deliverer, is worthy to rule (Judg. 8:22–23). Thus God is given the honor that is usually accorded the human hero. Whereas conventional hero stories glorify a human hero, the story of Gideon glorifies God.

The story of Gideon is not unique in this regard. We find something similar in numerous other hero stories of the Bible. One thinks at once of the stories of such national leaders as Moses and Joshua (whose conquest of Jericho in Joshua 6 is a particularly close parallel to Gideon's conquest of Midian), or such prophets as Isaiah and Jeremiah. The hero stories of Genesis focus on the pastoral and domestic life of heroes who find value in a way of life far removed from conventional standards of success found in other ancient literature. The preeminent example of the principle that I am discussing is the story of Jesus.

The technique is not limited to hero stories. In Psalm 18:31–42, for example, the conventional arming of the warrior and the warrior's boast treat God as the one who arms the hero and is worthy of honor. The beatitudes in Matthew 5:3–12 completely invert conventional standards of heroism. The song of the suffering servant in Isaiah 53 does the same.

What we have here is a biblical version of something common in modern literature, the anti-hero (the protagonist who displays a lack of the traits of the conventional literary hero). Gideon is an anti-hero in his lack of self-reliance, in his lack of any achievement that he can call his own, and in his unwillingness to aggrandize himself by assuming political rulership. But the anti-heroes of the Bible are themselves a parody of the anti-hero of modern literature. The latter express the nihilism of a faithless culture. But the biblical heroes, by relinquishing the claims of conventional heroism, achieve more than is humanly possible. Their weakness becomes strength, and their lack of conventional heroism embodies the heroism of trust in God.

The Story of Esther

The story of Esther is one of the world's favorites, and no wonder. It has all the ingredients of a good story. Although I will focus on the characterization of the heroine, I wish to begin by noting some of the richness of plot that the story possesses.

The Book of Esther tells two stories at the same time. At one level, it is a hero story that focuses on the central character, Esther. When viewed in this light, the action follows the Cinderella motif and falls easily into the framework of the well-made plot. The *exposition* or background for the main action consists of the dethronement of Queen Vashti, the enthronement of Esther, and Mordecai's saving of the king's life. The *inciting force* that introduces the plot conflict into this situation is Haman's rage at Mordecai's refusal to do obeisance before him. The *rising action* consists of the plot that Haman devises against the Jews. The *turning point* occurs with Esther's decision to confront the king with her appeal. The *further complication* consists of Esther's gradual and suspenseful execution of her plan. The *climax* comes with Esther's disclosure of her plight to the king, and the *denouement* consists of the deliverance of the Jews and the exaltation of Mordecai over Haman.

In addition to being a story about a beautiful and courageous heroine, the Book of Esther is a story of national deliverance. It is a rescue story that follows the U-shaped pattern of the conventional comic (happy-ending) plot. As in other stories built around a comic plot, the action consists of a series of obstacles that must be overcome. Here the obstacles stem from the intrigue of Haman to destroy the Jewish nation. The action descends into potentially tragic events, and then rises to a happy ending. The basic rhythm of a comic plot is the build-up and release of tension. Viewed thus, the plot of the story of Esther falls into a three-part pattern. Chapters 1 and 2, recounting the king's rejection of Vashti and marrying of Esther, are the necessary background to the conflict between Haman and the Jews. Chapters 3 through 7 narrate, step by step, how Haman plotted against Mordecai and the Jews, and how the latter developed a counterplot. Chapters 8 through 10 describe the aftermath of the struggle, the deliverance of the Jews.

Both of the foregoing plot outlines work well as a basic organizing framework for looking at the story. The story of Esther contains most of the ingredients that readers through the centuries have valued in a good story: heightened conflict between good and evil, a beautiful and courageous heroine, lurid scenes of banqueting and carousing, a palace complete with a harem, romantic love in the specific form of the Cinderella motif (an orphan girl from an enslaved nation who marries the king), a villain who makes the reader's blood boil, helpless victims who are rescued just in time, intrigue, suspense, decisive moral choice, climax, battle, and poetic justice. When we focus on this wealth of plot material, the dominant theme that emerges is the providence of God, who (even though he is not named in the story) controls events for his purposes of judgment and salvation.

Balancing all this richness of plot is an equally full emphasis on characterization. Although Esther is my interest, I will note in passing the framework that should be applied to the other characters.

The portrait of King Ahasuerus is a satiric portrait. In keeping with the tone of slave literature, the foreign king is held up to ridicule every time he enters the action. He is a bumbling, inept figure, the object of mocking by the Hebrew storyteller as he exchanges a gleeful wink with his audience. Queen Vashti is mainly a foil to the king, a moral norm that heightens the king's status as a playboy and dunce. Haman is the demonic villain—the person of uncontrolled pride and thirst for revenge. No wonder it became a convention for Jewish audiences to boo and hiss and rattle noisemakers whenever Haman's name was mentioned during oral readings of the story. Mordecai, a courtier by profession, is the conventional attendant on the protagonist, a character necessary to the action but for purposes of the story kept subordinate to the heroine.

We come, then, to Esther, after whom the story is accurately named. Let me emphasize that the human characters in the stories of the Bible are always on trial. We have to judge continuously whether their actions or traits in a given incident are good or bad. The storytellers of the Bible select details by two criteria: they give us positive models to follow and negative examples to avoid. With this as a working presupposition, we can see that the characterization of Esther is governed by two motifs. Esther is first portrayed as a young person caught in an identity crisis, and then as a heroic figure transformed through ordeal.

During the early stages of the action, Esther is a passive young woman who tries to live in two worlds. Once she is chosen to be part of the royal harem, she has an identity crisis. This is made clear when she enters the story in chapter 2. Esther comes from a religious background, but the whole emphasis in the king's harem is on physical beauty. Esther fits right into this pagan ethos.

Reinforcing this double identity is the fact that Esther goes by two names (2:7). Furthermore, we are told twice that no one at court knew about Esther's Jewish identity (2:10, 20). For her to have concealed such a fact, and for her to have won the admiration of everyone around her (2:15), she must have compromised her religious principles.[2] We read that Esther ate her portion of food (2:9), which almost certainly violated Jewish dietary laws and which contrasts starkly with the behavior of Daniel in a similar situation. And when Esther marries a pagan king, she marries outside of the Jewish faith.

What emerges from the opening chapter in which Esther figures, then, is a mixed picture. There is no doubt that Esther is strikingly beautiful, possessing "the eternal feminine" that electrifies the environment. She is

2. On this and other matters of characterization, I have particularly profited from the summary of scholarship in Carey A. Moore, *Esther*, vol. 7 of the Anchor Bible (Garden City, N.Y.: Doubleday, 1971).

so beautiful that she can trust her unadorned beauty to win the king when it is her turn to spend the night with him (2:15). But the spiritual principle of life is being submerged in all this glamor. And as the next key event will show, Esther cannot live forever in two worlds.

The pinch comes in chapter 4 when Mordecai sends word to Esther about Haman's plot against the Jews. Up to this point, Esther has been the beauty queen taking the path of least resistance in a pagan environment. Her first response to the message from her uncle is to perpetuate the pattern (4:10–11). When Mordecai appeals to Esther's self-interest in the matter (vv. 12–13), Esther realizes that she cannot continue to live in two worlds. At the moment of choice, both we and she sense the identity crisis in which she has lived. She makes a decisive choice in favor of her religious values (v. 16) and in that very moment is transformed from a moral nonentity into a person of heroic moral and spiritual stature. Esther thus belongs to a familiar literary type—the person transformed by ordeal.

Esther's behavior in chapter 5 exhibits some of the same tensions that have dominated the earlier action. It is true that she courageously enters the king's presence without having been summoned, but she then carries out her plan of disclosing her request to the king with suspenseful delay. Why does she twice refuse to state her real request? Perhaps she is so much in control of the situation that she senses it is not the right moment to make her move, but more likely she is frightened by the situation into which she has been thrust. In keeping with her ability to perpetuate a disguise, she is able to invite Haman to her banquet with the king without arousing Haman's suspicions (5:12).

The climax of the story, where Esther finally discloses her request for her nation (7:3–6), is rich in drama and paradox. Esther's unmasking of the villain is at the same time the unmasking of herself. Here she accepts her Jewish identity before the king, her husband. Having risen to the occasion with heroic courage, Esther masterfully controls the destiny of her nation in the concluding phases of the story.

To a superlative degree, Esther meets the requirements for a literary hero. Her conflicts reenact those of the religious community that produced and preserved the story. In fact, she is the representative of her nation. Although initially a beautiful young woman with a weak character, she becomes transformed into a person with heroic moral stature and political skill. She is able to act for good, and her story thus demonstrates the validity of a religious view of life. And she has captured the imagination of readers for centuries.

Ancient literature written about a heroine is relatively rare. The Book of Esther is one of several heroic narratives in the Bible that make a woman the engaging central figure. In addition to the story of Ruth, the stories of Deborah (Judg. 4–5), Hannah (1 Sam. 1), and Abigail (1 Sam. 25) are especially memorable.

The Story of Ruth

The Book of Ruth is perhaps the supreme masterpiece of narrative art in the Bible.[3] In it all the resources of storytelling combine—plot, characterization, setting, word patterns, imagery, archetypes, allusions, dialogue—to produce the total effect.

The story of Ruth is a narrative of idyllic romance: it is a short story describing a simple, pleasant aspect of rural and domestic life. The whole narrative world that we enter is part of the meaning, just as it is in the very different courtly world that prevails in the stories of Esther and Daniel. In contrast to those stories, the environment in the story of Ruth—pastoral, natural, elemental—provides an idealized setting that reinforces the love story that occurs within it.

Whereas the events in the stories of Daniel and Esther are permeated with the artificialities of court etiquette, the story of Ruth possesses an elemental quality. It depicts such basic human experiences as death and birth, family ties and motherhood, religious and romantic devotion. The human action occurs against a background of the natural cycles of famine and harvest. In the process, the romantic love that is the central action of the story emerges as something natural, not (as so often in classical literature) as an unwelcome disruption of the natural flow of things and as something that plunges people into crime and disgrace.

Most hero stories are comic, U-shaped plots, and the story of Ruth is an admirable example. The story begins in tragedy but then moves steadily toward a happy conclusion as various obstacles are overcome. The heroine begins in isolation from her society and gradually becomes assimilated into it, the usual pattern in comedy. The triumph at the end of the story is also the customary one for a comic plot, consisting of a marriage. More specifically, the comic plot is here conceived as a quest for a home (the pattern is hinted at in 1:9 and 3:1). There is even the familiar journey motif associated with the quest, as Ruth journeys from Moab to Bethlehem and from the house of Naomi to the farm of Boaz.

For all its simplicity, the plot is skillfully constructed in such a way as to build toward the climactic nighttime meeting between Ruth and Boaz on

3. For confirmation of this claim, and for a model of what a genuinely literary analysis of a biblical story looks like, see D. F. Rauber, "The Book of Ruth," in *Literary Interpretations of Biblical Narratives*, ed. Kenneth R. R. Gros Louis (Nashville: Abingdon, 1974), pp. 163–76. For a fuller explication of the story than I have space to provide, I especially recommend this essay.

the threshing floor. Each of the four chapters contributes a phase to the action. The first chapter provides the background to the story by narrating how the heroine came to be in Bethlehem. Chapter 2 narrates the early stages of the romance between Ruth and Boaz. Chapter 3 brings Ruth and Boaz together in betrothal, and the final chapter celebrates the central event just narrated and ties up the loose ends.

In addition to these elements of plot unity, the story is organized around image patterns. The controlling image for the story is that of harvest or ingathering. But even more pervasive is a tension between emptiness and fullness that is apparent from the beginning and finally resolved at the end of the story.

Ruth is above all a domestic heroine. She is twice married, devoted to her mother-in-law, the woman of the romance that is at the center of the story, a mother in the royal line of David and the messianic line. It is impossible to separate the domestic from the religious heroine, however. In fact, the domestic heroine draws much of her identity from her religious strength. The basis of her appeal as a woman is nowhere said to be stunning beauty but rather her gentleness and strength of character.

The domestic and religious strands merge in the most famous passage in the story, Ruth's statement of her commitment to her mother-in-law. In a lyric utterance made memorable by its rhetorical pattern of balance and parallelism, Ruth says,

> "Entreat me not to leave you
>   or to return from following you;
> for where you go I will go,
>   and where you lodge I will lodge;
> your people shall be my people,
>   and your God my God;
> where you die I will die,
>   and there will I be buried." [1:16–17]

The fact that Ruth here chooses Naomi's God shows her choice to be a religious as well as domestic one and explains why Milton, in his ninth sonnet, cites Ruth (along with Mary the sister of Martha) as an example of a woman who chose "the better part," that is, spiritual values.

Chapter 1 is expository in nature and narrates the tragic background to the story of love that will follow. It introduces the plot conflicts of the story—the human characters versus their environment, the family of Elimelech versus adversity and loss, Naomi versus depression.

Almost everything in the opening chapter, moreover, establishes domestic values as a leading concern of the story: references to family relations, the focus on the history of a family rather than a nation, the domestic titles or epithets for characters (husband, wife, sister-in-law), the parting wish between Naomi and her daughters-in-law in verse 9 ("The LORD grant that you may find a home"), and Ruth's eloquent decision to cling to her mother-in-law (vv. 16–17) all direct our attention to the domestic theme of the story.

The opening chapter also introduces us to the leading characters in the story, and the first thing we notice is that they are women rather than men. They are women for whom domestic values are of overriding importance and whose lives are threatened when their husbands die. The technique of the foil is also important, as we observe the youthful daughters-in-law versus the barren Naomi, the faithlessness of Orpah versus the loyalty of Ruth, Naomi's defeatism and bitterness versus the courage of Ruth in undertaking a new life.

Finally, the opening chapter clearly establishes the story pattern of emptiness versus fullness. On the one hand, we go through a spiral of emptiness that reaches out to the natural, social/domestic, and personal worlds. We read about famine, death, barrenness (vv. 11–12), and the ultimate emptiness—hopelessness. The cumulative effect is overpowering. But already in the opening chapter there is a countermovement. We read about an end to famine (v. 6), about Ruth's refusal to leave her mother-in-law, and about how Ruth and Naomi "came to Bethlehem at the beginning of barley harvest" (v. 22).

The rising action of the story in chapter 2 centers around the growing romance between Ruth and Boaz. The courtship begins and ends with balanced references to the harvest (1:22; 2:23). As this formal opening and close suggest, the story of growing love centers around the progress of the harvest. At one level, this story of harvest is a celebration of the fertility of the earth—a pastoral image of the good life. On another level, the progress of the harvest is a metaphor or symbol for the progress of the romance, a natural parallel to the human event. In both cases, the emphasis on the harvest is the working out of the theme of fullness or restoration.

As in other pastoral literature, the rural setting provides an idealized atmosphere for the love that takes root within it. In keeping with the pastoral world of the story, the woman in the romance is a gleaner of grain, while her husband-to-be is a farmer. As in other pastoral romances, the courtship is conducted in terms appropriate to the rustic milieu. Thus Boaz expresses his favor by inviting Ruth to glean with his own maidens (2:8) and drink the water of his workers (v. 9), as well as by his command to his workers to allow Ruth to glean among the sheaves and even to "pull some from the bundles for her" (v. 16).

In a happy love story, the lovers are worthy of each other, and here, too, the story of Ruth follows the conventions. Boaz is a successful farmer, a kind employer (v. 4), a religious and compassionate person, and (in terms of age) conspicuously older than Ruth, whom he calls "my daughter" (v. 8; see also 3:10, where Boaz is flattered that Ruth has "not gone after young men"). Ruth is energetic (2:7), modest, and gentle. In a comic plot built around the motif of overcoming the obstacles to the romance, the main obstacle at this point is simply the unawareness of Ruth and Boaz that they are likely candidates to marry each other. This unawareness creates the humorous irony at the end of the chapter (vv. 17–23), where Naomi rejoices as she grasps the potential of the situation, while Ruth mechanically records the external details of the day's events and senses no hidden significance.

The chief event of chapter 2, the initial encounter between Ruth and Boaz, is placed in the middle of the chapter (vv. 8–14), much as in a painting what is most important usually appears in the middle of the canvas. The whole encounter is staged as a delicate drama, combining dialogue and gesture as the two speakers gradually move toward agreement. The status of the heroine is highlighted when Ruth links herself with one of the most evocative of all biblical archetypes, that of the stranger or sojourner: "Why have I found favor in your eyes, that you should take notice of me, when I am a foreigner?" (v. 10). As D. F. Rauber comments, with the mention of *foreigner* "a nerve is touched in the consciousness, and our imaginations at once expand to draw into this outwardly simple story large portions of the total experience of the people" (pp. 167–68).

In the climactic third chapter, earlier narrative concerns move toward their completion. One of these motifs is the progress from emptiness to fullness. The chapter opens and closes with references to how the quest for a home is nearing its goal. The overabundance of grain with which Ruth returns to Naomi (vv. 15–17) is the triumphant rejoinder to the earlier emptiness.

Even more important is the growth in understanding that goes on between Ruth and Boaz. Full realization is forced on Boaz in an intense moment of encounter at midnight (vv. 6–11). Again the climactic encounter is placed in the middle of the chapter. The drama of the moment is presented with vividness and with latent humor:

Then she came softly, and uncovered his feet, and lay down. At midnight the man was startled, and turned over, and behold, a woman lay at his feet! [3:7–8]

Ruth's request that Boaz spread his skirt over her (v. 9) employs the same word that Boaz had used in their first encounter when he uttered the wish that Ruth would be rewarded by God, under whose *wings* she had taken refuge (2:12). It is true that God will spread his wings over Ruth, but in a way that Boaz had not been able to imagine. Rauber comments that "everything culminates in this image of ingathering. . . . It is a moment of imaginative splendor and depth" (p. 171).

The last chapter of the story is devoted to triumph and celebration. The focal point is verse 13: "So Boaz took Ruth and she became his wife; and he went in to her, and the LORD gave her conception, and she bore a son." Out of the context of the story, this would be no more than a bit of matter-of-fact reportage. In the context of the story and its images and interrelationships, the verse explodes with emotional and imaginative richness. It completes the quest for a home and resolves the struggle between emptiness and fullness. It is the human manifestation of the theme of harvesting that has dominated much of the story, with the fertility of Ruth's womb an implicit triumph over earlier references to barrenness and loss. This is reinforced by the picture of Naomi taking the infant into her bosom (v. 16).

To accentuate the importance of this story about a simple domestic heroine, the writer brackets verse 13 with two evocative allusions to Israelite history. On one side we find that wish of the townspeople that Ruth might be "like Rachel and Leah" (v. 11). For a moment the whole glory of Israel's patriarchal history focuses on the life of an obscure domestic heroine. This expansion into the past is matched by a later expansion into the future when we are told that the child was named Obed and that "he was the father of Jesse, the father of David" (v. 17). This is more than a patriotic appeal to national history. It also places the action of the story into the Bible's story of salvation history and Ruth into the messianic line.

A main purpose of heroic narrative is to suggest a sense of reality and values. Every storyteller gives us a picture of the world, and of what is right and wrong, valuable and worthless, in that world. The story of Ruth does so in an especially powerful way.

At the simplest level, the story celebrates the commonplace—nature, harvest, family, home, earth. It is not a story about the great public or national events of the time but about the domestic life of a family. It is in the commonplace that God works providentially in this story, and reading the story sends us back to ordinary life with renewed relish and appreciation.

More particularly, this heroic narrative celebrates domestic values. The unifying quest in the story is the quest for a home. The heroine of the story is offered to us as an image of fulfilled womanhood. In the story of Ruth, the whole glory of God's redemptive history rests on a mother in her domestic role.

Finally, the story of Ruth is a celebration of the ideal of wedded romantic love. Except for the Song of Solomon, it is the only canonical work dealing with romantic love. In this story, romantic love between man and woman is idealized and is placed in a strongly social and domestic setting. Boaz completes the marriage according to well-defined social regulations, and the marriage itself has full social sanction, as evidenced by the way in which the townspeople pronounce their blessing on the marriage.

The story of Ruth is a richly human story. The very complexity and artistry of the story resist the attempts I have seen to reduce the story to no more than a collection of historical facts or a theological platitude. I cringe every time I read a theologian's comment that "when the narrative 'trimming' is stripped away, the story of Ruth takes its place as simply one more bit of *Heilsgeschichte* [holy history], for it serves to trace the background of the great David."[4] Against such reductionism I offer the statement of a literary critic who holds up "a picture of the author of Ruth as an artist in full command of a complex and subtle art, which art is exhibited in almost every word of the story" (Rauber, p. 176). Heroic narrative exists to do justice to the humanity of our experience in the world, and this is true also of the religious hero stories that we find in the Bible.

4. Ronald M. Hals, *The Theology of the Book of Ruth* (Philadelphia: Fortress, 1969), p. 19.

5

Epic

Epic is a particular species within the class of heroic narrative. In the previous chapter I suggested that the considerations appropriate to the genre of hero story are an added grid of expectations and conventions that we need to apply beyond the more general narrative ones. Epic adds yet a third grid.

Epics are, of course, stories. In reading them, we need to apply the usual tools of narrative analysis and inquire into plot, setting, and characterization. Because an epic plot revolves around an epic hero, we can also use the framework of heroic narrative when analyzing an epic.

If, then, we ask what epic has in addition to stories in general and hero stories in particular, the first answer is simply *scope*. An epic is a long narrative, a hero story on the grand scale. One scholar lists amplitude, breadth, and inclusiveness as epic traits.[1] Epic is an encyclopedic form— a story with a proliferation of episodes and characters. Northrop Frye calls epic "the story of all things."[2] It is so expansive that it sums up what a

1. E. M. W. Tillyard, *The English Epic and Its Background* (London: Chatto and Windus, 1966), p. 6.
2. Northrop Frye, *The Return of Eden: Five Essays on Milton's Epics* (Toronto: University of Toronto Press, 1965), p. 3.

whole age or culture wishes to say. It focuses a society's attention on who it is and what it stands for.

Part of this expansiveness consists of the *nationalistic emphasis* of epic. Epic is the story of a nation. Although the plot focuses on a central hero, this hero is much more than a private person. He is a national or international figure. His destiny determines the destiny of a whole nation or of the world. Common narrative motifs include warfare, conquest, kingdom, and rulership. Often epics deal with the significant and formative events in the life of a nation. As one scholar puts it, the "great primary epics deal with their cultures at some primitive moment of crisis."[3]

Because of the national scope of epic, it exhibits a *historical impulse.* Epic takes history seriously. Allusions to key events in the life of a nation abound. The events that happen in epic are kept within the framework of broad historical movements in the life of the writer's nation. In one way or another, epic deals with the epoch-making events and movements of history.

Part of the expansiveness of epics is the *supernatural context* in which the action occurs. Literary critics have for centuries used the term *supernatural machinery* to refer to the supernatural beings who participate in the action in these stories. Miraculous events and otherworldly settings are common.

Despite its expansiveness, an epic is tightly structured. *Epic structure* includes both character and plot. Epic ordinarily possesses a unifying hero. The action focuses on a central epic feat, which is almost always some version of winning a battle and establishing a kingdom. The pattern of quest has been pervasive as an epic structure. Because of its scope, an epic plot is always to some degree episodic. We cannot possibly keep the entire story in our minds. Individual events do not form a seamless chain of cause and effect as they do in short stories. Despite this episodic flavor, however, the events can all be related to such overriding frameworks as the epic hero, the epic feat, and (usually) a quest toward a goal. The presence of *type scenes* (recurrent patterns or situations) also lends unity to most epics. The style in which all this exuberance is expressed is ordinarily a *high style.* Most epics have been written in poetry. Even when they are in prose, as biblical epic is, the style is a consciously exalted style. We find epithets (stately titles for persons or things, as when the land of Canaan is called "a land flowing with milk and honey"), pleonasm (taking more words than necessary in an effort to do justice to the grandness of the subject), repeated words and formulas, similes (in which a person or event in the

3. Hugh M. Richmond, *The Christian Revolutionary: John Milton* (Berkeley: University of California Press, 1975), p. 124.

story is compared to something in the world of history or nature), catalogues (lists of names or things), and allusions to history or literature.

The Epic Flavor of Biblical Narrative

Before I focus on specific biblical epics, it is important to note that the epic impulse is widespread in the Bible. Literary scholars who look at the Bible from the background of Western literature are likely to regard the whole Bible as at least epiclike, if not a full-fledged epic. The supernatural orientation, the rootedness in history, the national scope, the impulse to embody the basic values and rituals of a whole society, and the sheer expansiveness of the book make the Bible as a whole seem similar to Homer's *Iliad* and *Odyssey*, Virgil's *Aeneid*, and Milton's *Paradise Lost*, to cite the best known Western epics.

When we start to look at individual books within the Bible, the designation of epic also applies rather widely. The Book of Genesis lacks a single unifying hero, but in other respects it fits the definition. It is certainly about the formative early events in the life of the nation of Israel, since it tells the story of its ancestors. The constant emphasis on the theme of the covenant makes it a story of national and world destiny. The encounters between humans and God remind us continuously of events in the epics with which we are familiar. Genesis also possesses the quality of elemental human experience that is a hallmark of epic.

The historical chronicles of the Old Testament also frequently have the feel of ancient epic. Except for the Book of Joshua, with its unifying motif of conquest under the direction of Joshua, these books lack a unifying hero and single epic feat. But they have too many epic features to be regarded simply as collections of hero stories. They are stories of national history and destiny. They have an epic sweep and cumulative effect. They record the decisive events in the history of the nation. They embody the moral and spiritual values of the nation.

New Testament narrative also approximates epic effects. The Gospels are too expansive, too encyclopedic, and too momentous to strike us simply as hero stories. They have the weight and density and world-changing atmosphere of epics, and they serve a function akin to the epic function of summing up what a culture thinks most worthy of attention and preservation.

The Book of Acts has also rightly been compared to epic. It comes to focus on the journeys and quests of Paul. More importantly, it narrates the sustained action of the birth of the early church and its expansion across vast geographic stretches. It recounts bigger-than-life events and has a strong sense of destiny that sweeps us along as we read. To summarize, although I will give separate discussion to the three stories in the Bible that have the best claim to being regarded as epics, there is much to gain from realizing that the Bible as a whole is frequently epiclike. The framework of epic is continously relevant to the literary study of the Bible. The term *short story* is often applied by literary scholars to the stories of the Bible, but I find the attempt to compare Bible stories to modern short stories unconvincing. Epics are much more likely to yield genuine parallels.

The Epic of the Exodus

The part of the Bible that is most obviously epic in nature is what I will call the Epic of the Exodus. It spans the books Exodus, Leviticus, Numbers, and Deuteronomy. The main narrative sections are these: Exodus 1–20 and 32–34; Numbers 10–14, 16–17, and 20–24; and Deuteronomy 34.

The Epic of the Exodus meets the definition of epic on every score. It is a long narrative that recounts the journey of a nation from Egypt to Canaan, which is the central feat around which the story revolves. The story is nationalistic in emphasis, recording the formation of Israel as a nation and depicting *the* decisive event in the early history of the nation. A great deal of the story is devoted to stating the values and doctrine that were central to Old Testament religious culture. The story is set in history and filled with historical allusions.

Although the story is told in prose rather than poetry, its style is more embellished than is true of most hero stories in the Bible. Speeches tend to be recorded (and sometimes repeated) in full and leisurely detail. There are occasional epic catalogues and epic epithets. The writer is in no hurry to get to the next event. The use of allusions is important. One of the stylistic delights of epic is its ability to combine impressive big effects with intricacy in individual units. The individual episodes in an epic are usually more tightly packed than is true of the modern novel, for example.[4] Reading and pondering an epic is like touring a cathedral.

Unifying Frameworks

The Epic of the Exodus illustrates one scholar's contention that epic "exuberance . . . is not enough in itself; there must be a control commensurate with the amount included" (Tillyard, p. 8). One unifying element is

---

4. Given the constraints of space, I have limited my discussion to the big patterns in the Epic of the Exodus. As a superb example of what the individual units will yield, however, I particularly recommend the explication of the first two chapters of Exodus by James S. Ackerman, "The Literary Context of the Moses Birth Story," in *Literary Interpretations of Biblical Narratives*, ed. Kenneth R. R. Gros Louis (Nashville: Abingdon, 1974), pp. 74–119.

the epic hero, Moses. His birth stands at the beginning of the epic (Exod. 2) and his death brings it to a close (Deut. 34). He is the commanding central character throughout all of the events.

The story is also unified by the journey motif. We rarely lose sight of the idea of traveling, from the opening anticipation of a trip if Pharaoh ever allows it, through the forty years of wandering from one locale to another in the wilderness. As we read the story, we become fellow travelers with the characters, sharing their hardships and frustrations and longings for a fixed place.

Archetypes also help to unify the story. The master images of the story include water, fire, earth, rock, mountain, eating (especially manna), desert, meat, rod, and arm (especially the arm of God). Plot motifs that recur include the test and the rescue.

The story is unified partly by the prevailing atmosphere, as in Edmund Spenser's story *The Faerie Queene*. The world of the story is full of mystery and miracle and is a world alive with the intervening presence of God. We are given specimens of the supernatural acts of God in a world where this kind of thing is always going on. The multiplicity of events, far from impairing the unity of the story, actually reinforces it. This fullness of adventure and divine intervention is the essential quality of the world of the story. As we enter the world of the story, we observe humanity confronting the elemental aspects of its experience—the struggle for physical survival, the difficulty of relating to other people and to authority, life and death, the divine-human relationship, and the conflict within the human soul between good and evil.

Finally, the Epic of the Exodus has its own dominant type scene—a recurrent situation with a set of common ingredients that provides shape to the individual episodes. The pattern that is repeated throughout the epic is this sequence: a crisis threatens the Israelites; the people fail the test of their faith and complain to Moses; Moses cries to God; God rescues the people or provides for their need; God rebukes and/or reveals something to the people. This pattern begins at the Red Sea (Exod. 14) and thereafter punctuates the action—at the bitter water of Marah (Exod. 15:22–26), when the people lack food (Exod. 16:1–30), with the lack of water at Rephidim (Exod. 17:1–7), and so forth. Similar to this type scene is the conflict between human weakness and divine strength that I will discuss later.

The Story Itself

Few stories in the Bible can rival the Epic of the Exodus for sheer excitement and adventure. I find it one of the easiest Bible stories to read and lose myself in. There are narrative explanations for this.

The story itself is replete with suspense. In fact, it is one continuous narrow escape, like the stories of Tolkien. There is danger at every hand, in the form of foreign oppressors, a hostile environment, inadequate food and drink, and God's punishment of the people's disobedience. Life is momentous in the story. Much of the suspense takes the form of character testing. The Israelites generally fail the test, but we keep hoping that just once they will surprise us. Rescue from apparently certain disaster keeps the story lively.

Conflict also produces its share of fireworks. In the early phases of the story the conflict is international in scope, as the Egyptians oppress the Israelite slaves. Once the itinerary begins, the traveling community is often in conflict with its natural environment. Psychological conflict takes the form of conflict within the traveling community itself, particularly between the people and their leader Moses.

What is commonly called epic sweep partly accounts for the narrative success of the Epic of the Exodus. The journey from the land of slavery to the promised land "flowing with milk and honey" provides a strong sense of movement toward a goal. The sheer length of the ordeal grips us.

The story is also a supreme story of adventure and as such invites comparison with Homer's *Odyssey*, which also tells a story about a traveling community that encounters a series of tests and adventures on its journey. Variety of adventure is a virtue in both stories. As we progress through the Epic of the Exodus, it is quickly obvious that the writer has interspersed long and short episodes. The nature of the threat or conflict likewise changes from one episode to the next. So does the harshness or softness of the episode. As we read, we are led to wonder what will generate the conflict *this* time.

The Anti-Epic Motif

As suggested, the Epic of the Exodus invites comparison with other epics. Virgil's *Aeneid* is the closest parallel. Both epics tell about the formation of an empire and were a call to their original audiences to contemplate the early history of their nations. Both are quest stories in which a group of people travels from one geographic area to another in order to establish a stable nation in a promised land. Both stories are unified around a hero who is a leader of people and who embodies the values of the cultures from which the epics arose. Both epics are religious epics, filled with references to the proper worship of deity.

These parallels between the Epic of the Exodus and other epics should not be allowed to obscure the important way in which biblical epic differs from traditional epic. In fact, when we place biblical epic alongside conventional epics, it quickly sets up an intertext in which biblical epic both parallels and differs from conventional epic.

Conventional epic is humanistic in its basic premise: it exists to praise and glorify a human hero. The conventional epic hero is godlike in his accomplishments. He may even be of divine parentage, as Aeneas is. Heroes like Aeneas and Achilles and Beowulf merit praise by virtue of their own superhuman deeds. Their stories are essentially stories of human merit.

With this as the norm, the Epic of the Exodus, like Milton's *Paradise Lost*, emerges as an anti-epic as well as an epic. Everywhere we find the traditional epic values inverted. For the praise of people, the writer has substituted the glory of God. Instead of depicting human strength, this epic depicts human frailty and sinfulness. Instead of telling a story in which a human warrior leads his nation to victory through superhuman feats on the battlefield, this writer attributes the mighty acts of deliverance to God. In fact, the people in the story are usually passive spectators of God's acts.

In place of an epic leader who depends on his own abilities and strength, we find a reluctant leader who is unsure of his own claims to leadership, inarticulate, of obscure origin, and meek. Instead of exalting the nation about whom the epic is written, this epic continually stresses the imperfections of the Israelites—their rebelliousness, their lack of faith, their tendency to complain. Whereas traditional epic depicts physical warfare, the Epic of the Exodus is more concerned with spiritual conflict. Spiritual rebellion against God frequently replaces the conventional theme of armed conflict between nations. Common epic formulas (such as conquest and dominion) and epic virtues (such as power and worthiness) are attributed to God rather than to a human hero.

A brief look at some key events will illustrate the anti-epic strain in the story. The hero's hesitancy to assume leadership (Exod. 4) introduces the theme of human inadequacy. Moses' disclaimer that he is "not eloquent" (4:10) makes him a contrast to other epic heroes, who are unfailingly eloquent. Equally unconventional is his fear that others "will not believe [him] or listen to [his] voice" (4:1). Unlike other epic leaders, Moses is without external claim to prominence, being the son of a slave. His only real credential for leadership is that he has been called and equipped by God.

The events leading to the exodus from Egypt, especially the ten plagues, are solely the result of God's activity. The Israelites themselves remain spectators. At the conclusion of the ten plagues, we read regarding the Hebrews, "Thus they despoiled the Egyptians" (Exod. 12:36). This is the standard formula in heroic epic, but the usual expectations are completely denied. The conquest has not been won on the battlefield through human effort but has been given to the Israelites by God's miraculous intervention.

The speech of Moses to the people shortly after the departure from Egypt (Exod. 13:3–16) is filled with statements that attribute the epic acts to God rather than a human hero. This anti-epic note comes out in statements such as these: "by strength of hand the LORD brought you out from this place" (v. 3); "when the LORD brings you into the land of the Canaanites . . ." (vv. 5, 11); "and you shall tell your son on that day, 'It is because of what the LORD did for me when I came out of Egypt'" (v. 8); "by strength of hand the LORD brought us out of Egypt" (v. 14); "the LORD slew all the first-born in the land of Egypt" (v. 15). Thus the storyteller reserves his praise for God instead of a human hero.

God is also the epic hero in the events surrounding the deliverance at the Red Sea. In fact, God prompts Pharaoh to pursue the Israelites for the purpose of getting "glory over Pharaoh and all his host; and the Egyptians shall know that I am the LORD" (Exod. 14:4). When the Israelites are terrified by the approaching Egyptian army, Moses points to their divine deliverer with the words, "Fear not, stand firm, and see the salvation of the LORD, which he will work for you today. . . . The LORD will fight for you, and you have only to be still" (Exod. 14:13–14).

Subsequently we read about how "the LORD routed the Egyptians in the midst of the sea" (v. 27), how "the LORD saved Israel that day from the hand of the Egyptians" (v. 30), and how "Israel saw the great work which the LORD did against the Egyptians" (v. 31). It is small wonder that Moses, instead of singing a song exalting a human warrior in the manner of classical epic, leads the people in a song that praises God (Exod. 15). It is not surprising that the song portrays God as an epic warrior: "The LORD is a man of war" (Exod. 15:3).

The great disparity between God and people is emphasized not only by exalting God but also by exposing the unworthiness of the Israelites. The latter are depicted as chronic complainers. When the Egyptian army approaches, the people say to Moses, "Is it because there are no graves in Egypt that you have taken us away to die in the wilderness? What have you done to us, in bringing us out of Egypt? . . . For it would have been better for us to serve the Egyptians than to die in the wilderness" (Exod. 14:11–12). When they discover the bitter waters at Marah, they "[murmur] against Moses" (Exod. 15:24).

Lacking meat, the people "murmured against Moses and Aaron" and hankered after "the fleshpots" of Egypt (Exod. 16:2–3). When they lacked water at Rephidim, they "found fault with Moses" (17:2). On another occasion they wept and said, "O that we had meat to eat! We remember the fish we ate in Egypt for nothing, the cucumbers, the melons, the leeks, the onions, and the garlic" (Num. 11:4–5). In sum, the Israelites respond to physical hardship by displaying a lack of contentment with what God has sent, inability to live without luxuries, a complaining spirit, and unwillingness to postpone gratification until they reach the Promised Land.

The consistently unflattering view of the writer's own nation involves specifically spiritual sins as well as a complaining spirit. When God sends quail and manna, making it a test of obedience (Exod. 16:4–5), the people fail the test by showing themselves guilty of greed (16:20) and desecration of the sabbath (16:25–29). When Moses' return from the mountain is delayed, the Israelites resort to idolatry (Exod. 32). There are rebellions against legitimate authority, led by Miriam and Aaron on one occasion (Num. 12) and by Korah, Dathan, and Abiram on another (Num. 16).

The Israelites' supreme venture in shameful behavior occurs when they display a lack of faith by accepting the report of the ten spies who advise against entering the Promised Land (Num. 13–14). Even Moses, the highly idealized epic leader, is guilty of pride, impatience, and disobedience when he strikes the rock at Meribah instead of speaking to it (Num. 20:1–13).

As this survey of events suggests, the human record in the Epic of the Exodus is almost uniformly disastrous. At one point God speaks of how the people "have put me to the proof these ten times and have not hearkened to my voice" (Num. 14:22). If we go back over the story, we discover ten occasions when the Israelites as a whole are said to murmur against God, against God's chosen leaders, or against the circumstances into which God has brought them. It turns out to be a list of most of the key events in the epic: the oppression by the slavemasters in response to Moses' early activity (Exod. 5:20–21); the Red Sea crisis (Exod. 14:10–12); the bitter waters at Marah (Exod. 15:24); the lack of food near Elim (Exod. 16:2–3); the disobedience regarding the gathering of manna (Exod. 16:20, 27); the lack of water at Rephidim (Exod. 17:2–3); the incident of the golden calf (Exod. 32); the complaining at Taberah (Num. 11:1); the craving for meat (Num. 11:4–5); and the unbelief of the ten spies (Num. 13–14).

Whatever glory there is in the epic belongs to God, who repeatedly contends with human sinfulness and leads the Israelites to Canaan in spite of themselves. This anti-epic theme reaches its culmination in the song that Moses sings shortly before his death (Deut. 32), a song that praises God's faithfulness and dispraises Israel's waywardness.

The Epic of David

The story of David spans several Old Testament books. For representative episodes, 1 Samuel 16–17 and 2 Samuel 5–19 will suffice. Considered as a hero story, the account of the life of David is rather fragmented and lacking in unity, reading more like a historical chronicle than a literary narrative. But if we come to the story with the expectations of epic, placing the personal story of David into the broader context of national history, the expansiveness of the plot and complexity of the hero's characterization fall into place. David is the closest biblical parallel to such heroes of classical epic as Achilles and Odysseus and Aeneas and to the knights of medieval romance. He is the warrior who makes his mark in the world with his sword. His military heroism, aptly summed up in the shout of the crowds that "David [has slain] his ten thousands" (1 Sam. 18:7), puts him in a large group of ancient literary heroes for whom political kingship is the ultimate earthly reward and the battlefield is the scene of the decisive events of history. David is in every way one of the most complex characters in epic literature, rivaled only by Homer's Odysseus.[5] He is a hero of many roles, including shepherd, poet, warrior, subject, king, friend, husband, father, and religious leader. He is also a man of complex personal qualities. He is a man of both action and contemplation; the Old Testament narratives capture the first side of him, while his psalms show us the second side. The psalms show him to be a man of strong emotions, either in the pit of depression or in the ecstasy of praise.

Here is an epic hero who can display great self-restraint, as when he twice refuses a ready-made opportunity to kill his enemy Saul, while on other occasions he shows an equally unexplained tendency to give in to his passions, as when he commits adultery with Bathsheba and orders the innocent Uriah murdered in battle. Through all his tragedies and triumphs, the spiritual dimension is never absent from David's life. When he sins, he recognizes it as sin against God (Ps. 51). When he triumphs, he turns in praise to the God who has given him the victory (Ps. 18). All of this bespeaks a man for whom all of life is God's.

If we add David's relationships to this picture of his multiple roles and personal qualities, the epic quality of the story becomes even clearer. Because epics are built around a national leader, they combine the public and personal relationships of the hero. This is what we find in the story of David, where the hero relates to a wide array of friends and enemies, family members and state officials, religious leaders and ordinary people.

As epic hero, David combines two sets of values and two ways of life usually thought to be antithetical—the pastoral and the heroic. Pastoral writers ordinarily despise courtly values and show how much vice can be avoided by living the simple life of a shepherd. David begins his life as the humble shepherd, the sweet singer of Israel (2 Sam. 23:1), the man of spiritual introspection whom we know best from his psalms. But he becomes the leader of a nation, the man of heroic action, the courageous warrior defeating enemies on the battlefield. David's dual identity is highlighted when God says regarding him, "I took you from the pasture, from following the sheep, that you should be prince over my people Israel" (2 Sam. 7:8). We find here a primitive quality that pervades much of the

5. For a sampling of the amazing range of ways in which the character of David has been interpreted through the ages, see *The David Myth in Western Literature*, ed. Raymond-Jean Frontain and Jan Wojcik (West Lafayette, Ind.: Purdue University Press, 1980).

Bible, which takes us into a world where national leaders can walk without guards and where kings tend their flocks.

David first enters the heroic world of kingship when Samuel anoints him king over Israel (1 Sam. 16). The story belongs to the common biblical archetype of the unlikely hero. In fact, David, the youngest son of Jesse, is so obscure that he has to be fetched from the sheep before the anointing takes place (v. 11). Here is a variation on an important biblical theme—the unreliability of human standards of value in comparison with God's perspective. This theme is made explicit when "the LORD said to Samuel, . . . 'the LORD sees not as man sees; man looks on the outward appearance, but the LORD looks on the heart'" (v. 7).

The story of the anointing idealizes the future hero. He is described as being "skilful in playing, a man of valor, a man of war, prudent in speech, and a man of good presence; and the LORD is with him" (v. 18). We also read that the boy hero "was ruddy, and had beautiful eyes, and was handsome" (v. 12). Here, in short, is an epic hero.

The story of David and Goliath (1 Sam. 17) is one of the supreme moments in epic literature. The appeal of the story is to the most naive and least sophisticated of literary tastes. This story built around that perennial favorite, the boy hero, has all the ingredients of a good story. There is a vivid conflict between a pagan bully and the people of God, with the wartime setting heightening the effect. The single combat concentrates all of the hostility into a single event.

From the point of view of David and the narrator, the issue at stake is nothing less than "that all the earth may know that there is a God in Israel" (v. 46). The event thus becomes part of the holy war between the forces of God and evil, and we become participants in a conflict between obvious right and obvious wrong. The struggle between competing values stands out when David says to the giant, "You come to me with a sword and with a spear and with a javelin; but I come to you in the name of the LORD of hosts, . . . whom you have defied" (v. 45).

The contrast between the two principal actors in this epic drama is similarly heightened. One is a villain—a giant, no less, who evokes instinctive feelings of dread and moral revulsion when he defies the armies of God. On the other side we have a boy hero, a homespun underdog who fells the proud enemy of God with a slingshot. Here is one of many biblical stories that appeals to what is childlike and "romantic" in us. It fulfills our instinct for wish fulfillment, even though we realize that life is tragic as well as comic.

In terms of storytelling technique, the story of David and Goliath appeals to our imaginations. We can *hear* the giant defying Israel and *see* David picking up five smooth stones and *visualize* him running to meet Goliath. Along with this vividness, the story displays a firm sense of structure. The storyteller does not clutter the narrative with too many details. He begins with an exposition of background information, conveys a sense of rising action, constructs his story around a single climax, and once the climax has been reached quickly brings the story to a close.

In typical epic fashion, the main narrative concern in the story of David is David's kingship. The account of his reign begins in 2 Samuel 5, which shows David in a variety of roles—his role as the new king (vv. 1–12), his domestic role (vv. 13–16), and his role as warrior (vv. 17–25). Kingdom, home, war—these will be the dominant notes in the epic. David's heroic status is clearly established as a gift from God. The narrator asserts that "David became greater and greater, for the LORD, the God of hosts, was with him" (v. 10). In keeping with a conventional epic motif in which divine forces aid the hero, David inquires of God regarding his battle plans. (vv. 19, 23–25).

As epic hero, David is portrayed as a religious person, as chapters 6 and 7 of 2 Samuel make clear. David's dancing with abandon before the ark of God (6:14) shows him to be a man of strong religious emotions. His desire to build a temple for God (7:1–3) further establishes his piety, as does his prayer after God has rejected him as the one to build the temple (vv. 18–29). God's words about what he has done and will do for David (vv. 4–17) are sometimes called the Davidic covenant, and they, too, serve to establish David's favor with God.

Battlefield action is a staple in epic, and it is prominent in the story of David (see, for example, 2 Sam. 8 and 10). It makes David the clearest biblical parallel to the conquering heroes of classical epic and the old heroic code. In the conventional heroic formula, the hero wins fame for himself through prowess on the battlefield. David fits the pattern when we read that he "won a name for himself" (2 Sam. 8:13). The added dimension in biblical epic is that "the LORD gave victory to David wherever he went" (v. 14).

The story of David's adultery with Bathsheba (2 Sam. 11) is the first of several chapters dealing with the personal and domestic life of the hero. It shows the epic hero to be a man of strong passions and depicts the tragedy that engulfs him when he fails to control his sexual desire for a beautiful woman. The episode also exemplifies the way in which one sin leads to another in an attempt to conceal the original crime. In this case, the sin of adultery quickly leads to the premeditated murder in battle of Bathsheba's husband, Uriah. David's message to the captain ("Do not let this matter trouble you, for the sword devours now one and now another" [v. 25]) shows his inhuman callousness toward the murder.

For the writer of 2 Samuel, this event marks the turning point in David's career. Up to this point, the writer paints a sympathetic picture of David's successes. Beginning with the affair with Bathsheba, the action is dominated by the consequences of David's sin within his own family. A crime-

and-punishment motif comes to dominate the story, in contrast to the idealized interpretation that dominated the first half of the story. The writer thus interprets David's life as a tragedy based on a cause-effect view of the hero's suffering. David's family becomes a family under a curse, as in ancient Greek tragedy. The focus, moreover, is on David's failures as a father.

David is not the only epic hero who is diverted from his pursuits by sexual relations with a beautiful woman. Odysseus, whose fidelity to home and wife is unquestioned, has sexual relations with both Calypso and Circe. Unlike David, however, he is not morally reprehensible within the logic of the story because his relations are involuntary relations with goddesses, whose advances he cannot disregard with impunity. His sexual infidelity to his wife is not even considered objectionable by the narrator or by his wife, Penelope.

If we know Homer's story, we can scarcely read the story of David and Bathsheba without an intertext arising in our consciousness. The main discrepancy is not between the two human heroes but between the two conceptions of deity. In the Bible's epic, the holy God is displeased with the sin of adultery, as summarized in the narrator's statement that "the thing that David had done displeased the LORD" (2 Sam. 11:27). The underlying moral principle is clear: adultery is horrible because it is a perversion of something God-ordained and sacred, namely, faithful wedded love. The stories of classical mythology that depict gods and goddesses (such as Calypso and Circe in *The Odyssey*) as engaging in promiscuous sexual relations with each other and with humans reflect a low view of gods, who are made in man's image, and a low view of the sanctity of wedded love, the perversion of which is not notable because the thing itself is not regarded very highly in the first place.[6]

The story of David and Bathsheba also invites comparison with the most famous episode in Virgil's *Aeneid*. When Aeneas allows himself to be diverted from his duty by falling in love with Dido at Carthage, the act displeases Jupiter. To that extent the story parallels the story of David. But why does it displease Jupiter? It displeases him because the love affair diverts Aeneas from his political task. By contrast, God is displeased with David because David has committed an immoral act. The essential nature of Aeneas's sin is that he allowed passion to conquer his reason, the great transgression in classical ethics. The view of sin in the biblical epic is far different. Its essence is that David disobeyed the moral law of a holy God.

These differences explain the contrasting dynamics of restoration in the two epics. Aeneas resolves his lapse by simply allowing the light of reason

6. For comment on the unidealized view of romantic love in classical antiquity, see C. S. Lewis, *The Allegory of Love: A Study in Medieval Tradition* (New York: Oxford University Press, 1936), pp. 4–8.

to dispel the dark passions that have momentarily gained control of his sense of duty. He leaves on the very night after Mercury arrived to warn him of Jupiter's displeasure, and as the boat leaves Carthage his conscience is clear. David's restoration, however, involves his coming to terms with the past act. He cannot simply walk away from the act by a resolve to reform. His sin needs forgiveness from a holy and forgiving God, as is made particularly clear in Psalm 51, which was occasioned by David's conviction of his sin.

The story of David's adultery reaches its conclusion—and the hero's troubles begin—when the prophet Nathan tells a parable that convicts David of his sin (2 Sam. 12:1–15). The parable is itself an example of the indirectness by which great literature works. David convicts himself without knowing what he is doing. In performing an act of literary interpretation and civil and moral judgment, he is actually condemning himself. In keeping with the Bible's tendency to focus on the redemptive potential of tragic events, however, this story of personal failure is partly resolved by the hero's confession and God's forgiveness (2 Sam. 12:13).

David's sin results in family consequences, as Nathan had predicted (2 Sam. 12:11). This phase of David's story reminds us of Shakespeare's most famous tragedy, *King Lear*. In both stories, the action occurs on several levels at once—personal, family, and civil. The moral disorder within David, the father and king, quickly branches out and produces moral disintegration in both the family and state. Thus the incest of David's son Amnon (2 Sam. 13:1–19) and his murder by his brother Absalom (vv. 20–29) reenact David's two heinous sins. The narrative strategy here is that of the subplot.

With the story of Absalom's revolt (2 Sam. 15–19), the moral disorder moves outward from the individual and family into the state. These chapters are a self-contained story, cyclic in structure. They begin with the king fleeing for his life and conclude with his return as king. On a social and political level, disintegration and fragmentation are balanced by restoration and unity. Absalom emerges as a tragic figure—the archetypal usurper and overreacher who is punished in a gruesome manner.

The epic quality of David's story is well illustrated by the story of his flight (2 Sam. 15:13–16:14). The story is built around the procession motif that brings together a series of personal encounters in a context of war. The series of character vignettes begins with Ittai, who remains a loyal follower of the king even though it involves personal risk to him (2 Sam. 15:19–23). The Levites are the bewildered religious officials forced to comply with strange happenings now that war has arrived (vv. 24–29). Ahithophel plays the part of the traitor (v. 31), while Hushai is the person willing to risk his life for the rightful cause (vv. 32–37). Ziba is the opportunist, using war and treachery as a means of obtaining personal gain (2 Sam. 16:1–4). And Shimei is simply the enemy, glad for the misfortune that has engulfed the legitimate ruler (vv. 5–14). What realism and humanity we find painted with just a few telling brushstrokes.

In addition to the personal encounters, we find an amazing narrative ability to make the whole scene come alive with vivid details. Notice, for example, how the descriptive and affective technique makes the following picture of innocent suffering come to life in our imaginations:

> But David went up the ascent of the Mount of Olives, weeping as he went, barefoot and with his head covered; and all the people who were with him covered their heads, and they went up, weeping as they went. [2 Sam. 15:30]

Shimei's antagonism is captured not only by his curses ("Begone, begone, you man of blood, you worthless fellow!" [2 Sam. 16:7]), but also by the picture of his walking along the hillside opposite David, cursing as he went and throwing stones and flinging dust at David (v. 13). David's servants offer to make an end of Shimei, but David refuses the offer (vv. 9–12). Throughout the tragic scene of suffering, David rises in our estimation. Like other epic figures, he assumes grandeur as he wrestles with the great ordeals in his life.

The epic story of David is complemented by his lyric poems. They give an added dimension to his characterization that narrative by itself lacks. His lyric poems, which appear mostly in the Psalms, take us inside the hero's consciousness and give us a feel for the inner weather of his soul. Here we glimpse the psychological and spiritual realities behind the bustle of activities that made up David's life as king.

More than any other character in the Old Testament, David is an epic hero. The story of his life is so much more than the life of an individual. In his life we can see much of the life of his time and beyond that of all time, including our own experiences, both good and bad.

The Book of Revelation

Like the Epic of the Exodus, the Book of Revelation is both epic and counter-epic. It reenacts the familiar epic conventions, but it lifts them to a spiritual and heavenly level. The result is an intertext between conventional epic and the Book of Revelation.[7]

7. In the paragraphs that follow, I restate a view of the Book of Revelation that appears in my essay "*Paradise Lost* and Its Biblical Epic Models," pp. 75–79 in *Milton and Scriptural Tradition: The Bible into Poetry*, ed. James H. Sims and Leland Ryken (Columbia: University of Missouri Press, 1984).

The basic action in the Book of Revelation is an epic action. At the center of it all is a great and heightened battle conducted partly by spiritual beings using supernatural means of warfare. The setting for the action is cosmic and includes heaven as well as earth and hell. References to the earth often extend to the whole earth, not just a localized part of it. The following famous passage epitomizes the epic plot and setting of the book:

> Now war arose in heaven, Michael and his angels fighting against the dragon; and the dragon and his angels fought, but they were defeated and there was no longer any place for them in heaven. And the great dragon was thrown down, that ancient serpent, who is called the Devil and Satan, the deceiver of the whole world—he was thrown down to the earth, and his angels were thrown down with him. [12:7–9]

Other epic conventions also appear. There are scenes set in heaven where decisions are made that are then enacted on earth. These scenes resemble, both in construction and function, the epic councils of the gods. Epics usually include a preview or vision of future history, and this is the premise underlying most of the Book of Revelation. Epics recount the exploits of a hero who conquers his enemies and establishes an empire. The Book of Revelation is the story of Christ's conquest of Satan and evil and his establishing of his eternal spiritual kingdom.

The style of the book is an epic style. The writer uses similes in an effort to do justice to his vision and theme: "a loud voice like a trumpet" (1:10); "his head and his hair were white as white wool, white as snow" (1:14); "a sea of glass, like crystal" (4:6); "a loud voice, like a lion roaring" (10:3). Another feature of epic style is the exalted epithets (titles) that give the book much of its exuberance: "Jesus Christ the faithful witness, the first-born of the dead, and the ruler of kings on earth" (1:5); "the Lion of the tribe of Judah, the Root of David" (5:5); "King of kings and Lord of lords" (19:16).

The Book of Revelation contains epic catalogues—of churches, of the beings around God's throne in heaven, of the tribes of Israel, of the jewels in the heavenly city. There are allusions to the Old Testament (350 of them) and to events in the redemptive life of Christ. Epic style is exuberant and overflowing, and no part of the Bible possesses this quality more than the Book of Revelation:

> to him who loves us and has freed us from our sins by his blood and made us a kingdom, priests to his God and Father, to him be glory and dominion for ever and ever. Amen. [1:5–6]

The words are electric. The impression is grand.

But if Revelation is an epic, it is a unique epic. Everywhere we turn we find the familiar epic motifs transformed into a spiritual reality. The quest for a kingdom, for example, is a quest for the spiritual, heavenly, and eternal kingdom of Christ, not an earthly political kingdom, as is made clear midway through the book: "The kingdom of the world has become the kingdom of our Lord and of his Christ, and he shall reign for ever and ever" (11:15). Conquest in the Book of Revelation is not primarily national and military but consists rather of the defeat of Satan and the forces of spiritual evil. We see this during the war in heaven (chap. 12), during the millennial binding of Satan (20:1–4), and when Satan's forces are defeated and cast into the lake of fire (20:7–10).

Epics make much of the motif of glory, but they concentrate on human glory. In the Book of Revelation, glory is not the fame that human warriors win for themselves through victory on the battlefield but the spiritual glory that God confers on those who enter heaven through the merits of Christ. In the great battle of chapter 12, for example, we read that the saints conquer the dragon and his angels "by the blood of the Lamb and by the word of their testimony" (v. 11).

As part of this strategy of spiritualizing epic motifs, the Book of Revelation shifts the focus of epic formulas from the human to the divine. It dispenses with the classical paraphernalia of a semidivine or human hero and pictures instead a divine hero, Christ. Victory is not a human hero's victory but Christ's defeat of Satan and redemption of his church. Warfare is not primarily human and earthly but is conducted by supernatural beings. Human action often consists of the passive activity of patient endurance until Christ appears.

It is a rule of epic that the epic hero deserves fame for what he does. The pattern is present in the Book of Revelation, but it is God who deserves such honor: "Blessing and glory and wisdom and thanksgiving and honor and power and might be to our God for ever and ever!" (7:12). Revelation has the usual epic emphasis on history, but its focus is not on political or national history. Instead it brings to a climax what biblical scholars have taught us to call salvation history—the record of God's judgment and redemption throughout all history. Heroes in classical epic exert themselves to win or establish a city; the same motif appears at the end of Revelation, but it is not a human city. It is a supernatural and heavenly city—a "holy city . . . having the glory of God" (21:10–11).

The Book of Revelation, in its own way, is an anti-epic as well as an epic. It takes the best of the literary tradition of epic and transposes it into a different key. The result is something unlike anything else in the epic tradition.

6

Tragedy

From the time of Aristotle and the Greeks, tragedy has held an honored position among people who value literature. It is not a form that makes for light entertainment, but it has unusual ability to do justice to the serious side of life.

Tragedy is defined in terms of both plot and character. The one common denominator in all tragedies is the downward movement of the plot from positive experience to catastrophe. The tragic hero begins in an exalted position and ends in disgrace and usually death. The key element in this downward plunge in the action is some great mistake that the hero makes. The element of choice is essential to the tragic plot. The spectacle of a passive sufferer is not tragedy but pathos. Tragedy thus focuses on the destructive potential of evil in human experience.

The plot of tragedy is remarkably constant from one work to another and has six main phases. It begins with the hero's *dilemma*, the situation demanding or eliciting a choice. Caught in the difficult position, the tragic hero makes a moral *choice*. The choice plunges both the hero and his world into *catastrophe*. This is accompanied by the tragic hero's *suffering*. Most tragic heroes achieve some type of *perception* near the end of the action. It is an insight into what went wrong (a conviction of sin) and/or an awareness of what the hero has lost by his missing of the mark. The final phase of the tragic plot is normally the *death* of the tragic hero.

When we shift our attention from the tragic plot to the tragic hero, the first thing we notice is how conspicuous this person is in the world of the story. Tragedy focuses on the protagonist. The tragic hero is not a villain, though he may degenerate into such during the course of the story. A tragic hero is an initially good person who wins our general sympathy at the outset. He is a person with exalted social position. Until modern times, he was almost always a king or ruler—a person regarded as representative of his society, a strong and aggressive person willing to test the limits of his humanity, a person in the vulnerable position from which a great fall is possible.

Tragic heroes are what we loosely call bigger-than-life figures. They have a certain overflowing abundance of energy and possess that intangible quality that we call greatness of spirit. It follows, then, that ordinary misfortune or suffering is not what makes literary tragedy. Tragedy is the spectacle of exceptional calamity.

Despite all his greatness, however, the tragic hero is not exempt from moral criticism or the natural order of the world. The moral dimension of tragedy is especially bound up with the tragic flaw of character that afflicts the hero. Aristotle (in the *Poetics*) called it *hamartia*, a missing of the mark in archery. It is the New Testament word for sin. In Aristotle's terms, it is "some great error or frailty," some "defect which is painful or destructive." This means that tragedy deals with caused suffering, not the arbitrary buffetings of life.

By thus linking human choice and human suffering, tragedy depicts a hero who is *responsible for* his downfall. The tragic hero always initiates his own tragedy. Usually he is also *deserving of* his tragedy, since it grew out of a flaw of character. In literature generally, the calamity that engulfs the hero seems disproportionate, and the tragic hero gains a certain sympathy and grandeur as he struggles against the forces that punish him. Biblical tragedy is atypical in denying such sympathy to the tragic hero during his decline.

To summarize, tragedy can be defined as a story in which a protagonist of high degree and possessing greatness of spirit undertakes an action (makes a choice) and as a result inevitably falls from prosperity to a state of physical and spiritual suffering, sometimes attaining perception. This is the general literary definition that biblical tragedy both follows and breaks.

The Spirit of Tragedy in the Bible

It is common for literary scholars to speak of "the spirit of tragedy." That spirit is definitely present in the Bible. This is true even though there are very few full-fledged tragedies in the Bible.

We should note in this regard that the basic premises of literary tragedy correspond significantly with the theology and world view of the Bible. If we ask what features of human experience are captured with particular clarity in literary tragedy, the resulting list looks something like this: human limitation and fallenness (tragedy grounds itself on the bedrock of original sin), human choice, the dangerousness of life (human vulnerability and the knack for doing the wrong thing), justice, human suffering, wisdom through suffering (a redemptive potential in suffering), and human significance. Overall, tragedy is the story of human failure, and to read a tragedy or see it acted on stage is to participate in a ritual of confession, acknowledging that people are flawed creatures.

This is a long list, and it adheres strongly to the contours of the Bible's view of God, people, and the world. It is not surprising, therefore, that philosophers and theologians have lavished so much attention on the literary form of tragedy. Northrop Frye's comment that "the Bible is not very friendly to tragic themes" seems less accurate to me than it once did.[1] The tragic spirit pervades much of the Bible, even when it does not produce full-fledged tragedies.

That spirit makes its first appearance in the story of the fall in Genesis 3. Within the Bible, this is the source and model of all later tragedies. As such, it contains virtually all the ingredients of later biblical tragedies. The tragic heroes (Adam and Eve) are prominent and representative figures. They live in a world that demands moral choice—whether to obey or disobey God. They are not flawed characters to begin, but in their moment of tragic choice we can see their fatal missing of the mark as they disobey God. Reaching for everything, they lose all. They are both responsible for and deserving of their punishment. In typical tragic fashion, there are scenes of suffering and perception.

When we turn to the historical chronicles of the Old Testament, we also find tragic elements. There are numerous stories of characters who cast their lot with evil rather than good and who display character flaws in the process. The cause-effect link between sin and suffering runs strong throughout these histories. Cain commits a murder and dooms himself to a life of wandering (Gen. 4:1–16). Achan hides the spoil of silver and gold in his tent and dies for it (Josh. 7). Korah, Dathan, and Abiram rebel against the authority of Moses and Aaron, and the earth swallows them and their households (Num. 16). These are only specimens of the brief tragic narratives that we keep encountering as we read the Bible.

The lives of Old Testament kings display the same strand. I have already noted that in the account of David's life in 2 Samuel the overall pattern is

---

1. Northrop Frye, *The Great Code: The Bible and Literature* (New York: Harcourt Brace Jovanovich, 1981), p. 181.

tragic, with David's acts of adultery and murder providing the great watershed in his life between exceptional success and calamity. The life of his son Solomon is equally tragic, following a downward arc from initial prosperity and wisdom to apostasy, sensuality, and luxury.

Yet another source of literary tragedies in the Bible is the parables of Jesus.[2] In these dramas of the soul's choice we see the inevitable potential for either tragedy or comedy. The gallery of tragic figures is impressive: the slothful servant who hides his master's money, the five foolish virgins, the wedding guests who refuse the invitation, the elder brother who refuses the festivities of forgiveness, the rich man who ignored the beggar, the self-righteous Pharisee who is contrasted to the tax collector—the list goes on and on.

The element of suffering is so prominent in tragedy that many stories that are not tragic in their overall plot shape are smuggled into the canon of literary tragedies by virtue of their sensitive portrayal of human suffering. A biblical example is the story of Job. Overall, the plot of the story of Job is the usual U-shaped comic plot. But so much of the story focuses on human suffering that we can legitimately speak of the presence of the tragic spirit throughout much of the story. Much the same is true of the New Testament Gospels.[3] As a form, tragedy deals with the problem of evil and suffering. So does the Bible, so much so that one literary critic believes that "overriding all else" as we read the Bible is our awareness "of the problem, re-stated constantly and from many angles of experience, of evil and suffering: the theodicy which lies at the heart of all tragedy."[4] The spirit of tragedy is never far from the surface in the Bible, and occasionally it results in stories that are full literary tragedies.

The Tragedy of Samson

The story of Samson (Judg. 13–16) is one of the most complex stories in the Bible, despite its brevity. It is both a tragedy and a heroic folk narrative. The hero is both criticized and celebrated. As a result, most episodes are presented in an ambivalent light, depending on whether an event is viewed from the perspective of Samson as a tragic figure or a folk hero. On a public level, the story of Samson's heroism centers in his superhuman strength that makes him a deliverer of his nation from the enemy Philistines. At the personal level, Samson's tragedy revolves around his

2. For discussion, see Dan Otto Via, Jr., *The Parables: Their Literary and Existential Dimension* (Philadelphia: Fortress, 1967), especially pp. 110–44.

3. On the tragic element in the Gospels, see especially Roger L. Cox, "Tragedy and the Gospel Narratives," *Yale Review* 57 (1968): 545–70; and Gilbert G. Bilezikian, *The Liberated Gospel: A Comparison of the Gospel of Mark and Greek Tragedy* (Grand Rapids: Baker, 1977).

4. T. R. Henn, *The Bible as Literature* (New York: Oxford University Press, 1970), p. 257.

violation of his Nazirite vow to God. To add yet another complexity, this story of tragedy and heroism is also a story of temptation.

Like other tragic heroes, Samson has as great a potential as can be imagined. His birth is foretold by an angel (13:3). He belongs to the elite spiritual circle of Nazirites from birth (13:5). The prohibitions prescribed for a Nazirite (13:4–5) set Samson apart from ordinary humanity. In keeping with the tenor of the Bible, Samson's exalted position is given a strongly spiritual identity, as evidenced by statements that "the boy grew, and the LORD blessed him" (13:24) and that "the Spirit of the LORD began to stir him" (13:25).

With the hero thus elevated, the tragedy unfolds. It follows an atypical structure for tragedy. Instead of having a single linear cause-effect chain of events, this tragedy is based on the folk narrative principle of threefold repetition. We observe three falls of Samson, each one based on his involvement with a Philistine woman: the woman of Timnah, the prostitute at Gaza, and Delilah. Unifying this threefold cycle of events is Samson's violation of his Nazirite vow. Paradoxically, these tragic events are also occasions when the Israelites can laugh at how their hero has gotten the better of their enemies.

All these strands first come together in the account of Samson's marriage to the woman of Timnah (Judg. 14–15). The tragic element in Samson's command to his parents to get the woman as his wife ("for she pleases me well" [14:3]) resides in the fact that he allows his personal desire for a pagan woman to overcome God's command to keep himself holy (separate from evil). Samson's contact with the dead lion (14:8–9) was a betrayal of the Nazirite vow to avoid contact with dead bodies (see Num. 6:6–7) and the concern in ceremonial law to avoid touching unclean animals (Lev. 11:24–28). Quite apart from breaking the Nazirite vow, Samson exhibits foolish arrogance and greed in posing his riddle at the wedding feast. When he gives in to his wife's tears and entreaties by telling her the answer to the riddle, he already exhibits the tragic weakness that will eventually destroy him.

But from the perspective of heroic narrative, some of these same events are positive, since they led to the destruction of thirty enemies after Samson's riddle was guessed (14:10–19). Because God used the marriage for deliverance from the Philistines, the narrator counters the objections of Samson's parents to the marriage with the statement that "his father and mother did not know that it was from the LORD; for he was seeking an occasion against the Philistines" (14:4). So, too, we read that "the Spirit of the LORD came mightily" upon Samson when he killed the thirty men of the town (14:19).

A similar ambiguity pervades other events in the story. Samson's use of three hundred foxes to burn the fields of the Philistines (15:4–8) is an abuse of his strength in an act of personal vengeance. But when put into the context of international warfare between the Philistines and the Israelites, the event becomes another example of military deliverance by a national hero. Samson's tragic flaw of sensuality surfaces when he spends the night with the prostitute at Gaza (16:1), but the tragic aspect of the episode is again balanced by the heroic act of Samson's carrying off the heavy gates of the city (16:3). There is something of the comic trickster in this tragic figure.

The climax of Samson's tragedy is his liaison with Delilah (Judg. 16:4–21). The episode repeats motifs from the earlier marriage to the woman of Timnah: a liaison with a pagan woman, a devious wife who sides with her Philistine compatriots, a pleading wife whose entreaties lead Samson to divulge a secret about himself.

The temptation that ends in Samson's tragedy gains added force by being a highly patterned sequence. The overall design is the pattern three-plus-one (a series of three repeated events, with a crucial change introduced in the fourth instance). Each of the four episodes follows an identical pattern, consisting of five elements. First Delilah pleads with Samson (vv. 6, 10, 13, 15). Samson responds three times with trickery and then with the truth (vv. 7, 11, 13, 17). In the third phase of each episode, Delilah acts (vv. 8, 12, 14, 19). She then concludes her action with the shout, *The Philistines are upon you, Samson!* (vv. 9, 12, 14, 20). Finally, Samson exerts himself the first three times (vv. 9, 12, 14) but not the last time.

This pattern heightens the effect of a story that is shot through with conflict, suspense, temptation, and dramatic irony. There is a gradual movement to the climax, inasmuch as the third event revolves around Samson's hair. We laugh with Samson the trickster and sigh with relief during his first three lies, and then our hearts sink as we listen to the impossible. There is also number symmetry underlying the four episodes, as we read about seven bowstrings, an unidentified number of ropes, seven locks of hair, and (again) seven locks of hair.

The heart of Samson's tragedy is his violation of the Nazirite vow, which prescribed that "no razor shall come upon his head" (13:5). The catastrophe occurs when God leaves Samson (16:20), and the tragic suffering takes the form of Samson's having his eyes gouged out and being made a slave in the mill (16:21). In keeping with a common strategy in literary tragedy, the hero's tragedy is somewhat mitigated at the end. In the case of Samson, it consists of his renewed rapport with God (16:28) and the victory over the Philistines that Samson achieves in his death, "so the dead whom he slew at his death were more than those whom he had slain during his life" (16:30).

Samson is one of the most paradoxical heroes in the Bible. He is a folk hero, renowned for his physical strength and listed in the honor roll of the heroes of the faith in Hebrews 11 (v. 32). As a tragic figure, Samson is a type whom we have all known—the strong man and brawler who uses his strength for personal ends and whose sensual appetites and weakness for bad women are appalling.

The literary tragedy of Samson, despite its brevity, is packed with human experience. It is a story about the dangerousness of life. As such, it gives us an appraisal of the dangers of self-reliance, of physical strength and attractiveness, of sensuality and self-indulgence, of success and overconfidence, of spiritual levity and recklessness.

The Tragedy of Saul

The masterpiece of biblical tragedy is the Old Testament story of King Saul (1 Sam. 8–11; 13:8–15; 15–16; 18; 24; 26; 28; 31).[5] The tragedy of Saul is mingled with the story of the ascent of David, which occupies the intervening chapters in 1 Samuel. The details dealing with Saul have been selected by the storyteller in keeping with his tragic interpretation of the life of Saul. The story of Saul is par excellence a tragedy of calamity and self-caused suffering.

I will explicate the story from the viewpoint of the six-phase tragic pattern, but other structural patterns are also important. Most simply, this story of crime and punishment narrates the antecedents, occurrence, and consequences of Saul's tragic mistake. The storyteller has also organized the story around four memorable encounters between the hero and the prophet Samuel. When he anoints Saul, Samuel pronounces an oracle of blessing (1 Sam. 10:1–8). In the final three encounters, Samuel pronounces an increasingly sinister series of judgments against Saul—when Saul intrudes himself into the priestly office (13:11–14), when he spares the spoils of the Amalekites (15:10–29), and when he visits the witch of Endor to summon up the spirit of Samuel (28:15–19).

The story of Saul begins with a full-scale tragic prologue in the manner of Greek tragedy (1 Sam. 8). This story of the appointment of Saul as king sets up an interpretive framework against which we measure the action that follows at every stage of its unfolding. We learn three important things: the people's desire for a king is ill-founded (vv. 1–6), God disapproves of the nation's desire for a king (vv. 7–9), and human kingship in a fallen world is inevitably flawed (vv. 10–18).

The exposition or background of the tragedy is developed in full and

5. My discussion of the tragedy of Saul as a tragedy of weak leadership is indebted at every turn to the best discussion of a biblical tragedy that I have seen, that by Edwin M. Good, *Irony in the Old Testament* (Philadelphia: Westminster, 1965), pp. 56–80.

leisurely detail (1 Sam. 9–11). It introduces us to the givens of this particular tragic world. The main narrative business is to idealize the hero, showing the heights from which he subsequently fell. The list of Saul's attributes is staggering. It includes physical impressiveness (9:2), humility (9:21; 10:22–23; 11:12–13), anointing by Samuel and by God (10:1), confirming signs of God's favor (finding the lost horses and related incidents), spiritual endowment by God (10:6–7, 9; 11:6), selection by lot (10:21), good advisers (10:26), and initial military success (11:1–11). No tragic hero ever had a more promising start: "There was not a man among the people of Israel more handsome than he; from his shoulders upward he was taller than any of the people" (9:2), and "the spirit of God came mightily upon Saul" (11:6).

The unexpectedly large amount of space that the writer devotes to this background signals its importance. Surely Saul has the exalted status of the conventional tragic hero. After we have finished reading these three chapters, we sense that the story could as plausibly develop into a heroic narrative as a tragedy. Furthermore, Saul has every opportunity to succeed. He is fully equipped, physically, politically, and spiritually. His tragedy is not inherent in his external situation. He is not the victim of fate or of God. The whole idealized picture is ironic, however. As the tragedy unfolds, Saul becomes so much less than he might have been. All of his endowments, as described in these chapters, are the standard that Saul fails to measure up to.

With Saul now established as king, the story gives us a glimpse of his dilemma. Before we can understand Saul's tragic choice later in the story, we must see the tendency of character that will make possible this particular tragedy. This is the narrative business that occurs in 1 Samuel 12 and 13. In Samuel's farewell discourse as he relinquishes his judgeship in deference to the new king, he highlights the great either-or that now faces the nation: "If both you and the king who reigns over you will follow the LORD your God, it will be well; but if you will not hearken to the voice of the LORD, . . . the hand of the LORD will be against you and your king" (12:14–15).

This is followed by an early indication that the new king will not pass the test. When Saul intrudes himself into the priestly office and offers the sacrifice instead of obeying Samuel's command to wait until he arrives (1 Sam. 13), we see the hero's fatal tendency to take the path of expediency rather than obedience. Saul's tragedy is a tragedy of weak leadership—an attempt to win popularity with the people by doing what they want instead of obeying the commands of God. This is the interpretation of Saul's failure that Samuel gives when he arrives: "You have done foolishly; you have not kept the commandment of the LORD your God, which he commanded you" (13:13). As part of Saul's tragic flaw, we already see his tendency to rationalize his wrong choices with high-sounding piety (vv. 11–12).

Samuel's oracle of judgment ("now your kingdom shall not continue" [v. 14]) predicts that Saul's kingship will not be passed on to his descendants. Only after Saul's major tragic choice will Samuel announce that the kingdom has been taken from Saul himself, confirming that this earlier event is a prelude. As an individual, Saul still has a chance to succeed.

Chapter 15 is the narrative and psychological center of Saul's tragedy. The story is told in such a way as to make it one of the great dramas in the Bible. The tragic hero's dilemma is posed at the outset: God gives a command not to keep any spoils from the battle with the Amalekites (v. 3), but the people want to save the best of the spoils (v. 24). The tragic choice is told in a matter-of-fact style: "But Saul and the people spared Agag, and the best of the sheep and of the oxen and of the fatlings, and the lambs, and all that was good, and would not utterly destroy them" (v. 9). Drawn in two directions, Saul as tragic protagonist chooses downward rather upward in his world of allegiances, as he later admits to Samuel: "I have sinned; for I have transgressed the commandment of the LORD and your words, because I feared the people and obeyed their voice" (v. 24).

Here is a tragedy of weak leadership. Unlike the heroic leaders of the Bible, Saul is unwilling to risk himself by an act of faith in what God has directed. Saul is preoccupied with his image before the people and afraid of losing stature with them. There is even a touch of pride (the hubris of Greek tragedy) in Saul: he builds a monument for himself (v. 12) and spares the enemy king so he can take him home as a trophy of victory.

Despite these gestures toward greatness, Saul is actually "little in his own eyes" (v. 17), a dwarf compared to the figure who greeted us several chapters earlier. His tragedy is not inherent in his feeling of inadequacy, which simply provided the occasion for him to choose between competing ways of transcending his feelings of inadequacy. In retrospect, Saul's apparent modesty in hiding himself among the baggage turns out to be evidence of his fatal inability to rule in God's strength, and there is an ironic discrepancy between Saul's huge size and his childish act of hiding behind the luggage.

The actual encounter between Samuel and Saul is a packed drama. On Saul's side we find ironic and laughable attempts to evade the truth and rationalize his actions as acts of pious worship (vv. 13–16, 20–21). With the bleating of the sheep and the lowing of the oxen forming a background chorus, Saul expects Samuel to believe his story that he has destroyed everything. Samuel silences him with a dual interpretation of his tragic choice: it was a failure in leadership (v. 17) and an act of disobedience to God (vv. 18–19, 22–23).

Saul responds with superficial repentance (vv. 24–25), which is elicited only after Samuel has announced that the kingship will be taken from Saul himself (vv. 23, 28). Even in his act of repentance, Saul takes a business-as-usual attitude and is still preoccupied with saving face with the people: "I have sinned; yet honor me now before the elders of my people and before Israel" (v. 30). The scene closes with Samuel correcting Saul's act of omission by killing the king of the Amalekites (vv. 32–33), recalling David's similar role in slaying Goliath. Tragic lament (v. 35) rounds out the chapter.

The story next turns to the catastrophe and suffering phases of the tragedy. The important strands in Saul's tragic decline are fourfold. One is spiritual deterioration, as capsulized in the statement that "the Spirit of the LORD departed from Saul, and an evil spirit from the LORD tormented him" (1 Sam. 16:14). This is the effect, not the cause, of Saul's tragic choice. A second strand is Saul's psychological collapse, as he becomes a classic case of paranoia. Alienation from his family is also an important part of the story, as Saul even attempts to kill his own son Jonathan for befriending David (20:33).

Most importantly of all, the collapse of Saul is played off against the rise of David. These two stories now become intertwined in 1 Samuel. David's political and moral strength is the foil by which we measure the political and moral decline of Saul. The political contrast is rendered in memorable terms by the song of the women: "Saul has slain his thousands, / and David his ten thousands" (18:7). On the moral level, David twice refuses to carry out the expedient act of taking the king's life, even though his own men urge him to do so (1 Sam. 24, 26). The irony of Saul's tragedy is clear: his obsession with the threat posed by David is the construct of his own diseased mind.

Saul's tragedy reaches its climax when he consults the witch at Endor (1 Sam. 28). This is the fourth great encounter between Saul and Samuel. In effect, we return to earlier phases of Saul's life. Saul's disguise (v. 8) assumes a symbolic force: it recalls his earlier attempt to conceal his guilt from Samuel, and, like the ill-fitting garments of Shakespeare's Macbeth, it symbolizes how Saul has tried to fill a position of leadership in an ignoble way. The oracles of Samuel have been increasingly personal and confining, and the pattern is climaxed when this time Samuel predicts that Saul will lose his life the very next day (v. 19). Samuel also repeats his earlier insight into the tragic moment in Saul's life by reminding Saul of the incident involving the Amalekites (v. 18). Saul's tragedy ends on the conventional note of the hero's death, here a gruesome suicide (1 Sam. 31:4), after which the hero's body is displayed in the enemy's temple (vv. 9–10).

Edwin M. Good's statement of appreciation is an apt assessment of the story:

We have in the Saul story a masterpiece of structure, dramatic order and suspense, and tragic irony. Someday, someone will turn the story of Saul into a great tragedy for the stage. . . . Then perhaps Saul will be recognized as a tragic figure of the same stature as Oedipus or Othello (p. 80).

Further Reflections on Biblical Tragedy

I wish to conclude this analysis of literary tragedy in the Bible by placing the discussion into a broader context. One of the perennially unresolved questions of literary theory is whether tragedy and Christianity are compatible—whether there can even be such a thing as Christian tragedy. The critical consensus is that tragedy is incompatible with the major tenets of Christianity.[6] This is surely wrong, as demonstrated by the presence of literary tragedy in the Bible and by the presuppositions (noted earlier in my discussion) that Christianity and tragedy share. Jesus expressed a generally tragic view of human experience when he said, "The gate is wide and the way is easy, that leads to destruction, and those who enter by it are many. For the gate is narrow and the way is hard, that leads to life, and those who find it are few" (Matt. 7:13–14).

But on the subject of tragedy, the Bible also contains some distinctive features. To begin, we can profitably draw some contrasts between Greek tragedy and biblical tragedy. In Greek tragedy, the hero's tragic flaw is almost always some version of hubris or overweening pride. Biblical tragedy rings the changes on another root sin—disobedience to God. In Greek tragedy, the punishment of the heroes seems disproportionate to their offense, and they accordingly assume grandeur and elicit sympathy as they struggle against the cosmic forces that bring them to defeat. The tragedies of the Bible are degeneration stories in which the heroes do not gain stature during their decline.

Greek tragedy is generally said to be the tragedy of fate. As the curtain falls, we are left with the impression that the hero has been an unfortunate victim, either of the gods or of ignorance. In biblical tragedy, the responsibility falls completely on the tragic hero. The issues are always clearly defined beforehand. The tragic heroes know what choice they should make. Circumstances may test the heroes and make it understandable how they came to make their wrong choice. But in biblical tragedy the enemy is within. It does not reside in the tragic world. Moral choice, not external constraint or ignorance, is the crux of the matter.

In Greek tragedy, the ways of the gods often remain mysterious, and the heroes make their tragic choice without full awareness of the issues

6. For a survey of representative statements, see my book *The Literature of the Bible* (Grand Rapids: Zondervan, 1974), pp. 102–4.

involved. In biblical tragedy, the ways of God are known. The tragic heroes are without excuse for having violated God's commands. The impression left by classical tragedy is a pessimistic fear of doing anything, since the gods might destroy a person for it. In place of such passivity, biblical tragedy encourages an active obedience to what God has said.

In classical tragedy, the tragic hero is above all the sympathetic tragic victim. In biblical tragedy, the tragic hero is the unsympathetic sinner. The natural response in the first case is, Isn't it too bad that all this happened to the tragic hero? The natural response to biblical tragedy is, Isn't it too bad that the hero disobeyed God, when it might have been otherwise? In the words of W. H. Auden, "Greek tragedy is the tragedy of necessity; i.e., the feeling aroused in the spectator is 'What a pity it had to be this way'; Christian tragedy is the tragedy of possibility, 'What a pity it was this way when it might have been otherwise.' "[7]

This notion of biblical tragedy as the tragedy of possibility leads me to my final observation. It is surprising that in a book so preoccupied with sin and its judgment as the Bible is there are so few complete tragedies. The Bible is an anthology of aborted tragedies. The material for tragedy lies everywhere. Biblical narrative is full of incidents that are potentially tragic and that a writer could use as the basis for a tragedy. But in most of these stories the tragedy is averted through the protagonist's repentance and God's forgiveness. The story of David's repentance after his sin with Bathsheba and Uriah is the great paradigm.

The world of literary tragedy is usually a closed world. Once the hero has made the tragic choice, there is no escape. But the Bible is preoccupied with what is more than tragic—with the redemptive potential in human tragedy. In the stories of the Bible, there is always a way out, even after the tragic mistake has been made.

7. W. H. Auden, "The Christian Tragic Hero," in *Tragedy: Vision and Form*, ed. Robert W. Corrigan (San Francisco: Chandler, 1965), p. 143.

Part 2

Biblical Poetry

7

The Language of Biblical Poetry

The most important thing to know about poetry is that it is
a distinctive type of language. Poetry differs from ordinary prose by its
reliance on images and figures of speech, and by its verse form.

Poetry is heightened speech, far more compressed than prose. Whereas
expository prose uses the sentence or paragraph as its basic unit, and
narrative the episode or scene, the basic unit of poetry is the individual
image or figure of speech. Thus in the New Testament epistles we might
get a paragraph or chapter that explains godliness. In a historical narrative
we get a story in which a character exhibits godliness in action. But the
poet compresses godliness into an image or picture: "He is like a tree
planted by streams of water, that yields its fruit in its season" (Ps. 1:3).

Because prose rather than poetry is the standard form of speech that we
use in our daily lives, poetry can initially seem intimidating. There is no
doubt that poetry places greater demands on us than straightforward
prose. It requires a more contemplative approach and requires more
continuous interpretation than ordinary language.

Yet poetry developed before prose in virtually every culture that we
know. Small children love poetry. Furthermore, we speak a certain
amount of poetry every day, as we talk about the sun rising or a bear of a
test or our hopes being dashed. Despite what we have been conditioned to

159

think, biblical poetry is far from inaccessible. As we shall see, it has a power and beauty all its own.

Perhaps that is why poetry pervades the Bible. Some books of the Bible are wholly poetic: Psalms, the Song of Solomon, Proverbs, Lamentations. Others are mainly poetic: Job, Ecclesiastes (where even the prose passages achieve poetic effect), Isaiah, and numerous other prophecies. But even parts of the Bible that are written in prose use the resources of poetic language. We would be hard pressed to find a page of the Bible that does not require us to know the elements of poetry that I discuss in this chapter. That is why the ability to interpret poetry is a requirement, not an option, when we read the Bible.

My strategy in this chapter is to isolate and describe the things that make up poetry, and to accompany each of these with analysis of specimen passages of biblical poetry.

Thinking in Images (Ps. 91)

The simplest principle of poetic language is perhaps also the most important: Poets think in images. When the poetic imagination formulates reality, it does so in pictures. In a famous essay entitled "The Making of a Poem," the modern poet Stephen Spender said that the question facing a poet is, "Can I think out the logic of images?" To determine the logic of the images is one of the chief tasks facing the reader of biblical poetry.

Human emotions are perhaps the commonest subject of poetry in the Bible, and the typical strategy of the poet is to picture an emotion as a series of concrete images. Terror, for example, is not an abstraction but fire and water (Ps. 124:1–5):

> ¹If it had not been the LORD who was on our side,
>   let Israel now say—
> ²if it had not been the LORD who was on our side,
>   when men rose up against us,
> ³then they would have swallowed us up alive,
>   when their anger was kindled against us;
> ⁴then the flood would have swept us away,
>   the torrent would have gone over us;
> ⁵then over us would have gone
>   the raging waters.

When the poet-king prays for national prosperity, he thinks in concrete images (Ps. 144:12–14):

> ¹²May our sons in their youth
>   be like plants full grown,

> our daughters like corner pillars
> > cut for the structure of a palace;
> ¹³may our garners be full,
> > providing all manner of store;
> may our sheep bring forth thousands
> > and ten thousands in our fields;
> ¹⁴may our cattle be heavy with young,
> > suffering no mischance or failure in bearing;
> may there be no cry of distress in our streets!

The poet suffering from depression and loneliness does not give us a psychological analysis but a series of pictures (Ps. 102:3–11):

> ³For my days pass away like smoke,
> > and my bones burn like a furnace.
> ⁴My heart is smitten like grass, and withered;
> > I forget to eat my bread.
> ⁵Because of my loud groaning
> > my bones cleave to my flesh.
> ⁶I am like a vulture of the wilderness,
> > like an owl of the waste places;
> ⁷I lie awake,
> > I am like a lonely bird on the housetop.
> ⁸All the day my enemies taunt me,
> > those who deride me use my name for a curse.
> ⁹For I eat ashes like bread,
> > and mingle tears with my drink,
> ¹⁰because of thy indignation and anger;
> > for thou hast taken me up and thrown me away.
> ¹¹My days are like an evening shadow;
> > I wither away like grass.

Most of the images in this passage involve comparisons in the form of metaphors and similes, which I will discuss shortly. In the meantime, let us not overlook the obvious: metaphors and similes are first of all images and pictures.

The prevalence of images in poetry requires two activities from a reader. First they ask to be experienced *as images*. The more sensory and concrete these images become in our imagination, the richer will be our experience of poetry.

In addition to *experiencing* poetic images, we need to *interpret* them. The simplest form of interpretation is to note their connotations. The *denotation* of a word is its straightforward dictionary meaning. A word's *connotations* are what it communicates by way of additional overtones of meaning, especially emotional overtones. The word *home* denotes the house where one lives, but it connotes family, security, provision, and love.

The most elementary form of interpreting the connotations of an image is to decide whether it is positive or negative in association. Often there are additional connotations as well.

In addition to interpreting the connotations of images, we can profitably meditate on what I earlier called the logic of images. This entails observing the suitability or fitness of the images to the subject matter in a passage. Why did the poet use this particular image here? is always a helpful question to answer when contemplating a passage of poetry.

In summary, the prevalence of images in poetry requires us to read poetry with what psychologists call the right side of the brain. This is our mental capacity to think in pictures. We first need to experience poetry with our senses and then become analytic in determining the connotations and logic of the images in their context in a poem. To such a process we now turn.

Psalm 91 expresses the emotional confidence that springs from trusting in God. It is built around the rescue motif. The poet presents pictures of God's deliverance. The main structural principle in the poem is a catalogue or list of God's acts of protection and rescue. The three-part outline of the poem is as follows: introduction to the theme of the confidence that comes to the person who trusts in God (vv. 1–2), the catalogue of God's acts of deliverance (vv. 3–13), and God's confirmation that he will deliver as the poet has described (vv. 14–16).

Because the poet keeps changing the images, this psalm will illustrate what I have said about imagery in poetry. Two principles govern the poet's choice of images in Psalm 91 and account for the logic of the imagery. They are the impulses to give a *heightened* picture of terror and deliverance and demonstrate the *complete* range of God's protection. As the poet keeps changing his images, therefore, he gravitates to the most terrifying experiences that he knows, and he is careful to include both big and small areas of life.

The poet begins by defining the subject of his meditation, namely, the person who trusts in God. Already he thinks in images:

> [1]He who dwells in the shelter of the Most High,
>   who abides in the shadow of the Almighty,
> [2]will say to the LORD, "My refuge and my fortress;
>   my God, in whom I trust."

Trusting in God is not left an abstraction but becomes a picture of living in a house and resting in the shade of a tree or building and being in a military fortress. The logic of these images is not hard to define: in a poem that will deal with trust and protection, these images already give us concrete pictures of these realities. Living in a building, particularly if it is a home, connotes security and close relationship with others who live in the house, while the images of shade and refuge connote safety and protection. We might note in passing that the poet balances his four images of God (*shelter, shadow, refuge, fortress*) with four titles or epithets for God: *the Most High, the Almighty, the Lord,* and *my God.*

When the poet turns to his catalogue of God's acts of deliverance, the logic that determines his choice of images is the impulse to give us heightened pictures of danger or terror, accompanied by extraordinarily vivid pictures of rescue. The catalogue begins with balanced references to the natural and human worlds (v. 3):

> For he will deliver you from the snare of the fowler
> and from the deadly pestilence.

The picture of a bird in a trap is a picture of terror taken from everyday life in a culture where trapping birds was a familiar activity. The mention of *deadly pestilence* brings the terror even closer to home, being a reference to the helplessness a person feels before a plague or epidemic illness.

As the poet continues the catalogue of God's acts of provision, he again pairs references to the animal and human worlds (v. 4):

> he will cover you with his pinions,
> and under his wings you will find refuge;
> his faithfulness is a shield and buckler.

The comparison of God's protection to that of a parent bird is a picture of protection on the small scale, with connotations of warmth and intimacy. For a balancing picture of deliverance on a larger scale, the poet takes us to the terror of the battlefield. In contrast to the warmth of the mother bird, we feel the metal of military armor. We also notice the poet's impulse to cover the whole range of battlefield protection: the shield was a large piece of armor, while the buckler was a smaller, more easily maneuvered shield.[1]

As the poet keeps multiplying his images of danger and deliverance, he plays upon the complementary threats of night and day:

> [5]You will not fear the terror of the night,
> nor the arrow that flies by day,

1. Derek Kidner, *Psalms 73–150*, Tyndale Old Testament Commentary series (Downers Grove: Inter-Varsity, 1975), p. 333.

> [6]nor the pestilence that stalks in darkness,
>   nor the destruction that wastes at noonday.

The logic of this play upon night and day is to achieve the effect of fullness, as the poet covers all possible sources of danger in human life. The *terror of the night* is simply the fears that we archetypally associate with darkness and night—a mental or psychological threat. The *arrow that flies by day* is probably a picture of military attack, made specific with the image of the flying arrow. In verse 6, the pestilence or plague is rendered more terrifying by being personified and pictured as stalking a victim. What is the logic of linking epidemic diseases with night? It is a reference either to occasions when God sent deadly pestilence by night (Exod. 11:4–5; Isa. 37:36), or to early medical views that attributed the spread of plagues to bad air and evil smells as encountered in an enclosed room. In his search for ways to make the danger vivid, the poet rounds out the picture with *the destruction that wastes at noonday*, which may be sunstroke, here pictured as an attacking warrior who "lays waste" on the battlefield.

In verses 7 and 8 the poet amplifies his picture of protection on the battlefield:

> [7]A thousand may fall at your side,
>   ten thousand at your right hand;
>   but it will not come near you.
> [8]You will only look with your eyes
>   and see the recompense of the wicked.

This is a hyperbolic picture of deliverance on the grand scale, in keeping with the poet's intention to celebrate God's deliverance by reaching into the most vivid examples of it in his own experience and observation. We note also that this is a picture of *miraculous* protection, following the pictures of deliverance in the everyday routine.

The next two verses function as a kind of summary of the movement of the poem up to this point:

> [9]Because you have made the LORD your refuge,
>   the Most High your habitation,
> [10]no evil shall befall you,
>   no scourge come near your tent.

The logic underlying the images in these verses is that they echo images that have appeared earlier and gather up all the pictures of deliverance into a comprehensive generalization that *no evil shall befall you*.

Following the extended portrait of battlefield protection, the poet introduces another major image from his experience, that of a journey:

> ¹¹For he will give his angels charge of you
> > to guard you in all your ways.
> ¹²On their hands they will bear you up,
> > lest you dash your foot against a stone.
> ¹³You will tread on the lion and the adder,
> > the young lion and the serpent you will trample under foot.

Verse 11 introduces the journey motif (*he . . . will guard you in all your ways*), and the next two verses fill out the picture with concrete details. Verse 12 is an example of protection that reaches to the smallest possible mishap that could occur on a journey, stubbing one's foot on a stone. To heighten the vividness of the picture, the angels are pictured as lifting the person up with their hands. With verse 13 we move from the small to the great, as the traveler is powerful over such terrors as a lion and a snake.

By this point in the psalm the poet has given us the most vivid pictures of terror and deliverance that his experience afforded. What more could be added? Verses 14–16 provide the answer. Having stated his human confidence that comes from trust in God's protection, the poet ends with a confirming oracle from God himself:

> ¹⁴Because he cleaves to me in love, I will deliver him;
> > I will protect him, because he knows my name.
> ¹⁵When he calls to me, I will answer him;
> > I will be with him in trouble,
> > I will rescue him and honor him.
> ¹⁶With long life I will satisfy him,
> > and show him my salvation.

Here, too, we find the impulse toward concrete images. On the human side, we notice vivid terms of human relationship with strong connotations in the Old Testament: cleaving to someone in love, knowing someone by name, and calling to someone. To heighten the picture of God's activity on behalf of the person thus described, the speech uttered by God in these verses contains eight verbs to describe what God extends to those who trust in him. In effect, these verbs summarize the main action of the poem, which has been an ever-expanding vision of God's acts of protection.

Psalm 91 embodies a universal principle of poetry: Poets think in images. My analysis has demonstrated the corresponding activities that are required of us whenever we read poetry: we need to be active in recreating the pictures that the poem presents and in determining the logic of those images in the context in which they appear. In Psalm 91, the images were governed by the poet's desire to give us heightened pictures of terror and protection, and to show the sweep of God's protection, from the small to the large.

Metaphor and Simile

The Function of Metaphor and Simile

Metaphor and simile are as important to poetry as is the image. The essential feature of both metaphor and simile is comparison. Metaphor and simile establish a correspondence between two phenomena. They declare that *A* is somehow like *B*.

The difference between metaphor and simile is relatively minor. A simile always announces the comparison with the formula *like* or *as*: "your tongue is like a sharp razor" (Ps. 52:2); "as a hart longs for flowing streams, so longs my soul for thee, O God" (Ps. 42:1). Metaphor adopts a bolder strategy and asserts that one thing *is* another: "their teeth are spears and arrows" (Ps. 57:4); "thy word is a lamp to my feet" (Ps. 119:105). Both figures of speech assert a similarity between two things. A metaphor is simply an elliptical simile, with the "like" or "as" omitted.

Metaphor and simile thus secure an effect on one level and ask us to transfer that meaning to another level (in this they are like the New Testament parable). The very word *metaphor* suggests such a transfer, since it is based on the Greek words *meta*, meaning "over," and *pherein*, meaning "to carry." When the poet compares clouds to a chariot (Ps. 104:3), we first need to reflect on the qualities of a chariot. A chariot moves rapidly over roads and is under the purposeful direction of its driver. How are clouds like a chariot? They, too, move rapidly, and their movements serve the purposes of God (which is the point that the poet makes in this section of Psalm 104).

A metaphor or simile is bifocal, a split-level statement. Both ask us to keep two things in view. This at once disqualifies a lot of commentary that I have read on the poetry of the Bible. From the commentary I would get the impression that the text being discussed is a theological treatise. Far too much commentary obscures the process of transfer that even allows us to talk about the theological content of the poet's utterance. There is a pictorial dimension to metaphors and similes, and these should not be slighted. The metaphors and similes of the Bible constantly keep us in a world of grass and water and spears and lions and trees.

Metaphor and simile are a form of logic and can profitably be analyzed as such. The connection that a poet sets up between two phenomena is subject to validation on the basis of observation and rational analysis. Poets do not invent metaphors and similes; they discover them. The resemblances that a poet claims are rooted in reality. When the poet claims that God's law is like a light on a path, we can validate his statement by examining the logic of the connection that he claims. God's law does function in a person's moral life the way a light functions when a person walks down a dark path. So despite what may appear to be the far-flung fantasy of the poet's imagination, the poet is using logic in his discourse.

But if metaphor and simile are a form of logic, they also communicate something beyond logic, if by logic we mean abstract thought. Metaphors and similes ask us to *experience* the topic at hand by giving us a picture. They are an attempt to communicate total experience. Longing for God becomes much more than an abstraction when the poet compares it to physical thirst "in a dry and weary land where no water is" (Ps. 63:1). The meanings conveyed by metaphor and simile even go beyond what can be adequately described in words. They are affective as well as intellectual. When the experience of God's providence is pictured metaphorically as living in a house (Ps. 91:1), the meanings that we experience go beyond what we can express verbally.

Someone has said that metaphor and by extension simile are "both a thinking and a seeing."[2] The "seeing" occurs on the literal level of the image. The "thinking" happens when we trace the logic of the connection and transfer the meanings from one level to another. When the poet compares his soul to "a child quieted at its mother's breast" (Ps. 131:2), we first see and feel the domestic scene of mother and child, and then think about how that can be true of a state of soul.

What obligations do metaphor and simile place on a reader? They are double. The reader's first responsibility is to *identify* the literal reference of the statement. Without such identification, the whole purpose of speaking in metaphor or simile evaporates. We first need to let the literal picture sink into our consciousness. I once researched how commentaries treat the passages in the Psalms that talk about God "raising a horn" for his people. What I found was alarming: the whole purpose of the commentators was to interpret what the metaphor *means* without ever telling me what kind of horn the poet had in view.[3] What we need is commentaries that give us photographs to make the literal level of meaning come alive in our imagination.

The second task is to *interpret* metaphors and similes. Metaphors and similes are invitations to the reader to discover the meaning(s) of the poet's statement. There is no legitimate way to water down that statement. When

2. Paul Ricoeur, "The Metaphorical Process as Cognition, Imagination, and Feeling," in *On Metaphor*, ed. Sheldon Sacks (Chicago: University of Chicago Press, 1979), p. 145.

3. For details, see Leland Ryken, "Metaphor in the Psalms," *Christianity and Literature* 31, no. 3 (Spring 1982): 9–29.

a biblical poet states his meaning in the form of a metaphor or simile, he entrusts his utterance to the reader's ability to discover the meaning. In keeping with what I have already said about metaphor and simile, the process of interpretation involves discovering the nature of the similarity between the two halves of the comparison. More often than not, the connections are multiple, as we will see from an analysis of Psalm 23. The meanings, moreover, are affective and extraverbal as well as intellectual and conceptual.

Metaphor and simile place immense demands on a reader. They require far more activity than a direct, propositional statement does. They therefore involve far greater risk on the part of the writer, who entrusts a significant part of the act of communication to the reader. Taking the obligations of metaphor and simile seriously would revolutionize commentary on biblical poetry. As I read commentary from biblical scholars, I hear far too little about pastures and shields and horns, and about the multiplicity of meanings implied in the text.

In view of the risks, why do poets speak in metaphor and simile? There are several advantages. One is the vividness and concreteness of the appeal to the reader's imagination. Because metaphor and simile are distinctive ways of speaking, they achieve freshness of expression and overcome the cliché effect of ordinary discourse. Metaphor and simile possess arresting strangeness that both captures a reader's initial attention and makes a statement memorable. They also have another built-in tendency that accords well with a lyric poet's intention: they force a reader to ponder or meditate on a statement. They contain a retarding element that resists immediate assimilation. Like the parallelism of biblical poetry, they require a reader to pause on a thought before moving on.

Above all, poets use metaphor and simile for the sake of precision. Poets hate the approximate. They therefore use one area of human experience to shed light on another area. In Psalm 57:4, for example, the poet wants us to know exactly *how* destructive the slander directed against him is:

> I lie in the midst of lions
> > that greedily devour the sons of men;
> their teeth are spears and arrows,
> > their tongues sharp swords.

Among other things, the poet is thus able to communicate feelings and images and human experiences as well as ideas.

Metaphor and simile are basic to poetry. They are every bit as important as my long discussion of them indicates. From the time of Aristotle, experts have agreed that the thing that most distinguishes the true poet is the ability to think in metaphor. The poetry of the Bible confirms that insight.

Since my discussion of metaphor and simile occurs in a chapter on the language of biblical poetry, I need to underscore one further thing. Metaphor and simile are not "poetic devices"; they are a way of thinking and formulating reality. They are an important way in which the human race expresses meaning. Accordingly, they are not limited to the poetry of the Bible. They appear everywhere, including the prose sections. Here is a random example from a New Testament epistle:

> So then you are no longer strangers and sojourners, but you are fellow citizens with the saints and members of the household of God, built upon the foundation of the apostles and prophets, Christ Jesus himself being the cornerstone. [Eph. 2:19–20]

To read such a passage requires that we pay attention to everything I have said about metaphor and simile.

Psalm 23

I know of no better text from which to illustrate the dynamics of metaphor than Psalm 23. The topic of Psalm 23 is God's providence in the lives of people. The theme is the security and contentment of resting in God's providence. The approach to the topic, in other words, is affective, as the poet uses pastoral images to make us feel a certain way about God's providence.

The main structural principle in the poem is a catalogue of God's acts of provision. There is also an implied journey motif, as the sheep are led from their sheepfold to places of grazing and rest and then back to the sheepfold at the end of the day. The chronology of a typical day in the life of a shepherd thus also organizes the details in the poem. The poem is further unified by a controlling metaphor, as God's care for his people is compared to a shepherd's provision for his sheep. We can handle the poem very adequately by exploring this controlling metaphor.

The poem begins by announcing the central image: *The Lord is my shepherd.* The sheep-shepherd metaphor is the "lens" through which we contemplate God's providence at a human level. We can understand the message of the poem only by talking about sheep and shepherds. We might therefore begin by noting some general information about shepherding in ancient Palestine.

The conditions of shepherding were very different in ancient Palestine than they are in the United States and Britain, where sheep are usually fenced in and more or less take care of themselves. In Palestine, the shepherd had to find narrow strips of green grass and springs of water amid the drought of summer. The sheep had to be protected from attack by wild animals, as evidenced by David's account in 1 Samuel 17:34–36 of how he killed a lion and a bear that had attacked his flock. The narrow paths among rocky ledges also constituted dangers for the sheep as they moved from one locale to another. As the poem unfolds, we will find references to all of these conditions and shepherd's tasks.

On the basis of the literal picture of the shepherd's life that I have noted, we can already interpret a main meaning of the psalm. In ancient Palestine, sheep were totally dependent on their shepherd for sustaining their lives. By means of this metaphor, the poet will assert God's total control of the provision in our lives and of our utter dependence on God. Notice that I have moved naturally to speak of our lives. This suggests one of the advantages of metaphor: it is open-ended. Because David speaks metaphorically about sheep and shepherd instead of making his utterance directly autobiographical, any reader can make the poem his or her own.

Having introduced the controlling metaphor, the poet rounds out his statement by narrowing the focus specifically to the idea of provision: *I shall not want* (v. 1). The scope of the provision is left very general here. As the poem unfolds, the provision turns out to be comprehensive. It covers both physical and spiritual provision. It includes such tangible things as food and water, and such qualities as comfort, goodness, and mercy. We should also note that the poet claims only that he does not lack anything that he *needs*. This is consistent with the metaphor underlying the poem: sheep are not creatures of luxury but live in a context of basic needs being satisfied.

The catalogue of the shepherd's acts of provision begins in verse 2, which takes us squarely into the pastoral world of sheep, pastures, and water:

> he makes me lie down in green pastures,
> he leads me beside still waters.

This is one of the most pictorial and evocative verses in the whole Bible, and one that awakens our own imagination to picture the scene on the basis of our own experiences. Our first task is to get the literal picture. What kind of provision is here described? Not food, as we are first inclined to think. The sheep are not eating the grass but lying down in it. They are led not to the water but beside it.

The primary picture is one of rest and refreshment, and the scene is a kind of oasis. The background is the custom of starting a flock of sheep on rough herbage early in the day, leading the sheep to the richer, sweeter grasses as the morning progresses, and finally coming to a shady place for the noontime rest in lush, green pasture (compare Song of Sol. 1:7).[4] The

4. My explanations about the pastoral conditions underlying Psalm 23 are particularly indebted to William A. Knight, *The Song of Our Syrian Guest* (Boston: Tudor, 1907); and James K. Wallace, "The Basque Sheepherder and the Shepherd Psalm," *Reader's Digest*, July 1960, pp. 179–84. The latter article contains the interpretation of a Basque shepherd who claims access to an oral tradition lost to the modern reader.

green pastures and still waters, instead of being first of all a picture of food, simply add to the peacefulness of the scene. There is, however, probably no good reason to question that the sheep also drink from the stream. If so, there is a good reason why the waters are described as *still*: sheep will not drink from a fast-flowing stream. We might note in passing that the poem has implicitly introduced the metaphor of the daily journey or path from sheepfold to grazing area and back to the sheepfold at the end of the day.

So much for the literal picture. We next have to discover the human meanings of the metaphor. We need to carry over the meaning from level A to level B. If God is like a shepherd who leads his sheep to a resting place in an oasis, what does he do for people that is like such care for sheep? What human provisions are metaphorically pictured here? The answers are multiple: peace, contentment, beauty, rest, freedom from anxiety, the feeling of being safe and satisfied.

We might also note that even the literal picture, which I have described as it applies to sheep, is applicable at a human level. In all places and at all times, people have pictured perfection and contentment as a pastoral world—a green world where the grass is profuse, where the water flows gently and pleasantly, where the shade is cool and inviting, and where all is rest and quiet. It is a universal human longing and affects the human soul and imagination in deep and profound ways. With a few masterful words, the poet in Psalm 23 evokes our picture of this rural world of bliss.

The catalogue of the shepherd's acts of provision for his sheep continues in verse 3 with the comment, *He restores my soul.* The verb *restore* describes a bringing back to a previous condition. The reference to *soul* makes it appear that the figure of the sheep has been dropped and that the poet is here speaking in human terms about a person's spiritual life. In keeping with the controlling metaphor in the poem, however, the word is best translated *life* (the RSV lists this as an option, and most scholarly commentaries agree with this interpretation). The literal picture, then, is that of physical revitalization, and is probably a continuation of the picture of midday rest in the oasis.

If this is the literal picture, what transfers can we make to a human level? What does God do for people that is like a shepherd restoring the physical vitality of sheep at midday in a shady area? The key idea is restoration—a bringing back to an ideal condition. One area of application at a human level is physical: God restores physical life for people, too, through sleep, rest, food, and healing. We also experience emotional and psychological restoration after conditions of fear and anxiety, depression and sorrow. A third level of application is spiritual: God restores people by his forgiveness and reconciliation. In short, it is possible to see physical, psychological, and spiritual applications of the metaphor of life restored.

Now let me pause to note that at this point biblical scholars get very nervous and start talking gravely about curbs on interpretation. I grant that there is a danger here, but it is a risk that the writers of the Bible were willing to take. Metaphors and similes require a reader to discover meanings. They require a reader to become an active explorer. The curbs that I would suggest when we carry over the meaning from *A* to *B* are common sense, logical validation, and critical consensus (that is, we see what a wide range of responsible commentators say and then begin to weed out the aberrations).

Verse 3 contains this further picture of the shepherd's provision:

> He leads me in paths of righteousness
> for his name's sake.

This, too, looks like a human reference, but once again the English translation misleads us. A literal translation is *right paths*. On a pastoral level, the statement refers to the shepherd's guidance of his sheep on right or safe paths as opposed to dangerous ones when he leads his sheep between the sheepfold and the places of grazing. The image of the path or journey will become increasingly important as the poem unfolds.

If the literal picture is sheep being led on safe paths through the hills, what are the human applications of the metaphor? The main principle underlying the literal statement is guidance, and this provides the best clue in interpreting the human meanings of the metaphor. How does God guide people in a manner analogous to a shepherd leading sheep on safe paths? My answers include God's moral law, the Bible in general, the indwelling presence of the Holy Spirit, and the example and teachings of Christ.

Verse 4 presses the poem in a new direction with the statement,

> Even though I walk through the valley of the shadow of death,
> I fear no evil;
> for thou art with me;
> thy rod and thy staff,
> they comfort me.

Commentators familiar with the Hebrew language are virtually unanimous in saying that the common English rendering, *valley of the shadow of death*, goes beyond the original meaning of the phrase. As is true of many details in this poem, translators are too quick to abandon the literal references for a human meaning. The phrase conveys a sense of profoundest darkness, and its literal meaning is something like *death-shade* or (as the RSV puts it in a footnote) *the valley of deep darkness*.

The literal image is that of a dark valley through which a path leads. The phrase continues the image of a journey along a path. The poet is still contemplating the shepherd's leading his sheep over a path, and he here imagines the path as leading through the most fearful of all possibilities, a dark valley where dangers lurk. It is the place where sheep would be most fearful.

If the literal picture is a dark, dangerous valley through which fearful sheep must be led, what are the human applications? What are the dark valleys through which God leads us? Centuries of Christian experience, as well as most English translations, have fixed the meaning particularly on one answer, namely, death. There is, however, no good reason to limit the human meanings to just one. The dark valleys of our lives in the world include adversity, loneliness, depression, temptation, or sin.

The poet fills out the picture of the shepherd's protection at the point of greatest danger with the picture of the shepherd's rod and staff. The rod of the shepherd was the familiar crook that still makes its way into Christmas pageants. It was used for rescuing sheep from gullies or placing over the backs of the sheep to count them as they entered the sheepfold (Leviticus 27:32 contains a reference to "whatever passes under the rod" [NASB]). The staff was more of a protective weapon, being a club used to ward off attacking animals. In keeping with my belief that the images and metaphors of poetry require us to get the literal picture, let me quote a Basque shepherd's reading of verse 4:

> There is an actual Valley of the Shadow of Death in Palestine, and every sheepherder from Spain to Dalmatia knows of it. It is south of the Jericho Road leading from Jerusalem to the Dead Sea, and it is a narrow defile through a mountain range. Climatic and grazing conditions make it necessary for the sheep to be moved through this valley for seasonal feeding each year. . . . Travel through the valley is dangerous because its floor has gullies seven or eight feet deep. Actual footing on solid rock is so narrow in many places that a sheep cannot turn around and it is an unwritten law of shepherds that flocks must go up the valley in the morning hours and down toward the eventide, lest flocks meet in the defile. About halfway through the valley the walk crosses from one side to the other at a place where the path is cut in two by an eight-foot gully. One side of the gully is about 11 inches higher than the other; the sheep must jump across it. The shepherd stands at this break and coaxes or forces the sheep to make the leap. If a sheep slips and lands in the gully, the shepherd's rod is brought into play. The old-style crook circles a large sheep's neck or a small sheep's chest, and the animal is lifted to safety. . . . Many wild dogs lurk in the shadows of the valley, looking for prey. The shepherd, skilled in throwing his staff, uses it as a weapon (Wallace, pp. 183–84).

We might note in confirmation that in the psalm the references to the rod and staff do appear in connection with the threat posed by the valley of deep darkness. In other words, verse 4 hangs together as a single extended picture.

What does God do at a human level that is comparable to the shepherd's using his rod and staff? He protects from danger and destruction. This human meaning is rather easily stated, compared to all the description of the literal picture that I lavished on the verse. Is it really important to go into the literal level of a metaphor in such detail? Yes it is. Much of what literature communicates is communicated indirectly and by a rather mysterious process. The pictures of pastoral conditions that I have delineated do, in fact, become part of a reader's total experience of the poem. This is to say nothing of something that is equally important, namely, the immense asset it is to recognize and be able to show what an interesting book the Bible is and how close it is to human experience.

Verse 5 continues the catalogue of the shepherd's acts of provision with the statement,

> Thou preparest a table before me
> in the presence of my enemies.

Most commentators assume that beginning here and continuing to the end of the psalm the poet drops the sheep-shepherd metaphor and describes the provision that a human host makes for a guest. This may be a secondary level of meaning in the last two verses, but I am convinced, along with some other commentators, that the shepherd metaphor persists to the end of the poem. It is true that the terminology in verse 5 is human. But this is simply a metaphor through which the poet continues to describe what a shepherd does for his sheep. The Basque shepherd interprets the passage thus:

> David's meaning is a simple one when conditions on the Holy Land sheep ranges are known. Poisonous plants which are fatal to grazing animals abound. Each spring the shepherd must be constantly alert. When he finds the plants, he takes his mattock and goes on ahead of the flock, grubbing out every stock and root he can see. As he digs out the stocks, he lays them upon little stone pyres. . ., and by the morrow they are dry enough to burn. When the pasture is free from poisonous plants, the sheep are led into it and, in the presence of their plant enemies, they eat in peace (p. 184).

Even if we question this interpretation, the table could easily and even visually be strips of pasture and the enemies could be wild animals.

Regardless of how we interpret the statement about the table prepared in the presence of enemies, the type of provision is obviously grass at the pastoral level. If this is the literal picture, what are the applications at the human level? Surely the main provision is food. We might extend this slightly to cover daily physical provision in general, along the lines of the content that we give to the phrase *our daily bread* in the Lord's Prayer.

As the catalogue of the shepherd's acts of provision continues, we read,

> Thou anointest my head with oil,
> my cup overflows.

Anointed means literally "fattened," in reference to the richness and abundance of oil. The images of the oil and cup are pictures of what goes on in a sheepfold at the end of the day.[5] Each night as the sheep entered the sheepfold, the shepherd examined them for injuries. He would then anoint the scratches of injured sheep with olive oil. In each sheepfold there was a large vessel filled with water. From this the shepherd would fill a large two-handled cup, from which the sheep would drink and into which a fevered sheep might sink its nose. The image of the overflowing cup makes most sense at this level, since it evokes the picture of a sloppy host when applied at a human level.

If this is what the description means at the pastoral level, what meanings can we transfer to the human level? What does God do for people that is comparable to a shepherd's anointing the injury of a sheep and giving a fevered sheep water? We can legitimately see physical, emotional, psychological, and spiritual healing in the metaphor when applied at a human level.

The poem ends on a note of finality by opening outward into the future, and even here the poet continues to talk in terms of his pastoral metaphor:

> Surely goodness and mercy shall follow me
> all the days of my life;
> and I shall dwell in the house of the LORD
> for ever.

That the poet is still describing activities in the sheepfold becomes clear if we translate the word in the last clause as *return to* instead of *dwell*.[6] In other words, the sheepfold is metaphorically called a house. Underlying

---

5. For the details on which this interpretation is based, see Knight, *Song of Our Syrian Guest*, pp. 20–22, and Wallace, "Basque Sheepherder," p. 184.

6. The New American Standard Bible lists this as an alternate translation. According to William LaSor, "The Hebrew clearly uses the verb *to return*" ("What Kind of Version Is the New International?" *Christianity Today*, Oct. 20, 1978, p. 19).

the poem is the chronology of a typical day in the life of a shepherd and his sheep. We end the poem with nighttime activities. We might note also that the word translated *for ever* is parallel to *all the days of my life* and should be translated *for the length of days.*

The following commentary adequately sums up the composite picture of activities in the sheepfold in verses 5 and 6 of Psalm 23:

> The psalm has sung of the whole round of the day's wandering, all the needs of the sheep. Now the psalm closes with the last scene of the day. At the door of the sheepfold the shepherd stands and 'the rodding of the sheep' takes place. The shepherd stands, turning his body to let the sheep pass. . . . With his rod he holds back the sheep while he inspects them one by one as they pass into the fold. He has the horn filled with olive-oil and he has cedar-tar, and he anoints a knee bruised on the rocks or a side scratched by thorns. And here comes one that is not bruised but is simply worn and exhausted; he bathes its face and head with the refreshing olive-oil and he takes the large two-handled cup and dips it brimming full from the vessel of water provided for that purpose, and he lets the weary sheep drink. . . . And then, when the day is done and the sheep are snug within the fold, what contentment, what rest under the starry sky (Knight, pp. 22–24).

If the final picture in the psalm is thus the sheep within the sheepfold, what is the application at the human level? What do we experience that is like a sheep dwelling in the sheepfold of the shepherd? The answers include God's providence in our lives, God's presence with us, the church or family of believers, and ultimately heaven.

This exploration of Psalm 23 has shown how metaphors work and what they require of a reader or interpreter. They are first of all concrete images or pictures from life. Once we have the literal picture in our imagination, we need to draw the connections between it and the topic of the poem. This process is necessary whenever we encounter a metaphor or simile, whether in the Psalms or a biblical story or a New Testament epistle. It is also crucial to note that the discourses of Jesus are thoroughly rooted in the technique of metaphor and simile.

Other Figures of Speech

Image, metaphor, and simile are the backbone of biblical poetry. Other figures of speech, however, occur often enough that we need to become familiar with how they operate.[7]

7. Two excellent resources on the general subject of the language of biblical poetry are G. B. Caird, *The Language and Imagery of the Bible* (Philadelphia: Westminster, 1980); and E. W. Bullinger, *Figures of Speech Used in the Bible* (1898; reprint ed., Grand Rapids: Baker, 1968).

Hyperbole

Hyperbole is conscious exaggeration for the sake of effect. It does not claim to express literal truth but instead conveys emotional truth. Here are some specimens from the Psalms: "Yea, by thee I can crush a troop; / and by my God I can leap over a wall" (18:29); "My tears have been my food / day and night" (42:3); "My eye wastes away because of grief" (6:7).

Sometimes hyperbole consists of bigger units. For example, the Psalms contain a number of hyperbolic accounts of God's rescue, as in this portrait (Ps. 18:7–8):

> then the earth reeled and rocked;
>> the foundations also of the mountains trembled
>> and quaked, because he was angry.
> Smoke went up from his nostrils,
>> and devouring fire from his mouth;
>> glowing coals flamed forth from him.

Even more frequent are the exaggerated pictures of the speaker's enemies in the psalms of lament, as in Psalm 56:1–2:

> Be gracious to me, O God, for men trample upon me;
>> all day long foemen oppress me;
> my enemies trample upon me all day long.

Hyperbole obviously falls into the category of poetic license, and it is accordingly not intended to be interpreted as literal fact.

What is the rationale behind hyperbole? We might begin by noting that it is not only poets who talk this way. We all use hyperbole when we feel strongly about a matter or when we are trying to be persuasive. We speak about writing until our hand fell off or about how every appliance we own has broken down recently or about having a hundred things to do before we are ready for a trip or about how everyone is dissatisfied with a decision. In all these cases, hyperbole is a literal "lie" used for the sake of emotional effect. Since biblical poetry tends to express emotion, we should not be surprised to find hyperbole appearing frequently.

Apostrophe

An apostrophe is a direct address to someone or something absent as though it were present. It is frequently combined with personification, in which an abstract quality or physical object is treated as though it were a person. Lyric poetry such as we find in the Psalms is heightened speech, and we should not be surprised to find an abundance of apostrophe. Given this impulse toward poetic license, virtually anything can addressed in the form of apostrophe: "Depart from me, all you workers of evil . . ." (Ps. 6:8); "Lift up your heads, O gates" (Ps. 24:7); "Glorious things are spoken of you, O city of God" (Ps. 87:3); "Bless the LORD, O my soul" (Ps. 103:1). The most extended example is Psalm 148, which is a catalogue of apostrophes.

In real life we do not apostrophize objects in this way. It is one of the conventions and artificialities of poetry. Apostrophe is above all a way of expressing strong feeling and generating a sense of excitement. When apostrophes appear in poetry, they often erupt without warning, as though the poet were carried away with excitement and blurted out an address to something or someone who could not possibly reply. Apostrophes require a reader to be receptive of the emotional intensity that they represent and to respect the right of a poet to speak figuratively rather than matter-of-factly.

Personification

Personification is a figure of speech in which a poet treats something nonhuman (and perhaps even inanimate) as though it were a person. Here, too, the range of things that get personified in biblical poetry is immense. Abstractions are sometimes personified: "Oh send out thy light and thy truth; / . . . let them bring me to thy holy hill" (Ps. 43:3). On other occasions, forces of nature are apostrophized: "Let the floods clap their hands; / let the hills sing for joy together" (Ps. 98:8). Elsewhere groups of people or nations are treated as though they were a single person, as when the poet in the Song of Deborah describes various tribes as though they were individuals: "Gilead stayed beyond the Jordan; / . . . Asher sat still at the coast of the sea" (Judg. 5:17).

There are several reasons why poets so readily personify the things about which they write. It is a way of making a subject (especially if it is an abstraction) vivid and concrete. By personifying forces of nature, a poet suggests the close kinship between people and nature. And personification is a way of showing either the human community or the forces of nature acting with a unified purpose.

Personification requires several things of a reader. One is the ability to identify it when it appears. Another is the ability to relish and respond emotionally to the vividness that personification confers on a subject. It is also important to analyze the exact function that personification serves in a specific context. Finally, the presence of personification requires that a reader realize that truth is communicated by statements that are not factually true. Whenever a poet personifies something, he is playing the game of make-believe.

Psalm 114

Hyperbole, apostrophe, and personification are scattered throughout the poetry of the Bible. Poems are rarely built around these figures of speech the way Psalm 23 is constructed around a central metaphor. Psalm 114, however, is a compressed poem that relies heavily on the three figures of speech just discussed.

Psalm 114 is a patriotic poem that celebrates the miracles surrounding the exodus from Egypt and the entry into Canaan. The poet begins by identifying this as the subject of his poem, and in doing so he personifies the nation as though it were a person or family:

> [1]When Israel went forth from Egypt,
>   the house of Jacob from a people of strange language,
> [2]Judah became his sanctuary,
>   Israel his dominion.

This personification of the nation serves to show the unified purpose with which the people went through the events of the exodus.

Then, in an obviously hyperbolic account of what actually happened, the poet further personifies the forces of nature that were present on the occasion:

> [3]The sea looked and fled,
>   Jordan turned back.
> [4]The mountains skipped like rams,
>   the hills like lambs.

Personification here functions to heighten the vividness of the event and to add a spirit of celebration.

The next four lines of the poem repeat, line by line, the imagery of the four lines in verses 3 and 4, only this time the poet employs the technique of apostrophe:

> [5]What ails you, O sea, that you flee?
>   O Jordan, that you turn back?
> [6]O mountains, that you skip like rams?
>   O hills, like lambs?

Poets obviously use license. They express truth in terms that are not literally or factually true. The sea did not literally look, nor did the mountains and hills jump in high spirits.

At the poem's close, the poet offers a general conclusion about how people should respond to the God who has delivered his nation, and again he employs apostrophe and personification to make the point vivid:

⁷Tremble, O earth, at the presence of the LORD,
   at the presence of the God of Jacob,
⁸who turns the rock into a pool of water,
   the flint into a spring of water.

Figurative Language in Biblical Prose

I noted earlier that metaphor and simile appear in the prose of the Bible. The same thing is true of other figures of speech. The Bible is a very poetic book, even in its narrative and expository parts. This means that we must be ready to interpret figurative language at any point in our reading of the Bible.

Although the stories of the Bible are written in a spare, unembellished style, they are quite capable of containing figurative language. Consider the story of Cain and Abel (Gen. 4:1–16). God warns Cain with the statement, "If you do not do well, sin is couching at the door; its desire is for you, but you must master it" (v. 7). Sin is here personified as a monster (perhaps a wild animal) that through long acquaintance has become a domesticated pet comfortably resting at the door. Later in the story God personifies the blood of Abel by saying that it cries to him from the ground.

Figurative language is equally prominent in New Testament discourse. We find striking apostrophes, for example: "O death, where is thy victory?" (1 Cor. 15:55); "O Jerusalem, Jerusalem, killing the prophets and stoning those who are sent to you!" (Matt. 23:37); "Come now, you rich, weep and howl for the miseries that are coming upon you" (James 5:1). Equally vivid are the personifications scattered throughout the prose of the New Testament: "Then desire when it has conceived gives birth to sin; and sin when it is full-grown brings forth death" (James 1:15); "Love is patient and kind" (1 Cor. 13:4). Hyperbole was a favorite figure with Jesus: "It is easier for a camel to go through the eye of a needle than for a rich man to enter the kingdom of God" (Matt. 19:24).

I have taken this brief excursion into the narrative and expository sections of the Bible to underscore that there is no book of the Bible where we do not need to be able to recognize, interpret, and respond to figurative language.

Parallelism

In addition to figurative language, biblical poetry consists of a distinctive type of sentence structure. This, too, is part of the special language that biblical poets use. It is called parallelism and is the verse form in which all biblical poetry is written. Biblical parallelism is delightful and effective, but its *interpretive* importance has been generally exaggerated by biblical scholars. The first order of business with biblical poetry is to interpret figurative language, especially metaphor and simile. Parallelism adds greatly to the affective power and artistic beauty of an utterance, but in only a small number of cases does it add to the thought.

Parallelism is best defined as two or more lines that use different words but similar grammatical form to express the same idea. Whereas the basic element of recurrence in English poetry occurs at the level of rhyme and meter, which are lost in translation, recurrence in biblical poetry occurs at the level of thought or meaning, which survives in translation. C. S. Lewis describes the principle behind parallelism as "the practice of saying the same thing twice in different words."[8] The phrase *thought couplet* (or, if three clauses are involved, *thought triplet*) is a good synonym for parallelism. There are four main types of parallelism in the Bible.

Synonymous parallelism consists of expressing similar content more than once in consecutive lines in similar grammatical form or sentence structure:

> The LORD of hosts is with us;
>   the God of Jacob is our refuge. [Ps. 46:7]

> God has gone up with a shout,
>   the LORD with the sound of a trumpet. [Ps. 47:5]

In *antithetic parallelism*, the second line states the truth of the first in a contrasting way. Sometimes one line states the idea positively and the other negatively:

> My son, keep your father's commandment,
>   and forsake not your mother's teaching. [Prov. 6:20]

More often, the second line simply restates the idea in a contrasting way:

> Hope deferred makes the heart sick,
>   but a desire fulfilled is a tree of life. [Prov. 13:12]

> A righteous man turns away from evil,
>   but the way of the wicked leads them astray. [Prov. 12:26]

In *climactic parallelism*, the second line completes the first by repeating part of the first line and then adding to it:

> Ascribe to the LORD, O families of the peoples,
>   ascribe to the LORD glory and strength. [Ps. 96:7]

8. C. S. Lewis, *Reflections on the Psalms* (New York: Harcourt, Brace and World, 1958), p. 3. The best book-length treatment of biblical parallelism is James L. Kugel, *The Idea of Biblical Poetry: Parallelism and Its History* (New Haven: Yale University Press, 1981).

> The floods have lifted up, O LORD,
>   the floods have lifted up their voice. [Ps. 93:3]

> Thy right hand, O LORD, glorious in power,
>   thy right hand, O LORD, shatters the enemy. [Exod. 15:6]

A fourth type of parallelism is *synthetic parallelism* (*growing parallelism*). It consists of a pair of lines that together form a complete unit and in which the second line completes or expands the thought introduced in the first line (but without repeating part of it, as climactic parallelism does):

> Thou preparest a table before me
>   in the presence of my enemies. [Ps. 23:5]

> As a father pities his children,
>   so the LORD pities those who fear him. [Ps. 103:13]

To call this parallelism is something of a misnomer, since strictly speaking nothing in the second line parallels the first. But these units are obviously thought couplets in which the two lines together form a unit, as in the other types of parallelism.

The principle underlying all these forms of parallelism is balance or symmetry. The parts of a parallel construction in some sense balance each other and set up a rhythm. They require each other to complete the unit of thought. When we hear one shoe drop, as it were, we wait for the other one to do the same.

The effects of biblical parallelism are not monotonous. Along with symmetry, there is typically an element of asymmetry. Very rarely is there a complete grammatical similarity between the two lines. Consider, for example, these lines from Psalm 51:

> For I know my transgressions,
>   and my sin is ever before me.
> Against thee, thee only, have I sinned,
>   and done that which is evil in thy sight. [vv. 3–4]

The first two lines are similar in thought, but the key idea of transgression or sin appears as a direct object in the first line and as the subject of the verb in the second, and the order of the personal pronouns ("I," "me") is likewise reversed in the two lines. In the third and fourth lines, the subject of the sentence ("I") is not repeated in the second line, and the entire second line parallels a single word of the first, the verb *sinned*.

Biblical parallelism is not a rigid and confining thing. It is based on the premise of freedom within form. Someone has described it thus:

It is clear that there is repetition in the parallel lines. But almost invariably something is added, and it is precisely the combination of what is repeated and what is added that makes of parallelism the artistic form that it is. This intimate relation between the old and new elements is an important feature of Hebrew composition and Hebrew thought. On the one hand we observe form and pattern; on the other form and pattern are radically altered.[9]

The Functions of Parallelism

The liability of conducting an analysis of biblical parallelism such I have just done is that it can easily set up false expectations for readers of the Bible. Let me say emphatically, therefore, that there is no particular virtue in pigeonholing types of parallelism in a biblical poem. The important thing is simply to be receptive to the effects of the rhythm of thought that occurs with parallelism.

Nor should we try to get a lot of interpretive mileage out of parallelism. By itself, parallelism rarely affects the meaning of a statement or solves a problem of interpretation. Lewis rightly warns against the folly of the "effort to get a different meaning out of each half of the verse" (p. 3). In fact, the very principle of two statements being parallel should guard against the attempt to get something different from them. Occasionally, but only occasionally, one half of a parallel construction can help us interpret the meaning of the other half. At the end of Psalm 23, for example, the principle of parallelism alerts us that the phrase that is misleadingly translated "for ever" means the same thing as "all the days of my life."

With the foregoing cautions in mind, I turn to what I think are the chief functions and effects of parallelism. These also constitute my version of what parallelism requires of a reader.

The prime function of any verse form, including biblical parallelism, is artistic beauty and its enjoyment. Parallelism is an example of the skillful handling of language, and it satisfies the artistic urge for balance, symmetry, rhythm, and shapeliness. Biblical poets were artists with a love of beauty and eloquence. When the writer of Ecclesiastes stated that he "sought to find pleasing words" (12:10), he expressed a theory of writing that applies to all of the poets of the Bible.

One function of biblical parallelism is thus artistic enjoyment. Lewis has once again said it well:

In reality [parallelism] is a very pure example of what all pattern, and therefore all art, involves. The principle of art has been defined by someone as "the same in the other". . . . In a building there may be a wing on one side

9. James Muilenburg, "A Study in Hebrew Rhetoric: Repetition and Style," *Vetus Testamentum Supplements* 1 (1953): 98.

and a wing on the other, but both of the same shape. . . . "Parallelism" is the characteristically Hebrew form of the same in the other. . . . If we have any taste for poetry we shall enjoy this feature of the Psalms (pp. 4–5).

There is no need to press biblical poetry at once in a utilitarian direction. It is beautiful and delightful in itself.

A second effect of parallelism is to increase the impact of a statement. In particular, it produces a concentration of attention and is very much a meditative form. Parallelism focuses attention on a thought and resists immediate shift to another idea. Someone has said that biblical parallelism "has within it a retarding element, stemming the current of ideas. The poet allows himself plenty of time. A scene, before being succeeded by another, is presented twice, in different lights. All the content is squeezed out of it. Its finest nuances are utilized."[10] We thus look at an idea from at least two viewpoints as we look at the varied colors of light when a prism is turned. The complementary parts of a parallel construction reinforce an idea in our consciousness. There can be no doubt that if we read biblical poetry as slowly as it is meant to be read, it is a very affective form of discourse. The meanings sink into our consciousness with great force because of the element of repetition and retardation. The two parts of a parallel construction say more together than either would alone.

If we remember that much of the Bible was originally oral literature, we can also see parallelism as a mnemonic ("remembering") device. Parallelism makes it easier to memorize and recite a biblical passage, and it helps an audience to assimilate it when hearing rather than reading it. Lewis observes this in connection with the typical parallelism of Jesus' discourses, but it applies equally to all biblical poetry: "We may, if we like, see in this an exclusively practical and didactic purpose; by giving to truths which are infinitely worth remembering this rhythmic and incantatory expression, He made them almost impossible to forget" (p. 5).

Parallelism in Biblical Prose

Although this chapter is about the language of biblical poetry, I have already noted that figurative language is also common in the prose parts of the Bible. I need to conclude my discussion of parallelism by noting that it, too, is not limited to the poetic parts of the Bible.

Consider, for example, these specimens from two Old Testament prose passages:

"And now, Israel, what does the LORD your God require of you, but to fear the LORD your God, to walk in all his ways, to love him, to serve the LORD

10. Gillis Gerleman, "The Song of Deborah in the Light of Stylistics," *Vetus Testamentum* 1 (1953): 176.

your God with all your heart and with all your soul, and to keep the commandments and statutes of the LORD . . .?" [Deut. 10:12–13]

Again I saw that under the sun the race is not to the swift, nor the battle to the strong, nor bread to the wise, nor riches to the intelligent, nor favor to the men of skill. [Eccles. 9:11]

We know that this is prose rather than poetry because the recurrent unit is the sentence rather than the line, but the construction makes use of the same type of parallelism that we find in biblical poetry.

The discourses of Jesus are also saturated with parallelism:

"Judge not, that you be not judged. For with the judgment you pronounce you will be judged, and the measure you give will be the measure you get. . . . Ask, and it will be given you; seek, and you will find; knock, and it will be opened to you." [Matt. 7:1–2, 7]

The same rules apply here that apply to poetic parallelism, the chief of which is to note that the second half of a parallel construction "makes no logical addition; it echoes, with variation, the first" (Lewis, p. 5).

Finally, the style of the New Testament epistles is likewise characterized by a heavy reliance on parallelism. Here are two typical passages:

For I am sure that neither death, nor life, nor angels, nor principalities, nor things present, nor things to come, nor powers, nor height, nor depth, nor anything else in all creation, will be able to separate us from the love of God in Christ Jesus our Lord. [Rom. 8:38–39]

We are afflicted in every way, but not crushed; perplexed, but not driven to despair; persecuted, but not forsaken; struck down, but not destroyed. [2 Cor. 4:8–9]

The language of the Bible is powerful, majestic, impassioned. Its affective style, in its prose as well as its poetry, consists partly of the presence of parallelism.

8

Artistry in Biblical Poetry

P oetry, like the rest of literature, is the interpretive presentation of human experience in an artistic form. It differs from prose discourse and narrative in being a more concentrated form of writing. In general, poetry also aspires to be more consciously artistic—a thing of beauty.

It is the purpose of the present chapter to illustrate this artistic element in biblical poetry. I have chosen my examples from the Psalms. The elements of artistic form, whether in literature, visual art, or music, include these: pattern or design, unity, theme or central focus, balance, contrast, unified progression, recurrence or rhythm, and variation.

This artistic impulse is everywhere evident in biblical poetry. It exhibits itself in nuances and in the big effects of a poem. We should never forget that the poets who wrote the poetry of the Bible loved not only God and his truth but also poetry. They were interested in poetry as a craft. They knew that a psalm of praise had three main parts and a lament five main parts. No one automatically speaks in the form of parallelism; it is an acquired skill.

So far as the reader is concerned, artistry serves two main purposes. One is enjoyment and delight. Artistic beauty is one of God's gifts to the human race, whether in a tree or mountain or human face or poem. Secondly, the presence of artistry heightens the impact of an utterance. An

artistically excellent piece of writing communicates more effectively than a
flat piece of writing.

Theme and Variation (Ps. 103)

I will begin with big artistic effects, the most important of which is
unity. People have used several different formulas to express this principle.
They speak of "unity in variety" and "the whole-part relationship" and of
"the whole in every part." C. S. Lewis preferred the formulation *the same
in the other*.

I will use the designation *theme and variation*. The theme of a poem is
the idea that governs the entire development of the poem. It might be a
topic (such as God's providence in Psalm 23), an idea (such as that the
godly person is blessed in Psalm 1), or an emotion (such as praise in a
typical praise psalm). The variations are the successive units (either topical
units or imagistic units) that support this theme as the poem unfolds.

The principle of theme and variation in a poem imposes a double
obligation on a reader. The first is to identify the unifying theme and to
state it in sufficiently broad terms that it covers every detail in the poem.
The second is to divide the poem into its separate parts and to observe how
each of these units contributes to the main theme. A piece of practical
advice that I would offer is that it is a good idea to pencil horizontal lines
in one's Bible to demark the units of a poem.

Psalm 103 is a psalm of praise. It is a moderately long psalm, but the
principle of theme and variation insures that it will produce a unified
impression in our mind as we read and ponder it.

The unifying theme of the psalm is that God is worthy of praise for his
wonderful acts. The main structural principle in any praise psalm is the
catalogue or listing of the praiseworthy acts and attributes of God. Having
thus identified the element that remains constant throughout the poem,
we are ready to observe the changes that the poet rings on that theme.

The poem begins, as all lyric poems begin, by introducing the theme:

> [1]Bless the LORD, O my soul;
>   and all that is within me, bless his holy name!
> [2]Bless the LORD, O my soul,
>   and forget not all his benefits.

Often a poem will contain within it words or phrases that explicitly state
the controlling theme, either for the whole poem or for a specific unit. The
phrase *all his benefits* summarizes what this psalm of praise is about.

The first variation on that theme is a catalogue of God's acts in the life of the speaker:

> [3]who forgives all your iniquity,
>   who heals all your diseases,
> [4]who redeems your life from the Pit,
>   who crowns you with steadfast love and mercy,
> [5]who satisfies you with good as long as you live
>   so that your youth is renewed like the eagle's.

Several things contribute to the artistry within the unit. One is the very precise parallelism of clauses. We get a series of five consecutive "who" clauses. At the end of the series, just as monotony threatens, the poet varies the pattern (v. 5): instead of yet another "who" clause, he shifts from synonymous parallelism to synthetic parallelism, adding to rather than restating the idea in the previous line. We might also note the cumulative effect of the evocative verbs in the series: *forgives, heals, redeems, crowns, satisfies.*

The next variation on the theme of God's praiseworthy acts and attributes broadens the scope by listing God's acts in the believing community, or in history:

> [6]The LORD works vindication
>   and justice for all who are oppressed.
> [7]He made known his ways to Moses,
>   His acts to the people of Israel.

The abstractions of verse 6 are balanced by the specific historical allusion in verse 7.

The next section focuses on the attributes of God's character:

> [8]The LORD is merciful and gracious,
>   slow to anger and abounding in steadfast love.
> [9]He will not always chide,
>   nor will he keep his anger for ever.
> [10]He does not deal with us according to our sins,
>   nor requite us according to our iniquities.

Here is a prime illustration of the artistic impulse to balance one thing with another. Verse 8 names four positive *attributes* of God, and verses 9–10 state four negatives (things that God does not do). Furthermore, the four attributes in verse 8 are balanced by four parallel clauses that describe God's *actions.*

Verses 11–13 constitute a unit that uses the technique of simile to praise God's actions:

> ¹¹For as the heavens are high above the earth,
>   so great is his steadfast love toward those who fear him;
> ¹²as far as the east is from the west,
>   so far does he remove our transgressions from us.
> ¹³As a father pities his children,
>   so the LORD pities those who fear him.

Even within a unit like this, the principle of theme and variation is at work. The element that remains constant in the three verses is that each one expresses a comparison that says something about God. But there is also an element of contrast. The first two comparisons are pictures of measureless space that make us feel the bigness of God and the magnitude of his grace. By contrast, the simile that compares God to a father who pities his children makes God's mercy intimate, warm, personal, and relational.

The unit that follows continues to praise God. It is built on a contrast in which the mortality of people heightens the permanence of God's love:

> ¹⁴For he knows our frame;
>   he remembers that we are dust.
> ¹⁵As for man, his days are like grass;
>   he flourishes like a flower of the field;
> ¹⁶for the wind passes over it, and it is gone,
>   and its place knows it no more.
> ¹⁷But the steadfast love of the LORD is from everlasting to everlasting
>   upon those who fear him,
>   and his righteousness to children's children,
> ¹⁸to those who keep his covenant
>   and remember to do his commandments.

As part of the patterned coherence of the poem, we might note that the mention of children in verse 17 echoes the image in verse 13 of a father who "pities his children."

The final movement of the poem rises to a crescendo of praise. The controlling image for these verses, the universal kingship of God, is announced at the outset and then elaborated:

> ¹⁹The LORD has established his throne in the heavens,
>   and his kingdom rules over all.
> ²⁰Bless the LORD, O you his angels,
>   you mighty ones who do his word,
>   hearkening to the voice of his word!

> [21]Bless the LORD, all his hosts,
>   his ministers that do his will!
> [22]Bless the LORD, all his works,
>   in all places of his dominion.
> Bless the LORD, O my soul!

The unity of the passage is amazing. The image of kingship is introduced with the image of *throne* and then echoed with the images of *kingdom* and *dominion*. The opening line of the section also introduces the ideas of transcendence and universality with the phrase *in the heavens*. Once introduced, the motif pervades the passage, with such phrases as *over all*, *all his works*, and *in all places*. The apostrophes are appropriately addressed to angels in God's heavenly court.

The strategy of ending the poem with the same line as that which opened it is brilliant. By thus returning to the beginning, the poet gives his poem an envelope structure that conveys a sense of shapeliness and completeness. By repeating the opening sentiment, the poet reminds us of how much ground the meditation has covered. And after the expansiveness of the catalogue of God's acts, after the heightened emotions and exalted images, we subside again into quiet introspection. From the world of space and history, after the heights of heaven and depths of "the Pit" (meaning the grave), we reenter what Richard G. Moulton calls "the world within."[1]

Pattern and Design

Pattern and design are important to all of the arts. Sometimes, as in the abstract art of a Persian carpet or music without words, the beauty of the pattern is the whole purpose of a work. A poem, because it consists of words, always communicates an intellectual content, but there is something that every carefully crafted poem has in common with a Persian carpet. Someone has said in this regard,

> Art, ultimately, is organization. It is a searching after order, after form. The primal artistic act was God's creation of the universe out of chaos, shaping the formless into form; and every artist since, on a lesser scale, has sought to imitate Him—by selection and arrangement to reduce the chaotic in experience to a meaningful and pleasing order.[2]

1. Richard G. Moulton, *The Literary Study of the Bible* (Boston: Heath, 1898), p. 150.
2. Laurence Perrine, *Sound and Sense: An Introduction to Poetry*, 5th ed. (New York: Harcourt Brace Jovanovich, 1977), p. 217.

The parallelism in which biblical poetry is written is of course its most obvious element of artistic patterning. It is the purpose of the next several pages to explore other examples of the artistic impulse to arrange poems in carefully designed patterns.

Psalm 19

Psalm 19 is one of the high points in the Psalms—so much so that Lewis calls it "the greatest poem in the Psalter and one of the greatest lyrics in the world."[3] It happens to be one of the most highly patterned psalms as well.

The poem falls into two carefully balanced halves, each of which, in turn, is divided into two units. The unifying subject of the poem is the excellence of God's revelation. That revelation occurs in two spheres— nature and the law—and the poem praises both. The symmetrical arrangement of the poem is this:

Verses   1–6: God's revelation in nature:
                    1–4a: praise of the heavenly bodies in general;
                    4b–6: praise of the sun.
Verses   7–14: God's revelation in the law:
                    7–11: description of God's law;
                    12–14: prayerful response to God's law.

If the idea of God's revelation of himself is the big idea in the poem, the idea of law also binds the two halves together. In addition, the poem begins on a cosmic scope and gradually narrows down to the personal level, moving from *the heavens* to *my heart*.

The impulse to arrange things in an artful way is as evident in the individual parts of the psalm as in the overall structure. We begin, for example, with a particularly beautiful instance of synonymous parallelism:

> The heavens are telling the glory of God;
>   and the firmament proclaims his handiwork.

These lines announce the theme of the first six verses, namely, what the heavenly bodies tell us about God. The poet expresses the idea metaphorically by portraying the silent stars and planets as engaged in an ongoing act of speech.

The careful parallelism of the opening verse is matched in the second:

3. C. S. Lewis, *Reflections on the Psalms* (New York: Harcourt, Brace and World, 1958), p. 63.

> Day to day pours forth speech,
>   and night to night declares knowledge.

Within the pattern of recurrence set up by the synonymous parallelism, we note as well the antithesis between day and night. These are not opposites but complementary halves of an unbroken cyclic succession that adds up to a harmonious whole.

Having asserted that the heavenly bodies are energetically proclaiming God's glory in an unbroken succession, the poet next provides a countermovement (v. 3):

> There is no speech, nor are there words;
>   their voice is not heard.

This comes as something of a surprise, since on the surface it refutes what the poet has said in the previous verses. Actually, this further description serves the purpose of calling attention to the fact that the earlier description had been figurative. The heavenly bodies are literally silent and nonverbal. In their very movements and splendor they communicate something about God, a fact that led the poet to speak metaphorically of how they *tell, proclaim, pour forth speech,* and *declare.* But then the poet balances his figurative picture with a reminder of the literal facts of the matter, that the stars and moon do not speak in words.

One countermovement quickly gives way to another, however, for in the very next verse (v. 4) the poet is back to his bold, imaginative idea that the heavenly bodies "speak" about God:

> yet their voice goes out through all the earth,
>   and their words to the end of the world.

We note again the strict parallelism of the utterance, quite an appropriate technique in a poem about the artistry and beauty of nature. Putting verses 3 and 4 together, it is obvious that the poet is playing on the idea of a silent message: the heavenly bodies do not literally speak, but they silently communicate information, hence figuratively can be said to have a *voice* and *words.* The main idea in verse 4 is that nature's witness to God is a universal witness, a theme that the poet accentuates by the balanced phrases *through all the earth* and *to the end of the world.*

Halfway through the opening movement of the poem, the poet narrows the focus from the skies in general to the sun in particular: "In them [that is, the heavens] he has set a tent for the sun" (v. 4b). The course of the sun is then described in two balanced similes:

> which comes forth like a bridegroom leaving his chamber,
> and like a strong man runs its course with joy.

Like the Romantic nature poets of the nineteenth century, this poet wishes to awaken us to the glory of the commonplace. He personifies the sun and surrounds its daily course with all the excitement and emotion of a wedding and a race. Like a runner, moreover, the sun follows a prescribed course or track.

Verse 6 then elaborates the picture of the daily cycle of the sun:

> Its rising is from the end of the heavens,
> and its circuit to the end of them;
> and there is nothing hid from its heat.

This is a descriptive verse, but as was true in the two previous similes, the poet's real purpose is not to convey information but to express wonder at the mystery and majesty of the sun's daily circuit. Part of the design in a carefully crafted poem consists of inner coherence, which is often achieved by echoing motifs that have been introduced earlier. In this verse, the ideas of cycle and universality, already introduced in verse 4, are reinforced by the balanced references *from the end* and *to the end*.

In a poem that on the surface is built around two very distinct ideas (nature and law), how will the poet get from one topic to the other while retaining the unity of his poem? The last line of verse 6 provides the transition. The comment by Lewis on this line is matchless:

> The key phrase on which the whole poem depends is "there is nothing hid from the heat thereof." [The sun] pierces everywhere with its strong, clean ardour. Then at once, in verse 7 he is talking of something else, which hardly seems to him something else because it is so like the all-piercing, all-detecting sunshine. The Law is "undefiled," the Law gives light, it is clean and everlasting, it is "sweet." No one can improve on this and nothing can more fully admit us to the old Jewish feeling about the Law; luminous, severe, disinfectant, exultant (p. 64).

The two halves of the poem are thus linked by the theme of God's revelation of himself and the idea of law (in nature as well as morality).

The description of the moral law that follows is one of the most intricately patterned passages in the Bible:

> The law of the LORD is perfect,
> reviving the soul;
> the testimony of the LORD is sure,
> making wise the simple;

> the precepts of the LORD are right,
>   rejoicing the heart;
> the commandment of the LORD is pure,
>   enlightening the eyes;
> the fear of the LORD is clean,
>   enduring for ever;
> the ordinances of the LORD are true,
>   and righteous altogether.

Each pair of lines constitutes a unit, and each of these six units follows the same pattern, consisting of three parts: first the law is named by a title, then a quality is attributed to it, and finally an effect of the law is named (slightly modified in the last two units, where the second line adds another quality to the description instead of naming an effect). The number of words remains generally constant from unit to unit, reinforcing the patterned effect. As was true in the first half of the poem, the poet describes a subject not primarily as a way of informing us but as a way of praising.

Just as the poet had earlier introduced two comparisons for the glory of the daily circuit of the sun, he now brings in two comparisons to assert the value and desirability of God's law:

> More to be desired are they than gold,
>   even much fine gold;
> sweeter also than honey
>   and drippings of the honeycomb.

As is common in the poetry of praise, the poet refers to recognized standards of excellence in nature, only to declare the object of his praise (here, God's law) even better.

Verse 11 completes the first half of the praise of God's law by returning to the idea of the beneficial effects of the law:

> Moreover by them is thy servant warned;
>   in keeping them there is great reward.

Even here there is a note of transition that anticipates the final movement of the poem, inasmuch as the poet for the first time addresses God directly, in preparation for his final prayer of petition.

The final verses of the poem move from lyric praise to petitionary prayer:

> [12]But who can discern his errors?
>   Clear thou me from hidden faults.

¹³Keep back thy servant also from presumptuous sins;
   let them not have dominion over me!
Then I shall be blameless,
   and innocent of great transgression.
¹⁴Let the words of my mouth and the meditation of my heart
   be acceptable in thy sight,
O LORD, my rock and my redeemer.

Throughout the second half of the poem the poet has asserted that God's law produces results, and here we see it demonstrated in the poet's own prayer. Furthermore, the piercing ray of the sun, so dazzling in the first half of the poem, now finds its counterpart in the poet's desire for the law to find and purge his *hidden faults*.

The sheer beauty and artistry of a psalm like this are not extraneous to its meaning. They are part of the total effect of the poem. In a poem like this, all the details work together to produce the total effect, and the careful design binds everything together. "But when I read a psalm I don't see all these things," people say to me. As is true of every topic I cover in this book, we need to learn what to look for. Beyond that, we need to take the time to stare at a biblical text. When we do these things, we will see what is there.

Psalm 107

Psalm 107 is too long to permit a complete discussion here, but it is so carefully crafted that it deserves comment as an example of design in biblical poetry. Psalm 107 is an ode that praises God's ability to deliver from danger. After an opening call to praise (vv. 1–3), the poem unfolds in five clear units: rescue from the desert (vv. 4–9), rescue from prison (vv. 10–16), rescue from illness (vv. 17–22), rescue from the sea (vv. 23–32), and a catalogue that praises God's power to reverse conditions (vv. 33–43). In each of these sections, God is pictured as reversing a situation.

The first four units narrate four great rescues, and they all unfold according to the same pattern. The poet begins each of these sections by naming a group of people caught in a great crisis and by briefly portraying their desolation. Then follows a refrain that recurs in exactly the same form: "Then they cried to the LORD in their trouble, / and he delivered them from their distress." In the third section of each unit, the poet describes God's deliverance, using the imagery that had been used in the initial account of each group's misery. Finally, each short narrative concludes with a call to thank God for his deliverance, beginning with the fixed refrain, "Let them thank the LORD for his steadfast love, / for his wonderful works to the sons of men!"

The symmetry of the plan is artistically satisfying, and the cumulative effect of such an oratorical passage is overwhelming. The pictures of human predicaments and divine interventions follow a common pattern of calamity—cry—deliverance—thanksgiving.

The fifth section is a more miscellaneous catalogue of God's acts of power, but even here the element of conscious design is striking. The four-part scheme is now dropped, but the acts of God that are catalogued involve the same principle of reversing natural forces and human fortunes that prevailed in the four narratives. Here is an excerpt from the catalogue:

> [33]He turns rivers into a desert,
>   springs of water into thirsty ground,
> [34]a fruitful land into a salty waste,
>   because of the wickedness of its inhabitants.
> [35]He turns a desert into pools of water,
>   a parched land into springs of water.

What a psalm like this illustrates is the powerful effect that artistic patterning produces.

Acrostic Poems

If we are in any doubt about whether the poets of the Bible were self-consciously artistic, we should consider a group of acrostic or "alphabet" psalms. These are poems in which the successive units (either lines, verses, or groups of verses) begin with the successive letters of the Hebrew alphabet.

In Psalms 9, 10, 25, 34, and 145, the verses begin with words whose first letters are, consecutively, the letters of the Hebrew alphabet. The same is true of the encomium in praise of the virtuous wife in Proverbs 31:10–31. In Psalm 37, the opening letters of alternate verses are arranged according to the sequence of the alphabet. Another variation occurs in Psalm 111, where each line (rather than each verse) begins with the successive letters of the Hebrew alphabet.

The most elaborate acrostic biblical poem is Psalm 119. This artistically shaped poem consists of twenty-two sections, each comprised of eight verses. These units feature, in order, the twenty-two letters of the Hebrew alphabet, with all eight verses of a given unit beginning with the same letter of the alphabet. This orderliness reinforces the subject of the poem, which is the law of God.

Three-Part Lyric Form (Ps. 121)

In later chapters I will say more about the dynamics of lyric poems (that is, short meditative or emotional poems). This chapter on poetic artistry, however, is a good place to talk about the three-part form that lyrics possess.

Lyrics begin with a statement of the controlling theme. This unifying umbrella in the poem can be an emotion, an idea, or a situation to which the poet is responding. There are various ways to establish the theme. The poet can describe a situation (Ps. 12:1–2), invoke God (Ps. 55:1), address a human audience (Ps. 66:1), or state an idea (Ps. 32:1). No matter how the theme is introduced, it comes early and serves the purpose of giving the poem a focus from the very beginning.

The main part of any lyric is the development of the controlling theme. There are four main ways by which a poet can go about this. One is *repetition,* which consists of restating an idea or emotion in different words or images. Psalm 133, for example, uses different images to flesh out the idea "how good and pleasant it is / when brothers dwell in unity." Often a lyric theme is developed through *contrast,* as when Psalm 1 develops an extended contrast between the ways of the righteous and the wicked. The *list or catalogue* is very common in lyrics. It occurs when the poet names or responds to various aspects of the theme. All of the praise psalms, for example, list God's praiseworthy acts or qualities. Finally, some poems are structured on the principle of *association.* Here the poet branches out from one topic to a related one, as when Psalm 19 moves from God's revelation in nature to his revelation in the law.

Lyric poems do not simply end. They are rounded off with a note of finality as the poet resolves the meditation or emotion into a concluding thought, feeling, or attitude. In the Psalms this is often a brief prayer or wish. Whatever form it takes, this last phase of a lyric is a moment of closure:

> So will I ever sing praises to thy name,
>   As I pay my vows day after day. [Ps. 61:8]

> May the LORD give strength to his people!
> May the LORD bless his people with peace! [Ps. 29:11]

> Blessed be God! [Ps. 68:35]

The presence of a formal close like these reinforces the point I wish to make with this discussion of lyric form: it is part of the shapeliness that we should come to expect and admire in the lyric poems of the Bible.

Psalm 121 illustrates the shapeliness of good lyrics. It is one of fifteen psalms that bear the title "A Song of Ascents," which means that it was a pilgrim psalm that Old Testament worshipers sang en route to Jerusalem to worship God in the temple. The topic of the psalm is the pilgrimage itself. The theme, or interpretive slant that the poet takes toward the topic, is God's ability to protect the traveler.

Several organizing patterns in the poem reinforce its identity as a pilgrim poem. The motif of a journey pervades the references in the poem. We also sense an underlying conflict between the dangers of the journey and the protecting acts of God. The chief structural principle in the poem is the catalogue of God's acts of protection. The poet introduces his theme by establishing a particular situation that we can visualize:

> ¹I lift up my eyes to the hills.
>   From whence does my help come?
> ²My help comes from the LORD,
>   who made heaven and earth.

The very first line plants in our imagination the picture of a traveler ready to undertake a perilous journey through the hills. At a more symbolic level, it is a memorable example of the biblical urge toward transcendence. Faced with the danger, the poet asks and answers, in catechismlike manner, the pressing question of the moment. The repeated phrase *my help* announces the unifying idea of the psalm. We might also say that verse 1 establishes the need for God's protection, while verse 2 asserts that protection is a fact to be relied on.

The development of the theme is a catalogue of God's protecting acts (vv. 3–6). The first variation on the theme is an instance—a proof or demonstration—of God's protection: *He will not let your foot be moved* (or *slip*), a vivid picture of the physical journey. To elaborate this idea, the poet moves from an instance of God's protection of him to a more general comment about God's character:

> he who keeps you will not slumber.
> Behold, he who keeps Israel
>   will neither slumber nor sleep.

These lines repeat a common idea for the sake of emotional emphasis. In fact, this is a very affective unit. The second and third lines add nothing to the thought of the first, just as we get no addition to our store of information when we read that God will not sleep after we have already been told that he will not slumber. But these repetitions have an emotional impact and make us feel the reliability of God. Another stylistic technique that heightens the security that we feel as we read the lines is the presence of titles or epithets for God: *he who keeps you* and *he who keeps Israel*.

Verse 5 combines an epithet that names a role of God and a concrete illustration of protection:

> The LORD is your keeper;
>   the LORD is your shade
>   on your right hand.

To call God a *shade* is to draw a picture of a tree that protects a traveler from the scorching heat of the sun. The additional statement that God is a shade on a person's *right hand* combines another evocative image of protection with the first one. A warrior who accompanied his lord into battle customarily stood on his right hand, holding his master's protective weapons in readiness. The psalmist has given us an intensified picture of protection by reaching into the two most vivid areas of danger and protection that his world provided.

The next verse (6) returns to the literal, physical rigors of the journey to Jerusalem:

> The sun shall not smite you by day,
>   nor the moon by night.

The first line refers to protection from the very real dangers of sunstroke and heat exhaustion. The second line balances this picture of peril by day with a reference to peril by night. How can the moon smite a person? It is probably a reference either to an ancient notion that the moon causes disease, or to a persistent human association of the moon with mental disorders (compare the instance in Matthew 17:15, where the father of an epileptic boy tells Jesus that his son is a lunatic, that is , "moonstruck").

With the catalogue of God's protecting acts finished, the poet now completes his lyric with the customary note of finality. In many psalms, this final movement involves moving from something specific to something general, or from the present moment to a vision of the future. In Psalm 121 the poet does both of these:

> [7]The LORD will keep you from all evil,
>   he will keep your life.
> [8]The LORD will keep
>   your going out and your coming in
>   from this time forth and for evermore.

The physical journey to Jerusalem here expands into the archetypal journey of life. God's protection from the dangers of the trip have broadened to protection *from all evil*. The focus on the present experience of the pilgrimage has enlarged in scope to *for evermore*. As part of this expansiveness, we might note that a characteristic biblical way to express totality was to name a pair of opposites, with the implication that this covered everything between. In verse 6 this took the form of balancing the sun by day and the moon by night; here at the end it encompasses *going out* and *coming in.*

Something does not have to be big and embellished in order to qualify as an example of the beautiful. Psalm 121 is one of my favorite examples in all of literature of the beauty of the simple. This moving poem illustrates to perfection three time-honored principles of artistic form—unity, coherence, and emphasis. And it exhibits the seamless, apparently artless movement of three-part lyric form.

Composite Artistry (Ps. 139)

Many things go to make up the artistry of biblical poetry. The effects range from the big to the small. The skillful handling of language is everywhere evident and is seen especially in the ease with which biblical poets speak in the verse form of parallelism. Big artistic effects include unity (with theme-and-variation the best way to deal with the subject in analysis), pattern and design, and three-part lyric form.

Much could also be said about the stylistic excellence of biblical poetry. Biblical poetry is written in the high style. Poets take more words than necessary to express an idea (as the technique of parallelism itself requires). The handling of language and the mastery of figurative language result in a style far removed from the ordinary speaking voice. Also noteworthy is the frequent presence of epithets for a person or thing: *Lord God of hosts, the Mighty One of Jacob, the house of the LORD our God* (an epithet for the temple in Psalm 122:9), *a people of strange language* (an epithet for Egypt in Psalm 114:1).

To illustrate the composite artistry that biblical poetry exhibits, I have selected Psalm 139. This is the most exalted psalm in the Psalter. In terms of genre we should call it an ode—the loftiest type of lyric poem, written in an elevated style on a exalted subject. Because of its sheer magnitude, an ode often breaks down into a series of somewhat self-contained units.

Psalm 139 is a prayer addressed to God. Its unifying focus, in fact, is highlighted in the very opening address: *O LORD . . . .* The theme of the majesty of God will govern the entire development of the poem that follows. The variations that the poet weaves on this theme are these:

    Verses 1–6: God's omniscience.
    Verses 7–12: God's omnipresence.
    Verses 13–18: God's omnificence (all-creating power).
    Verses 19–24: God's holiness.

The architectonics of the poem insure that we will never lose sight of the central focus on the greatness of God.

The opening movement of the poem praises God because he knows all things:

> ¹O LORD, thou hast searched me and known me!
> ²Thou knowest when I sit down and when I rise up;
>   thou discernest my thoughts from afar.
> ³Thou searchest out my path and my lying down,
>   and art acquainted with all my ways.
> ⁴Even before a word is on my tongue,
>   lo, O LORD, thou knowest it altogether.
> ⁵Thou dost beset me behind and before,
>   and layest thy hand upon me.
> ⁶Such knowledge is too wonderful for me;
>   it is high, I cannot attain it.

The first thing to note is the overall design of the passage. The very vocabulary keeps the focus of the idea that God knows everything: *searched, known, knowest, discernest, searchest out, art acquainted with, knowledge.* The passage is also unified by the catalogue technique, as the poet lists examples and proofs of God's omniscience. Within the catalogue, we should note the range of things mentioned, including both the thoughts of the speaker and his outward movements.

Underlying the catalogue of God's acts is a controlling image, that of physical movement in a house and on a path. In effect, God is pictured as watching or following the speaker from a vantage point. A second spatial image is also implied in verse 5, where the speaker pictures himself as being boxed in or enclosed by God's knowledge.

The thoroughness of God's knowledge is conveyed by the word pattern *all my ways* and *altogether.* This is reinforced by the biblical technique of suggesting comprehensiveness by naming opposites, with the implication that everything between is therefore included: *sit down* and *rise up, path* and *lying down, behind and before.*

The overall impression that reading the passage produces is the *thoroughness* of God's knowledge of the speaker and the *control* that God exercises over the speaker's life by means of this omniscience. The very form of the passage helps to create this impression, which results from the abundance of balance, antithesis, and parallelism.

With verse 7 we move to the second motif in the ongoing symphony, God's omnipresence:

> ⁷Wither shall I go from thy Spirit?
>   or wither shall I flee from thy presence?

⁸If I ascend to heaven, thou art there!
  If I make my bed in Sheol, thou art there!
⁹If I take the wings of the morning
  and dwell in the uttermost parts of the sea,
¹⁰even there thy hand shall lead me,
  and thy right hand shall hold me.
¹¹If I say, "Let only darkness cover me,
  and the light about me be night,"
¹²even the darkness is not dark to thee,
  the night is bright as the day;
  for darkness is as light with thee.

This passage is as carefully unified as the opening unit was. The pair of rhetorical questions (questions whose answers are self-evident and which are asked for the sake of effect) in verse 7 introduces the controlling image for the entire unit, as the speaker pictures an attempt to escape from God's presence. A journey through space underlies this quest (actually an anti-quest) to hide from God.

Verse 8 balances two pictures of escape, first upward to the heights of heaven and then down to the depths of the earth. Verses 9 and 10 complete the futile journey by picturing movement outward in a horizontal direction. Having exhausted the possibilities of escape through movement, the poet completes his futile quest to escape God's presence by seeking the cover of darkness (vv. 11–12), archetypal agent of secrecy. Underlying the quest is a sense of surprised discovery, as captured in the "even ..." exclamations of verses 10 and 12.

In this passage, then, the poet contemplates an ironic impossibility. It is well summarized (v. 11) by the folly of trying to reverse the process by which God created light from darkness in Genesis 1.

Such is the general pattern. Again the poet embellishes his statements in the details. The horizontal movement of the sun is embellished by picturing the sun as a being with wings. The closeness of God is pictured through anthropomorphism, as God is pictured (v. 10) as leading and holding with his *hand*. And verses 11 and 12 present a series of plays upon the words *light* and *darkness*.

The poet's third variation on the theme of God's greatness is a meditation on the fact that God is omnific (all-creating):

¹³For thou didst form my inward parts,
  thou didst knit me together in my mother's womb.
¹⁴I praise thee, for thou art fearful and wonderful.
  Wonderful are thy works!
  Thou knowest me right well;
¹⁵ my frame was not hidden from thee,

> when I was being made in secret,
>   intricately wrought in the depths of the earth.
> [16]Thy eyes beheld my unformed substance;
>   in thy book were written, every one of them,
> the days that were formed for me,
>   when as yet there was none of them.
> [17]How precious to me are thy thoughts, O God!
>   How vast is the sum of them!
> [18]If I would count them, they are more than the sand.
>   When I awake, I am still with thee.

As is inevitable in psalms of praise, the chief structural principle in the passage is a catalogue of God's acts. In keeping with the personal focus of this psalm, we do not get a catalogue of God's acts of cosmic creation but of the development of the speaker's fetus in his mother's womb.

The chief means by which the poet makes his thought poetic in this passage is metaphor. In the metaphor in verse 13, the control of God over the developing fetus is described in terms of someone's knitting a garment with conscious labor and design. Verse 15 makes metaphoric use of an ancient myth that all living things were produced in the middle of Mother Earth. (There is no possibility of this poet's literal belief in the myth; verse 13 shows that he knows very well where a living person is formed.) A fetus is as hidden and its growth as mysterious as was creation in the myth of things growing in the middle of the earth. God is metaphorically pictured in human terms—as having *eyes* and reading a *book*. Finally, there is the figurative picture of thoughts being like numbers that can be added, and the simile comparing the sum of those numbers to the numberless sand on a shore or in a desert.

The final movement of the poem, in which the poet denounces wicked people who defy God, might seem at first glance to break the unity of the poem. But I have come to conclude that this is the poet's way of praising yet another of God's attributes, his holiness. Here is the passage:

> [19]O that thou wouldst slay the wicked, O God,
>   and that men of blood would depart from me,
> [20]men who maliciously defy thee,
>   who lift themselves up against thee for evil!
> [21]Do I not hate them that hate thee, O LORD?
>   And do I not loathe them that rise up against thee?
> [22]I hate them with perfect hatred;
>   I count them my enemies.
> [23]Search me, O God, and know my heart!
>   Try me and know my thoughts!
> [24]And see if there be any wicked way in me,
>   and lead me in the way everlasting!

Many poems contain key words and phrases that highlight their own unity. I believe that the next-to-last line of the poem serves such a function for the last unit. *Purging out the wicked way* is the controlling motif here at the end of the poem. This, in turn, is an indirect way of praising God's holiness, since anything that detracts from that holiness does not deserve to exist.

This motif takes two forms. First the poet expresses a wish that evil people who defy God—who are an affront to God's holiness—be defeated. To intensify the picture of these wicked people, the poet speaks in epithets: *the wicked, men of blood, men who maliciously defy thee.* This is balanced by descriptions of conflict between evil and God: *hate, loathe, enemies.*

The violence and energy of these verses form a contrast to the quiet ending of the poem in the last two verses. Here the poet applies the motif of purging the wicked way to himself, making it clear that he places himself under the same judgment that he has just applied to people who hate God.

Part of the artistry of the poem is the way in which the poet ties the end of the poem to the beginning by echoing the language of the opening. *Search me* balances the opening *thou hast searched me. Know my heart* echoes the earlier *thou knowest. Know my thoughts* calls to mind the statement *thou discernest my thoughts.* The double reference to the *way* in the last verse repeats the controlling image of the *path* in the poem's first movement. While thus taking us back to the beginning, the last line of the poem also expands outward into the future: *lead me in the way everlasting.*

We could not ask for a better illustration of the whole-part relationship in a long poem. The simplicity of the overall design is balanced by amazing intricacy of detail, a balance that perfectly pictures the greatness of God and his simultaneous control of details in the world. Finally, the poem, despite its length and multiplicity of subthemes, follows three-part lyric structure, from the opening address to God (the subject of the poem), through the specific attributes for which God is praised, to the poet's humble submission before God's greatness in the closing lines.

9

Explicating Biblical Poetry
What to Say About a Poem

*E**xplication* is the literary term used to denote the close reading of a text, whether a story or a poem. It implies more than analysis for one's own benefit. To explicate ordinarily means to analyze a text and then arrange the material in the most effective way for presentation to an audience, whether in oral or written form. The methodology that I outline in this chapter is equally appropriate for an expository approach and an inductive approach based on a series of questions accompanied by group discussion.

The keys to formulating a good explication are easy to identify. A good explication is *systematic, thorough,* and *logical or orderly in its progression.* Furthermore, it is important for an audience that an explication possess *a discernible strategy.* Jumping from one isolated detail to another, or from one part of a poem to another, is a sure path to an ineffective explication.

The Dynamics of Explicating Poetry

There are four indispensable things to do in a good explication, and at least one additional topic that is worthy of mention. The logical way to progress through these elements is to move from the big to the small.

Genre and Implied Situation

An explicator is a tour guide or traveling companion. The goal is to help a reader see what is really present in the poem. A good explication is a lens that brings a text into focus.

The lens that most quickly brings a poem as a whole into initial focus is identifying the genre. Unless a person knows the general category to which a psalm (for example) belongs, detailed information about its religious ideas still leaves one with a very hazy picture of the text. On the other hand, to be told that a given psalm is a psalm of praise or a lament psalm or meditative lyric at once creates a picture of the shape and content of the poem.

An awareness of the form or genre of a work programs our encounter with it. To know the literary family of a poem at once tells us how the poem is organized and what its general purpose is. The basic form of a poem carries with it a whole set of expectations or things for which to look, and it at once provides initial handles for dealing with the poem.

Closely akin to genre is the implied situation that might be assumed in a poem. As we learn more and more about what is happening in a poem, we often come to sense an underlying situation—a set of givens that are essential to understanding the dynamics of the poem.

This, too, is important early information to state in an explication. It is useful to know that the speaker in Psalm 10 is in the middle of a crisis in which his enemies have slandered him. Psalms 42–43 will make a lot more sense if we realize that the speaker is living in exile and is therefore prevented from worshiping God in the temple in Jerusalem. Psalm 121 presupposes a pilgrimage to Jerusalem.

The Intellectual Core

Once we have put a poem into its literary family and made explicit any situation that it implies or presupposes, the next logical procedure is to summarize what the poem says. I call this the intellectual core of a poem—the big paraphrasable element consisting of topic and theme.

The *topic* of a poem is what the poem is about. The topic of Psalm 23 is God's providence, and that of Psalm 1 the godly person. The *theme* is what the poet asserts or implies about the topic. A statement of theme narrows the topic down to a specific thesis. Thus the theme of Psalm 23 is the contentment that comes from resting in God's providence, and that of Psalm 1 is the blessedness of the godly person. I should note in passing that the two-stage process of first identifying the broad topic and then narrowing it down to a particular interpretive slant or theme usually produces greater precision than when we obscure the two-stage process.

Structure and Unity

With the genre and main idea of the poem identified, the next logical step is to lay out the *unity and structure* of the poem. Here the aim is to give an overview of the entire poem and to provide clear pathways through it. There are several dimensions to the structure of a poem. Every poem has its own topical units based on either changing ideas or changing images. It is important to mark out the successive units in a poem, thereby showing the flow of thought or feeling.

Structure also depends on the type of material that dominates a poem. There are four possibilities. If a poem is mainly a description of either a character or a scene, it has a *descriptive structure*. If it presents a sequence of ideas or emotions, it has an *expository structure*. *Narrative structure* occurs if the main material is a sequence of events. If the dominant element is an address by the speaker to a listener, the poem has a *dramatic structure*. Many poems consist of a combination of these, but there is great merit in choosing one of them as the way in which an explicator has chosen to organize the poem for a given occasion. We are not in quest for the one right way to formulate the structure. What we need is a clear pathway through the poem, even when it is selected from two or more options.

Other structural schemes may be important for a given poem. In the previous chapter I noted that lyrics tend to have a three-part structure. In the next chapter we will see that praise psalms have their own version of three-part structure and that lament psalms have five main elements. If a poem is strongly repetitive, in effect maintaining a single principle in different guises, the term *repetitive structure* is helpful. If a poem consists of a series of ideas that march by a process of logic to a conclusion, we can speak of *logical structure*. A poem that mainly lists various aspects of a topic can best be identified as structured on the *catalogue* principle.

Many lyric poems are written at the white heat of emotion. They follow the very flow of a speaker's consciousness and jump abruptly from one subject to another. It is futile to look for a logical flow of ideas in such a poem. The point of unity is that it is all happening in the mind and consciousness of the speaker. The best designation for such a structure is *psychological structure*. Many lament psalms furnish examples.

One of the most helpful things that was ever pointed out to me about poems was that most of them are organized around one or more *contrasts*. Perhaps this is the poetic equivalent of plot conflict in a story. In any case, one should always look for the principle of contrast in a poem. Psalm 1 is organized around a contrast between two ways of life. Lament psalms contrast the helpless victim and the oppressive foe, as well as portraying a tension between the speaker's emotional terror and confidence in God.

Psalm 121 is built around the contrast between the dangerous journey and the protection of God.

I should guard against the impression that it is wise to mechanically grind every poem through all the structural schemes I have noted. My advice is simply to use whichever ones yield the most for a given poem.

If we do justice to the structure of a poem, we have already provided a sense of its unity. There may, however, be additional elements of overall unity in a poem that need to identified. Some poems have a *unifying image pattern* or *controlling image* (an image or metaphor that underlies an entire poem). Thus Psalm 23 is unified partly by the controlling metaphor of the sheep-shepherd relationship, and Psalm 121 by the journey motif. Imagery of a storm unifies Psalm 29 and images of rescue Psalm 91.

Poetic Texture

All of my previous categories have concerned the overall effects of a poem. But poems also consist of details. The best language we have for talking about these matters is an architectural metaphor. The structure of a poem is like the two-by-fours that hold up a wall. But the walls that we actually see are covered with (let us say) wallpaper. The details in a poem—the actual words and figures of speech—are like the wallpaper. The customary term is *poetic texture*.

Poetic texture consists of words (including their connotations or overtones), images, metaphors, similes, apostrophes, personifications, hyperboles, and any other figures of speech. These are what actually communicate the meanings. Exploring their meanings, in fact, is almost certain to take by far the most space in an explication of a poem, as will be evident in my demonstrations later in this chapter. One good format under which to explore these meanings is to ask what the *logic* or *function* or *aptness* of a given figure of speech is in a given context. Why is this poetic device here? is a good stock question to keep in mind. Another is, What is the logic or explanation of this particular device in this context?

The best way to organize running commentary on poetic texture is to begin at the beginning of a poem and march steadily through the poem, organizing the discussion by whatever unit seems to lend itself to separate discussion (whether an image, a line, a verse, or a group of verses). This way of proceeding recreates how we actually experience a poem as we read it. It also insures that we will not confuse people who are reading or listening to our explication. In this sequential reading of a poem, the framework of theme and variation usually works well, as we consider how each unit contributes to the unifying theme of the poem.

Artistry

The first four categories I have discussed are the basics of a good explication. One cannot understand what a poem says without doing these things. Having done all this, however, there is likely to be a category of things that did not get adequately covered. Much of this falls under the heading of artistry—the sheer beauty of the poem, quite apart from what it says.

There would be no biblical poetry without the verse form of parallelism, for example, yet parallelism may not have found its way into the discussion of poetic texture. At many points one would simply wish to say something about the eloquence and beauty represented by parallelism.

The same is true of the types of pattern and design that I discussed in the previous chapter. The poets who wrote the poetry of the Bible regarded these things as important. So should we.

What Does a Good Explication Do?
Psalm 1 as a Test Case

I wish to apply the methodology I have outlined by going through Psalm 1, reconstructing the process that I think best for formulating the meaning and beauty of the poem. I will explicate Psalm 1 under the format, What does a good explication do?

The first thing that a good explication does is establish some big labels that a reader or listener would find useful right at the outset. The *genre* of Psalm 1 is the meditative or reflective lyric. In effect, we contemplate various aspects of the announced subject.

There are two equally valid ways to formulate the *topic and theme* of Psalm 1, alerting us that we are not necessarily in search of the one right formulation. The version that I prefer is that the topic is the godly person, with the theme (interpretive slant) being the blessedness of the godly person. It is true that the poem devotes nearly as much space to portraying the wicked person, but I believe that this is a foil that sets off the blessedness of the godly person. But for people who prefer the second approach, it would be equally accurate to regard the poem as dealing with the contrast between the two ways. The theme might then be that godliness leads to blessing and wickedness leads to judgment.

Despite its surface simplicity, Psalm 1 is one of the most structurally intricate poems in the Bible. This predominantly descriptive poem is structured as a prolonged contrast between two types of people and two ways of life. The poem also divides into three topical units of two verses each. The first two verses introduce two types of people, the next two verses further describe them with a pair of harvest images, and the final two verses move to a final verdict on the two people by describing their future destiny.

Psalm 1 is also structured as a system of alternating positive and negative descriptions. Verse 1 opens the poem with enormously positive connotations in the form known as the beatitude and then quickly shifts to an account of the what the godly person does not do:

> Blessed is the man
> who walks not in the counsel of the wicked,
> nor stands in the way of sinners,
> nor sits in the seat of scoffers.

This negative description is balanced in verse 2 by a positive description:

> but his delight is in the law of the LORD,
> and on his law he meditates day and night.

Verse 3 contains a sequence of positive-negative-positive statements:

> He is like a tree
> planted by streams of water,
> that yields its fruit in its season,
> and its leaf does not wither.
> In all that he does, he prospers.

Verse 4 has a negative-positive pattern:

> The wicked are not so,
> but are like chaff which the wind drives away.

This is followed in verse 5 by a negative description:

> Therefore the wicked will not stand in the judgment,
> nor sinners in the congregation of the righteous.

Verse 6 culminates the pattern of alternating statements by describing the positive results of godliness and the negative results of wickedness:

> for the LORD knows the way of the righteous,
> but the way of the wicked will perish.

Wherever possible, an expositor should draw interpretive conclusions about data, including structural data. The pattern of alternating statements between positive and negative, as well as the prolonged contrast that organizes the poem, conveys the sense of life that it is the purpose of the psalm to communicate. The sense that life is a struggle, that it requires choice, and that it involves both doing and avoiding certain actions, are all implied by the very structure of the poem.

Having thus clarified the unifying elements in the poem, we are ready to do running commentary on the poetic texture. The wrong metaphor to use for this is "tearing the poem apart." The right image is that of exploring and discovering the poem. Running commentary on the texture consists mainly of identifying and interpreting the meanings of images and figures of speech. Merely identifying a figure of speech is only the starting point. The really important thing is to explore what meanings are conveyed by it.

Verse 1 communicates its meaning chiefly through metaphor. We are told, for example, that the godly person *walks not in the counsel of the wicked*. Wicked people do not literally take walks down a path called "the counsel of the wicked," nor do they literally publish handbooks of advice entitled *The Counsel of the Wicked*. The statement tells us metaphorically that godly people do not follow the way of life of the wicked. How is walking down a path an apt metaphor for a person's lifestyle? Points that they have in common include a long-term, continuous activity, progress or change, and arrival at a destination. The word *counsel* is a legislative word, and it, too, is an apt comparison. The wicked do not literally pass their own legislation, but they exercise such things as peer pressure and cultural influence that are as influential as the laws that an assembly passes.

The statement that the godly person does not *stand in the way of sinners* is also metaphoric. Sinful people do not literally stand together in a field or room called "the way of sinners." They do, however, participate together in evil activities, which is the main meaning of the metaphor.

The third descriptive clause—*nor sits in the seat of scoffers*—is likewise figurative rather than literal. People in a scoffing mood do not take turns sitting in a chair with a sign over it that reads "The Seat of Scoffers." The terminology is again legislative. In the Old Testament, to "sit in the seat" (or its variant "sit in the gate") means to be a member of the town council or the policy-making body of a community.

Normally the verse form of parallelism does not contribute strongly to one's interpretation of the meaning of an utterance, but the verse at which we have been looking is an exception. There is a subtle progression at work in these three parallel clauses. There is a progressive paralysis of evil, as we move from walking to standing to sitting. More significantly, there is a progressive identification with evil. To walk down a path implies individual compliance with evil. To stand in the way implies participation as a member of a group. And to sit in the seat implies active involvement in determining the evil that pervades a society.

Verse 2, with its comment that the godly person meditates on God's law day and night, also requires interpretation. I should underscore that a good explication makes an attempt to interpret every statement that is not utterly clear. What does it mean to meditate on God's law day and night? We know that no one consciously ponders God's law twenty-four hours a day. Perhaps it is a hyperbole that we realize is not literally true but that conveys the intense devotion of the godly person to God's law. Alternately, we might interpret the word *meditate* to mean that the godly person's whole life is guided, unconsciously as well as consciously, by God's law. Or perhaps *day and night* means "in the morning and in the evening." A good explication alerts an audience to the best interpretations of a passage and normally commits itself to what the explicator thinks is the most convincing one. I think verse 2 is a hyperbole.

In verse 3, which pictures the godly person as *a tree planted by streams of water*, the chief business of the explicator is to explore the meanings embodied in the image of the tree. These meanings include productiveness (*that yields its fruit in its season*), stability (especially as contrasted with chaff [v. 4]), closeness to a source of nurture (*planted by streams of water*), and endurance (*and its leaf does not wither*). As I stressed in a previous chapter, the comparisons of poetry require us to *carry over* the meaning from one level to another. We need to apply what verse 3 says about the tree to a human level.

Verse 4 gives us a second harvest image when it compares the wicked to *chaff which the wind drives away*. The meanings that this image communicates depend partly on our contrasting it with verse 3. I might note in passing that a well-constructed poem creates its own small world of details. Images or words often have a meaning in the context of a poem that they might otherwise lack. Because the image of the chaff driven by wind is set over against the image of the productive tree planted by streams of water, we can see all the more clearly the essential meanings of the image: transience, worthlessness, deadness, instability. The literal picture of chaff that the verse paints says exactly what the poet believes to be true of wicked people.

In the last two verses of the poem, the verb tense shifts to the future. Here is the final verdict on the two ways of life that have been described. The poem also returns to the metaphoric mode of the first two verses, and the same meanings that we applied to the metaphors of the path and assembly are now true at an ultimate level.

With the structure and poetic texture of Psalm 1 thus explicated, there are some points of artistry and craftmanship that are simply worthy of note. This, too, is part of the poem's artistic meaning—part of the beauty that it communicates, quite apart from its meaning or as a reinforcement of that meaning. Such artistic beauty is one of the excellencies of the Bible and something that sets it apart from other sacred books of the world.

In connection with Psalm 1, for example, we might simply relish the parallelism. Every verse falls into either synonymous, synthetic, or antithetic parallelism. The progression in the three parallel clauses in verse 1 is particularly striking and clever.

Another element of pattern is the envelope structure that the imagery forms. The imagery comes from three areas of life, arranged in a pattern of *A-B-A*. The imagery of the path or way and of the assembly occurs in the first and last pairs of verses. The middle two verses form a separate unit that uses imagery about nature, specifically the harvest.

To sum up, a good explication is systematic and thorough and has a discernible strategy or plan of attack. The right strategy is to move from the large to the small—from genre and implied situation to topic and theme to structure and unity, and then to a sequential reading of the images and figures of speech, followed by appropriate comments about artistry.

Specimen Explications

Poetry is intricate and complex, and its compressed style requires an analytic and meditative approach. To explicate a biblical poem as I have described it is to spend more time on a passage than we do in a straight reading. This is a step in the right direction. Biblical poetry is a meditative mode. The point in reading it is not to finish as quickly as possible but to let the fullness of the meanings filter into our consciousness. To put oneself through the discipline of literary analysis is one of the biggest assets in reading the Bible in keeping with its meditative purpose.

How does one find all that there is in a biblical poem? I would offer three answers. First, we need to acquaint ourselves with how poetry works. My entire treatment of biblical poetry is designed to convey the essential information. Secondly, we can consult reliable commentaries in order to appropriate the insights of others. When we do so, we absolutely need to fit those insights into our own organizing framework, which I have described in this chapter. Finally, a good reader or explicator is never ashamed of staring at a poem. In fact, in my lexicon explication is synonymous with staring—with looking closely, long, and repeatedly at a poem until the patterns and meanings of the figures of speech start to reveal themselves.

Having theorized about the right method for explicating a poem and asked what a good explication does, I want to conclude this chapter with specimen explications of selected Old Testament psalms. In each case, I have not tried to be exhaustive but simply to provide a good initial explication.

Psalm 97

Psalm 97 is representative of what I call the simple lyrics of the Psalter. It is short enough (twelve verses) to produce a single impression, and it progresses by clear units. Its topic is God's kingship over the world. The theme is that God's kingship causes the righteous to rejoice in the Lord. This topic and theme are announced in the opening verse:

> The LORD reigns; let the earth rejoice;
> let the many coastlands be glad!

The unifying images are already introduced here. Images of kingship and rule will continue to describe God's actions throughout the poem. The scope of those who are subject to that kingship will be nature and all people, as suggested here by the images of *the earth* and *the many coastlands*. And the dominant emotion of the poem is well summarized by the phrase *be glad*.

The theme of the poem is elaborated by three variations. The first is a description of God's power over nature:

> [2]Clouds and thick darkness are round about him;
>> righteousness and justice are the foundation of his throne.
> [3]Fire goes before him,
>> and burns up his adversaries round about.
> [4]His lightnings lighten the world;
>> the earth sees and trembles.
> [5]The mountains melt like wax before the LORD,
>> before the LORD of all the earth.
> [6]The heavens proclaim his righteousness;
>> and all the peoples behold his glory.

The purpose of the poet is to convey an exalted sense of the power of God. He does this in one of the conventional ways that biblical poets used for the purpose: he merges the big and awe-inspiring forces of nature into a single composite picture. To heighten the effect still more, the poet uses hyperbole. The result is a picture that, while not literally true in all its details, *suggests* the power of God to do anything he wishes.

I might also note that one should not be overly influenced by the stanzaic divisions (called strophes) as we find them in printed versions of the Psalms. Verse 6, for example, is clearly a summary of the unit that precedes it, yet it is printed with the next section.

The second variation on the theme of how God's universal kingship causes the righteous to rejoice shifts the focus from the actual power of God to the human response to that power:

> [7]All worshipers of images are put to shame,
>> who make their boast in worthless idols;
>> all gods bow down before him.
> [8]Zion hears and is glad,
>> and the daughters of Judah rejoice,
>> because of thy judgments, O God.
> [9]For thou, O LORD, art most high over all the earth;
>> thou art exalted far above all gods.

God is superior not only to the forces of nature but also to other gods. I have noted that lyric poets often develop their theme by means of contrast, and this passage is an example. The sovereign greatness of God produces two human responses. Worshipers of idols are forced to admit that they have chosen an inferior deity, while worshipers of God rejoice.

The final variation on the main theme is a portrayal of the blessings of God on the righteous:

> ¹⁰The LORD loves those who hate evil;
>   he preserves the lives of his saints;
>   he delivers them from the hand of the wicked.
> ¹¹Light dawns for the righteous,
>   and joy for the upright in heart.
> ¹²Rejoice in the LORD, O you righteous,
>   and give thanks to his holy name!

Verse 10 achieves its effects through contrasts—between *loves* and *hate*, *saints* and *the wicked*. Verse 11 uses a metaphor from nature in picturing the favor and blessing of God on the righteous. This metaphor, incidentally, illustrates the commonest method by which we can tell when to interpret a statement figuratively, namely, when it does not make adequate sense at a literal level. We know that physical light dawns for everyone, not just the righteous. Hence the light of verse 11 must symbolize something besides the light of the sun.

Verse 12 illustrates the way in which lyric poems reach closure. As is common in the Psalms, the final resolution of this meditative poem is an apostrophe urging a response from those who believe in God. Such a concluding note, like the opening statement of theme, could be isolated from the preceding unit in an outline of the psalm. I have kept it with the larger unit as a way of keeping the outline simpler.

As we look back over the poem, we see that Psalm 97 has unfolded in a way so natural that we could imagine its being the actual thought process of a speaker, even though we know that people do not spontaneously speak in parallel verse form and in the form of theme and variation. The logic of the flow of thought could not be clearer. From the opening statement of theme, the poet paints a picture of God's power over nature. He then branches out to declare that God also rules over the gods of the earth, a fact that makes the righteous rejoice in their God. From this thought it is a natural development to celebrate the blessings that come to those who fear God. And the final verse states in the form of a command what the poem has already declared to be the situation: *Rejoice in the LORD, O you righteous*.

Psalm 90

Psalm 90 is a famous poem on the subject of time. Its specific theme is human mortality, which is viewed in the light of God's eternity and power.

The poem, in other words, is a moving meditation on human vulnerability in the world, a vulnerability that is muted by an awareness of God's sovereign power over the believer's life.

Although the poem is brief, it does not possess the simplicity of thought that we have seen in Psalm 97, and I have selected it for this reason. To the very end of his meditation, this poet will balance positive and negative attitudes toward his subject. Some biblical poems preserve the ambiguities that we feel in many of our experiences, and Psalm 90 is one of these poems.

The poem is primarily expository, as the poet presents a series of thoughts on the theme of human transience. The movement is strongly repetitive, as the poet mainly restates the central idea in different words and images. The entire poem, moreover, is structured as a contrast between God's sovereign eternity and power on the one hand and people's physical and spiritual weakness on the other.

This poem illustrates particularly well the dynamics of a meditative poem. As the poem unfolds, we witness a mind in action, moving from an initial reflection to a series of related thoughts. The sequence of ideas pushes constantly forward, creating its own momentum and capturing the sense of a person engaged in the very process of thinking and reflecting and responding.

The poem begins with a famous picture of God's transcendence that is often taken out of context and considered by itself:

> [1]Lord, thou hast been our dwelling place
>   in all generations.
> [2]Before the mountains were brought forth,
>   or ever thou hadst formed the earth and the world,
>   from everlasting to everlasting thou art God.

This opening might lead us to expect that the poem will be a meditation on the character of God, but the poem turns out to be much more about the mortality of people. What is the logic of beginning with an evocative picture of God's eternity? This is the perspective from which we will look at our own mutability and weakness in the poem. The overall strategy in the poem is to make us feel humble before God. Furthermore, the poem as a whole will show how homeless people are in their earthly life. As the poem unfolds, we are led to acknowledge that nothing earthly is secure against the changes of time. The picture of God as an eternal dwelling place therefore stands at the very outset as the antidote or solution to the problem of human mutability that the poem will pose.

The next unit in the poem, verses 3 and 4, provides a transition from the opening picture of God's eternity and power to human transience:

> ³Thou turnest man back to the dust,
>   and sayest, "Turn back, O children of men!"
> ⁴For a thousand years in thy sight
>   are but as yesterday when it is past,
>   or as a watch in the night.

Poets love to work with contrasts, and here is one of the most memorable—a contrast between time-bound people who die and the God who transcends time. Verse 3 deflates any illusion of human sufficiency by picturing the ease with which God terminates human life. And verse 4 shows that God is exempt from human limitations of time by a juxtaposition of big and small units of time: a span of time that to human thinking is vast (a thousand years, the old way of denoting the biggest span of time imaginable) is to God like the smallest measurements of time that people use—the fleeting memory of a day already past or a mere watch in the night (which in ancient times was virtually the smallest unit of time).

The poem is built on an incremental ("growing") principle in which human mortality becomes more and more terrifying in our consciousness. The powerlessness of people in the face of God's control over time becomes even more pronounced in verses 5 and 6:

> ⁵Thou dost sweep men away; they are like a dream,
>   like grass which is renewed in the morning:
> ⁶in the morning it flourishes and is renewed;
>   in the evening it fades and withers.

Lyric poems give us a heightened version of a given experience and in the process highlight that subject with clarity. In these verses, the poet reaches into the most evocative examples of fleetingness with which he was familiar—a flood that quickly sweeps objects away, a dream that we forget as quickly as we have had it, grass that withers in less than a day in the drought of summer. T. S. Eliot called this lyric strategy "the objective correlative," meaning that the poet conveys an emotion (in this case a feeling of vulnerability in the face of human transience) by presenting a series of images or situations that *correlate* with the feeling and universally elicit that feeling from readers.

The vision of human mortality rises to something far more tumultuous in the next unit, where it is given a spiritual identity and becomes more than physical:

> ⁷For we are consumed by thy anger;
>   by thy wrath we are overwhelmed.
> ⁸Thou hast set our iniquities before thee,
>   our secret sins in the light of thy countenance.

> [9]For all our days pass away under thy wrath,
>   our years come to an end like a sigh.
> [10]The years of our life are threescore and ten,
>   or even by reason of strength fourscore;
>   yet their span is but toil and trouble;
>   they are soon gone, and we fly away.

The characteristic lyric way to conduct an argument or convince us of the truth of something is affective—to repeat the idea so often that we finally feel its truth. In the passage just quoted, the verse form of parallelism adds a haunting weightiness to the human misery that the lines assert. Some of the mood pieces in Ecclesiastes come to mind as parallels.

Having diagnosed the human predicament (mortality) and assigned a spiritual cause to it (God's wrath over human sinfulness), the poet next offers an appropriate response:

> [11]Who considers the power of thy anger,
>   and thy wrath according to the fear of thee?
> [12]So teach us to number our days
>   that we may get a heart of wisdom.

The rhetorical question in verse 11 implies that part of the human predicament is a prevailing unawareness of, or indifference to, God's wrath. Verse 12 mentions but does not elaborate the possibility of a proper response to the problem of human mutability that the poem has posed. Perhaps such wisdom *to number our days* (that is, consider our mortality in its physical and spiritual dimensions) is what the poem as a whole dramatizes. A major function of poetry is to raise the reader's consciousness about the issues of life. Reading a poem is a moment of awareness. Surely we can say that Psalm 90 raises our consciousness about the problem of human mortality, and such awareness constitutes *a heart of wisdom* on the issue.

It is a rarity for the poems of the Bible to end on a wholly negative note. Psalm 90 has been a growing vision of anxiety about human life lived under the disapproving eye of God. But the concluding section mutes that anxiety with a prayer to God:

> [13]Return, O LORD! How long?
>   Have pity on thy servants!
> [14]Satisfy us in the morning with thy steadfast love,
>   that we may rejoice and be glad all our days.
> [15]Make us glad as many days as thou hast afflicted us,
>   and as many years as we have seen evil.
> [16]Let thy work be manifest to thy servants,

> and thy glorious power to their children.
> ¹⁷Let the favor of the Lord our God be upon us,
> and establish thou the work of our hands upon us,
> yea, the work of our hands establish thou it.

There is mingled optimism and pessimism in these humble petitions. The awareness of human affliction continues, but it is now mitigated by the note of God's love and favor.

The mingled effect is achieved partly by echoing words from earlier parts of the poem. A prayer for God to satisfy *in the morning* would ordinarily connote the certainty and promptness of God's help (as in Ps. 46:5), but here the statement carries the melancholy awareness from verse 6 that man is like grass that flourishes *in the morning* and then *fades and withers* by evening. The picture of rejoicing and being glad *all our days* (v. 14) is subdued because of the earlier assertion that *all our days pass away under thy wrath* (v. 9). And the wish for God's work to be manifest (v. 16) cannot be made without recalling that part of God's work is to turn man back to dust (v. 3) and sweep him away (v. 5).

But if much is carried forward from earlier in the poem, there is also a new note of assurance. Like the writer of Ecclesiastes, the writer of this poem is an optimistic realist. With an awareness of the givens of life in a fallen world, he nonetheless harbors the conviction that with God's grace something can be made of life. God is a God of *pity* (v. 13) as well as wrath. Although nothing earthly is secure, God can satisfy human longings (v. 14). One can ask for days of gladness that will be as many as the days of affliction (v. 15). A sense of human continuity is suggested by the statement that God's glorious power will be manifest to the believer's children (v. 16), and we remember the opening assertion that God is *our dwelling place in all generations* (v. 1). Finally, there is reason to hope that not only God's work will endure (which is never in doubt) but also human work—*the work of our hands* (v. 17).

In terms of the dynamics of explicating poetry, I would offer Psalm 90 as an example of the need for constant alertness on the part of the reader. Because the opening and closing verses of this psalm are so often quoted out of context, it is easy to come to the poem thinking that it will be a simple psalm of comfort. But the opening picture of God as a secure dwelling place quickly gives way to an ever-expanding vision of how homeless we are in the world. Even the vision of hope at the end is mingled with an awareness of the contrary facts of our existence. The best advice that I can give, therefore, is to be an alert reader, to be prepared for a shifting flow of thought and feeling in a poem, and to follow the poem's own course of development instead of imposing our own set of expectations on it.

Psalm 32

I have stressed the need to discern and state the unity of a psalm. I do not mean to imply that it is always easy to do so, but with enough patience we will find that most of the psalms have a firm logic of development underlying and pervading them. But some psalms are seemingly miscellaneous in their content and structure. I would not abandon the quest to find unity in these poems, but I would operate on the premise that such poems will have to be wrestled into a rather general framework, and that I might have to do some streamlining (overlooking of details for the sake of general clarity) when formulating the structure and unity.

Psalm 32 illustrates what I mean by a miscellaneous poem whose unity needs to be wrestled into shape. The first five verses, dealing with the forgiveness of sins, could not possibly be more unified than they are. But then the poem takes off in directions that could never have been predicted from the opening and that seem quite miscellaneous. With such a poem, I would keep a firm rein on the idea of variations on a central theme, and I would look carefully for references to that theme scattered throughout the poem, not simply at the beginning.

Psalm 32 is one of the penitential psalms (the others are 6, 38, 51, 102, 130, and 143). The general framework under which all of these poems can be approached is that the speaker confronts his own sin and establishes a strategy for finding relief from the crisis of his guilt. The speaker in these poems is on a quest, and the goal of the quest is to be at one with God. In some sense each of these poems tells us about a deliverance or rescue made possible by God's grace. The personal note is strong, and appeals to the speaker's own experience are prominent.

With these features of the genre in mind, I would take the big idea in Psalm 32 to be *what to do when trouble comes*. This is the idea that surfaces in the early, middle, and late phases of the poem (see vv. 6–7, 10). The specific theme is that God is the source of rescue for those who trust in him. I do not think that the theme can be successfully formulated as dealing specifically with forgiveness. We will see that the sentiments in the second half of the poem are simply too general to be pinned down only to the crisis described early in the poem (sin that requires forgiveness), and I would therefore reiterate my earlier caution that a poem should be allowed to set its own agenda, even if that agenda does not accord with familiar interpretive schemes that have grown up around a psalm. The first variation on the theme of God's ability to rescue from distress is couched in the form of two beatitudes:

> [1]Blessed is he whose transgression is forgiven,
>   whose sin is covered.

> [2]Blessed is the man to whom the LORD imputes no iniquity,
>   and in whose spirit there is no deceit.

Here is the goal at which the speaker has arrived, namely, fellowship with God unclouded by unforgiven sin. Forgiveness of sin is the first act of rescue that is asserted and celebrated in the poem. The opening verses convey a tremendous feeling of relief and openness and a sense of the slate wiped clean. This is the positive statement of the theme. We might note also the sense of completeness that comes when the poet first states his idea positively (v. 1) and then negatively (*no iniquity, no deceit*).

Having shown us the goal at which he arrived, the poet next takes us back in time to his great crisis of soul that pushed him to undertake his quest for forgiveness:

> [3]When I declared not my sin, my body wasted away
>   through my groaning all day long.
> [4]For day and night thy hand was heavy upon me;
>   my strength was dried up as by the heat of summer.

Here is the proof by negative example of the truth asserted in the opening beatitudes. Here, too, is the motif of distress that is part of the poem's unifying theme. There is plenty of realistic psychology in this portrait of unrelieved guilt: psychosomatic ailments, loss of appetite and sleep, emotional and physical enervation.

Verse 5 continues the personal reminiscence and is the positive counterpart to the malaise just described:

> I acknowledged my sin to thee,
>   and I did not hide my iniquity;
> I said, "I will confess my transgressions to the LORD";
>   then thou didst forgive the guilt of my sin.

The deadlock that had been so vividly described is here broken in an equally dramatic way. In a poem dealing with deliverance, here is the first rescue.

Taken together, verses 3–5 have been a personal narrative about guilt and its relief. From this point, however, the poem becomes decidedly general in its statements. The effect is to make the speaker's experience of sin and forgiveness a specific example of the larger principle of rescue from distress:

> [6]Therefore let every one who is godly
>   offer prayer to thee;
> at a time of distress, in the rush of great waters,

> they shall not reach him.
> [7]Thou art a hiding place for me,
>   thou preservest me from trouble;
>   thou dost encompass me with deliverance.

Here is the general principle that the poet's personal experience has illustrated. At the level of technique, the poem effectively balances abstractions with concrete images and metaphors. Thus the abstraction *time of distress* becomes vivid with the metaphor of a flood *of great waters* that sweeps objects along. The abstraction *thou preservest me from trouble* is fleshed out with the concrete picture of *a hiding place* where a person is safe from enemies.

At this point the poem could be considered to be complete. But as in some other psalms, the poem keeps going after it has reached a point of apparent completeness. The next variation is a general exhortation to heed instruction:

> [8]I will instruct you and teach you
>   the way you should go;
>   I will counsel you with my eye upon you.
> [9]Be not like a horse or a mule, without understanding,
>   which must be curbed with bit and bridle,
>   else it will not keep with you.
> [10]Many are the pangs of the wicked;
>   but steadfast love surrounds him who trusts in the LORD.

What possible relevance does this have to the context of this particular poem? Some commentators claim that these words are imagined as being spoken by God to the poet, but this strikes me as totally arbitrary, nor do I see that it resolves the question of unity.

These verses have all the earmarks of a didactic exhortation to be attentive, in the manner that we so often find in the wisdom literature of the Bible. I would suggest that the logic at work here is that the speaker wishes to share the discovery that he has made about God's ability to save. And so he adopts the stance of a teacher of wisdom, drawing upon personal experience, exhorting others to listen, and distilling the wisdom that he has learned. That wisdom repeats yet again the unifying theme of the poem, that we can depend on God to deliver those who trust in him.

The final verse of the psalm rounds off the poem by urging a response to the specific truth that has been stated in the poem:

> Be glad in the LORD, and rejoice, O righteous,
>   and shout for joy, all you upright in heart!

In view of God's forgiveness and deliverance, here is the appropriate human response.

Psalm 32 illustrates several things about explicating biblical poems. One is that with some poems it is inevitable that a major part of one's critical energies will be expended on finding and describing the unity and structure of the poem. A second thing to note is that not all of the psalms are equally laden with poetic texture. This poem is not lacking in vividness and affective power, but it is rather largely a poem of direct statement rather than a highly metaphoric or figurative expression.

Finally, a good expositor of the Bible needs to have flexibility and an openness to the possibility that one's perception of a poem can change and be revised. While working out the explication of Psalm 32, I had to revise it completely after having written most of an earlier draft (and after having been misled by some commentaries). Poems do not carry all their meaning on the surface, nor are their patterns always clear. The more often one reads the Bible, the more likely he or she will find it necessary to revise earlier understandings of passages. Some insights into such seemingly cut-and-dried matters as unifying theme or structure come only after years of contact with a text. Overall, I would say that if one wants to master a biblical poem, there is no substitute for staring at it long and hard.

10

Types of Biblical Psalms

What I have said about biblical poetry in the three previous chapters applies to poetry generally, wherever we find it. But there are various genres or subtypes of poems. Since any study of biblical poetry will naturally come to focus on the Book of Psalms, it is essential that we be aware of the most important types of psalms. This chapter discusses and illustrates the salient features of the five main poetic genres to be found in the Psalms.

A generic approach is particularly appropriate to the Psalms because their most significant grouping is by kind, not by author. There is nothing to distinguish the style of one author from another. The Psalms are virtually anonymous. All of the poets use parallelism and take their imagery from conventional sources, such as nature, religious worship, hunting, war, farming, and family life. The thing that makes the Psalms fall into groupings is various genres.

Lyric Poems

When we use the term *poem*, we usually mean lyric poem. Briefly defined, a lyric poem is a short poem containing the thoughts or feelings of a speaker. In ancient times, including biblical times, lyric implied something in addition: it was musical in form, intended to be either sung or accompanied by musical instruments (usually a lyre, hence the name lyric). For our purposes, three features of lyric are important: lyrics are personal or subjective, they are reflective or emotional in basic content, and they are brief.

The Personal Element

Lyric is essentially a private mode. In effect we overhear the poet address someone other than us—God, self, a group, enemies, or no one in particular. The lyric poet usually speaks in his own voice, using the "I" form of the pronoun. Since Old Testament religion was strongly communal, the Psalms present a variation on the first-person technique: instead of speaking only in the first-person singular form ("I"), the psalmists frequently use the plural form, in effect speaking as representatives for the whole religious community.

This concept of the "representative I" helps to resolve a question that arises with lyric. If lyric poems are so obviously the direct personal, private, and even autobiographical sentiments of the poet himself, how can we as readers relate to the utterance? The answer is that we should read such poems as giving expression to our own experiences also. It is an example of the commonplace that the poet is our representative, saying what we want said, only saying it better. A good lyric is like a public prayer, both personal and public, expressing what both the speaker and a larger group want to affirm.

Emotion or Reflection

The emotional element in a lyric poem is usually considered its chief identifying trait. It is not easy to express emotion in poetry. The means of doing so include the use of exclamation, hyperbole, emotive words, and vivid description (since sensory images often evoke emotion). A common lyric strategy has always been to project human feelings onto external nature. Mainly, though, the psalmists make religious and psychological feelings the subject matter of their poetry. Praise, adoration, awe, terror, joy, sorrow, fear, depression—these are what the Psalms are about and therefore lend an emotional aura to them.

Although in literature generally lyrics are predominantly emotional, I would make a qualification in regard to the Psalms. It is noteworthy how many of them are meditative or reflective in content and tone. These poems present a series of ideas or thoughts rather than a sequence of impassioned feelings.

Regardless of whether a lyric is emotional or reflective in content, we should not go to such poetry looking for a story line. We will not find a story. At most, we will find occasional snatches of narrative to explain the poet's emotion or to elaborate his feelings. Lyric poets are much more interested in creating a mood than in presenting action. As a result, it is always a legitimate procedure to analyze how a lyric passage makes us feel. If we then proceed to ask by what techniques it makes us feel that way, we are on the road to a good explication of a poem.

Lyrics are heightened speech used to express intensified feeling or thought. Because of this, they often contain abrupt shifts and generally (though not always) lack the smooth transitions that we find in stories. C. S. Lewis speaks of "the emotional rather than logical connections" in lyrics.[1] Such shifts demand alertness on the reader's part, and they may require some interpretive creativity in determining how one unit in a poem fits with another.

Regardless of whether a lyric is emotional or reflective, it is usually conceived as the speaker's *response to a stimulus*. There is frequently an implied situation underlying a lyric. In the Psalms, the poets are nearly always responding to something that has moved them—a personal crisis, malicious enemies, the greatness of God, a victory or defeat, the beauty of nature. One of the helpful things to do with a lyric is therefore to identify as precisely as possible the stimulus to which the poet is responding. This may require reading between the lines, but it is usually possible.

Lyric Brevity

Lyrics are short poems. Since a lyric often expresses a single feeling at the moment of greatest intensity, it is necessarily brief. After all, it is impossible to prolong an emotional pitch indefinitely. The fact that the Psalms were originally intended to be sung is perhaps another reason for their prevailing brevity.

Because of their brevity, lyrics must be regarded as self-contained units. Even when they appear in collections, as they do in the Psalms, they are not chapters of a single book but entities in themselves, separate from the psalms that precede and follow them. Some poems in the Psalter are too long to meet my criterion of brevity. But a close look at what happens in these poems reveals that they actually break down into a series of separate lyric units, each one governed by its own controlling thought.

Lyric brevity means that these poems are concentrated and compressed. They capture a feeling at its moment of greatest intensity or a thought at its moment of greatest insight and conviction. Because of this compression, we must emphatically not regard a lyric as expressing the whole truth on a given subject. Lyric poems capture a moment and do not

1. C. S. Lewis, *Reflections on the Psalms* (New York: Harcourt, Brace and World, 1958), p. 3.

represent a systematic and reasoned philosophy of the subject. It would be particularly foolish to isolate a hyperbolic statement from its context and treat it as a universal truth.

Because of the brevity of a lyric poem, unity of effect is an essential feature. The overwhelming majority of lyric poems have a single focus, which may be either an emotion or an idea. This unifying theme is almost always stated early, and it controls all of the details that follow. Nothing is more debilitating to a lyric poem than for a reader to allow it to remain a series of fragments. The verse divisions of our modern Bibles do us a great disservice here. We would be much better off with line numbers, since they do not prejudge the question of where to make the divisions into topical units and also make a more unified visual impression.

The most effective ways of formulating the unity of a lyric have been covered in previous chapters, and I will only review them here. Outlining a poem's topical or imagistic units is essential to grasping its unified progression. The framework of theme and variation is a useful tool in this outlining process. The three-part lyric form of introduction-development-resolution is of course a good thing to look for. Finally, it is helpful to identify which of the four possible ways a poet has used to develop the theme. Those possibilities are repetition of an idea, a listing or catalogue, contrast, and the principle of association in which one thought leads to a related one.

Lyric as the Basic Form

Lyric is the umbrella genre in the Psalms. All of the psalms are lyric poems. The forms that I discuss later in this chapter are all subtypes of lyric poetry. This means that the lyric features that I have discussed apply to any psalm that we might read. They are the first items on the agenda when we come to explicate a psalm.

The explications in the three previous chapters have already illustrated helpful strategies to use when analyzing a psalm as a lyric poem. Instead of repeating that material here, I have chosen to explicate three poems that I think represent three common lyric impulses in the Psalms—the "tiny lyric," the reflective lyric, and the emotional lyric.

Psalm 133

Scattered throughout the Psalms are a number of very short lyrics, three to six or seven verses in length. They are often the neglected poems of the Psalter because they seem too short to explicate or use in a Bible study. Yet they illustrate particularly well one aspect that I have stressed in connection with lyric—the ability to zero in on a specific thought or emotion and silhouette it with heightened clarity and impact. In actual reading, the appeal of these tiny lyrics is great. They prove that the simple is one of the forms of beauty.

Psalm 133 is such a lyric. It is one of the "Songs of Ascents," which at once links it with the Old Testament pilgrimages to the temple in Jerusalem. In fact, the poem itself is about the pilgrimage:

> [1]Behold, how good and pleasant it is
>   when brothers dwell in unity!
> [2]It is like the precious oil upon the head,
>   running down upon the beard,
> upon the beard of Aaron,
>   running down on the collar of his robes!
> [3]It is like the dew of Hermon,
>   which falls on the mountains of Zion!
> For there the LORD has commanded the blessing,
>   life for evermore.

The simplicity of the poem is breathtaking. The design consists of an opening statement of theme, which is then elaborated with a pair of similes.

The first verse expresses the unifying theme and mood as concisely as it is possible to do. Given the context of pilgrimage, a specific kind of fellowship is in view, namely, the unity that comes to people who are joined together by their mutual worship of God. To call these worshipers *brothers* is a metaphor that first awakens our feelings about family love and unity and security and a sense of belonging and then asks us to transfer those associations to people joined by a shared religious commitment.

To elaborate this controlling theme, the poet first compares group unity to the oil that ran down Aaron's robe. How is fellowship like that? Oil has qualities of spreading and covering, as fellowship engulfs a group of like-minded people. As the fragrance of oil permeates the space around it, so unity pervades a religious group.

But there is more than this in the verse, which refers specifically to the oil used to anoint Aaron. In other words, verse 2 combines allusion (a reference to something in history or literature) with simile. The verse alludes to some facts of Old Testament worship recorded in Exodus 30:22–33. We learn there, for example, that the oil was sacramental and holy. It was part of a religious ritual that set Aaron apart. In fact, no one other than the priests was allowed to mix this oil. It was so special as to be unique, one of a kind. Its purpose, moreover, was to consecrate Aaron and the tabernacle utensils as a preparation for worship. The dynamics of simile are such that we are asked to transfer all these qualities of consecration, preparation for worship, and holiness to the group of traveling pilgrims joined in the worship of God.

The second simile takes us from the world of religious worship in the tabernacle to the world of nature: "It is like the dew of Hermon, / which falls on the mountains of Zion!" We all know that dew has the ability to cover and spread, thereby reinforcing some of the same meanings as we noted in the previous verse. But dew is also an archetype of refreshment and beauty. Perhaps the idea of overflowing abundance is also present, since Mount Hermon, the highest in Israel, was known for its heavy dews. Here too, then, is the motif of superlative, one-of-a-kind quality. This is how the poet feels about the unity of religious worshipers preparing to encounter God.

At the end, the poet rounds off his meditation by invoking the authority of God for the experience that he has celebrated and by pointing from the present moment to an eternal future: "For there the LORD has commanded the blessing, / life for evermore."

Here, we might say, is the lyric impulse in its pure form. We overhear the speaker expressing a single thought in highly charged images or word-pictures. The mood created by the images of the family, the priestly oil of consecration, and the dew of Hermon, as well as by the concluding appeal to the command of God, is strongly unified. As we read the poem, we experience a moment of heightened awareness about religious fellowship.

Psalm 8

Psalm 8, one of five nature poems in the Psalter, is representative of the reflective or meditative lyric. As the poet contemplates the glory of God in the creation, he moves through a series of related thoughts and reaches a conclusion. In fact, there is at least a hint of a problem-solution structure to the poem, as the poet seeks to understand how God could value such a small creature as himself.

The poem begins and ends with the same thought, the majesty of God in the whole earth:

> O LORD, our LORD,
> how majestic is thy name in all the earth!

This is the theme—the interpretive slant that the poet takes toward his subject. That subject is nature and humanity's place in the scale of nature.

The poet's first reflection follows naturally from the opening assertion about God's universal majesty. It is the idea that God's glory as revealed in nature is so universally recognized that even infants "chant" it in their response to nature:

> ¹Thou whose glory above the heavens is chanted
> ² by the mouth of babes and infants,
>   thou hast founded a bulwark because of thy foes,
>   to still the enemy and the avenger.

This is obviously a reflective poem requiring our best powers of thought. The meaning here is that the natural world created by God elicits such universal human responses, even from children, that it is enough to silence God's enemies. I should add that although verses 1 and 2 do not refer explicitly to nature, this is the dominant subject of the poem as a whole and is certain to be what the poet is talking about from the beginning of the poem.

Having mentioned God's glory *above the heavens*, the poet moves his gaze downward *to* the heavens:

> ³When I look at thy heavens, the work of thy fingers,
>   the moon and the stars which thou hast established;
> ⁴what is man that thou art mindful of him,
>   and the son of man that thou dost care for him?

Verse 3 has a contemplative cast to it. In effect we observe the speaker as he contemplates the heavens on a starry night. Even to picture an anthropomorphic creator molding the heavenly bodies with his *fingers* is a highly imaginative act of contemplating God's creation of the world.

Then we follow the leap of the poet's mind as he moves from the impressiveness of the moon and stars to himself, and is led to wonder how God can care for such a small creature as him. It is as though we follow the speaker from observation to a discovery. That discovery, moreover, is something of a problem or riddle that requires a solution.

As the speaker continues to meditate on the matter, he comes to a conclusion about the place of people in the scale of nature:

> ⁵Yet thou hast made him little less than God,
>   and dost crown him with glory and honor.
> ⁶Thou hast given him dominion over the works of thy hands;
>   thou hast put all things under his feet,
> ⁷all sheep and oxen,
>   and also the beasts of the field,
> ⁸the birds of the air, and the fish of the sea,
>   whatever passes along the paths of the sea.

This passage, too, is contemplative, with the poet picturing to himself the ways in which people have dominion over various facets of nature. In keeping with its reflective nature and intellectual cast, the poem is based on a grand paradox that we are asked to grasp with our minds: people are simultaneously small and great. Their greatness is kept firmly within the framework of God's grace, however. It is something that God has conferred upon the human race, as the poem reiterates: *thou . . . dost crown him, thou hast given him, thou hast put.* The proper response is combined humility and confidence before God.

This psalm, incidentally, invites comparison with the "Wonders of Man" speech in the Greek playwright Sophocles' play *Antigone.* That speech, too, catalogues the ways in which people are masters over nature and becomes a magnificent expression of Greek humanism. In Psalm 8, human mastery of nature is not a self-accomplishment but is something conferred by God. Even the envelope structure of the poem, which encloses the body of the poem within exclamations about God's majestic name, shows that for this nature poet any meditation on nature and humanity's place in it must begin and end with God.

Here, then, is an example of a reflective or meditative lyric. There are a number of such in the Psalter. The basic strategy is to think through a topic in several of its dimensions. As readers, we recreate the meditative process of the speaker and share the discovery of an insight.

Psalm 46

I have chosen Psalm 46, a worship psalm or song of Zion, as representative of an emotional lyric. The main strategy in such a poem is affective: it aims to make the reader feel a certain way. I am therefore going to explicate the poem under a format that once made me cringe but that I now think is thoroughly legitimate for an affective lyric. As I go through the various units, I am going to ask, "How does this passage make us feel, and why?"

Psalm 46 is a strongly unified poem. The main idea is stated three times—at the very outset (*God is our refuge and strength, / a very present help in trouble*) and in the refrain that appears in the middle and at the end (*The LORD of hosts is with us; / the God of Jacob is our refuge*). The poem gives us variations on this theme of the certainty of God's presence amid the uncertainties of life, and the confidence that this instills in people who trust in God.

A look at the image patterns, refrains, musical interludes (as noted by the Hebrew word *Selah* in the margin), and stanzaic units shows that the poem has a clear three-part structure. Verses 1–3 describe God's presence in the midst of natural upheavals. Verses 4–7 assert God's presence in the midst of political or military threats. And verses 8–11 accompany an account of God's power over warring nations with God's own statement of his power. As already noted, each unit is accompanied by a statement of the idea that governs the poem as a whole.

Psalm 46 is also structured around underlying contrasts: God versus forces of disruption or chaos, the stability of God's presence versus instability in other areas of life, peace of mind versus the things that would induce fear, the destructiveness that characterizes the worlds of nature and human history versus the salvation of God's acts in history.

As I turn now to commentary on the poetic texture of the poem, my concern will be first to note the effect that a given unit has on a reader and then ask what stimulates such a response. The Bible as a whole is an affective book, and the lyric poems in it are so preeminently. To become self-conscious about our responses as we read is one step toward becoming a better reader of the Bible. To ask what there is in the text to produce that effect serves as a check on the accuracy of our responses and can itself enhance those responses.

The opening statement of theme at once evokes a feeling of confidence in the power and character of God:

> God is our refuge and strength,
>   a very present help in trouble.

The technique here is metaphor. The poet reaches into the most vivid experience of protection that his world provided, the world of warfare, to picture the protecting power of God. The images of *refuge, strength,* and *help* together build up in our modern Western imaginations the picture of a castle or fort, with all the connotations that these have for us. To define the help as being *present* defines the constant availability of the help, and the added modifier *very* is a lyric intensive that heightens the effect. In an affective lyric like this, every word is likely to add something to the growing effect.

The imagery in the rest of the opening movement takes us to the world of cataclysmic upheaval in nature:

> [2]Therefore we will not fear though the earth should change,
>   though the mountains shake in the heart of the sea;
> [3]though its waters roar and foam,
>   though the mountains tremble with its tumult.

The magnitude of the forces of nature described here produces a concentrated picture of terror. Here are the uncontrollable forces of nature that we most fear: earthquake, erosion, tidal waves, sea storms. The extended synonymous parallelism (four successive lines instead of the customary two) greatly reinforces the effect of fear in the face of cataclysm.

A passage like this awakens the primitive and instinctual fears that we all feel toward storms or upheavals in nature. The objects of nature that are affected by the attacks described in these lines are themselves portrayed as helpless victims through the technique of personification: the mountains *shake* and *tremble*, the sea has a *heart* where things are in turmoil, and the waters *roar*. The usual lyric strategy is for the poet to present images and describe situations that indirectly evoke rather than name the feelings that the poet wishes to communicate. At the very beginning of verse 2, the poet breaks that pattern and directly names the dominant mood of the entire poem: *therefore we will not fear.*

Verse 4, which begins a section that portrays God's protection of his holy city, at once strikes a new note of calm:

> There is a river whose streams make glad the city of God,
> the holy habitation of the Most High.

The sudden note of calm enters with the mention of a river. The river, with its flowing, life-giving water and peacefulness, is one of the powerful archetypes of the human imagination. It is filled with connotations that make us feel good, and some evocative hymns have capitalized on those connotations ("Like a River, Glorious Is God's Perfect Love," and "Shall We Gather at the River?"). The archetype of the city is likewise an archetype that embodies connotations of security, community, safety, and much more. Stately epithets idealize this city yet further: *the city of God* (meaning Jerusalem, the place where God dwelt in the temple), and *the holy habitation of the Most High*. Everything considered, verse 4 of this psalm is one of the most evocative verses in the Bible, on a par with Psalm 23:2 ("He makes me lie down in green pastures, / He leads me beside still waters").

The next verse (5) continues the picture of security that has been introduced:

> God is in the midst of her, she shall not be moved;
> God will help her right early.

In a verse like this, it is the nuances that evoke a response. To picture God as being *in the midst* of the city gives an added reason to feel secure: the source of protection is at the very power center of the capital city, not on the periphery in the suburbs. The assertion that the city *shall not be moved* gains its impact by virtue of its vivid contrast to the changing earth and shaking mountains and foaming sea earlier in the poem. The city is personified (*her, she*), making the protection that God extends more personal and intimate.

Finally, in a poem where virtually every statement is heightened, it is not enough to say that *God will help her*. The poet intensifies the picture by showing God's eagerness to help: he will help her *right early*. This phrase also conveys the meaning *at the break of dawn*, which is when attacks on a city were likely to occur. Everything in the poem works together to produce the confidence that God will be present to help exactly when help is needed.

Verse 6 completes the narrative of God's deliverance and once again makes us feel safe in the assurance that God is in control of events:

> The nations rage, the kingdoms totter;
>   he utters his voice, the earth melts.

These four brief clauses of reportage convey the certainty and decisiveness of God's intervention. There is a hammerlike effect as two brief clauses narrate what the warring nations do, followed by two more brief clauses that state what God does to counter their efforts. By personifying the nations that rage and totter, the poet in effect diminishes them, treating them as single entities. There is another effect as well: the warring nations become reduced to a person disintegrating physically and emotionally in the face of fear, cowering and trembling. To enlarge the effect of God's power, the poet uses hyperbole as he pictures the earth melting before the voice of God.

As the poet concludes his picture of divine protection of the holy city against the attacking enemies, he ties the poem to its controlling theme with the first appearance of the poem's refrain (v. 7):

> The LORD of hosts is with us;
>   the God of Jacob is our refuge.

Here is what the images and brief narrative fragments have added up to. The refrain, too, makes us feel safe and secure, and it achieves this effect by discernible means. First there is the exalted epithet *the LORD of hosts*. God is the commander of vast *hosts*, of either angels or warriors. It is an image of power and authority. The protection of this powerful king extends not simply to a city but personally to *us*. The second epithet, *the God of Jacob*, is a historical allusion to the patriarchal past. It brings to bear on the present situation all the glorious associations of providential care that we read about in the story of patriarchs in Genesis (and by extension in the broader history of the nation of Israel).

The final movement of the poem is similar in tone and imagery to the second, but now the scope of God's power over the warring nations extends from his protection of a single city to the entire earth:

> [8]Come, behold the works of the LORD,
>   how he has wrought desolations in the earth.

> [9]He makes wars cease to the end of the earth;
>   he breaks the bow, and shatters the spear,
>   he burns the chariots with fire!

Verse 8 is a transition verse that both summarizes the middle of the psalm and points forward to the last section. In this verse the poet uses apostrophe, suddenly directing an anonymous audience to survey with him what God has done. We know that apostrophe is a standard lyric procedure for expressing and generating strong feeling. Here the feeling is the sense of awe and relief that we feel when looking over a scene of destruction when the threat has passed.

Verse 9 makes us feel safe. It evokes a mood of gratitude that peace has finally arrived. The abstraction of the first line is made vivid with the terminal images of the broken bow and shattered spear in the next two lines. The energetic verbs (*breaks, shatters, burns*) make us feel the finality of God's victory over the warring nations.

These feelings of safety and security reach their climax when God himself speaks and exerts his authority over the earth (v. 10):

> "Be still, and know that I am God.
>   I am exalted among the nations,
>   I am exalted in the earth!"

The opening line here strikes the keynote for the entire psalm. It puts the powerful feelings into a single focus. The authority of God is conveyed by the fact that he utters a command. The force of his command to "be still" is to "leave off striving, stop your warfare." The line is a good example of a biblical statement that affects us at our deepest level and in ways that we cannot verbalize. The very line produces the effect that it commands. The power of God is amplified by our awareness that it extends universally—*among the nations, in the earth.*

To conclude the poem on a note of finality, the poet repeats the earlier refrain at the end:

> The LORD of hosts is with us;
>   the God of Jacob is our refuge.

The poem as a whole has been calculated to make us feel secure in the confidence of God's presence in a world of uncertainty. The refrain summarizes these motifs.

At an interpretive level, the affective power of Psalm 46 is expanded when we realize that it can be read at several levels of meaning simultaneously. On one level of meaning, it is a song of Zion—a worship psalm that celebrates God's presence in Jerusalem and his protection of that city (see Ps. 48:4–8 for a parallel). The poem also belongs to an Old Testament genre known as the song of victory—a celebration and thanksgiving on the occasion of deliverance on the battlefield.

For a modern reader, it is even more evocative to place the poem into the literary family of an apocalyptic or eschatological vision of the last time. In the Olivet discourse (Matt. 24–25), Jesus answered his disciples' questions about what it would be like at the time of his coming and the close of the age by describing the last times as a period of chaos on earth:

> "You will hear of wars and rumors of wars. . . . For nation will rise against nation, and kingdom against kingdom, and there will be famines and earthquakes in various places. . . . Immediately after the tribulation of those days the sun will be darkened, and the moon will not give its light, and the stars will fall from heaven, and the powers of the heavens will be shaken; then will appear the sign of the Son of man in heaven, and then all the tribes of the earth . . . will see the Son of man coming. . . . " [Matt. 24:6–7, 29–30]

This passage describes the last days as a time of international chaos and cataclysmic upheaval in nature, followed by the appearance of Christ. Psalm 46 follows an identical movement. The reference to the melting of the earth in verse 6 parallels the eschatological statement in the New Testament that in the "coming of the day of God . . . the elements will melt with fire" (2 Peter 3:12).

An apocalyptic interpretation of the reference to the city (vv. 4–5) is likewise possible. In Revelation, heaven is called "the holy city, new Jerusalem" (Rev. 21:2). God is pictured as being in the midst of the city, as he is in Psalm 46, and there is a river flowing through the holy city of Revelation as there is through the city of God in Psalm 46: "Then he showed me the river of the water of life, bright as crystal, flowing from the throne of God and of the Lamb through the middle of the street of the city" (Rev. 22:1–2). We should note in this regard that the river of Psalm 46 has to be a symbolic river, since there was no river flowing through Jerusalem, the city's water being supplied by an aqueduct (see Isa. 7:3).

Psalm 46 is an example par excellence of the emotional lyrics that frequent the Book of Psalms. In such poems, the poet communicates what he knows by affecting the reader. Readers, in turn, comprehend by being receptive to effects.

Lament Psalms

The Framework of Lament Psalms

All of the psalms are lyric poems. What I have said about lyric, the dominant form, is always important as a framework for analyzing a psalm.

The remainder of this chapter will explore the generic features of subtypes of lyric. These more specific considerations do not replace the more general lyric considerations, but they will yield a more precise understanding of the poems that fall into these subtypes than the lyric framework by itself will provide.

The most numerous category of psalms is the lament or complaint. These poems comprise about one-third of the Psalter. Complaint poems contain the poet's strategy for mastering a crisis, and they can be either private or public (communal) in focus.

Lament psalms are a fixed form consisting of five elements, which (note well) *can occur in any order* and *can occur more than once* in a given poem:

1. *An invocation or introductory cry to God.* This usually (but not always or only) comes at the very beginning of a lament psalm. It may be accompanied by exalted epithets for God, and it often already contains an element of petition. Here is a typical invocation: "Hear my voice, O God, in my complaint" (Ps. 64:1).

2. *The lament or complaint.* This is a definition of the crisis, a description of the speaker's direful situation. It is the stimulus behind the entire poem, the thing to which the poet is responding. This means that lament psalms are what we call *occasional poems*— poems that arise from a specific occasion in the poet's life. This occasion is usually hinted at in the complaint, though some of the lament psalms paint the crisis in very general terms. Some common occasions for laments in the Psalter are mockery or slander by personal enemies, military threat, disease, the burden of sin and guilt (as in the penitential psalms), or drought.

3. *Petition or supplication.* Here the poet outlines what he is asking God to do to remedy the distressing situation.

4. *Statement of confidence in God.* This means that lament psalms are built on a principle of reversal. The poet begins by convincing us that his situation is hopeless and that he is about to be destroyed. But at some point he recants: it turns out that he will not be destroyed after all, for God can be trusted to act on his behalf. Here is a typical statement of confidence in God (Ps. 54:4–5):

> Behold, God is my helper;
>   the Lord is the upholder of my life.
> He will requite my enemies with evil;
>   in thy faithfulness put an end to them.

5. *Vow to praise God,* or its variant of simply praising God. Psalm 35
   ends with a typical vow to praise God:

> Then my tongue shall tell of thy righteousness
> and of thy praise all the day long.

Such is the general pattern. Lament psalms are easy to recognize
because of the fixed form that they follow. They are also evidence that
biblical poets wrote as self-conscious artists aware of the conventions or
"rules" of their craft. Nothing else will account for the constancy of the
form and the unexpected regularity with which the statement of confidence and vow to praise God are included, since these elements cannot be
considered inevitable when a poet writes a complaint. Besides, biblical
poets sometimes refer to their poems with the technical generic label
complaint.

Lament psalms are too numerous to list. Typical specimens of the form
include Psalms 10, 35, 38, 51, 54, 64, 74, and 77. I will explicate the first
of these as the prototypical lament psalm, exploring especially the logic of
the specific devices that the writer of a complaint employs.

Psalm 10

Psalm 10 begins with a cry to God:

> Why dost thou stand afar off, O LORD?
> why dost thou hide thyself in times of trouble?

The logic behind such a cry to God is easy to discern. God has obviously
not delivered the speaker from his crisis. The speaker therefore pictures
himself as having to persuade and arouse God to act. Hence the urgent
appeals to God and the anthropomorphic picture of God as a person who
needs to be awakened to do something. In the opening questions we can
catch the notes of both helplessness and accusation.

Having invoked God, the poet is ready to define the crisis. In Psalm 10
this consists of an extended portrait (vv. 2–11) of evildoers who oppress the
helpless. Writers of lament psalms lavish their attention on painting an
intensified and frequently exaggerated picture of their enemies and their
own helplessness. The logic behind such pictures is the affective purpose of
making us feel the terror of the situation. There is also some psychological
realism at work here, since to give shape to a problem at such length is
already a way of mastering it. Let us explore, then, the range of resources
that the poet uses in Psalm 10 to express the danger posed by wicked
people in his society.

First the poet names the problem (evil people with power on their side) and elicits negative feelings toward the people involved by means of a metaphor taken from either hunting or warfare (v. 2):

> In arrogance the wicked hotly pursue the poor;
>> let them be caught in the schemes which they have devised.

With the problem now defined, the poet begins to ring his changes on the theme as he gives us an ever-expanding vision of evil. The overall device is the literary form known as "the character"—a character sketch of a moral type. Here we get a many-sided portrait of the wicked oppressor of the poor and helpless in society. The sketch begins with a description of the evil person's actions and thoughts:

> [3]for the wicked boasts of the desires of his heart,
>> and the man greedy for gain curses and renounces the LORD.
> [4]In the pride of his countenance the wicked does not seek him;
>> all his thoughts are, "There is no God."

What emerges from these brushstrokes is a portrait of the incorrigibly hardened and profane person, greedy, proud, and untouched by a sense of moral conscience—the most dangerous kind of person a society can harbor.

But this is not the extent of the problem that troubles the poet. The real problem is that God's justice is not evident in the face of such a moral monstrosity (v. 5):

> His ways prosper at all times;
>> thy judgments are on high, out of his sight;
>> as for all his foes, he puffs at them.

The poet assumes that the reader's moral sensibility is healthy. His persuasive strategy is therefore to make the reader feel sympathy with the underdog, hence the repulsive picture of the proud person's gesture of contempt toward the helpless. There is also an element of protest in this account of the prosperity of evil people. Everything in a lament psalm is a strategy to move the reader, just as the poet himself is strongly moved.

From the external actions of the enemy, we move to his thoughts (v. 6):

> He thinks in his heart, "I shall not be moved;
>> throughout all generations I shall not meet adversity."

By taking us inside the very consciousness of the wicked person, the poet shows us how coldly premeditated his plans are. In effect, the poem gives us deeper and deeper layers of evil.

In keeping with his strategy of making his portrait of the enemy vivid, the poet next returns to the physical reality of the terror:

> [7]His mouth is filled with cursing and deceit and oppression;
>   under his tongue are mischief and iniquity.
> [8]He sits in ambush in the villages;
>   in hiding places he murders the innocent.
> His eyes stealthily watch for the hapless,
> [9] he lurks in secret like a lion in his covert;
> he lurks that he may seize the poor,
>   he seizes the poor when he draws him into his net.

The people about whom the poet writes are not abstractions. They are real people, hence the technique of making them palpable with the images of *mouth* and *tongue*. I assume that the portrait in verse 8 is hyperbolic, as the oppressors are pictured as wielding weapons as a warrior or hunter does. It is likely that the literal crisis involves social and economic oppression. But if the poem uses exaggeration, it nonetheless expresses truth—not literal truth but truth about the oppressiveness of the wicked and the utter helplessness of their victims.

The metaphors from hunting in verse 9 (where the enemies are both predatory lions hunting for prey and human hunters using traps) paint a picture of both the power of evil and the helplessness of innocent people in the face of it. The poet generates sympathy for the weak by his pattern of epithets: *the innocent, the hapless, the poor*.

Earlier the poet made us feel the oppressive power of the wicked by describing their actions and taking us inside their very thought process. Now he does the same for the victims:

> [10]The hapless is crushed, sinks down,
>   and falls by his might.
> [11]He thinks in his heart, "God has forgotten,
>   he has hidden his face, he will never see it."

Ironically, the innocent victims have the same view of God that the evildoers do: God does not observe the evil that people do.

As we conclude the actual lament, we are left with the impression that the poet has used all the resources of his imagination to define the crisis and evoke appropriate responses. The poem has taken us through a kaleidoscope of descriptive details, metaphors, dramatized speeches or interior monologues, epithets, and snatches of plot conflict. The sheer fullness of technique captures the conviction and feeling of the speaker, convincing us that there is substance to his crisis. Nor should we overlook the universality of such a lament psalm. The crisis that the poet laments is always going on in societies.

The next unit of the poem alternates petition (vv. 12, 15) and statements of confidence in God (vv. 13–14, 16–18):

> [12]Arise, O LORD; O God, lift up thy hand;
>   forget not the afflicted.
> [13]Why does the wicked renounce God,
>   and say in his heart, "Thou wilt not call to account"?
> [14]Thou dost see; yea, thou dost note trouble and vexation,
>   that thou mayest take it into thy hands;
>   the hapless commits himself to thee;
>   thou hast been the helper of the fatherless.
> [15]Break thou the arm of the wicked and evildoer;
>   seek out his wickedness till thou find none.
> [16]The LORD is king for ever and ever;
>   the nations shall perish from his land.
> [17]O LORD, thou wilt hear the desire of the meek;
>   thou wilt strengthen their heart, thou wilt incline thy ear
> [18]to do justice to the fatherless and the oppressed,
>   so that man who is of the earth may strike terror no more.

Here is the upward movement toward which lament psalms nearly always move. What is the logic of concluding a lament psalm with statements of confidence in God and with petitions that presuppose that God will act? We might remember that a lament psalm is a strategy for mastering a strongly felt crisis. Turning to God in prayer, expressing confidence in the power and character of God, vowing to praise God for his deliverance—all of these are an important part of the psychological and spiritual dynamics of encountering and mastering the crisis.

We might note in passing that the mingling of petition and statements of confidence in God in the last section of Psalm 10, along with the absence of a vow to praise God, shows that the elements of the lament psalm are something that the psalmists use flexibly. There is no prescribed order or form in which these elements appear.

As we stand back from Psalm 10, we can generalize about the logic of the form. The form is highly affective. It aims to move the reader and God, and to express adequately the feelings of the speaker himself. In a lament psalm, the poet encounters and tries to master a crisis in his life. This involves doing justice to the problem itself and not hiding the painful truth. Naming the crisis is itself part of the strategy for coping with the problem. These functions explain the five elements that comprise the lament psalm and the emotions that we find portrayed.

Finally, psalms of lament rest on at least two assumptions: that there is a right and a wrong, and that God can be trusted to vindicate the cause of the right. Usually the poet makes a third assumption as well: that he is on the side of the right (an assumption that is reversed in the penitential psalms, where the speaker takes God's side against himself). Without these premises, the lament psalm as we find it would be impossible.

The Psalm of Praise

The Elements and Form of Praise Psalms

The second largest grouping of psalms is the psalm of praise. This label is generally limited to psalms that praise God specifically. The English word *praise* originally meant to set a price on, or to appraise. From this came the idea that to praise means to commend the worth of, or to express approval and admiration of. Praise is thus a response to the worthiness of someone or something. The psalms of praise, being strongly theocentric in focus, direct the praise to God.

The elements of praise, not to be confused with the form of the praise psalm that I will note later, help to define the content of a psalm of praise. One of these is the elevation of the object of the praise. A corresponding second element is the direction of the praiser's whole being away from himself or herself toward the object of praise. This means, paradoxically, that although the psalms of praise are filled with the speaker's emotions, we do not look at the speaker. We look *with* the poet *at God*. The poet in a praise psalm is someone who says, "Look at that," and points. A third ingredient of praise is testimony. This means that praise has a communal dimension to it, with the praise ordinarily occurring in a group of people and serving as the speaker's witness to what God has done. Thus we are aware of simultaneous vertical and horizontal planes in praise, which is directed both to God and to a human community.

The psalm of praise has a fixed form, just as the lament psalm does. It consists of three parts, actually particularized versions of the three-part lyric structure that I discussed earlier.

The psalm of praise almost always begins with a formal *call to praise*. This call might consist of as many as three elements: an exhortation to sing to the Lord, to praise, to exalt; the naming of the person or group to whom the exhortation is directed; mention of the mode of praise. Psalm 149:1–3 is an introduction possessing all three elements:

> Praise the LORD!
> Sing to the LORD a new song,
>   his praise in the assembly of the faithful!
> Let Israel be glad in his Maker,
>   let the sons of Zion rejoice in their King!
> Let them praise his name with dancing,
>   making melody to him with timbrel and lyre!

I should note in passing that some psalms of praise intersperse such calls to praise throughout the psalm.

The main element in any psalm of praise is the actual praise of God. This normally consists of a *catalogue* or listing of God's praiseworthy acts and attributes. A much less frequent technique is the *portrait* that praises God. Given the central importance of the catalogue, a main feature of explicating a praise psalm is to divide the list into its topical units. This may have more to do with content than form, but it is bound to loom large. A good strategy is to pay attention to repetition of words, images, or ideas within a unit, and to use these as the basis for dividing the catalogue into its constituent parts.

The catalogue of praise typically praises God for his character or attributes and his acts. These two are related, with the comments about God's character and attributes serving as a commentary on his acts. In the Psalms, moreover, God's praiseworthy acts occur in three main arenas: nature or creation, history, and the personal life of a believer. Common actions for which God is praised include acts of creation, providence or provision, judgment, and redemption or salvation. The technique of allusion is always potentially important in a catalogue of praiseworthy acts.

The final element in a typical praise psalm is the *concluding resolution* that ends the praise on a note of finality and closure. It often takes the form of a brief prayer or wish. Here are a few specimens:

O LORD my God, I will give thanks to thee for ever. [Ps. 30:12]

God has blessed us;
   let all the ends of the earth fear him! [Ps. 67:7]

Rejoice in the LORD, O you righteous,
   and give thanks to his holy name! [Ps. 97:12]

It is customary to make some further classifications in regard to the psalms of praise. These psalms, for example, can be either private psalms (praising God for personal blessings) or public psalms (praising God for blessings on the community or nation). Another distinction is between declarative praise (praise for a specific act that God has done) and descriptive praise (praise of God for what he is or does perpetually). But these are mainly tools of classification, not analysis. They have been elevated to a position all out of proportion to their usefulness by some biblical scholars, who multiply the classifications far beyond what I have noted. I would urge against the mania for pigeonholing the psalms of praise into highly specialized types.

The psalms of praise are among the most exalted in the Psalter. If we are looking for the literary quality of the sublime in the Bible, here is where we will find it in abundance. Here, too, are the purest examples of the poetic portrayal of God—of the imagination as a vehicle for expressing supernatural reality. Here is the kind of effect that we encounter repeatedly (Ps. 93:1–4):

> The LORD reigns; he is robed in majesty;
>   the LORD is robed, he is girded with strength.
> Yea, the world is established; it shall never be moved;
>   thy throne is established from of old;
>   thou art from everlasting.
> The floods have lifted up, O LORD,
>   the floods have lifted up their voice,
>   the floods lift up their roaring.
> Mightier than the thunders of many waters,
>   mightier than the waves of the sea,
>   the LORD on high is mighty!

Praise was a way of life for the psalmists and the believing community that they represented. The best analysis of the phenomenon is that of Lewis.[2] He observes that "all enjoyment spontaneously overflows into praise," that, in fact, enjoyment is incomplete until it issues forth in praise. Praise, writes Lewis, is "inner health made audible." And just as people praise what they value, they urge other people to join in their praise. Also excellent is Claus Westermann's observation that praise belongs to life and life without praise in inconceivable.[3] This is so because to praise means to extol, and everyone extols one thing or another. In the Psalms, people extol God.

Knowing that my space was limited, I decided to explicate Psalm 33 as the prototypical psalm of praise. Other typical specimens are Psalms 18, 30, 65, 66, 96, 97, 103, 107, 124, 136, and 139.

Psalm 33

Psalm 33 is less rich in poetic texture than are most of the praise psalms, but since I have devoted attention to explicating poetic language in previous chapters, this will allow me to focus on the specific generic features of the praise psalm. Word patterns count for a lot in Psalm 33, and I have accordingly italicized the dominant word cluster in each section as I quote it.

The opening call to praise includes all three of the possible ingredients:

> [1]*Rejoice* in the LORD, O you righteous!
>   Praise befits the upright.

2. "A Word about Praising," in *Reflections on the Psalms*, pp. 90–98.

3. Claus Westermann, *The Praise of God in the Psalms*, trans. Keith R. Crim (Richmond: John Knox, 1961), p. 76.

> [2]*Praise* the LORD with the lyre,
>   *make melody* to him with the harp of ten strings!
> [3]*Sing* to him a new song,
>   *play skilfully* on the strings, with loud shouts.

Here we find an exhortation to praise, the naming of the audience to whom the exhortation is directed, and identification of the mode of praise (lyre, harp, singing, and shouting). The word pattern that dominates is a series of energetic verbs that express commands.

A common transition from the opening call to the catalogue of praise is a motivatory "for" conjunction, and this is what we find in Psalm 33:

> [4]For the word of the LORD is *upright*;
>   and all his work is done in *faithfulness*.
> [5]He loves *righteousness* and *justice*;
>   the earth is full of the *steadfast love* of the LORD.

The dominant word pattern this time is a series of conceptual images (abstractions) that name qualities of God. This means that this section praises the character and attributes of God. Two other key words are *word* and *work*, both in verse 4. These serve as an umbrella for the entire catalogue that follows, where the word and work of God will dominate the action.

The next unit of the catalogue, for example, alludes to God's creation of the world by his creating word:

> [6]By the word of the LORD the heavens were *made*,
>   and all their host by the breath of his mouth.
> [7]He *gathered* the waters of the sea as in a bottle;
>   he *put* the deeps in storehouses.
> [8]Let all the earth fear the LORD,
>   let all the inhabitants of the world stand in awe of him!
> [9]For he spoke, and it *came to be*;
>   he commanded, and it *stood forth*.

The main focus is obviously on God's creation of the world, and the main word pattern is a series of verbs that name God's creating acts. The language of the entire passage echoes Genesis 1. A secondary word pattern, therefore, consists of references to God's creating word: *the word of the Lord, he spoke, he commanded*. The poem domesticates the wonder of God's creative power by picturing God's creation of the vast forces of nature as being as easy as performing a household chore: he gathered the waters of the sea as though he were filling a bottle with water or filling a storage room.

The next unit shifts the focus from the creation to the nations of the world, and the key word pattern celebrates God's counsel:

> [10]The LORD brings the *counsel* of the nations to nought;
>   he frustrates the *plans* of the peoples.
> [11]The *counsel* of the LORD stands for ever,
>   the *thoughts* of his heart to all generations.
> [12]Blessed is the nation whose God is the LORD,
>   the people whom he has chosen as his heritage!

What does the terminology of *counsel* and its synonyms mean? It refers to God's providence and planned control of events. By evoking a picture of a policy-making assembly, this word pattern ties in with a secondary word pattern: *nations, peoples, nation, people.* The section itself is based on a contrast or foil between God's counsel and the futile counsel of the nations, and between nations who pursue their own designs and the nation whose God is the Lord.

God's omniscience is the next thing for which the poet praises God:

> [13]The LORD *looks* down from heaven,
>   he *sees* all the sons of men;
> [14]from where he sits enthroned he *looks* forth
>   on all the inhabitants of the earth,
> [15]he who fashions the hearts of them all,
>   and *observes* all their deeds.

In keeping with the theme of God's omniscience, the main word pattern repeatedly describes God's ability to see and observe. That he sees everything is accentuated by the recurrence four times of the adjective *all.*

The next unit of the catalogue is based on an extended contrast and concerns God's ability to save or deliver:

> [16]A king is not *saved* by his great army;
>   a warrior is not *delivered* by his great strength.
> [17]The war horse is a vain hope for *victory*,
>   and by its great might it cannot *save.*
> [18]Behold, the eye of the LORD is on those who fear him,
>   on those who hope in his steadfast love,
> [19]that he may *deliver* their soul from death,
>   and *keep them alive* in famine.

The contrast within the unit is between the inability of human resources to deliver a person and the ability of God to do so. The first half of this contrast, pointing out the impotence of human resources, is a series of negatives: *not saved, not delivered, vain hope, cannot save.* These negatives become the backdrop against which the salvation of God stands out with resolute energy.

With the catalogue of God's praiseworthy traits and acts finished, the poet completes his poem with a resolution to hope in God. The key word pattern is a series of prepositional phrases indicating relationship:

> [20]Our soul waits *for the LORD*;
>   he is our help and shield.
> [21]Yea, our heart is glad *in him*,
>   because we trust *in his holy name.*
> [22]Let thy steadfast love, O LORD, be upon us,
>   even as we hope *in thee.*

Here is the logical conclusion of the preceding catalogue: If God is truly as the poet has portrayed him, the natural response is to place one's trust in him.

The overall strategy or logic of a psalm of praise is to exhort people to praise God and then to offer a rationale for the command. The rationale normally consists of a catalogue of praiseworthy traits and acts. As we look back over the catalogue in Psalm 33, we can see that it is governed by the motif of God's roles—as creator, as ruler, as deliverer. A chief task in explicating a praise psalm is to lay out the catalogue into its constituent parts, thereby noting the things for which God is praised.

Nature Psalms

Although there are five nature psalms (psalms that take nature as their chief subject) in the Psalter, nature finds its way less directly into dozens of psalms. In fact, the Psalms keep us rather continuously rooted in the world of nature. Many of the sublime pictures of God in the Psalms draw upon the awe-inspiring forces of nature. In the praise psalms, nature is one of the arenas where God is portrayed as acting. Nature is also one of the commonest sources of metaphor and simile in the Psalms: "he is like a tree planted by streams of water"; "the Lord is my rock"; "deliver me, lest like a lion they rend me."

The best discussion of nature in the Psalms is the chapter on that subject by Lewis in *Reflections on the Psalms*, where he makes the following points. Two factors determine the approach of the psalmists to nature. The first is that they were a nation of farmers. As such, they had both a utilitarian and an aesthetic appreciation of nature. Secondly, the Jews were unique in having a clear and thoroughgoing doctrine that a transcendent God had created nature. To view God as the creator of nature empties nature of deity in the sense that there is no trace of the pagan and pantheistic belief that various objects in nature are divine. God and nature are separate, and there is no attempt to populate the streams and trees with local deities, as in pagan mythology. In another sense, the Hebrew conception fills nature with God, making it a revelation or manifestation of God. Even more unique is the Hebrew appreciation for aspects of nature that are indifferent or hostile to people (such as the snow and hail [Ps. 148]). This appreciation stems from an awareness that people and all the rest of nature are fellow dependents, having been created by the same God. It is easy to document these generalizations both from the scattered references to nature throughout the Psalms and from the five nature poems.

The five nature psalms are 8, 19, 29, 104, and 148. I have already explicated the first two of these (see pp. 232 and 192), although I did not take the time to analyze the attitudes toward nature that they embodied. It so happens that the nature psalms are among the best poems in the entire Psalter.

Psalm 29

Psalm 29 is "The Song of the Thunderstorm."[4] The topic and occasion of the poem are a thunderstorm in the Mediterranean region. The theme—the perspective from which we experience the storm—is the presence and grandeur of God. Specifically, the poem praises the glory of God, as verse 9 makes clear ("in his temple all cry, 'Glory!' ").

The poem has a firm three-part structure, and its emotional sequence is shaped like a pyramid, corresponding to the progress of a storm. Verses 1 and 2 are a call to praise and awaken a sense of anticipation. Verses 3–9 describe the progress of the storm and are governed by a feeling of awe. Verses 10 and 11 are a concluding comment on the character of God and end the poem with subdued calm and assurance.

The poem begins with a threefold ascription of praise to God:

> [1]Ascribe to the LORD, O heavenly beings,
>   ascribe to the LORD glory and strength.
> [2]Ascribe to the LORD the glory of his name;
>   worship the LORD in holy array.

The language is so exalted that it actually creates the feeling of exuberance that it calls the angels to express. Verse 1 happens to be the most frequently cited example of climactic parallelism in the Psalms.

---

4. This designation comes from Richard G. Moulton, *The Literary Study of the Bible*, 2d ed. (Boston: Heath, 1900), p. 163.

Corresponding to the threefold ascription of praise to God is a sevenfold series of descriptive clauses that begin with the subject *the voice of the Lord* in the middle of the poem. The phrase *voice of the LORD* is a metaphor based on the tremendous sound that a storm makes. This sound is ascribed to God because he is the one who governs the entire sequence of events portrayed in this psalm.

The storm is pictured as arising in the Mediterranean Sea (v. 3):

> The voice of the LORD is upon the waters;
> the God of glory thunders,
> the LORD, upon many waters.

Verse 4 follows this initial description with what I call a lyric interlude (common in the Psalms)—a passage of commentary that simply expresses how the poet feels about what he is portraying:

> The voice of the LORD is powerful,
> the voice of the LORD is full of majesty.

As the storm progresses, it moves eastward from the Mediterranean Sea to the land, where it breaks the branches (v. 5):

> The voice of the LORD breaks the cedars,
> the LORD breaks the cedars of Lebanon.

In an imaginative stroke, the poet compares the wild waving of the tree branches to the jumping of animals (v. 6):

> He makes Lebanon to skip like a calf,
> and Sirion like a young wild ox.

In addition to the descriptions of the sound and the wind, the poet paints a picture of the lightning: "The voice of the LORD flashes forth flames of fire" (v. 7).

As the storm progresses still further eastward, it moves beyond the forests of Lebanon to the wilderness of Kadesh (v. 8):

> The voice of the LORD shakes the wilderness,
> the LORD shakes the wilderness of Kadesh.

The obscure ninth verse is apparently a flashback to the forest scene:

> The voice of the LORD makes the oaks to whirl,
> and strips the forest bare;
> and in his temple all cry, "Glory!"

How did the temple slip into the poem? I think it is a metaphoric statement. The temple in Jerusalem was the place where God was palpably present and where the Old Testament worshiper encountered God most directly. In Psalm 29, the storm has been so permeated with the presence of God that the scene of the storm itself can metaphorically be called the temple. All who see the storm have come face to face with the glory of God, just as thoroughly as if they had visited the temple in Jerusalem.

Following the ecstasy of the thunderstorm, the poem subsides into quietness at its close. First there is a generalization that grows logically from the storm just described, namely, that God is king over nature (v. 10):

> The LORD sits enthroned over the flood;
>   the LORD sits enthroned as king for ever.

So far as the doctrine of nature is concerned, the key term here is the preposition *over*. It implies God's transcendence over creation. The whole poem has asserted the immanence of God—his closeness to nature and his intimate involvement in it. But God and nature are ultimately separate. One made the other.

Finally, in typical lyric fashion, the poet concludes by expressing a wish or prayer (v. 11):

> May the LORD give strength to his people!
>   May the LORD bless his people with peace!

This is the logical implication of God's kingship. If he is indeed enthroned over the earth, he is also the sovereign God who alone can bless his people.

The full meaning of Psalm 29 emerges when it is interpreted as a parody. In its general outline, this psalm is parallel to some Canaanite poetry on the same topic. Underlying the Canaanite poetry was a myth involving Baal, god of the storm and of fertility (since rain caused vegetation to grow). According to the myth, there was an annual battle between Baal and the god of death or of the salt sea. Baal always defeated his foe and brought rain to the land. In response, he was enthroned as god over the earth, and in some versions Baal built a palace for himself on the land.

Psalm 29 is in some ways a parallel to this mythological theme of Canaanite poetry, though the parallel is not as close as is sometimes claimed.[5] As in the Canaanite poetry, the storm begins in the Mediterra-

---

5. For a discussion of the similarities between Psalm 29 and pagan poetry, especially the *Canaanite Poem of Baal*, see Theodor H. Gaster, *Myth, Legend, and Custom in the Old Testament* (New York: Harper and Row, 1969), pp. 747–51. Further description of the Baal myth can be found in John Gray, *The Canaanites* (New York: Praeger, 1964), pp. 127–37.

nean Sea. It then moves eastward over the land, but not over the land of the Israelites. In fact, the geographic references in the psalm are not really Jewish, belonging instead to the region farther north. There is also a conspicuous emphasis on the enthronement of God, who is said to be *enthroned over the flood* and *king for ever*.

As a parody, Psalm 29 is argumentative in nature. It substitutes God for Baal and makes the point that what the pagans serve as Baal is really God. Jehovah, not Baal, is the one who deserves to be enthroned and praised in song.

Psalm 104

Psalm 104 is the most exalted nature psalm and can be classified as an ode. Its focus is on God's worthiness to be praised for what he does in the natural creation. The organization of the poem is a piece of magnificent architectonics:

> Verses 1–4: the function of nature.
> Verses 5–9: the origin of nature.
> Verses 10–30: the provision of nature:
> > Verses 10–18: earth.
> > Verses 19–23: sky.
> > Verses 24–26: sea.
> > Verses 27–30: summary.
> Verses 31–35: lyric response to the God of nature.

The strategy of all the nature psalms is to praise the God of nature rather than nature itself. In effect, the poet of Psalm 104 begins his nature poem by talking about God (v. 1):

> Bless the LORD, O my soul!
> O LORD my God, thou art very great!
> who art clothed with honor and majesty.

Here is the commentary that tells us in advance what the poet's description of nature will add up to. The last line of the opening verse, with its mention of how God is *clothed*, is a transition to the next three verses, which also humanize God and picture him as wearing and using the forces of nature the way a person uses things:

> 2 who coverest thyself with light as with a garment,
> who hast stretched out the heavens like a tent,
> 3 who hast laid the beams of thy chambers on the waters,
> who makest the clouds thy chariot,
> who ridest on the wings of the wind,

> [4]who makest the winds thy messengers,
>   fire and flame thy ministers.

The main idea of this highly metaphoric passage is the function of nature, which is repeatedly shown to serve God. Throughout the description, God controls nature, which as a result is infused with the energy and purpose that God gives it. The immanence of God emerges strongly from the description. Paradoxically, so does his transcendence, since in the very process of humanizing God, the poet shows that God controls the forces of nature as easily as people set up a tent or ride in a chariot.

The meaning of the passage is embodied in metaphor and simile. It is up to us to discover the connections that the poet has in mind. The covering properties of light make it like a garment. If the heavens are over the world in which we live, they can be compared to a tent. The sheer permanence and solidity of land next to water leads the poet to compare it in an architectural metaphor to the beams of a house built on the edge of a stream or sea. Clouds and wind move rapidly across the skyline, hence the comparison to a chariot and a bird with wings. And since the wind and lightning communicate God's power, they are like royal messengers.

From the function of nature the poet turns to its origin. The passage is a creation story in miniature and is again highly figurative and imaginative:

> [5]Thou didst set the earth on its foundations,
>   so that it should never be shaken.
> [6]Thou didst cover it with the deep as with a garment;
>   the waters stood above the mountains.
> [7]At thy rebuke they fled;
>   at the sound of thy thunder they took to flight.
> [8]The mountains rose, the valleys sank down
>   to the place which thou didst appoint for them.
> [9]Thou didst set a bound which they should not pass,
>   so that they might not again cover the earth.

Once again the poet domesticates the transcendent power of God by comparing God's creation of the world to common human activities. Thus the act of creating the earth was like laying the foundations of a building (v. 5), with associations of careful planning, permanence, and solidity. Having created the earth, God is pictured as covering it with the sea the way people cover themselves with a garment (v. 6). The personification of the waters in verse 7 makes their actions comparable to the behavior of a scolded child or pet, as a kind of conflict is set up between the forces of nature and God's *rebuke*. The harmony and order of creation emerge in the pictures of the mountains rising and (symmetrically) the valleys sinking, accompanied by the boundary that keeps the sea in its place.

The longest section of this nature psalm is devoted to cataloguing the provision that nature gives. The poet begins with the part of nature that an agrarian society knows best, the plants and animals in the earthly landscape, and paints a series of word-pictures:

> [10]Thou makest springs gush forth in the valleys;
>   they flow between the hills,
> [11]they give drink to every beast of the field;
>   the wild asses quench their thirst.
> [12]By them the birds of the air have their habitation;
>   they sing among the branches.
> [13]From thy lofty abode thou waterest the mountains;
>   the earth is satisfied with the fruit of thy work.
> [14]Thou dost cause the grass to grow for the cattle,
>   and plants for man to cultivate,
>   that he may bring forth food from the earth,
> [15]   and wine to gladden the heart of man,
>   oil to make his face shine,
>   and bread to strengthen man's heart.
> [16]The trees of the LORD are watered abundantly,
>   the cedars of Lebanon which he planted.
> [17]In them the birds build their nests;
>   the stork has her home in the fir trees.
> [18]The high mountains are for the wild goats;
>   the rocks are a refuge for the badgers.

The imagery of this marvelous descriptive passage puts us solidly into a world of elemental nature. The passage shows a farmer's point of view in its strongly functional attitude toward nature. Every facet of nature that the poet describes is good for something. Plants and animals, earth and water all serve each other, and nature emerges finally as a single, all-embracing organism governed by God's providence. All aspects of nature are fellow dependents of God and of each other. Nature is orderly and purposeful, operating according to a divine plan that provides for the needs of every part.

From the earth the focus shifts to the sky:

> [19]Thou hast made the moon to mark the seasons;
>   the sun knows its time for setting.
> [20]Thou makest darkness, and it is night,
>   when all the beasts of the forest creep forth.
> [21]The young lions roar for their prey,
>   seeking their food from God.
> [22]When the sun rises, they get them away
>   and lie down in their dens.
> [23]Man goes forth to his work
>   and to his labor until the evening.

According to this passage, the heavenly bodies provide us with time—the orderly succession of day and night to divide our daily existence. Again a sense of the harmonious interaction of all creation comes through.

In typical lyric fashion, the poet momentarily interrupts his catalogue for a lyric exclamation (v. 24):

> O LORD, how manifold are thy works!
> In wisdom hast thou made them all;
> the earth is full of thy creatures.

Here, in effect, is a piece of commentary that ties the wealth of descriptive detail to the unifying theme of the whole poem.

Having surveyed the earth and sky, the poet completes his survey with a look at the sea:

> 25Yonder is the sea, great and wide,
> which teems with things innumerable,
> living things both small and great.
> 26There go the ships,
> and Leviathan which thou didst form to sport in it.

The Jews were not a seafaring people, and this passage shows the results. Compared with the minute realism and firsthand observation evident in the section describing the creatures of the earth, the description of what goes on in the sea in verse 25 is laughably vague. Verse 26 adds a new idea, though, with its suggestion that one of the provisions of nature is sport or recreation.

The catalogue of provisions that nature supplies reaches its climax in a summary that binds earth, sky, and sea together:

> 27These all look to thee,
> to give them their food in due season.
> 28When thou givest to them, they gather it up;
> when thou openest thy hand, they are filled with good things.
> 29When thou hidest thy face, they are dismayed;
> when thou takest away their breath, they die
> and return to their dust.
> 30When thou sendest forth thy Spirit, they are created;
> and thou renewest the face of the ground.

Here is a beautiful expression of the poet's God-centered conception of nature. In this view, nature is obviously not self-sufficient but is totally dependent on God.

The concluding phase of the poem is a lyric response to the God who is revealed in nature. We get a miscellany of responses, unified by the motif of glorifying God:

> [31]May the glory of the LORD endure for ever,
>   may the LORD rejoice in his works,
> [32]who looks on the earth and it trembles,
>   who touches the mountains and they smoke!
> [33]I will sing to the LORD as long as I live;
>   I will sing praise to my God while I have being.
> [34]May my meditation be pleasing to him,
>   for I rejoice in the LORD.
> [35]Let sinners be consumed from the earth,
>   and let the wicked be no more!
> Bless the LORD, O my soul!
> Praise the LORD!

The first line in verse 31 states the theme of the poem (*the glory of the LORD*), and the second line states the topic (*his works*). The picture of the earth trembling (v. 32) refers to an earthquake, while the mountains that smoke (v. 32) are either volcanoes or hilltops shrouded in fog. In contrast to most nature poetry that has been written throughout history, the nature poetry of the Psalms does not ultimately praise nature but instead *rejoices in the Lord*.

Psalm 148

Psalm 148 consists almost entirely of a series of doxologies (commands to praise). The poet recreates his excitement as we read this series of apostrophes. The implied theme of all these commands addressed to various forces of nature is that all nature is unified by its obligation to praise the Creator.

The poem begins and ends with the same exclamation (*Praise the LORD!*), which sounds the keynote for the whole poem. Within the envelope provided by this repeated exclamation, the poem's catalogue follows a firm progression down the scale of nature from the angels in heaven to people on earth. As we move through the three main units, a phrase in the opening line of each announces the group to whom the apostrophes in that unit will be addressed: *from the heavens* (v. 1), *from the earth* (v. 7), *all peoples* (v. 11). Twice the poet interrupts his apostrophes to offer a reason for his commands to praise God; these come in verses 5b–6 and 13b–14.

The opening series of doxologies focuses on the heavens, including both angels and the heavenly bodies that are visible in the sky:

> [1]Praise the LORD from the heavens,
>   praise him in the heights!
> [2]Praise him, all his angels,
>   praise him, all his host!
> [3]Praise him, sun and moon,
>   praise him, all you shining stars!
> [4]Praise him, you highest heavens,
>   and you waters above the heavens!
> [5]Let them praise the name of the LORD!

Here, obviously, is what we mean by affective poetry. The apostrophes actually create the response that they command.

Having uttered his first barrage of doxologies, the poet offers a rationale for his boldness (vv. 5b–6):

> For he commanded and they were created.
> And he established them for ever and ever;
>   he fixed their bounds which cannot be passed.

In such a passage the doctrine of creation that pervades the Psalms comes through strongly. What joins all of creation is not a common divinity, as in pantheistic nature poetry, but a common origin and a common providence under God.

The second phase of the catalogue concentrates on nonhuman earthly creatures:

> [7]Praise the LORD from the earth,
>   you sea monsters and all deeps,
> [8]fire and hail, snow and frost,
>   stormy wind fulfilling his command!
> [9]Mountains and all hills,
>   fruit trees and all cedars!
> [10]Beasts and all cattle,
>   creeping things and flying birds!

The noteworthy thing about this list is that it includes not only things beneficial to people but also natural forces that are indifferent or actively hostile to them. The psalmist reaches such a viewpoint from the doctrine of creation, which makes all creatures fellow dependents on God.

In a poem that proceeds through the entire order of nature, it is significant that the poet places people alongside the clouds and cattle:

> [11]Kings of the earth and all peoples,
>   princes and all rulers of the earth!

> [12]Young men and maidens together,
>   old men and children!
> [13]Let them praise the name of the LORD.

People, too, are under obligation to praise God.

But the reason that the poet gives for people to praise God is not the same as he earlier stated for other forces of nature (vv. 13b–14):

> for his name alone is exalted;
>   his glory is above earth and heaven.
> He has raised up a horn for his people,
>   praise for all his saints,
>   for the people of Israel who are near to him.

For an Old Testament believer, this is the language of redemption or salvation. People have a reason to praise God that angels and nonhuman nature do not. For the psalmists, nothing, including nature, exists apart from their salvation. With the statement that God's glory is *above* nature, we again see the doctrines of transcendence and creation that remove the Bible's view of nature from many other views.

The Psalms as Nature Poetry

Nature poetry is one of the biggest categories in the world's poetry. Almost any poetry anthology will have a significant amount of it. If we compare the nature poetry of the Psalms with other nature poetry, we discover some interesting things.

Nature poetry generally has displayed two contradictory (on rare occasions complementary) interpretations of nature. Nature has sometimes been equated with law, rule, order, and reason. In other ages and by other writers it has been identified with impulse, instinct, spontaneity, and energy. These two tendencies might be called the classical and romantic strains, respectively. The classical view regards people as part of nature, while the romantic view sees people and nature as hopelessly out of joint with each other.

It is much easier to put the nature poetry of the Bible into the first tradition. In the Psalms, nature is pictured as being orderly, law-bound, and operating according to God's purposeful plan.[6] People and nature exist harmoniously together. By implication, some passages affirm nature to be instinctive, impulsive, and spontaneous, but there is very little of what we

---

6. Psalm 148, in fact, fits right into the notion of the great chain of being that was so prominent in English literature from the Middle Ages through the eighteenth century.

would call the typical romantic view of nature. It is not, of course, a question of enthusiasm for nature, since both views are equally appreciative of nature.

The closer we scrutinize the nature poetry of the Bible, however, the less similar it seems to either the classical or romantic tradition. The psalmists are preoccupied with God rather than nature. They certainly talk more about God's creation of nature and his revelation of himself in nature than they do about either rule or energy, the common themes elsewhere.

Poets who have written about nature outside the Hebraic-Christian tradition have tended to deify it. If they are what we call nature poets, they have tended to treat nature as the highest value. They have been either naturalists (nature itself is the ultimate reality) or pantheists (nature is divine). The biblical poets are simply in another category. Their concern with nature is part of their broader concern with God. To them, the nature poetry of other traditions would be empty, as though the most important thing had been left out.

Psalms of Worship

Worship is another dominant subject in the Psalms. The conventional title for a worship psalm is "song of Zion," which I will use as a synonym for "psalm of worship." When the Israelites were led into Babylonian captivity, they were taunted with the command, "Sing us one of the songs of Zion!" (Ps. 137:3).

The background against which all the psalms of worship must be viewed is the pervasive awareness of the Israelites that God dwelt in the temple in Jerusalem. Psalm 11:4 states, "The LORD is in his holy temple." Similar statements abound: "O LORD, I love the habitation of thy house, / and the place where thy glory dwells" (Ps. 26:8); "so I have looked upon thee in the sanctuary, / beholding thy power and glory" (63:2); "for the LORD has chosen Zion; / he has desired it for his habitation: 'This is my resting place for ever; / here I will dwell' " (132:13–14). Because of the presence of God in the temple, the Jews attached overwhelming importance to the place.

In the background of the Psalms is yet another phenomenon, the practice of religious pilgrimages. Most of these journeys were made to the temple in Jerusalem. All males were required to go to Jerusalem three times annually, at the festival of unleavened bread (the passover), the feast of weeks, and the feast of tabernacles (feast of booths). The prevalence of such pilgrimages in Hebrew culture undoubtedly accounts for much of the emphasis on worship that we find in the Psalter. In important ways the Psalter can be called a temple collection, an anthology of songs used in worship at the temple.

Poetic Pictures of Worship

One of the functions of literature is to take us from our own world and transport us to another world that we enter by means of our imagination. From that world we can see our own experience with renewed clarity and zest. One of the chief values of the worship psalms is that they give us concrete pictures of worship, including its emotions, that the psalmists experienced. The actual pictures of temple worship and pilgrimages are remote from our own experience. As we live in that poetic world, however, we experience much that is true to our own experience of worship as well.

A complete explication of numerous psalms is beyond the scope of this book, and I have accordingly limited my full-scale explications to Psalms 84 (pp. 266–69) and 121 (pp. 197–201). But a look at some of the pictures of worship scattered throughout the songs of Zion will give a feel for how these passages create a whole world of worship in our imagination.

A verse in Psalm 27 provides a good entry into the subject:

> One thing have I asked of the LORD,
>   that will I seek after;
> that I may dwell in the house of the LORD
>   all the days of my life,
> to behold the beauty of the LORD,
>   and to inquire in his temple. [v. 4]

The poet opens his statement with hyperbole: he obviously asks for many things from God, not just one. But by means of this technique he forcefully conveys the supremacy that he accords the worship of God. In a similar vein is the comment about wishing to live in God's house *all* the days of one's life.

We notice secondly the important role that the place of worship plays. Worship occurs preeminently in the temple (or its predecessor the tabernacle). The most customary metaphor by which the psalmists express their feelings toward the temple is that of a house. References in the Psalms to *dwelling in the house of the Lord* are of course metaphoric, since no worshiper literally lived in the temple. Nor should we overlook the word *beauty.* The aesthetic dimension of worship keeps coming to the fore in the Psalms, in a manner like the comment of a disciple of Jesus recorded in Mark 13:1: "And as he came out of the temple, one of his disciples said to him, 'Look, Teacher, what wonderful stones and what wonderful buildings!' "

Psalms 42 and 43, printed separately but actually comprising a single poem, are a concise record of the longing for worship that we find in the Psalms. The situation underlying the poem is that the speaker is living in exile, in pagan territory, and is therefore prevented from traveling to

Jerusalem to worship God. This strongly psychological poem runs the gamut of emotions associated with worship at the temple.

The poem opens with a memorable simile that pictures longing for God (42:1–2):

> As a hart longs
>   for flowing streams,
> so longs my soul
>   for thee, O God.
> My soul thirsts for God,
>   for the living God.
> When shall I come and behold
>   the face of God?

The poetic equivalent for strong feeling is often a sensation, and this is what we find here.

Writing from deep depression, the speaker is nevertheless sustained by the hope of someday returning to Jerusalem to worship God, a hope captured in the famous refrain that occurs three times:

> Why are you cast down, O my soul
>   and why are you disquieted within me?
> Hope in God; for I shall again praise him,
>   my help and my God.

Equally evocative is the poet's personification of light and truth as guides to Jerusalem (43:3–4):

> O send out thy light and thy truth;
>   let them lead me,
> let them bring me to thy holy hill
>   and to thy dwelling!
> Then I will go to the altar of God,
>   to God my exceeding joy;
> and I will praise thee with the lyre,
>   O God, my God.

Permeating the whole passage is the note of joy in worship that has such a restorative effect when we read the worship psalms.

A number of worship psalms recreate for us the excitement of the pilgrimages, with Psalm 121 being the supreme example. Psalms 120–134 are a group of psalms that bear the common heading "A Song of Ascents," meaning that they were sung on the pilgrimage to Jerusalem. They are therefore an interesting index to the range of things (many of them dealing with everyday life rather than something specifically related to worship) toward which the pilgrims' minds gravitated on the occasion of family and group trips to Jerusalem.

By putting poetic fragments from the worship psalms together, we can trace the sequence of emotions associated with worship all the way from the anticipation of worship to the final feelings as the pilgrim left Jerusalem. Psalm 122 begins with the anticipation and ends with the concluding feelings:

> I was glad when they said to me,
>   "Let us go to the house of the LORD!"
> . . . .
> Pray for the peace of Jerusalem!
>   "May they prosper who love you!
> Peace be within your walls,
>   and security within your towers!"
> For my brethren and companions' sake
>   I will say, "Peace be within you!"
> For the sake of the house of the LORD our God,
>   I will seek your good.

These concluding feelings illustrate what a wide range of experiences converged for the Old Testament worshiper in a trip to Jerusalem: city (and by extension country), peace, security, fellow believers, temple, and God.

As for the actual worship that occurred at the temple, the songs of Zion provide us vivid and kaleidoscopic glimpses, all of them suffused with high excitement:

> Enter his gates with thanksgiving,
>   and his courts with praise!
>   Give thanks to him, bless his name! [100:4]

> I will offer in his tent
>   sacrifices with shouts of joy;
> I will sing and make melody to the LORD. [27:6]

> We have thought on thy steadfast love, O God,
>   in the midst of thy temple. . . .
> Walk about Zion, go round about her,
>   number her towers,
> consider well her ramparts,
>   go through her citadels;
> that you may tell the next generation
>   that this is God,
> our God for ever and ever.
>   He will be our guide for ever. [48:9, 12–14]

These things I remember,
    as I pour out my soul:
how I went with the throng,
    and led them in procession to the house of God,
with glad shouts and songs of thanksgiving,
    a multitude keeping festival. [42:4]

If we remember how thoroughly the Old Testament worshiper felt the presence (*Shekinah*) of God in the temple in Jerusalem, we are in a better position to understand the sacred aura that surrounds the city of Jerusalem in the songs of Zion. Nor should we forget the patriotic feelings that were part of the matrix. Here are specimens of the sentiment:

If I forget you, O Jerusalem,
    let my right hand wither!
Let my tongue cleave to the roof of my mouth,
    if I do not remember you,
if I do not set Jerusalem
    above my highest joy! [137:5–6]

Those who trust in the LORD are like Mount Zion,
    which cannot be moved, but abides for ever.
As the mountains are round about Jerusalem,
    so the LORD is round about his people. [125:1–2]

Our feet have been standing
    within your gates, O Jerusalem!
Jerusalem, built as a city
    which is bound firmly together,
to which the tribes go up,
    the tribes of the LORD,
as was decreed for Israel,
    to give thanks to the name of the LORD.
There thrones for judgment were set,
    the thrones of the house of David. [122:2–5]

Great is the LORD and greatly to be praised
    in the city of our God!
His holy mountain, beautiful in elevation,
    is the joy of all the earth,
Mount Zion, in the far north,
    the city of the great King.
Within her citadels God
    has shown himself a sure defense. [48:1–3]

With the kind of poetry at which we have been looking, it is the cumulative effect—the total world that builds up in our imagination—that is important. As we enter that world, we confront much that is foreign to our religious experience—

pilgrimages to Jerusalem, worship in a temple, strong religious sentiment associated with a city, and a merging of patriotic and religious spheres. What, then, is the value of entering the world of the songs of Zion? My answer is that through the particulars we can identify universal experiences. These experiences include awe before the greatness and love of God, fellowship with others who share the same spiritual experiences and values, and a sense of joy and praise.

Psalm 84

The informal tour that I have taken through the worship psalms in the preceding section turns out to be exactly the right context for explicating Psalm 84. Virtually everything in the songs of Zion as a whole converges in this supreme example of the type.

Psalm 84 is an occasional poem about a pilgrimage to the temple. The outline of the poem is clear and firm: statement of theme (v. 1), initial responses to the temple upon arrival (vv. 2–4), the joy of the journey (vv. 5–7), a prayer uttered at the temple (vv. 8–9), and the concluding feelings of the worshiper (vv. 10–12). If the topic of the poem is worshiping God in the temple, the theme, as suggested in the opening exclamation (*How lovely is thy dwelling place*), is the loveliness or delight of that worship. The poem follows a repetitive pattern as it states in different ways how satisfying it is to worship God.

The poem begins with the pilgrim's cry of joy as the temple comes into view:

> How lovely is thy dwelling place,
> O LORD of hosts!

This announces the theme and sets the tone of ecstasy that will prevail throughout the psalm. It also introduces the controlling image or metaphor in which the temple is compared to a home. The word *lovely* is a hugely evocative word, combining a sense of the aesthetic beauty of the sight with overtones of romantic love.[7]

The first variation on the theme is an expression of the longings that arise in the pilgrim upon arrival at the temple (v. 2):

> My soul longs, yea, faints
>   for the courts of the LORD;
> my heart and flesh sing for joy
>   to the living God.

---

7. Derek Kidner, *Psalms 73–150*, Tyndale Old Testament Commentary series (Downers Grove: Inter-Varsity, 1975), p. 303, comments, "*How lovely* is more exactly 'How dear' or 'How beloved'; it is the language of love poetry."

Here is an instance where the parallelism of the statement adds a lot to our understanding. Just notice what the poet equates: *my soul* is paired with *my heart and flesh*, and to enter *the courts of the LORD* (that is, the temple area) is to meet *the living God*. In each case, the one thing is indistinguishable from the other. We are looking at a thoroughly wholistic experience, with the spiritual and the physical joined together. It is, of course, a strongly emotional statement, with words like *longs*, *faints*, and *sing*. The speaker's heart and flesh, moreover, are personified and pictured as doing the singing, as though it were a spontaneous rather than conscious act.

Verse 3 is one of the great verses in the Psalms:

> Even the sparrow finds a home,
>   and the swallow a nest for herself,
>   where she may lay her young,
>   at thy altars, O LORD of hosts,
>   my King and my God.

The poet here fuses the small and the great—a sparrow and God. Numerous psalms indicate that no part of God's creation is unimportant. Whereas in the nature psalms all creatures are said to praise God, here they find their sanctuary in God. The very fact that the pilgrim would include this description in his account of noteworthy events at the temple shows the very real part that physical sensation and observation played in the religious experience of the worshiper.

But the reference to the sparrow's nest is more than a bit of striking realism. It assumes a metaphoric meaning. The poet repeatedly insists on the domestic associations of the image: *a home, a nest, where she may lay her young*. The point becomes unmistakable: the temple is a home, not only for the bird, but also for the worshiper of God. Psalm 84 is filled with stately epithets for God (for example, *O LORD of hosts, my King and my God*), but in this verse God is pictured as being fatherly as well as awesome.

Having portrayed the temple as a home for the sparrow, the poet underscores those associations in the first of three beatitudes in the psalm (v. 4):

> Blessed are those who dwell in thy house,
>   ever singing thy praise!

The privileged people who *dwell* in the temple are either priests who minister there or (more likely) those who worship their heavenly Father there. In either case, the nature of God's house is clear—it is a house of praise.

Having expressed his initial feelings upon arrival at the temple, the poet
next recalls the joys of the pilgrimage:

> ⁵Blessed are the men whose strength is in thee,
>   in whose heart are the highways to Zion.
> ⁶As they go through the valley of Baca
>   they make it a place of springs;
>   the early rain also covers it with pools.
> ⁷They go from strength to strength;
>   the God of gods will be seen in Zion.

The motif of this passage is announced in the phrase *the highways to
Zion*. Palestine was a mountainous and thirsty land. The suffering involved
in the journeys to Jerusalem was very real. This passage describes,
figuratively and literally, God's provision for the needs of the pilgrims as
they made their trips through desert areas. To *go from strength to strength*
is the kind of biblical aphorism that communicates spiritual meaning
without our being able to exactly verbalize what it means. In the Bible, we
often find that words have become more than words.

Verses 8 and 9 are a prayer uttered by the pilgrim upon reaching the
temple:

> O LORD God of hosts, hear my prayer;
>   give ear, O God of Jacob!
> Behold our shield, O God;
>   look upon the face of thine anointed!

This is almost certainly a prayer for the king and is another index to how
closely the nation of Israel was tied to the religious experience of the
people.

The concluding movement of the psalm expresses the final feelings of
the worshiper. In this packed passage where everything is eloquent and
moving, we find a memorable picture of the life-creating power of the
worshiper's experience. First the poet declares the supreme value that he
attaches to the worship of God (v. 10):

> For a day in thy courts is better
>   than a thousand elsewhere.
> I would rather be a doorkeeper in the house of my God
>   than dwell in the tents of wickedness.

By what means does the statement gain its affective power? The basic
strategy involves comparison in the form of antithesis: one day versus a
thousand days, God's courts versus other places, a doorkeeper versus an

owner of tents, and God's house versus human tents. By choosing the smaller thing (one day, being a doorkeeper) over what in ordinary thinking is the larger (a thousand days, dwelling in tents), the poet subverts conventional standards of value and shocks us into considering a whole different vision of what is most worthwhile.

Having made his subversive claim, the poet offers an explanation (v. 11):

> For the LORD God is a sun and shield;
>   he bestows favor and honor.
> No good thing does the LORD withhold
>   from those who walk uprightly.

The metaphor of the *shield* means protection. To call God a *sun* is more undefined, but we at least know that the sun is the source of light and energy and therefore of life itself. The aphorism stating that *no good thing does the LORD withhold from those who walk uprightly* is hyperbole, expressing the strength of the worshiper's feeling at a moment when he is particularly close to God.

The poem ends with a strongly felt beatitude or benediction (v. 12):

> O LORD of hosts,
>   blessed is the man who trusts in thee!

This is a fitting conclusion and response to the worship of God that the poem has portrayed and celebrated.

Psalm 84 is the prototypical song of Zion. It includes all of the motifs that we find in the psalms of worship—the sense of longing and anticipation that precedes worship, the ecstasy of the actual worship at the temple, pictures of the combined physical and spiritual details of temple worship, the pilgrimage or journey, a strong sense of place, the link between nation and religion, and (permeating it all) a delight in the presence of God.

11

The Song of Solomon

The Song of Solomon has been extravagantly misinterpreted throughout the centuries and continues to be so today. To demonstrate why the book should not be considered a spiritual allegory, or a drama, or a story about a love triangle, would usurp all the space that I have available, so I have simply treated the book as my literary intuitions lead me, leaving my readers to decide how well this accounts for the book.

What Kind of Book Is It?

Placing the Song of Solomon into its right literary family is the most helpful thing we can do in making sense of the book. If we simply place it alongside other types of literature that are like it, we will see that there is nothing unusual about the book. It is a totally recognizable form of literature, and there is no reason to make abnormal interpretations of it.

Love Poetry

There really can be no doubt that the Song of Solomon is a collection of love poems. When we read in the second verse of the book, "O that you would kiss me with the kisses of your mouth!" it is obvious that the main characters in the book are rapturously in love and that the main action of the book is romantic love between a man and a woman.

As in other love poetry, the main subject matter is the emotions of love. The book covers a whole range of romantic emotions: the rapture of falling in love, impatience for the love to progress to marriage, longing to be with the beloved, the frustration of separation between lovers, and above all the voice of romantic passion satisfied (as in the matchless, "My beloved is mine and I am his" [2:16]).

To say that the content of the poem is human passion is to say that this is a collection of love lyrics, not a story or a drama. As we read the book, we participate in a series of moods. The *content* of the book is far too thoroughly interior and psychological for this to be regarded as narrative or drama. It is almost continuously an outpouring of feelings, not a likely strategy for a story or drama. The *structure* of the book is even farther removed from narrative. The basic structure is what in modern literature we call the stream of consciousness, meaning that it follows the shifting flow of actual thought and feeling. The rapid shifts, the flashbacks, the lack of a clear progression—all these push us in the direction of reading the book as a collection of love lyrics.[1]

In a story, the focus of our attention is on what happens next. This is not how we read the Song of Solomon. The right question to ask with lyric is, How does this passage make me feel? The Song of Solomon is primarily affective in this way. That is why the dramatic cast of the book, with speakers addressing an implied audience, does not make it a drama. Lyric poetry is often organized on a dramatic principle and even as a dialogue between two speakers without implying that it is meant to be staged. Furthermore, many of the poems in the Song of Solomon have a dramatic structure but are really monologues or apostrophes, not dramatic speeches delivered to a live audience, just as in the psalms of lament the speaker's enemies were not really on hand to hear him denounce them.

To read the book as a collection of love lyrics is liberating in several key regards. Commentators have agonized over the problem of assigning the units to the right speaker. When the book is read as drama, everything hinges on who is doing the talking. When we read the book as a collection of lyrics, it is not all that important to decide who is talking, and we are free to concentrate instead on the love sentiments themselves. When the book is read as either story or drama, interpreters are faced with monumental

1. The best discussion of why the Song of Solomon should be read as a collection of separate love lyrics is by Marcia Falk, *Love Lyrics from the Bible: A Translation and Literary Study of the Song of Songs* (Sheffield: Almond, 1982). This is also a good bibliographic source. Also helpful is Robert Gordis, *The Song of Songs* (New York: Jewish Theological Seminary, 1954).

struggles to decipher the exact flow of events. When the book is read as a collection of lyrics, we can be relaxed about the organization of the book. We do not have to force any of the lyrics to fit a story line or assumed situation. Nor does it matter greatly whether a given lyric pictures love before or after marriage.

The best introduction to the Song of Solomon is simply to read an anthology of Renaissance love poems.[2] Such an excursion will show at once that the specific lyric types or genres that we find in the Song of Solomon are common in love poetry. They include courtship lyrics, poems in praise of the beauty and virtue of the beloved, expressions of longing to be with the beloved, invitations to the beloved, songs of separation, vows of eternal constancy, and poems that celebrate the joys of being with the beloved—of seeing, hearing, touching, kissing, and so forth. The Song of Solomon contains all of these.

The middle chapters of the Song of Solomon, moreover, are an epithalamion, or wedding poem. Common motifs include impatience over the slow arrival of the wedding, a picturing of the events of the wedding, and a celebration of the sexual joys of the marriage. In ancient literature, such poems were always written by a court poet in praise of an aristocratic wedding. The Song of Solomon contains examples of all these motifs of the epithalamion. (The Bible contains one other epithalamion, Psalm 45.)

The lyrics that make up this collection portray a single romance. Although, as C. S. Lewis has insisted,[3] a collection of love lyrics is not a way of telling a story, such a collection usually alludes to events in a romance. If we simply take the references in the Song of Solomon at face value, the implied situation revolves around a courtship and marriage between a king named Solomon, called "the beloved," and a Shulamite girl, called "love." We can infer that Solomon met and fell in love with a beautiful rustic girl. Alternately, the rustic identity of the girl might be a fictional disguise, since the king's rustic identity in the work is obviously fictional and since it is a common technique in pastoral literature. Solomon invited the girl to the palace to be part of the royal harem in Jerusalem. The love progressed and was consummated in marriage. The references in the book will make most sense if we simply assume that the king fell in love with and married a farm girl. It is as simple as that.

These are simply the givens that emerge from a straightforward reading of the text. Confusion at once sets in when we try to explain them away

2. It is equally possible to supply a context for the Song of Solomon from ancient Egyptian love poetry. See John B. White, *A Study of the Language of Love in the Song of Songs and Ancient Egyptian Poetry* (Missoula: Scholars Press, 1978).

3. C. S. Lewis, *English Literature in the Sixteenth Century Excluding Drama* (Oxford: Oxford University Press, 1954), p. 327.

(and the attempt seems to be perennial). We have no way of knowing how historically factual the details in the book are, but the book does not pretend to be a history. Obviously the poet has transformed any real-life romance into a highly idealized and poetically embellished piece of literature. *No one* in real life talks the way the speakers in the Song of Solomon do. The book makes no attempt to tell us the factual history of a romance. Its truthfulness consists of truthfulness to the emotions of romantic love, presented as ideal norms. While scholars argue about the real-life persons behind the book, the subject and purpose of the book lie dead. It is time to bring them to life.

I might note in passing that to suppose the book depicts a love triangle strikes me as far-fetched. In this interpretation, the love of Solomon is held up to satiric rebuke, while that of an assumed rustic lover back home is idealized. For this to be accurate, there would have to be a clear differentiation between the love of the two men. But the imagery and sentiments are cut from the same cloth throughout the book. They are uniformly passionate and sensuous. Furthermore, there are two named lovers in the book, and we have no right to arbitrarily assign speeches to more than these. In short, this interpretation "founders on the difficulty of separating the male speakers on the basis of the text itself."[4] Finally, the book is said to be Solomon's (1:1), and it is impossible that a court poet would have written a poem that celebrates the king's having been rejected by a woman he wooed.

Pastoral Poetry

A great deal of the love poetry of the world has been pastoral poetry, and here, too, the Song of Solomon runs an expected course. In pastoral poetry the characters are shepherds, the setting is rustic, and the actions are those customarily done by shepherds. The very landscape counts for a lot in such poetry, and descriptions of the setting are prominent.

Such poetry is metaphoric from start to finish. No one pretends that it portrays literal events. In fact, most pastoral poetry in ancient times was written by city poets about court figures. The shepherd paraphernalia is sometimes a disguise for actual people, but in any event the life portrayed is a metaphor for the realities of love. Failure to realize the essentially fictional mode of pastoral has been debilitating to the interpretation of the Song of Solomon. When the woman asks where her beloved pastures his

---

4. G. Lloyd Carr, *The Song of Solomon: An Introduction and Commentary,* Tyndale Old Testament Commentary series (Downers Grove: Inter-Varsity, 1984), p. 48. This is the best commentary on the Song of Solomon that I have found, and the author has a firm grip on interpreting the book as a collection of love lyrics.

flock (1:7), there is no reason to assume the existence of a rustic lover back home. In pastoral poetry, such language often refers to court people.

In pastoral love poetry, various aspects of the romance are described in rustic imagery. A standard genre, for example, is the pastoral invitation to love, in which the speaker invites his or her beloved to a life of mutual love. It is in effect a proposal of marriage. But in pastoral literature the invitation is expressed metaphorically as a request to go for a walk in the country-side. The Song of Solomon contains two pastoral invitations to love (2:10–15; 7:10–13).

Another pastoral form is the blazon, in which the speaker praises the beauty and virtue of the beloved by comparing them to objects in nature. There are numerous examples in the Song of Solomon, including 2:1–3; 4:1–5, 12–15; 5:12–16; and 7:1–9. Yet another strategy is simply to describe the delights of the love relationship in rural images and meta-phors, a technique that pervades the Song of Solomon:

> My beloved is to me a cluster of henna blossoms
> in the vineyards of En-gedi. [1:14]

> With great delight I sat in his shadow,
> and his fruit was sweet to my taste. [2:3b]

Many pastoral love poems fall into the category of the lament or complaint, in which the speaker bemoans the frustrations of separation. In the Song of Solomon, for example, we find this lover's complaint about how hard it is for the woman to find time alone with her man (1:7):

> Tell me, you whom my soul loves,
> where you pasture your flock,
> where you make it lie down at noon;
> for why should I be like one who wanders
> beside the flocks of your companions?

Why have poets through the centuries used pastoral as a way of writing about love? Pastoral is a ready-made vehicle—an accepted language for love poetry and a storehouse of poetic motifs. Another gift of pastoral is that it is open-ended or universal in application. Love poetry that is directly biographical or autobiographical is too particularized and topical to last, whereas the metaphoric mode of pastoral allows anyone to make the poem his or her own. Pastoral is a way to distance and objectify an experience that may be too personal to write about directly. The pastoral mode, being conventional and surrounded with rich traditional associations, also con-fers dignity and status to love poetry.

Finally, the pastoral setting idealizes the love that is portrayed. Pastoral transports us to an ideally flowery and fruitful world populated by ideally attractive and ardent lovers. It puts love into a world where it can flourish without the pressures that exist in ordinary life. The positive qualities of the natural environment reinforce the beauty of the love that is depicted, and sensory delight in nature is transmuted into romantic sentiment. To this day, love poets often use nature as the source of their imagery.

The Style of the Book

The style of the book is the most purely poetic thing in the Bible. It is one of the delights of the book, but most modern readers are scared off by the very abandonment of the poetic style. Is something this poetic really appropriate in the Bible? Yes it is. The right way to read the Song of Solomon is to abandon oneself to the poetry. It is a poetry full of emotional and imagistic fireworks, but this is in keeping with the subject matter of the book. Not to abandon oneself to the poetry is to cut against the grain of the book.

We can appropriately call the style of this book a golden style. I get the term from Lewis's description of English Renaissance poetry.[5] The main effort of such poetry is directed toward richness of imagery, metaphor, and emotion. Golden poetry uses words that invite sensory and emotional response. There is a delight in nature, and the imagery is filled with references to flowers and trees, the moon and the sun. The subject matter that goes along with this style is equally golden, claims Lewis; it consists of ideally ardent lovers in an ideally flowery and fruitful landscape.

Golden poetry is obviously at the opposite end of the stylistic spectrum from realism. It could never be mistaken for the ordinary speaking voice. It is a consciously poetic style, and one which modern readers, conditioned to expect realism, may have to learn to enjoy. Reading Renaissance love poetry is the quickest way to become acclimated.

As a specimen of the golden style, I have selected verses 9–14 of the opening chapter:

> [9] I compare you, my love,
>   to a mare of Pharaoh's chariots.
> [10]Your cheeks are comely with ornaments,
>   your neck with strings of jewels.
> [11]We will make you ornaments of gold,
>   studded with silver.
> [12]While the king was on his couch,
>   my nard gave forth its fragrance.

5. Lewis, *English Literature*, pp. 64–65, 323. The best discussion of the imagery of the Song of Solomon, and especially its nonliteral nature, is by Israel Baroway, in *Edmund Spenser: Epithalamion*, ed. Robert Beum (Columbus: Merrill, 1968), pp. 81–103. Baroway's conclusions were, in turn, indebted to Richard G. Moulton, *The Modern Reader's Bible* (New York: Macmillan, 1895), pp. 1448–50.

>¹³My beloved is to me a bag of myrrh,
>   that lies between my breasts.
>¹⁴My beloved is to me a cluster of henna blossoms
>   in the vineyards of En-gedi.

What words might we use to describe the style of such a passage? It is obviously a *sensuous* style, and we had better get clear at once what this abused word really means. *Sensuous* is a word positive in connotation that means "sensory, having to do with the senses." It is a particular vexation to me that this word is confused with the term *sensual*, which means having to do with the illicit gratification of the appetites, especially the sexual. The style of the Song of Solomon is sensuous, but not sensual. In fact, its metaphoric or symbolic mode has in it a built-in sense of reserve.

Other descriptive terms also help us identify the style of the passage at which we are looking. It is a *pictorial* style that often creates scenes that we imagine (even though the text does not spell out the specific details). In this passage, we picture or imagine the woman's jewels, the king on his couch, and the woman's perfume. Although other passages may illustrate the point better, the style is also *passionate*. The style is *hyperbolic*, giving us an exaggerated version of the attractiveness of the two lovers. The style is *pastoral*, deeply rooted in the world of nature and growing plants.

Finally, it is obviously a *metaphoric* or *symbolic* style. The woman is not literally a horse, nor is the man literally a bag of perfume or a cluster of blossoms. Such metaphors and similes require us to make a transfer from one level to another, and it is essential to the interpretation of the Song of Solomon to realize that the transfer is rarely a visual one. What the comparisons in the Song of Solomon ask us to transfer is the *value* or *excellence* of an object. When the man compliments his beloved by comparing her to a mare of Pharaoh's chariots, he does not expect us to visualize the woman as being like a horse. A mare of Pharaoh's chariots is the best and most beautiful of its kind. It is the idea of superlative quality that the woman shares with the horse. The vineyards of En-gedi (v. 14) were on a shore of the Dead Sea in a region famous for lush gardens and vineyards. Like the horses of Pharaoh, the vineyards of En-gedi were the best of their kind, a standard of excellence. The whole cluster of images in the quoted passage adds up to a picture of wealth and excellence, which is what the lovers represent to each other.

While the transfer of value is usually the main point of the comparisons, secondary meanings are often possible. The horses of Pharaoh's chariots no doubt created an aura of beauty that attracted attention when they passed. The same is true of the woman. The perfume that the woman wears not only is valuable but also gives sensory pleasure when one is in its presence. So does the beloved.

A final thing to note about the style of the Song of Solomon is that it proceeds chiefly by an association of images and feelings. It is, indeed, a stream-of-consciousness style, not a narrative style. We can follow the poet's association of images as we progress through the quoted passage. The mention of the adorned horses of a king's chariot (v. 9) leads to a picture of the jewelry that adorns the woman (vv. 10–11). From the picture of the woman royally adorned we move to the picture of the king in his courtly setting (v. 12). Recalling the perfume that she wore on that occasion, the woman turns it into a metaphor: the king is her perfume (v. 13). Having mentioned perfume, the poet makes a natural leap to the smell of blossoms in a vineyard (v. 14). Another evidence of the fluidity of the style is the way in which we move from one speaker to another without transition.

I return to my earlier point about abandoning oneself to the delights of the poetry. Unless we decide to allow ourselves the luxury of simply enjoying the fireworks of poetry at its most imaginative, we will not really care for the Song of Solomon. Here is a work that will yield its meaning only if we are willing to accept it on its literary terms.

What Kind of Love?

The Song of Solomon is the largest repository of biblical teaching on the subject of romantic love. This alone would make it a necessary part of the Bible. Without the view of love presented here, the Bible's teaching on the subject would be incomplete. What kind of love is offered for our approval in the Song of Solomon?

To begin, the love celebrated in the Song of Solomon is *erōs*, not *agapē*. Its keynote is *love because of* (which is partly what I mean by *erōs*), not *love in spite of* (the standard translation of the word *agapē*). On this basis alone I would reject the attempt to allegorize the book to mean God's love for people, whom God loves in spite of their sinfulness. Although in modern usage the adjective *erotic* often implies sexual lust, in its essence the word means "having to do with sexual love; amatory." The love portrayed and celebrated in the Song of Solomon is erotic in the sense that it exists between a man and woman and has a strong physical dimension to it. The clear implication of the poem is that the mutual physical attractiveness that a man and woman feel toward each other is good and ennobling.

The love in the poem is also *romantic*. It is highly refined and conducted according to an elaborate social pattern of compliments, wooing, acceptance, and so forth. This romantic strain removes the love from two perversions. Despite its frank acceptance of sexual passion, the romantic love here portrayed could not possibly be mistaken for mere animal or

physical appetite. This distinctly human identity of the love removes it
from lust. On the other side, the romance of it all removes it equally from
any matter-of-fact, routine, unromanticized relationship between husband
and wife.

A third characteristic of the love depicted in the work is that it is
idealized, that is, held up as an ideal. The love of the couple is portrayed
as an ennobling human sentiment. It awakens such moral qualities as
gentleness, humility, modesty, high regard for another person, and loyalty
in love. This idealization of romantic love removes the poem from
asceticism, which holds that romantic love is never a good thing in itself.

Finally, the romantic love that is celebrated in the poem is *married love*.
Its assumed context is marriage. As the love deepens, it becomes directed
toward marriage. The physical consummation of the love is described as
occurring after the wedding. In chapters 4 and 5 the lady is six times
referred to as Solomon's *bride*.

To summarize, the ideal that is celebrated in the Song of Solomon is
wedded romantic love. This love is not put into a spiritual context of faith
in God. What do we make of this? Simply that a work of literature never
says everything there is to say on a subject. A work of literature is a
distillation of life. In this poem, the poet distills the attractiveness of the
lovers and the serene joy of their relationship. We all know that there are
other sides to a romance and marriage. In fact, one of the questions I like
to pose for discussion is whether the picture of the busy wife in Proverbs
31:10–31 is a companion poem, a sequel, or a contrast to the Song of
Solomon.

Structure of the Book

To make sense of the book at all, we have to determine to our
satisfaction the topical units. As I have worked with the book over the
years, I have become increasingly confident that the following scheme
does justice to the content of the book. Let me reiterate that if we read the
book as a collection of love lyrics, the pressure is off so far as the specifics
of the structure are concerned. We do not need to agonize over whether a
given unit goes with the section before it or after it, or what title we should
give it. What is important is the love sentiment that is expressed, not who
is talking. Thus numerous other ways of dividing the material may be
equally acceptable as the one I present here.

I remain convinced that the book is not structured on a chronological
principle. We might expect that the wedding poems would come at the
end, but in fact they come in the middle. Some of the late lyrics strike me
as more appropriate to the courtship phase of the romance. This suggests
that the book is structured on the principle that biblical scholars call

chiastic ("crossing") structure but that literary critics are more likely to call ring composition. In such a structure, the second half of the work takes up the same motifs as were present in the first half, but in reverse order.

This is what we find in the Song of Solomon. The first and last chapters (approximately) portray sentiments appropriate to falling in love—early phases of a romance. They are also the most crowded with a variety of people. In the very middle is the wedding. Between those two points is a collection of love lyrics that generally could occur at any stage of a courtship or marriage.

We will make more sense of the book if we free ourselves from the need to tie every unit down to a narrative progression. In the words of Lewis, a collection of love lyrics does not tell a story but "exists for the sake of prolonged lyrical meditation, chiefly on love. . . . External events—a quarrel, a parting, an illness, a stolen kiss—are every now and then mentioned to provide themes for the meditation . . . [These are] not there to in order to interest you in the history of a love affair, after the manner of the novelist" (p. 327).

Here, then, is an outline of the book, accompanied by brief commentary:[6]

1. *Title of the book* (1:1). Identifies the book as belonging to Solomon, not necessarily as author, but certainly as one of the two lead characters.
2. *Expository or introductory lyrics* (1:2–8). A kaleidoscope of lyric fragments that introduces us to the characters, pastoral setting, basic situation (a romance in which the lovers are in quest for satisfaction in love), and style of the work. These verses pluck us from our familiar world and abruptly transport us to a world of heightened emotions and idealized love. We move from the woman's statements of longing for her lover (vv. 2–4), to her apology for her suntanned complexion (vv. 5–6), to her desire for her beloved's companionship (vv. 7–8). The "daughters of Jerusalem" who appear in the work from time to time are like the chorus in a Greek drama—townspeople who provide a social setting for what happens.
3. *The lovers' dialogue* (1:9–2:2). The two lovers celebrate their mutual love and their delight in each other. Solomon praises the woman's beauty in figurative terms (1:9–11), the lady replies, praising the king as her beloved (1:12–14), the two exchange exclamations about the other's beauty (1:15–16a) and praise their pastoral surroundings,

6. For a brief trip through the book, it is hard to better the outline by Johannes G. Vos in *The Expositor's Bible*, ed. Carl F. H. Henry (Philadelphia: Holman, 1960), 2:105–12.

apparently a bower in a court garden (1:16b–17), and the woman compares herself to flowers (2:1), with the man repeating the image (2:2).

4. *The marriage poems, or epithalamion* (2:3–5:1). Here we begin a sequence of longer units, as follows:

   a. 2:3–7. The lady meditates, praising her beloved, recalling the past delights of their romantic relationship, and expressing her longing for the wedding (in the refrain that first appears in verse 7 and that has as its main meaning a plea for patience in waiting for the love to reach maturity).

   b. 2:8–17. Excitement over the groom's arrival for the wedding. A hyperbolic passage in which the woman imagines or fantasizes that her beloved comes to claim her and utters a pastoral invitation to love.

   c. 3:1–5. The woman dreams in anticipation of the marriage. This little narrative pictures separation from the beloved followed by finding him and bringing him into her parental home; it is a metaphoric picture of her quest to find satisfaction in love, ending in marriage.

   d. 3:6–11. A very pictorial lyric that describes the king's appearance in the wedding procession.

   e. 4:1–15. Solomon praises the beauty and virtue of his bride.

   f. 4:16–5:1. The groom claims his bride. A highly sensuous passage that metaphorically describes the sexual consummation of the marriage. The controlling metaphor compares the bride to a garden that the groom enters and claims as his possession. The last two lines ("Eat, O friends, and drink: drink deeply, O lovers!") is a choral address to the couple, and it is an apt summary of one of the things that makes the Song of Solomon so peerless, namely, its ability to express satisfied desire.

5. *Songs of two people in love* (5:2–7:13). A collection of beautiful love lyrics, not tied to a specific chronology. With one exception, they could as well be before or after the wedding.

   a. 5:2–8. Balancing the woman's earlier dream of anticipation, we have this fantasy of separation, expressing the frustrations of separated lovers. As so often is the case in the Song of Solomon, the poetic equivalent of an emotion is a picture, as in the passage "my hands dripped with myrrh, / my fingers with liquid myrrh." Because of the implied sexual intimacy in the passage (with imagery of knocking and opening), I would judge this to be a poem dealing with married life.

   b. 5:9–6:3. The woman's praise of her beloved.

   c. 6:4–12. The man's praise of his lady's beauty.

    d. 6:13–7:9. Another lyric that praises the woman's beauty and erotic attractiveness.

    e. 7:10–13. A pastoral invitation to love, this time uttered by the woman.

6. *Courtship lyrics* (chap. 8). In keeping with the ring construction of the book, the last chapter is much like the first—a kaleidoscope of fragments tossed together in rapid-fire, stream-of-consciousness succession. Furthermore, the first and last chapters share the quality of being the most crowded with diverse characters. Like the opening chapter, too, is the way in which this chapter evokes the world of courtship before the marriage; in fact, both chapters place the woman in her family in a rural milieu (recall the references in the opening chapter to the woman's brothers' displeasure at her suntanned complexion). I called the opening sequence expository or background lyrics. The last chapter is also background material to the romance that occupies center stage in the book.

    a. 8:1–5. The woman's wish that her lover's affection might be acknowledged in her parental home and that she might marry him. A hyperbolic account of inviting one's boy friend home for the weekend!

    b. 8:6–7. The moment of epiphany toward which the entire book moves: a request for permanence in love—the most beautiful such request in all the world's love poetry.

    c. 8:8–10. A brief history of the woman's chastity. The girl's brothers are pictured as guardians of her chastity as she grows up (v. 8). If she is *a wall* (that is, chaste), they will arrange a marriage and dowry for her (v. 9a). If she has been morally loose (*a door*), they will take measures to guard her (v. 9b). Now that she is mature, the woman declares that she has kept herself pure for her beloved (v. 10).

    d. 8:11–14. A concluding dialogue between the lovers. First the lady expresses her contentment with her lover: whereas Solomon has many vineyards, Solomon himself is the woman's vineyard (vv. 11–12). Then Solomon, on the verge of departure, requests to hear his beloved's voice (v. 13), and she replies with a wish that he return speedily (v. 14).

Explications of Selected Lyrics

Knowing that I did not have space to explicate the entire book, I have selected passages on the basis of their being either representative or the most important lyrics in the book.

The Emblematic Blazons

I take the term *emblematic blazon* from Renaissance love poetry. In ancient Egyptian love poetry the same genre was called a *wasf*. Such a poem praises (blazons forth) the beauty or virtue of the beloved (hence the term *blazon*) by cataloguing his or her attractive features and comparing them to objects or emblems in nature. There are four emblematic blazons in the Song of Solomon, three praising the woman (4:1–5; 6:4–7; 7:1–5) and one praising the man (5:10–15). The pattern in the first three is downward movement, beginning with the eyes or hair, with the pattern reversed in the last one. I have selected the first one that appears in the book (4:1–5):

> [1]Behold, you are beautiful, my love,
>   behold, you are beautiful!
> Your eyes are doves
>   behind your veil.
> Your hair is like a flock of goats,
>   moving down the slopes of Gilead.
> [2]Your teeth are like a flock of shorn ewes
>   that have come up from the washing,
> all of which bear twins,
>   and not one among them is bereaved.
> [3]Your lips are like a scarlet thread,
>   and your mouth is lovely.
> Your cheeks are like halves of a pomegranate
>   behind your veil.
> [4]Your neck is like the tower of David,
>   built for an arsenal,
> whereon hang a thousand bucklers,
>   all of them shields of warriors.
> [5]Your two breasts are like two fawns,
>   twins of a gazelle,
>   that feed among the lilies.

What is going on here? What is *not* going on? The poet is not painting a picture of the woman's body, and the main point of the comparisons is not primarily visual correspondence. The main point of the comparisons is the *value* that the woman represents. Beyond that, I see merit in three different interpretations that have been given to the imagery of the Song of Solomon, interpretations that I see as complementary, though others might wish to choose among them.

One good explanation is that the imagery in such passages is primarily *affective* rather than visual or pictorial. Thus one critic theorizes that "we can only explain these images satisfactorily by interpreting them as being drawn not on the visual plane but on the emotional."[7]

A second explanation is that the imagery appeals primarily to the *nonvisual senses*. Here is how one scholar has developed the argument:

> The images seem ludicrous. They lack unity and coherence. They mix the most extravagant and dissimilar metaphors which distract from and in no way describe what they are intended to represent. . . . Hebrew poetry . . . is not primarily visual, but appeals to a wide range of associations and senses. When we read "your two breasts are like two fawns," we think of a visual picture, in this case, a jarring absurdity. When we realize that the image in not visual but *tactile*, the sensuousness of the description is nearly over-whelming. . . . The description of the teeth stresses . . . their wetness, and in the characteristic Hebrew concern for how things are built, how they match each other, how even and well formed they are.[8]

Yet another interpretation is that the imagery is *symbolic* rather than sensory. My chief source takes the comparison of the woman's neck to a tower with weapons as his point of departure:

> The Western reader seizes upon the colossal disparity in proportions, the monstrous incongruity in size, and is tempted to smile. Not so the Oriental reader. He sees nothing ridiculous in the comparison, for his aesthetic realization is independent of close sensory congruity. . . . The tower is a symbol to him—a symbol of excellence, a recognized standard of value . . . , a tower raised to transcendent value through glorious historic and functional associations. . . . He rivets his attention upon the transference of value, or preeminent quality to the body of the girl. . . . Knowing that the poet is not attempting to paint a picture of the girl's body, but to identify it with excellence, his imagination is perfectly satisfied with the most shadowy, the most partial, the most superficial physical or qualitative correspondence to the standard of value.[9]

What is true of the individual comparisons applies also to the catalogue of comparisons in a blazon. The effect of such a grouping is a general one. The result is not a picture of the beloved but an affective impression of value and desirability. As an attempt at a unified and coherent picture, these blazons are contradictory (in 5:11 the man's hair is both blond and

---

7. Murray Roston, *Prophet and Poet: The Bible and the Growth of Romanticism* (Evanston, Ill.: Northwestern University Press, 1965), p. 64.

8. Gene Edward Veith, Jr., *The Gift of Art: The Place of the Arts in Scripture* (Downers Grove: Inter-Varsity, 1984), pp. 64–65. The entire discussion, which I have only excerpted, is well worth consulting.

9. Baroway, "Imagery of Spenser," pp. 83–84. Here, too, the entire discussion is most helpful.

black!).[10] But as a combination of acknowledged standards of excellence, they evoke a strong feeling of the worth of the person.

Pastoral Invitations to Love

There are two pastoral invitations to love in the Song of Solomon (2:10–15; 7:10–13). Here are four verses from the first one, which epitomizes the Song of Solomon as a whole:

> [10]My beloved speaks and says to me:
> "Arise, my love, my fair one,
>   and come away;
> [11]for lo, the winter is past,
>   the rain is over and gone.
> [12]The flowers appear on the earth,
>   the time of singing has come,
> and the voice of the turtledove
>   is heard in our land.
> [13]The fig tree puts forth its figs,
>   and the vines are in blossom;
>   they give forth fragrance.
> Arise, my love, my fair one,
>   and come away. . . ."

The strategy in such a poem is to invite the beloved to go for a walk in the countryside and to use the appeals of the landscape as a way of making the invitation persuasive. There is a metaphoric overtone to the invitation, which in effect becomes a marriage proposal—an invitation to share a life together. The most famous pastoral invitation to love in English literature was written by the Renaissance poet Christopher Marlowe and begins with the evocative line, "Come live with me and be my love."

More generally, the style of the excerpt takes us to the heart of the Song of Solomon. The style is sensuous, evocative, and pastoral. The world that it creates in our imagination is an ideally beautiful and fruitful world, far removed from asphalt parking lots at hamburger stands. The short lines and parallel clauses produce a musical, songlike quality. Even when reading the lines silently, we hear the overtones of singing. The voice of satisfied desire is strong. An aphoristic line like "the time of singing has come" sums up the mood of the book.

The Refrain

The Song of Solomon contains a refrain that occurs three times (2:7;

---

10. The December 1977/January 1978 issue of the *Wittenburg Door* spoofed the literal interpretation of the Song of Solomon with a composite visual sketch of the woman as described in the poem. It is most entertaining.

3:5; 8:4), each time in a similar context. The refrain is a plea for patience in situations where the anticipation is almost overpowering:

> I adjure you, O daughters of Jerusalem,
>> by the gazelles or the hinds of the field,
> that you stir not up nor awaken love
>> until it please.

The form of the utterance is a command, in effect a self-rebuke (even though it is addressed to the daughters of Jerusalem) for impatience. Gazelles and hinds are mentioned because they are timid creatures, hence appropriate in a plea to be nonaggressive. The contexts in which this refrain appears are similar: the woman's longing for the wedding as she recalls the delights of the romance (2:3–7), her fantasy about claiming Solomon as her husband (3:1–5), and her desire during the courtship to have her beloved accepted as part of her family (8:1–4). The main point of the refrain, then, is that love must be allowed to take its course and should not be rushed.

The Consummation of the Love

The epithalamion that comprises the middle of the Song of Solomon reaches its climax with a figurative description of the lovers' consummation of their love. The passage begins with a long address by the groom to his bride in which he praises her beauty and chastity (4:9–15):

> You have ravished my heart, my sister, my bride,
>> you have ravished my heart with a glance of your eyes,
>> with one jewel of your necklace.
> How sweet is your love, my sister, my bride!
>> how much better is your love than wine,
>> and the fragrance of your oils than any spice!
> Your lips distil nectar, my bride;
>> honey and milk are under your tongue;
>> the scent of your garments is like the scent of Lebanon.
> A garden locked is my sister, my bride,
>> a garden locked, a fountain sealed.
> Your shoots are an orchard of pomegranates
>> with all choicest fruits,
>> henna with nard,
> nard and saffron, calamus and cinnamon,
>> with all trees of frankincense,
> myrrh and aloes,
>> with all chief spices—

> a garden fountain, a well of living water,
>   and flowing streams from Lebanon.

We obviously move to a riot of sensations as we approach the consummation of the love. The controlling metaphor compares the bride to a precious
spice garden. The emphasis on the enclosed nature of the garden praises
the bride's chastity. In this passage the poetic equivalent for emotion is a
picture. The claim that the beloved's love is better than wine appears
several times in the Song of Solomon and means that the beloved is
(figuratively speaking) more intoxicating than wine. The overall impression is the extreme value of the garden and hence of the bride.

The bride responds to the groom's description by expressing her wish to
be desirable to her husband (4:16):

> Awake, O north wind,
>   and come, O south wind!
> Blow upon my garden,
>   let its fragrance be wafted abroad.
> Let my beloved come to his garden,
>   and eat its choicest fruits.

The imagery of the spice garden continues to be the basic frame of
reference, but the locked garden is now opened to the beloved. We cannot
read the passage without getting a strong impression of the worth of happy
sexual love in marriage.

The passage reaches its climax as the husband claims his garden, that is,
his bride (5:1):

> I come to my garden, my sister, my bride,
> I gather my myrrh with my spice,
> I eat my honeycomb with my honey,
> I drink my wine with my milk.

This barrage of metaphors creates a sense of love as an appetite and
marriage as the thing that satisfies it. There is no attempt at providing a
coherent picture. Instead, the poet mixes the most evocative sensory
images he has at his disposal. To eat a honeycomb with the honey is to
possess the very source of life's sweetness. We might note in passing that
the symbolic mode of the Song of Solomon, in which sexual consummation, for example, is pictured as claiming a sensuous garden, has built into
it a certain reserve that keeps the poem far from pornography.

The Request for Permanence in Love

The most customary way to structure a long work of literature is to
move it toward some climactic moment of epiphany or insight near the

end. Verses 6 and 7 of the last chapter are such a moment in the Song of Solomon, as the woman makes an eloquent request for permanence in love:

> Set me as a seal upon your heart,
>   as a seal upon your arm;
> for love is strong as death,
>   jealousy is cruel as the grave.
> Its flashes are flashes of fire,
>   a most vehement flame.
> Many waters cannot quench love,
>   neither can floods drown it.
> If a man offered for love
>   all the wealth of his house,
>   it would be utterly scorned.

Here is the interpretive framework that explains what kind of love we have been looking at throughout the book. Love songs the world over are full of vows of eternal constancy, since love at its most intense wants to be bound to the beloved. True or permanent love is the subject of the Song of Solomon.

The imagery of this poem is powerful. The request to be set as a seal upon either the heart or arm has two meanings. In ancient times, a seal was an engraved stamp for making an imprint, which carried the force of an official signature. To put a seal upon something was to claim it as a possession. Seen thus, the lady's request is, "Stamp me on your heart and thereby claim me as yours."

There is a second meaning as well. Seals were worn on either the hand (see Gen. 41:42; Jer. 22:24) or on a chain around the neck (see Gen. 38:18; Prov. 3:3), where they would be easily accessible when needed to stamp a document. Seen thus, the meaning of the images is not simply possession but closeness. In asking to be set as a seal on the man's heart or arm, the woman is asking to be always close to her beloved.

Following her request, the woman explains why she has made it: *for love is strong as death.* How strong *is* death? No one can conquer it. It is both irresistible and permanent. The same is true of love. The next line is parallel in meaning, as is made clearer in the translation offered by the New English Bible: "passion [is] cruel as the grave."

True love is next compared to fire. This is an archetypal image for love, because both fire and love are uncontrollable. The fire of love, in fact, is so powerful and uncontrollable that floods of water cannot *quench* or *drown* it, defying the laws of nature. To close this impassioned definition of true love, the poet declares its supreme value: it is so valuable that all of a person's wealth is tawdry when put beside it. Such love is not for sale.

The Song of Solomon is the most thoroughly poetic book in the Bible, but it need not be a closed book. It pains me to see what interpreters have done with it, and how people steer away from it because they do not know what to do with it. My advice is simple: read it as love poetry and abandon yourself to the rapture of the images and sentiments. The moment an interpretation requires us to be on our guard, seeing some of the characters and sentiments as bad and others as good, the spell is already broken and we have lost the impact of the book. The Song of Solomon is affective, not analytic, in its approach to love. Both its style and its lyric content require a sense of abandonment on the reader's part.

Other Biblical Literary Forms

12

Encomium

The encomium is one of the most refreshing and artistic forms in the Bible. For whatever reasons, the encomia of the Bible led their writers to write in highly intricate rhetorical and poetic patterns.

An *encomium* is a work of literature written in praise of an abstract quality or general character type. In elaborating their theme, writers of encomia draw upon the following motifs:

1. Introduction to the subject that will be praised. This may include a brief definition of the subject.
2. The distinguished and ancient ancestry of the subject; praise "by what kind he came of."
3. A catalogue or description of the praiseworthy acts and qualities of the subject.
4. The indispensable or superior nature of the subject. The superiority of the subject might include a description of the rewards that accompany it (something distinctively important in biblical encomia).
5. A conclusion urging the reader to emulate the subject.

All encomia have a lyric quality comparable to what we find in a psalm of praise. Some biblical encomia are in prose rather than poetry, but these are so imagistic and patterned in their arrangement that they produce a poetic effect.

Old Testament Encomium

Psalm 1

Psalm 1 (already explicated on pp. 211–15) is an encomium praising the godly person. The praise is conducted by describing both the inner quality and outward actions of such a person. The praise of the godly person is heightened by the presence of the foil of the wicked person.

The poem begins with a positive evaluation of the godly person in the evocative form of a beatitude: "Blessed is the man. . . . " Three parallel clauses then narrate what the godly person avoids (v. 1). Positively, "his delight is in the law of the LORD, / and on his law he meditates day and night" (v. 2). An encomium can be trusted to give a precise definition of the subject that it praises, as the first two verses of Psalm 1 already demonstrate.

From the catalogue of activities the poet turns to a portrait of the godly person. It takes the form of a simile that pictures a productive tree growing by streams of water (v. 3), with the meanings of that picture elaborated by a contrasting simile that compares the wicked to chaff (v. 4). These similes are not merely decorative. They require us to analyze *how* godly and wicked persons are like these phenomena.

To complete the praise of the godly person, the poet shifts the focus to the future judgment of both the wicked and the godly (vv. 5–6). What emerges from this final verdict is a strong impression of the superiority of the godly way of life, a standard formula in an encomium.

Psalm 15

Psalm 15 is similar to Psalm 1, taking as its object of praise the holy person. When an encomium praises a general character type, it is likely to take the literary form known as "the character," a form that can be traced all the way back to the Greek writer Theophrastus. It is a brief descriptive sketch of a character type who exemplifies a single dominant principle. The portrait can be either a moral type (e.g., the proud person), a social type (the overdressed person), or a vocational type (the preacher). The sketch can include both external appearance and actions and inner character traits. The basic structure of a character sketch is repetitive—we see a single principle maintained under a variety of different forms. The person is not individualized but treated as a common type.

Not surprisingly (given the biblical emphasis on the primacy of the spiritual), the encomia in the Psalms praise spiritual and moral qualities. Psalm 15 paints a picture of the holy person. The sketch, in fact, is couched as the answer to a question of far-reaching importance, namely, who can worship God acceptably? The question is addressed to God:

> O LORD, who shall sojourn in thy tents?
> Who shall dwell on thy holy hill?

The imagery of the tent and hill refers to worshiping God in the tabernacle or the temple.

The answer to these questions, which also constitutes the encomium, is a catalogue of the acts of the holy person. The list alternates between positive and negative descriptions in a manner reminiscent of Psalm 1:

> [2]He who walks blamelessly, and does what is right,
>   and speaks truth from his heart.
> [3]who does not slander with his tongue,
>   and does no evil to his friend,
>   nor takes up a reproach against his neighbor;
> [4]in whose eyes a reprobate is despised,
>   but who honors those who fear the LORD;
> who swears to his own hurt and does not change;
> [5]who does not put out his money at interest,
>   and does not take a bribe against the innocent.

In analyzing such a list, one should look for patterns or clusters of related ideas, and I leave it to my reader to do so.

The conclusion of the encomium, syntactically isolated from the catalogue, is a comprehensive generalization about the person just described: *He who does these things shall never be moved.* The effect of this concluding assertion is to make the reader want to be such a person, which is always the final impression left by an encomium. An encomium is an affective form. Its hidden agenda is always to persuade or move the reader to emulate the thing being praised.

Other Encomiastic Psalms

The genre of the encomium appears in at least three additional psalms. I leave the details of the analysis to my readers.

Although Psalm 112 begins with the statement, "Praise the LORD," it is not a psalm of the praise of God. This opening line is simply the interpretive framework within which the poet conducts an encomium that praises "the man who fears the LORD" (v. 1). Again one should analyze the catalogue to determine the traits, typical actions, and rewards that characterize this person.

Psalm 128 is part of the "Song of Ascents" and as such is part of the many-sided picture of what went through the pilgrims' minds as they took stock of their spiritual lives en route to worship God at the temple. It is interesting to note, therefore, the family focus of this encomium. The concluding prayer or wish (vv. 5–6) has the effect of describing the *rewards* that come to "every one who fears the Lord."

Psalm 119 is far too long to be a typical encomium. Yet its general content and shape are those of the encomium. Its subject is the law of God, which is also called by numerous synonyms throughout the course of the psalm. Reading portions of the psalm will at once show that it is made up of the conventional motifs of an encomium: definition and description of the subject, praise of its qualities and effects, its superiority and indispensable nature, its divine origin, and numerous commands to follow it.

The Praise of Wisdom in Proverbs

The spirit of the encomium pervades the Book of Proverbs, especially the first nine chapters, even when the praise of wisdom does not have the precise form of the encomium. The general idea of many passages is to praise the quality known as wisdom, to personify it as a woman and thereby treat it as a general character type (the wise person), to praise its attributes, worth, and actions, and to give a detailed account of the benefits of following wisdom. What is all this if not an encomium?

At least two poems in the Book of Proverbs have the formal pattern of the encomium. One of these is Proverbs 3:13–20. This poem introduces the topic of wisdom by declaring the happiness of people who find it (v. 13):

> Happy is the man who finds wisdom,
> and the man who gets understanding.

The first variation on this theme is the supreme value of wisdom:

> [14]for the gain from it is better than gain from silver
> and its profit better than gold.
> [15]She is more precious than jewels,
> and nothing you desire can compare with her.

Here is a technique of personification that is such a hallmark of the first nine chapters of Proverbs, with wisdom pictured as an attractive woman.

The next section lists the qualities that Wisdom hands out as gifts to people:

> [16]Long life is in her right hand;
> in her left hand are riches and honor.

> [17]Her ways are ways of pleasantness,
>   and all her paths are peace.
> [18]She is a tree of life to those who lay hold of her;
>   those who hold her fast are called happy.

Here, in a highly imaginative and attractive picture, is the indispensability of wisdom to the good life.

One of the conventions of an encomium is to praise the ancient and distinguished ancestry of the subject. The conclusion of the encomium in praise of wisdom shows us exactly *how* distinguished the ancestry of wisdom is:

> [19]The LORD by wisdom founded the earth;
>   by understanding he established the heavens;
> [20]by his knowledge the deeps broke forth,
>   and the clouds drop down the dew.

Wisdom is obviously a quality of God himself, and its ancestry is therefore from eternity.

The other encomium in early Proverbs is chapter 8, an exalted poem too long to quote. It begins with the narrator's call to emulate or follow wisdom (vv. 1–3). The encomium itself is put into the mouth of the personified woman Wisdom. It, too, begins with a call to heed (vv. 4–5) and then proceeds to list the qualities and acts of wisdom, along with its superiority over other things and the beneficial results of following it (vv. 6–21). Then comes a little creation story in which Wisdom pictures herself as being the first created thing and therefore present when God created the world (vv. 22–31). Such is the distinguished ancestry of the subject. The encomium concludes (vv. 32–36) with an extended and moving call to possess the wisdom that the poem has described.

The Virtuous Wife

The Book of Proverbs concludes (31:10–31) with another encomium, this one in praise of the virtuous wife, a general character type. (A student observed the unfortunate proximity of this poem to the caution earlier in the chapter, "Give not your strength to women.") The poem is an acrostic, with the successive verses beginning consecutively with the letters of the Hebrew alphabet.

As a way into the subject, the poet asks a rhetorical question (v. 10): *A good wife who can find?* The import of this question is to suggest that such a woman is rare, hence of great value, as the next line asserts: *She is far more precious than jewels.* Here is the comparative technique that is common in encomia.

Verse 11 begins the catalogue of the virtuous wife's character traits and acts. The catalogue as a whole (vv. 11–27) describes the wife in an ever-widening context of activity, from family relations to domestic business to social concern. At the end (vv. 28–29) the scope again constricts to the family. The poet first describes the ideal wife in relation to her husband, thereby suggesting the primacy of the marital role for a wife:

> [11]The heart of her husband trusts in her,
>   and he will have no lack of gain.
> [12]She does him good, and not harm,
>   all the days of her life.

The wife is next seen in a domestic role, with emphasis on how she provides for the physical needs of her household:

> [13]She seeks wool and flax,
>   and works with willing hands.
> [14]She is like the ships of the merchant,
>   she brings her food from afar.
> [15]She rises while it is yet night
>   and provides food for her household
>   and tasks for her maidens.
> [16]She considers a field and buys it;
>   with the fruit of her hands she plants a vineyard.
> [17]She girds her loins with strength and makes her arms strong.
> [18]She perceives that her merchandise is profitable.
>   Her lamp does not go out at night.
> [19]She puts her hand to the distaff,
>   and her hands hold the spindle.

The tone of this composite, consciously overdrawn picture of domestic activities is mildly humorous. *No* wife is the kind of dynamo who can do all these things, apparently requiring virtually no sleep and yet having the energy to pump iron in the weight-lifting room (v. 17)!

In the ever-widening sphere of activity that is ascribed to the wife, she is next shown in a social role in the community, though the things that she does for herself and her family continue to be present in the catalogue:

> [20]She opens her hand to the poor,
>   and reaches out her hands to the needy.
> [21]She is not afraid of snow for her household,
>   for all her household are clothed in scarlet.
> [22]She makes herself coverings;
>   her clothing is fine linen and purple.
> [23]Her husband is known in the gates,

> when he sits among the elders of the land.
> [24]She makes linen garments and sells them;
>   she delivers girdles to the merchant.
> [25]Strength and dignity are her clothing,
>   and she laughs at the time to come.
> [26]She opens her mouth with wisdom,
>   and the teaching of kindness is on her tongue.
> [27]She looks well to the ways of her household,
>   and does not eat the bread of idleness.

A strong moral note enters the portrait in verses 20 and 26, balancing the economic picture of the career woman in verse 24. What a person praises is always an index to values and morality. A passage such as this is therefore a comment about the proper role of a wife. With it we might profitably compare current notions of the wife as liberated woman.

The catalogue of praiseworthy traits has continually kept the home and family in focus, and at the end the poet returns to the family role of the wife. In fact, the climactic praise of the wife is put in the mouth of her husband and children:

> [28]Her children rise up and call her blessed;
>   her husband also, and he praises her:
> [29]"Many women have done excellently,
>   but you surpass them all."

But the concluding note is higher even than the domestic; it is spiritual (v. 30):

> Charm is deceitful, and beauty is vain,
>   but a woman who fears the LORD is to be praised.

This verse establishes a hierarchy of values in which spirituality ranks higher than physical beauty, which can (as the narrator notes) be misleading. The concluding wish (v. 31) is a variation on the conventional motif of the rewards that come to the subject of praise:

> Give her of the fruit of her hands,
>   and let her works praise her in the gates.

New Testament Encomium

The encomia of the Old Testament tend to praise character types. They convey a picture of the good life as lived under God's law in this world. In the New Testament, the encomium tends to be more theological, with a focus on such topics as love and faith. It is also frequently Christocentric.

John 1:1–18

The Gospel of John opens with an exalted encomium in praise of the incarnate Christ. It is one of the most patterned units in the Bible, and since I cannot explore the poem in detail, I invite my readers to stare at the passage until the repeated words and phrases start to emerge into view.[1]

The passage is printed in our Bibles as prose, but this obscures the sheer poetry of the passage. I have therefore printed the passage as a poem, dividing it into the units suggested by the form of encomium and commenting on it unit by unit. To highlight the patterns of repetition (for example, such word patterns as *in the beginning, through him, the world, received him, grace and truth*), one should type the entire poem on a single page, using the line arrangement suggested in my discussion. There are eight stanzas.

The first stanza praises the ancient and distinguished ancestry of the subject:

> In the beginning was the Word,
>   and the Word was with God,
>   and the Word was God.
> He was in the beginning with God.

Whereas other Gospel writers begin their accounts with a human genealogy of Christ, John begins with a divine genealogy. For his language he reaches all the way back to our very archetype of beginnings, Genesis 1:1 ("In the beginning God created . . ."). To call Christ a *Word* is, of course, to use a metaphor whose chief meaning is the idea of revelation.

Already in the opening stanza the poet uses rhythm and repetition of phrases to create the incantatory and oracular effect and emotional compulsion that will pulsate through the entire section. The repeated phrases include *in the beginning, the Word,* and *with God.*

Stanza 2 praises Christ by declaring him indispensable to everything that exists, since he actually created all things:

> All things were made through him,
>   and without him was not anything made that was made.

---

1. For good commentary on the matter, see the excerpts from literary critics in *The New Testament in Literary Criticism,* ed. Leland Ryken, A Library of Literary Criticism (New York: Ungar, 1984), pp. 182–87.

The rhetorical effect of the statement depends on antithesis; in fact, the line is an example of antithetic parallelism. *All things* is set over against *not anything*, and *through him* against *without him*.

The third stanza praises Christ's life-giving quality:

> In him was *life*,
>   and the *life* was the *light* of men.
> The *light* shines in the *darkness*,
>   and the *darkness* has not overcome it.

Here the writer begins to speak in the evocative symbols of light and darkness for which the entire Gospel of John is famous. To heighten the effect, he sets light and darkness into conflict. This stanza also uses the rhetorical pattern known as gradation, which consists of a series of clauses in which the last key word in a clause becomes the first key word in the next clause (as highlighted by my italics).

Stanza 4 exalts the dignity of the incarnate Christ by describing his forerunner, sent from God:

> There was a man sent from God,
>   whose name was John.
> He came for testimony,
>   to bear witness to the light,
>   that all might believe through him.
> He was not the light,
>   but came to bear witness to the light.

The implied metaphor in the passage is that of kingship, since kings had heralds who went before them to proclaim their arrival. The imagery of light continues from the previous stanza, and it is of course a physical symbol for such realities as spiritual truth and illumination. As in the rest of the poem, the parallel clauses in the stanza produce an overpowering chantlike effect, and we are carried along by the great stream on which we have embarked (as with Milton's epic style). Patterns of repetition reinforce the effect: *to bear witness, the light, came.*

The fifth stanza praises the incarnate Christ for his redemptive work in bringing to spiritual life all who receive him and believe in his name. This is the greatest of the praiseworthy acts of the subject and accordingly is given the most space:

> The true light that enlightens every man
>   was coming into the world.
> He was in the world,
>   and the world was made through him,

> yet the world knew him not.
> He came to his own home,
>   and his own people received him not.
> But to all who received him,
>   who believed in his name,
>   he gave power to become children of God;
> who were born
>   not of blood
>   nor of the will of the flesh
>   nor of the will of man
> but of God.

The passage is full of contrasts, and the general effect is to praise the superiority of Christ. He is *the true light,* in implied contrast to false or lesser lights. The world is held up to satiric rebuke because it *knew him not* even though he is far superior to it, having *made it.* Those who *received him not* are the background that heightens the attainment of those *who received him* and thereby became *children of God.* And as for the superiority of this new birth, it is *not of blood . . . ,* but *of God.*

The controlling metaphor in the passage also contributes to the impact. Pervading the passage is the imagery of birth and creation (echoing the Genesis imagery of the first and second stanzas). A spirit of life-giving energy breathes through the passage, and we catch the excitement of a superior quality that transcends the deadness of the people who *received him not.*

Stanza 6 praises the fact of the incarnation itself:

> And the Word became flesh
>   and dwelt among us,
>   full of grace and truth;
> We have beheld his glory,
>   glory as of the only Son from the Father.

The stanza combines the human, earthly imagery of *flesh* and *dwelt among us* with exalted heavenly imagery of *glory, grace and truth, from the Father.* The effect is to exalt the divine attributes of one who became flesh.

The seventh stanza uses the words of John the Baptist to assert Christ's superiority:

> (John bore witness to him, and cried,
>   "This was he of whom I said,
> 'He who comes after me ranks before me,
>   for he was before me.' ")

This unit has seemed like an oddity to some commentators, but the genre of the encomium offers an explanation for it. The herald of the king here voices the conventional praise of the subject's superiority. He does so by means of a striking paradox: the one who *comes after* is actually *before*, both in worth and time. The passage also echoes earlier stanzas. The assertion that *he was before me* recalls the claim to divine ancestry at the very beginning of the poem. The description of how John *bore witness* echoes similar terminology in the third stanza.

The last stanza of the encomium praises the revelatory acts of the incarnate Christ:

> And from his fulness have we all received,
>> grace upon grace.
> For the law was given through Moses;
>> grace and truth came through Jesus Christ.
> No one has ever seen God;
>> the only Son,
>> who is in the bosom of the Father,
> he has made him known.

The first half of the stanza uses the technique of comparison to declare the superiority to the great Hebrew lawgiver Moses, while the second half uses the equally conventional strategy of declaring the subject of praise indispensable.

Colossians 1:15–20

Embedded in the first chapter of Colossians is another encomium that praises the person and work of Christ. It presents the gospel in miniature. The hymn is built on the principle of balance. The first half praises the supremacy of Christ in the cosmos, and the second half praises his supremacy in the church. Joining the two halves is the imagery of Christ's being *first*.

The best way to see the elaborate system of parallels between the two halves is to type them side by side and then start drawing lines between the parallels. Our Bibles obscure the poetry of the passage by printing it as prose. I have put it into the parallelism that it actually possesses.

The poem begins the praise by declaring Christ's divinity, which makes him supreme over the creation (v. 15):

> He is the image of the invisible God,
>> the first-born of all creation.

The metaphor *first-born* denotes supremacy. It also adheres to the conventional motif of emphasizing ancient ancestry that we often find in encomia.

Having introduced the motif of creation, the writer next elaborates the point by listing Christ's acts of creation (v. 16):

> For in him all things were created,
>   in heaven and on earth,
>   visible and invisible,
>   whether thrones or dominions
>   or principalities or authorities—
> all things were created through him and for him.

Here we see the supremacy of Christ over the physical creation, since he is both prior to it and the creator of it. Already the writer makes use of an elaborate rhetoric of antithesis and parallelism of clauses.

Verse 17 climaxes the first movement of the poem by praising Christ for being indispensable to the existence of all things:

> He is before all things,
>   and in him all things hold together.

The supremacy of Christ over the world is comprehensive and complete.

In the middle of the poem the focus shifts to the church, but we find that the writer retains the motif of Christ's being first and therefore supreme:

> He is the head of the body, the church;
>   he is the beginning,
>   the first-born from the dead,
>   that in everything he might be pre-eminent.

Here begins the elaborate system of cross-references to the first half of the poem, with the phrase *the first-born from the dead* balancing the earlier *the first-born of all creation*.

Corresponding to the comments about Christ's creative acts in the first half is the praise of him for his acts of redemption (vv. 19–20):

> For in him all the fulness of God was pleased to dwell,
>   and through him to reconcile to himself all things,
> whether on earth or in heaven,
>   making peace by the blood of his cross.

To accentuate the parallels between Christ's original creation of the world and his subsequent redemption or reconciliation of it, the writer balances the statement *all things . . . in heaven and on earth* from the first half with *all things, whether on earth or in heaven* in the second.

The keynote of the poem is the idea of supremacy. Christ is praised by being declared supreme over everything else. The whole spirit of the writer's ecstatic praise is captured by the motif of "allness": *all creation* (v. 15), *all things* (v. 16 [twice], v. 17 [twice], v. 20), *in everything* (v. 18), *all the fulness* (v. 19).

1 Corinthians 13

With 1 Corinthians 13 we come to an encomium that praises an abstract quality, love. It is a rhetorical tour de force, replete with balance, parallelism, and contrast. The entire chapter, moreover, is built on an intricate system of threefold patterns, and I have decided to retain this system in the layout of the chapter.

The encomium begins (vv. 1–3) with a triad of three successive clauses in which the basic pattern is the formula (itself having three parts) *If I . . . but have not love, . . . nothing.* Within this formalized structure, we find further repetition and contrast:

> If I speak in the tongues of men and of angels,
>> but have not love,
> I am a noisy gong or a clanging cymbal.
> And if I have prophetic powers,
>> and understand all mysteries and all knowledge,
> and if I have all faith,
>> so as to remove mountains,
> but have not love,
> I am nothing.
> If I give away all I have,
>> and if I deliver my body to be burned,
> but have not love,
> I gain nothing.

Considered as part of an encomium, the opening movement obviously praises love as being indispensable to the Christian life. This indispensability is highlighted by the contrast between *all* and *nothing: all mysteries, all knowledge,* and *all faith* become *nothing* in the absence of love. Similarly, giving away *all I have* gains *nothing* if not accompanied by love.

The next section (vv. 4–7) praises love by listing its qualities and acts. Love is personified in the passage, which becomes poetic with the parallelism of the utterance:

> Love is patient and kind;
>> love is not jealous or boastful;
>> it is not arrogant or rude.
> Love does not insist on its own way;

it is not irritable or resentful;
it does not rejoice at wrong,
    but rejoices in the right.
Love bears all things,
    believes all things,
    hopes all things,
    endures all things.

There is an envelope structure underlying the passage, which moves from the description of positive acts to an account of things that love avoids, and then back to a report of the positive acts of love. Thematically, there is an emphasis on the fact that love avoids misdeeds and actively performs good deeds.

The third movement (vv. 8–13) praises love by declaring its permanence, as opposed to the transience of three spiritual gifts. This is a variation on the common motif of the superiority of the subject. The passage begins by announcing the theme, immediately followed by a triad of contrasts (v. 8):

Love never ends;
    as for prophecies, they will pass away;
    as for tongues, they will cease;
    as for knowledge, it will pass away.

This is elaborated by an extended contrast between love and the three spiritual gifts just mentioned. The main idea is the transience of the three gifts and the permanence of love (vv. 9–12):

For our knowledge is imperfect
    and our prophecy is imperfect;
but when the perfect comes,
    the imperfect will pass away.
When I was a child,
    I spoke like a child,
    I thought like a child,
    I reasoned like a child;
when I became a man,
    I gave up childish ways.
For now we see in a mirror dimly,
    but then face to face.
Now I know in part;
    then I shall understand fully,
    even as I have been fully understood.

For the moment, we may seem to have lost sight of the actual subject of the encomium, but the poem returns to the superior permanence of love in the great aphorism at the end (v. 13):

> So faith, hope, love abide, these three;
> but the greatest of these is love.

Out of an illustrious trinity of spiritual virtues, love is praised as *the greatest*. The first sentence of the next chapter actually belongs with the encomium, since it represents the familiar command to emulate: *Make love your aim.*

Hebrews 11

The biblical encomium is such a glorious form that as one reads through these pieces each one seems better than the previous one. We might well feel that way about Hebrews 11, in praise of faith.

We begin with a definition of the subject to be praised (v. 1):

> Now faith is the assurance of things hoped for,
> the conviction of things not seen.

Once again we notice that although this chapter is printed as prose, it is so rhythmic that it easily falls into the verse form of parallelism. The opening definition announces what the ensuing catalogue will focus on, namely, that faith enables a person to believe something in the absence of empirical proof. The whole chapter emphasizes the theme of the two worlds, and how faith enables a person to live in both worlds simultaneously. This encomium celebrates the feats of people who live by the primacy of the unseen spiritual world.

The second verse praises faith by showing that it has divine approval: "For by it the men of old received divine approval." This focus on people *of old* hints at the encomiastic formula of ancient and distinguished ancestry.

We are now ready for the catalogue of the mighty acts of faith. Since most of the catalogue will be based on a chronological principle, we begin (v. 3) at the beginning—in Genesis 1:

> By faith we understand
>   that the world was created by the word of God,
> so that what is seen
>   was made out of things which do not appear.

One way to organize the encomium is to view it as an ever-expanding list of the things that faith enables a person to do. The first such act is to believe the Genesis account of creation.

The main part of the catalogue (vv. 4–31), too long to reprint here, assumes an overpowering cumulative effect. The chief element of artistic patterning is a series of statements beginning with the formula *by faith*. . . . The structural principle that organizes the list is historical chronology. Having begun with the creation of the world (v. 3), we march straight through Old Testament history: Abel (v. 4), Enoch (vv. 5–6), Noah (v. 7), Abraham (vv. 8–19), Isaac (v. 20), Jacob (v. 21), Joseph (v. 22), Moses (vv. 23–28), the Israelites who lived through the exodus and conquest (vv. 29–31), the judges and kings (v. 32).

From time to time this onward sweep of mighty acts is momentarily arrested when the writer tosses in brief asides that explain something about faith (vv. 6, 13–16, 19, 26). The overall movement thus becomes one of ebb and flow.

Interspersed with the catalogue of praiseworthy acts of faith are several other encomiastic formulas. One is the indispensability motif in verse 6: "And without faith it is impossible to please him." From time to time we encounter a comparison that declares faith superior to other things: faith leads to *a better country* (v. 16), *greater wealth* (v. 26), *a better life* (v. 35).

The catalogue ends with a rhetorical flourish that carries us along. The passage begins (v. 32) with the inexpressibility motif: the acts of faith are so numerous, the writer protests, that he cannot even try to recount them all: "And what more shall I say? For time would fail me to tell of Gideon, Barak, Samson, Jephthah, of David and Samuel and the prophets." It is a classic case of eating one's cake and having it too. Then, in a passage replete with parallelism, we get a whole list of mighty acts of faith (vv. 33–38). Individual names now cease to appear and instead we get general categories of events.

The first two verses of Hebrews 12 complete the encomium with the conventional command to emulate:

> Therefore, since we are surrounded
> by so great a cloud of witnesses,
> let us also lay aside every weight,
> and sin which clings so closely,
> and let us run with perseverance
> the race that is set before us,
> looking to Jesus
> the pioneer and perfecter of our faith,
> who for the joy that was set before him
> endured the cross,
> despising the shame,
> and is seated at the right hand
> of the throne of God.

In a brilliant stroke, the writer here allows the reader to place herself or himself in a long and distinguished line of heroes. To call these heroes of the faith *witnesses* is to use a metaphor from the courtroom, with the implication that these witnesses testify to the power of faith.

In calling these witnesses a *cloud*, the writer alludes to the pillar of cloud used by God to guide the Israelites through the wilderness. The implication is clear: the heroes of faith listed in Hebrews 11 serve as guides and models for believers of later ages. Appropriately, Jesus is held up as the crowning example of faith, the one to whom the reader is urged to look for guidance and for the very perfection of his or her faith.

The Song of the Suffering Servant

With the foregoing encomia serving as background, we are in a position to turn to the most unusual and paradoxical encomium ever written, the song of the suffering servant in Isaiah 52–53. This poem both employs and inverts the usual conventions of the encomium. The parallelism of the song is truly impressive, itself embodying the paradox that the suffering of the messianic servant is beautiful because of what it accomplishes.

The encomium opens with a paradox, as the *servant* is said to be *exalted* (52:13):

> Behold, my servant shall prosper,
>   he shall be exalted and lifted up,
>   and shall be very high.

A paradox is an apparent contradiction that we need to resolve. In this case, the servant is of low social standing, but spiritually exalted.

The next two verses employ a simile to asert that just as many people were shocked by this anti-hero's marred appearance, so they will be shocked when they understand who he is:

> As many were astonished at him—
>   his appearance was so marred, beyond human semblence,
>   and his form beyond that of the sons of men—
> so shall he startle many nations;
>   kings shall shut their mouths because of him;
> for that which has not been told them they shall see,
>   and that which they have not heard they shall understand.

The author here praises the subject for the unlikely reason that his body was mutilated, much as the Book of Revelation praises the Lamb because he was slain.

   The next section of the poem continues the idealization of the anti-hero
but does so by reversing the usual motif of distinguished ancestry (53:1–3):

> Who has believed what we have heard?
>   And to whom has the arm of the LORD been revealed?
> For he grew up before him like a young plant,
>   and like a root out of dry ground;
> he had no form or comeliness that we should look at him,
>   and no beauty that we should desire him.
> he was despised and rejected by men;
>   a man of sorrows, and acquainted with grief;
> and as one from whom men hide their faces
>   he was despised, and we esteemed him not.

We might say that this protagonist is praised for all the wrong reasons.
Instead of coming from prominent social rank, he grew up by a natural,
unspectacular process (*like a young plant*) and came from an unpromising
source (*like a root out of dry ground*). Whereas the beauty of Odysseus
and Telemachus and Aeneas is compared by epic poets to the gods, this
suffering servant is explicitly denied any kind of impressive appearance.
Instead of being socially exalted, he is despised. Here, indeed, is the
apotheosis of the anti-hero.
   The next section praises the suffering servant by listing the acts that he
performed. Verses 4–6 stress the redemptive nature of the acts, 7–9 their
tragic nature. Again we are forced to note how the acts reverse the usual
standards of success. To be *wounded* and *bruised*, for example, is not
usually the kind of behavior that merits heroic status. Whereas the
conventional hero wins rewards for himself, the suffering servant inverts
that formula by enduring pain for the benefit of others (v. 5):

> But he was wounded for our transgressions,
>   he was bruised for our iniquities.

   The picture of how the suffering servant *was oppressed, and afflicted, /
yet he opened not his mouth* (v. 7) is exactly the opposite of the heroic ideal
in classical epic. To be silent *like a sheep before . . . its shearers* (v. 7) is to
display a humility that is the opposite of what the heroes of classical epic and
medieval romance display. The fact that the suffering servant dies as a man
condemned by the law and the courts of justice (v. 8) should be an index to
criminality, yet here it is one of the acts for which the subject is praised. The
fact that *they made his grave with the wicked* (v. 9) is similarly held up for
praise, and the way in which his death was unnoticed by others (v. 8) is in stark
contrast to the elaborate funeral rites for epic heroes.

The last section of the poem (vv. 10–12) praises the suffering servant by describing what his suffering accomplished for the salvation of sinners. Here, too, there are some paradoxical inversions of conventional literary expectations. God is recorded as saying (v. 12),

> Therefore I will divide him a portion with the great,
>   and he shall divide the spoil with the strong;
> because he poured out his soul to death,
>   and was numbered with the transgressors;
> yet he bore the sin of many,
>   and made intercession for the transgressors.

The picture of the hero dividing the spoils on the battlefield is straight from the heroic world of ancient literature, but the heroic values have been completely inverted. Conventional heroes divide the spoil because they have killed their enemies, and for their own benefit. This anti-hero divides the spoil (that is, celebrates spiritual victory) because he has been killed for the sake of others, who are ignoble people at that (v. 6).

What we see highlighted here is something that one keeps encountering with biblical literature. In terms of its literary techniques and forms, the Bible invites comparison with other literature. Yet when we see the specific meaning and values that these forms carry in the Bible, we are struck as much by the contrast as by the similarity. The most consistent pattern of inversion involves exalting the primacy of the spiritual over conventional human standards of value. When we set the Bible alongside other literature in this way, there is no way to deny that often the Bible refutes its counterparts.

13

Proverb

The proverb or aphorism (a concise, memorable statement) is a major biblical form. The Bible as a whole is the most aphoristic book ever written. The English poet Francis Thompson spoke about the Bible as "a treasury of *gnomic* wisdom. I mean its richness in utterances of which one could, as it were, chew the cud. This, of course, has long been recognised, and Biblical sentences have passed into the proverbial wisdom of our country."[1]

Wisdom literature is the name given to parts of the Bible that are made up wholly or largely of proverbs. The Old Testament books of Ecclesiastes and Proverbs are the indisputable examples. Much of the Book of Job is expressed in the form of aphorisms, and the Epistle of James is also strongly proverbial in its statements.

But we cannot limit the proverb as a biblical form to wisdom literature. Proverbs occur throughout the Bible. From the stories of the Bible have come proverbs about *being our brother's keeper* (Gen. 4:9), about working by *the sweat of your brow* (Gen. 3:19), and about how your *sin will find you out* (Num. 32:23). The other major repository of biblical

1. Quoted in *Literary Criticisms*, ed. Terence L. Connolly (New York: Dutton, 1948), p. 543.

prose, the New Testament epistles, have supplied even more proverbs, such as those about *the powers that be* (Rom. 13:1, KJV), about how *whatever a person sows, that he will also reap* (Gal. 6:7), and about *a labor of love* (1 Thess. 1:3).

The poetry of the Bible, whether in the lyric or prophetic parts, is continuously aphoristic: *thy word is a lamp to my feet / and a light to my path* (Ps. 119:105); *a little child shall lead them* (Isa. 11:6); *his mercies . . . are new every morning; / great is thy faithfulness* (Lam. 3:22–23). The sayings and discourses of Jesus are also essentially proverbial: *come to me, all who labor and are heavy laden, and I will give you rest* (Matt. 11:28); *render to Caesar the things that are Caesar's, and to God the things that are God's* (Mark 12:17).[2]

The proverb is obviously a major literary form of the Bible. We should therefore resist attempts to trivialize the form. I refer to condescending statements of the type that tell us that "proverbs are catchy little couplets designed to express practical truisms," or that "proverbs are worded to be memorable, not to be theoretically accurate."[3]

No form is more central to the teaching of the Bible than its proverbs. The aphoristic style is powerful and affective, a form that "not only represents insight but compels it."[4]

The Proverb as a Literary Form

Our understanding of proverbs and wisdom literature will be enhanced if we consider the nature of the individual proverb. Upon analysis, this brief form is governed by several leading principles.

Memorable Conciseness

A proverb is always a brief utterance. This is part of the key to its memorability. Even the first time we encounter a proverb we know that it is worthy of memory. Its very conciseness makes it striking and attention-getting. The proverb overcomes the cliché effect of ordinary discourse

2. Good sources on the proverbial nature of Jesus' sayings include Robert C. Tannehill, *The Sword of His Mouth: Forceful and Imaginative Language in Synoptic Sayings* (Philadelphia: Fortress, 1975), and the selections excerpted under "Proverb as a Literary Form" in *The New Testament in Literary Criticism*, ed. Leland Ryken, A Library of Literary Criticism (New York: Ungar, 1984), pp. 295–301.

3. R. C. Sproul, *Knowing Scripture* (Downers Grove: Inter-Varsity, 1977), p. 89; Gordon Fee and Douglas Stuart, *How to Read the Bible for All It's Worth* (Grand Rapids: Zondervan, 1982), p. 201.

4. Norman Perrin, *The New Testament: An Introduction* (New York: Harcourt Brace Jovanovich, 1974), p. 296.

by being more concentrated and more tightly packed. To create an aphorism requires a skill with words and syntax that most people lack. It is, in other words, a literary gift.

The aim of such verbal concentration is to make an insight permanent. In the words of a literary critic, "to epigrammatize an experience is to strip it down, to cut away irrelevance, to eliminate local, specific, and descriptive detail, to reduce it and fix it in its most permanent and stable aspect, to sew it up for eternity."[5]

Proverbs are moments of epiphany—high points of human insight. As the modern short-story writer James Joyce put it, they are moments when a spiritual or intellectual eye adjusts its vision of truth or human experience to an exact focus. A proverb captures the clearest and most affective moment and the point of greatest light.

Two Paradoxes About Proverbs

Proverbs are more complex than their surface simplicity might suggest. One of their paradoxes is that they are simultaneously simple and profound. Proverbs are short and easily grasped at a surface level. They simplify experience by focusing on a single aspect of it and omitting everything extraneous to the topic at hand.

But proverbs are also profound. For one thing, what they say usually touches on the most important issues of life. Their very seriousness of subject makes them profound. Then, too, they have a way of being universal and open-ended in their application, so that what looked like a simple idea keeps expanding in its significance and applicability to life. *He who loves money will not be satisfied with money,* the writer of Ecclesiastes tells us (5:10). What could be simpler than that? It is actually a double comment about money: the appetite for money grows by indulgence and is therefore insatiable, and material things do not satisfy permanently and at the deepest level. And as for the application of this truth, we never get to the end of it in our own lives and in our observations of others.

Another paradoxical quality of proverbs is that they are both specific and general, both particularized and universal. Proverbs are often filled with concrete images: *through sloth the roof sinks in, / and through indolence the house leaks* (Eccles. 10:18). But this proverb is not primarily about leaking roofs. It uses the particular image to capture a universal quality, namely, laziness of any type and in any area of life.

Poetic Form

Proverbs rely heavily on poetic techniques. Foremost are metaphor and

5. Barbara Herrnstein Smith, *Poetic Closure: A Study of How Poems End* (Chicago: University of Chicago Press, 1968), p. 208.

simile: *the tongue is a fire* (James 3:6); *the path of the righteous is like the light of dawn* (Prov. 4:18). Figurative statements like these require us to perform the kind of analysis that we do with poetry of any type. In the process, proverbs become a meditative form that requires us to ponder them.

In addition to using figurative language, biblical proverbs are often expressed in the form of parallelism:

> Trust in the LORD with all your heart,
>   and do not rely on your own insight. [Prov. 3:5]

Such parallelism is of course one of the things that make biblical proverbs so memorable. Particularly prominent in the lists of proverbs in the Old Testament Book of Proverbs is antithetic parallelism, which one literary critic calls "the very life blood of the proverb."[6] Here is an example:

> Hope deferred makes the heart sick,
>   but a desire fulfilled is a tree of life. [Prov. 13:12]

The Voice of Human Experience

Someone has rightly said that the wisdom teachers are the photographers of the Bible.[7] The one indisputable confirmation of a proverb is a long hard look at daily reality. In biblical cultures, there were three main classes of religious leaders—priests, prophets, and wise men. Jeremiah 18:18 refers to all three and ascribes a distinctive type of literature to each one: *law* for the priest, the *word* for the prophet, and *counsel* for the wise men. The first two have the stamp of being God's direct word to people, while wisdom literature comes to us as a person's word to fellow humans. The truth that a proverb conveys is truthfulness to life and to human experience.

The experiential richness of proverbs means that the environment where they really come to life is the everyday situation where they apply. Proverbs ordinarily lose a lot of their impact when they appear in a collection. They are most effective when we can take them to a situation in life. But of course we would not have them at our disposal if we did not have literary collections of them. The best way to teach or study biblical

6. Richard G. Moulton, *The Modern Reader's Bible* (New York: Macmillan, 1895), p. 1457.

7. Robert Short, *A Time to Be Born—A Time to Die* (New York: Harper and Row, 1973). A book of photographic commentary on the Book of Ecclesiastes, this is one of the first sources one should consult to gain an appreciation of biblical proverbs.

proverbs is to supply a context for each one from someone's actual experiences or from observations of what is going on in society and the world.

The proverb is part of the human urge for order. By using conciseness, simplicity combined with profundity, particularity merged with universality, poetry, and an appeal to human experience, makers of proverbs help to master the complexity of life and the elusiveness of truth. The writers accurately observe human experience, and by doing so help to explain it.

The Book of Proverbs

Individual proverbs, because of their brevity, represent literature at its most rudimentary. In the Book of Proverbs we can observe the evolution of the individual proverb into larger literary units. The first step is the proverb cluster—a series of individual proverbs on a common theme. Thus we find clusters about the king (25:2–7), the fool (26:1–12), the sluggard (26:13–16), and various social pests (26:17–28).

Various types of descriptive sketches represent a further stage of complexity. One is the portrait—of the drunkard (23:29–35), the sluggard or lazy person (26:13–16), and an evil society (30:11–14). Another form is the vignette (short sketch) on subjects ranging from the industrious ant (6:6–8) to good farming (27:23–27). The brief narrative is yet another form. In Proverbs we find brief stories of an adulterous woman seducing a young man (7:6–23) and Wisdom's preparation of a feast (9:1–6).

More complex yet is the collection of proverbs molded into a single literary work. The Book of Ecclesiastes and the first nine chapters of Proverbs are the biblical examples. They are unified at the levels of overriding structure, image patterns, characters, settings, and theme.

Proverbs 1–9

The unifying plot of Proverbs 1–9 is a prolonged conflict between two women, Wisdom and Folly. Within that battle we find a number of individual skirmishes that reach out to include a varied cast of characters, chiefly a father figure and his son, which in the context of ancient wisdom teaching are metaphoric for teacher and pupil. We also find conflicts at the level of theme, chiefly between good and evil and wisdom and folly. The presence of so much conflict naturally makes moral choice the unifying action in these chapters. Faced with competing values and lifestyles, the "son" (and by extension the reader) is repeatedly urged to choose one and reject the other.

The unifying topic of the work is wisdom. Various subordinate themes appear, including the origin of wisdom, the benefits or rewards of wisdom, the tragic results of rejecting wisdom for folly, the necessity to choose wisdom, and the characteristics and acts of wisdom.

We also find a unifying viewpoint and tone. The repeated addresses to *my son* give these chapters a single viewpoint. It is that of a narrator, an old person, an authority figure who has seen life and is qualified to explain its meaning to the young person whom he addresses. The wise man often speaks in the imperative as he gives instructions and advice. We find repeated formulas that in one way or another command the listener to be attentive. A typical example is this: "My son, do not forget my teaching, / but let your heart keep my commandments" (3:1). The effect is to instill in us the conviction that the narrator possesses urgently needed information.

Even the imagery of Proverbs 1–9 falls into unifying patterns. The master images are two personified abstractions named Wisdom and Folly, the son, jewels, the path or way, and sexual imagery.

In the midst of all this unity, the writer has incorporated a diversity of literary techniques and forms. In fact, the artistry of the author or compiler is seen as much in his ability to handle a variety of forms as it is in his achievement of unity. At the level of individual proverb, there is a welcome variety in the kinds of parallelism (in contrast to the monotonous drumbeat of antithetic parallelism that prevails in some later lists of proverbs). We also find examples of descriptive lyric, dramatic monologue (in which a single speaker addresses an implied audience), encomium, narrative, and dramatized scene. The writer seldom relies solely on the sentence proverb, usually managing to present a larger poetic unity.

The Structure of Proverbs 1–9

The following list shows the general flow of this unified piece of wisdom literature.

1. A prologue introducing the author, purpose, and theme of the work (1:1–7). A motto or superscription that rings the changes on the theme of wisdom.
2. A dramatic monologue in which the father advises his son to avoid getting gain by violence (1:8–19). The conventional wisdom formula of mingling commands with statements of motivation is introduced, as is the metaphor comparing the teacher to a father and the pupil to a son.
3. An oration in which Wisdom, stationed in the most conspicuous places of the city (which is where the teachers of wisdom did their teaching), warns against the neglect of wisdom (1:20–33).
4. A dramatic monologue in which the teacher urges his pupil to follow wisdom and describes the rewards of doing so (2:1–3:12).

The archetype of the path or way dominates chapter 2. With chapter 3 the mode shifts to the common wisdom formula of stating a command and immediately following it with a description of the reward for obeying the command.

5. An encomium in praise of the abstract quality of wisdom (3:13–20).
6. A dramatic monologue in which the father again commands his son to follow wisdom and describes the rewards that accompany such a life (3:21–4:27). The first nine verses of chapter 4 combine the common wisdom motifs of a summons to listen, motivation, admonition, and consequences of choosing wisdom. The next ten verses are a descriptive lyric that contrasts the ways of the righteous and the wicked.
7. A dramatic monologue that warns against unchastity and offers marriage as the God-given way of satisfying the sexual urge (chap. 5).
8. Miscellaneous instructions (6:1–19). Highlights include descriptions of the industrious ant (vv. 6–8) and the lazy person who sleeps in when the alarm clock rings (vv. 9–11).
9. A dramatic monologue in which the father warns against adultery (6:20–7:27). The temptation story in chapter 7 is the longest sustained story in Proverbs and comes alive as a result of the vivid descriptive detail.
10. An oration by Wisdom extolling the quality for which she is named (chap. 8). The entire speech is governed by the motifs of an encomium.
11. A narrative describing the rival feasts to which Wisdom and Folly invite people (chap. 9). A fitting conclusion to the work, summing up its main issues and leaving the reader with a choice.

Ecclesiastes

The Book of Ecclesiastes is one of the greatest masterpieces in all of literature and also one of the most misunderstood books in the Bible. Herman Melville called it "the truest of all books," while the American novelist Thomas Wolfe described it as "the highest flower of poetry, eloquence, and truth" and "the greatest single piece of writing I have known."[8] It is one of the few works in the Bible where the author states his theory of writing:

Besides being wise, the Preacher also taught the people knowledge, weighing and studying and arranging proverbs with great care. The Preacher sought to find pleasing words, and uprightly he wrote words of truth. [12:9–10]

8. Quoted in Short, p. ix.

This self-characterization is accurate: the writer of Ecclesiastes is a great organizer and stylist committed to the intellectual quest for truth.

The Double Theme of the Book

The Book of Ecclesiastes espouses the most basic theme of the Bible—that life lived by purely earthly or human values, without faith in God and supernatural values, is meaningless and futile. The key to this theme is the phrase *under the sun* (or its equivalent *under heaven*), which occurs thirty times in the book and denotes life lived by purely earthly standards. To be under the sun is to be earth-bound, cut off from supernatural values.

In developing this theme, the writer uses a common literary strategy. He demonstrates at length the inadequacy of any world view other than a God-centered one, and he combines with this demonstration a series of affirmations of an alternate world view. This means that individual passages must be accurately placed into either a negative or positive context. If we read every passage as being equally indicative of the writer's settled philosophic position, we are left with a meaningless collection of contradictory statements.

A valid interpretation of the book is one that adequately explains the contradictions between passages that declare life meaningless and those that extol life. Such an interpretation is not difficult: the book is structured on a dialectical principle in which opposites are contrasted to each other. There are "under the sun" passages and "above the sun" passages. The writer's negative pictures of life are the conclusions that emerge when life is lived only on an earthly plane. When the narrator voices despair over the futility of life under the sun, he is not affirming this as his final view of life. Throughout the work (and not just at the end, as some commentators wrongly claim) he offers exuberant pictures of the God-centered life.

Passages of negation and passages of affirmation follow each other in a predictable rhythm throughout the book. My tabulation ends up with fifteen negative passages, thirteen positive ones, and three mixed ones. The phrase *under the sun* or an equivalent occurs in twelve of the fifteen passages that are wholly negative in tone, but in only four of the thirteen positive sections. The positive passages, in turn, have something that is lacking in the negative ones—a conspicuous emphasis on the God-centered life and a divine perspective to earthly life. The structure and word patterns thus combine to produce the dialectical principle on which the whole book is based.

Why would the writer mingle the two instead of first giving the bad news and then the good news? His mingling of negative and positive is realistic and faithful to the mixed nature of human experience. The technique keeps the reader alert. It also creates the vigor of plot conflict for this collection of proverbs, as the writer lets the two viewpoints clash. The dialectical pattern of opposites is a strategy of highlighting: the glory of a God-centered life stands out all the more brightly for having been contrasted to its gloomy opposite.

Although the book is a collection of what I call mood pieces, it reads much like a story. The writer steps forward as our traveling companion on an archetypal *quest*. The narrative transitions keep alive the idea that the speaker is searching relentlessly: *again I saw, then I saw, so I turned to consider, I have also seen, I turned my mind to know and to search out and to seek*. The quest is not a physical journey but a journey of the mind and soul. It is the most crucial of all quests—the quest to find satisfaction in life. The negative passages describe the labyrinth of dead ends that writer ran into as he pursued his quest and sampled all the offerings of a godless life. The positive passages picture the goal at which he finally arrived, and the settled position from which he recalls his restless past.

The negative passages give the book its modern flavor. The element of protest is strong in these poems and reminds us continuously of modern protest literature. As the writer pursues his quest to find satisfaction, he samples all the things that people in our own culture seek—money, sex, work, material things, knowledge, hedonism, power. The Book of Ecclesiastes is a satire against the acquisitive and commercial spirit of modern life. But equally modern is the tendency of commentators to read right past the positive alternative that is embodied throughout the book.

The Negative Theme

It is time to explicate a few representative passages to show how all this is worked out in the text. As the narrator devotes separate sections to describing the various places he looked for satisfaction, he includes this account of his futile quest to find meaning in his work:

> I hated all my toil in which I had toiled under the sun, seeing that I must leave it to the man who will come after me; and who knows whether he will be a wise man or a fool? Yet he will be master of all for which I toiled and used my wisdom under the sun. This also is vanity. So I turned about and gave my heart up to despair over all the toil of my labors under the sun, because sometimes a man who has toiled with wisdom and knowledge and skill must leave all to be enjoyed by a man who did not toil for it. This also is vanity and a great evil. What has a man from all the toil and strain with which he toils beneath the sun? For all his days are full of pain, and his work is a vexation; even in the night his mind does not rest. This also is vanity. [2:18–23]

We should notice first how tightly unified the individual units of the book are. The framework of theme and variation is the best way to approach a passage like this. The quoted passage uses a word pattern of *toil* and *labor* to keep the focus on the experience of work.

The passage also illustrates the affective style of Ecclesiastes. The characteristic Hebrew way of conducting an argument is to repeat the main point so many times that we begin to feel its truth. In the quoted passage, we feel the utter impotency of work to give satisfaction in life. The four occurrences of the phrase *under the sun* (or *beneath the sun*) confirm my interpretation that the negative sections describe an attempt to find meaning solely within the earthly sphere, without any attention to a supernatural world and scale of values.

The Positive Theme

To illustrate the positive side of the argument, I offer this passage that appears immediately after the complaint about work:

> There is nothing better for a man than that he should eat and drink, and find enjoyment in his toil. This also, I saw, is from the hand of God; for apart from him who can eat or who can have enjoyment? For to the man who pleases him God gives wisdom and knowledge and joy. [2:24–26]

The first thing to note about this rapturously positive passage is where it appears. It appears already in the second chapter of the book, showing how wrong the prevalent interpretation is that the book offers a positive alternative only at the very end.

In place of the negative phrase *under the sun* (which does not appear here), we get an outpouring of phrases that paint a picture of the God-centered life: *from the hand of God, apart from him, God gives.* Whereas the negative passages deny the possibility of finding enjoyment, the God-centered passages constantly hold it out as a possibility. Ecclesiastes could not possibly have been penned by a nihilist. The author is full of zest for life. For him the great tragedy is a person's inability to find enjoyment in life.

Equally important is the fact that the writer finds enjoyment in the very areas of life (eating, drinking, working) where he had denied it in the passages that have preceded. The Book of Ecclesiastes is not escapist. It brings a supernatural perspective down into the earthly sphere instead of seeking to escape to another world.

Since it is the positive passages that usually get slighted, let me look briefly at another specimen. In the middle of a section dealing with the problem of time, the author gives us these variations on the theme "the right view of time":

> I have seen the business that God has given to the sons of men to be busy with. He has made everything beautiful in its time; also he has put eternity into man's mind . . . I know that there is nothing better for them than to

be happy and enjoy themselves as long as they live; also that it is God's gift
to man that every one should eat and drink and take pleasure in all his toil.
I know that whatever God does endures for ever; . . . God has made it so,
in order that men should fear before him. [3:10–14]

Again we notice the strongly theocentric perspective of the passage: *God
had given; he had made; it is God's gift; whatever God does; God has
made it so.* This is obviously an "above the sun" passage.

The supernatural perspective does not, however, substitute another
world for this one. We remain in the world of eating and drinking and
working. But that world is not enclosed as it is in the "under the sun"
passages. Instead of the stock phrase *under the sun* we find the key
assertion that God *has put eternity into man's mind.* Here is the antidote
to life under the sun, and it consists of the human capacity for transcendence—for something spiritual beyond the earthly sphere. Given this
supernatural perspective, the problem of time has a many-sided solution:
it is God's gift, it is part of God's beautiful order, it is the arena within
which people can enjoy earthly life, and the fact that its meaning does not
reside in itself, instead of being a frustration, means that people can find
ultimate meaning in God (*God has made it so, in order that men should
fear before him*).

The Outline of the Book

Space does not permit me to give a detailed reading of the entire book.
With the basic pattern of negative and positive units already illustrated, I
turn to a brief outline of the book.[9]

1. 1:1–3. Introduction to the narrator and theme (negative). The word
   translated *vanity* in English versions is a controlling image in the book,
   appearing more than thirty times. In the original it is a concrete image
   meaning "vapor" or "breath," with connotations of fleetingness and
   insubstantiality (which can be compared with later references to
   striving after wind).
2. 1:4–11. A descriptive lyric on the theme of the meaningless cycle of life
   under the sun (negative). The unifying theme is stated in verse 8: *all
   things are full of weariness.* Since life itself does not offer satisfaction,
   the protagonist is ready to undertake an active quest to find it.
3. 1:12–2:23. Four dead ends on the journey toward satisfaction in
   life, with the phrase *under the sun* sprinkled throughout the four
   units.

9. For commentary on the individual passages, I benefited particularly from Derek
Kidner, *The Message of Ecclesiastes* (Downers Grove: Inter-Varsity, 1976).

    a. 1:12–18. The futility of trying to find meaning in human wisdom (negative).

    b. 2:1–11. The futile quest to find satisfaction in pleasure and wealth (negative).

    c. 2:12–17. The inability to find meaning in permanent achievement that will survive death (negative). A protest against death.

    d. 2:18–23. Failure to find meaning in work (negative).

4. 2:24–3:22. The human quest satisfied.

    a. 2:24–26. Enjoyment of life as a gift from God (positive).

    b. 3:1–8. Time viewed from a human perspective as orderly (positive). Although the passage implies human limitation, it is not a passage of despair. Implicitly rejecting such perennial solutions to the problem of time as hedonism, fatalistic despair, and asceticism, this passage encourages acceptance and realistic optimism (realizing that time brings both good and bad).

    c. 3:9–22. Time viewed from God's perspective (positive). The assertion that God *has made everything beautiful in its time* (3:11) casts a retrospective positive light on the preceding poem on "a time for everything." The passage gives variations on the theme of how God controls time for his purposes. The overall intent is to encourage acceptance of time as the arena within which people can find meaning and enjoyment.

5. 4:1–8. Categories of social groupings (negative). The groups include the weak who are oppressed by the strong (4:1–3), the competitive, success-oriented person (v. 4), the dropout (v. 5), the golden mean between the two preceding extremes (v. 6), and the compulsive moneymaker (vv. 7–8). The section is an implied satire against the futile quest to find satisfaction in money.

6. 4:9–12. Human companionship (including marriage) as a solution to the misery of life (positive). Perhaps the *threefold cord* is God and the partners in marriage.

7. 4:13–16. The fickleness of fame (negative).

8. 5:1–7. Man as worshiper, an alternative to life under the sun (positive). Instead of a series of melancholy observations about the futility of life, we get a series of commands about the proper worship of God. One of the key assertions in the whole book appears in the statement that *God is in heaven, and you upon earth.* Here is the alternative to life under the sun.

9. 5:8–17. The futile quest to find satisfaction in wealth (negative). A satiric passage against the acquisitive urge for money: the futility of greed among public officials (vv. 8–9), the inability of money to satisfy (v. 10), the relative uselessness of money (v. 11), the anxieties that

attend wealth (v. 12), the self-destructiveness that money can bring (v.13), the fleetingness of money (v. 14), and the inability of wealth to survive one's death (vv. 15–17).

10. 5:18–20. The human quest satisfied (positive). A typical God-centered passage, with emphasis on the earthly enjoyment that is possible when life is lived with God at the center.

11. Chapter 6. A recap of life under the sun (negative). The ultimate tragedy for this writer is not being able to enjoy life. References to appetite not being satisfied (v. 7) and to the wandering of desire (v. 9) remind us that the voice of unsatisfied desire is strong in Ecclesiastes, in a manner similar to the odes of John Keats.

12. 7:1–8. The wisdom of seeing life as mainly tragic (negative). A series of eight comparative proverbs, adding up to a protest against any frivolous optimism about life.

13. 7:9–14. The wisdom of accepting life's adversity (positive). The person who has not placed ultimate allegiance in life under the sun has *the protection of wisdom* (v. 12) and is not destroyed by the tragedies of life. Prosperity and adversity are both under the control of God (v. 14).

14. 7:15–19. Two lifestyles contrasted.
   a. 7:15–17. Disillusionment with life (negative). An ethic of noninvolvement by which many people wrongly live.
   b. 7:18–19. The alternative to such an ethic—a zestful involvement with life based on wisdom (positive).

15. 7:20–29. The evil that people do apart from God (negative). The unifying theme is stated at the outset: *surely there is not a righteous man on earth who does good and never sins*. The rest of the passage then catalogues ways in which the assertion is true.

16. 8:1–9. How to live with authorities (in the Book of Ecclesiastes, the king). Positive, because although the passage ends with a rather pessimistic picture of the limitations under which people live, the bulk of the section contains positive advice for living successfully under those limitations.

17. 8:10–15. A strategy for coping with the injustices that prevail under the sun. A mixed passage: negative pictures of the injustices of life (vv. 10–11, 14) are balanced by a great venture in faith (vv. 12–13) and an endorsement of life as something to be enjoyed (v. 15).

18. 8:16–9:6. Two great protests. A negative passage in which the writer acknowledges the failure of human wisdom to find truth (8:16–17), as well as lamenting the finality of death (9:1–6).

19. 9:7–10. A command to enjoy earthly life (positive).

20. 9:11–18. The great antithesis, yet once more.
   a. 9:11–15. The fickleness of fortune and fame (negative).
   b. 9:16–18. Another venture in faith (positive).

21. Chapter 10. A miscellaneous catalogue of proverbs. A mixed passage

that repeats the dual theme of the whole book: the ways in which people manage to mess up under the sun, combined with a conviction that *wisdom helps one to succeed* (v. 10).

22. 11:1–8. Variations on the theme that one should approach life expectantly, knowing that not everything will succeed (positive). The unit progresses by pairs of verses in which earthly limitation is countered by the advice to be decisive even in the face of such limitation.

23. 11:9–12:8. A call for righteous and purposeful living in the time of one's youth, with the specter of old age serving as the background that lends urgency to the command. A mixed passage, since the extended portrait of old age dominates the passage and counterbalances the call for righteous living in our final impression.

24. 12:9–14. The conclusion, in which the writer explains his purpose in writing and restates the goal at which he arrived on his quest (positive).

One pattern that we might note is that in the later stages the positive and negative strands become more and more closely fused. Here is where the mixed sections appear. The positive affirmations are made in a context of realistic glances at life in the world. The effect is to insure that the affirmations are not facile; as in all great literature, the writer earns the right to affirm by doing justice to the negative side of life.

Although the book is structured as a series of lyric meditations or mood pieces, it need not remain fragmented in our minds. In addition to the dialectical structure of opposites and the progressive quest toward a goal, the imagery of the work unifies the whole. Repeated formulas include *vanity of vanities, this also is vanity, eat and drink,* and the ever-present *under the sun.* The imagery, moreover, is elemental, with references to sun and food, the cycles of nature, death and God.

Two Famous Lyrics

Two lyrics in the book are so famous that they deserve to be noted in detail. The most famous poem ever penned on the subject of time appears in the first eight verses of chapter 3:

> [1]For everything there is a season,
>   and a time for every matter under heaven:
> [2]a time to be born, and a time to die;
>   a time to plant, and a time to pluck up what is planted;
> [3]a time to kill, and a time to heal;
>   a time to break down, and a time to build up;

^{4}a time to weep, and a time to laugh;
     a time to mourn, and a time to dance;
^{5}a time to cast away stones, and a time to gather stones together;
     a time to embrace, and a time to refrain from embracing;
^{6}a time to seek, and a time to lose;
     a time to keep, and a time to cast away;
^{7}a time to rend, and a time to sew;
     a time to keep silence, and a time to speak;
^{8}a time to love, and a time to hate;
     a time for war, and a time for peace.

The theme is announced at the outset; the rest of the poem is a series of variations on the theme. The word *time* occurs twenty-nine times in eight verses. The eloquence of the passage is achieved by its strict parallelism, combined with antithesis.

There is no overall progression in the catalogue, but generally the two lines of a verse are parallel in subject matter. In verse 2, for example, being born and planting are similar to each other, and dying and plucking up what was planted belong together. In verse 5, I should also note, "casting stones" was an ancient euphemism for sexual intercourse and is parallel to the embrace of the next line; "gathering stones" means refraining from sexual intercourse. The pattern of pairing items in the same order is dropped just when it threatens the poem with monotony: in verse 7, the second line does not repeat the same topic as the first, while in verse 8 the order of the parallel items is reversed in the second line (an example of the rhetorical device known as chiasmus, or "crossing").

This poem on "a time for everything" illustrates the affective style and cumulative effect of Ecclesiastes. By the time we finish reading the poem, we feel that there is, indeed, a time for everything. Equally characteristic of the book is the author's way of surveying all aspects of life.

The portrait of old age near the end of the book (12:1–8) is equally moving. The genre of the piece is "the character," or character sketch. Here it is a composite picture of the physical symptoms of advancing age. It is a rule of literature that whenever the subject matter is painful or threatening, writers find ways of distancing it so we can contemplate it with some degree of detachment. In this portrait, the author uses a highly metaphoric style for his description of old age.

The passage begins with a generalized description of old age as a time of *evil days . . . when you will say, "I have no pleasure in them"* (v. 1). Then begins the physical description. Descriptions of how *the sun and the light and the moon and the stars are darkened* (v. 2) refer to weak eyesight (and perhaps also to a general oblivion to the flow of ordinary events). The *clouds* that *return after the rain* (v. 2) is a picture of tears from eyestrain (and perhaps also the more general phenomenon of a loss of resilience in rallying back after a crisis, so that it is like one storm after another).

The *keepers of the house* that *tremble* (v. 3) are shaking hands and arms, while the *strong men* that *are bent* (v. 3) depicts stooping shoulders. The loss of teeth is figuratively described as *grinders* that *cease because they are few* (v. 3), and weak eyes are pictured in the figure of *the windows* that *are dimmed* (v. 3). Weak hearing is evoked by *the doors on the street* that *are shut* (v. 4). Three successive details illustrate, respectively, the loss of appetite, of sleep, and of the ability to speak: *the sound of the grinding is low, and one rises up at the voice of a bird, and all the daughters of song are brought low* (v. 4).

Fear of high places and walking is pictured in the account of how *they are afraid also of what is high, and terrors are in the way* (v. 5). The picture of *the almond tree* that *blossoms* (v. 5) is a description of white hair, while the account of how *the grasshopper drags itself along* (v. 5) refers to loss of sprightliness in walking. The physical portrait is summarized in conceptual fashion by a concluding statement about how *desire fails* (v. 5).

After the failure of physical powers, death itself is pictured, again through concrete metaphors of cessation of activity and final dissolution (v. 6). The *silver cord* that *is snapped* is the cord from which a household lamp was suspended. The *golden bowl*, another household object, *is broken*. Two other domestic catastrophes complete the picture: *the pitcher is broken at the fountain* and *the wheel broken at the cistern*.

The whole portrait is unified by the submerged image patterns of storm, a disintegrating house, and household objects broken beyond repair. As Richard G. Moulton rightly comments, "The poetic beauty of the passage is marvellous" (p. 1645).

The Book of Ecclesiastes is a literary masterpiece. It is one of the most moving books in all of literature. It achieves its power by remaining close to human experience as we know it. It is the easiest book in the Bible to illustrate with photographs or slides (and the book by Robert Short is an invaluable model to follow). Instead of being a problem book, the Book of Ecclesiastes espouses basic biblical truth. In it we can find the voice of unsatisfied desire, but also the voice of the deepest human longings satisfied.

14

Satire

Satire is the exposure, through ridicule or rebuke, of human vice or folly. It becomes literary when the controlling purpose of attack is combined with a literary method such as story, description, or metaphor. Satire can appear in any literary genre (such as lyric, narrative, or drama) and can be either a minor part of a work or the main point of an entire work. Although satire usually has one main object of attack, satiric works often make a number of jabs in various directions, a feature that can be called "satiric ripples." It is a convention of satire that satirists feel free to exaggerate, overstate, and oversimplify to make their satiric point.

Satire is a subversive form. It assaults the deep structure of our thinking and aims to make us uncomfortable. It questions the status quo and unsettles people's tendency to think that their behavior is basically good. The satirist is a bearer of bad tidings.

The Ingredients of Satire

There are four main ingredients in satire. These are the things around which we can organize an analysis or discussion of a piece of satire.

The thing that makes a passage satiric is the presence of *an object of attack*. The attack might focus on a single thing, as when Jesus' parable of the Pharisee and the tax collector attacks the Pharisee's self-righteousness. When the subject is as broad as the wicked society that the prophet Amos attacks, the object of rebuke is many-sided. The object of attack might be something as universal as greed or pride, but it is more likely to be a historical particular. Satire is thus a predominantly topical form of literature, and to understand biblical satire frequently requires the help of historical scholarship to reconstruct the cultural situation that is the assumed frame of reference.

The second ingredient of satire is the *satiric vehicle*. This is the literary construct in which the attack is embodied. Story is perhaps the commonest satiric vehicle. When satirists do not tell a whole story, they still might give brief snatches of action or short descriptions of people in their typical behavior. The portrait technique is also common. Even briefer units can suffice: an individual metaphor, as when Amos calls the wealthy women of Jerusalem "cows of Bashan" (4:1), or a derogatory epithet, as when Jesus calls the Pharisees "blind guides" (Matt. 23:16), or an uncomplimentary simile, as when Jesus compares the Pharisees to whitewashed tombs (Matt. 23:27–28). Direct vituperation or attack is also common in biblical satire, with the "woe formula" heading the list of devices: "Woe to those who are at ease in Zion" (Amos 6:1).

The third ingredient in satire is *tone*. This is the satirist's attitude toward his subject. There are two main techniques in satire, and literary critics name them after two Roman satirists who practiced them. Horatian satire (named after Horace) is light, urbane, and subtle. It uses a low-pressure approach in influencing an audience toward a negative assessment of the thing being attacked. Juvenalian satire (named after Juvenal) is biting, bitter, and angry. One type of satire attempts to laugh vice out of existence, the other to lash it out of existence. Biblical satire tends to have a serious and angry tone.

Finally, satire always has a stated or implied *satiric norm*. This is the standard of virtue or normalcy by which the satirist criticizes the object of attack. Sometimes the satirist states the norm, as when Jesus accompanies his satiric parables with a saying that states an alternative to the behavior attacked in the parable. On other occasions, it is up to the audience to infer the standard by which the criticism has been conducted.

If this is what satire is, it is obvious that satire is pervasive throughout the Bible. The biggest repository is prophetic writing, where we encounter continuous attacks on the evils of the prophet's society. The second largest category belongs to Jesus—his discourses, his parables, and the dialogues in which he participates.

Satire can also be an ingredient in works that are not primarily satiric. In many of the stories of the Bible, for example, the bad behavior of people is exposed in a satiric manner. In the story of Jacob, the greedy aggressiveness of the protagonist is satirized. Some of the lyric poetry of the Bible is satiric. In the psalms of lament, for example, the poet paints satiric portraits of his enemies. Satire is also prominent in the proverbs of the Bible: "Like a gold ring in a swine's snout is a beautiful woman without discretion" (Prov. 11:22).

Jesus as Satirist

The sayings and discourses of Jesus are a good starting point for looking at biblical satire. In the narrative parts of the Gospels, Jesus often attacks the Pharisees in a satiric manner. In some of the discourses and parables, we find more literary examples of the satiric impulse.

The Parable of the Rich Fool

We know that the parable of the rich farmer who tore down his barns to build bigger ones (Luke 12:13–21) is a satire because it has an object of attack. That object of attack is not a historical particular but something universal—greed for material things and the state of soul that it engenders. The parable is a concise study in the psychology of covetousness.

The overall satiric vehicle is a fictional story about a farmer. Within this narrative framework, Jesus paints a portrait of the protagonist in terms of both his actions and his thoughts. The main action is an exercise in futility: the farmer channels all his energies into a building project that he never lives to enjoy. The story makes its satiric point with a surprise ending. More telling is the way in which Jesus makes the farmer lay bare his soul by means of an inner dialogue: *Soul, you have ample goods laid up for many years; take your ease, eat, drink, be merry* (v. 19). Here is the real object of attack: spiritual complacency and false earthly security.

The satiric norm appears in two forms, one within the story, the other in the aphorisms with which Jesus surrounds the parable. Within the story, God's judgment against the farmer is dramatized to show us the folly of the complacent and materialistic farmer: *Fool! This night your soul is required of you; and the things you have prepared, whose will they be?* (v. 20). In keeping with Jesus' typical practice, moreover, the parable is accompanied by sayings that also state the standard by which the farmer in the parable is blameworthy. One satiric norm is the principle that a person should *beware of all covetousness; for a man's life does not consist in the abundance of his possessions* (v. 15). This opening proverb is balanced by a concluding one in which Jesus states, *So is he who lays up treasure for himself, and is not rich toward God* (v. 21).

The satiric tone of the parable is Horatian. When God rebukes the farmer with the address *Fool!* it is obvious that the action of the farmer has been an example of laughable folly, in the mode of Old Testament wisdom literature. The very procedure of the farmer is ridiculous: why would anyone tear down existing barns instead of simply building additional ones?

The Parable of the Rich Man and Lazarus

The object of attack in the parable of the rich man and Lazarus (Luke 16:19–31) is twofold—unconcern for the poor and refusing to believe the revelation that God has given. The former motif governs the first half of the story, while the second motif concludes the story.

The main narrative strategy by which Jesus embodies this attack is a prolonged foil between two characters. One of them is the object of attack: in the unconcern of the rich man for the beggar at his gate, we see the immoral behavior that Jesus wishes to denigrate. With a few vivid brushstrokes, Jesus paints a stark contrast between luxury (with its *purple and fine linen*) and poverty (*a poor man . . . full of sores*). Although one of these two polarized characters is the object of attack, it would be wrong to conclude that Lazarus is the satiric norm. He simply provides the occasion for the rich man to make his moral choice.

With the central contrast thus established, the scene quickly shifts to the afterlife. The motif of reversal of fortune in the afterlife is an important part of the satire. By showing us God's judgment against the rich man, the story influences us to reject such behavior. Once the judgment has occurred, the request of the rich man that Abraham send messengers to warn his brothers leads to the further satiric point about the folly of not heeding the revelation that God has given.

The tone is serious. The norm is not contained within the parable but is something that we have no difficulty in supplying. With the negative behavior of the rich man so plainly attacked, we know that the positive message is moral compassion for the poor and taking God's revelation seriously.

The Parable of the Pharisee and the Tax Collector

To round out this sketch of the range of satiric strategies that appear in Jesus' parables, I have chosen another parable built around a pair of polarized characters, the parable of the Pharisee and the tax collector (Luke 18:9–14). This time the object of attack is not a general trait like greed or moral unconcern but a recognizable historical particular—the self-righteous behavior of the Pharisees.

Two character portraits—foils to each other—are the satiric vehicle. One of the characters is the object of satiric attack, and the other is the satiric norm (the standard of good behavior that we are intended to follow). Scene, gesture, and dramatized speech are the chief narrative devices, and they, too, are based on the technique of foil. The Pharisee, we infer, stood in a conspicuous place in the temple area to pray, while the tax collector was so ashamed of his sin that he stood *far off.* Instead of lifting his eyes to heaven (which we infer the Pharisee did), the tax collector *beat his breast.*

The content of the two prayers completes the contrast. The Pharisee prayed, not to God, but *with himself.* He rehearsed his own virtuous acts for his own benefit (vv. 11–12). By contrast, the tax collector realized his spiritual poverty and prayed a single brief prayer of confession: *God, be merciful to me a sinner* (v. 13). The theological issue around which the parable revolves is highlighted with Jesus' statement that the tax collector *went down to his house justified rather than the other* (v. 14).

The tone of the parable is serious and sharp in its implied denunciation of the Pharisee's self-righteousness. The aphorism with which Jesus concludes the parable hints at the satiric norm—the principle that is violated by the Pharisee: *every one who exalts himself will be humbled, but he who humbles himself will be exalted* (v. 14).

A Denunciation of the Pharisees

The satiric discourses of Jesus are epitomized by his denunciation of the Pharisees in Matthew 23. Satire falls naturally into two categories on the basis of its form. The satiric parables illustrate the formal tradition. They are skillfully crafted literary works, and the attack is subtly embodied in the literary form itself. The other type is the informal tradition. Here the satirist is the plain-spoken person who employs direct rebuke instead of giving a polished literary performance. The style is random and disjointed, the structure loose and fragmented.

The object of satiric attack throughout Matthew 23 is the gap between the Pharisees' doctrine and their practice, as Jesus makes clear at the outset: *The scribes and the Pharisees sit on Moses' seat; so practice and observe whatever they tell you, but not what they do; for they preach, but do not practice* (vv. 2–3). What follows is a very loosely structured series of attacks on the practices of the Pharisees. The result is a kaleidoscope of customary practices of the Pharisees, mingled with reminders of the satiric norm by which the Pharisees are being judged. The list of offenses includes religious ostentation (vv. 5–7), unbiblical distinctions regarding oaths (vv. 16–19), neglect of the important moral issues (vv. 23–24), hypocrisy (throughout the discourse), and hostility to God's prophets (vv. 29–36).

What are the resources of the plain-style satirist? One is the catalogue of abuses—an ever-expanding vision of vice. It is a feature of satire for the satirist to exhibit a kind of overflowing abundance of energy, which usually takes the rhetorical form of accumulation of examples. Direct rebuke or vituperation is another resource: *You traverse sea and land to make a single proselyte, and when he becomes a proselyte, you make him twice as much a child of hell as yourselves* (v. 15). Name-calling is a standard form of vituperation: *you blind men* (v. 19). Description and portraiture of what the satirist is attacking are also a standard technique: *They love the place of honor at feasts and the best seats in the synagogues* (v. 6).

Hyperbole and exaggeration are virtually synonymous with satire, as illustrated by Jesus' account of the Pharisees' *straining out a gnat and swallowing a camel* (v. 24). The "woe formula" is a hallmark of biblical satire: *woe to you, scribes and Pharisees, hypocrites!* (v. 13). Finally, metaphor and simile are standbys: *You are like whitewashed tombs, which outwardly appear beautiful, but within they are full of dead men's bones and all uncleanness* (v. 27).

The Book of Amos

The Old Testament Book of Amos is the major work of informal satire in the Bible. The satirist is the plain-spoken person of simple piety. He is not even a professional prophet but a shepherd (1:1; 7:14–15). He is fired by a spirit of religious outrage and uses invective, abuse, and direct attack to convey this bitter tone.

As is usually the case in informal satire, the object of attack is not human folly but religious, social, and political vice. Equally conventional is the way in which Amos champions the cause of a whole group (the socially oppressed), and the way in which he attacks social classes instead of individuals. He is especially concerned with the sins of greed, social injustice, luxury, and moral callousness, and particularly as these are practiced by those who profess to be models of righteousness. The focus is on public evils, not private foibles. Political and ecclesiastical satire are prominent.

The informal tone corresponds to the structure of the book. The book is not a single sustained flow. It is an encyclopedic collection of fragments, loosely structured and somewhat unliterary in development (except for the intricately patterned oracles against the nations that comprise the first major unit in the book).[1] The book contains such varied literary forms as the saying, narrative, predictive prophecy, vision, dialogue, doom song, dramatic monologue, lyric, and pronouncement of woe. In short, the book illustrates one literary critic's description of informal satire: "It is clear that satire never offers that direct, linear progression which is ordinarily taken as plot. Instead, we get collections of loosely related scenes and busyness

---

1. These oracles (1:3–2:8) follow a repeated rhetorical pattern with five ingredients: an opening formula (*thus says the Lord*); a balanced pair of clauses (*for three transgressions . . . and for four*); a set formula for judgment (*I will not revoke the punishment*); a statement of indictment; a list of judgments, beginning with the statement *So I will send a fire upon*. . . .

which curls back on itself. . . . Disjunctiveness and the absence of change" are the chief ingredients.[2] Like the medieval English poem *Piers Plowman*, the Book of Amos displays evidence of a lively literary imagination, not in its structure (which is random), but in the use of such devices as imagery, metaphor, simile, epithet, poetic parallelism, rhetorical questions, paradox, sarcasm, and parody.

Space does not allow a detailed explication of the book, but here is a specimen of the things I have been noting:

> They hate him who reproves in the gate,
>   and they abhor him who speaks the truth.
> Therefore because you trample upon the poor
>   and take from him exactions of wheat,
> you have built houses of hewn stone,
>   but you shall not dwell in them;
> you have planted pleasant vineyards,
>   but you shall not drink their wine.
> For I know how many are your transgressions,
>   and how great are your sins—
> you who afflict the righteous, who take a bribe,
>   and turn aside the needy in the gate.
> Therefore he who is prudent will keep silent in such a time;
>   for it is an evil time.
> Seek good, and not evil,
>   that you may live;
> and so the Lord, the God of hosts, will be with you,
>   as you have said.
> Hate evil, and love good,
>   and establish justice in the gate. [5:10–15a]

The first thing we notice is the many-sided portrait we get of an evil society—a society that rejects the truth, lives in luxury, engages in exploitation, and perpetuates a corrupt judicial system. The attack takes the form of not only naming these vices but also predicting a coming judgment against them. The positive norm (the antidote to these abuses) appears in the commands at the end of the passage.

The literary skill of Amos is best seen in the technique of parody in the book. Amos repeatedly evokes a common literary genre or formula, only to give us a shocking reversal of its ordinary meaning. This is a major weapon of subversion in this prophet's arsenal.

The arming of the hero is a moment of high drama in epic literature. Amos reverses the pattern:

> Flight shall perish from the swift,

2. Alvin Kernan, *The Plot of Satire* (New Haven: Yale University Press, 1965), p. 100.

> and the strong shall not retain his strength,
>   nor shall the mighty save his life;
> he who handles the bow shall not stand,
>   and he who is swift of foot shall not save himself,
>   nor shall he who rides the horse save his life;
> and he who is stout of heart among the mighty
>   shall flee away naked in that day. [2:14–16]

Or consider what happens to the familiar psalm of praise in the hands of Amos. Amos, too, catalogues the mighty acts of God in nature and history (4:6–13). This catalogue, however, lists not a series of blessings but a series of disasters that God sent in an effort to bring Israel back to himself.

Priestly exhortations to come and worship God in sacred places were a familiar part of Old Testament religion. Amos evokes the form with shocking effect: "Come to Bethel, and transgress; / to Gilgal, and multiply transgressions" (4:4). Another favorite sermon topic was the coming "day of the Lord," which complacent religionists liked to think would be the day on which God would destroy their enemies. Amos gives quite a different version of the day of the Lord:

> Woe to you who desire the day of the LORD!
>   Why would you have the day of the LORD?
> It is darkness, and not light;
>   as if a man fled from a lion,
>   and a bear met him;
> or went into the house and leaned with his hand against the wall,
>   and a serpent bit him.
> Is not the day of the LORD darkness, and not light,
>   and gloom with no brightness in it? [5:18–20]

Rescue stories are a perennial favorite, but who would consider the following to be a satisfactory rescue: "As the shepherd rescues from the mouth of the lion two legs, or a piece of an ear, so shall the people of Israel who dwell in Samaria be rescued, with the corner of a couch and part of a bed" (3:12).

Obituaries are written for dead persons, but Amos writes one for his nation when it shows no signs of being on the verge of collapse:

> Hear this word which I take up over you in lamentation, O house of Israel:
>   "Fallen, no more to rise,
>   is the virgin Israel;
>   forsaken on her land,
>   with none to raise her up." [5:1–2]

The effect is like reading one's own obituary in the newspaper.

The Book of Amos typifies a large biblical category of satiric prophecy. Prophetic writing is made up of two major genres—the oracle of salvation and the oracle of judgment. The latter is a short unit in which the prophet denounces the sins of a person or nation and predicts a coming judgment. The best literary format for making sense of these oracles of judgment is satire. They possess an object of attack, which is embodied in literary forms ranging from descriptive portraits to metaphors to statements of woe. There is a discernible tone to these oracles (usually biting), and there is a stated or implied norm (either the character of God or God's moral law).

The Book of Jonah

The greatest satiric masterpiece in the Bible is the Old Testament Book of Jonah. In contrast to the Book of Amos, the Book of Jonah belongs to the formal tradition of satire. The satirist is not the plain-spoken person who is unable to disguise his anger in the name of politeness. Instead he is completely submerged in the story itself. The attack is skillfully embodied in a well-told story.

The object of attack is the kind of nationalistic zeal that made God the exclusive property of Israel and refused to accept the universality of God's grace. This attitude is embodied in the protagonist of the story, the reluctant prophet Jonah. The dual theme that emerges from the satire is that God is a God of universal mercy and that bigotry or ethnocentrism is sin.

The satirist uses narrative as the satiric vehicle. The setting of the story encompasses both elemental nature (the sea, the belly of a fish, a tree on a hillside) and the sprawling metropolis of Nineveh. The simplicity of the plot is striking: in four successive chapters we read about Jonah's flight, Jonah's rescue, Jonah's sermon, and Jonah's rejection of God's mercy. Plot conflicts pit Jonah against God, against his physical environment, and against the obligations of his prophetic office.

The story has two main characters. Jonah embodies the attitudes that are held up to ridicule in the satire. God functions in the story as the satiric norm who exposes what is wrong with Jonah's attitude. Jonah is a static character. Events that should produce change in his life fail to do so. Jonah only becomes hardened in his ill-tempered bigotry and nationalism. The scope of God's saving love serves as a foil to Jonah's hatred of everything non-Jewish.

The satiric tone is light rather than biting. Jonah is held up to scorn by being rendered ridiculous. He is the small-time operator with big ideas who thinks he can run away from God. He is a laughable figure who pouts like a child when he fails to get his sadistic way.

Three motifs unify the book. One is the characterization of the two principal characters. On one side we have the motif of the surly prophet; on the other, the pattern of God's universal mercy. The second point of unity is the sequence of four chapters, devoted to Jonah's flight, rescue, sermon, and rejection of God's grace. A final pattern is the giantesque motif—the pattern of the unexpectedly large or the extravagantly unlikely occurrence.

Jonah's Flight from God

My commentary on the details of the story will be necessarily brief.[3] The story of Jonah's flight is based on an ironic impossibility: no one can run away from God, as the poet of Psalm 139 expressed in memorable terms (vv. 7–12). Even the prophet's name is ironic: *Jonah* means "dove," symbol of hope and peace, which are the farthest things from Jonah's mind. Almost everything that Jonah does in the opening chapter is ignominious, from his attempt to run away from the obligations of his prophetic office to speak God's word, to his sleeping while the ship is endangered, to the self-incriminating answer he gives to the sailors' questions (vv. 8–9), to his being cast into the sea as a guilty sinner while the erstwhile pagan sailors are converted (vv. 15–16). The story is an anti-quest, appropriate for the anti-hero around whom it is built.

Intensifying the irony is the fact that in the very act of denying his prophetic office Jonah continues to talk the language of religious ortho-doxy. His statement that *I fear the LORD, the God of heaven, who made the sea and the dry land* (v. 9) is a theological cliché in the Bible—a stock way of identifying God (for parallels, see Ps. 121:2; 146:6; Exod. 20:11; Neh. 9:6; Acts 14:15). As Edwin M. Good comments, "Jonah's theology is unexceptionable, but, like so much theology, it seems to make no dif-ference to his action. We are certainly intended to perceive the incongruity between the prophet's confession of [God] as creator of the sea and his attempt to escape on the sea" (p. 45).

Jonah's Rescue

Jonah's lyric prayer from the belly of the fish (chap. 2) belongs to a familiar Old Testament type, the psalm of praise. It celebrates deliverance from watery death. Written in the conventional verse form of parallelism, the poem would fit in the Book of Psalms.

When we turn from description to interpretation, several conclusions emerge. This prayer shows Jonah in a repentant frame of mind and is the

---

3. The best literary commentary I have encountered on the Book of Jonah is Edwin M. Good's discussion in *Irony in the Old Testament* (Philadelphia: Westminster, 1965), pp. 39–55.

most favorable light in which we see him. Having conceded this, I must add that it is not hard to fit this implicit idealization of the protagonist into the overall satiric design of the book. By making Jonah such a miraculous recipient of God's mercy, this poem serves to render inexcusable and repulsive Jonah's later rejection of God's salvation when it is extended to others. The poem expresses an insight into God's redemptive nature that serves as a standard by which we judge Jonah's later attitude. Nor should we overlook the temporary nature of Jonah's repentance. He repudiates God until it becomes personally feasible to submit to God.

Jonah's Sermon

The first three verses of chapter 3 echo the language of the opening of the story, concluding the cycle of futility that Jonah has enacted. The dominant motif in the account of Jonah's sermon is the giantesque motif. The city and by extension the task are amplified when we read that *Nineveh was an exceedingly great city, three days' journey in breadth* (v. 3). This is either satiric exaggeration or (more likely) a reference to the entire city-state (the city and surrounding district). In either case, we can agree with Good's interpretation of why the author chose this strategy of amplification: "In the author's mind, Nineveh is not a quantity but a quality, not a mere metropolis but an immorality. He takes the symbol of the ancient world's most impressive evil, magnifies and intensifies it by mass, and sends his timorous prophet into the middle of it" (p. 48).

Not only is the task amplified; so is the evidence of God's grace. Jonah preaches an eight-word sermon (*Yet forty days, and Nineveh shall be overthrown*) that leads to the repentance of the most evil city of its time. To highlight the unexpected success of the prophet, we read that even the animals fasted and were covered with the symbolic sackcloth (vv. 7–8).

Jonah's Rejection of God's Grace

The final chapter of the book brings the leading concerns of the story to completion. The first is the satiric characterization of Jonah. As we stand at the threshold of the last chapter, it is obvious that the story could take two directions: it might become a conversion story in which the prophet reforms his attitude, or it might reinforce the satire that dominated the opening chapter. When the ill-tempered Jonah rejects God's mercy, the satiric design of the work is confirmed.

Jonah's problem is not theological. In fact, his theology is impeccable: *I knew that thou art a gracious God and merciful, slow to anger, and abounding in steadfast love, and repentest of evil* (v. 2). This is a theological formula that occurs in nearly verbatim form six other times in the Old Testament (Exod. 34:6; Ps. 86:15; 103:8; 145:8; Joel 2:13; Neh. 9:17). In the words of Good, "Jonah is mouthing—not for the first time—

a liturgical cliche, a rote theology . . . . He speaks the pious and well-worn words, but he thoroughly disapproves of their being true" (p. 50).

A second narrative concern brought to its conclusion in the closing chapter is the characterization of God. The book ends, in fact, with the focus on the satiric norm, the compassion of God:

> "And should not I pity Nineveh, that great city, in which there are more than
> a hundred and twenty thousand persons who do not know their right hand
> from their left, and also much cattle?" [4:11]

Finally, the giantesque motif makes its final appearance. Balancing the earlier miraculous fish is a miraculous plant that grows up overnight. It is intended to teach the prophet the illogic of his anger over the salvation of the city of Nineveh, but it only turns Jonah into a rancorous pouter. Here at the end Jonah becomes the archetypal refuser of festivities and the incorrigibly cantankerous person.

The Book of Jonah epitomizes the satire in the Bible. It is a subversive work that challenges the human tendency to rest content with its prejudices. It is built around a discernible object of attack and a satiric norm consisting of the character of God. This satiric purpose is embodied in a skillfully told story notable for an economy of words in which every detail counts.

15

Drama

No book in the Bible was written for the stage. Yet the dramatic impulse permeates the Bible. Everywhere we turn we find an abundance of quoted speeches, snatches of dialogue, stationing of characters in a setting, and gestures by characters. It is even easy to imagine the inflection of characters' voices as we read the stories of the Bible. The biblical imagination is strongly dramatic.

This is most evident in the narrative parts of the Bible. Again and again we find stage directions written into the text. The following specimen is typical of what we find throughout biblical narrative:

> And the LORD appeared to [Abraham] by the oaks of Mamre, as he sat at the door of his tent in the heat of the day. He lifted up his eyes and looked, and behold, three men stood in front of him. When he saw them, he ran from the tent door to meet them, and bowed himself to the earth, and said, "My lord, if I have found favor in your sight, do not pass by your servant. . . ." So they said, "Do as you have said." [Gen. 18:1–5]

Such dramas in miniature are common in the stories of the Bible.

The dramatic impulse is also strong in the poetry of the Bible. The Psalms are filled with apostrophes in which the poet suddenly begins to address someone or something: "Depart from me, all you workers of evil"

(Ps. 6:8); "Why are you cast down, O my soul?" (Ps. 42:5). The same impulse to address an implied audience is common in the prophetic books, where either God or his prophets accost people in dramatic fashion: "Hear this word, you cows of Bashan" (Amos 4:1). In similar manner, the New Testament epistles are cast into a form that assumes an assembled audience: "Brethren, do not be children in your thinking" (1 Cor. 14:20). And the Book of Revelation is so filled with heavenly scenes and dialogues that it has frequently been viewed as a drama, probably influenced by the author's knowledge of Greek drama.

The Bible is from start to finish a dramatic book. One book comes close to being a staged drama—the Book of Job.

Literary Elements in the Book of Job

The Book of Job has been extravagantly praised for its literary qualities, but there are several reasons why it is a rather closed book to most modern readers. We have been told much about the theological and philosophical weightiness of the book, but there are so many speeches and sentiments expressed that we despair of keeping track of the arguments. Knowing that the book is a story, we read it with the usual narrative interest in finding out what happens next, but there is so little action and so much leisurely repetition that we are constantly frustrated.

Three things can make the Book of Job an enjoyable reading experience, all them related to the dramatic nature of the book. The first step toward salvaging the book is a welcome awareness that the argument is not intricate and detailed. We need not agonize over following the ideas that are presented. The debate repeats a few common ideas. The real focus is character conflict. The story is much less a philosophic discussion than an argument—the friends against Job and Job against his comforters and against God. The dynamics of dialogue and character conflict should absorb our interest. We should listen for the voices of people who are angry with each other, not the voices of philosophic argumentation. The work more closely resembles what happens on the stage of a theater than what happens in a philosophy or theology class.

Until the modern era, most drama was written in poetic form, and so is the Book of Job. A second avenue to the enjoyment of the book is therefore a relish for the artistry of Hebrew poetry. If we read the book as story, looking for a fast-moving plot, we will be endlessly frustrated. We need to respect the leisurely pace of Hebrew poetry. This means being receptive to the poetic effects of figurative language, the skillful way of stating the same truth at least twice in different ways, and striking imagery.

A third aspect of the book considered as a drama is its irony.[1] There are two major ironies. The so-called friends of Job demonstrate the irony of orthodoxy. They spout the received wisdom of Old Testament religion. They could adduce many biblical parallels for their sentiments, as indicated by the large number of marginal cross-references that modern study Bibles show. Their statements fall into the familiar formulas and rhetorical techniques of Old Testament wisdom literature, showing that they not only have the right doctrine but also can express it in the right clichés.

The irony of their orthodoxy is that it happens not to apply to the situation of Job. The friends' "wisdom" consists of a few favorite sermon topics: sinners bring suffering on themselves; God will punish sinners for their wrongdoing; if Job will repent, God will restore him. In uttering these platitudes, the friends speak theoretic truth. In general, these things are true. But as we know from the prologue, Job is not being punished for any misdeed. Given this discrepancy, virtually everything the friends say is enveloped in irony.

But once we get beyond the prologue, the speeches of Job are also filled with irony—the irony of rebellion against God. Based on what we know from the prologue, we know that God is not inflicting the suffering on Job in sadistic delight. Yet Job will make this and other wild charges against God in his early speeches. This explains why God rebukes Job at the end of the story, and why Job repents.

In sum, the Book of Job is a drama—a "closet drama" intended to be read rather than acted, as even the length of the speeches suggests. Instead of looking for a sustained philosophic argument or the excitement of a fast-moving plot, we should look for characters in conflict, oratorical outbursts as characters lose control of their emotions, and leisurely poetic embellishment of virtually everything that is said.

Unifying Frameworks in the Book of Job

A main obstacle to the reading of the Book of Job is the tendency of a work this long to break down into a confusing collage of unrelated fragments. To guard against this happening, we need to keep the overriding framework in our minds as we read.

One element of unity is the overall story of Job. It possesses the usual beginning-middle-end shapeliness that we expect of a plot, as well as the conventional unity, coherence, and emphasis. There is even a moment of epiphany where we expect it—near the end of the story. By the literary

---

1. A good source on the irony of the Book of Job is Edwin M. Good, *Irony in the Old Testament* (Philadelphia: Westminster, 1965), pp. 196–240.

criterion of plot wholeness, we can see at once that the prose prologue and prose epilogue are integral to the work, not extraneous additions.

A second organizing framework for the book is the symmetrical arrangement of the speeches. The main principle of organization is three cycles of speeches in which the speakers follow each other in the same order each time. This arrangement is not only orderly but also highly artistic, as the outline of the book in figure 3 demonstrates.

A third unifying framework revolves around patterns of irony already mentioned. At any point in the book, we will benefit from knowing that the orthodox sentiments of the friends and the rebellion of Job against God are wide of the mark.

Fourthly, the obtuseness or wrong-headedness of the friends is a static background that persists throughout the drama and helps to unify our impression. Their lack of insight actually *elicits* Job's growing perception. The more they repeat their favorite sermon topics of God's justice and Job's sin, the farther they push Job on his quest to understand the meaning of his suffering.

The spiritual and intellectual progress of Job is another big unifying factor in the work. Following the prologue, we observe how far Job is from perception. The story as a whole is thus structured as a *quest* for understanding and union with God. Combined with this is the fact that the story is structured as a *test* that Job gradually passes. Job's growth in understanding is not a steady progress, but in each cycle of speeches his ebb and flow of understanding occurs at a progressively higher level, and in the battle between faith and despair the balance gradually changes.

Figure 3   **The outline of the Book of Job**

Prologue (chaps. 1–2)
Dialogue or debate (3–31)
   Job's lament (3)

Cycle 1 (4–14)	Cycle 2 (15–21)	Cycle 3 (22–27)
Eliphaz (4–5)	Eliphaz (15)	Eliphaz (22)
Job's reply (6–7)	Job's reply (16–17)	Job's reply (23–24)
Bildad (8)	Bildad (18)	Bildad (25)
Job's reply (9–10)	Job's reply (19)	Job's reply (26–27)
Zophar (11)	Zophar (20)	– – – – – – –
Job's reply (12–14)	Job's reply (21)	– –.– – – – –

   Job's concluding monologue (28–31)
Elihu's speeches (32–37)
Confrontation between God and Job (38–42:6)
Epilogue (42:7–17)

Finally, the ideas around which the drama is built help to unify it. The Book of Job is like the modern "problem play" in which a philosophic or social problem is posed and then various characters offer their solutions. At the end a definitive answer is established. The main problem around which the Book of Job revolves is why the righteous suffer. A secondary question is whether disinterested religion is possible. That is, can a person remain faithful in allegiance to God without any guarantees of personal benefit as a reward? A third question that therefore lurks in the background throughout the story is, What is God like? If we keep these questions in mind as we read, we will find that the individual units are continuously tied to a unifying frame of reference.

The Prologue

The prologue (Job 1–2) is essential to the ironic strategy of the book. It establishes the givens of the narrative world of this story. The irony stems from the fact that only we as readers know about what has transpired in heaven, while the characters in the story make their statements in ignorance of it. We thus measure their ignorance against our superior fund of information. What, then, do we learn from the prologue?

We learn first about the complete innocence of Job. He is a "blameless and upright man, one who fear[ed] God, and turn[ed] away from evil" (1:1, 8; 2:3). We see this innocence in action when we read about how Job sacrificed on behalf of his children "continually" (1:5) and when we observe Job's ideal patience in his initial suffering (1:22; 2:10). We can see with our eyes that Job is not guilty of sin, though the friends will assume that he is. The prologue thus highlights the specific problem posed in the drama, namely, why do *the righteous* suffer? The premise on which the testing of Job is based is that it is "without cause" (2:3).

A second thing that we learn in the prologue is that God is allowing but not causing the suffering of Job. The cause of Job's suffering—the one who inflicts it on him—is Satan (1:10–12; 2:4–6). Nor has God relinquished his providential control over Job's life: in the first testing Satan is prevented from touching Job himself (1:12), while in the second he may not take Job's life (2:6). Of course, Job operates in ignorance of all this, and there is a resulting irony when he starts accusing God of being the one who inflicts misfortune on him.

The prologue thus shows, thirdly, that Job's suffering is designed as a test of his faith, not as a punishment for sin. Against this we will be able to measure the irony of both orthodoxy and rebellion. The friends will assert incorrectly that Job is being punished for his sins, while Job, although he passes the test in the two scenes of suffering described in the prologue, will shortly channel his emotional energies into anger instead of faith.

In terms of narrative vividness, the prologue is one of the great stories of literature. In a memorable scene, Job's domestic world disintegrates (1:13–19). The scene unfolds visually and is a drama in miniature. It has four phases, like four hammer blows, as each of four messengers appears to describe an episode of woe. Job's response is to place his adversity in a supernatural context, even though he does not know all that has taken place in heaven: "Naked I came from my mother's womb, and naked shall I return; the LORD gave, and the LORD has taken away; blessed be the name of the LORD" (1:21).

The main structural principle of the prologue is twofold repetition. Chapter 2 thus reenacts the pattern of the first chapter, as the misfortune is this time directed against Job personally instead of against his children. To highlight Job's ideal patience, his wife enters the action as a foil. She advises her husband to "curse God, and die" (2:9), advice which reminds us that the penalty for cursing God was death (Lev. 24:10–16). Job, however, "did not sin with his lips" (2:10), though this will certainly not be true in the ensuing action.

The drama of the opening reaches its climax when the friends arrive. Here, indeed, is a spectacle of exceptional suffering in the manner of literary tragedy. When the friends approached Job, "they did not recognize him; and they raised their voices and wept. . . . And they sat with him on the ground seven days and seven nights, and no one spoke a word to him, for they saw that his suffering was very great" (2:12–13).

Thus ends the prologue of the drama. A memorable scene in itself, it also raises the chief premises of the story that follows. They include the total innocence of the protagonist before his suffering begins, the permissive theory of evil (God permits but does not cause human suffering), and our awareness that the problem of human suffering cannot be completely understood on a purely earthly or human level but requires a supernatural context for its explanation.

Job's Complaint

Job's complaint or lament (chap. 3) is the first development after the prologue. It is a speech of complete despair, as Job utters a formal curse against the day of his birth. This is a very different Job from the person who in the prologue "did not sin or charge God with wrong" (1:22) and who did not "sin with his lips" (2:10). The irony of the monologue is that we know from the prologue that God did not consent to Job's suffering for the purpose of sending Job into this type of despair. Another irony is that Job asks for the one thing (death) that we know from the prologue will be denied to him.

Job's opening monologue also establishes the quest motif in the story by showing us the things that Job needs to discover. One of these is simply the cause and purpose of his suffering. The other is the need for understanding about the supernatural world, especially the world of the afterlife. Here at the outset Job's view of the afterlife is a negative picture of oblivious inactivity, much as Homer portrays it in the *Odyssey*: "There the wicked cease from troubling, / and there the weary are at rest" (3:17). From this picture of gloomy nonexistence Job will progress to visions of God in heaven and resurrection from the dead.

The First Cycle of Speeches

My commentary on the cycles of speeches will necessarily be brief, and I will be content with very selective illustrations of representative passages. On the side of the friends, the key thing to notice is the irony of their orthodox sentiments. Those sentiments revolve around the ideas that suffering is punitive, that God is just and Job guilty of sin, and that suffering can be redemptive in Job's life if he will only repent. Out of many expressions of these ideas, I offer these lines by Eliphaz as a summary statement:

> "Think now, who that was innocent ever perished?
>   Or where were the upright cut off?
> As I have seen, those who plow iniquity
>   and sow trouble reap the same.
> By the breath of God they perish." [4:7–9]

As Job replies in turn to each of the three friends, the dominant strain is his rebellion and accusations against God. Job ironically charges God with causing his suffering and with taking a sadistic pleasure in it:

> "For he crushes me with a tempest,
>   and multiplies my wounds without cause. . . .
> When disaster brings sudden death,
>   he mocks at the calamity of the innocent." [9:17, 23]

When Job catalogues the mighty acts of God (12:13–23), the acts are all acts of calamity, a parody of the psalms of praise and a bitter man's creed praising a sadistic God. As he enumerates his charges against God, Job introduces the informing metaphor of the whole book, that of the trial: "For he is not a man, as I am, that I might answer him, that we should come to trial together" (9:32).

Another motif that is picked up from the earlier monologue is the need for Job's growth in understanding. "Teach me, and I will be silent," Job says (6:24), unwittingly foreshadowing the whole plot of the story. "Lo, he passes by me, and I see him not," Job complains (9:11), but at the end Job *will* see God. "Let me know why thou dost contend against me," Job requests (10:2), and we are reminded that he has in fact embarked on a quest to learn why. We sense also that Job is at the very beginning of his quest to know the truth about the afterlife; at this point it remains "the land of gloom and chaos, / where light is as darkness" (10:22).

In keeping with my earlier claim that the book is governed more by the drama of character clashes than by philosophic argument, we should also note the drama of increasing hostility between Job and his counselors. It comes out chiefly in the lead-ins to the speeches of the debate. Name-calling is one of the strategies of insult. Bildad calls Job a windbag: "How long will . . . the words of your mouth be a great wind?"(8:2). Zophar is equally insulting: "Should your babble silence men?" (11:3). In one of the masterpieces of sarcasm in the whole Bible, Job exclaims about his "comforters," "No doubt you are the people, / and wisdom will die with you" (12:1).

A number of points are covered in the opening cycle of speeches, but basically the issues have been narrowed to the two questions of Job's guilt or innocence and God's justice or injustice. The friends maintain that Job is guilty and God just. Job asserts that he is innocent and God unjust. Neither side is correct. The irony of orthodoxy and of rebellion have both been exposed.

The Second Cycle of Speeches

A curiously modern example of failure in communication overshadows the second cycle of speeches. In the first cycle Job repeatedly asserted his innocence and integrity. As far as he is concerned, that point has been established. Job's friends give no evidence of having heard what Job has said about his innocence. They continue to *assume* Job's guilt and thereby completely miss the problem to which the Book of Job calls such significant attention, namely, why do *the righteous* suffer? The friends become increasingly pitiless in their attacks on Job as they stubbornly cling to their misunderstanding.

Job, however, makes significant progress on his quest to understand the meaning of his suffering. He continues to assert his own innocence, but he expresses new insights into the character of God. Despair and faith wage an even battle within Job during the second cycle of speeches.

On the negative side, Job continues to make wild accusations against God:

> "He has torn me in his wrath, and hated me;
>   he has gnashed his teeth at me. . . .
> He slashes open my kidneys, and does not spare;
>   . . . he runs upon me like a warrior." [16:9, 13–14]

But balancing these accusations are statements of confidence in God's integrity: "Even now, behold, my witness is in heaven, / and he that vouches for me is on high" (16:19). Even more impressive is Job's "supreme venture in faith," as one commentator calls it:[2]

> "Oh that my words were written!
>   Oh that they were inscribed in a book!
> Oh that with an iron pen and lead
>   they were graven in the rock for ever!
> For I know that my Redeemer lives,
>   and at last he will stand upon the earth;
> and after my skin has been thus destroyed,
>   then from my flesh I shall see God,
> whom I shall see on my side,
>   and my eyes shall behold." [19:23–27]

Job does not have all the details, but he has attained a blessed hope. And in contrast to the friends, Job decisively dissociates suffering from sin in chapter 21.

Toward the Whirlwind

By now we sense that it is futile to expect any intellectual progress from Job's friends. Throughout the third cycle of speeches, they repeat their repertoire of orthodox ideas about God's justice and human sinfulness. Although some commentators believe that the youthful Elihu advances the argument into more positive realms (chaps. 32–37), I cannot see that he does. Instead he reenacts in an inverse way the Hebrew literary pattern of three-plus-one: we expect the fourth speaker to add something new, but he fails to do so. He is even more abrasive and arrogant than the three friends, but after the smoke has cleared, we are back where the three friends had started.

Job, however, continues to make spiritual and intellectual progress. In the third cycle of speeches he is still capable of holding his early attitude

2. Edgar Jones, *The Triumph of Job* (Naperville, Ill.: Allenson, 1966), p. 89. I found this commentary particularly helpful in working my way through Job.

toward God: "the soul of the wounded cries for help; / yet God pays no attention to their prayer" (24:12). On the other side, we find a statement of faith like this:

> "Oh, that I knew where I might find him,
>   that I might come even to his seat! . . .
> I would learn what he would answer,
>   and understand what he would say to me.
> Would he contend with me in the greatness of his power?
>   No; he would give heed to me.
> There an upright man could reason with him,
>   and I should be acquitted for ever by my judge." [23:3–7]

Such progress continues in Job's monologue that follows the third cycle of speeches (chaps. 28–31). It begins with the lyric poem about wisdom (chap. 28). The poem unfolds in three movements: the ability of people to find "every precious thing" hidden in the earth (vv. 1–11), the inability of people, however, to find wisdom (vv. 12–22), and an assertion that "God understands the way to it," combined with the logical conclusion that "the fear of the Lord, that is wisdom" (vv. 23–28). In the context of Job's intellectual progress, this famous poem about wisdom shows a new appreciation for transcendence, as opposed to the human knowledge that was Job's earlier basis for entering into argument with God. Job's great oath of innocence (chap. 31) is a highly oratorical speech in which Job asserts his ethical integrity in the areas of sexual purity (vv. 1, 9–10), honest dealing (v. 7), treatment of servants (v. 13), benevolence to the poor (vv. 16–23), use of money (vv. 24–25), idolatry (vv. 26–28), attitude toward enemies (vv. 29–30), hospitality (vv. 31–32), and confession of sins (vv. 33–34).

The Voice from the Whirlwind

The climax of the drama comes when the silent God finally speaks to Job from the whirlwind (Job 38–42:6). The content of the two speeches focuses on the deity of God. The first speech (chaps. 38–39) is a catalogue of scientific questions about the natural creation. Their effect is to demonstrate the superior knowledge of God. The second speech (chaps. 39–40) paints graphic pictures of Behemoth (perhaps a hippopotamus) and Leviathan (a crocodile embellished by the poetic imagination). It chiefly dramatizes God's ability to "do all things" (42:2).

Irony pervades the speeches. After Job has repeatedly called God to account, God now reverses the situation: "I will question you, and you shall declare to me," he says to Job (38:3). Even more surprising is the fact that God does not mention the chief subject of the drama as a whole, the suffering of Job. On the surface, the speeches are a sublime irrelevance and a great non sequitur. There are several effects. One is that we are made to feel that God is superior to people. Another effect is that if Job cannot answer these questions of relative insignificance, he cannot possibly resolve an ultimate philosophic mystery like the problem of evil.

The speeches of God are not as negative as they have often been interpreted as being. They do, of course, show God's transcendence over his creation. But paradoxically they also show his immanence—his closeness to his creatures. God's care extends to objects of nature about which Job does not even think. The import is like that of Jesus' "how much more" statements in the Gospels: if God's providence extends to the relatively insignificant world of nature, will God not much more care for his human creature?

There is an element of rebuke in the speeches of God, as the lead-ins make clear. "Who is this that darkens counsel by words without knowledge?" God asks Job in rebuke of Job's earlier charges (38:1). Job later quotes this very question by God and admits, "I have uttered what I did not understand" (42:3). "Will you even put me in the wrong?" God asks Job in reference to Job's statements during the debate (40:8). "Shall a faultfinder contend with the Almighty?" God asks the person who had charged him with being sadistic (40:2). To whitewash the behavior of Job in the early stages of his quest is to misinterpret the book, as the conclusion makes clear.

This is confirmed when we look at the responses of Job to the voice from the whirlwind. After the first speech, Job acknowledges that he had said things beyond his knowledge:

> "I lay my hand on my mouth.
> I have spoken once, and I will not answer;
> twice, but I will proceed no further." [40:4–5]

Even more drastic is Job's response after the second speech: "I despise myself, and repent in dust and ashes" (42:6). In retrospect, Job sees that he complained because he did not know enough about God. A new humility has replaced the earlier assurance that Job could answer the problem of innocent suffering.

The goal of Job's quest toward understanding is also the ultimate goal of human existence—to see God: "I had heard of thee by the hearing of the ear, / but now my eye sees thee" (42:5). God does not give a direct answer to the question of why the righteous suffer, but he has used Job's suffering as the occasion to reveal himself to Job in a new way. It turns out that God was more interested in Job's faith and spiritual growth than in making Job comfortable in life.

The Epilogue

The epilogue to the story (42:7–17), in which the fortunes of Job are restored, has been much misunderstood. In terms of plot, it is exactly what we can expect in a comic U-shaped plot. In fact, the story would be incomplete without this denouement (tying up loose ends). The restoration of Job's earthly fortunes comes across as anticlimactic, and this is exactly the right effect. The important thing in Job's life is his faith in God.

The main narrative premise of the epilogue is poetic justice. Significantly, Satan is not even mentioned, his case having been disproved by Job's eventual triumphs of faith. The friends are rebuked by God and told to ask Job to pray for them (vv. 7–9). After all that he has endured from friends who behave like enemies, Job is finally vindicated. The final element of poetic justice is the motif of virtue rewarded, as Job's fortunes are restored and his family "ate bread with him in his house" (v. 11). The final statement of the book is a bit of eloquent understatement for which biblical narrative is so famous: "And Job died, an old man, and full of days."

Part **4**

The New Testament

16

How Literary Is the New Testament?

The New Testament has suffered from a notable neglect by literary critics. Anthologies of the Bible as literature tend to omit or slight it. The Old Testament is normally felt to be much more literary than the New Testament. Yet when I collected excerpts of literary commentary for a reference book on the New Testament, I was left with the strong impression that the New Testament is no less literary than the Old, and that literary approaches are equally indispensable for understanding both Testaments.[1] The purpose of this opening chapter is to explore what it means that the New Testament is a work of literature and how this affects the way we read and interpret it.

Is the New Testament "Literature"?

The literary status of the New Testament has elicited contradictory claims nearly from the beginning. One of the church fathers, Origen, claimed that the New Testament did not measure up to Greek stan-

1. For a treasury of literary commentary on the New Testament, see Leland Ryken, ed., *The New Testament in Literary Criticism*, A Library of Literary Criticism (New York: Ungar, 1984).

dards of literary style, offering as a reason for this that God wanted it to be clear that the power of the gospel did not rest in human eloquence.[2] Augustine disagreed, stating that Paul's "wisdom is his guide, eloquence his attendant."[3]

Modern Viewpoints

Opinions in our century have followed three main paths. The view that the writers were unlettered people without literary intention or ability, and that they were interested only in the religious content of their utterances, has been prominent. Martin Dibelius writes, for example, that the writers of the New Testament were "men without special education" and that "what they wrote down was either completely unliterary . . . or else half-literary and thus unpretentious writing intended for a certain class of people."[4]

Another major viewpoint is that the New Testament is indeed literary but that its forms are so unique that ordinary literary criteria are powerless to deal with what we find there. The most forceful statement on the uniqueness of New Testament forms is by Amos N. Wilder, who believes that "early Christian literary arts were different from those that ancient paganism produced, and that Greek and traditional humanist categories are inadequate as measuring rods."[5]

Still other commentators have simply operated on the premise that the New Testament has much about it that resembles familiar literary forms of the period in which it was written, or of literature generally. Critics in the former category have lavished attention on trying to identify existing literary models that New Testament writers followed. Critics in the latter camp do not care where or when the literary forms that they find in the New Testament originated, as long as they are genuinely present in the New Testament.

The Approach of This Book

My own approach to the New Testament will stress its literary primacy and show that its literary traits are a mingling of convention

2. Origen, *Against Celsus*, in *The New Testament in Literary Criticism*, p. 16.

3. Augustine, *On Christian Doctrine*, in *The New Testament in Literary Criticism*, p. 17.

4. Martin Dibelius, *A Fresh Approach to the New Testament and Early Christian Literature* (New York: Charles Scribner's Sons, 1936), pp. 16–17. Among the fallacies evident in this viewpoint is the assumption that folk literature cannot be truly literary and artistic. The New Testament proves that it can be.

5. Amos N. Wilder, *Early Christian Rhetoric: The Language of the Gospel* (Cambridge: Harvard University Press, 1971), p. 36. Although Wilder's theory of the uniqueness of New Testament forms is wrong, this book is an excellent source of generalizations about the literature of the New Testament.

and innovation, of the familiar and the new. The four dominant genres of the New Testament—Gospel, Acts, Epistle, and Apocalypse—are unique. We do not find these same generic labels in an anthology of English or American literature, for example. I would insist, though, that the thing that makes these New Testament books unique has a great deal more to do with their content and theological claims than with their form.

To say that New Testament forms are unique obscures an important point. Their uniqueness actually stems from modifications that their writers have made on familiar literary forms. The stories of the Gospels and Acts, the conventions of letter writing in the Epistles, and the visions of the Book of Revelation all draw upon recognizable literary techniques. Old Testament models are particularly relevant for all New Testament forms except the Epistles, where contemporary Greek letters are the basic form on which New Testament writers worked their innovations.

What Makes the New Testament Literary?

The New Testament is literary by the same criteria that we apply to any other canon of literature. The New Testament is more than a work of literature, but it is not less. The writing that we find in the New Testament is a mixture of three types of writing that we find in the Old Testament as well.

One of these is what we might call expository or theological writing, exemplified by the following passage:

> Count it all joy, my brethren, when you meet various trials, for you know that the testing of your faith produces steadfastness. And let steadfastness have its full effect, that you may be perfect and complete, lacking in nothing. [James 1:2–4]

The implied purpose of such theological exposition is to convey information as clearly and directly as possible. The structure and logic of the passage are mainly conceptual; the passage is a sequence of ideas. The vocabulary is predominantly abstract.

A second type of writing in the New Testament is historical writing. The following example is typical:

> After this Paul stayed many days longer, and then took leave of the brethren and sailed for Syria, and with him Priscilla and Aquila. At Cenchreae he cut his hair, for he had a vow. And they came to Ephesus, and he left them there; but he himself went into the synagogue and argued with the Jews. [Acts 18:18–19]

It is not hard to infer that the intended purpose of such a passage is to record the facts of events. I call this the documentary impulse. It is pervasive in the narrative parts of the New Testament (the Gospels and the Book of Acts).

But there is a third type of writing as well, one that with good reason we can call literature. It is usually mingled with the two impulses already noted—the didactic impulse to teach theological and moral truth and the historical impulse to state what actually happened. Although this mixture makes the Bible a unique book, this should not be allowed to obscure the ways in which the New Testament is a literary book by ordinary literary standards. Not to recognize this is to impoverish and misunderstand the New Testament. My purpose in the remainder of this chapter is to suggest the ways in which the New Testament is literary in nature.

Experiential Concreteness

To begin, it is common to define literature partly by its content. The subject of literature is human experience. Literature images reality. It incarnates its meaning in the form of images, characters, and events. Its aim is not to state ideas but to recreate experiences. It accomplishes this aim by appealing to our imagination (the image-making and image-perceiving capacity that we all possess). Literature recreates an experience in sufficient detail and concreteness to enable a reader to relive it.

Because the New Testament shows the characteristic biblical tendency toward the brief unit, it is easy to overlook how concrete its writing is and how many appeals to the imagination it contains. Here is an illustration:

> On that day, when evening had come, [Jesus] said to them, "Let us go across to the other side." And leaving the crowd, they took him with them in the boat, just as he was. And other boats were with him. And a great storm of wind arose, and the waves beat into the boat, so that the boat was already filling. But he was in the stern, asleep on the cushion; and they woke him and said to him, "Teacher, do you not care if we perish?" And he awoke and rebuked the wind, and said to the sea, "Peace! Be still!" And the wind ceased, and there was a great calm. [Mark 4:35–39]

The first thing to note about the passage is that it communicates its truth by means of a story. Meaning is here incarnated or embodied in characters doing things in a particular setting. Despite its brevity, this story is filled with appeals to our image-making capacity. It is full of precision. We know when the action occurs, for example: *when evening had come.* The realism is enhanced by the detail that Jesus joined the others *just as he was.* The waves, we are told with equal vividness, *beat into the boat.* Jesus, moreover, was *asleep on the cushion.* The whole scene comes alive in our imaginations as we read.

All of this concreteness makes it easy to find recognizable human experience in the story. One level of truth in the story is truthfulness to human experience, and this is always a touchstone of literature. We recognize the physical reality of the storm, for example. The psychological experience of terror in the face of physical threat is equally apparent. A literary narrative like this is primarily interested in getting us to relive an experience, not to grasp an idea.

This impulse to image the truth and draw upon everyday experience in the process is not limited to the stories of the New Testament but is just as characteristic of many of the expository sections. Jesus' usual style of preaching or teaching, for example, was heavily anecdotal and poetic (imagistic). The idea of being heavenly-minded becomes as tangible as a drawer full of valuables when Jesus says,

> Do not lay up for yourselves treasures on earth, where moth and rust consume and where thieves break in and steal, but lay up for yourselves treasures in heaven, where neither moth nor rust consumes and where thieves do not break in and steal. [Matt. 6:19–20]

What about the Epistles? Aren't they predominantly abstract? They are much more concrete and experiential than we ordinarily think. For one thing, they are occasional letters written on specific occasions and dealing with specific situations that had arisen in the lives of a church or an individual. They are rarely systematic treatises on a theological issue. This at once gives them an experiential feel.

Beyond this, the very language of the Epistles is frequently concrete and imagistic:

> Share in suffering as a good soldier of Christ Jesus. . . . An athlete is not crowned unless he competes according to the rules. It is the hard-working farmer who ought to have the first share of the crops. [2 Tim. 2:3, 5–6]

The concept of Christian living is much more than an abstraction in such a passage. In a manner typical of literary authors, the writer here uses everyday experiences to express his idea.

When measured by the familiar literary criterion of experiential content, the New Testament is a literary book. It continuously appeals to our intelligence through our imagination. It is abstract in some parts, but its more characteristic mode is presentation of human experience.

Literary Genres

The most customary way to define literature is by its genres (types). Through the centuries, people who deal with literary texts have agreed that certain genres should be classified as literary.

The New Testament is made up of three main genres: narrative or story, letter or epistle, and vision or apocalypse. All three of these tend to be literary rather than expository in nature. Within these broad categories, moreover, we find an abundance of familiar literary forms: parable, oration, proverb or saying, lyric, hymn, and satire.

I noted earlier that the four main classifications of books in the New Testament—the Gospels, Acts, the Epistles, and Revelation—do not have exact parallels in the familiar landscape of English and American literature. But each of them has enough affinities with familiar literary forms to allow us to apply many of the usual categories of story and poetry to them. The Book of Revelation, for example, is hardly a typical story, but the standard narrative questions of who does what, and where, and with what results, are the right ones to ask when dealing with the book.

The uniqueness of the New Testament lies not so much in the individual genres but in the mixture of forms that we find. The Gospels, for example, mingle history, story, drama, oratory, proverb, parable, and poetry in a way that is without exact parallel elsewhere in literature. The Sermon on the Mount combines the techniques of oratory, satire, parable, and poetry. The Book of Revelation combines features of the epistle, poetic symbolism, apocalyptic and visionary writing, drama, and lyric.

Artistry

Literature is an art form. One of the criteria by which we classify something as literary is the presence of form, beauty, craftsmanship, and technique. These qualities can characterize a whole work or only a part of it, but wherever they are strongly in evidence, we rightly consider a text to have literary properties.

In its grandest design, such artistry is evident in the overall structure of individual New Testament books. The Gospel of Matthew, for example, alternates blocks of narrative with blocks of teaching material, and the sections of teaching end with a formula to the effect, "When Jesus had finished these sayings. . . ." In the Gospel of Mark, both the chronology and the symbolic use of setting are based on a principle of Christ's acceptance in Galilee and eventual rejection in Jerusalem, with a literal and symbolic journey between the two. The Book of Acts is structured as a successive series of expanding waves of church movement from Jerusalem to Rome. The Epistles are built on a principle of salutation-thanksgiving-body-moral exhortation-conclusion. The Book of Revelation is structured as an intricate series of sevenfold units.

From such grand architectonics we can move to artistry on a small scale. Here we can note the adherence of individual stories, as well as the parables of Jesus, to such narrative principles as unity, completeness, repetition, and contrast. The discourses of Jesus and many passages in the Epistles are arranged so rhythmically and rhetorically as to qualify as Hebrew poetry:

> What is sown is perishable,
> what is raised is imperishable.
> It is sown in dishonor,
> it is raised in glory.
> It is sown in weakness,
> it is raised in power.
> It is sown a physical body,
> it is raised a spiritual body. [1 Cor. 15:42–44]

Patterned writing like this is common in the New Testament. Word patterns and image patterns are customary.

What functions are served by such artistry in the New Testament? It heightens the impact of utterance, giving it a force that it would otherwise lack. But it is also delightful in itself. It adds to the enjoyment of our reading of the New Testament. Such writing calls attention to itself by its skill and eloquence. A literary approach differentiates itself from other approaches by placing a high value on the artistic quality of the writing. It is not hesitant to speak of the authors' craftsmanship and to delight in it.

Literary critics assume self-conscious artistry and composition on the part of New Testament writers. In this they differ from many biblical scholars, who either doubt that the writers had literary abilities or are indifferent to the evidence that they did. A common bias of New Testament scholarship is that "we must assume unliterary beginnings of a religious unpretentious 'literature'. . . . We should look in vain for analogies in literature proper."[6]

But why would we make such an assumption? The New Testament

---

6. Martin Dibelius, *From Tradition to Gospel* (New York: Charles Scribner's Sons, 1935), p. 39.

was written by people steeped in the Old Testament, which is one of the most literary books in the world. These same writers lived in a cultural setting that included the influence of Greek civilization. Paul quotes from Greek writers in the New Testament.[7] Since he did not have *Bartlett's Familiar Quotations* to aid him, we can conclude that he had a firsthand acquaintance with Greek literature and knew some of it by heart. Everywhere we turn in the New Testament we find similarities to Greek literature as well as to Old Testament literature, despite the innovations that we find worked on these conventional forms. The New Testament epistles bear resemblances to Hellenistic letters, the Epistle of James to the Greek form known as the diatribe, the Book of Revelation to Greek dramatic conventions. The prologue to the Gospel of John is partly a parody of the Greek *Hymn to Zeus*. The speeches of Paul in Acts are similar to classical orations and defense speeches.[8]

Literary Language

Literature in general, and poetry in particular, use special resources of language in a way that we can recognize as literary. The most obvious category is figurative language. We can consider a passage to be literary whenever the writer makes use of metaphor, simile, symbol, hyperbole, apostrophe, personification, allusion, paradox, pun, or irony. New Testament writing is continuously figurative in these ways.

The most famous example is the discourses of Jesus:

> Beware of false prophets, who come to you in sheep's clothing but inwardly are ravenous wolves. You will know them by their fruits. Are grapes gathered from thorns, or figs from thistles? So, every sound tree bears good fruit, but the bad tree bears evil fruit. [Matt. 7:15–17]

But such a reliance on figurative language, especially metaphor and symbol, is also common in the Epistles:

> For the sun rises with its scorching heat and withers the grass; its flower falls, and its beauty perishes. So will the rich man fade away in the midst of his pursuits. [James 1:11]

7. See, for example, 1 Corinthians 15:33, which is quoted from the play *Thais* by the Greek dramatist Menander; the speech to the Areopagus in Acts 17, where Paul alludes to Homer, Cleanthes, Aratus, and Epimenides; and Titus 1:12, where he quotes with approval from the Cretan poet Epimenides.

8. These and similar points are made by the authors in *The New Testament in Literary Criticism*.

And as for the Book of Revelation, its essential mode is symbolism:

> " 'He who conquers, I will make him a pillar in the temple of my God;
> ... and I will write on him the name of my God, and the name of the
> city of my God....' " [3:12]

The language of the New Testament is generally much more concrete in its original than it is in modern English translations. A literary approach is sensitive to these energies of language. In 2 Peter 1:5, for example, we are commanded to "supplement" our faith with various virtues. This looks abstract until we learn that the term had a special meaning in its original usage.[9] Wealthy patrons of Greek plays had a practice of paying the expenses for equipping and training actors. To "supplement" faith with virtues is far from an abstraction. It means generous and costly cooperation and is as palpable as lavishly equipping a group of actors.

The special resources of language employed by New Testament writers also include rhetorical patterns and devices. I have noted that many prose passages are so patterned and display such parallelism that they should be printed in the form of Hebrew poetry. In addition to such symmetry of clauses, we find rhetorical questions, question-and-answer constructions, imaginary dialogues, and patterns of repetition. Most notable of all is the aphoristic tendency of the New Testament—its richness in proverbs or "sayings," often figurative in expression, that compress a great deal more meaning into them than ordinary discourse does.[10]

The important principle at work here is that such language patterns allow writers to communicate more than ordinary language conveys. Such writing stands out. It has arresting strangeness. It overcomes the cliché effect of ordinary language. Skill with language is a literary feature that is prominent in the New Testament.

A corollary of this special use of language is that style can become an avenue for a literary approach to the New Testament. The letter or epistle, for example, may not be an inherently literary form, but the stylistic excellence of the New Testament epistles invites a literary approach (among other approaches). Many of the individual episodes

---

9. My information comes from Michael Green, *The Second Epistle General of Peter and the General Epistle of Jude*, Tyndale New Testament Commentaries series (Grand Rapids: Eerdmans, 1968), pp. 66–67.

10. For more on the ways in which the sayings of Jesus use literary resources to convey more than ordinary discourse does, I especially recommend Robert C. Tannehill, *The Sword of His Mouth: Forceful and Imaginative Language in Synoptic Sayings* (Philadelphia: Fortress, 1975).

in the Gospels are too brief and unembellished to seem like literary narratives, but their realistic style and the presence of Jesus' memorable sayings in them makes them literary.

Master Images or Archetypes

The literary imagination organizes reality around recurrent master images known as archetypes. An archetype is an image, character type, or plot motif that recurs throughout literature (as well as throughout life). Archetypes are the building blocks of literature and the ingredients of our own lives.

Here, too, the New Testament adheres to literary principles. Images such as light and darkness, bread and water, blood and cross pervade the pages of the New Testament. Archetypal character types are equally prominent. For example, the suffering servant, the outcast, the refuser of festivities (usually in the form of the Jews and the Pharisees), master and servant, and the pilgrim are recurrent figures in the New Testament. Among plot motifs, images of journey, quest, initiation, the lost and found, death and resurrection are prominent. Jesus' parables are especially rich in archetypes.

The importance of these archetypes is multiple. They are a leading means by which the New Testament emerges in our imagination and thinking as a unified book. They also help to familiarize modern readers with a book that in many ways seems remote from their own lives. They enhance our understanding of the universal human implications of what is recounted in the New Testament. Finally, these master images embody much of the religious meaning that the New Testament writers wished to express.

A Literary Approach to the New Testament

The New Testament is inherently literary at the levels of both form and content. At the level of content, its authors show more interest in recreating experiences and conveying truth by means of particular images than in developing abstract ideas. At the level of form, it shows its literary allegiance by the prevalence of literary genres, a high degree of artistry, special resources of language, and the presence of unifying master images.

These literary features do not guarantee a literary approach to the New Testament. As I noted earlier, the New Testament is a hybrid form that mingles history, theological exposition, and literature. It invites a multiplicity of approaches. What, then, characterizes a literary approach to the New Testament?

Literary commentary is alive to the images and experiential concreteness of the New Testament. It resists the impulse to reduce literary texts to abstract propositions or to move beyond the text to the history behind it. This means a willingness to accept the text on its own terms and to concentrate on reliving the experiences that are presented. A literary approach assumes that much of the meaning of the New Testament is communicated by means of characters, events, and images.

This literary stance implies a whole methodology. It assumes that a text invites us to enter a whole world of the imagination and to live in that world before we move beyond it. A basic premise of literary interpretation is that, in the words of novelist Flannery O'Connor, "the whole story is the meaning, because it is an experience, not an abstraction."[11] To read in a literary way is to use our imaginations to enter a whole world having its own settings, characters, events, customs, ideas, and symbols. These are the means by which a literary text communicates its meanings. They appeal to what modern psychology calls the right side of the brain—our capacity to take in the truth imagistically, experientially, intuitively, and wholistically.

Believing that the subject of literature is human experience, a literary approach is particularly attuned to the universal meanings in a text. It operates on the premise that whereas history tells us what happened, literature tells us what happens. A literary approach assumes that characters in a story have a burden of meaning larger than themselves. They are representatives of the human condition generally. A main purpose of literary criticism of the New Testament is therefore to build bridges between the New Testament world and our own experiences.

Literary critics also believe that a text must be approached in an awareness of its genre. An awareness of genre, in fact, programs how we assimilate and organize a text. The right interpretation of a text, writes a literary critic, is the one "that conforms to the intentionality of the book itself and to the conventions it assumes and requires."[12] The key idea here is the emphasis on intentionality of the book, implying a generic approach, in contrast to the usual claims of biblical scholars to know the intention of the author.

A literary approach is equally interested in artistic form, both as something that enhances the impact and meaning of an utterance and as something that is beautiful and delightful in itself. To the literary

11. Flannery O'Connor, *Mystery and Manners*, ed. Sally and Robert Fitzgerald (New York: Farrar, Straus and Giroux, 1957), p. 73.
12. Northrop Frye, *The Great Code: The Bible and Literature* (New York: Harcourt Brace Jovanovich, 1981), p. 80.

critic, it is not a matter of indifference that the parables and discourses of Jesus are among the most beautiful literary passages in the world. The eloquence of many passages in the Epistles, the storytelling ability of the writer of Acts, and the imagistic splendors of the Book of Revelation are things in which the literary critic is interested.

An attention to the nuances of language is also part of a literary approach to the New Testament. Literary critics believe that much of the language of the New Testament is essentially poetic, consisting of images, metaphors, and other figurative expressions that require ordinary tools of poetic analysis for the unfolding of their meanings. In addition to individual images and metaphors are the overriding master images that both unify the New Testament and convey important aspects of its religious meaning.

Much of what I have said about a literary approach to the New Testament can be summarized under the formula *meaning through form*. This simply asserts that we cannot derive the meaning of the New Testament without first examining its form. "Form" should be construed broadly in this context. It includes anything that involves how a writer has expressed his content, as distinct from what he has said. Without form (beginning, of course, with language itself), no meaning is conveyed.

While this is true for all forms of writing, it is especially crucial for literature. Literary discourse has its own forms or "language," and these tend to be more complex, subtle, and indirect than ordinary discourse. The storyteller, for example, speaks with characters, action, and setting. This means that before we can understand what storytellers are saying about reality we must first interact with the form, that is, the story. In a similar way, poetry conveys its meanings through figurative language. It is therefore impossible to talk about what a poetic statement means without first encountering the form (metaphor or simile, for example).

The literary critic's preoccupation with the "how" of New Testament writing is therefore not frivolous. It is evidence of an aesthetic delight in artistic form, but it is more than that. It is also evidence of a desire to understand what is said in the New Testament, in keeping with its tendency to incarnate meaning in literary forms that require careful scrutiny.

Distinctive Literary Features of the New Testament

I hope that this book will show readers that the New Testament is in many ways like the literature with which they are familiar. A story is a story, after all, wherever we encounter it. One reason why many modern readers lack the antennae to respond to the New Testament is that it has traditionally been isolated from the familiar landscape of their reading experience. Along with these familiar features, however, it is also beneficial to note at the outset some distinctive features that characterize the New Testament as a literary book.

For example, the New Testament is from start to finish a religious book. It represents literature in the service of a didactic purpose. There is a strong rhetorical or persuasive purpose behind the writing. The New Testament is a literature of encounter and confrontation, presupposing response as a condition of reading it. Erich Auerbach long ago noted the prevalence (without parallel in other ancient literature) of face-to-face dialogues in the New Testament.[13]

The New Testament shares this religious quality with the Old Testament, but what is distinctive to the New Testament is its specifically Christocentric focus. The most obviously distinctive feature of the Gospels, for example, is their consistent concentration on the person and work of Christ. The Book of Revelation, which in its opening statement of theme announces that it is the revelation or unveiling of Jesus Christ, is likewise constructed around Jesus as protagonist. The Book of Acts and the Epistles focus on the world-changing impact of the redemptive life of Christ in the early church.

Another distinguishing literary feature of the New Testament is its simplicity and realism. The simplicity is a simplicity of majesty, but both the language and the style are relatively unembellished (with some passages in the Epistles serving as exceptions). Combined with this simplicity is realism. The writers of the New Testament deliberately include everyday details in their accounts. The New Testament keeps us firmly rooted in our familiar world, not only in the narratives but in the discourses of Jesus and the Epistles as well. As we read the New Testament we live in a world of farming and nature and buying and selling and journeying. Auerbach describes it as "a world which is . . . entirely real, average, identifiable as to place, time, and circumstances" (p. 43).

But by some mysterious transformation, these realistic and precise images point beyond themselves to spiritual realities. In the New Testament, words become more than words. There is an incipient symbolism at work. Sowing seed and baking bread and putting on armor become more than physical activities. The concrete sensory world con-

13. Erich Auerbach, *Mimesis: The Representation of Reality in Western Literature*, trans. Willard R. Trask (Princeton: Princeton University Press, 1953), p. 46. Wilder, *Early Christian Rhetoric*, pp. 40–54, also has good comments on the confrontational quality of the New Testament.

tinuously opens into a spiritual world, usually conceived as the kingdom of God. The New Testament is preeminently a literature of "second meanings" in which there is almost always more than meets the eye.

The New Testament is also strongly oral. Most of what we read almost certainly existed first in oral form. Jesus himself wrote nothing of what we find in the New Testament. Oral forms such as addresses, sayings, and dialogues dominate the narrative parts of the New Testament (the Gospels and Acts), whose individual units probably circulated orally before being collected in written documents. The Epistles, though they were written, are strongly oral in their rhetoric and were for the most part intended for public reading. The same is true of the Book of Revelation. Wilder summarizes the situation aptly: "Oral speech is where it all began. . . . Even when [the writers] did come to write we can overhear the living voices, speaking and praising. This kind of writing is very close to speech" (p. 40).

The oral roots of New Testament literature help to explain another literary feature—the fact that the New Testament is popular or folk literature. It speaks to the common person. In the words of a biblical scholar, the New Testament is "the Book of the People."[14] Its language is for the most part the language of everyday speech. Its writers show a preference for the brief unit that is easily grasped. The Gospels and the Book of Acts, for example, are not single sustained stories but collections of stories. The informal nature of the Epistles—indeed, even the choice of the letter as a form—shows that they arose from real-life situations and were addressed to ordinary people. And the Book of Revelation, replete with animal characters and battles and dragons, sprang "not from the professional scribes or the official class," being rather "for the most part folk-literature."[15] The folk-literature quality of the New Testament reaches its high point with the parables of Jesus, which are the very touchstone of the popular imagination as it has existed through the centuries.

A final trait that we might notice is that the New Testament is not a self-contained book. It presupposes the Old Testament as a condition of understanding it. Its writers repeatedly treat the events about which they write as the fulfillment of Old Testament prophecies. The New Testament is filled with echoes of the Old Testament. Northrop Frye has expressed the situation accurately when he notes that New Testament references to the Old

14. Adolf Deissmann, *Light from the Ancient East*, trans. Lionel R. M. Strachan (New York: Harper and Brothers, 1927), p. 145.

15. Isbon T. Beckwith, *The Apocalypse of John: Studies in Introduction with a Critical and Exegetical Commentary* (New York: Macmillan, 1919), p. 171.

extend over every book—not impossibly every passage—in the New Testament; and some New Testament books . . . are a dense mass of such allusions, often with direct or oblique quotations. . . . The New Testament . . . claims to be, among other things, the key to the Old Testament, the explanation of what the Old Testament really means (p. 79).

The New Testament, then, emerges as a combination of the familiar and the unfamiliar. At many points it invites comparison with familiar literature. Elsewhere, especially at the level of content, it is a unique book.

17

The Gospels

The four New Testament Gospels contain the same three ingredients that are intermingled throughout the Bible: the historical impulse to record the facts, the theological and didactic impulse to teach religious truth, and the literary impulse to recreate experiences in our imaginations. In this important sense they are thoroughly similar to other narrative parts of the Bible. The Gospels' distinctiveness within the Bible has a great deal more to do with content (especially the characterization of Jesus and the nature of his message) than with literary form.

The Gospel as a Literary Form

It is generally claimed that the Gospels are a unique form and that there is no model to which they can be adequately compared. The claims for the uniqueness of the Gospels are not misguided, but they have been overstated. The Gospels are encyclopedic forms, and it is the precise combination of literary elements that converge in them that is without precise parallel outside of the Bible.

The combination of individual forms that make up the Gospels is truly striking. The list of genres represented in the Gospels keeps expanding as we analyze these books. Historical narrative, parable, drama or dialogue, sermon or oration, and saying or proverb are especially prominent. In addition, the Gospels remind us at various points of biography, diary or journal, tragedy, comedy, satire, and poetry. There is nearly equal emphasis on what happened (narrative) and what was said (discourse). Where else in our literary experience, or even within the Bible, do we find exactly this combination?

How Literary Are the Gospels?

A good starting point for a literary approach to the Gospels is to explore what makes them literary. If we simply apply the criteria for determining literariness that I discussed in the opening chapter of this book, we will see at once that the Gospels are very literary in nature.

To begin, they are filled with vivid details that appeal to our imaginations and allow us to recreate experiences as we read. The writers consistently go beyond the documentary impulse to record the bare historical facts. They also want us to experience the events. Here is the type of passage that epitomizes the Gospels:

> On another sabbath, when he entered the synagogue and taught, a man was there whose right hand was withered. And the scribes and the Pharisees watched him, to see whether he would heal on the sabbath, so that they might find an accusation against him. But he knew their thoughts, and he said to the man who had the withered hand, "Come and stand here." And he rose and stood there. And Jesus said to them, "I ask you, is it lawful on the sabbath to do good or to do harm, to save life or to destroy it?" And he looked around on them all, and said to him, "Stretch out your hand." And he did so, and his hand was restored. [Luke 6:6–10]

We see here the usual biblical preference for the brief unit rather than the embellished story, but it is amazing how many appeals there are to our imagination. We visualize the setting and events. There is a wealth of specific detail regarding human gestures and what the characters actually said. Like many another passage from the Gospels, this episode is ready for filming. It comes alive in our imaginations and thereby obeys the most primary of all literary impulses.

Literature does not present its material objectively but always offers an interpretation of the human experiences that it presents. Here, too, the Gospels show a literary inclination. Each of the four Gospels has its distinctive world, its own preoccupations, its own assumed audience, its own picture of Jesus and his teaching. The story of Jesus is told from four different points of view, as scholars have repeatedly shown.

A third criterion of literature is that it presents its content in a highly artistic form. In stories, such artistry consists of pattern, unity, balance, symmetry, contrast, foil, repetition, foreshadowing, and echo. In the Gospels, this artistry is plentiful. It ranges from such small things as the arrangement of individual units into a meaningful pattern, to such large matters as the overall structure of a Gospel.

As an example of the former, the genealogy that opens the Gospel of Matthew (1:1–16) falls into three segments of fourteen names each, a pattern that the writer himself points out (v. 17). For artistry on a grand scale, we can observe the structure of Matthew as a whole. It is a symphonic design in which units of narrative and units of teaching alternate. The five blocks of teaching material, moreover, end with a refrain along the lines of "when Jesus had finished these sayings" (see 7:28; 11:1; 13:53; 19:1; 26:1). The instances of such careful patterning in the Gospels are truly impressive.[1]

To sum up, the Gospels are thoroughly literary in nature. They have been such a frequent source for sermons that we tend to think of them as collections of unrelated fragments. The best antidote to this misconception is to read whole Gospels at a single sitting, conscious of the definition of literature that I have given.

Narrative as the Primary Form

It came as quite a surprise to me to learn that biblical scholarship in our century has generally regarded the discourse or saying as the primary form of the Gospels. This no doubt stemmed from the preoccupation of scholars with the original form that the Gospels took. That form was oral and consisted of the preaching of the apostles about Jesus. From these oral fragments the Gospels as we now find them evolved.

But if we simply look at the four Gospels as we now have them, it is obvious that above all they tell a story. Narrative is the organizing framework within which the sayings and discourses are arranged. The reason the Gospels remain collections of incoherent fragments in most people's minds is that not enough attention has been given to their story qualities.

As stories, the Gospels are episodic rather than unified around a single progressive action in which one event leads to the next. Once we become accustomed to this arrangement, its virtues as a way of telling the story of Jesus become obvious. The apparent randomness effectively portrays Jesus in his manifold roles. The writers show us

---

1. For a sampling, see the entries on the individual Gospels in Leland Ryken, ed., *The New Testament in Literary Criticism*, A Library of Literary Criticism (New York: Ungar, 1984).

the many sides of Jesus, which would be hard to do by portraying a single action.

This same randomness also conveys a general sense of the life Jesus lived. The variety of scenes, events, and characters captures the nature of the world in which Jesus lived and acted. Stop to consider Jesus' life during the years of his public ministry: he traveled, preached, led a group of disciples, performed miracles, engaged in dialogue with people, defended his actions and beliefs in open debate, and was finally put on trial and crucified. Given the many-sided nature of his life, the mixture and arrangement of ingredients that we find in the Gospels capture the reality of Jesus' life better than more traditional conceptions of plot.

The sheer variety, instead of impairing the unity of the Gospels, actually supports it. All that appears in the Gospels bears the stamp of Jesus' life and world. An inner consistency emerges in our imaginations. We come to expect that something different will happen every few minutes as we read.

Unity in the Gospels

The most important unifying factor in the Gospels is unity of hero. Everything in the Gospels focuses on the person, acts, and sayings of Jesus, and this is one of the chief identifying traits of the genre.

Although the Gospels are not strictly chronological, they are loosely so. The general pattern is a movement from Jesus' birth (which is recorded only in Matthew and Luke), through his three-year earthly ministry, to his death, followed by his resurrection. All four Gospels are structured in such a way as to make the passion of Jesus (the events surrounding his crucifixion) the climax toward which the story moves.

Within this general chronological framework, the individual Gospel writers arranged their material to fit their specific thematic and narrative purposes. Matthew and Mark, for example, both record a day of teaching in parables, but Mark places it near the beginning of his story (chap. 4) and Matthew halfway through his (chap. 13). Some of the events in Jesus' life appear in different places in the different Gospels. John, for example, placed Jesus' cleansing of the temple near the beginning of his story (chap. 2), whereas the three synoptic Gospels have it near the end of the book during the Passion Week.

The arrangement of material in the Gospels will seem more unified if we pause to consider that it reflects how the memory recalls events. Memory was important in the composition of the Gospels, which no doubt represent the final molding of material that first circulated orally in the form of individual units. How does the memory work? It recalls broad outlines, it remembers single incidents, and it strings together certain sequences of events. This is exactly what we find in the Gospels. The Gospels are structured on the principle of memory.

The Gospels are further unified by recurrent situations or type scenes. Jesus is always the central figure in the scene. Next to him in importance is the group of disciples. Almost as prominent are the Pharisees, a nearly constant force of hostility. Another rather constant group is the crowd of ordinary people, sometimes a nameless mass, at other times represented by a particular named person.

The crowds are normally caught between the claims of Jesus and the authority of the religious establishment. As a result of this middle position, the crowds are typically poised at a moment of choice. Jesus is usually shown trying to persuade them, either by word or miracle or disparagement of his enemies. Given this implied struggle for the minds of the onlookers, we can see why Jesus and the Pharisees so often initiated conflict with each other.

If characters help to unify the Gospels, so does geography. In each Gospel we enter a narrative world replete with place names. We are constantly in the world of Palestine as we travel with Jesus from one locale to another. Sometimes the geography is used for structural purposes. The Gospel of Mark, for example, is structured on a grand contrast between Galilee, place of acceptance, and Jerusalem, which symbolizes rejection of Jesus.

Individual episodes within the Gospels are unified by the same principles of narrative unity that we find in any story. The right questions to ask are the usual ones of setting, characterization, and plot, namely, Where? Who? What happens? The commonest structural principle in the individual episodes of the Gospels is that of conflict moving toward resolution. Even if there is not a conflict, we should be alert for a progression toward a final resolution or moment of epiphany, as in the story of Jesus' encounter with the woman at the well (John 4:1–30).

Because the Gospels contain so much dialogue and encounter, it is also a helpful procedure for many of the episodes to lay out the action into separate dramatic scenes, as though it were a play, focusing on each segment and also noting the sequence or positioning of scenes as we move through the episode. As a variation on this procedure, we might profitably approach some of the episodes as though the event were being photographed by a television crew. We will find distant or overview shots, close-ups, shifts from one speaker to another, shots of the crowd, and so forth.

Still more unity emerges if we pay attention to the narrative world around which each Gospel is constructed. It is a literary principle that works of literature create their own consistent world of interrelated details. The individual Gospels have their own characteristic ideas, images, settings, and emphases. In Matthew's Gospel, for example, we move in a Jewish world where Old Testament prophecies and religious customs are consistently present, where Jesus is repeatedly portrayed in terms of royalty, and where the teaching of Jesus is organized into blocks interspersed between sections of narrative. With Luke's Gospel we enter a different narrative world—a cosmopolitan world in which people on the social and religious fringes (women, the poor, outsiders, people in shady occupations) are the ones who receive God's grace. Knowing that individual Gospel writers build their own world in this way can go a long way toward unifying our experiences of the Gospels.

The Portrait of Jesus

The Gospels exist to explain the life and message of Jesus. It is possible, however, to misinterpret how the writers went about their task. There are three theories on the matter. We might compare them to three types of visual art—a photograph, a painted portrait, and an abstract painting.[2] A photograph records everything about a subject and is virtually objective. Its limitation is that it cannot be very interpretive of the subject, nor can it highlight a given aspect of the subject. A painted portrait is selective in details, highlighting certain aspects of a subject while omitting others. An abstract painting conveys only a vague impression of its subject and depends almost wholly on what the viewer is able to make of impressionistic details and broad outlines on the canvas.

The Gospels give us portraits of Jesus. Far too much has been omitted from the life of Jesus for the accounts to be considered photographs. The writers not only were selective in what they included; they also gave a particular interpretation of the person and work of Jesus, making no attempt to give a wholly objective recording of the facts. Verbal portraits always leave a lot to the imagination of the reader, and those in the Gospels are no exception. Each Gospel gives us a distinctive portrait of Jesus in which certain things are highlighted and others omitted.

One scholar has proposed the television sports replay as a model for what we find in the Gospels:

> In these replays the action can be dramatically slowed down so that one
> is able to see much more than one was able to see in the action as it

2. I am indebted for this comparison to Robert A. Guelich, "The Gospels: Portraits of Jesus and His Ministry," *Journal of the Evangelical Theological Society* 24 (1982): 117–25.

actually occurred. If one is given the full treatment—close-up, slow-action, forward-and-reverse, split-screen, the same scene from several perspectives, and with the verbal commentary and interpretation of an expert superimposed—one has a fair analogy of what the evangelists do. . . . One might add to the significance of the analogy by pointing out that the true significance of certain plays can only be known after the game is over.[3]

Most of the alleged discrepancies among the Gospels have resulted from an inaccurate understanding of the literary principles on which they are founded.

The Style of the Gospels

The most notable stylistic trait of the Gospels is their economy of words and details. This was nothing new, since it is also the norm for storytelling in the Old Testament. But the tendency is perhaps even more pronounced in the Gospels. As in the Old Testament stories, we find a preference for the brief unit, a relatively self-contained quality to the individual episodes, a prevailing realism, an impulse toward dialogue and dramatic techniques, and a simple, unembellished style.

Anyone who has tried his or her hand at writing a story will sense at once the skill with which the Gospel writers managed to select the significant detail that embodies the maximum meaning. In this kind of narrative artistry, what the writers omit is as important as what they include, and the Gospels are notable for their understated approach to the world-changing events they record. It is a tribute to their success that so few words can produce such a vivid impression in our imaginations.

Because of their prevailing brevity and conciseness, the Gospels combine simplicity and difficulty. Despite the surface simplicity, the individual units are often perplexing when we move from description to interpretation. Many passages tease us into trying to discover their significance without giving us the kind of help that would make that discovery easy. Yet the overall message of the Gospels is easily grasped.

Subtypes Within the Gospels

All of the Gospels share a reliance on certain subtypes or subgenres. Each of these has its governing ingredients and traits. Knowing the range of possibilities will help us make more sense of individual pas-

3. Donald A. Hagner, "Interpreting the Gospels: The Landscape and the Quest," *Journal of the Evangelical Theological Society* 24 (1981): 34.

sages when we come upon them. I should also note that my list of subtypes focuses on narrative units, leaving the material in discourses (including parables, sayings, and addresses) for treatment elsewhere.

Annunciation and Nativity Stories

The Gospels of Matthew and Luke begin with a series of stories that deal with events surrounding the birth of Jesus. Some of these are annunciation stories in which angels appear to people and make predictions about the birth of Jesus or related incidents. A feature of these stories is the inclusion of lyric poems embedded in the narrative. Nativity stories recount what happened when Jesus was actually born, including stories of his early infancy. Luke adds the boyhood story of Jesus in the temple at age twelve (2:41–52).

The main purpose of these stories is to accentuate the uniqueness of Jesus, to explain his significance, to validate the historical facts of the matter, to record the supernatural occurrences surrounding the events, and to document the fulfillment of Old Testament prophecies about the coming Messiah. The main literary feature of these stories is the excitement that they convey about the world-changing events that they narrate.

Calling or Vocation Stories

The Gospels contain a number of stories in which Jesus called people to follow him or to respond to a specific command. Such calling stories include (but are not limited to) the calling of the disciples. The four ingredients and corresponding questions to ask of the text are these:

1. The *characters* involved: who is called?
2. The *circumstances* in which the call occurs: where does the call of Jesus come to people?
3. The *nature* of the call: to what does Jesus call people?
4. The *response* to the call: what constitutes the right or wrong response to the call of Jesus?

In reading these stories, we should remember the basic narrative principle that characters in a story carry a burden of meaning larger than themselves. They are representatives of the human race generally. When Jesus calls a character in the Gospels, he also calls us.

This is a good place to note another feature of the Gospels. Usually when we read stories we identify with the protagonist or hero. In the Gospels, the one character with whom we do not identify in the sense of equating ourselves with him is Jesus. We identify with other characters. They are our substitutes and represent us as they respond to Jesus. Roland Frye has said that the characters in the Gospels

> are sketched with sure strokes, but not so fully as to preclude our identifying ourselves with them. Their faces are never so completely drawn that we cannot place our own heads on their shoulders: we could be blind man, neighbor, parent, or Pharisee, and it can be instructive for us to assume each role in turn as we read.[4]

Recognition Stories

In recognition stories a character discovers who Jesus is. These stories dispense with plot conflict and keep the focus instead on the movement toward the character's moment of recognition or insight.

Two ingredients assume importance in these stories. One is the circumstances of the recognition, including the occasion, setting, and characters involved. The important question here is *how* the circumstances lead to the recognition. The second major element is the precise nature of *what* a character comes to recognize about Jesus. As readers we identify with characters in these stories. Their moment of epiphany is one that we share with them.

These stories contribute in a particularly direct way to the central purpose of the Gospels, which is to explain the person and work of Christ. It is natural to focus, therefore, on what these stories tell us about Jesus.

Witness Stories

In witness or testimony stories, either Jesus or another character testifies about who Jesus is or what he has done. These stories are similar to recognition stories, but instead of moving toward a moment of recognition, we listen to someone's proclamation about Jesus.

Witness stories usually consist of three main ingredients. We can phrase them as three questions:

1. *Who?* (The witness.)
2. *What?* (The testimony.)
3. *Why?* (The proof, which might include circumstances.)

When the witness is Jesus himself, the focus is on the second of these elements rather than the third. Because the question of evidence is

---

4. Roland Frye, "The Jesus of the Gospels: Approaches Through Narrative Structure," in *From Faith to Faith: Essays in Honor of Donald G. Miller, on His Seventieth Birthday*, ed. Dikran Y. Hadidian, Pittsburgh Theological Monographs, no. 31 (Pittsburgh: Pickwick, 1979), p. 79.

important in these stories, it is usually profitable to explore the logic between the claim that is made about Jesus and the evidence on which it is based.

Encounter Stories

In his most characteristic pose in the Gospels, Jesus is encountering a character or a group. The story of Zacchaeus (Luke 19:1–10) shows the genre on a small scale, the story of the Samaritan woman (John 4:1–42) on a grand scale. These stories should be approached as dramas. We can divide them into scenes and speeches. The essential action usually consists of dialogue rather than external events.

Encounter stories follow a predictable rhythm of movement. They have a firm progression and wholeness. They begin when either Jesus or another character initiates the encounter. Jesus asks the Samaritan woman for a drink, for example, and tells Zacchaeus that he plans to stay overnight at his house. Once the encounter has been initiated, we can trace the progress of the dialogue toward its goal. In retrospect, at least, we can identify the purpose or goal toward which Jesus builds the encounter. Encounter stories are strongly goal-oriented, being essentially quest stories.

At the end, the person encountered either accepts or rejects the claim that Jesus has made on his or her life. The outcome of these stories is crucial. The people who are encountered by Jesus in effect undergo a test that they either pass or fail.

As elsewhere in the Gospels, we should regard the people who encounter Jesus as representative of people generally. The premise in these stories is that everyone must face the claims of Jesus. Encounter stories are parables of the human condition and of how Jesus speaks to that condition.

Conflict or Controversy Stories

Conflict stories are the prototypical Gospel story—most like ordinary stories and also among the most numerous in the Gospels. These stories pit Jesus against an opposing person or group. They give the Gospels much of their color and excitement, and they move the overall action inexorably toward the eventual trial and death of Jesus.

Jesus is always the protagonist in a conflict story, regardless of whether he or his opponents originate the conflict. We need to identify the antagonists or villains in such a story, as well as the reason for their antagonism against Jesus and the exact means by which they try to trap or defeat Jesus.

As for the progress of the action, we can usually plot the steps by which the conflict between Jesus and his opponents proceeds. In particular, we can note Jesus' strategies of defense and offense or coun-terattack. These stories are built on a back-and-forth rhythm in which Jesus always gets the advantage. We also need to interpret how the conflict is finally resolved, and determine the lesson we are intended to learn from this resolution.

Pronouncement Stories

One of the distinctive subtypes in the Gospels is the pronouncement story. This is a brief story in which an event in Jesus' life is linked with a memorable saying or proverb by Jesus. Usually the event leads up to and culminates in the saying. The saying is embedded in the narrative in such a way that the two are remembered together.

The important principle in pronouncement stories is that the story is related to the saying as a stimulus is related to a response. The saying either interprets or illustrates the event. The interpretation of such a story will in large part be an exploration of how the two parts correlate. Pronouncement stories can themselves be subdivided into six categories—stories of correction, objection, commendation, quest, test, and inquiry.[5]

Pronouncement stories are a Gospel hallmark. In fact, memorable sayings are often an ingredient in other Gospel subtypes (especially conflict stories), resulting in what might be called hybrid forms.

Miracle Stories

Another form that we especially associate with the Gospels is the miracle story. The typical structure of a miracle story is this:

1. A need is established.
2. Jesus' help is sought.
3. The person in need (or his acquaintances) expresses faith or obedience.
4. Jesus performs a miracle.
5. Characters in the story respond to the miracle and/or to Jesus.

A given miracle story might omit one or more of these elements.

There is a remarkable variety in the miracle stories. Some are skel-etal outlines of what happened, while others are narrated in leisurely and full detail. Sometimes the miracle is the center of attention, while at other times it is subsidiary to another issue (thereby making the

5. For more on these classifications, see Robert C. Tannehill, "Attitudinal Shift in Synoptic Pronouncement Stories," in *Orientation by Disorientation: Studies in Literary Criticism and Biblical Literary Criticism Presented in Honor of William A. Beardslee*, ed. Richard A. Spencer, Pittsburgh Theological Monographs, no. 35 (Pittsburgh: Pickwick, 1980), p. 184.

story a hybrid). Sometimes the physical miracle attests the power of Jesus, while on other occasions the miracle takes on a symbolic meaning or is told in such a way as to teach a lesson (about faith, for example).

Passion Stories

The events surrounding the trial, death, and resurrection of Jesus form the climax of all four Gospels. If we count chapters, the percentages of each Gospel devoted to the passion of Jesus are as follows: Matthew, 29; Mark, 38; Luke, 25; and John, 38. Increasing specificity of detail characterizes the storytelling method as the writers reach the passion account. Obviously this is what the Gospel writers regarded as most important in their stories.

If we view the four passion stories as a composite whole, we can further subdivide them into discernible stories: arrival in Jerusalem, the Passover and the upper room, suffering in Gethsemane, arrest, trial, crucifixion, burial, resurrection, and postresurrection appearances. Here, too, we find the convergence of both tragedy and comedy as the Gospels move through suffering to their happy ending.

Hybrid Stories

The narrative genres I have discussed often converge in individual stories. When they do, it is possible to discuss stories in terms of two or more of these types. Miracle stories often become recognition stories as well. Memorable sayings by Jesus are so customary in the Gospel narratives that the criteria of the pronouncement story are often relevant to stories that overall would be classified as something else. When Jesus called his followers, the call often included a miraculous element, and the story accordingly has the ingredients of both a calling story and a miracle story. Despite the combination of elements in these hybrid stories, however, the way in which the writer handles the story often makes one of the story types the dominant element.

The Gospel of John

The dominant pattern of the Gospels is story or narrative, but this becomes obscured when we read them piecemeal. The full narrative sweep of a Gospel dawns on us only when we read it continuously the way we read a short story or novel. To illustrate the narrative features of a Gospel, I have selected the most literary Gospel, the Gospel of John.[6]

6. Among book-length literary analyses of individual Gospels, I recommend David Rhoads and Donald Michie's book *Mark as Story: An Introduction to the Narrative of a Gospel* (Philadelphia: Fortress, 1982).

A narrative approach to a Gospel will concern itself, among other things, with the overall unity and design of the work. The impact of any long narrative depends in part on the overriding structure that the writer is able to impose on the details. The Gospel of John is built on several unifying principles that span the book.

Structure and Unity

In its general outline, the book follows the chronology of the protagonist's public career. It thus begins with an account of Jesus' divine origin. It then proceeds through the preparatory ministry of John the Baptist, the early events of Jesus' public ministry, some main incidents of his career as an itinerant religious teacher, and finally his trial, death, and resurrection. This is clearly a story with a beginning, middle, and end.

In fact, the self-conscious shaping by Jesus of his own life has all the shapeliness of a carefully constructed story. At every stage it is evident that Jesus was controlling his life according to a plan. The climax toward which his entire life was slanted was his death and resurrection. This movement toward a climax can be traced through the successive references to the "hour" of Jesus, an allusion to the time of his death and resurrection.

Early in the book there are references to the fact that Jesus' hour has not yet come (2:4; 7:30; 8:20). We also encounter statements that "the hour is coming" (4:21; 5:28). Late in the narrative there are reminders that Christ's hour has definitely arrived (12:23; 31:1; 17:1). As the final confrontation with the Jews approaches, Jesus begins to speak more openly of his coming death, and in his last public discourse he defines his whole purpose on earth as being his death as the Savior of the world (12:20–36).

Another element of narrative structure is the progressive intensification of plot conflict and a corresponding movement toward the climax of the story. The writer begins his story with events that evoked no conflict (the miracle at Cana, the discourses with Nicodemus and the Samaritan woman, the healing of the official's son), and then moves to acts of Jesus that elicited extreme conflict (the healing on the sabbath, the argument over Christ's claims to be the bread of life, the controversy at the Feast of Tabernacles, and so forth). Finally there is the overt conspiracy to kill Jesus and at last the crucifixion itself.

The only exception to this pattern of increasing hostility is the cleansing of the temple (2:13–16), a scene of violent conflict that appears early and serves the narrative function of foreshadowing the eventual struggle between Jesus and the Jews and the ultimate victory of Jesus in this struggle. We might note, too, that in the cleansing of the temple Jesus initiates the conflict, whereas later chapters about the ongoing struggle feature the antagonism of the Jews against Jesus.

The Gospel of John is also structured on the principle of expansion followed by constriction. The action begins with an account of Jesus' relations with a small circle of believers, including John the Baptist, the disciples he called to follow him, and his family and friends, seen with Jesus at the wedding of an acquaintance in Cana. From this intimate circle of friends, Jesus' public ministry quickly expands throughout Palestine and encompasses huge crowds of people, as Jesus becomes one of the most talked-about public figures of his time. As the conspiracy to kill Jesus grows, his contacts again become constricted. During the last week of his life, he spends his time with the disciples, and his postresurrection appearances likewise involve the small inner circle of friends.

Yet another aspect of the structural unity of the Gospel of John is the overriding conflict between belief and unbelief. Keeping Jesus always in the center of the action, the writer presents a series of responses by people who come into contact with the protagonist. At root, these responses show either belief or unbelief in the saving work of Jesus. In John's Gospel, the unbelief is concentrated in "the Jews," that is, the religious leaders.

Many individual episodes are specifically tied to this ongoing struggle, which is based on Jesus' clash with his social and religious environment. In the words of G. Wilson Knight, the Gospel pictures Jesus "silhouetted against a world of formalized religion, hypocrisy, envy, evil and suffering."[7] The writer's purpose in presenting this conflict between belief and unbelief is to instill belief in the reader, as he makes clear at the end of the book: "Now Jesus did many other signs in the presence of the disciples, which are not written in this book; but these are written that you may believe that Jesus is the Christ, the Son of God, and that believing you may have life in his name" (20:30–31).

Patterns

John's skill in organizing the material is evident not only in his management of the overall narrative structure but also in his construction of smaller units. One of these elements of design consists of combining an event that involves Jesus with a discourse that interprets the meaning of the event. Typical examples include Jesus' request for a drink from the Samaritan woman followed by his statements about the water of life (chap. 4), the healing on the sabbath linked to Christ's words about his divine authority (chap. 5), the feeding of the five thou-

7. G. Wilson Knight, *The Christian Renaissance* (New York: Norton, 1962), p. 169.

sand related to the discourse on the bread of life (chap. 6), and the raising of Lazarus accompanied by Jesus' remarks about his being the resurrection and the life (chap. 11).

An elaboration of this narrative technique is the linking of a single discourse to two events. For example, the discourse on Christ as the light of the world (chap. 8) is flanked by references to attendance at the Feast of Tabernacles, where the burning of huge torches was part of the ritual (chap. 7), and the giving of sight to the blind man (chap. 9). The same pattern occurs with the discourse on the bread of heaven, which is placed in the context of both the Passover and the feeding of the five thousand (chap. 6).

Yet another variation of this pattern is the relation of a single event to two discourses. For example, the healing of the blind man (chap. 9) illustrates Jesus' preceding discourse about the light of the world (chap. 8), while the expulsion of the healed man from the synagogue leads immediately into Jesus' discourse about the good shepherd and bad shepherds (chap. 10). The author's sensitivity to symbolism is obvious in all this, since the events that he narrates are external symbols of the theological truths that Christ proclaims in his accompanying discourses.

A similar type of narrative pattern that underlies a number of individual episodes is the motif of the misunderstood statement. These dramas in miniature unfold in three stages: Jesus makes a pronouncement, a bystander expresses a misunderstanding of the utterance, and Jesus proceeds to explain the meaning of his original statement. This narrative pattern occurs no fewer than nine times in the book.[8] Usually the misunderstanding arises when Jesus' statement calls for a figurative or symbolic interpretation and is given a literal meaning by the bystander, a fact whose significance for interpreting the Gospel should not be overlooked.

The fourth Gospel also makes use of number patterns in a manner similar to that which pervades the Book of Revelation. Patterns of three are prominent. The narrator records three Passovers and three other feasts that Jesus attended. Early in the book John the Baptist three times witnesses to Christ's messiahship. Late in the narrative Jesus is three times condemned. He also speaks three times from the cross. There are three denials by Peter and three stages in Christ's restoration of Peter.

There is a similar use of the number seven. The writer structures the central part of his narrative around seven great miracles or "signs"

8. The passages are as follows: 3:3–8; 4:10–15; 4:31–38; 6:47–58; 7:33–36; 8:21–30; 8:31–47; 8:56–58; 11:11–15. The pattern appears with slight modification in 2:17–22.

that Jesus performed. The list includes turning the water into wine (2:1–11), the healing of the official's son (4:46–54), the cure of the paralytic (5:1–18), the feeding of the five thousand (6:5–13), walking on the water (6:16–21), the healing of the blind man (9:1–7), and the raising of Lazarus (11:1–44).

Equally important is the pattern of seven statements by Jesus beginning with the formula *I am* and followed by a metaphoric description of Jesus' person and work: the bread of life (6:35), the light of the world (8:12), the door of the sheep (10:7), the good shepherd (10:11), the resurrection and the life (11:25), the way, the truth, and the life (14:6), and the true vine (15:1). As the book unfolds there is also a sevenfold witness to Christ: the witness of the Father (5:37; 8:18), of the Son (8:14; 18:37), of Christ's works (5:36; 10:25), of Scripture (5:39–46), of John the Baptist (1:7; 5:35), of the disciples (15:27; 19:35), and of the Spirit (15:26; 16:14).

The Flow of the Story

A literary approach to the Gospels is concerned not only with the elements of narrative pattern and design but also with the sequential unfolding of the story. The progress of the story from beginning to end—the sequential ordering of the material—is of prime importance if we read the book as a story. The following survey of the Gospel of John thus attempts to reconstruct the linear development of the story as we actually read the book.

John begins his story with a lyric prologue (1:1–18). The narrative function is to introduce the reader to the protagonist or hero of the story. He is introduced to us as the incarnate Christ, both divine and human, both heavenly and earthly. Two chief functions are ascribed to Christ in the prologue: he is the revelation of God to people, and he is the bringer of spiritual life.

The prologue also introduces some stylistic traits that will permeate the story to follow. Already we see a reliance on symbol and metaphor as the form through which the nature of God's unprecedented disclosure in Christ is conveyed. Thus Christ is presented as "the Word" and as "the light" that "shines in the darkness" and "enlightens every man." We are also introduced to the great conflicts around which the story will be built—conflicts between light and darkness, Christ's being in the world and yet rejected by the world, his coming to his own home and not being received there.

The remainder of the first chapter is devoted to a few brief narratives that introduce us to the protagonist by showing his impact on other people. One of these people is John the Baptist, who regards his successful ministry as only the prelude to the even greater ministry of the coming Messiah (1:19–34). Already as we read we can see that the essential purpose of the story will be to portray, explain, and exalt the central character. This reaches its early climax in the story of Christ's baptism, which is accompanied by the supernatural sign of the descent of the Spirit in the form of a dove (1:29–34).

These early witness and recognition stories are followed by several calling or vocation stories (1:35–51). Here, too, the protagonist is characterized by the loyalty and worship that he elicits from his followers. Dialogue is the basic mode of these stories, as we hear voices calling, responding, and explaining. The effect is to place us as participants and spectators of the world-changing events that make up the essential material of the Gospels.

Variety of episode is necessary to any good story. Monotony dulls the effect. After viewing the kaleidoscope of brief scenes and characters that makes up chapter 1, we enter a slower-paced world in chapter 2, which is devoted to just two events, the miracle at Cana and the cleansing of the temple. Having shown the protagonist indirectly by dramatizing how he influences those around him, the writer now moves to a more direct presentation of Jesus in action.

The miracle of turning water into wine (2:1–11) is the first of seven great miracles that Jesus performs in the Gospel of John. In terms of storytelling technique, John here draws upon his staple—a combination of summarized narrative (in which the writer tells us what happened) and dramatized dialogue. This early episode belongs to the familiar archetype of the initiation, as the author emphasizes that it was "the first of his signs" (v. 11).

The precise term *sign* is important in this Gospel. John uses the term to draw attention to the significance inherent in Jesus' miracles. They are not simply factual events or physical phenomena but symbols of spiritual reality. This fusion of event and symbolic meaning is one of the most distinctive features of John's Gospel. It is an essentially literary approach in which truth is imaged in concrete form.

What meaning, then, did this great sign embody? This is an interpretive question that the Gospel of John continuously requires us to answer. John himself makes one meaning explicit when he states that Christ's miracle "manifested his glory" in such a way that "his disciples believed in him" (v. 11). But even when the narrator tells us the truth about his great symbols, he does not necessarily tell us the whole truth.

Another meaning is implicit in this parabolic miracle of Jesus. The six stone jars contained water that was used for the ceremonial rituals that would have accompanied a Jewish wedding. By turning this water into wine, Jesus was announcing, through a symbolic act, that he had come to fulfill and supersede the ceremonial laws of Old Testament religion. In the background of the episode is another biblical archetype, the messianic banquet, in which the kingdom of God is compared to a feast. The quantity of water changed to wine is symbolic of the abundance of the messianic banquet, a fact that the narrator himself makes explicit by emphasizing that each of the jars held "twenty or thirty gallons" (v. 6).

As we conclude this early event in the story, then, we can rest assured that as readers we have been initiated into the storyteller's essential method of narration. We now know that his story exists to tell us the truth about the protagonist, Jesus. Much of the meaning of the story, moreover, will be embodied in symbolic images and events. The main intent of the story (to acquaint the reader with the person and work of Christ) will be clear—in fact, the narrator can be trusted to provide interpretive signposts to guide us. But much of the meaning of the story will depend on our ability to see deeper meanings in the surface details. Those meanings, moreover, will have a lot to do with Christ's fulfillment of Old Testament foreshadowings.

Up to this point in the narrative, Jesus has been shown in his relations with a small circle of friends and relatives. With the episode of the cleansing of the temple (2:13–25), the scope of the action broadens as Jesus enters the public spotlight. Here is the first conflict or controversy story in a Gospel that will rely heavily on this form. Like many events in the Gospels, this one is narrated with vivid and dramatic detail. It is as though we are witnessing the event in person or on television.

As elsewhere in the Gospels, we are asked to interpret the meaning of the event in terms of the mission of Christ. In cleansing the temple, Christ asserts his authority by challenging the religious establishment of his day. The event also introduces a note of revolution into the story as Christ uses physical force to single-handedly drive the moneychangers out of the temple. This is not a private campaign but a messianic gesture in which God himself enters his temple with divine authority to cleanse it. In this episode we also find the first misunderstood statement of Jesus when he utters the enigmatic statement, "Destroy this temple, and in three days I will raise it up" (2:19).

Jesus' dialogue with Nicodemus about the new birth (3:1–15) is typical of the self-contained nature of the narrative pieces that the Gospel writers compiled as they told their stories of Jesus. The basic model of action is threefold: a character enters the life of Jesus, encounters the claims of Jesus, and then drops out of the story. Dialogue is the means of encounter in these stories.

In the story of Nicodemus we find Jesus in a new role in the Gospel of John, the role of teacher. The story itself is an encounter story built around another of Jesus' misunderstood utterances. Nicodemus misinterprets Jesus' statement that "unless one is born anew, he cannot see the kingdom of God" (3:3) when he interprets the statement literally. He asks, "How can a man be born when he is old? Can he enter a second time into his mother's womb and be born?" (3:4). Jesus responds by interpreting his original statement as referring to a spiritual birth (3:6–8). This dialogue about spiritual birth becomes linked to the overriding plot of John's Gospel when Jesus defines the new birth in terms of belief: "that whoever believes in [me] may have eternal life" (3:15).

Several common strategies of the Gospels converge in an episode like the story of Nicodemus. The Gospels are a series of epiphanies (revelations or disclosures leading to spiritual insight) in which we as readers share a character's gradual movement toward perception regarding Jesus. This pattern corresponds to what we can infer about the formation of the Gospels: they are composed of units that grew up around the disciples' early (oral) proclamation about Jesus. No doubt the stories about Jesus that were used most in the preaching of the disciples were those that could most easily be used to teach the basic outlines of the Christian faith.

The writers who compiled the stories and put them into the collections known as the Gospels molded their material according to their purposes. They kept their history about Jesus in a clearly discernible interpretive framework. This is well illustrated when the account of Christ's discussion with Nicodemus is followed by the narrator's commentary that elaborates the statements made by Jesus (3:16–21). These verses, beginning with the famous statement that "God so loved the world that he gave his only Son, that whoever believes in him should not perish but have eternal life," are both theological teaching and the writer's personal testimony. The Gospels were written by people who had been transformed by their experience with Christ and who wanted others to share the same experience.

Jesus' conversation with the Samaritan woman at the well (4:1–30) is one of the most famous of the elaborated Gospel stories. It is the classic encounter story in the Gospels. As with other encounter stories, this one is a drama in miniature. The physical stage is set with realistic details: "So he came to a city of Samaria. . . . Jacob's well was there, and so Jesus, wearied as he was with his journey, sat down beside the well. It was about the sixth hour." Dialogue carries the essential meaning of the encounter that follows. As so often is true in the Gospels, drama is the mode of presentation.

The story is also a masterpiece of narrative art. Encounter stories are essentially quest stories in which Jesus initiates a conversation and slants it toward the goal of bringing a person to belief. The sense of progression toward the goal is overpowering in this story as we trace the back-and-forth movement between the two speakers. It is a classic case of one thing leading to the next. The plot has the usual beginning-middle-end shapeliness that we associate with well-made stories. It begins with Jesus' apparently casual request for a drink of water. It proceeds to Christ's progressive self-disclosure as the promised Messiah about whom the woman herself speaks. The story ends with the woman's belief and testimony. The story even has the moment of reversal that Aristotle liked in stories: the woman thinks to dismiss the religious claims that Jesus has just made with the comment that "when [Messiah] comes, he will show us all things" (4:25), but Jesus shocks her by saying, "I who speak to you am he" (4:26).[9]

The characterization of the Samaritan woman also makes the story memorable. She is the archetypal outcast who comes to the well at noon when no one else would be present. She is a moral drifter, having had five divorces and now living with a lover. When the subject turns to religion, she tries to evade the real issue by raising a point of theological dispute: "Our fathers worshiped on this mountain and you say that in Jerusalem is the place where men ought to worship" (4:20). The Gospels are rich in recognizable human experience. We have all met the Samaritan woman in the routine of our lives. In fact, we can see much of ourselves in her.

The story of Jesus and the Samaritan woman epitomizes the Gospel as a literary form. If we are looking for the standard ingredients of the Gospel, we can find them here: the focus on Jesus as protagonist, the travel motif, the prominence of nature as a setting for the action, realism of description, the prominence of dialogue, the presence of archetypal symbols (in this case, water as a symbol of eternal life), a miraculous element (Jesus knows the woman's entire marital history without having met her before), the presence of mysterious sayings by Jesus (e.g., "whoever drinks of the water that I shall give him will never thirst"), a preoccupation with spiritual salvation as the central issue, and a crowd of onlookers drawn into the action.

The individual stories that make up the Gospels exist on a continuum based on length or shortness. The story of the Samaritan woman is an embellished story, told in a leisurely pace and filled out with realistic description and dialogue. But this literary impulse is mingled

9. I mention Aristotle by design: his *Poetics* remains the definitive starting point on the subject of plot in stories and is an excellent source of terms for discussing the Gospels.

with the starkest documentary impulse to record the facts and no more. This is well illustrated by the fragment that immediately follows the drama at the well of Jacob:

> After the two days he departed to Galilee. For Jesus himself testified that a prophet has no honor in his own country. So when he came to Galilee, the Galileans welcomed him, having seen all that he had done in Jerusalem at the feast, for they too had gone to the feast. [4:43–45]

Such fragments serve as reminders that the degree of literary intention in the Gospels varies.

The healing of the official's son (4:46–54) is another miracle story. We find the usual ingredients: a need established, the help of Jesus sought, an expression of faith, the performance of a miracle, and a response from those involved in the miracle. In terms of the bigger movement of the Gospel as a whole, a miracle story such as this shows Christ's supernatural power, his compassion for the physical needs of people, and the way in which those who realized Christ's divine power were brought to belief.

The healing of the paralytic man at Bethesda on the sabbath (chap. 5) is a miracle story on the grand scale. Although it is a healing story like the episode preceding it, the differences between the two miracles show the narrative principle of variety that is almost always at work in the Gospels. In the place of a brief narrative, we have an elaborated story. Whereas the healing of the official's son led to belief, this miracle ends in conflict with the Pharisees over the issue of whether the healing had violated the law about keeping the sabbath and over Christ's claims of authority (5:10–18). In the healing of the official's son, the account of the miracle was followed by a one-sentence summary of the belief of those who witnessed the miracle. Here the description of the miracle is accompanied by the extended discourse of Jesus about his divine authority (5:19–47). This fusion of act and discourse, event and spiritual significance, is of course a chief differentiating feature of John's Gospel. In this instance, Jesus' discourse is devoted to his self-characterization, as he explains who he is. The frequent self-characterization of the protagonist is one of the things that makes the Gospels unique as stories.

The miraculous feeding of five thousand people (6:1–14) perpetuates the narrative pattern of variety in unity. The basic elements of the miracle story persist, but there are changes as well. The miracle itself involves sustaining life instead of healing disease. It encompasses a huge crowd of people; earlier miracles involved individuals. Along with the differences is an element of sameness, as the story winds its way back at the end to the overriding plot of the Gospel as a whole, the struggle between belief and unbelief: "When the people saw the sign which he had done, they said, 'This is indeed the prophet who is to come into the world!' " (6:14).

In keeping with the basic narrative strategy in the Gospel of John, the miracle of the feeding of the crowd is a sign that reaches its culmination in an interpretive discourse, in this case Jesus' discourse on his status as the bread of life (6:22–40). The Gospel of John is famous for its symbolism, and here is a prime example. The physical image of bread becomes symbolic of a spiritual reality. The very rhetoric that Jesus uses in talking about bread shows this mingling of the physical and the spiritual: "food which endures to eternal life (v. 27), "the true bread from heaven" (v. 32), "the bread of life" (v. 35), "the living bread which came down from heaven" (v. 51). Here, truly, the physical becomes transformed into something more than physical.

Many of the episodes in John's Gospel begin with narration of an event and then expand by showing the repercussions of the initial stimulus. The story we have just considered is typical. It begins with a miracle, followed by a discourse in which Jesus elaborates the physical miracle, transforming it into a spiritual symbol. The discourse, in turn, generates disagreement, first among the Jews (6:41–59) and then among the disciples (6:60–71). Belief versus unbelief continues to hold center stage as the Gospel unfolds.

In summary, the long sixth chapter illustrates the typical structure of the embellished stories found in the Gospels. The storyteller's impulse in these stories is to linger on an event, not simply to give the bare outline. In the center of the action are the person and work of Jesus. The story begins with an event that is then elaborated in a discourse. Then both become transmuted into a conflict between belief and unbelief.

The Gospels use two chief means of characterizing the protagonist. One is Jesus' self-characterization through deed and word. The other is the response of others to Jesus' claims about himself. The account of Christ's appearance at the Feast of Tabernacles (chap. 7) illustrates the interplay between these two types of characterization as we witness a bewildering variety of responses to Jesus' claims about himself. One response is the hostility of the Jewish leaders. In keeping with the plot structure of increasing antagonism against Jesus, the earlier intellectual debate now intensifies into a conspiracy to kill Jesus (7:1, 25), and even an unsuccessful attempt to arrest him (v. 32). The sheer danger and adventure of the story should not escape us as we read the Gospels.

Another response of people is uncertainty about the claims of Jesus:

"And there was much muttering about him among the people. While some said, 'He is a good man,' others said, 'No, he is leading the people astray' " (7:12). A third response is belief in Jesus as Savior, as evidenced by the report that "many of the people believed in him" (7:31). Behind this pattern of varied response is the clear call of Jesus for people to believe in him: "If any one thirst, let him come to me and drink" (v. 37). Like so many other chapters in the Gospels, this one is full of voices—voices arguing and voices expressing perplexity, hostility, and belief.

Debate and conflict also govern the next chapter (8), in which Jesus defends his claims against the Pharisees. The chapter begins with the Pharisees placing a woman caught in adultery in front of Jesus "to test him, that they might have some charge to bring against him" (8:6). It ends with the Jews taking up stones to throw at Jesus (v. 59). Sandwiched between these two conflicts is a prolonged altercation between Jesus and the Pharisees. It should be obvious how much is lost if we do not approach the Gospels as stories. They are fast-paced and action-filled, having much more in common with a novel or a television drama than a sermon.

Earlier I called the Gospel of John the most literary of the Gospels. This claim is not based only on John's poetic sensitivity to image and symbol. It also stems from John's tendency to work with relatively long episodes and to embellish them with literary technique. John is rarely content simply to record what happened. He recreates events in such a way as to tell us how things happened so we can relive them.

The story of the healing of the man born blind (chap. 9) illustrates to perfection this literary inclination.[10] The story is conceived dramatically, with virtually all the action embodied in the form of dialogue among various characters. The action shifts from scene to scene in a way that makes us feel as though we are watching it on television. The drama is shot through with realism, humor, and controversy. It is as recognizably chaotic as a committee meeting that has gotten out of control.

To lend purpose and design to the story, John includes an interpretive framework at the outset. The disciples ask Jesus, "Rabbi, who sinned, this man or his parents, that he was born blind?" (9:2). Jesus challenges their conventional way of thinking by replying that the man's blindness was not the result of sin but that "the works of God

10. For a fuller explication than I attempt here, and as an excellent illustration of the type of literary analysis to which the Gospels lend themselves, I commend James L. Resseguie's essay "John 9: A Literary-Critical Analysis," in *Literary Interpretations of Biblical Narratives, Volume II*, ed. Kenneth R. R. Gros Louis (Nashville: Abingdon, 1982), pp. 295–303.

might be made manifest in him" (v. 3). The miracle that follows, then, will be another of the revealing signs of John's Gospel, manifesting the power and compassion of God. The sign itself is a thoroughly physical event, as Jesus "spat on the ground and made clay of the spittle and anointed the man's eyes with the clay" (v. 6).

The elaboration of the miraculous sign follows a now familiar pattern. The actual miracle begins an ever-widening series of ripples in the community. True to life, the first people to hear of the miracle are the healed man's neighbors (vv. 8–12). From the neighborhood the action moves to the religious leaders (vv. 13–34), who finally cast the man out of the synagogue. There is humor as well as pathos in the episode, with the Pharisees inflexibly denying the obvious healing of the man and the equally obvious divine power of Jesus. This is a good episode with which to note, therefore, the pervasive satiric element in the Gospels. Satire is the exposure, through ridicule or rebuke, of human vice or folly. In the events of the Gospels, as well as the parables and discourses of Jesus, there is continuous satire, usually directed against the Jewish religious leaders.[11]

At its end, the story of the healing of the blind man winds its way back to the unifying plot conflict of the Gospel as a whole. It is the conflict between belief and unbelief. After Jesus seeks out the man who has just been thrust out of the synagogue, the man believes and worships Jesus (vv. 35–38), while the Pharisees who witness this scene of belief remain the archetypal refusers of festivity (vv. 39–41). Jesus charges them with blindness, a concluding reminder that this is another episode in John's Gospel that is unified around a controlling image that symbolizes the spiritual meaning of the main event.

The culminating belief of the man who was healed shows how strongly oriented toward a goal the individual stories of the Gospels are. There is an incipient quest motif underlying most episodes in the Gospels. Jesus initiates action and utters discourses with a view to bringing people to a response. Knowing that this is how the episodes are structured, we are in a better position to organize the movement and details of a Gospel story around its appointed goal. Beginning at the end is usually a helpful way of analyzing a Gospel story.

The organizing pattern of John's Gospel is to combine events with accompanying discourses that seize upon a central image from the event. Jesus' famous discourse about his being the good shepherd (10:1–21) perpetuates this pattern. The comments about the ignoble

11. For more on satire in the New Testament, see chapter 14, above. On the element of humor in the Gospels that is usually overlooked, the classic source is Elton True-blood, *The Humor of Christ* (New York: Harper and Row, 1964).

shepherds who are motivated by greed and who abandon their sheep cast a retrospective look at the behavior of the Pharisees who rejected the healed man. The care of the good shepherd described in the discourse likewise explains the actions of Jesus in his dealings with the healed man.

The importance of the discourse about the good shepherd reaches out to other contexts as well. The discourse comes in the middle of John's Gospel, for example, and by summarizing the redemptive life of Jesus it sounds the keynote for the entire Gospel. Within the larger context of the Bible as a whole, the discourse climaxes the tradition of pastoral literature in which religious issues are portrayed metaphorically in terms of shepherds and sheep (see, for example, Ezek. 34).

The next episode, the account of Jesus' appearance at the Feast of Dedication (10:22–42), parallels the earlier appearance at the Feast of Tabernacles (chap. 7). In fact, John refers to Jesus' attendance at six Jewish religious festivals. As a narrative principle, repetition of any type functions as a device of disclosure by which a storyteller signals what is important in the story. In keeping with John's strategy of attaching symbolic meanings to events, it is not hard to see the importance of Jesus' attendance at Jewish religious festivals. He is the fulfillment of Old Testament ceremonial laws and rituals. Not surprisingly, Jesus' attendance at these events generates controversy and conflict, as well as occasional belief.

The raising of Lazarus from the grave, coming near the middle of the Gospel of John, is a climactic episode. It is accordingly told in full circumstantial detail. To give the story a sense of unity and purpose from the beginning, John provides an interpretive framework at the outset: Jesus announces to his disciples that the death of Lazarus "is for the glory of God, so that the Son of God may be glorified by means of it" (11:4). Here, in fact, is the hidden agenda of all the Gospels. In terms of narrative classification, the Gospels are admiration stories in which the selection of material and storytelling technique are designed to exalt the hero of the story.

John's Gospel puts us in touch with a number of archetypes, such as light and darkness, water and bread, sight and blindness. The controlling archetype in the story of Lazarus is the death-rebirth pattern. It is combined with another common motif of John's Gospel, the misunderstood statement of Jesus. When Jesus tells his disciples that "our friend Lazarus has fallen asleep, but I go to awake him out of sleep" (v. 11), the disciples' perplexed response shows that for them the remark is a puzzle requiring a solution (vv. 12–16).

The story itself, in fact, is structured like a suspense story. First

Jesus delays his trip to Bethany for two days. His mysterious comments that Lazarus is only sleeping likewise seem to raise doubt that he plans to do anything about the death. As Jesus approaches the village, the friends and relatives of Lazarus come out to meet Jesus. Instead of moving quickly to the miracle, John takes time to record the conversations of Jesus with both Martha (vv. 20–27) and Mary (vv. 28–34). Then we picture the grief of Jesus and the responses it elicits from onlookers (vv. 35–37).

The drama at the grave site is similarly suspenseful. Jesus commands that the stone be taken away, but having done so he has to contend with Martha's objection that the body has begun to decompose. After the stone is removed from the grave, Jesus prays to his heavenly Father and cries out with a loud voice, "Lazarus, come out." Then, almost beyond belief, we watch as "the dead man came out, his hands and feet bound with bandages, and his face wrapped with a cloth" (v. 44). As elsewhere in the Gospels, we have been participants in an awe-inspiring event.

Individual episodes like this have a double allegiance. They are first of all stories in themselves, built on a principle of beginning-middle-end. But they are also building blocks in the overall edifice of the Gospel. The Gospels adhere to the time-honored principles of good composition: unity, coherence, and emphasis.

The story of the raising of Lazarus contributes in exactly this way to the bigger story of John's Gospel. As elsewhere, a physical event becomes symbolic of a spiritual reality. Usually this transformation is explained in a discourse of Jesus, and this is true here as Jesus tells Martha, "I am the resurrection and the life" (v. 25). Here, too, is one of seven "I am" self-characterizations of Jesus around which John builds his Gospel. As with the previous great signs recorded in the Gospel, Jesus' raising of Lazarus generates resistance from the religious authorities (vv. 45–57).

In keeping with his practice of narrative variety, John follows the embellished story of Lazarus with two brief narrative fragments. One is the story of Mary of Bethany's anointing of Jesus (12:1–8). Mary's act is a symbolic gesture, capturing as with a camera click the leading Gospel theme of the supreme worthiness of Jesus. The episode also reenacts the usual narrative pattern of event leading to conflict, as Judas Iscariot and Jesus disagree on the appropriateness of the anointing (vv. 4–8). From another perspective, the contrast is between the responses of Mary and Judas to the person of Jesus.

The triumphal entry into Jerusalem (12:12–19) is another simple narrative. We might note that a Gospel writer's choice of whether to use simple or embellished narrative does not depend on the significance of an event in the life of Jesus. The Gospel of Luke, for example, treats the same event in much more detail. The decision regarding the length of an episode seems to have been a storyteller's decision rather than a theologian's. John uses the event of the triumphal entry to embody two themes—the imperfect understanding that the disciples had of the event until after Christ's glorification (vv. 14–16) and the popularity that Jesus enjoyed with the crowd at the height of his earthly career (vv. 17–19). The latter motif is continued in the ensuing narrative fragment about the Greeks who came to hear Jesus (vv. 20–22).

In terms of overall plot, the Gospel writers succeed splendidly in moving their stories progressively and inexorably toward a climactic conflict between Jesus and his enemies. In John's Gospel, we can trace, step by step, the development from the Jews' early debates with Jesus to a general plan to kill him. In the later phases of the story, the threat to Jesus is so dire that he travels secretly (11:54). As noted earlier, the same movement toward the climactic encounter can be seen in the references to the coming "hour" and to the actual arrival of the "hour." Following the triumphal entry, therefore, Jesus utters a discourse on the theme, "The hour has come for the Son of man to be glorified" (12:23–36).

As the story approaches the events of Christ's death, the focus constricts from Jesus' ministry in the world to his last days with his loyal disciples. The very details of the story reflect this constriction. Instead of miraculous signs that generate belief and unbelief in the crowds and religious leaders, Jesus now performs a sign for his disciples by washing their feet (13:1–20). The foot washing is another of Jesus' parabolic acts, combining action and meaning to teach spiritual truth in a manner similar to what we find in the miracles and parables of Jesus. The sin of unbelief, which had earlier involved large numbers of Jews, now becomes narrowed to unbelief within the disciples, as embodied in the dismissal of the traitor Judas Iscariot (13:21–30) and the prediction of Peter's denial (vv. 36–38). And in contrast to the earlier public discourses, Jesus now delivers a private address to the inner circle of disciples in the upper room (chaps. 14–16).

The discourse in the upper room belongs to the Hebraic literary form of the farewell address that an important person gives to his children or followers on the eve of his death.[12] Jesus' farewell address

---

12. The adherence of Jesus' discourse in the upper room to the Old Testament and intertestamental form of the farewell address is discussed by Raymond E. Brown, *The Gospel According to John, Thirteen to Twenty-one*, vol. 29A of the Anchor Bible (Garden City, N.Y.: Doubleday, 1970), pp. 597–601. Old Testament examples include the discourses of Jacob (Gen. 48–49), Moses (the Book of Deuteronomy), Joshua (Josh. 23–24), and David (1 Chron. 28–29). In the New Testament, 2 Peter shows some of the same motifs.

includes the following conventional motifs: the speaker's announcement of his imminent departure, the listeners' sorrow and accompanying words of comfort from the speaker, the directive to keep God's commandments, a command to the listeners to love one another, a prediction of what will happen to the listeners in the future, the invocation of peace upon the listeners, the naming of a successor (in this case, the Holy Spirit), and a concluding prayer for the listeners. The tone of Jesus' farewell address is intimate, loving, and full of compassionate concern for the disciples. In the background is the initiation motif, as the disciples are being introduced to the mission they will carry out in the absence of their master. The symbolic "I am" pronouncements that Jesus makes in John's Gospel here reach their culmination in the discourse about the true vine (15:1–6).

As is true of the other Gospels, the Gospel of John devotes a disproportionately large amount of space to the events surrounding the death of Jesus. In terms of narrative structure, the passion story in the Gospel of John unfolds in three stages—the betrayal (18:1–11), the trial (18:12–19:16), and the crucifixion (19:17–42). The betrayal is narrated summarily, while the trial is described in full circumstantial detail. The trial, in fact, is staged like a drama, and it is accordingly full of voices—voices questioning, accusing, denying, and demanding crucifixion.

One avenue to appreciating the storytelling technique of the passion stories is to note how skillful the writers were in selecting the significant detail in a style characterized by conciseness, economy, and understatement. A literary critic has described it thus:

> Mark tells of the crucifixion in twenty short verses, and even John does not go beyond thirty. Instead of attempting to portray what was impossible of description, they gave the effect upon the different observers—what the two robbers said, the mocking of the crowd, the testimony of the centurion, the weeping women, a convulsed earth and a black sky. This, with a few lines describing what was done, and a few words from the cross, paints the world's supreme tragedy. Note how noble is the restraint of the writers. There is no outburst of wrath against Judas, no condemnation of Herod, of Pilate, of the priests. The world's mightiest figure is set forth with no word of eulogy, with no attempt at heroics, no analysis of the feeling of the actors in events charged with emotion.[13]

The resurrection of Jesus from the grave (chap. 20) is the climax of John's Gospel, as it is of the others. It is the ultimate triumph of the

13. Charles Allen Dinsmore, *The English Bible as Literature* (Boston and New York: Houghton Mifflin, 1931), p. 265.

protagonist, proof of his uniqueness and divinity. It is also the ultimate example of the death-rebirth archetype. In terms of plot structure, the resurrection is the final phase of the U-shaped comic plot of the Gospel. The gradual isolation of the protagonist is now followed by his re-integration into society. It is evident that the inherent form of the New Testament Gospels is not tragedy but comedy.

The postresurrection appearances of Jesus are all structured as en-counters with individuals. In terms of Gospel subtypes, they are rec-ognition stories in which Jesus' followers come to recognize Jesus as their resurrected master. These are moments of high drama. Mary Magdalene's moment of surprised recognition is captured by her ex-clamation "Rabboni! [Master!]" (20:16). The story of the appearance to Thomas (20:24–29) is equally memorable, as Thomas's initial skep-ticism becomes muted in his exclamation of recognition and adora-tion, "My Lord and my God!" With this story, incidentally, the plot conflict between belief and unbelief that has unified John's Gospel reaches its final resolution.

The last event recorded in the story, the postresurrection appear-ance in which Jesus restores Peter (21:1–19), echoes key events in the Gospel and serves as a conclusion to the story that John has told. The mystery of Jesus' appearance at daybreak reminds us of a supernatural mystery that has pervaded the story from the prologue that gives a divine genealogy for the hero. The miraculous haul of fishes echoes an equally pervasive miraculous element in the story. The threefold res-toration of Peter repeats the pattern of Peter's denial of Jesus and underscores the importance of patterns of repetition in John's Gospel.

John's Gospel in Retrospect

As we look back over the whole story that John has told, we might well ask what principle of organization accounts for the arrangement of the individual parts in their final form. If the Gospel writers were compilers of stories and sayings already in circulation, what pattern did they follow in weaving the individual units into the completed fabric? Although the general outline of events is chronological, the writers do not claim that each event is strictly chronological in its relation to other details. The Gospel of John, in particular, may delib-erately dislocate chronology in order to achieve its ends. The arrange-ment of parts is not determined by theological considerations, since the theology would remain unchanged with other arrangements.

We can infer that the organization of John's Gospel is based on narrative principles. One of these is the principle of variety of episode. With a storyteller's instinct, John mingles long and short episodes, as well as mighty acts and spoken discourses. Events that carry their own meaning, such as the healing of the official's son, are interspersed with acts that are accompanied by interpretive discourses. Jesus' encounters with individuals are balanced by appearances to large crowds. Stories that end in belief are juxtaposed to episodes that lead to conflict and unbelief.

A second narrative principle that governs John's story is progression. We have observed the intensification of plot conflict as the story unfolds, the movement toward the climactic event of the execution of Jesus, and an expansion of Jesus' career from a private circle to the public arena, followed by a constriction to his disciples and friends.

Nor should we overlook the way in which John's Gospel is composed on the principles of unity, coherence, and emphasis. The unity consists of the presence of a central protagonist in every episode, as well as the existence of a plot conflict between Jesus and his opponents, and between belief and unbelief. The coherence of the story is enhanced by recurrent patterns, including the linking of a mighty sign by Jesus with a discourse that elaborates the same sign, the symbolic use of images such as bread and light to embody spiritual truth about Jesus, the motif of misunderstood sayings of Jesus, a series of "I am" pronouncements by Jesus, and number patterns. Out of these unifying elements emerges the emphasis on the worthiness and power of Jesus and the call to belief in him.

The Gospels as Stories

What is gained by reading the Gospels as complete and unified stories? To begin, such a reading is the only good corrective to the fragmentation that characterizes most people's experience of the Gospels. In most readers' minds, the Gospels are bewildering collections of fragments in which the individual units lack coherence with each other. How can this be right, when it is obvious that each Gospel writer took pains to arrange the individual units to best advantage and to cast them into a carefully designed narrative flow?

Once we accept the principle that a Gospel is a literary whole, we will find the total impact greatly enhanced. Individual units in the Gospel of John, for example, will have much more meaning for us if we can relate them to such overriding frameworks as the conflict between belief and unbelief, or the technique of matching Christ's great "signs" with discourses that expand them into symbols of spiritual realities, or the very human and moving story of Christ's worsening conflict with the Jewish authorities until they finally execute him.

It is an axiom of educational theory that isolated facts have little meaning until people can place them into a bigger unifying framework. The only adequate framework that I have found to unify the Gospels is to read them as continuous and whole stories. They are like modern serial stories in which the individual episodes are relatively self-contained but in which the units fit together in a movement toward a final goal.

Reading the Gospels as stories also gives us more accurate tools for analyzing them and talking about them. The Gospels are not a series of essays or sermons, though it is common to treat them as if they were. The Gospels are above all series of events performed by characters in specific settings. A basic principle of interpretation is that meaning is communicated *through* specific literary forms. Before we know what the Gospels teach, we need to ask the prior question of what happens to characters in a story.

Even the sayings and addresses embedded in the Gospels are placed in a narrative context. The famous sayings of Jesus are almost always linked with a specific narrative situation. The reason most people find it hard to think in terms of any larger literary unit than the individual proverb is that they have not been encouraged to think of the Gospels as whole stories.

Finally, the kind of narrative analysis I have urged opens the way for an artistic response to the Gospels. The Gospels are literary masterpieces that exhibit such artistic qualities as unity, coherence, and emphasis. They possess the adventure, excitement, and human interest of a novel or television drama. There is no reason to apologize for taking the time and effort to demonstrate that the Gospels are beautifully told stories that also contain beautiful poetry and proverbs. In fact, something is lacking if we do not find such beauty in them.

18

The Parables

The parables of Jesus are at once thoroughly literary and thoroughly laden with religious meaning. As for their literary dimension, they are the indisputable example of fiction in the Bible. They incarnate their meaning in story or metaphor in such a way that we cannot possibly ignore their literary nature. Yet they are a didactic genre that Jesus used to teach basic Christian doctrine and morality.

The parables also illustrate to perfection the double quality of much biblical literature. They require both a naive and a sophisticated response. On the surface they are the very touchstone of simplicity. They deal with the most realistic situations imaginable: a farmer sowing seed, a shepherd caring for sheep, a woman baking bread. But their complexity is such that scholars have produced an endless succession of books and articles on their meaning.

The parables exist on a continuum ranging from the simple to the complex. On the one end of the spectrum is the single metaphor or simile in which Jesus compares the kingdom of heaven to a mustard seed or lost coin or hidden treasure. At the other end is a relatively complex story with a skillfully designed plot, elaboration of setting and dialogue, and subtle characterization. In this chapter I will concentrate on the more complex parables that tell a story. To interpret the simple parables requires an ability to deal with metaphor and simile in the usual manner.

Literary Features of the Parables

Before explicating selected parables, I wish to note the literary features of the parables in general.[1] My excursions into the volumes of commentary that biblical scholars have produced on the parables in recent years have convinced me that the scholars have obscured the parables and isolated them from ordinary readers of the Bible. A genuinely literary approach can go a long way toward rehabilitating them for the people to whom Jesus gave them—ordinary people.

Folk Stories

The narrative appeal of the parables is the appeal of the folk story. These simple narratives exhibit virtually all of the features that have characterized popular storytelling through the ages.

One of these traits is the homespun realism that appeals to the most naive of literary tastes. The world of the parables is the world of the common people to whom Jesus preached—a world of fields, harvest, wedding invitations, household routine, or traveling to a neighboring town. The people who perform these actions are equally recognizable: they are farmers, migrant workers, fathers and sons, embezzlers, widows on a pension, merchants. Jesus has given us an unforgettable picture of peasant and bourgeois life in first-century Palestine. Corresponding to this thoroughgoing realism is the absence of fantasy elements such as talking animals or haunted forests.

The parables, in short, are based on the literary principle of verisimilitude (lifelikeness). They hold the mirror up to life. Reliance on precise, vivid illustrations is a standard technique in such literature, and here, too, the parables run true to form. "It is 'things' that make stories go well," writes a literary critic; in the parables everything "is concrete and vigorous ... [and] described in solid terms."[2] The Jesus of the parables reveals the gift of the master storyteller—"an amazing power of observation."[3]

1. For elaboration of the points I make in this section, see Leland Ryken, *How to Read the Bible as Literature* (Grand Rapids: Zondervan, 1984), pp. 139–53; and the excerpts from leading biblical scholars and literary critics in Leland Ryken, ed., *The New Testament in Literary Criticism*, A Library of Literary Criticism (New York: Ungar, 1984), pp. 255–72.

2. P. C. Sands, *Literary Genius of the New Testament* (New York: Oxford University Press, 1932), p. 86.

3. Geraint V. Jones, *The Art and Truth of the Parables* (London: S.P.C.K., 1964), p. 113. This is one of the best literary studies of parables.

This power shows itself also at the level of characterization. Only one of the characters in the parables (Lazarus) is named. This anonymity helps to make the characters universal types. We know that we have met them, like the characters of Chaucer and Dickens, before. As Geraint V. Jones has aptly said, Nowhere else in the world's literature has such immortality been conferred on anonymity" (p. 124).

The realism of the parables is an important part of their religious meaning. There are so few references to religious practices or to the religious professionals of the day that the surface world of the parables is decidedly "secular." On the basis of their literal level, we could not possibly guess that they are designed to teach religious truth. The parables thus assault any "two-world" outlook that divides the spiritual and earthly realms. In the world of the parables, it is in everyday experience that people make their spiritual decisions and that God's grace works.

The parables are oral folk stories, not only by virtue of the realism of their content, but also in their composition. They adhere to the rules or principles of folk stories through the centuries. Since I will apply these when I explicate selected parables, I will only list them here.

1. The rule of plot conflict.
2. The rule of suspense (generating curiosity about outcome).
3. The rule of contrast or foil.
4. The rule of simplicity or the single plot (absence of complicated situations or multiple actions). Part of the simplicity is the "dramatic rule of two," in which only two characters (or a character and a group) take part in the action at a given time (as in Greek drama).
5. The rule of repetition, especially threefold repetition.
6. The rule of end stress (the crucial element comes last, often as a foil to what has preceded).
7. The rule of universality, especially universal character types.

A final feature of the parables that links them to folk literature is their reliance on archetypes. Considered only as stories, the parables are too simple and brief to interest us. The presence of archetypes counteracts this effect. When Jesus tells stories about father and son, or about two sons, or about master (employer) and servant (employee), or about lost and found, our interest is assured.

Persuasion and Response

The parables are oral literature, which no doubt explains their brevity and simplicity. Their context in the Gospels makes it clear that

Jesus spoke the parables in the course of his teaching and debates with his opponents. In fact, some of the parables are Jesus' half of an argument.

Because of this context, the parables possess a strong persuasive element. They were addressed to specific audiences and designed to move listeners to a response. The parables are invitations and even traps designed to elicit a response. Knowing that listeners cannot absorb everything that they hear, Jesus told brief, memorable stories that do not carry all their meaning on the surface. They were intended to be carried away and pondered as a means of providing delayed-action insight (see Jesus' explanation of his method in Matthew 13: 10–17).

Satire and Subversion

There is a strong satiric element in the parables.[4] A number of them have a discernible object of attack. Sometimes the satire is the main point (e.g., the parables of the rich man and Lazarus and the Pharisee and the tax collector), while in others it is only one part of the overall design (as in the ecclesiastical satire against the priest and the Levite in the parable of the good Samaritan).

Even when the parables are not satiric, they tend to be subversive. This subversive quality stems particularly from the element of reversal of conventional values that underlies most of the parables. Regardless of what the specific theme of a parable is, there is often a deeper meaning as well. By introducing so many reversals of expectation, Jesus makes us question the reliability of our whole mindset.

For example, if Jesus wished simply to tell an example story about being compassionate to those in need, *any* character might have sufficed in the parable of the good Samaritan. But Jesus shocks us by making help come from the least likely source. Similarly, in the parable of the workers in the vineyard, the pay scale that takes no account of how long a person has worked runs counter to everything that we assume about fair employment practices. By means of these shocking reversals, Jesus conveys a sense of the completely new standards that prevail in the spiritual kingdom of God.

This element of reversal is signaled within the parables themselves by elements of unreality or exaggeration in predominantly realistic stories. Many of the parables contain a crack in the realism—some element that does not fit and that therefore teases us into seeing more in the parable than the literal level. Examples include a wedding feast

4. For more on satire in the parables, see chapter 14, above.

for which all the invited guests find excuses not to come, an employer who pays the same wage regardless of how long his employees have worked, and a merchant who sells all his property to buy a single pearl.

Allegory in the Parables

Are the parables allegorical? Yes—they are. Despite all that some (though not all) biblical scholars have said to the contrary, the parables fit any standard literary definition of allegory. Elsewhere I have argued this in more detail,[5] and here I will simply discuss *how* the parables are allegorical.

The essential feature of allegory is that of double meaning: a detail in the story also stands for something else. If the term *allegory* has the wrong connotations because it smacks of the arbitrary and frivolous allegorizing that prevailed in the Middle Ages, we can use the synonym *symbol*. It is as simple as that.

There are several reasons why we cannot keep allegorical meanings out of the parables. Many of the images that Jesus used in the parables already had inherited symbolic meanings. Thus the owner of a vineyard is God, sowing seed is teaching or preaching the word of God, and a master who judges is God. Secondly, once we know that a parable is about a spiritual reality like the kingdom of God, the logic of the story itself demands that we interpret some of the details allegorically (symbolically). Most conclusive of all is the fact that Jesus himself interpreted two of his parables in an allegorical way (Matt. 13:18–23, 36–43).

Jesus' interpretation of these parables shows that he intended them as allegories. We should therefore note the crucial difference between *interpreting an allegorical text* and *allegorizing a text* that is not intended as allegory. When we ascribe corresponding other meanings to some of the details in a parable, we are interpreting a text that was intended to be allegorical.

A biblical scholar has devised a simple scheme for determining the allegorical content of the parables.[6] As he went through the parables, he listed the main details in each story and then counted how many of them have a corresponding other meaning. His conclusions: the allegorical content of the parables in the Gospel of Matthew is 82 percent, that in Mark 75 percent, and that in Luke 60 percent.

5. See Ryken, *How to Read the Bible as Literature*, pp. 145–51, 199–203.

6. M. D. Goulder, "Characteristics of the Parables in the Several Gospels," *Journal of Theological Studies* n.s. 19 (1968): 58–62.

The most helpful literary framework for discussing the allegory of the parables is Northrop Frye's idea of an allegorical continuum.[7] According to this scheme, *every* work of literature has an allegorical dimension to it. Furthermore, all commentary on the meaning of a literary work is allegorical in the sense that it translates the details of the story into a corresponding meaning. What we need, then, is not an approach that enables us to divide allegorical from nonallegorical works, but a framework that enables us to talk about the *degree* to which works of literature are allegorical.

This is where the concept of a sliding scale or continuum comes into play. At one end of the scale we find continuous allegory, in which virtually every detail has a corresponding meaning. In the middle we find incarnation, in which there is an obvious thematic intention but in which the ideas have been completely embodied in the story as a whole. At the far end of the spectrum we find realistic works with an abundance of surface detail with little obvious thematic intention. The allegorical continuum can be pictured as it is in figure 1.

The parables of Jesus range over the left half of this continuum. In the parable of the sower, for example, virtually every detail has a corresponding meaning. In the parable of the prodigal son, some of the details have an allegorical meaning (the father = God, the elder brother = the Pharisees), while others do not (the shoes and robe that the father gives to his son upon his return). In the middle of the spectrum we can place a parable like the story of the good Samaritan, in which the whole story embodies the meaning.

The basic principle of the parables is analogy or metaphor. A parable "elicits a judgment in one sphere in order to transfer it to another."[8] The metaphoric nature of the parables has sometimes been contrasted to allegory, but this is misleading. Allegory, too, is a bilevel

Figure 1 **The allegorical continuum**

Continuous allegory   Incarnation

Stories with obvious thematic design   Realistic reportage with minimal thematic import

7. Northrop Frye, *Anatomy of Criticism: Four Essays* (Princeton: Princeton University Press, 1957), pp. 89–92.

8. A. T. Cadoux, *The Parables of Jesus: Their Art and Use* (London: James Clarke, 1930), p. 56.

form. Indeed, as C. S. Lewis rightly points out, "every metaphor is an allegory in little."[9]

In both metaphor and allegory, one thing is compared to another. As Amos N. Wilder states, "there is the picture-side of the parable and there is the meaning or application."[10] The very word *parable* suggests allegory, since it literally means "to throw alongside." In the parables of Jesus, we do just that: we attach a corresponding meaning to some of the details in the story, either continuously or to the story as a whole. Allegorical reading of the parables actually enhances their metaphoric nature by introducing additional metaphors—God as father, for example, or the word of God as seed. Nonallegorical readings tend to reduce every parable to a single, very general meaning (recently the theme of reversal of values has been popular), and in the process they fail to do justice to the specificity of the text.

Explicating the Parables

The process of analyzing the parables and organizing a discussion of them falls naturally into the following four steps:

1. Narrative analysis (interacting with the story as a story).
2. Interpreting the allegory or symbolism of details that call for such interpretation.
3. Determining the theme(s) of the parable. This should not be confused with interpreting the allegory. In the parable of the talents, for example, to say that the owner of the talents is God and the return after a long journey is Christ's coming at the end of history is to interpret the allegory. To say that the parable teaches the need for good stewardship is to find the theme of the parable.
4. Application of the theme. Granted that a given theme is present, to whom does it apply, and how? There are two possible levels of application: how did it apply *then* (that is, in Jesus' day), and how does it apply *now?*

Knowing that I could explicate only a few of the parables, I have selected ones that illustrate something of the range of techniques that we find in the parables of Jesus.

9. C. S. Lewis, *The Allegory of Love: A Study in Medieval Tradition* (New York: Oxford University Press, 1936), p. 60.

10. Amos N. Wilder, *Early Christian Rhetoric: The Language of the Gospel* (Cambridge: Harvard University Press, 1971), p. 74.

The Parable of the Sower or Soils

The parable of the sower (Matt. 13:1–9, 18–23), more accurately called the parable of the soils, epitomizes the parable as a genre. The realism of the parable is fully evident. The kinds of soil that are the chief focus of the parable are exactly the ones that a farmer in Palestine would have encountered: the road that bordered the field and on which some seed invariably fell when the farmer broadcast it, the corners of a field where weeds dominate, the soil with an underlay of limestone, and the fertile soil. Nothing could have been more familiar to the experience of Jesus' original audience.

The story is too simple to interest us only on the surface level, yet it possesses enough narrative technique to make it effective for its didactic purpose. Three ingredients figure in the action—a sower, seed, and four kinds of soil. The types of soil are the variable in the story and are accordingly the key to its meaning. The main organizing principle is common in folk stories—threefold repetition. Further symmetry stems from the way in which the three unsatisfactory soils are balanced by three degrees of success in the fertile soil. An element of plot conflict is provided by the environment of struggle in which the seeds play out their destiny—an environment in which seeds are *devoured* and *choked* and *scorched*. The situation of entrusting seed to the earth also possesses the quality of an archetypal risk whose outcome is uncertain and therefore suspenseful.

Jesus himself provides an interpretation of the allegorical details in the parable (vv. 18–23). The seed is God's message of salvation and righteous living ("the word of the kingdom"). We infer (though this is the one detail in the story that Jesus does not allegorize) that the sower is the evangelist, or Jesus himself. The kinds of soil symbolize the responses of people who hear the word of God, which Jesus differentiates very specifically.

Several themes are embodied in this allegorical story. The preaching of the gospel is shown to occur in a context of spiritual warfare, with the result that it will inevitably meet with resistance. One cannot expect uniformly successful results from the preaching of the word. The parable shows, moreover, that salvation depends on the responses of people who hear the gospel (witness how the variable element is the soils). There is an assurance that the gospel will produce positive results in the lives of some listeners. Mainly, though, this is a parable about hearing. Its chief message is, *Take care how you listen and obey*.

What applications might this classification of responses by various types of listeners have had in Christ's day? Most interpreters of the parable believe that Jesus intended the parable as an encouragement to his disillusioned disciples. When the disciples saw the resistance that Jesus encountered, this theory states, they became discouraged and doubtful. Jesus told a parable that had the concept of fruitfulness and success as its climax in order to counteract their disillusionment.

I find this interpretation misleading. Matthew 13:2 makes it clear that Jesus was speaking to a large crowd of people, not simply to the disciples. The parable, moreover, concentrates on the kinds of soil, not the sower. The whole interest is focused on the soils, that is, the hearers of the gospel. This is a parable about how we listen, not about how we preach.

The parable was a challenge to those who were listening to the claims of the gospel to respond adequately to the message of the kingdom. Jesus delineates three inadequate responses to the message of the kingdom. The parable is thus a warning to the hearers of the gospel to avoid these errors. The harvest produced by the seed that fell in the fertile soil indicates an opportunity to choose a better way.

This application of the parable is timeless. The options are the same today as they were in Jesus' day. The choices with which Jesus confronted his first listeners are the same ones that he puts before people today.

The Parable of the Generous Employer

The parable of the sower belongs to the category of parables of action, inasmuch as the point of the parable turns on what happens to the seed that is sown, not on the character of the sower. But other parables hinge on the dynamics of human character. The parable of the workers in the vineyard and their generous employer (Matt. 20: 1–16) typifies the parables of character.

The plot is simply a framework on which Jesus hangs his character study. It is based on the principle of fivefold repetition, as the owner of the vineyard, harried by the pressure of harvest, goes to the marketplace at five different times of the day to enlist workers for his vineyard. The motif on which the plot is based is simply labor and its reward. Hiring the workers in the first part of the parable is balanced by payment at the end.

The pressure point of the parable comes at the end and centers on the character of the employer. He pays everyone the same wage, regardless of how long people had worked. This is equivalent to giving every student the same grade in a course, with no questions asked. Given conventional standards of fair play, the employees who had worked longest naturally complained. The insight into human psychology is thoroughly realistic at this point.

But more important is the question of what kind of person the employer is. Is he just? If not, what is he? He is just because he has fulfilled the conditions of his contract with the workers: *Did you not agree with me for a denarius?* (v. 13). But the parable is not primarily about justice: it is about generosity, as the employer's parting shot in the parable suggests: *Or do you begrudge my generosity?* (v. 15). A denarius was a living wage, and the fact that the employer was concerned that everyone, even those who worked only one hour, would receive a denarius proves his compassion. Within the logic of the parable, the owner of the vineyard emerges as a generous man, with the grumbling workers functioning as a foil that heightens his generosity. (Conversely, the generosity and compassion of the employer point out the moral failure of the workers who complain.)

As a literary form, the parable "elicits a judgment in one sphere in order to transfer it to another" (Cadoux, p. 56). This parable is a good example. We are intended to transfer what the parable demonstrates about the owner of the vineyard to God. In fact, several details in the parable must be interpreted allegorically. The owner of the vineyard is God, the workers in the vineyard are believers, working in the vineyard is doing God's work in the world, the payment is salvation, and the equality of payment means that all believers will be glorified in heaven. The theme hinges particularly on this last item: salvation depends on the generosity of God, not on human merit.

Viewed thus, the parable illustrates the subversive reversal of conventional values that pervades the parables. Who ever heard of a pay scale that pays no attention to how long the workers have been on the job? The aphorism with which Jesus concludes the parable focuses exactly on this rejection of conventional human standards: *So the last will be first, and the first last* (v. 16). That is, in the kingdom of God where generosity is the foundational premise, ordinary human standards have been abolished.

The application to Jesus' original audience is fairly obvious. Jesus here anticipates what would become one of the great issues in the early church: the Gentiles could be saved without the encumbrances of the ceremonial laws that the Jews had performed for centuries. Was this fair? The parable at least provides a perspective from which an answer might emerge.

But the application of the parable is more extensive than that. In any religious group, the disparity of commitment and spiritual exertion among members is immense. Do the slackers deserve salvation? Here, too, the parable of the generous employer, with its implicit rejection of human merit as a criterion for salvation, provides an answer.

The Parable of the Good Samaritan

The parable of the good Samaritan (Luke 10:25–37) provides a contrast to the previous parables. In it, Jesus avoids continuous allegory and instead tells an example story that falls in the middle of the allegorical continuum. The whole story is the meaning, and we do not translate individual details into a corresponding meaning. We simply observe examples of virtue to follow and vice to avoid. The theme of the parable, moreover, is not (as in most of the parables) theological but ethical.

Jesus tells the parable as part of a debate with an opponent, as the introduction makes clear with its explanation that *a lawyer stood up to put him to the test* (v. 25). It is important to our understanding of the parable to realize, therefore, that this story is Jesus' answer to the lawyer's question, *And who is my neighbor?* (v. 29). Jesus does, however, subtly shift the focus from defining who the lawyer's neighbor is to the more personal question of how to *be* a neighbor.

The story as a whole epitomizes the folk qualities of the parables. The main narrative premise is the *test* motif, as the wounded man on the road becomes a test of the compassion of three passersby. The story opens with some violent *plot conflict* to grab our attention: "he fell among robbers, who stripped him and beat him, and departed, leaving him half dead" (v. 30). The plot pattern of *threefold repetition* also provides structure, as we see a common event (a passerby observes the wounded man) three times, with a crucial change introduced the third time. The technique of *foil* is therefore also important to the dynamics of the story, as we observe a heightened contrast between virtue and vice.

The parable begins with precise realism. The violence that occurred on the road between Jerusalem and Jericho was notorious. We read that the lone traveler *was going down from Jerusalem to Jericho* (v. 30). The trip does, in fact, involve a drastic descent in altitude. Similar realism underlies the account of a priest going down the same route as the victim had taken. In Christ's day many priests who served in Jerusalem actually lived in Jericho. We are not told why the priest passed by on the other side. He may have simply lacked compassion. In the background lies the practice of robbers who used supposedly wounded people as decoys, putting travelers at a disadvantage if they stooped over the decoy to investigate. Whatever the reason for the priest's action, he introduces the element of satire into the parable, as Jesus exposes the moral failure of a religious leader.

The Levite who passes by reinforces the ecclesiastical satire against the religious elite of Jesus' day. Levites were also ministers in the temple. There was a Jewish ceremonial law (Num. 19:11) that made anyone who touched a dead body unclean for seven days. If the Levite was en route to a stint of service in Jerusalem, he may have been deterred from helping the wounded man by the fact that he would have been unable to carry out his religious function for a whole week. If this is the drift of the parable, we can begin to see its complexity, despite its surface simplicity: established religious rules are in conflict with moral compassion for people in need.

The pattern of threefold repetition reaches its climax with the behavior of the Samaritan, and here, too, we see the subversive assault on the deep structure of conventional thinking. Jesus makes compassion come from the least likely (and most despised) source. The unexpectedness of the situation is heightened by the fact that the Jews of Jesus' day thought in terms of the triad priest-Levite-Israelite. Here the third person is a Samaritan, a race so hated that when the lawyer is asked to identify the neighbor in the parable, he cannot bring himself to name the Samaritan and instead replies, *the one who showed mercy on him* (v. 37).

To accentuate the basic shock of the situation, Jesus uses the rule of proportionate space to focus our attention on the virtuous behavior of the unlikely benefactor. A biblical scholar notes that

> in Greek, there are forty-six words given to what precedes the arrival of the Samaritan on the scene but sixty words devoted to his arrival and, step-by-step, to his reaction. Since this reaction is so unexpected, it must be spelled out in explicit detail. The hearer must not be able to shrug it off by saying: No Samaritan would act that way! He must feel instead: I have just seen the wine and the oil, the donkey, and the inn. I have just seen the two denarii exchange hands.[11]

This is obviously a parable of action. It was occasioned by the lawyer's question, "What shall I *do* to inherit eternal life?" (v. 25). Jesus' final words underscore that the parable has, indeed, been a parable of doing: "Go and *do* likewise" (v. 37).

As this parting statement suggests, the parable of the good Samaritan is an example story that pictures a model of virtue to emulate. There is no better illustration of how the dominant aim of Jesus' parables is the persuasive one of moving the listener to a response. The parable itself is Jesus' literary definition of *neighbor* and as such shows how the imagination embodies truth instead of telling us about

11. John Dominic Crossan, *The Dark Interval: Towards a Theology of Story* (Niles, Ill.: Argus, 1975), pp. 107–8.

it abstractly. We do not have to turn this parable into a proposition in order to assimilate its truth. All we need to do is recognize the neighborly behavior of the Samaritan and the moral deficiency of the priest and the Levite.

The Parable of the Prodigal Son and the Forgiving Father

The most literary of Jesus' parables is the one commonly known as the parable of the prodigal son but perhaps better called the parable of the forgiving father (Luke 15:11–32).[12] Here we have a fully developed story with complication of action and subtlety of characterization. The three-phase story concentrates on the relationships among the three main characters.

Like many of Jesus' parables, this one is his half of an argument. The context of the parable is that "the Pharisees and the scribes murmured, saying, 'This man receives sinners and eats with them' " (v. 2). In replying, Jesus told two short parables (the parables of the lost sheep and lost coin) that stress God's joy in receiving repentant sinners into fellowship. The story of the lost son, the forgiving father, and the older brother who refuses reconciliation is the climax of this triad of parables on a common theme.

This is the most archetypal of Jesus' parables. The journey of withdrawal and return is common among the stories of the world. It is a death-rebirth story and a story of initiation (into sin and its consequences). The prodigal is an archetypal character who represents an impulse that lies within each of us. It is the impulse away from the domestic, the secure, and the governed, toward the distant, the adventurous, the rebellious, the indulgence of forbidden appetites (including the sexual), the abandonment to unrestraint. The older brother of the parable represents an equally recognizable part of our psychological make-up: the voice of duty, restraint, self-control, and self-righteousness, cold and rigid when it encounters its opposite. It is no wonder that one of these is the *younger* son (a figure of youth with its thirst for experience and abandonment to appetite) and the other the *older* son (with its middle-aged mentality).

Also important to our response to the literal level of the parable is the fact that it is a family situation. There are feelings of parent toward child, for example, that cannot be put into words but that are accurately portrayed in the picture of the father's relationship to both of his sons. We also know experientially what happens at the end of the parable. It is called sibling rivalry and here takes the form of hurt

12. For some superb commentary and appreciative statements on this parable, I recommend the excerpts in *The New Testament in Literary Criticism*, pp. 285–94.

from a feeling that a parent has unfairly favored one's sibling. In short, almost everything that happens in the parable taps deep springs of archetypal feeling.

The realistic description and dialogue in the parable enhance its archetypal richness. Everything is concrete and tangible. We picture poverty as hunger for hog feed, forgiveness as a father embracing a son and putting a robe, ring, and shoes on him, and jealousy as the charge that the father never gave the older son *a kid, that [he] might make merry with [his] friends.* Here emotions are translated at once into action and image. The movement of the plot is quick and decisive, as are the speeches of the characters.

There are many famous first sentences in the stories of the world, but none more famous than this one: *There was a man who had two sons . . .* (v. 11). It is one of the memorable moments of literature. The opening action is equally memorable: the younger son arrogantly asks for his share of the inheritance, which in its cultural setting was equivalent to saying that he wished that his father were dead. Once we have assimilated this opening shock, we encounter another: the father takes it all in stride and gives his son the money he has requested.

The son's *journey into a far country* (v. 13) is archetypal. It is a primordial image of human experience whose application is never exhausted. We are all "lost children." The spectacle of immoral indulgence of appetites is told with stark simplicity: *he squandered his property in loose living* (v. 13). At this point the son's fortunes take a turn that we could predict, given the archetypal pattern at work here: *and when he had spent eveything, a great famine arose in that country, and he began to be in want* (v. 14).

As in the story of the fall itself, loss leads to initiation, here an initiation into the adult world of labor and deprivation. A few details portray the depths into which the son falls as a consequence of his sin and folly: *So he went and joined himself to one of the citizens of that country, who sent him into his fields to feed swine. And he would gladly have fed on the pods that the swine ate; and no one gave him anything* (vv. 15–16). Not only were hogs unclean animals for the Jews: to eat the food of hogs would reduce the prodigal to a subhuman level, yet even this is denied him. No wonder the father will twice describe his son as having been *dead.* Here is the essence of human tragedy.

Equally true to the pattern of literary tragedy is the way in which the son's suffering leads to his moral and intellectual growth. The turning point in his development comes when he reaches a perception of his moral failing. The parable puts it in unforgettable terms: *he came to himself* (v. 17) and was ready to admit to his father, *Father, I have sinned against heaven and before you; I am no longer worthy to be*

called your son (vv. 18–19). This awareness of bankruptcy is combined
with a resolve to return to his father: *he said, "How many of my father's
hired servants have bread enough and to spare, but I perish here with
hunger! I will arise and go to my father"* (vv. 17–18). Here is the moment
of recognition that is common to narrative in general and tragedy in
particular.

The surface realism of this parable is as striking as the spiritual
realities that it embodies. The son's comment about his father's *hired
servants* must be understood in terms of the three kinds of employees
in the Jewish culture of the day. The categories were bondmen (slaves
with good family standing), servants (subordinates of the slaves), and
hired servants (hired for the occasion). The son who reached for everything has bottomed out on the social scale of his society.

As impressive as the realism of the opening phase of the story is,
we are aware as we read it of the enormous human realities being
portrayed by it. We have here an analysis of freedom abused, moral
degeneracy, human accountability, estrangement, loss, anguish, longing, self-laceration over one's failure, physical suffering, and (at the
end) the courage to confess and repent. Where have so few sentences
ever captured so much of the human condition?

In the second phase of the action, the character and actions of the
father become the focus of interest. The father reverses our expectations of disapproval by showing forgiveness and exuberant compassion toward his wayward son before the latter has even had a chance
to confess. Following the formal confession speech (which we hear for
the second time in the parable in verse 21), the father rejects the son's
offer to be accepted as a hired servant and instead commands, *Bring
quickly the best robe, and put it on him; and put a ring on his hand, and
shoes on his feet; and bring the fatted calf and kill it, and let us eat and
make merry* (vv. 22–23).

All of these details convey deeper meanings rooted in the cultural
context assumed in the parable. The robe symbolizes (in a sense distinct from allegory) the honor with which the son is received into
family fellowship. The ring, a signet ring, signifies the exalted status
of the son, who is granted the rights and authority of the ruling family
instead of being subordinated as a slave. The shoes also represent his
status as a son, since slaves went barefoot. And as for the fatted calf
that is slain, it is an evocative biblical archetype, with connotations
of honor, hospitality, and extravagant celebration.

In the third act of this drama, Jesus turns the parable into a satiric
attack on the scribes and the Pharisees. The occasion for the parable,
we should remember, was the Pharisees' complaint that Jesus associated with sinners. This is exactly the attitude that is embodied in

the elder brother. As a literary character, he belongs to a familiar archetype from literature, the unsympathetic refuser of festivities. The father tries to mediate between his two sons, but the elder brother remains incorrigibly self-centered and unforgiving, isolated from the drama of forgiveness in which he is invited to participate. Each of the sons thus misbehaves in his own way, while the father emerges as the generous and forgiving central figure in the picture.

The parable communicates rich meanings simply at a human level. But that is not its only purpose. Jesus told this parable in a specific context that helps us to interpret the allegory. The persuasive purpose of the parable as a reply to Jesus' accusers emerges only if we make the equations of the father as God, the prodigal as human sinner, the older brother as scribe and Pharisee, the son's return as an illustration of repentance, and the father's acceptance of his son as God's forgiveness of sinners. Furthermore, the language of the father's speech explaining his joy (a speech that we hear twice) is unmistakably theological: *for this my son was dead, and is alive again; he was lost, and is found* (v. 24; see also v. 32).

By interacting with the story at its narrative and allegorical levels, we have already observed its themes. This parable is a marvelously compressed picture of such universal psychological and spiritual realities as sin, guilt, repentance, and forgiveness. And the application is universal and timeless.

The parable of the prodigal son epitomizes Jesus' parables. It exhibits the narrative qualities of the parable as a literary form—the realism, the folk conventions, the archetypal richness, the sheer humanity, the allegorical or symbolic overtones of many of the details in the story. Here we find literary artistry, profundity combined with simplicity, elemental emotion, and spiritual intensity.

19

The Book of Acts

It is an easy step from the Gospels to the Book of Acts. Both are collections of relatively self-contained stories with interspersed speeches. A loose chronological principle organizes the individual units. We also find the familiar mingling of three dominant impulses—the didactic impulse to teach religious truth, the documentary impulse to record historical information about events, and the literary impulse to recreate experiences in vivid and concrete detail.

The Book of Acts provides a good test case for the underlying thesis of this book—that the New Testament literary forms are not totally new but represent a modification of traditional literary types. The Book of Acts is much closer to our familiar literary experiences than we have been led to think.

Unique Features of the Book of Acts

The title of the book—*The Acts of the Apostles*—itself suggests something of the novelty of what we find here. As the title suggests, the book lacks a single protagonist. But of course so do many of the Old Testament narrative books. If we streamline slightly, we might say that Peter dominates the first half of the book and Paul the second half. Or perhaps we might view either the church or the Holy Spirit as the central character who is present from beginning to end. In any case, the multiplicity of focus makes this story unusual. We are reminded of the genre of biography at many points in the book, though the book as a whole is not biographical.

The content of the book, secondly, makes it different from the stories that we read elsewhere. It is filled with unique, once-only events, unlike the more universal or representative occurrences that most stories present. The history of the early church by eyewitnesses is a unique subject for a story. The writer keeps the focus very steadily on this subject, so that the events we encounter strike us as unusual material for a story.

The Book of Acts as Story

The things that make the book unique are minor compared with the familiar literary features of the book. In such areas as unified structure, narrative techniques, dramatic scenes and speeches, and unifying images, the Book of Acts emerges as a thoroughly recognizable literary phenomenon.[1]

Structure and Unity

The structure of the book can be plotted in several ways, depending on how simple or detailed we wish the arrangement to be. The simplest scheme is twofold. In the first half of the book, the church discovers its identity. In the second half, it reaches out into the world. The latter story is synonymous with the missionary journeys of Paul.

A threefold outline sees the book as falling into the following units: events in Jerusalem (1–5), the church's mission in Palestine and Syria (6–12), and the mission and imprisonment of Paul (13–28). There is a gradual constriction from a crowded background of characters and events to the journeys of a single person.

Even more customary is the sixfold arrangement of the book: the founding of the church in Jerusalem (1:1–6:7); the dispersal of Christians throughout Palestine after the martyrdom of Stephen (6:8–9:31); the spread of the church to Syria (9:32–12:25); Paul's first missionary journey, to Asia Minor (13:1–16:5); Paul's journeys to Macedonia and Greece (16:6–21:14); Paul's carrying of the gospel to Rome as a prisoner (21:15–28:31). Seen thus, the organizing principle of the story is

1. For a wealth of literary commentary on the Book of Acts, see the collected excerpts in Leland Ryken, ed., *The New Testament in Literary Criticism*, A Library of Literary Criticism (New York: Ungar, 1984), pp. 42–61. My commentary in this chapter is indebted at every turn to these sources.

a succession of waves by which the Christian gospel advances from Jerusalem to Rome.

The journey and quest motifs are obviously important in the patterns I have noted. The outward expansion of the church is not a random wandering but a purposeful quest to conquer the world with the Christian gospel. There is a strong sense of movement toward a goal. Of course, there is a surprise at the very end of the book. The story ends abruptly, with Paul's mission to Rome left incomplete. This open-ended conclusion is an impressive version of the technique of the serial story, with its premise "to be continued." The story told in the Book of Acts did not end but is still continuing.

All this emphasis on travel and geography helps to supply some of the master images that unify the story. Chief among these are the journey and the city. The journeys of the apostles and missionaries assume the symbolic force of "the Way" (see 9:2; 16:17; 18:26; 19:9, 23; 24:14, 22). The journey of Paul as a prisoner bound for Rome has the overtones of a Via Dolorosa (the way of sorrow; that is, the way of the cross), a journey of suffering for Christ. The image of the city also recurs in the story and is one of the things that gives the Book of Acts its modern flavor.

Along with the progressive element in the story, the book is structured on a cyclic principle. The following pattern is repeated throughout the book in an ever-widening spiral: Christian leaders arise and preach the gospel; God performs mighty acts through them; listeners are converted and added to the church; opponents (usually Jewish) begin to persecute the Christian leaders; God intervenes to rescue the leaders or otherwise protect the church.[2]

Geography is a major organizing principle in the Book of Acts. I have already noted that the progression of the plot involves geographic expansion outward from Jerusalem. The story begins in Jerusalem and ends in Rome, and there is a symbolic importance in this strategy. Jerusalem represents the Jewish roots from which Christianity arose. Rome is the capital of the Gentile world. The geographical transfer that occurs in the Book of Acts is also a theological transfer.

The foregoing discussion of the structure of the book suggests why some commentators have ascribed an epic quality to Acts. The story has epic sweep. It is the story not of an individual but of a whole group. The epic sense of destiny breathes through the book. Equally epic is the expansion of the action over vast stretches of geography.

2. M. D. Goulder's *Type and History in Acts* (London: S.P.C.K., 1964) is a book-length treatment of Acts in terms of this cyclic structure.

Storytelling Technique

The Book of Acts is not an ecclesiastical history filled with names and dates. It is a story. Its preoccupation is not with institutions and church organization but with personalities and events. The story of Acts is built around a gallery of character portraits and a series of memorable events. In this story we meet such varied characters as kings and rulers, rabbis and high priests, ordinary people like Simon the tanner and Lydia the seller of cloth, and the intellectual elite of the Greeks known as the Areopagus.

The story, moreover, is an adventure story. The Book of Acts gives us twenty-eight chapters packed with trials, riots, persecutions, escapes, martyrdoms, voyages, shipwrecks, and rescues. And all of this action takes place in the major cities of the ancient world—Jerusalem, Antioch, Philippi, Corinth, Athens, Ephesus, and Rome. There is an equal variety in the settings: temples, prisons, courts, deserts, ships, seas, barracks, and theaters. To catch the full effect of this adventure, we need to read the whole book in one or two sittings.

As an adventure story, the Book of Acts makes use of a narrative pattern that is familiar in stories wherever they are told—the narrow escape. "Paul's story," writes William A. Beardslee, "is made up of a whole series of narrow escapes," with "further depth . . . given to the narrow escape theme by the fact that Paul's career is paralleled on a smaller scale by the narrow escapes of Peter."[3]

Storytellers select their material carefully, often with a view toward making the few details that they include add up to a total picture. There can be little doubt that the writer of Acts chose events that are *representative*. Examples include preaching in the temple (3), the apostles before the Sanhedrin (4:13–22; 5:17–32), the working of signs (3), the election and ordination of church officers (6:1–6), and a martyrdom (7).

Similarly, we attend a sabbath service in a synagogue (13:13–52), a church assembly to settle an issue of church policy (15:1–21), and a Christian worship service (20:7–12). We listen to a typical sermon to Jews (2:14–42), a typical address to Greek philosophers (17), a typical appeal to pagans ignorant of the Christian message (14:8–18), and a typical defense before a Roman govenor (24). We also witness a riot in Ephesus (19:23–41). Storytellers cannot include everything that happened, but they can select the significant particular that suggests the bigger picture.

---

3. William A. Beardslee, *Literary Criticism of the New Testament*, Guides to Biblical Scholarship: New Testament series, ed. Dan Otto Via, Jr. (Philadelphia: Fortress, 1970), p. 51.

Despite the uniqueness of its events, the story of Acts is built around universal or archetypal patterns. Archetypal motifs include imprisonment, attack, rescue, journey, quest, trial, sea voyage, and the city. Recent literary commentary on Acts has uncovered a host of parallels in the literature of ancient Greece and Rome.

The Book of Acts is famous for its drama. Its dramatic flavor is evident in the prevalence of oral forms (dialogue, address, sermon, courtroom defense), emphasis on the settings in which events occur, and attention to the dramatic gestures of characters. In the Book of Acts, we find an abundance of all these. In fact, dramatized speeches in their settings account for nearly 75 percent of the book. The setting for Paul's defense before Agrippa is typical of the dramatic flavor of the book as a whole:

> So on the morrow Agrippa and Bernice came with great pomp, and they entered the audience hall with the military tribunes and the prominent men of the city. Then by command of Festus Paul was brought in. . . .
> Agrippa said to Paul, "You have permission to speak for yourself." Then Paul stretched out his hand and made his defense:
> "I think myself fortunate that it is before you, King Agrippa, I am to make my defense today against all the accusations of the Jews. . . ." [25:23; 26:1–2]

"The story of Paul before Agrippa," writes P. C. Sands in his invaluable book on the literary aspects of the New Testament, "is as stirring as that of Elijah on Mount Carmel."[4]

A final thing to note about the storytelling technique of Acts is the realism with which the story is told. Sands catches the essence of the style with these examples:

> Converts in Athens *'glued themselves'* to Paul . . . , and Paul and his company *'tear themselves away'* from the elders of Ephesus. . . . Apollos was *'boiling'* in spirit or *'fervent'*, the audience at Pentecost were *'pricked* in their heart', and Stephen's hearers were *'cut to the heart'* (lit. sawn asunder), Paul *'makes havoc of'* (lit. 'sacks') those who believed (pp. 121–22).

The Book of Acts combines the familiar and the unfamiliar. Its subject matter is unique, and as a story it is more miscellaneous than we ordinarily expect a story to be. But in terms of narrative structure and storytelling technique, it is a thoroughly recognizable literary work.

4. P. C. Sands, *Literary Genius of the New Testament* (New York: Oxford University Press, 1932), p. 116.

Luke's narrative and dramatic abilities so impressed Ernest Renan
that he spoke of "a new Homer."

The Story of Peter's Rescue

To illustrate the narrative and artistic qualities of Acts, I have chosen to explicate the story of Peter's rescue from prison as told in chapter 12. The reading that I give to this specimen will illustrate the kind
of richness that other parts of the book also possess.

The appeal of the story derives partly from the story pattern itself,
the rescue motif. This archetype provides the structure for the story,
which can be organized around the threefold pattern of the antecedents, occurrence, and aftermath of the rescue. The opening paragraph
of the story establishes the situation that makes the rescue possible:

> [1]About that time Herod the king laid violent hands upon some who
> belonged to the church. [2]He killed James the brother of John with the
> sword; [3]and when he saw that it pleased the Jews, he proceeded to arrest
> Peter also. This was during the days of Unleavened Bread. [4]And when
> he had seized him, he put him in prison, and delivered him to four
> squads of soldiers to guard him, intending after the Passover to bring
> him out to the people. [5]So Peter was kept in prison; but earnest prayer
> for him was made to God by the church.

Here is the first necessary ingredient of a rescue story—the danger or
threat that renders the hero of the story helpless. To heighten the
danger, this story locates the threat in a villain, the archetypal evil
king with absolute power to annihilate people whom he dislikes.

Almost every detail in the first four verses adds to the threat and
the seeming helplessness of the situation. In the New Testament, the
very name *Herod* is synonymous with terror, with the epithet *Herod
the king* adding the connotations of anti-Christian tyranny. To say that
this king *laid violent hands upon* Christians is to give us a physical
sense of the terror. The mention in the opening verse of the antagonism
between Herod and *the church* introduces the plot conflict between
other religions and Christianity, between the power structure of the
state and a small, persecuted religious minority.

In verse 2, the account of the murder of James is callously brief,
suggesting something of the swiftness of the murder itself. The execution is made vivid to our imaginations when we are told that James
was killed *with the sword.* Verse 3 enlarges on this hostility against the
Christians by indicating the Jews' approval of Herod's crime. All the
Jewish hostility delineated in the Gospels and the Book of Acts here

becomes aimed against Peter, the leader of the Christian church in Jerusalem. Herod is suddenly the most dangerous type of villainous king—the one who hopes to win favor with his constituency by killing leaders of a religious minority.

Verse 4 adds to the spectacle by locating us within the echoing walls of a prison, with the hopelessness of Peter's situation intensified by the enormous safeguard of *four squads of soldiers to guard him.* There may be a hint of foreshadowing here, making us wonder if Herod suspected that something might thwart his plans to kill Peter when the Passover was finished. The further reference to Herod's waiting until the Passover was over *to bring him out to the people* draws the terror to a crescendo, with the dread reinforced by our awareness that this desire to avoid bloodshed on the Passover was what happened at the execution of Jesus.

The first four verses of the story have been an ever-expanding vision of terror and helplessness. Verse 5 has a sudden calming effect. Counteracting all the terror are such spiritual resources as prayer, a caring group of Christians, and God in heaven. The evocative last clause introduces a solemn note of hope into the vision of terror: *but earnest prayer for him was made to God by the church.*

From the general situation we move to the critical last night of the Passover, the night before the planned execution. In verse 6 the writer renders the helpless plight of Peter in full visual detail:

> The very night when Herod was about to bring him out, Peter was sleeping between two soldiers, bound with two chains, and sentries before the door were guarding the prison.

It is no wonder that painters have seen the visual potential of the moment. Escaping is obviously the last thing that Peter expected. We notice also the inspiring picture of the hero peaceful in the face of death.

Verse 7 introduces the third essential ingredient in a rescue story, in addition to the threat and the helpless victim, namely, the agent of rescue. In this story, it is an angel, resplendent in supernatural light:

> And behold, an angel of the Lord appeared, and a light shone in the cell; and he struck Peter on the side and woke him, saying, "Get up quickly." And the chains fell off his hands.

The shining divine light is one of the great archetypes of the Bible. Here that supernatural aura is mingled with something as mundane as striking a sleeping person to awaken him.

The description of the rescue continues in the next two verses:

[8]And the angel said to him, "Dress yourself and put on your sandals."
And he did so. And he said to him, "Wrap your mantle around you and
follow me." [9]And he went out and followed him; he did not know that
what was done by the angel was real, but thought he was seeing a vision.

The very details that the storyteller gives us here convey how the
benumbed Peter moves as if in a dream. Peter is childlike in the scene.
With just a few details the writer makes the event come alive.

In verse 10 the supernatural or miraculous merges with the everyday physical world:

When they had passed the first and the second guard, they came to the
iron gate leading into the city. It opened to them of its own accord, and
they went out and passed on through one street; and immediately the
angel left him.

We have all stood in an empty city street in the darkness and know
something of the feelings of fear, vulnerability, loneliness, and exposure that drive one to seek refuge. This is the situation of Peter in his
state of semiconsciousness.

Only in verse 11 does the recipient of this miraculous rescue come
to full consciousness:

And Peter came to himself, and said, "Now I am sure that the Lord has
sent his angel and rescued me from the hand of Herod and from all that
the Jewish people were expecting."

It has taken Peter about as long to gain awareness as it does a teen-
ager at the breakfast table. Here is his moment of epiphany (insight)
into the meaning of the event. The very brevity of the account of the
rescue, with everything concentrated in a few vivid details, takes us
through the swift excitement of the event itself.

The story of what happens next is likewise so famous that it is
impossible to retell the story of the rescue without this sequel. It is
the story of the interrupted prayer meeting:

[12]When he realized this, he went to the house of Mary, the mother of
John whose other name was Mark, where many were gathered together
and were praying. [13]And when he knocked at the door of the gateway,
a maid named Rhoda came to answer. [14]Recognizing Peter's voice, in
her joy she did not open the gate but ran in and told that Peter was
standing at the gate. [15]They said to her, "You are mad." But she insisted

that it was so. They said, "It is his angel!" [16]But Peter continued knocking; and when they opened, they saw him and were amazed. [17]But motioning to them with his hand to be silent, he described to them how the Lord had brought him out of the prison. And he said, "Tell this to James and to the brethren." Then he departed and went to another place.

What we have here is a delightful foil (contrast and echo) to the story of the rescue. After the terror of the prison, we have the safe and homey associations of the house of Mary. Instead of the sinister gates and soldiers of the prison, we have a maid named Rhoda answering the door of the gateway. (A student, incidentally, identified Rhoda as the archetypal airhead, though other characters in the episode qualify for the same title.)

After all the tension of what happens in the prison during the rescue, we have the undercurrent of humor in this episode, climaxing in the absurd suggestion that it is Peter's angel knocking at the door. After the swift, purposeful actions of the rescue, we now witness confusion of action at the prayer meeting. The opened gates of the prison contrast with the gate that remains closed to Peter here, as Peter finds it easier to get out of prison than into a prayer meeting. The angel had led Peter out of prison; here the hapless Peter is momentarily identified as his own angel. In the first story, Peter was amazed; here the people around him are said to be amazed.

Putting these two episodes beside each other, we find the epitome of two tendencies that recur throughout the Bible. On the one hand we encounter miraculous, more-than-earthly activity. On the other, we recognize actions so familiar to our own experience that they could have happened in our own family or neighborhood or church during a typical week. The Bible as a whole is filled with both types of material.

At first sight we might think that the story of Peter's rescue is complete with his exit from the scene. But it is a narrative principle that an action is complete only when the issues that have been introduced are resolved. The story opened not with Peter, but with the wicked Herod and his elaborate intentions to persecute the church. At the end of the story, therefore, we return to Herod. The first piece of narrative business is to show us the aftermath of the rescue back at the prison the next morning:

[18]Now when day came, there was no small stir among the soldiers over what had become of Peter. [19]And when Herod had sought for him and could not find him, he examined the sentries and ordered that they should be put to death. Then he went down from Judea to Caesarea, and remained there.

As readers, we are naturally curious to know the repercussions of the miraculous rescue in the camp of the enemy. In keeping with the logic of a miracle story, this scene helps to authenticate the miracle. We note, too, another element in the coherence of the story: Peter's appearance had caused commotion at Mary's house, and now his disappearance causes commotion at the prison and court.

Balancing the opening reference to Herod's grand and evil schemes against the church, the story ends with an account of Herod's untimely death:

> [20]Now Herod was angry with the people of Tyre and Sidon; and they came to him in a body, and having persuaded Blastus, the king's chamberlain, they asked for peace, because their country depended on the king's country for food. [21]On an appointed day Herod put on his royal robes, took his seat upon the throne, and made an oration to them. [22]And the people shouted, "The voice of a god, and not of man!" [23]Immediately an angel of the Lord smote him, because he did not give God the glory; and he was eaten by worms and died.

There is a good narrative rationale for the inclusion of this material. The chapter began with Herod's wicked experiment in living, which consisted of an attempt to exalt himself by killing Christian leaders. In order for this story to be complete, we need to see the outcome of the experiment.

Here at the end, Herod's plan of action is put into the supernatural framework of the Book of Acts as a whole, where God is the chief actor and where the great conflict between good and evil is more than earthly and human. Suddenly the story takes on the coloring of the holy war in Old Testament Israelite history, where pagan kings are portrayed as God's enemies. We notice also the appearance of an angel in these verses, another link with the story of Peter's rescue. The angel appeared to Peter and smote him to initiate deliverance; he smites Herod to initiate judgment. Similarly, Peter had earlier dressed for a rescue, whereas Herod dresses for a condemnation.

The picture that Luke draws of Herod in these verses may have been influenced by his familiarity with Greek tragedy. Greek tragedy is always about a powerful figure, usually a king, who is guilty of some great flaw of character. In Greek tragedy, moreover, this flaw is almost always some form of *hubris*, or overweening pride. God-like pride is the most acute form. It was a spectacle that moved the ancient Greeks deeply, and here we find it in brief but vivid form. Josephus recorded the same event, but in more detail. Luke's account seems more governed by the literary pattern of tragedy than the physician's viewpoint.

In this account of a king eaten by worms, Herod becomes a physical as well as moral monstrosity, a walking piece of rotten flesh covered by a symbolic robe.

The story ends with a brief and understated counterpoint to the story of judgment that precedes it: *But the word of God grew and multiplied* (v. 24). Here, in fact, is the hidden or spiritual plot in the story of Acts—the mighty acts of God contending with forces hostile to the Christian gospel.

The narrative logic of Acts 12 is impeccable. There is no detail that does not belong to the overall action. We see here in microcosm the type of narrative artistry that permeates the entire book.

What themes, finally, emerge from this well-told story? The truth that literature conveys is often representational truth—truth to the way things are in human experience. At least four themes are embodied in the story we have been considering:

1. The reality and availability of a God who is more powerful than the threats that befall his followers.
2. The power of evil in the great spiritual warfare of the ages.
3. The smallness of human faith and expectation in the daily routine of Christian living.
4. The monstrosity of human rebellion against God and his purposes.

These realities are conveyed not as ideas, but as images—images of prison and light, an open gate and a closed door, a maid named Rhoda, and royal robes glittering with gold over rotten flesh.

The story of Peter's rescue epitomizes the Book of Acts. It is an adventure story that combines everyday realism with a miracle. The story features the heroic character Peter and is a chapter in the ongoing struggle between the early Christian church and its opponents. The artistry with which the story is told is amazing.

20

The Epistles

The letter or epistle is such an amorphous literary category that it would be hard to define the conventional form by which to measure specific examples. Letters exist on a continuum in terms of their content and purpose. At the expository end we find letters intended for the utilitarian purpose of conveying information. At the other end of the spectrum we find letters that go beyond this practical purpose and assume literary qualities. The literary term *epistle* is normally reserved for letters that lean toward this end of the continuum. Often they are written with publication or at least oral reading in view.

Further categories also show the letter or epistle to be elusive. There is no determined subject matter that would help us to define the genre. Letters can tend toward either the private or public direction, with respect to both writer and audience, and these distinctions apply to both expository letters and literary epistles. Given the range of available options, writers of literary epistles are free to follow their own designs, and the resulting letters will inevitably be somewhat distinctive.

Biblical scholarship has generally taken letter writing in the ancient Greco-Roman world as a model by which to describe the New Testament epistles.[1] The conclusions support my own approach in this chapter: the New Testament epistles are rooted in familiar conventions of letter writing in the ancient world but also show many original features. In terms of content, Greek and Roman letters tended to be informational and expository, and virtually every subject can be found among these letters. The basic purpose was to exchange information between two people. The language tended to be stereotyped. The basic structure consisted of three parts—introduction (salutation and greetings), text or body, and conclusion (final wish, greetings, or prayers).

Conventional Features of the Epistles

If we compare the New Testament epistles with their Hellenistic counterparts, we find that they follow the familiar conventions in their broad outlines. At the level of content, they serve the familiar purposes of conveying information and maintaining personal acquaintance. Their opening and closing formulas resemble those in other letters of the ancient world.

They also show the usual range of formality and informality. In the New Testament epistles we find personal notes and news. Sections of travelogue are common in Paul's letters. The person addressed in New Testament letters is often an acquaintance. But we also find letters with a public, formal tone addressed to groups of people, some of whom the sender did not know personally. Some of the letters are private communications, while others were intended for oral reading and circulation (the forerunner of our "open letter" intended for publication).

Equally conventional is the occasional nature of the New Testament epistles. The Epistles are not essays. They are letters addressed to specific people and situations. Taken together, they give us a realistic picture of the varied life of the early Christian church.

It would be wrong, therefore, to regard the Epistles as systematic and expository. One scholar has described their occasional nature thus:

> Since these are letters, the points argued and stressed are often not those of the greatest importance. They are usually points about which differences of opinion existed.... The churches addressed ... knew [the author's] views on the great central facts; these he can take for granted. It is to show them their mistakes in the application of these central facts

1. See especially William G. Doty, *Letters in Primitive Christianity*, Guides to Biblical Scholarship: New Testament series, ed. Dan Otto Via, Jr. (Philadelphia: Fortress, 1973); and Leland Ryken, ed., *The New Testament in Literary Criticism*, A Library of Literary Criticism (New York: Ungar, 1984), pp. 66–77, 273–81.

to their daily life, to help their doubts, that he writes. . . . Many of the questions he discusses are those propounded by the perplexed church. He answers the question because it has been raised.[2]

Like letters generally, the New Testament epistles (with the exceptions of Romans and Hebrews) are not systematic arguments. Instead the writers assume an epistolary context in which they respond to the actual situations of their audiences. Like other letters, the epistles allude to a context.

Distinctive Features of the Epistles

If the New Testament epistles are in many ways conventional for their era, what makes them distinctive? They are more thoroughly religious and more literary in technique than most Hellenistic letters were, as the following discussion will suggest.

The Religious Emphasis

At the level of content, the New Testament epistles are almost completely theological and moral. They are very similar to the Gospels in their basic content. The concern with doctrinal truth and moral living is identical in both genres. It is this preoccupation with doctrinal and moral issues that has made the letters seem more systematic than they really are.

The religious orientation of the Epistles gave rise to innovations of form. One of these is the strongly oral cast of the Epistles. They are sermonic or homiletic in tone and style. Their writers were orators and preachers. The Epistles are accordingly full of impassioned pleading. The note of direct address to an assembled audience pervades the more public epistles. The element of confrontation is prominent.

The religious content of the Epistles also resulted in modifications of the conventional structure of the letter. While retaining the three basic elements of the ordinary letter, the New Testament epistolary form features two other significant elements, as table 1 shows at a glance.

The most notable difference is the addition of two items in the New Testament epistles, but even the conventional elements are modified in these epistles. In Paul's letters, for example, the conventional Greek formula for the salutation ("Greetings!") becomes the theologically charged "grace and peace." Whereas the subject matter covered in the body of a conventional letter might be virtually anything, the focus of

2. Morton Scott Enslin, *The Literature of the Christian Movement* (New York: Harper and Row, 1938), p. 214.

Table 1 **Epistolary form**

Hellenistic Letters	New Testament Epistles
Opening (sender, addressee, greeting)	Opening (sender, addressee, greeting)
	Thanksgiving (prayer for spiritual welfare and remembrance or commendation of the spiritual riches of the addressee)
Body	Body
	Paraenesis (exhortations)
Closing (greetings and final wishes)	Closing (final greetings and benediction)

the New Testament epistles is single-mindedly on theological and moral issues. The concluding benediction gives the conventional closing a warmly spiritual note:

> Peace be to the brethren, and love with faith, from God the Father and the Lord Jesus Christ. Grace be with all who love our Lord Jesus Christ with love undying. [Eph. 6:23–24]

The most innovative element in the New Testament epistles was the inclusion of a thanksgiving and a section of moral exhortations. The thanksgiving is a liturgically formulated statement of thanks and praise for spiritual blessings. In Paul's epistles, these thanksgivings often become small essays in the grand style. The thanksgiving in Second Thessalonians is briefer and simpler than most:

> We are bound to give thanks to God always for you, brethren, as is fitting, because your faith is growing abundantly, and the love of every one of you for one another is increasing. Therefore we ourselves boast of you in the churches of God for your steadfastness and faith in all your persecutions and in the afflictions which you are enduring. [1:3–4]

The section of moral commands, technically called *paraenesis*, is another innovation of the New Testament epistle. It is built around such motifs as proverbial wisdom, lists of vices and virtues, catalogues of commands, and extended exhortations on a single moral topic. Here is a brief specimen:

> Therefore, putting away falsehood, let every one speak the truth with his neighbor, for we are members one of another. Be angry but do not sin; do not let the sun go down on your anger, and give no opportunity to the devil. Let the thief no longer steal, but rather let him labor. . . . Let no evil talk come out of your mouths, but only such as is good for edifying. . . . [Eph. 4:25–29]

The paraenesis normally comes after the doctrinal middle section of an epistle. When we reach this moment in an epistle, we are conscious that a pivot has been made. Here is a typical transition from the doctrinal section to the moral exhortations:

> I appeal to you therefore, brethren, by the mercies of God, to present your bodies as a living sacrifice, holy and acceptable to God. . . . [Rom. 12:1]

Even when the pivot is not as clearly marked as this, the general movement of a New Testament epistle is from doctrinal instruction to moral application.

Literary Techniques

If the Epistles are more religiously oriented than most other ancient letters were, they are also more literary. They are literary first of all by virtue of how they accentuate their own set of conventions or artifice. The elaborate structural patterns that I have just noted prove that these epistles were not randomly composed. The writers were following an established genre of letter writing. To fill out the categories in the expected way and the standard order required self-conscious artistry on the part of the writers.

In addition to falling within the overall epistolary genre, the New Testament letters incorporate distinctly literary genres within them. One of these is the saying or proverb, with the most extended collection of proverbs occurring in the Epistle of James. Brief liturgical statements and creedal affirmations are also embedded in some of the Epistles. Usually a formal introduction and parallel construction will identify such units, as in Ephesians 5:14:

> Therefore it is said,
>
> > "Awake, O sleeper, and arise from the dead,
> > and Christ shall give you light."

We also find lyric poems or hymns incorporated into the Epistles, and they, too, advertise themselves by their poetic parallelism.[3] A famous example is 1 Timothy 3:16:

> Great, indeed, we confess, is the mystery of our religion:
>
> > He was manifested in the flesh,
> > vindicated in the Spirit,
> > seen by angels,
> > preached among the nations,
> > believed on in the world,
> > taken up in glory.

3. For more on the liturgical and hymnic genres in the Epistles, see *The New Testament in Literary Criticism*, pp. 142–46, and chapter 6 of this book.

The style of the Epistles is as literary as their generic traits. For example, the style is very poetic. The leading manifestation of this poetic impulse is the prevalence of concrete images and metaphors, as in Peter's portrait of false teachers:

> These are waterless springs and mists driven by a storm. . . . They themselves are slaves of corruption; for whatever overcomes a man, to that he is enslaved. . . . It has happened to them according to the true proverb, The dog turns back to his own vomit, and the sow is washed only to wallow in the mire. [2 Peter 2:17, 19, 22]

The Epistles, for all their theology, appeal continually to our imagination. We cannot get their meaning without analyzing metaphors and similes. As P. C. Sands puts it, Paul's diction "is continually enlivened by metaphor, '*glueing* yourselves to the good', '*boiling* with the spirit', '*buying up* the opportunity', 'let the love of Christ *make its home* in you', let the peace of Christ *be umpire* in your hearts'. . . ."[4]

Other figures of speech also make the style of the Epistles continuously poetic and literary. We find paradox, as when Paul writes that Christians are treated

> as imposters, and yet are true;
> as unknown, and yet well known;
> as dying, and behold we live;
> as punished, and yet not killed;
> as sorrowful, yet always rejoicing;
> as poor, yet making many rich;
> as having nothing, and yet possessing everything. [2 Cor. 6:8–10]

Equally poetic in such a passage is the elaborate parallelism of the lines.

Other poetic touches are also present. We find rhetorical questions that draw us into their orb and move us toward assent:

> If God is for us, who is against us? He who did not spare his own Son but gave him up for us all, will he not also give us all things with him? [Rom. 8:31–32]

Dramatic apostrophes are also one of the affective forms found in the Epistles: "O death, where is thy victory?" (1 Cor. 15:55). There are some memorable personifications, including James's statement that "desire when it has conceived gives birth to sin; and sin when it is full-grown brings forth death" (1:15). We also find question-and-answer constructions for dramatic effect:

4. P. C. Sands, *Literary Genius of the New Testament* (New York: Oxford University Press, 1932), p. 153.

What then? Are we to sin because we are not under law but under grace? By no means! [Rom. 6:15]

The Epistles of course share the aphoristic tendency of the whole Bible. In keeping with the practice of the Old Testament wisdom teachers and Jesus, the writers of the Epistles fill their letters with concise, memorable statements: *we are more than conquerors through him who loved us* (Rom. 8:37); *the greatest of these is love* (1 Cor. 13:13); *be doers of the word, and not hearers only* (James 1:22).

Finally, the Epistles are consistently literary, not only in their figurative language and proverbial style, but also in their highly patterned rhetoric. This artistry consists of repetition, balance, antithesis, and parallelism. Almost any page from the Epistles will illustrate this conscious design. To get the full effect, we need to print the phrases and clauses like poetry. Printed thus, the wavelike motion of the prose style is truly affecting:

> There is one body
>   and one Spirit,
> just as you were called
>   to the one hope
>   that belongs to your call,
> one Lord,
> one faith,
> one baptism,
> one God and Father of us all,
>   who is above all
>   and through all
>   and in all. [Eph. 4:4–6]

The effect of such a passage is incantatory, with the parallelism of the clauses reinforcing the repetition of the key words *one* and *all*.

Here is another memorable specimen out of many that might be quoted:

> Finally, brethren,
>   whatever is true,
>   whatever is honorable,
>   whatever is just,
>   whatever is pure,
>   whatever is lovely,
>   whatever is gracious,
> if there is any excellence,
>   if there is anything worthy of praise,
> think about these things. [Phil. 4:8]

Antithesis is a marked characteristic of Paul's mindset and world view. He perceives the world as a battleground between good and evil, God and Satan. There is, moreover, the tension between this world and the spiritual world. Paul's rhetoric is the natural vehicle for his outlook:

> What is sown is perishable,
>   what is raised is imperishable.
> It is sown in dishonor,
>   it is raised in glory.
> It is sown in weakness,
>   it is raised in power.
> It is sown a physical body,
>   it is raised a spiritual body. [1 Cor. 15:42–44]

To illustrate the combination of parallelism and antithesis that is Paul's trademark, the conclusion to Romans 8 will suffice (vv. 38–39):

> For I am sure that neither death,
>   nor life,
>   nor angels,
>   nor principalities,
>   nor things present,
>   nor things to come,
>   nor powers,
>   nor height,
>   nor depth,
>   nor anything else in all creation,
> will be able to separate us
>   from the love of God
>   in Christ Jesus our Lord.

The exalted and highly patterned style in such a passage is not simply an embellishment. It is part of the meaning. The Epistles are affective as well as intellectual. Their style conveys an ecstasy and an emotional conviction that are an important part of their meaning.

Even the customary salutation of a letter becomes transformed into something grand and eloquent in the New Testament epistles:

> Paul, a servant of Jesus Christ,
>   called to be an apostle,
>   set apart for the gospel of God
> which he promised beforehand
>   through his prophets
>   in the holy scriptures,

the gospel concerning his Son,
  who was descended from David
  according to the flesh
and designated Son of God in power
  according to the Spirit of holiness
  by his resurrection from the dead,
Jesus Christ our Lord,
  through whom we have received grace and apostleship
to bring about the obedience of faith
  for the sake of his name
  among all the nations,
  including yourselves
  who are called to belong to Jesus Christ;
To all God's beloved in Rome,
  who are called to be saints:
Grace to you and peace
  from God our Father
  and the Lord Jesus Christ. [Rom. 1:1–7]

We have heard too much about the "unliterary" quality of the New Testament. Even if in the original the vocabulary tends to be that of ordinary speech, there is no way in which we can consider the rhetorical patterning of clauses to be ordinary.

The New Testament epistles represent a mingling of the traditional and the innovative. Like ordinary letters, they exist to convey information to an audience and are prompted by a specific occasion. Their religious focus makes them distinctive. They also differ from other ancient letters by being more consistently literary in their form and style, but this very quality makes them similar to other literature and actually enhances their accessibility for a modern reader.

21

Poetry, Proverb, and Hymn

In this chapter I am not concerned so much with specific books of the New Testament as with some general literary qualities that pervade the New Testament. I will have fulfilled my aim if I alert my readers to these general tendencies.

Poetry

When I speak of poetry in the New Testament I refer to the prevalence of concrete images and figurative language. It is a commonplace that poets speak a language all their own.[1] The language of the New Testament is often poetic.

Poetic Language

The most basic poetic unit is the image that names a concrete object or sensation. Such imagery requires of a reader the ability to *imagine* as much as possible. Poetic language is based on the premise that we can picture the truth as well as conceptualize it. Images also tend to be an *affective* medium.

1. For a more complete analysis of poetic language than I attempt here, see chapter 7, above.

The next most prevalent ingredients in poetic language are metaphor and simile. Both compare one thing to another. A simile does so by announcing the comparison with the formula *like* or *as:* "the kingdom of heaven is like treasure hidden in a field" (Matt. 13:44). Metaphor is also a comparison, but it adopts a bolder strategy by dropping the comparative formula and simply asserting that one thing *is* another: "you are the light of the world" (Matt. 5:14).

Briefly stated, metaphor and simile require the following interpretive actions from us. They first require us to identify and experience the literal level of the comparison. Before we determine how the kingdom of God is like hidden treasure or a Christian like light, we need to experience the phenomena of treasure and light. Having experienced the phenomenon at the literal level, we need to carry over the appropriate meaning(s) to the subject that is being discussed. The very word *metaphor* suggests what we need to do. It is based on the Greek words *meta*, meaning "over," and *pherein*, meaning "to carry." With metaphor and simile, we need to *carry over* meaning from one subject to another.

Simile and metaphor assert a correspondence between two things. It is up to the reader to discover what the correspondence is (and it might be multiple). Metaphor and simile are obviously meditative forms that ask us to ponder how one thing is like another.

A number of other figures of speech fill out the poet's repertoire. A *symbol* is a concrete image or event that represents meanings in addition to itself. An *allusion* is a reference to past literature or history. *Apostrophe* consists of addressing someone or something absent as though it were present and is usually a sign of strong feeling on the part of the speaker. *Personification* occurs when a writer or speaker attributes human qualities to something nonhuman. *Hyperbole* is conscious exaggeration for the sake of effect, usually emotional effect. Most figurative speech is based on the premise of *poetic license*, meaning that the poet departs from fact to achieve an effect.

Parallelism

Most poetry is written in a discernible verse form. In the Bible, this verse form is called *parallelism*. It consists of two or more phrases that express an idea in different words but in similar grammatical form. With *synonymous parallelism*, two or more lines express a truth in the same grammatical form:

> Ask, and it will be given you;
> seek, and you will find;
> knock, and it will be opened to you. [Matt. 7:7]

With *antithetic parallelism,* the second unit introduces a contrast:

> all things were made through him,
>> and without him was not anything made that was made. [John 1:3]

Synthetic [or growing] parallelism consists of a two-line unit in which the second line simply completes the meaning of the first:

>> Blessed are the poor in spirit,
>>> for theirs is the kingdom of heaven. [Matt. 5:3]

In *stairstep parallelism,* the last key word in a line becomes the first main word in the next line:

>> In him was *life,*
>>> and the *life* was the *light* of men.
>> The *light* shines in the *darkness,*
>>> and the *darkness* has not overcome it. [John 1:4–5]

Several functions are served when an utterance falls into poetic rhythm. Parallelism beautifies a passage by adding artistry to it. Parallelism also heightens the impact of a statement. It has an aphoristic quality and makes a statement memorable. It focuses our attention and creates a sense of compulsion. Furthermore, emotional utterances have a natural tendency to be more rhythmical than ordinary speech. Sometimes parallelism identifies a passage as being a poem or hymn, and it always implies a certain formality. Overall, parallelism helps to produce the effect of heightened speech.

Poetry in the New Testament

Why all this talk about poetry? Because the New Testament is continuously poetic in the ways I have noted. This is somewhat obscured from us because most of it is printed as prose. But there is nothing to prevent speakers or writers from using figurative language in prose, and whenever they do, their statements require that we interpret them poetically. As I will show in a later chapter, the Book of Revelation is continuously poetic. It communicates the truth about the spiritual world and the future by means of evocative images and symbols. The Epistles are not this continuously figurative, but we certainly cannot interpret their message without knowing how to interpret figures of speech at many points as we read. Verses like this abound: "I beseech you as aliens and exiles to abstain from the passions of the flesh that wage war against your soul" (1 Peter 2:11).

As for parallelism, much more of the New Testament should be printed in poetic lines than is usually done. Regardless of how we print it, much of it is couched in parallel clauses:

> Let every man be quick to hear, slow to speak, slow to anger. [James 1:19]

> When I was a child, I spoke like a child, I thought like a child, I reasoned like a child. [1 Cor. 13:11]

> Worthy is the Lamb who was slain, to receive power and wealth and wisdom and might and honor and glory and blessing! [Rev. 5:12]

> Whoever receives this child in my name receives me, and whoever receives me receives him who sent me. [Luke 9:48]

The flow of clauses and phrases in the New Testament is often rhythmic in this way, and as such its effect can appropriately be called poetic.

Jesus as Poet

The leading poet of the New Testament is of course Jesus.[2] In fact, Jesus is one of the world's most famous poets. His sermons and discourses are essentially poetic in style.

Jesus' speech, for example, is saturated with metaphors and similes, as he repeatedly uses one area of human experience to cast light on another area. Calling people to belief in God is like gathering a harvest (Matt. 9:37–38). Sending the disciples to minister in a hostile world is similar to sending "sheep in the midst of wolves" (Matt. 10:16). Living a life of self-sacrifice for the sake of Christ becomes a picture of someone picking up a cross and bearing it (Matt. 10:38), while the ordeal of Jesus' own death is a cup whose contents must be drunk (Matt. 26:39).

Jesus compared the hypocritical Pharisees to "whitewashed tombs, which outwardly appear beautiful, but within . . . are full of dead men's bones and all uncleanness" (Matt. 23:27), and to "graves which are not seen, and men walk over them without knowing it" (Luke 11:44). Many of Jesus' comparisons are archetypal symbols, as when he speaks about living water (John 4:10), the bread of life (John 6:35), the light of the world (John 8:12), and the good shepherd (John 10:11). Jesus' reliance on analogy as the most effective way to explain his saving ministry reaches its climax in the parables, where the kingdom of God is compared to such things as a field, a mustard seed, a treasure, a pearl, a vineyard, a banquet, and a wedding.

Jesus also used bold paradoxes to startle his listeners. He spoke of

2. For more commentary on Jesus as poet, see the selections in Leland Ryken, ed., *The New Testament in Literary Criticism*, A Library of Literary Criticism (New York: Ungar, 1984), pp. 152–63.

a burden that was light (Matt. 11:30), of saving one's life by losing it (Matt. 16:25), of the first being last and the last first (Mark 10:31). Such paradoxes are not merely rhetorical devices; they are essential to Jesus' message. From start to finish, Jesus came to subvert conventional ways of thinking. The language of the gospel is shocking because the coming of Christ's kingdom reverses earthly standards of value. In Jesus' teaching, a revolutionary message naturally produced its own revolutionary discourse.

This explains another characteristic feature of Jesus' speech, his use of hyperbole or exaggeration. Elton Trueblood calls it the giantesque motif.[3] The most famous example is Jesus' statement that "it is easier for a camel to go through the eye of a needle than for a rich man to enter the kingdom of God" (Matt. 19:24). On a par is the satiric picture of the Pharisees "straining out a gnat and swallowing a camel" (23:24). And then there is the hilarious picture of someone wildly swinging a log from his own eye while claiming to be able to get a speck of dirt out of someone else's eye (Luke 6:42).

Such overstatements are of course not intended to be taken literally. Jesus was not stating a reasoned ethical position when he said that "if any one comes to me and does not hate his own father and mother and wife and children and brothers and sisters, yes, and even his own life, he cannot be my disciple" (Luke 14:26). He was using hyperbole to assert the priority that a person must give to God over other relationships.

The speech of Jesus was essentially poetic. He spoke in images rather than theological abstractions. He thought in pictures. As Oliver Cromwell put it, Jesus spoke *things*. When we read the words of Jesus, we are not in a world of systematic theology but in a world of everyday objects—of chickens and lilies and lamps. To understand the message of Jesus in the Gospels, we need to apply all that we know about how poetry works.

Proverb

In addition to being poetic, the New Testament is also proverbial or aphoristic.[4] An aphorism is a concise, memorable statement of truth. Like poetry, it is heightened speech and requires a skill with words

3. Elton Trueblood, *The Humor of Christ* (New York: Harper and Row, 1964), p. 47. This is the topic that Trueblood handles most expertly in his small classic.

4. For commentary on the proverb as a New Testament form, see the excerpts collected in *The New Testament in Literary Criticism*, pp. 295–301; and Robert C. Tannehill, *The Sword of His Mouth: Forceful and Imaginative Language in Synoptic Sayings* (Philadelphia: Fortress, 1975).

that most people lack. In both form and content, the proverbial literature of the New Testament shows affinities to Old Testament wisdom literature, which in biblical times was both folk literature and a form of instruction.

The Sayings of Jesus

When we think of proverbial literature in the New Testament, we naturally think first of the sayings of Jesus. Even more of Jesus' teaching is encapsulated in his sayings than in his parables. Everywhere we turn in the Gospels, the words of Jesus fall continuously into the concise, chiseled form of proverbs that are almost impossible to forget: "a prophet is not without honor, except in his own country" (Mark 6:4); "no one can serve two masters" (Matt. 6:24); "where your treasure is, there will your heart be also" (Luke 12:34). Many of Jesus' sayings have passed into the storehouse of common proverbs.

Proverbs have a power beyond that of ordinary speech. They are a product of the literary imagination. Perhaps this explains why the proverbs of Jesus often merge with figurative language. Many of them make use of metaphor: "you are the salt of the earth" (Matt. 5:13); "I am the vine, you are the branches" (John 15:5). Some of Jesus' proverbs depend on hyperbole for their impact: "when you give alms, do not let your left hand know what your right hand is doing" (Matt. 6:3). Other proverbs are based on paradox: "whoever would save his life will lose it" (Mark 8:35). Still others reinforce the compelling effect of proverbs with a rhetorical question: "for what does it profit a man, to gain the whole world and forfeit his life?" (Mark 8:36).

In these specimens we can catch the subversive quality of Jesus' sayings. In the Old Testament, proverbs tend to be statements of worldly wisdom that reinforce conventional religious thinking. They do not shock our sensibilities. To be told that "a good man obtains favor from the LORD, / but a man of evil devices he condemns" (Prov. 12:2) confirms what a religious person already believes. But the sayings of Jesus often challenge conventional thinking. They reverse ordinary expectations and therefore employ such speech patterns as paradox and hyperbole. Their goal is to jolt us into a new judgment about values and ourselves.

Another reason proverbs occur frequently in the Gospels is that they are often linked with narratives and parables, so that we remember event and saying together. One of the subtypes in the Gospels is the pronouncement story in which a saying of Jesus is paired with an event that it explains or illustrates:

> And as he sat at table in his house, many tax collectors and sinners were sitting with Jesus and his disciples. . . . And the scribes of the Phar-

isees . . . said to his disciples, "Why does he eat with tax collectors and sinners?" And when Jesus heard it, he said to them, "Those who are well have no need of a physician, but those who are sick; I came not to call the righteous, but sinners." [Mark 2:15–17]

Even when a Gospel unit is not primarily a pronouncement story, the sayings of Jesus are often part of the episode. The story of the woman taken in adultery, for example, is a conflict story, but in the middle of the account Jesus utters a memorable proverb: "Let him who is without sin among you be the first to throw a stone at her" (John 8:7).

As with the narrative parts of the Gospels, so with the parables. They are often preceded and/or followed by an aphorism of Jesus. The parable of the marriage feast, for example, ends with the proverb, "For every one who exalts himself will be humbled, and he who humbles himself will be exalted" (Luke 14:11). In addition to these aphorisms surrounding the parables, much of the actual parabolic material is phrased in such a memorable way that we can call it aphoristic: "Go out to the highways and hedges, and compel people to come in, that my house may be filled" (Luke 14:23).

Proverbs in the Epistles

The second great repository of proverbs in the New Testament is the Epistles. The style of Paul, for example, is marked by an epigrammatic tendency: "the wages of sin is death, but the free gift of God is eternal life in Christ Jesus our Lord" (Rom. 6:23); "the love of money is the root of all evils" (1 Tim. 6:10); "for to me to live is Christ, and to die is gain" (Phil. 1:21). Sometimes Paul incorporates an existing proverb into his writing: "a little leaven leavens the whole lump" (Gal. 5:9; 1 Cor. 5:6); "bad company ruins good morals" (1 Cor. 15:33).

Throughout the Epistles we note a tendency to include proverbial sayings; the Epistle of James as a whole falls into the genre of wisdom literature. The very structure of this epistle—a series of small, self-contained units that follow each other in rapid-fire succession—is that of wisdom literature. The subject matter—practical Christian morality—is likewise what we expect in wisdom literature. Everywhere we find the aphoristic gift of stating the truth with memorable terseness: "be doers of the word, and not hearers only" (1:22); "draw near to God and he will draw near to you" (4:8).

A common strategy in biblical wisdom literature is to draw extensively upon the world of nature for similes and analogies to human behavior. The Epistle of James makes frequent use of the technique:

If we put bits into the mouths of horses that they may obey us, we guide their whole bodies. Look at the ships also; though they are so great and are driven by strong winds, they are guided by a very small rudder wherever the will of the pilot directs. So the tongue is a little member and boasts of great things. How great a forest is set ablaze by a small fire! And the tongue is a fire. [3:3–6]

Part of the genius of wisdom literature like this is its ability to put us in touch with ordinary human experience. The proverbs of the New Testament are one of the things that make the New Testament a book of the people.

Interpreting Proverbs

The proverbial nature of much of the New Testament requires that we know how to interpret proverbs. It is important to note in the first place that the proverb is *a meditative form*. It invites us to pause and consider it carefully. It is very much an oral form, which perhaps helps to explain why Jesus chose it so consistently for his discourses. He wanted to give his hearers something to ponder as they left him. Nor should we forget that the disciples who followed Jesus were the designated recorders of Jesus' teaching after his death—recorders for whom memory was crucial in their preaching and composition of the Gospels.

The important principle of interpretation that follows from this is that *a proverb does not put an end to thought on a subject*. It is designed rather to stimulate further thought and application. Its very terseness helps to insure that we will take note of it. A good proverb is so striking that it not only expresses an insight but compels it. Those who hear or read a proverb, writes a biblical scholar, "receive it somewhat in the way one receives a curious object which one must examine in order to find out how it can be used. They are given a text upon which they can ruminate and discuss with one another in an effort to clarify its meaning."[5]

A second rule for interpreting a proverb is to realize that it states *a universal principle about life*. A proverb is an insight into the repeatable situations of life. This means that proverbs are open-ended in their application to life. This is part of their inexhaustibility. The proverb that "whatever a man sows, that he will also reap" (Gal. 6:7) applies to many situations of life. The truth that "men loved darkness rather than light" (John 3:19) is always being confirmed by our observations of life. Part of interpreting a proverb is therefore to ponder what it means and how it applies. Proverbs organize our understand-

5. Birger Gerhardsson, *The Origins of the Gospel Tradition*, in *The New Testament in Literary Criticism*, p. 156.

ing of reality, but we have to supply the data from experience that they organize.

A third thing to note about the proverbs of the New Testament is that they *are often figurative rather than literal.* I noted that proverbs often use the resources of metaphor, simile, paradox, and hyperbole. When they do, we need to apply all that we know about interpreting figurative language. When Jesus says, "My yoke is easy, and my burden is light" (Matt. 11:30), he uses metaphor and paradox rather than literal statement and requires us to interpret them.

Finally, we will do a better job of interpreting proverbs if we realize the impulse behind them. Proverbs are part of *the human urge for order.* Proverbial thinking enables us to master the complexity of life by bringing human experience under the control of an observation that explains it and unifies many similar experiences. Proverbs are a way of organizing what we know to be true of life. A New Testament scholar expresses it thus: "The essence of a proverbial saying is that it is based on observation of how things are in the world. . . . In the context of a firm belief in God, the proverb comes to express insight into the way things are, or should be, in the world ordered by God and a challenge to behaviour that God will reward."[6] New Testament proverbs are high points of insight into reality—moments of spiritual focus in which we see life clearly in God's terms.

New Testament Hymns

In the New Testament, poetic language and proverbs do not exist by themselves but are intermingled with the prose that is the dominant form. The same is true of the lyric quality that I discuss in this section. Prose and poetry, narrative and lyric, are not kept separate in the New Testament. Lyric poetry is mingled with narrative in the Gospels and the Book of Revelation, and with expository prose in the Epistles, where the prose itself often becomes lyrical.

Lyrical discourse is either meditative/reflective or emotional/ affective in nature. It is writing that creates a mood and often has a singing quality. It is intense, unified, compressed, and highly patterned. Often it is poetic in its use of images and regular rhythm (in the Bible, parallelism). Lyric is heightened speech and is always *a response* to the subject about which the speaker or writer speaks.

This lyric *quality* is pervasive in the New Testament epistles and

6. Norman Perrin, *The New Testament: An Introduction* (New York: Harcourt Brace Jovanovich, 1974), p. 296.

the Book of Revelation. As an example of the former, here is Paul's charged description of the confidence that comes to those who have been saved by Christ:

> What then shall we say to this? If God is for us, who is against us? He who did not spare his own Son but gave him up for us all, will he not also give us all things with him? Who shall bring any charge against God's elect? It is God who justifies; who is to condemn? Is it Christ Jesus, who died, yes, who was raised from the dead, who is at the right hand of God, who indeed intercedes for us? Who shall separate us from the love of Christ? Shall tribulation, or distress, or persecution, or famine, or nakedness, or peril, or sword? . . . No, in all these things we are more than conquerors through him who loved us. [Rom. 8:31–37]

A similar ecstasy is just below the surface in the Book of Revelation, where the true lyric voice often asserts itself:

> To him who loves us and has freed us from our sins by his blood and made us a kingdom, priests to his God and Father, to him be glory and dominion for ever and ever. Amen. [1:5–6]

In addition to this general lyric *quality*, the New Testament possesses a number of lyric *genres*. The purpose of the discussion that follows is to identify these genres and to offer a few critical comments that I leave my readers to develop.

Nativity Hymns

Passages of lyric poetry alternate with narrative in the account of the annunciation and birth of Christ in Luke's Gospel. One of these lyrics is the Magnificat (so called after the opening word of its Latin translation) of Mary in Luke 1:46–55. Modeled on the Old Testament psalm of praise and more specifically on the song of Hannah (1 Sam. 2:1–10), the hymn unfolds as a catalogue of God's acts of grace to Mary herself (vv. 48–53) and to the nation of Israel (vv. 54–55).

The Benedictus (also named after its Latin opening) of Zechariah (Luke 1:68–79) likewise has two parts. The first (vv. 68–75) praises God for having fulfilled his promises to his people Israel. The second half (vv. 76–79) is an address to Zechariah's own infant child John the Baptist. The hymn combines the retrospect of Old Testament prophecy with the prospect of fulfillment in the immediate future.

The nativity itself is also accompanied by songs. One is the song of the angels to the shepherds (Luke 2:14). Another is the song of Simeon in the temple (Luke 2:29–32), which is a brief version of the same motifs as the song of Zechariah had developed.

Poetic Fragments Used in Worship

When we move to the Epistles, we find brief poetic passages that modern scholars believe were part of early Christian worship. Leaving aside some of the overly speculative and ingenious attempts to find hymns in the New Testament, there remain stylistic criteria for discerning poetic or liturgical passages. These criteria include introductory or concluding formulas that identify a passage as confessional or hymnic, the presence of parallelism or other unusual grammatical features, a pronounced rhythmical and/or lyric quality, and poetic vocabulary.

Ephesians 5:14 illustrates these features:

Therefore it is said,

> "Awake, O sleeper,
> and arise from the dead,
> and Christ shall give you light."

The formula in the first line identifies the utterance as one that is commonly repeated in Christian circles. By being couched as a direct address to a generalized Christian audience ("O sleeper"), the statement uses the poetic device of apostrophe. In addition to this bit of poetic license, the lines contain parallel clauses, as well as metaphors (sleep, death, light). This imagery leads most scholars to claim that this brief passage is a hymn or chant used in early Christian baptism services.

Hymnic criteria are met in 2 Timothy 2:11–13 as well:

The saying is sure:
> If we have died with him,
>   we shall also live with him;
> if we endure,
>   we shall also reign with him;
> if we deny him,
>   he also will deny us;
> if we are faithless,
>   he remains faithful—
> for he cannot deny himself.

Scholars who are familiar with the original Greek of the New Testament place Hebrews 1:3 in the same category:

> He reflects the glory of God
>   and bears the very stamp of his nature,
> upholding the universe
>   by his word of power.

In the Greek, 1 Peter 1:18–21 and 2:21–25 also qualify.

Sometimes a passage that seems like ordinary prose is accompanied by a formula that suggests that the passage may have been a liturgical unit. For example, Titus 3:5–7 is followed by the statement *the saying is sure* (v. 8). Similarly, Titus 2:11–14 is followed by the comment *declare these things* (v. 15).

Hymns in the Book of Revelation

The Book of Revelation, in which the main impulse is to exalt the work of Christ, contains numerous lyric fragments. They are identifiable by their parallelism and lyric content. Their subject is usually adoration, and the context in which they appear is ordinarily heavenly worship. The fourth chapter of Revelation contains two examples:

> Holy, holy, holy, is the Lord God Almighty,
>   who was and is and is to come! [v. 8]

> Worthy art thou, our Lord and God,
>   to receive glory and honor and power,
>   for thou didst create all things,
>   and by thy will they existed and were created [v. 11]

Similar passages include 5:9–10; 7:12; 11:17–18; 15:3–4; and 19:1–8.

Christ Hymns

We come, finally, to a genre of New Testament lyrics that are so stylistically exalted and poetically great that they deserve a section by themselves. They are known today as Christ hymns. They are written in the verse form of parallelism and are highly patterned in their arrangement. In content, they are Christocentric and fraught with theological themes.

John 1:1–18

The prologue with which the Gospel of John opens is an encomium that praises the incarnate Christ.[7] The poem consists of eight stanzas. In this version I have used italics to draw attention to patterns of repetition within stanzas. Even more repetition emerges if one studies the whole poem to see and hear key words and phrases.

The poem begins by announcing the divine origin of Christ:

> *In the beginning* was *the Word,*
>   and *the Word* was with God,
>   and *the Word* was God.
> He was *in the beginning* with God.

---

7. For explications of this poem and Colossians 1:15–20 in terms of the encomium, see chapter 12, above.

When John wrote these lines, pagan Greeks had for three centuries sung Cleanthes' *Hymn to Zeus*, which also praised a divine word— "the universal Word, that flows through all, and the light celestial. . . . One Word—whose voice alas! the wicked spurn."[8] By echoing the familiar pagan vocabulary, John's poem assumes the status of a parody (a work that echoes an earlier one, but with inverted effect). What the pagans ascribed to Zeus, John attributes to Christ.

The brief second stanza uses antithetic parallelism to assert the cosmic importance of Christ:

> All things were made through him,
> and without him was not anything made that was made.

Christ is here praised for being indispensable to the entire cosmos. To heighten the impact, the writer speaks in terms of absolute contrasts: *all things* versus *not anything, through him* versus *without him.*

The third stanza gains its eloquence through the use of stairstep parallelism:

> In him was *life,*
> and the *life* was the *light* of men.
> The *light* shines in the *darkness,*
> and the *darkness* has not overcome it.

Here, too, is the poetic impulse to think in images and symbols, in this case light and darkness and warfare. This is not incidental but rather integral to the total meaning of the utterance. Ralph P. Martin has written in this regard,

> It may be thought that the classification of parts of the New Testament according to the basic patterns of poetic and hymnic form is an interesting exercise but nothing more. This is not so. . . . Much of the hymnic language is poetic and suggestive of deep spiritual reality rather than prosaic and pedestrian. The early Christians . . . were seeking to interpret their understanding of God's salvation in a way which defied rational and coherent statement. Hence they had recourse to the language of symbol.[9]

8. I have quoted these brief excerpts from William M. Ramsay, *The Layman's Guide to the New Testament,* Layman's Bible Commentary series (Atlanta: John Knox, 1980), p. 243.

9. Ralph P. Martin, "Approaches to New Testament Exegesis," in *The New Testament in Literary Criticism,* pp. 145–46.

The imagery of light becomes fused with the image of kingship in the next stanza:

> There was a man sent from God,
>   whose name was John.
> He came for testimony,
>   *to bear witness* to *the light,*
>   that all might believe through him.
> He was not *the light,*
>   but came *to bear witness* to *the light.*

In ancient cultures, kings had heralds who went before them to proclaim their arrival. Here Christ is portrayed as such a king.

The fifth stanza, the longest in the poem, praises Christ's lifebringing power:

> The true light that enlightens every man
>   was coming into *the world.*
> He was in *the world,*
>   and *the world* was made through him,
>   yet *the world* knew him not.
> He came to his own home,
>   and his own people received him not.
> But to all who received him,
>   who believed in his name,
> he gave power to become children of God;
> who were born,
>   not of blood
>   nor of the will of the flesh
>   nor of the will of man,
> but of God.

The unity and coherence of the poem are amazing. Christ as light continues to be a dominant motif. Christ's creation of the world is echoed from earlier parts of the poem. So is the motif of conflict, as Christ is rejected and has to overcome the impotence of nature in order to bring people to spiritual life.

The famous sixth stanza praises the fact of the incarnation itself:

> And the Word became flesh
>   and dwelt among us,
>   full of grace and truth;
> We have beheld his glory,
>   glory as of the only Son from the Father.

Along with exalted spiritual abstractions (grace, truth, glory), we find more metaphor. Christ is a *Word* that reveals God to people. The thoroughness with which the incarnate Christ identified with humans is forced upon our consciousness when Christ is said to have *dwelt among us*.

The poem proceeds much as a piece of music does. It introduces motifs, abandons them temporarily, and then resumes them. In the seventh stanza, the poem reintroduces John the Baptist for purposes of declaring the superiority of Christ:

> (John bore witness to him, and cried,
>   "This was he of whom I said,
> 'He who comes *after me* ranks *before me*,
>   for he was *before me*.' ")

There is a paradoxical play on the words *after me* and *before me* in the passage. Though born after John, Christ is *before* him, by virtue of both his deity and his having been with God *in the beginning* (stanza 1).

The final stanza praises the subject of the poem by first declaring his superiority and then asserting his indispensability:

> And from his fulness have we all received,
>   *grace* upon *grace*.
> For the law was given through Moses;
>   *grace* and truth came through Jesus Christ.
> No one has ever seen God;
>   the only Son,
>   who is in the bosom of the Father,
> he has made him known.

What Christ brought to the human race is *superior* to the law that Moses brought, and Christ is the *indispensable* revealer of God to people, who cannot see God but who can know him through the incarnate Son.

This great hymn is a prime illustration of Northrop Frye's claim that "the simplicity of the Bible is the simplicity of majesty."[10] The vocabulary and syntax of the hymn are simple. The images are those of the primitive or unsophisticated imagination: light, darkness, combat, kingship, birth. Out of these simple ingredients the poet weaves a tapestry that has a moving grandeur.

10. Northrop Frye, *The Great Code: The Bible and Literature* (New York: Harcourt Brace Jovanovich, 1981), p. 211.

1 Timothy 3:16

From the grandeur of John's prologue we can move to the quiet simplicity of 1 Timothy 3:16. It has the classic form of a hymn embedded in a New Testament epistle, complete with an introductory formula and parallel construction:

> Great indeed, we confess,
>   is the mystery of our religion:
>
> He was manifested in the flesh,
>   vindicated in the Spirit,
> seen by angels,
>   preached among the nations,
> believed on in the world,
>   taken up in glory.

The poem is structured in couplets, each of which is built on the principle of contrast. The nouns that conclude the lines in the English translation are the key to this: they contrast two world orders—divine and human, heavenly and earthly. Here, in kernel form, is the essence of the incarnation itself.

Philippians 2:5–11

Philippians 2:5–11 likewise begins with a formula, this time the command, familiar in the encomium, to emulate:

> Have this mind among yourselves,
>   which is yours in Christ Jesus.

The hymn that follows consists of six stanzas that fall thematically into three movements—Christ preexistent, incarnate, and exalted.[11]
The first stanza opens the drama with Christ in heaven:

> who, though he was in the form of God,
>   did not count equality with God
>   a thing to be grasped.

The image of *grasping* in this stanza is a metaphor from the battlefield. It meant to plunder or seize a spoil of war. In its context in the poem,

11. For a complete treatment of the hymn and scholarship on it, see Ralph P. Martin, *Carmen Christi: Philippians 2:5–11 in Recent Interpretation and in the Setting of Early Christian Worship* (Grand Rapids: Eerdmans, 1983).

it means that Christ did not cling to his right or privilege of deity the way a soldier insists on keeping what he has won in battle.

The next two stanzas advance us from heaven to earth with their account of the incarnation itself:

> but emptied himself,
>   taking the form of a servant,
>   being born in the likeness of men.
> And being found in human form
>   he humbled himself,
>   and became obedient unto death,
>   even death on a cross.

The controlling metaphor in these two stanzas is that of the slave. The word *servant* here means a slave without rights or privileges in society. The last phrase, *even death on a cross*, belongs with this image as well, since the Romans reserved crucifixion for slaves and fomenters of revolutions.

The first half of the poem has been a downward spiral from the greatest possible height to the lowest possible depth. At this midpoint, the drama of Christ's humiliation is reversed by a corresponding ascent. First Christ is described as receiving an exalted name:

> Therefore God has highly exalted him
>   and bestowed on him the name
>   which is above every name.

What Christ refused to cling to or claim is now bestowed on him.

Next we catch a glimpse of the cosmic power that accompanies the exalted name:

> that at the name of Jesus every knee should bow,
>   in heaven
>   and on earth
>   and under the earth.

Here is the image of lordship that reverses the earlier servanthood.

Because a Christ hymn like this was probably part of early Christian worship, it appropriately ends on a note of confession:

> and every tongue confess
>   that Jesus Christ is Lord,
>   to the glory of God the Father.

The climax of this hymn's drama of redemption is the believer's confession that a new age has already begun.

Colossians 1:15–20

The traits of both form and content that I have noted in the Christ hymns of the New Testament are epitomized in the hymn found in Colossians 1:15–20. This Christ hymn consists of two companion poems. The first exalts Christ's supremacy over creation, while the second extols his headship over the church. The impact of companion poems depends on our tracing the parallels between the two parts. In this hymn, everything in the first poem corresponds to something in the second. In figure 2 the two poems are printed with lines that show the connections, and I leave it to my readers to ponder what those correspondences are.

The keynote of the companion poems is the idea of supremacy. The best index to this emphasis is the recurrence of the words *all* and *everything: all creation, all things* (a total of five times), *in everything, all the fulness.*

The companion poems of Colossians 1 encapsulate the New Testament forms I have discussed in this chapter. They are poetic in form. Their lines have the concise, memorable quality that we associate with the proverbial quality of New Testament literature. The passage shares the lyric quality of much of the New Testament and falls into the specific New Testament genre of the Christ hymn.

Figure 2 **Parallels within Colossians 1:15–20**

Christ over Creation	*Christ over the Church*
He is the image of the invisible God, the first-born of all creation;	He is the head of the body, the church.
for in him all things were created, in heaven and on earth, whether thrones or dominions or principalities or authorities— all things were created through him and for him.	He is the beginning, the first-born from the dead, that in everything he might be preeminent.
	For in him all the fulness of God was pleased to dwell, and through him to reconcile to himself all things,
He is before all things, and in him all things hold together.	whether on earth or in heaven, making peace by the blood of his cross.

22

Oratory

Two features of New Testament literature provide the context for my treatment of oratory as a major form in the New Testament. One is the context from which the New Testament originally came. Much of the New Testament first existed in oral form. Jesus, for example, did not write his words as we find them in the Gospels. He spoke them. The Epistles and the Book of Revelation were read aloud in the churches. In cultures that relied on the spoken rather than the written word, the forms of the spoken word are prominent in the literature that is produced. To read the New Testament is to become a listener of the spoken word.

A second literary framework into which I wish to place New Testament oratory is drama. Although the New Testament is not written in the form of a play, the dramatic impulse is everywhere evident. In the narrative sections and the Book of Revelation, we are hard pressed to find pages on which we do not observe characters speaking and acting in the manner of drama. Directly quoted speeches and dialogue suffuse the New Testament, as in this typical passage:

> Then they seized [Jesus] and led him away, bringing him into the high priest's house. Peter followed at a distance; and when they had kindled a fire in the middle of the courtyard and sat down together, Peter

459

sat among them. Then a maid, seeing him as he sat in the light and gazing at him, said, "This man also was with him." But he denied it, saying, "Woman, I do not know him." And a little later some one else saw him and said, "You also are one of them." But Peter said, "Man, I am not." And after an interval of about an hour still another insisted, saying, "Certainly this man also was with him; for he is a Galilean." But Peter said, "Man, I do not know what you are saying." And immediately, while he was still speaking, the cock crowed. And the Lord turned and looked at Peter.... And [Peter] went out and wept bitterly. [Luke 22:54–62]

This is a drama in miniature. The characters are stationed in definite settings. Stage directions for the movements and gestures of characters are written into the script. In effect, the account begins with the familiar "enter Peter" and ends with "exit Peter." In addition, we listen to the actual dialogue in which the characters engage in their face-to-face encounters.

In this chapter I propose to look at a specific genre within the general categories of literature and drama. It is the extended formal address of a speaker to a specific audience. Such addresses comprise more of the New Testament than we may be aware. I have chosen to explicate specimens from the three main repositories of such New Testament oration. Those repositories are the discourses of Jesus recorded in the Gospels, the speeches in the Book of Acts, and the Epistles (which are often written speeches). My aim is to uncover some of the rhetorical techniques and artistry that help to give these orations their power.

Jesus' Sermon on the Mount

Jesus' Sermon on the Mount (Matt. 5–7) will illustrate the typical features of his addresses. Five of these features will be especially prominent.

One characteristic is *an aphoristic tendency.* Because a proverb stays with an audience, it lent itself to the oral nature of Jesus' sermons. After all, the proverbs of Jesus do not put an end to thought on a subject. They stimulate further thought and application.

The style of Jesus' addresses is *poetic* as well as proverbial. Jesus relies heavily on concrete imagery, metaphor, simile, paradox, and hyperbole. In addition, much of his speech falls naturally into the poetic form of Hebrew parallelism.

Recent commentators on the Gospels have also shown how *intricately patterned* the discourses of Jesus are. The key ingredient in such patterning is some form of repetition, recurrence, or balance. Here is an example of patterning on a small scale from Jesus' Olivet Discourse (Matt. 24:40–41):

> Then two men will be in the field;
> one is taken and one is left.
> Two women will be grinding at the mill;
> one is taken and one is left.

We will see the same impulse toward intricate patterning on a grand scale when we observe the outline of the Sermon on the Mount.

A fourth trait of Jesus' discourses is *a strong subversive element.* Jesus repeatedly assaults our patterns of deep thought and undermines our conventional way of thinking and valuing. The famous Beatitudes will highlight the tendency.

Finally, Jesus' discourses often show a literary sophistication by being *a fusion of literary genres.* The Sermon on the Mount, for example, brings together such diverse genres as the beatitude, the character sketch, proverb, satire, lyric, and parable. The sermon as a whole has affinities with utopian literature. It is an inaugural address in which Jesus outlines the principles of his ideal society, conceived as a spiritual kingdom governed by personal spirituality and morality. The sermon is also an example of wisdom literature, in which the wise authority figure sits in the middle of his disciples and instructs them.

The Structure of the Sermon

The principle of organization in Jesus' sermon is relatively simple and highly artistic. Units are either extended passages on a single topic, or fall into a threefold pattern in which three similar items are listed in succession. Here is the pattern that Jesus followed:

1. Prologue: setting and audience (5:1–2).
2. A portrait of the Christian:
   a. the Beatitudes (5:3–12);
   b. two metaphors—salt and light (5:13–16).
3. Jesus' interpretation of the Old Testament law (5:17–48).
4. Instructions on three religious observances:
   a. giving alms (6:1–4);
   b. prayer (6:5–15);
   c. fasting (6:16–18).
5. A threefold exhortation about choosing right values:
   a. choosing between earthly and heavenly treasure (6:19–21);
   b. choosing between light and darkness (6:22–23);
   c. choosing between God and mammon (6:24).

6. The discourse on not being anxious (6:25–34).
7. Instruction on three practices:
   a. judging others (7:1–5);
   b. witnessing (7:6);
   c. prayer (7:7–12).
8. Three great contrasts, or a threefold challenge to act on what Jesus has said:
   a. the wide and narrow gates (7:13–14);
   b. true and false prophets (7:15–23);
   c. the wise and foolish housebuilders (7:24–27).
9. Epilogue: the response of the crowd (7:28–29).

The artistry of the design is apparent. There is no reason why the sermon as it stands could not be exactly the form that Jesus' longer sermons took.

The Portrait of the Christian

The beatitudes that begin the sermon (5:3–12) are a character portrait of the ideal follower of Jesus. They are one of the most patterned passages in the Bible:

> ³"Blessed are the poor in spirit,
>   for theirs is the kingdom of heaven.
> ⁴Blessed are those who mourn,
>   for they shall be comforted.
> ⁵Blessed are the meek,
>   for they shall inherit the earth.
> ⁶Blessed are those who hunger and thirst for righteousness,
>   for they shall be satisfied.
> ⁷Blessed are the merciful,
>   for they shall obtain mercy.
> ⁸Blessed are the pure in heart,
>   for they shall see God.
> ⁹Blessed are the peacemakers,
>   for they shall be called sons of God.
> ¹⁰Blessed are those who are persecuted for righteousness' sake,
>   for theirs is the kingdom of heaven.
> ¹¹Blessed are you when men revile you and persecute you
>   and utter all kinds of evil against you falsely on my account.
> ¹²Rejoice and be glad,
>   for your reward is great in heaven,
>   for so men persecuted the prophets
>   who were before you."

The most obvious element of artistry is the parallelism of statements. Each beatitude follows a similar grammatical pattern consisting of three parts: an initial pronouncement of blessing (*Blessed are . . .*), the naming of a character type, and a rationale for the pronouncement of blessing (starting with the statements *for they shall* or *for theirs is*). This parallelism of expression, which comes straight from the Hebrew poetry that Jesus loved, lends an aphoristic quality to the individual beatitudes and links them with the proverbs of wisdom literature.

The subversive quality of Jesus' message also comes through strongly. For proof, we can first look at the type of person that Jesus considers happy or blessed. The character traits that Jesus names are spiritual and moral and as such run counter to conventional ideas of what makes a person happy. Once we are alerted to this spiritual orientation, we can see that the rewards that Jesus promises are likewise spiritual. In fact, they adhere to the common pattern of the beatitude in the New Testament, where beatitudes tend to be eschatological in content, pronouncing a blessing on those who will share in the coming kingdom of Christ.

To complete his portrait of the Christian, Jesus utters two of his most famous metaphors (5:13–16). God's ideal person has the preserving and flavoring influence in society that salt has with food, and the ability to reveal truth to people that a lighted lamp has in a dark room.

The Discourse About the Law

From his opening portrait of the ideal Christian Jesus moves to a long explanation of his relationship to the Jewish law (5:17–48). First we should notice the rhetorical patterning that makes the passage easy to follow. Jesus discusses six Jewish laws and follows a similar pattern in each unit. He begins with the formula, *You have heard that it was said . . .*, followed by his repetition of a familiar law. Having summarized the traditional command, Jesus counters it with his own teaching, beginning with the formula *but I say to you. . . .* The rhetorical pattern is based on a principle of antithesis.

The actual content of this passage has often been distorted. A careful look at what Jesus says shows that he is not abolishing the Old Testament moral law. In fact, he announces at the outset that "whoever then relaxes one of the least of these commandments and teaches men so, shall be called least in the kingdom of heaven" (5:19). Jesus simply calls his followers to go beyond what the moral law requires in their dealings with other people.

The law, for example, prohibited murder (5:21). But Jesus expects his followers to live by a higher morality than that. He expects them to refrain from uncontrolled anger and hatred (vv. 22–26). Again we can see the subversive nature of Jesus' message: instead of encouraging people to be satisfied with obeying the letter of the law, Jesus tells them to obey the spirit of the law as well. His theme is that "unless your righteousness exceeds that of the scribes and Pharisees, you will never enter the kingdom of heaven" (5:20).

Three Observances and Three Choices

Following the extended passage dealing with the law, Jesus moves to two sections built out of brief units. The organizing rhetorical pattern in both passages is a threefold pattern.

The first unit deals with three religious practices—giving alms (6:1–4), prayer (6:5–15), and fasting (6:16–18). Here, too, Jesus' statements fall into a rhetorical pattern of antithesis, as he contrasts ostentatious religion with religion practiced in secret. The pivot in each unit comes when Jesus concludes his portrait of people who practice their religion ostentatiously with the sarcastic refrain, *Truly, I say to you, they have received their reward* (vv. 2, 5, 16). The second half of each section, in which Jesus states postively his antidote to the abuse he has described, also ends with a refrain: *and your Father who sees in secret will reward you* (vv. 4, 6, 18).

This section uses the literary resources of satire, as Jesus begins each unit by ridiculing the way in which ostentatious people go about practicing their religion to be seen by people. As is typical of satirists, Jesus exaggerates the practices of those he is attacking, picturing them as having a band of trumpet players precede them when they make their offering (6:2) and as disfiguring their faces to make sure that people know they are fasting (6:16). The positive advice that Jesus offers as a corrective also employs hyperbole, as in the picture of not letting one's right hand know what the left hand is doing when giving alms (6:3), or going into a closet to pray (6:6, KJV).

It is in the middle of this satiric section that Jesus places "the Lord's Prayer" (6:9–13). In its original context, this prayer is offered as a satiric norm—a model of short prayer instead of the *empty phrases* that the Gentiles *heap up* (6:7). The prayer itself adheres to two principles of Jesus' speech: it is in poetic form, and it is aphoristic.

The instruction on practicing religion secretly in the presence of God instead of openly to impress people has as its sequel a threefold exhortation to choose heavenly or spiritual values over earthly values (6:19–24). Jesus does not speak in abstractions but in images of treasure, rust, thieves, light, darkness, servants, and masters. Antithesis underlies the contrasts between earthly and heavenly treasures, light and darkness, and the two masters (God and mammon). Each of the contrasts is climaxed by a memorable proverb that clinches the point: *for where your treasure is, there will your heart be also* (v. 21); *if then the light in you is darkness, how great is the darkness* (v. 23); *you cannot serve God and mammon* (v. 24).

The Discourse Against Anxiety

From two passages dealing with multiple subjects Jesus moves to another extended passage, the famous warning against being anxious (6:25–34). The passage is a lyric meditation in which we contemplate the futility and evil of worry from every possible angle. If we are looking for a masterpiece of persuasive rhetoric, here it is. Jesus pours out reasons and affective appeals to make us *feel* how wrong and useless it is to worry.

Jesus begins by stating his thesis, which he applies to two areas of life (food and clothing):

> Therefore I tell you,
> do not be anxious about your *life*,
>   what you shall *eat*
>   or what you shall *drink*,
> nor about your *body*,
>   what you shall *put on*.

Then Jesus asks a twofold rhetorical question that repeats the two subjects that have been introduced:

> Is not *life* more than *food*,
>   and the *body* more than *clothing*?

Jesus next takes up the first of the two topics that he has introduced, the subject of food. He bases his argument on an analogy from nature and clinches the point by persuasively adding a rhetorical question with which we cannot possibly disagree:

> Look at the birds of the air:
>   they neither sow nor reap nor gather into barns,
>   and yet your heavenly Father *feeds* them.
> Are you not of more value than they?

Still more persuasion follows as Jesus asks another rhetorical question, which this time forces us to acknowledge how ineffectual worry is:

> And which of you by being anxious
>   can add one cubit to his span of life?

Having disposed of the conventional reasons for worrying about food, Jesus proceeds to his second announced topic, clothing. Again he uses an analogy from nature, saying, in effect, "Take a look around you and observe God's providence":

> And why are you anxious about *clothing*?
> Consider the lilies of the field, how they grow;
>   they neither toil nor spin.

Not only are the lilies clothed without effort on their part, but the beauty of their clothing is even greater than that of Solomon, the Old Testament touchstone for magnificence:

> yet I tell you,
> even Solomon in all his glory
> was not *arrayed* like one of these.

Then Jesus proceeds to apply a second analogy, also taken from nature:

> But if God so *clothes* the grass of the field,
>   which today is alive
>   and tomorrow is thrown into the oven,
> will he not much more *clothe* you,
>   O men of little faith?

In a summary statement, Jesus returns to the categories of experience in which, as he has proved, worry is useless:

> Therefore do not be anxious, saying,
>   "What shall we *eat*?" or
>   "What shall we *drink*?" or
>   "What shall we *wear*?"

Two further reasons explain why these questions are so ignominious:

> For the Gentiles seek all these things;
> and your heavenly Father knows that you need them all.

The positive antidote to the anxiety about physical provision that Jesus has attacked is stated as a proverb:

> But seek first his kingdom and his righteousness,
> and all these things shall be yours as well.

Having refuted all possible counterarguments, Jesus states with finality the conclusion toward which his argument has been pointing:

> Therefore do not be anxious about tomorrow,
> for tomorrow will be anxious for itself.

To conclude the entire discourse, Jesus offers an aphorism that implies a note of gentle cynicism and compassionate realism about what life in a fallen world is like:

> Let the day's own trouble
> be sufficient for the day.

In this meditation on the futility of worry we see the *affective* nature of Jesus' discourses. By the time we finish listening to Jesus' case against worry, we are left feeling that it is the last thing in the world that we would care to do.

Three Religious Practices

In the next section we return to the threefold arrangement. Jesus here provides instruction about judging others (7:1–5), witnessing (7:6), and prayer (7:7–12). The aphoristic and poetic tendencies of Jesus' discourses here combine to achieve an effect that is both memorable and eloquent:

> with the judgment you pronounce
> you will be judged,
> and the measure you give
> will be the measure you get. [7:2]

> Do not give dogs what is holy;
> and do not throw your pearls before swine. [7:6]

> Ask, and it will be given you;
> seek, and you will find;
> knock, and it will be opened to you.
> For every one who asks receives,
> and he who seeks finds,
> and to him who knocks it will be opened. [7:7]

Who can doubt that Jesus is one of the world's most famous poets? No poet has been more quoted than Jesus.

Three Great Contrasts

As Jesus concludes his oration (7:13–27), he sharpens the issues and begins to force a response from his listeners. He leaves his audience with a challenge, urging them to make sure that they are members of God's kingdom. In order to make his point with impact, Jesus uses three memorable contrasts—the narrow gate that leads to life versus the wide gate that leads to destruction (vv. 13–14), true prophets versus false prophets (vv. 15–23), and the wise man who builds his house on a rock versus the foolish man who builds on the sand (vv. 24–27).

Jesus' mastery of metaphor and simile is much in evidence here at the end of his most famous public speech. Life is a path with a gate at the entrance. False prophets are ravenous wolves in sheep's clothing. Prophets are like fruit trees that can be judged by their fruit. Hearing or rejecting the words of Jesus is like building a house. Jesus the teller of parables here merges with Jesus the poet.

We do not need the epilogue (7:28–29) to tell us that Jesus was a master orator. It does, however, confirm my earlier claims about the strongly dramatic cast of much of the New Testament. The prologue to the Sermon on the Mount situates the speaker in a definite landscape and before a specific audience: "Seeing the crowds, he went up on the mountain, and when he sat down his disciples came to him" (5:1). As the curtain falls at the end of the sermon, we observe the crowd again: "And when Jesus finished these sayings, the crowds were astonished at his teaching" (7:28).

Jesus' Sermon on the Mount epitomizes his oratorical style. That style is proverbial, poetic, and patterned. Jesus did not scorn literature but flaunted his mastery of it.

Paul's Address in Athens

The second major repository of orations in the New Testament is the Book of Acts. In fact, three-fourths of the book consists of speeches and their immediate settings.[1] Modern scholarship has repeatedly shown that the orations of Acts are cast into the rhetorical forms common in classical culture of the time. F. F. Bruce divides the speeches of Acts into four main categories—evangelistic, deliberative, apologetic, and hortatory.[2]

One of the most memorable speeches in Acts is Paul's address to the Areopagus in Athens (Acts 17:16–33). The Athenian address has evoked disagreement from modern scholars. In particular, scholars have been troubled by the need to reconcile Paul's seeming approval of the pagan assumptions of his audience with the uncompromising

1. I take this figure from Paul Schubert, "The Final Cycle of Speeches in the Book of Acts," *Journal of Biblical Literature* 87 (1968): 16.
2. F. F. Bruce, *The Speeches in the Acts of the Apostles* (London: Tyndale, 1942).

Christian witness that is customary in his preaching. I believe that the key to the interpretation of the Athenian address lies in a literary approach, that is, one which pays close attention to the narrative details given in Acts and which places the oration in the context of the rules of classical rhetoric and oratory.

The Context of the Oration

The narrative tells us what we need to know about the circumstances in which the oration occurred. We learn, for example, that the thing that prompted Paul to speak was his horror at the idolatry that he saw around him: "Now while Paul was waiting . . . at Athens, his spirit was provoked within him as he saw that the city was full of idols" (v. 16). The people who cleared the way for Paul to speak were "the Epicurean and Stoic philosophers" (v. 18). This means that Paul was addressing an intellectual audience, not the people on the street with their crude idolatry.

There has been disagreement about what is meant by the statement that Paul was brought "to the Areopagus" (v. 19) to deliver his address. The Areopagus was both a hill and a council of men who exercised control over the public speaking that went on in Athens. There would seem to be good evidence for concluding that Paul spoke before this council or court, having been asked to demonstrate his credentials as a speaker in the marketplace. We read that Paul stood "in the middle of the Areopagus" (v. 22). At the end "Paul went out from among them" (v. 33), indicating that Paul stood before a group of men known as "the Areopagus."

If we realize that the address was delivered to a dignified council, we are in a better position to understand the drama of the occasion and the reason for the dignity of Paul's address. His oration adheres to the best form of classical oration and includes allusions to Homer, Plato, and other Greek writers.

The narrative framework also informs us that the oration was cut short by the interruption of the audience. It is often claimed that the address as it has been recorded in Acts is a summary of a much longer address. If we look closely at the text, however, this conclusion appears doubtful. The dignified opening of the address shows no sign of being condensed. The style is leisurely and drawn out. The sentences and clauses are long and include parallel constructions (vv. 24–25, 29). The address as we have it even includes Paul's quotations from Greek poets. Furthermore, verse 32 states clearly that *"when* they heard of the resurrection of the dead, some mocked." In other words, at a specific point in the address the audience made it impossible for Paul to continue.

Classical Rhetoric in the Address

The narrative context, when combined with an awareness of the structure of a classical oration, gives us the key to interpreting the Athenian address. According to classical rhetoric, the first part of an address was the *exordium*. This was the introduction to the main part of the speech. According to Quintilian, a contemporary of Paul, the aim of the exordium was "to prepare the hearer to listen to us more readily in the subsequent parts of our pleading. This object, as is agreed among most authors, is principally effected by three means, by securing his good will and attention, and by rendering him desirous of further information."[3] The introduction, in short, was designed to ingratiate the speaker with his audience. A common way of gaining the attention of the listeners was to cite some anecdote that would interest them.

The recorded oration of Paul to the Areopagus is virtually all exordium. In it, Paul pours his energies into establishing rapport with his listeners—saying things with which they agreed, finding a common base with them, making his audience feel that they had begun their quest for God with the right conception. Having done all this, Paul intended to add the Christian distinctives to this introduction. But he never had a chance to develop the main part of his address, as we shall see.

Paul begins his dignified oration with the formula that the famous Athenian orator Demosthenes used to open his addresses: *Men of Athens* (v. 22). Paul's intellectual audience would have felt on native ground with such an opening.

Paul next gives an assessment of the character of the Athenians, appealing to the interest that every audience has in how a visitor views them: *I perceive that in every way you are very religious* (v. 22). This is a commendation and an attempt to find common ground between Paul and his audience. The word translated "religious" could mean either "superstitious," with negative connotations, or "religious," with positive connotations. Obviously Paul is using it in the favorable sense as part of his strategy of gaining a sympathetic hearing.

Paul next uses the time-honored technique of recounting an anecdote, in this case one that involved the listeners themselves: *For as I passed along, and observed the objects of your worship, I found also an altar with this inscription, "To an unknown god"* (v. 23). Then Paul announces his topic: *What therefore you worship as unknown, this I proclaim to you* (v. 23). Paul here defines his audience very carefully. He

---

3. Quoted from Kenneth Myrick, *Sir Philip Sidney as a Literary Craftsman* (Lincoln: University of Nebraska Press, 1965), p. 55.

is addressing philosophers or anyone else for whom the altar to the unknown god summed up their religious state of mind. An altar to an unknown god implies people who have religious sensitivity, who believe that there is a god, but who have not yet found this god. The inscription would appeal to someone dissatisfied with, and skeptical of, the existing religious climate. Paul is appealing to such people, playing on their dissatisfaction and building upon it.

As Paul proceeds to talk about the God who he and his audience agree exists, he first stresses something with which his intelligent audience would agree—that God cannot be confined in physical idols:

> The God who made the world and everything in it, being Lord of heaven and earth, does not live in shrines made by man, nor is he served by human hands, as though he needed anything, since he himself gives to all men life and breath and everything. [vv. 24–25]

We must bear in mind that Paul is addressing persons who are dissatisfied with the existing idol worship, as evidenced by their declaration that their god is still an unknown god.

As Paul continues, he talks about what we might call universal theism. He claims that there is a universal divine being, that people have a religious consciousness, and that people who seek God can find him:

> And he made from one every nation of men to live on all the face of the earth, having determined allotted periods and the boundaries of their habitation, that they should seek God, in the hope that they might feel after him and find him. Yet he is not far from each one of us. [vv. 26–27]

There is nothing distinctively Christian about Paul's remarks thus far. Paul is simply closing ranks with his audience, assuring them that they share with him an awareness that there is a God and that together they can know this God. The word translated "feel after" may have struck a familiar note in Paul's Greek audience. Homer had used the word to describe the groping of the blinded Cyclops Polyphemus as he sought the entrance of his cave, while Plato had used it in the *Phaedo* to describe people's guesses at the truth.[4]

By now Paul's audience is hearing what it likes to hear in the style it likes best. As Paul proceeds, he continues to emphasize that he

4. Based on E. M. Blaiklock, *The Acts of the Apostles: An Historical Commentary* (Grand Rapids: Eerdmans, 1959), pp. 144–45. My subsequent references to Paul's allusions come from the same source.

shares the theism of his audience. In fact, he quotes with approval from several Stoic poets who had expressed the same idea:

> "In him we live and move and have our being";
> as even some of your poets have said,
> "For we are indeed his offspring." [v. 28]

One source to whom Paul may be alluding here is Cleanthes, who had written, "Thou, Zeus, art praised above all gods. . . . The origin of the world was from thee: and by law thou rulest over all things. Unto thee may all flesh speak, for we are thy offspring." The Greek poet Aratus had written, "Always we have need of Zeus. For we are also his offspring. . . ." And the poet Epimenides had written about Zeus, "For in thee we live and are moved and have our being." The fact that the brief exordium of Paul's oration contains so many echoes of Greek authors is testimony to Paul's Greek education and to the dignity of the occasion. It also makes very doubtful that we have a shorthand summary of his speech.

As Paul nears the end of his exordium, he summarizes the general points that he has made:

> Being then God's offspring, we ought not to think that the Deity is like gold, or silver, or stone, a representation by the art and imagination of man. [v. 29]

The style of the speech up to this point has been exalted, leisurely, allusive, and repetitive—the opposite of what it would be if the speech as recorded in Acts were a condensation.

Having completed the exordium, Paul moves to the part of his oration that Latin rhetoricians would have called the *propositio*—the statement of thesis. Here at last Paul begins to declare the distinctives of the Christian faith—things such as repentance, judgment, Jesus, and eternal life. As a transition between the exordium and the Christian thesis that he hopes to develop, Paul says, *The times of ignorance God overlooked, but now he commands all men everywhere to repent* (v. 30).

The next verse continues the statement of the thesis that Paul has come to defend:

> because he has fixed a day on which he will judge the world in righteousness by a man whom he has appointed, and of this he has given assurance to all men by raising him from the dead. [v. 31]

Paul has now warmed to his theme and is ready to develop his Christian message. And what happens? He is interrupted and cannot continue: "Now when they heard of the resurrection of the dead, some mocked; but others said, 'We will hear you again about this' " (v. 32). The next verse confirms that Paul's speech was cut short: "So Paul went out from among them" (v. 33), with the word *so* connecting Paul's departure from the group with the mocking of some of his listeners.

The Aftermath of the Speech

The epilogue to the story of Paul's address hints that the interrupted oration was not a total failure: "But some men joined him and believed, among them Dionysius the Areopagite and a woman named Damaris and others with them" (v. 34). One of Paul's converts was "Dionysius the Areopagite," a member of the Areopagus, whose name was also used by famous mystic of the early Christian church.

How did Paul evaluate his oratorical performance before the Areopagus? There is evidence that he may have been disillusioned with his attempt to impress his listeners with his high-flown address that never got beyond the introduction. Paul's next stop on his missionary journey was Corinth (Acts 18:1). In a letter that he later wrote to the Corinthian church, Paul described two kinds of preaching: "When I came to you, brethren, I did not come proclaiming for you the testimony of God in lofty words or wisdom. For I decided to know nothing among you except Jesus Christ and him crucified" (1 Cor. 2:1–2).

Although we cannot be certain about the point, Paul might well be alluding to this address before the Areopagus. He describes how when he came to Corinth he made a conscious decision not to preach in "lofty words or wisdom" (that is, purely human wisdom) and not to preach about anything except the distinctively Christian subject of "Jesus Christ and him crucified."

We must not be misled, however, into thinking that Paul's sermons and writing are not rhetorically accomplished. He may have bid a farewell to the embellishments of classical rhetoric in his preaching, but his defense speeches recorded later in Acts adhere to the conventions of similar orations in the classical world.[5] Furthermore, Paul's style, even in passages where he repudiates human wisdom and eloquence, is a rhetorically sophisticated style, as we shall see in the next section.

5. See Fred Veltman, "The Defense Speeches of Paul in Acts," in *Perspectives on Luke-Acts*, ed. Charles H. Talbert, Special Studies, no. 5 (Danville, Va.: Association of Baptist Professors of Religion, 1978), pp. 253–56.

1 Corinthians 13

The gap between New Testament oratory and the Epistles is very small. The authors of the Epistles were preachers whose sermonic rhetoric carried over into their writing. The audiences of their sermons and letters were essentially the same. The New Testament epistles circulated in oral form among the churches, and many of them were written with such a context in mind.

To illustrate the oratorical style of the New Testament epistles, I have chosen to explicate 1 Corinthians 13. My governing purpose is to show how patterned, how eloquent, and how artistic the passage is. The implied thesis of this entire book is that the New Testament is a literary and artistic book, and that we have heard far too much about its unliterary nature. My analysis of 1 Corinthians 13 should demonstrate that Paul's pejorative comments about human eloquence do not mean that his own writing is anything less than very eloquent.

The genre of 1 Corinthians 13 is the encomium, a lyric passage that praises an abstract quality. The subject of this encomium is love. The passage praises its subject by means of the usual formulas of an encomium: the indispensability of the subject (vv. 1–3), a catalogue of its praiseworthy acts and attributes (vv. 4–7), the superiority of love (vv. 8–13), and a concluding command to emulate the subject (14:1— "Make love your aim").

The poem of praise comes to us in an oratorical, wavelike style in which the organizing principle is repeated patterns of three. Balance, parallelism, and contrast are also much in evidence.

The passage opens with three parallel statements, each of which falls into a threefold formula. The formula is this: (1) *If I* . . ., (2) *but have not love*, (3) *nothing* (or an equivalent). Each of the units is thus based on an all-or-nothing contrast:

> If I speak in the tongues of men and of angels,
>   but have not love,
>   I am a noisy gong or clanging cymbal.
> And if I have prophetic powers,
> and understand all mysteries and all knowledge,
> and if I have all faith,
> so as to remove mountains,
>   but have not love,
>   I am nothing.
> If I give away all I have,
> and if I deliver my body to be burned,
>   but have not love,
>   I gain nothing.

This is both highly artistic and oratorical. It is the kind of passage that asks to be read aloud.

The next movement, the catalogue of love's acts and attributes, is also based on a rhetorical pattern of three. In three successive clauses, the noun *love* is the subject of verbs that follow it:[6]

> Love is longsuffering,
>   is kind;
> love envieth not;
> love vaunteth not itself,
>   is not puffed up,
>   doth not behave itself unseemly,
>   seeketh not its own,
>   is not easily provoked,
>   imputeth not the evil;
>   rejoiceth not at unrighteousness,
>   but rejoiceth with the truth;
>   beareth all things,
>   hopeth all things,
>   endureth all things.

An oratorical passage like this enters our consciousness in a series of waves. It is rhythmic and affective, sweeping us along with its eloquence.

The pattern of threes continues in the next unit, which contrasts the permanence of love with the transience of three spiritual gifts (which, incidentally, have already been introduced in the opening movement of the passage):

> Love never ends;
>   as for prophecies, they will pass away;
>   as for tongues, they will cease;
>   as for knowledge, it will pass away.

The same contrast is elaborated in the next unit, where the word *imperfect* occurs three times as well:

> For our knowledge is imperfect
>   and our prophecy is imperfect;
> But when the perfect comes,
>   the imperfect will pass away.

6. English translations tend to obscure the rhetorical pattern in this section. My version is based on Henry Alford, *The New Testament for English Readers* (Chicago: Moody, n.d.).

For further elaboration of the motif that the imperfect is inferior to that which is perfect and therefore permanent, Paul introduces the analogy of what he was like as a child as contrasted with what he is like as an adult:

> When I was a child,
>   I spoke like a child,
>   I thought like a child,
>   I reasoned like a child.
> When I became a man,
>   I gave up childish ways.

Balance and contrast continue as Paul applies the analogy to the announced topic of spiritual gifts that will pass away, as opposed to love, which endures:

> For now we see in a mirror dimly,
>   but then face to face.
> Now I know in part,
>   then I shall understand fully,
>   even as I have been fully understood.

The threefold pattern accompanied by contrast reaches its climax in the famous aphorism with which the discourse concludes:

> So faith, hope, love abide, these three;
>   but the greatest of these is love.

What this shows, I trust, is that the oratorical style of the New Testament epistles deserves some of the epithets that we commonly ascribe to literature: beautiful, eloquent, and artistic. Augustine was right when he said that "wisdom was [Paul's] guide, eloquence his attendant."

23

The Book of Revelation

The Book of Revelation is the most thoroughly literary book in the Bible. It is filled with images, characters, and events.[1] Ironically, it is also the book of the Bible that commentators have tried the hardest to translate out of its literary mode into an expository or propositional mode.

The Literary Genres of the Book of Revelation

The Book of Revelation is an anthology or compendium of literary genres. The combination of literary forms that converge in the book makes it unique, but this should not be allowed to obscure the fact that the forms themselves are familiar ones. If we simply take the time to piece together the separate strands in the book, there is no reason why we should find it a perplexing book.

The two broadest categories of literature are story and poetry. In any strict sense, the Book of Revelation is neither, but an easy familiarity with narrative and poetry are the best preparation for under-

---

1. Some excellent commentary on the literary nature of the Book of Revelation can be found in various sources collected in Leland Ryken, ed., *The New Testament in Literary Criticism*, A Library of Literary Criticism (New York: Ungar, 1984), pp. 302–28.

standing the book. Also prominent are the genres of drama, epistle, apocalypse, and epic.

The Book of Revelation as Story

Overall, the Book of Revelation is conceived on a narrative principle. This is partly obscured by the fact that the story is told as a series of visions instead of in a smooth narrative flow. But the visions fit together the way episodes in a story do.

As in any story, there is a unifying plot conflict in the Book of Revelation. The overarching conflict is a spiritual struggle between good and evil. Within this general framework, we find a whole system of contrasts at work. There are many character conflicts, for example: Christ versus Satan, the saints versus the followers of the beast, the bride of Christ versus the whore of Babylon, the Lamb versus the dragon, Michael's angels versus the dragon's angels. Scenic contrasts are equally pervasive: heaven versus the sinful earth and the bottomless pit, the city of God versus "the great city" of evil, New Jerusalem versus Babylon.

There are also conflicting actions. The establishment of the New Jerusalem is set against the destruction of Babylon. The sealing of the saints has as its counterpart the receiving of the mark of the beast. Most of the individual visions, moreover, are structured as a conflict between forces of good and evil. Nor should we overlook a basic temporal contrast that underlies the book, a contrast between timeless eternity (associated with deliverance for believers) and temporal history (associated with various types of misery).

The linear sequence of the book corresponds to what happens in a story. There are few works of literature that have such a strong onward pressure as the Book of Revelation. We are continually being propelled to the next event as we read. The linear movement is not a smooth narrative flow from one event to the next. The movement is much closer to some of the effects in modern cinema—a kaleidoscopic sequence of visions, pictures, sounds, images, and events, ever shifting and never in focus for very long. The lack of a smooth narrative sweep, combined with the repetitive structure of the book, makes it impossible to arrange the book according to a rigid chronology in which each event is regarded as following the preceding event or scene.

Despite this lack of a single chronology, the Book of Revelation has the sense of progression that we associate with stories. As we progress through the book, we are caught up in a movement through increasingly intense conflicts between good and evil. With the fourth of the seven seals, for example, a fourth of the earth is judged (6:8); with five of the judgments introduced by the seven trumpets, a third (8:7–12);

and with the plagues resulting from pouring of the seven bowls of wrath, the entire earth, "for with them the wrath of God is ended" (15:1). As we near the end of the book, we have the strong sense that the great conflict between good and evil is moving toward its final resolution.

Even more important than the overall plot structure of the book is the way in which the organizing framework for the individual units is a narrative framework. The most helpful way to make sense of the individual units is to ask the following questions, which are the standard narrative questions:

1. The question of setting: *where* does the action occur?
2. The issue of character: *who* are the actors or agents?
3. The question of plot or action: *what* happens?
4. The issue of plot outcome: what is the *result* of the action?

This basic narrative framework will enable us to organize virtually any individual passage in the Book of Revelation.

The Book of Revelation as Drama

Reinforcing the narrative thread of Revelation are its strong affinities with drama.[2] The format of the book—a number of visions—makes it a series of dramatized scenes. Again and again we find characters placed into elaborately described settings. Speeches, songs, and snatches of dialogue punctuate the action. The book is not, of course, a single sustained drama. It is more like a pageant, with brief scenes following each other to produce an overall story of the end of history.

We might remember in this regard that the New Testament world was essentially a Greek world. Greek civilization had for centuries been known for its drama. People were familiar with the conventions of the theater. Although never intended for the stage, the Book of Revelation is cast into a form that would be familiar to anyone who thought in terms of the theater. The book should also seem accessible to a century (our own) in which people automatically have the right antennae to assimilate works that resemble television dramas and films.

The Epistolary Framework

Although story and drama provide the dominant organizing framework for the book, these are not the first things to greet us as we start

2. See John W. Bowman, "The Revelation to John: Its Dramatic Structure and Message," *Interpretation* 9 (1955): 436–53.

to read. John chose as his portal into the book a familiar New Testament form—the epistle or letter. "John to the seven churches that are in Asia," we read in the fourth verse of the book. This is the customary salutation of the New Testament epistles. Following the prologue, moreover, we find a total of seven letters to the churches (chaps. 2–3). John has obviously adapted a popular form of early Christian literature.

The epistolary framework reappears at the very end of the book (22:6–21). The miscellaneous admonitions and concluding thoughts resemble those at the end of most New Testament epistles. Balancing the opening salutation of the book is the concluding benediction: "The grace of the Lord Jesus be with all the saints. Amen" (22:21). Someone has rightly said that "Revelation is, in fact, the first book to show the influence of the collected and published letters of Paul."[3]

The Book of Revelation as Apocalypse

The literary family into which the Book of Revelation is most customarily placed is the form known as apocalypse. This form, too, was familiar to a Hebrew audience of the early Christian era, although it often seems strange to modern readers. Apocalyptic works are visionary works that transport us to an alternate world from the one in which we live. Literally the word *apocalypse* means "unveiling," or a *revelation* of something that is hidden.

Apocalyptic writing has a number of identifiable characteristics, virtually all of them fully evident in the Book of Revelation. Apocalyptic works are dualistic in the sense that they divide the world decisively into good and evil. Apocalyptic writing is also eschatological, being primarily concerned with future events, especially those at the end of history. The basic unit of presentation is the ecstatic vision of a world remote from our own, either in time or in the sense of being a supernatural world.

Biblical apocalypse tends to be messianic, centering in the appearance and work of a divine Messiah. Angels and demons are prominent. Also common are animal symbolism (use of animals to stand for human characters, movements, or events) and numerology (use of numbers with symbolic meanings). Apocalyptic writing tends to be judgmental, with the writer denouncing an existing system of values and predicting its miserable end. There can be no doubt that the apocalyptic genre is the dominant form of the Book of Revelation.

Apocalyptic writing is not as remote from our own literary experience as it may seem at first. It has many of the traits of folk literature.

3. Edgar J. Goodspeed, *How to Read the Bible* (Philadelphia: Universal Book and Bible House, 1946), p. 201.

The presence of animal characters, for example, is something with which we have resonated from childhood. In the Book of Revelation we encounter such animal characters as the Lamb, horses of various colors, warriorlike locusts, a dragon, and terrifying beasts from the sea and earth.

Color symbolism is something else that the popular imagination has always relished. In the Book of Revelation, the color white is associated with Christ (1:14), the saints of God (3:18; 4:4; 7:9, 14; 19:8), the armies of heaven (19:14), and God's throne of judgment (20:11). Red, by contrast, usually appears in contexts of evil—warfare (6:4), the appearance of the satanic dragon (12:3), and the whore of Babylon and her beast (17:3–4).

Even the element of deliberate strangeness in apocalyptic writing has parallels in modern writing. Someone has compared such writing to underground writing in which oppressed people develop a code language of obscure and indirect symbols, which in the case of Revelation "were necessary for the safety of both writer and readers at a time when the church was driven underground by the Roman Gestapo."[4] Someone else believes that the closest parallel in our day is the political cartoon, in which nations or their leaders are represented as animals (the eagle for the United States or the dragon for China) or an stereotyped figures (such as Uncle Sam).[5] It seems reasonable to believe that the "caricatures" in the Book of Revelation would have been immediately recognized by John's original audience. The whore of Babylon, for example, obviously stood for the Roman empire.

The Book of Revelation as Epic

The Book of Revelation is also similar to the narrative genre known as epic. As such, it reminds us of such familiar epics as Homer's *Odyssey*, Virgil's *Aeneid*, and Milton's *Paradise Lost*. Its style, for example, is an epic style. The writer uses epic similes in an effort to do justice to his vision and theme: "his feet were like burnished bronze, refined as in a furnace" (1:15); "a great star fell from heaven, blazing like a torch" (8:10); "a loud voice, like a lion roaring" (10:3).

Another feature of epic style is the exalted epithets (titles) that convey a sense of exuberance: "Jesus Christ the faithful witness, the first-born of the dead, and the ruler of kings on earth" (1:5); "the Lord God Almighty, who was and is and is to come" (4:8); "King of kings and Lord of lords" (19:16). There are also epic catalogues—of churches, of

---

4. Charles F. Wishart, "Patmos in the Pulpit," *Interpretation* 1 (1947): 459.

5. G. R. Beasley-Murray, *The Book of Revelation* (London: Marshall, Morgan and Scott, 1974), pp. 16–17.

the beings around God's throne in heaven, of the tribes of Israel, of the jewels in the heavenly city. Epic style achieves grandeur and depth through the presence of allusions, and Revelation is no exception. It contains some 350 allusions to the Old Testament, as well as many references to the redemptive life of Christ.

Epic style is exuberant and overflowing, and here, too, Revelation meets the standard:

> Grace to you and peace from him who is and who was and who is to come, and from the seven spirits who are before his throne, and from Jesus Christ the faithful witness, the first-born of the dead, and the ruler of kings on earth. [1:4–5]

C. S. Lewis has written that "continuity is an essential of the epic style," and he speaks of "the enormous onward pressure of the great stream on which you are embarked." Such a style, adds Lewis, can be described with such terms as "ritualistic," "incantatory," possessing "grandeur," capable of creating "the true epic exhilaration."[6] Such designations describe exactly what we encounter as we read the Book of Revelation.

The content of Revelation is as thoroughly epic as is the style. Epics are stories of great and heightened conflict. They portray battles in which at least some of the participants are spiritual beings using supernatural means of warfare. The setting for the action is cosmic and includes heaven as well as earth and hell. The whole tendency is expansive. The following excerpt from Revelation is thoroughly recognizable as an epic event:

> Then I saw another amighty angel coming down from heaven, wrapped in a cloud. . . . And he set his right foot on the sea, and his left foot on the land, and called out with a loud voice, like a lion roaring; when he called out, the seven thunders sounded. [10:1–3]

Epic abounds in bigger-than-life characters and events.

Other epic conventions are also present in Revelation. There are scenes set in heaven where decisions are made that are then enacted on earth. In function and construction, these scenes are like the epic councils of the gods. Epics usually include a preview of future history, and this is the premise underlying most of the Book of Revelation. Epics recount the exploits of a hero who conquers his enemies and establishes an empire. The Book of Revelation is the epic story of

6. C. S. Lewis, *A Preface to Paradise Lost* (New York: Oxford University Press, 1942), pp. 40, 45–46.

Christ's conquest of Satan and evil and his establishing of his eternal spiritual kingdom.

Symbolism in the Book of Revelation

Cutting across all the genres of the Book of Revelation is the basic literary mode of symbolism. This means that concrete images and events are constantly used to represent something else. Instead of Christ's being pictured as a spirit or man, for example, he is portrayed as a lion and lamb. To interpret such symbols literally is to misread the book.

To insist that the mode is symbolic is not to deny that the Book of Revelation describes historical events that really happen. The question is not whether the events are historical but whether they are described *literally*. The events described by John are historical events that really happen (or will yet happen), but *how* will they happen? Fortunately we have a passage within the book that does not portray future events but is instead a flashback that portrays past events. By observing how the writer handles these recognizable events, we can determine the basic pattern of interpretation that we are intended to apply elsewhere in the book.

This passage occurs in chapter 12 and describes the incarnation of Christ. Here is an excerpt:

> [1]And a great portent appeared in heaven, a woman clothed with the sun, with the moon under her feet, and on her head a crown of twelve stars; [2]she was with child and she cried out in her pangs of birth, in anguish for delivery. [3]And another portent appeared in heaven; behold, a great red dragon, with seven heads and ten horns, and seven diadems upon his heads. [4]His tail swept down a third of the stars of heaven, and cast them to the earth. And the dragon stood before the woman who was about to bear a child, that he might devour her child when she brought it forth; [5]she brought forth a male child, one who is to rule all the nations with a rod of iron, but her child was caught up to God and to his throne.

The writer himself twice calls this brief drama a portent or sign, not a literal account. On the basis of the Old Testament symbols for the tribes of Israel (vv. 1–2), we can identify the woman as Israel. The child who is to rule all the nations is obviously Christ. The dragon, we know, is Satan (12:9), who was unable to destroy Christ during his earthly life and redemptive ministry.

Here, then, we can see the symbolic mode of Revelation: it does not literally describe the circumstances of Christ's birth, *but it calls those circumstances to mind.* This is the interpretive key to the whole book.

We can find this same exegetical key in the visions of the four horses (6:1–8). These four visions together form a unit and are based on the procession motif. Four horses with riders move across our field of vision, and we get a progressively more sinister pageant of warfare. The first horse, a white horse whose rider "went out conquering and to conquer," symbolizes the spirit of warfare, initially somewhat attractive. The next horse is "bright red," the color of blood, and its rider "was permitted to take peace from the earth." This is more sinister than the white horse with a conquering warrior.

The third horse is black, the color of death, and its rider "had a balance in his hand." This is an unusual weapon for a warrior to be carrying, but it is explained by a voice that says, "A quart of wheat for a denarius, and three quarts of barley for a denarius." These prices for the weights of grain make the scene a picture of famine (see Ezekiel 4:9–10 and Leviticus 26:26 for parallels). This surrealistic picture of the destructiveness of war reaches its climax with the fourth horse, yellowish-green in color, "and its rider's name was Death, and Hades followed him."

What does this nightmare vision of warfare really mean? It is a symbolic account of what Jesus predicted directly and propositionally in his Olivet Discourse: "You will hear of wars and rumors of wars. . . . For nation will rise against nation, and kingdom against kingdom, and there will be famines and earthquakes in various places" (Matt. 24:6–7). The four visions have been symbolic of events or movements that really happen, but that do not happen literally as the Book of Revelation pictures them. What Jesus predicted will not literally take the form of four warriors riding on horses, but the symbolic picture of the four horsemen calls those realities to mind.

This symbolism is already present in the seven letters to the churches, which are the most historically rooted part of the Book of Revelation. We read there about the sword of Jesus' mouth (2:16), people not having soiled their garments (3:4), glorified believers becoming a pillar in a temple (3:12), some Christians having become lukewarm (3:16), and Christ standing at a door and knocking (3:20). No one takes these statements literally. They are symbolic of *spiritual* realities. If there is this much symbolism already in the seven letters to the churches, how much more can we not expect in the more visionary chapters that follow?

This symbolic mode is customary throughout the prophetic writings of the Bible. The youthful Joseph dreamed that the sun, moon, and stars bowed down to him. This prophecy was, indeed, fulfilled, but not in the form in which it occurred in the dream. The second chapter of Daniel contains an account Nebuchadnezzar's dream of a human figure composed of various minerals. This symbolic figure stood for political realities, but these realities did not literally consist of various minerals. Isaiah 13:10–13 predicts the fall of Babylon in symbolic terms of the sun and moon being darkened, the heavens trembling, and earth being shaken. The surrounding context makes it clear that the destruction really consisted of military defeat, which verses 10–13 describe symbolically.

This customary biblical mode of symbolism makes a reappearance in the apocalyptic Book of Revelation. A lot of interpretive nonsense will be avoided if we follow the interpretive method that the Bible itself suggests for this type of prophetic writing.

Interpreting the Symbols

If there are this many symbols in the book, how do we know what they mean? This is the central problem in the interpretation of the Book of Revelation. Our best equipment is a keen eye for the obvious. We need to make use of what we know on the basis of our experiences in life and our acquaintance with literature in general. It is important to remember that literary symbolism is a largely conventional and universal language. The purpose of the symbols of Revelation is to reveal, not to conceal. Since the allusions and techniques used in the Book of Revelation are so thoroughly rooted in the Bible as a whole, we should also use what we know about biblical symbolism in general.

Earlier I said that the Book of Revelation gives us symbolic pictures of historical characters, events, and movements. Although the book does not give us a literal account of these things, it does *call them to mind.* A good stock question to ask of any passage in Revelation is therefore this one: *Of what theological fact or event in salvation history does this passage seem to be a symbolic version?*

As an example, consider this passage:

> Then I saw another angel ascend from the rising of the sun, with the seal of the living God, and he called with a loud voice to the four angels who had been given power to harm earth and sea, saying, "Do not harm the earth or the sea or the trees, till we have sealed the servants of our God upon their foreheads." [7:2–3]

What does this picture of the sealing of the believers mean? In biblical symbolism, a seal was a mark of ownership. The sealing of the servants of God on their foreheads is a symbolic picture of believers being claimed and saved by God. Here is the theological fact or event from salvation history that the passage calls to mind.

Or consider this brief picture:

> The fourth angel poured his bowl on the sun, and it was allowed to scorch men with fire; men were scorched by the fierce heat, and they cursed the name of God who had power over these plagues, and they did not repent and give him glory. [16:8–9]

The first thing that we should do with this surrealistic picture of torture is to experience the physical sensations of the event portrayed. The Book of Revelation is a book of images. We need to read it with what modern psychology calls the right side of our brain (our ability to think by means of images and intuition). Having done so, we can ask what recognizable fact of history is pictured here. It is obviously a picture of God's judgment against human sinfulness and of the unrepentant heart as it exists throughout human history. It is as simple (and as profound) as that.

We do not need esoteric road maps to take our journey through the Book of Revelation. We need a firm grip on human experience in the world, on the obvious meanings of literary symbols, and on the theological framework of the Bible as a whole. Whenever something more specific is intended, the book itself will provide the interpretation (for examples, see 1:20; 4:5; 17:7–18; 19:8).

What kind of historical events does the Book of Revelation describe by means of its symbols? There have been four major approaches to the book. One regards the book as arising out of the situation of the first-century church and interprets the events as having occurred in the early centuries of history after Christ. A second interpretation considers the book as forecasting the whole of human history from the time of Christ to his return. A third approach, the futurist, believes that except for the first few chapters the book is exclusively concerned with happenings at the end of history. Finally, the idealist view minimizes the historical particulars of the book and holds that it depicts principles and theological ideas on which God operates throughout history.

I think that the book is a combination of all of these. We should begin with the situation of the church to which the book was written. Because of the literary form of the book, which portrays events symbolically, its relevance extends throughout the history of the world. Babylon, for example, may have been the Roman empire for John's first-century audience, but in Old Testament times it was literally Babylon, and it has taken many forms throughout history. The literary mode of symbolism means that the events portrayed in Revelation are perpetually relevant and will be ultimately relevant at the end of history.

The Nonpictorial Mode of the Book

To insist on the symbolic mode of the book is not to say that it is a strongly pictorial book. The book is strongly sensory and even visual (in the sense that we visualize images and symbols), but not predominantly pictorial. The harder we try to visualize the scenes, the more incomprehensible and grotesque they become. One scholar has put it this way:

> Symbolic writing . . . does not paint pictures. It is not pictographic but ideographic. . . . The skull and crossbones on the bottle of medicine is a symbol of poison, but not a picture. . . . The fish, the lamb, and the lion are all symbols of Christ, but never to be taken as pictures of him. In other words, the symbol is a code word and does not paint a picture.[7]

Thus the description of a sun-clothed, star-crowned woman in chapter 12 is a symbol of the church, not a picture of it.

The description of Christ in the opening chapter is a good test case in this regard:

> [12]Then I turned to see the voice that was speaking to me, and on turning I saw seven golden lampstands, [13]and in the midst of the lampstands one like a son of man, clothed with a long robe and with a golden girdle round his breast; [14]his head and his hair were white as white wool, white as snow; his eyes were like a flame of fire, [15]his feet were like burnished bronze, refined as in a furnace, and his voice was like the sound of many waters; [16]in his right hand he held seven stars, from his mouth issued a sharp two-edged sword, and his face was like the sun shining in full strength.

We do not experience this description as a single composite figure. We assimilate it piecemeal, interpreting each detail in a symbolic way.

The *golden lampstands* amid which Christ stands symbolize the churches to whom the seven letters are about to be addressed. The *long robe* that Christ wears indicates a person of priestly and kingly distinction. The *white hair* suggests ancientness, with the detail modeled on Daniel's picture of the "Ancient of Days" (Dan. 7:9).

---

7. Donald W. Richardson, *The Revelation of Jesus Christ: An Interpretation* (Richmond: John Knox, 1939), p. 16. For more comments along this line, see the excerpts in *The New Testament in Literary Criticism*, pp. 315–20.

The images of eyes *like a flame of fire* and *feet like burnished bronze*
indicate the supernatural or transcendent nature of Christ. They are
the first occurrence in the book of enamelled imagery—imagery (especially of jewels and glass) that makes us think of hardness of texture
and brilliance of light. Such imagery suggests a spiritual realm whose
permanence transcends our cyclic vegetative world. The picture of
Christ holding *seven stars* in *his right hand* reinforces this atmosphere
of mystery and more-than-earthly magnitude. The *two-edged sword*
that protrudes from Christ's mouth symbolizes his judgment against
evil. The face *like the sun shining in full strength* likewise resists our
picturing it visually and instead *suggests* the power and supernatural
splendor of Christ.

This portrait of Christ is primarily a symbolic rendition in which
individual details stand for some quality of Christ. It is intended to be
not representational but impressionistic. It conveys a sense of Christ's
awesomeness, eternity, splendor, power, judgment, and mystery, but
cannot be said to be a picture of those things. The theological significance of this technique is important. A literary critic analyzed the
difference between the statues of Greek gods and the impressionistic
description of God in Revelation and came to this conclusion:

> When one thinks of the serenity of the Greek representations of the gods
> beside these visions of the Hebrew and Christian seers, the latter at first
> may seem confused and turgid. Then as one thinks it over the very clarity
> and definiteness of outline in these wonderful marbles stand out as a
> limitation: in comparison with these vague and mystical imaginings of
> the Christian seers the representations of Greek art are impotent. In the
> end the Greek statue of a god, for all its gracious beauty, is only a glo-
> rified and idealized man. The visions of the apocalypse, on the other
> hand, transcend once for all the limitations of human nature.[8]

Archetypes

Many of the images and symbols in the Book of Revelation belong
to the familiar archetypes of literature. The world of the book is an
elemental world of life, death, blood, lamb, dragon, beast, light, darkness, water, sea, sun, war, harvest, white, scarlet, bride, throne, jewels,
and gold. There are many references to rising, usually associated with
spiritual goodness, and falling, associated with evil. Heaven is high
and light, while the bottomless pit is low and dark.

The last half of the book is a spiritualized version of familiar archetypes: a woman in distress who is marvelously delivered, a hero

---

8. J. H. Gardiner, *The Bible as English Literature*, in *The New Testament in Literary
Criticism*, p. 320.

on a white horse who kills a dragon, a wicked prostitute who is finally exposed, the marriage of the triumphant hero to his bride, the celebration of the wedding with a feast, and the description of a palace glittering with jewels in which the hero and his bride live happily ever after. Underlying the entire book is a submerged journey motif, as human history painfully winds its way toward its goal and consummation.

Structure and Unity in the Book of Revelation

Despite its multiplicity of individual visions, the Book of Revelation is the most carefully structured long work in the Bible. I have already suggested some pathways through the book: a unifying plot conflict between good and evil, a progressive movement toward the final resolution, and a repeated pattern consisting of scene/agent—action—result.

Although the work is constructed on a repetitive principle in which we retrace a similar cycle of events, the background story that these cycles reenact has a definite organization to it. It is the same pattern of events that Jesus outlines in the Olivet Discourse (Matt. 24–25). We can organize the pattern into five phases:

1. Wars, earthquakes, famine, and false teachers (Matt. 24:5–8).
2. Persecution of Christians (Matt. 24:9–22).
3. False Christs and false prophets (Matt. 24:23–28).
4. Natural disasters, the appearance of Christ, and the harvesting of the elect (Matt. 24:29–31).
5. Final judgment (Matt. 24:32–25:46).

The Book of Revelation tells the same story as this, and does so a number of times. It fills in the details beyond what Jesus does in the Olivet Discourse, but we can make sense of what is happening in any given unit of Revelation simply by relating the foreground events to this general pattern in the background.

There are so many details in Revelation that we might well despair of being able to keep it in our mind as a single entity. But upon analysis the book turns out to have a simple and manageable structure. The outline of the book consists of a prologue, a series of six sevenfold units, and an epilogue. Here is the outline of the book:

1. Prologue (chap. 1).
2. Letters to the seven churches, climaxed by a vision of heaven (2–4).

3. The seven seals:
   a. prologue (5).
   b. warrior on a white horse (6:1–2).
   c. warrior on a red horse (6:3–4).
   d. rider on a black horse (6:5–6).
   e. Death riding on a pale horse (6:7–8).
   f. martyrs in heaven (6:9–11).
   g. cosmic dissolution, associated with God's judgment (6:12–17).
   h. interlude: sealing of the 144,000, a picture of the glorified saints (7:1–17).
   i. silence (8:1).
4. The seven trumpets:
   a. prologue (8:2–6).
   b. hail, fire, blood on the earth (8:7).
   c. the sea becomes blood, and destruction at sea (8:8–9).
   d. the falling star, bringing bitter water (8:10–11).
   e. darkening of sun, moon, and stars (8:12).
   f. locusts from the pit (8:13–9:12).
   g. the cavalry of judgment (9:13–20).
   h. interlude: John eats the scroll; the history of the two witnesses, persecuted and triumphant (10:1–11:14).
   i. judgment and glorification of believers in heaven (11:15–19).
5. The seven great signs:
   a. the dragon's war against the Son, the woman, and the woman's offspring (12).
   b. the beast from the sea (13:1–10).
   c. the beast from the earth (13:11–18).
   d. the Lamb on Mount Zion (14:1–5).
   e. angelic messages of judgment (14:6–13).
   f. the reaping of the earth (14:14–16).
   g. reaping and judgment of the wicked (14:17–20).
6. The seven bowls of wrath:
   a. prologue (15).
   b. sores on men (16:1–2).
   c. sea becomes blood (16:3).
   d. rivers become blood (16:4–7).
   e. fierce heat of the sun (16:8–9).
   f. darkness (16:10–11).
   g. the foul spirits prepare for Armageddon (16:12–16).
   h. earthquake and final judgment against evil (16:17–21).
7. The seven events of final judgment and consummation:
   a. judgment of Babylon (17–18).
   b. marriage supper of the Lamb (19:1–10).

    c. Christ defeats the beast and the false prophet (19:11–21).
    d. the binding of Satan and the millennial reign of Christ (20:1–6).
    e. the loosing of Satan and his defeat (20:7–10).
    f. final judgment (20:11–15).
    g. description of the new heaven and new earth (21:1–22:5).
  8. Epilogue (22:6–21).

This scheme is like a road map through the book. No matter where we are, we can locate ourselves somewhere in a landscape of sevenfold events.

But the unity is even tighter than this. Each of the sevenfold units is composed of two basic ingredients—fallen human history, closely associated with evil and judgment, and the consummation of history, often linked particularly with the glorification of believers in heaven. Furthermore, the general movement within each unit is from fallen human history with its evil and misery to consummation (in the form of either the end of history or the glorification of believers in heaven). From earth to heaven, from history to its end—this is the recurrent movement in the units that make up the Book of Revelation. No matter where we dip into the book, we know where we are.

The Book of Revelation is one of the easiest books to read in the Bible. It is an affective book. It feeds our imaginations with heightened images of judgment, splendor, redemption, mystery, good and evil, battle, heaven, and worship.

Reading the Book of Revelation

Although the Book of Revelation has a strongly repetitive or cyclic structure in which we repeatedly encounter the same sequence of events, it is also a progressive book. In fact, we are unlikely to read another book where so much happens so quickly. The purpose of the running commentary that follows is to capture something of the flow of the action, as well as to provide some preliminary interpretation of the events and symbols.

The Epic Prologue

The opening chapter of the book is an epic prologue or introduction. Any grand event begins with ritual and formality. The Book of Revelation begins in exactly this way and in a manner that resembles the openings of epics. The opening chapter is a fourfold introduction to the book. First we are introduced to the theme and source (vv. 1–3). Then the writer greets his audience with a formal salutation (vv. 4–8). Finally we are introduced to the narrator of the book (vv. 9–11) and to the hero (vv. 12–20).

Epic writers begin by announcing their theme or subject. "Of man's first disobedience," writes Milton at the beginning of *Paradise Lost*. John begins his book with a similar announcement: *The revelation of Jesus Christ* (1:1). In the story that follows, Christ will stand revealed in all his glory. This is the content of John's book. Epic poets also begin by invoking a deity or muse to inspire them. John does not invoke God but does the equivalent by identifying God as the divine source for his work: *The revelation of Jesus Christ, which God gave him to show to his servants . . . by sending his angel to his servant John, who bore witness to the word of God* (1:1–2). The next verse pronounces a blessing (one of seven beatitudes scattered throughout the book) on the person *who reads aloud the words of the prophecy, and . . . those who hear.* Oral performance is yet another epic feature of Revelation.

With the formal salutation (vv. 4–8) the epic style and content of the book come into fuller view. I have already noted the exuberance and grandeur of the style of the passage. At the level of content, epic motifs such as *kingdom, glory,* and *dominion* are now fully established as the expectations that we bring to the ensuing action.

In the final two units of chapter 1, the narrator and hero step forward. The narrator is like that in other epics—a mediator between his audience and a vision of supernatural characters and events, a representative of his audience ("John, your brother, who share with you in Jesus the tribulation and the kingdom and the patient endurance"), an agent of divine inspiration. And in keeping with the opening promise that the book will reveal Jesus Christ, in the symbolic portrait of Jesus that concludes the chapter the hero stands revealed in all his power and splendor.

The Letters to the Churches

As his gateway into the main part of his revelation, John chose the familiar New Testament form of the epistle. Chapters 2 and 3 are letters to seven representative churches. The artistry of the letters is amazing. In keeping with the pattern of seven that typifies the book as a whole, the individual letters fall into a sevenfold pattern, as follows:

1. *A greeting* ("To the angel of the church in . . .").
2. *A title for Christ* (with all but the last one taking some detail from the description of Christ in chapter 1).
3. *A commendation of the church* (beginning, "I know . . .").
4. *A criticism of the church* (omitted in the cases of Smyrna and Philadelphia).
5. *A warning.*

6. *An exhortation to be attentive* (beginning with the statement "he who has an ear, let him hear . . .")
7. *A promise* (beginning with a formula to the effect "to him that overcometh will I give . . ." [KJV]).

In the last four letters, the order of items 6 and 7 is reversed, introducing an element of variety into the overall pattern.

Although the letters are addressed to particular churches, their content is timeless and universal. Together the letters embody the themes that are important to the Book of Revelation as a whole. The letters show that there is a great spiritual conflict going on in the world. Everyone is involved. The forms of evil differ from one church to another, but they are essentially variations on the theme of good versus evil, Christ versus Satan. In one way or another, some kind of positive choice for Christ is demanded in every letter. People's response to the call to godly living is a matter of momentous importance, with a person's eternal welfare at stake.

Another theme in the letters is that God is the sovereign judge who is concerned about what people are doing in the world. People are urged to live in an awareness of God's presence, and the certainty of God's judgment is repeatedly offered as the rationale for repentance while there is time. There is, finally, a repeated emphasis on the fact that Christ is coming again. In the letters, Christians are enjoined to live in an eschatological awareness, ordering their lives around the certainty of Christ's return. Because life has a goal, patient endurance becomes a chief mark of the Christian in these letters.

In terms of the narrative framework that we can apply to any section of Revelation, the main scene of action is earth, more specifically seven representative cities (an archetype that will be important throughout Revelation, incidentally). The agents are the followers of Christ and the followers of Satan. The action consists of the church encountering conflict, persecution, and false doctrine. The result, as implied in the concluding promise "to him that overcometh," is that people choose their eternal destiny.

Taken together, the letters speak of the same events that Jesus outlines in his Olivet Discourse. There are references to persecution of believers, false teachers within the churches, the return of Christ, and final judgment. The individual letters also reveal the general movement that I have claimed for all the sevenfold sections of Revelation— a movement from history, associated with trial and misery, to the spiritual realities that will be ushered in at the end of history.

Chapter 4, a scene of heavenly worship, is often considered to be an independent interlude or a prelude to the opening of the seals in the

next chapter. It can more plausibly be interpreted as the climax of the
movement that underlies the letters to the seven churches. These letters have ended with brief but undeveloped pictures of heavenly reward for the faithful. In chapter 4, these foreshortened visions of heaven
finally receive their consummation. The opening verse of chapter 4
confirms this: the vision that follows is a picture of *what must take
place after this,* that is, after the events described in the letters.

Chapter 4 itself is one of the great visions of Revelation, suffused
with supernatural splendor. The imagery and symbolism convey a
general aura of glory but also invite more specific interpretation. There
is combined specificity and vagueness in the opening vision of *a throne
... in heaven, with one seated on the throne* (v. 2). Enamelled images
dominate our impression:

> And he who sat there appeared like jasper and carnelian, and round the
> throne was a rainbow that looked like an emerald. [v. 3]

Modeled on a similar vision in Ezekiel (1:27–28), the light and rainbow
convey the impression of an encircling brightness around the throne.
Again we move between clarity and vagueness, specific description
and reticence.

With God established as the still center around which heavenly
ritual occurs, the description moves to the surrounding action. First
a heavenly court is assembled in our imaginations as we read:

> Round the throne were twenty-four thrones, and seated on the thrones
> were twenty-four elders, clad in white garments, with golden crowns
> upon their heads. [v. 4]

Then we see *flashes of lightning* and hear *peals of thunder* (v. 5), archetypes for the presence and power of God. To climax the effect, we see
in our imaginations *a sea of glass, like crystal* before the throne (v. 6).

And this is only the beginning. As our gaze moves still further outward from the throne, we see *four living creatures, full of eyes in front
and behind* (v. 6). At such a point we become acutely aware that the
descriptive mode is symbolic, not pictorial. These are obviously symbols of watchfulness and omniscience. The four creatures are then
specifically identified with the lion, ox, man, and eagle (v. 7). The important thing about these creatures is probably their superlative power
and excellence, as in a rabbinic saying that "the mightiest among the
birds is the eagle, the mightiest among the domestic animals is the
bull [ox], the mightiest among the wild beasts is the lion, the mightiest
among all is man." We have here the best in God's creation, offering
praise to God.

With the dramatic stage props now assembled, heavenly praise is introduced into the scene (vv. 8b–11). Brief lyric fragments like this will recur throughout the Book of Revelation and add a note of emotional response appropriate to the content of the book. Indeed, heavenly experience would be incomplete without this note of singing that makes the Book of Revelation, in its own way, the New Testament book of psalms.

The Seven Seals

The next sevenfold unit in Revelation is the series of seven seals that are opened as predictions of future events. The unit begins with a prelude set in heaven (chap. 5). Chapter 5 is a self-contained unit with a single setting (the heavenly court), a central action (the declaration of the worthiness of the Lamb to open the scroll), and a unifying theme (the worthiness of Christ). Applying the narrative framework of scene/agent—action—result, we can say that the scene is heaven, the chief agent is Christ, the action is that by a process of elimination only Christ is able to open the seals of the scroll, and the result is that with the obstacle overcome we are propelled into the actual series of visions. In function and construction, the scene resembles the heavenly council in epics, where action is initiated in heaven and then enacted on earth.

Symbolism pervades the scene, and there is no attempt at a single consistent picture. In one verse (5) Christ is pictured as a lion and in the very next verse (6) he is a lamb. These are symbols of Christ, not pictures of him. The lion symbolizes power and kingship, while *the Lamb standing, as though it had been slain* (v. 6) symbolizes the atonement of Christ. This scene of heavenly ritual rises to a crescendo of praise, beginning with the four creatures and twenty-four elders around the throne (v. 8), then encompassing all the heavenly hosts of angels and saints (v. 11), and finally extending to *every creature in heaven and on earth and under the earth and in the sea* (v. 13). The passage has a strong linear movement and is conceived dramatically (with elaborate attention to both scene and dialogue). Like the other visions of Revelation, this one mingles the familiar and the unfamiliar to produce its supernatural effect.

We next move to the opening of the seven seals. The first four visions (6:1–8) form a unit. As suggested in my earlier discussion of this passage, the four vignettes of horse and rider are a pageant or procession in which the spirit of warfare, initially attractive, becomes a nightmare of misery and destructiveness on earth. These visions present in visual and symbolic form the warfare and famine that Jesus predicted in his Olivet Discourse.

From this vision of catastrophe on earth, the focus suddenly shifts to heaven, where the martyrs are pictured awaiting God's vengeance against the forces of evil (6:9–11). The martyrs, whom I take to be symbolic of believers in general, are placed in a symbolic setting (under a heavenly altar). The souls of these believers ask for justice on earth, but the justice that they request is postponed. The souls are consoled by being given *a white robe*, symbolic of their victory in heaven. The overarching conflict between good and evil in the book as a whole here takes the form of a prediction that justice will not occur *until the number of their fellow servants and their brethren should be complete, who were to be killed as they themselves had been.*

The sixth seal (6:12–17) brings the shift from fallen history, with its miserable warfare and famine, to the consummation of history. We get a vision of cosmic collapse replete with powerful archetypes of the end—a great earthquake, a black sun and bloody moon, stars falling to the earth, the sky vanishing like a scroll, and every mountain and island being removed from its place. The inhabitants of the earth respond by fleeing from the wrath of the Lamb. It is not hard to identify the reality that is pictured by means of these images and symbols. This is the end of history and the final judgment that we read about throughout the Bible.

The subsequent interlude in which believers are *sealed* (chap. 7) completes the movement from earthly history to heavenly bliss. The sealing of the believers is a symbolic action that identifies these persons as belonging to God. It is the great opposite of the receiving of the mark of the beast by unbelievers (13:16). The sealing is dramatized as occurring on a heavenly stage. It unfolds in two stages: first John hears the number of the sealed (v. 4) and then he sees the multitude of the redeemed (v. 9). The number of those sealed (144,000) is symbolic of completeness and hugeness. All twelve tribes are present, with the foursquare symbolism of twelve times twelve reinforcing the sense of completeness that we feel with the number 144,000. The number of a thousand was the ancient equivalent for the largest number imaginable.

The scene of heavenly celebration that concludes chapter 7 typifies the scenes of celebration and worship that are interspersed throughout the book. We are greeted with a flood of idealized archetypes, which are uniquely powerful in the Book of Revelation. There are white robes of triumph and joy, a throne of God to suggest his kingly rulership in heaven, a temple to symbolize God's presence, springs of living water to express the satisfaction of every human need, and much in addition.

The seventh seal (8:1) surprises us: instead of a further vision, there is simply *silence in heaven for about half an hour.* The Book of Revelation is full of surprises and mysteries like this. Throughout the book clarity and mystery mingle. We are given enough to satisfy us, but enough is also withheld to leave us with a longing to know more.

Looking back over the vision of the seven seals, we can see how manageable the units in Revelation are. A great deal happens, leading me to note that in the Book of Revelation the sheer amount of what happens is out of proportion to the brevity of the text. The account of the seven seals began with the vision of four horses, then the martyrs were comforted in heaven and told of more persecution on earth, then the earth dissolved before the judgment of Christ, and finally the complete host of the redeemed was glorified in heaven.

One pattern underlying the section is the movement from history, associated with misery, to the consummation of history, associated with judgment against unbelievers and the glorification of believers in heaven. A second pattern is the outline of events that Jesus gives in the Olivet Discourse: first wars, famine, and persecution; then natural disasters and the appearance of Christ; then final judgment and glorification. A third organizing framework is the narrative framework that pervades the book: the scene is earth and heaven, the agents are God and all people, the action is the destruction of earth and the glorification of believers in heaven, and the result is the end of evil and the perfection of good.

The Seven Trumpets

The vision of the seven trumpets (chaps. 8–11) follows the same general pattern as that of the seven seals, emphasizing the cyclic structure of the book as a whole. Again there is a preliminary scene set in heaven, where God's judgment against the evil earth is decreed (8:3–6). The four visions of horses here have their parallel in four visions involving the elemental aspects of nature—earth, sea, rivers, sun, moon, and stars (8:7–12). These elemental forces are used to convey the impression that something basic is happening in the earthly sphere. The sense of calamity is more terrifying than with the fourth seal, for the fourth part of the earth affected there (6:8) is now replaced by a third part of the earth, sea, rivers, and sun, moon, and stars.

The fifth trumpet (9:1–11), involving the opening of the bottomless pit, is the most terrifying image of evil yet to appear in the unfolding drama of Revelation. This pit, with its archetypal associations of descent (it is bottomless), smoke, and darkness (9:2), is an image from our nightmares and evokes primitive feelings of horror and revulsion. Pictured as an abyss with a narrow opening at the top, the pit is a hell-like place, if not a picture of hell itself.

The locusts that ascend from the pit are agents of God's judgment against unbelievers (9:4). They are a biblical archetype, recalling similar judgments of God in the eighth plague against the Egyptians and against the Israelites in the prophecy of Joel. In one of the most amazing imaginative feats of a book filled with them, the terror of the locusts is amplified when the writer links a literal locust with other threatening forces (9:7–11). The locusts are *like horses arrayed for battle*, not in terms of size, but because they come in droves and with destructive effect, just as war-horses do. Their teeth are *like lions' teeth*, not literally, but in their destructive potential as they devour standing grainfields. The hard shell of a locust's body becomes amplified into *iron breastplates*, and the literal noise with which plagues of locusts sweep the countryside becomes amplified by the writer's imagination into *the noise of many chariots with horses rushing into battle.*

The sixth trumpet, which pictures a cavalry of warriors (9:13–21), is one of the most mysterious episodes in the book. The purpose of the cavalry is clear: the troops are agents of God's judgment to *kill a third of mankind* (v. 15). They are thus part of the overriding conflict between good and evil. But much is left unexplained. The cavalry is introduced into the narrative abruptly (v. 16), as though we already know who they are, but in fact we do not know whether they are human or angelic warriors. The war-horses, like the locusts of the previous vision, become transformed into bigger-than-life apocalyptic creatures. Their mouths eject fire, smoke, and sulfur (vv. 17–18), and their tails are like serpents with heads (v. 19). Balancing this physical terror is the moral and spiritual terror of unrepentant humanity with which the vision concludes (vv. 20–21).

The interludes introduced into the visions of the seals and trumpets are major passages, in effect small, self-contained apocalypses. The interlude of the two witnesses between the sixth and seventh trumpets (10:1–12:13) is an example. Its narrative effect, like that of the interlude between the sixth and seventh seals, is to generate suspense, as the climactic seventh vision is momentarily withheld. Perhaps we are to see in this that repentance is possible while God withholds his final judgment.

The interlude in the section about the trumpets begins with one of the "giantesque" scenes of Revelation: a mighty angel descends from heaven and stands with his right foot on the sea and his left foot on the land. His voice is like that of a lion roaring. The mystery of all this is reinforced when John is told to eat the scroll that the angel carries. The mystery hardly dissipates when we know that there are parallel moments with the Old Testament prophets Jeremiah (15:16) and Ezekiel (3:1–3). Many of the events and images of Revelation apparently exist to reveal the sheer mystery of the spiritual world. The simultaneous bitterness and sweetness of the scroll when John eats it (10:9–10) underscore the dual nature of John's prophecy, which is comforting to believers but bitter in its pronouncement of judgment upon evil.

The story of the two witnesses (11:1–13), also part of the interlude, is itself a reenactment of the history of believers that occurs elsewhere in Revelation. These two figures, symbolizing the believing church, are given the task of proclaiming God's word in a degenerate time of history. They are associated with olive trees (see Zechariah 4:14 for the source of the symbol), symbolizing life in the midst of death, and lampstands, symbolizing light in the midst of darkness. The two figures are also linked by way of allusion with Moses and Elijah, as evidenced by their ability to prevent rainfall, to turn water into blood, and to bring about plagues (11:6). The symbolism of all this is clear: the church in persecution has the same resources available to it as the Old Testament prophets had.

From the opening description of the two prophets we move to their epic feat. It consists of proclaiming God's word (v. 7). Following an epiclike battle in which the beast kills the two witnesses (v. 7), there is a scene of exultant evil followed by the miraculous revival of the witnesses. This sequence of events either pictures a single event that will occur near the end of history, or it is a vision of the archetypal pattern of what happens whenever the defeated church revives. In either case, the story of the two witnesses has reenacted the basic motif of Revelation—persecution of the church in a corrupt world followed by eventual triumph. In the words of Austin Farrer, the interlude of chapter 11 "is a foreshortened and premature conclusion, cancelled, and yet permitted to stand by way of interlude."[9]

The seventh trumpet (11:15–19) brings this section of the book to an expected climax, modeled along the lines of earlier climaxes. History is consummated when *the kingdom of the world has become the kingdom of our Lord and of his Christ* (v. 15). The coming of Christ to establish his kingdom is accompanied by the judgment of all the dead, good and evil (v. 18), in the manner predicted by Jesus in his Olivet Discourse and his eschatological parables. A riot of sensations forms the conclusion of the episode:

> Then God's temple in heaven was opened, and the ark of his covenant was seen within his temple; and there were flashes of lightning, loud noises, peals of thunder, an earthquake, and heavy hail. [v. 19]

The Book of Revelation never fails to fill our imaginations. In the terms

9. Austin Farrer, *A Rebirth of Images: The Making of St. John's Apocalypse* (London: Dacre, 1949), p. 44.

popularized by contemporary psychology, here is a book that speaks to the right side of the brain (the hemisphere that assimilates images).

The Seven Great Signs

Chapter 12, which initiates the section of the seven great signs, in several ways summarizes the whole Book of Revelation. It opens with a symbolic account of the birth of Christ (vv. 1–5) and a description of how a great red dragon (symbolizing Satan) attempts to destroy him. The child's miraculous ascension into heaven (v. 5) is a symbolic way of depicting Satan's inability to destroy Christ during his earthly life. As I suggested earlier, this section is a flashback, not a forecast. Because it deals with recognizable historical events, it serves as the interpretive key for Revelation, showing us that the writer uses symbols that bring literal events to mind.

As the defeat of Satan continues to unfold in this first great sign, the scene shifts from earth to heaven. The picture of a war in heaven, with *Michael and his angels fighting against the dragon* (v. 7), epitomizes both the epic quality of the Book of Revelation and the overriding plot conflict of the Bible as a whole. Satan's being cast out of heaven (v. 9) might well be a symbolic account of Christ's victory at Calvary, along the lines of Christ's prediction before his crucifixion that "now shall the ruler of this world be cast out" (John 12:31). Having been cast out of heaven, the dragon concludes the episode by going off *to make war* on the offspring of the woman (that is, the church), and *on those who keep the commandments of God and bear testimony to Jesus* (v. 17). Here is the flashback that explains what happens elsewhere in the Book of Revelation.

This vision involving the woman and dragon alerts us to the essentially imaginative mode of Revelation. It is a book that requires a childlike response. A woman clothed with the sun, with the moon under her feet and a crown on her head, a great red dragon who is cast out of heaven, a dragon pouring water out of its mouth and thereby threatening a woman who is miraculously rescued when the earth opens its mouth and swallows the stream—these are events that speak to what is childlike in our imaginations. We have encountered this type of thing in our reading of fantasy literature.

Chapter 13 is divided between two further signs, those involving a beast from the sea (vv. 1–10) and a beast from the earth (vv. 11–18). The symbolism associated with the beasts shows that they are counterfeits of Christ. One of the heads of the beast from the sea, for example, *seemed to have a mortal wound, but its mortal wound was healed, and the whole earth followed the beast with wonder* (v. 3). This is the demonic counterfeit of the dying and reviving Christ. Similarly, the beast from the earth *had two horns like a lamb* (v. 11), giving it a resemblance to the Lamb of God depicted elsewhere in Revelation. In addition, the mark that is put on the right hand or the forehead of the beast's followers (v. 16) echoes the earlier sealing of the believers as a mark of their possession by God.

I said in my introductory remarks that the symbolic mode of the book requires us to ask, Of what theological reality or event in salvation history does this detail seem to be a symbolic version? The two beasts of chapter 13, with their ability to counterfeit, to persecute, and to lead people astray, should remind us of a prediction that Jesus made in the Olivet Discourse: "For false Christs and false prophets will arise and show great signs and wonders, so as to lead astray, if possible, even the elect" (Matt. 24:24).

As we have come to expect, the sequence of seven great signs in the middle of Revelation moves from what will happen on earth to a vision of ultimate victory for believers in heaven. Chapter 14 accordingly opens with a vision of the Lamb on Mount Zion, symbolic of Christ in heaven. The redeemed, the great opposite of the followers who bear the mark of the beast, are described by means of two evocative symbols. They are compared to chaste men *who have not defiled themselves with women* (14:4). This male image complements the more familiar image of the church as a chaste bride. As with the image of the bride later in Revelation, we find here a metaphor in which sexual purity symbolizes that believers are pure in their devotion to Christ. The believers in heaven are also described as those who have been *redeemed from mankind as first fruits for God and the Lamb* (14:4). In Hebrew sacrifices, the first fruits were the choicest part of a harvest, set aside as a special offering to God. The body of the redeemed is said to be set aside to God in a similar manner.

The remainder of chapter 14 is devoted to scenes connected with the end of history. They include messages predicting God's coming judgment of evil (vv. 6–13), Christ's reaping of the earth (vv. 14–16), and the final judgment of the wicked (vv. 17–20). These visions come alive in our imaginations by means of some of the great archetypes of evil and judgment—Babylon the great, the wine of God's wrath, the smoke of torment, the reaping of the earth with a sickle, and the winepress of God's wrath, with blood flowing from it so deep that it reaches a horse's bridle. Here is the essential mode of Revelation—a phantasmagoria of images, some of them possessing all the terror of a surrealistic nightmare.

Chapters 12–14, beginning with the incarnation of Christ and concluding with his second coming, "provide a complete apocalypse."[10] Like the seven letters, seals, and trumpets, these chapters display a

10. Ibid., p. 53.

movement from the flow of history to events that will culminate history and bring triumph to believers. It is evidence of the cyclic structure of the book as a whole, and of its tendency to repeat common themes and patterns in new ways. As I said at the outset, once we grasp the essential movement of the individual units of the book, we are never at a loss. We can step into any section of the book and know our way around.

The Seven Bowls of Wrath

The section about the seven bowls of wrath (chaps. 15–16) repeats the usual pattern. The judgments are described briefly so as not to belabor the issue. This vision is prefaced with a heavenly council (chap. 15), just as the visions of the seals and trumpets were. As in the earlier sequences, moreover, the plagues center on elemental nature and human warfare. Along with this repetitive element, there is progression, as we are informed of the finality of judgment this time: these plagues *are the last, for with them the wrath of God is ended* (15:1).

This vision is devoted wholly to the theme of God's judgment, both during history and at its consummation. The pouring out of the first five bowls (16:1–11) pictures God's judgment on elemental nature, with most of the details resembling those of the ten plagues against Egypt in the Book of Exodus. Pouring of the sixth bowl (16:12–16) describes, without giving the details, a climactic battle between good and evil that will occur at Armageddon. Here is another of the epic events in the Book of Revelation. From history we move to its consummation, as pouring the seventh bowl (16:17–21) echoes such eschatological images from elsewhere in the Bible as earthquake, lightning, thunder, cities splitting apart, and islands and mountains vanishing.

The Seven Last Events

Chapters 17–22 bring to a conclusion all of the smaller, tentative cycles that have preceded. Because of the progressive intensification that has accompanied the unfolding action in Revelation, we read this last sevenfold cycle with a strong impression that this is the final version of judgment against evil and the triumph of good.

This great drama of judgment begins with the single most extended vision in Revelation—the judgment of the whore of Babylon (chaps. 17–18). The drama unfolds in three stages, as we move from an opening description of the harlot (17:1–6a) through an explanation of her significance (the remainder of chap. 17) to a prediction of her punishment (chap. 18). The whore of Babylon is another of the great symbols of Revelation. On the literal level, she is described as *seated upon many waters* (17:1). She is also pictured as a city. Since in the Old Testament Jeremiah had addressed the city of Babylon as "you who dwell by many waters" (Jer. 51:13), it is evident that John is modeling his symbolic Babylon along the lines of the Babylon of ancient times.

In Revelation, however, it is the symbolism that counts. Babylon emerges in our imaginations as both a corrupt city and a monstrous woman. The color symbolism of red (17:3–4) already sets up negative connotations, which become reinforced when the woman is described as a prostitute *with whom the kings of the earth have committed fornication* (v. 2). And these are only the beginning. As the recital of immoralities continues, the kings are also described as having become drunk with the wine of fornication (v. 2). Cannibalism is the climactic detail: *And I saw the woman, drunk with the blood of the saints and the blood of the martyrs of Jesus* (v. 6). Even the harlot's name elicits horror: *Babylon the great, mother of harlots and of earth's abominations* (v. 5).

Now that we have encountered the whore of Babylon as concrete image and symbol, we are ready for a more analytic account of her. In the remainder of chapter 17, John interprets her significance in both spiritual and political terms. Spiritually she is linked with Satan, as evidenced by the way in which she rides on a beast identified as Satan (v. 7). Politically she is associated with the Roman empire, as suggested by the detail that *the seven heads are seven mountains on which the woman is seated* (v. 9). This was undoubtedly the chief contemporary significance of the symbol for the original audience of the book. By making the heads and horns symbolic of political rulers (vv. 10–12), the angelic interpreter gives this image of evil an ever-expanding set of meanings. And when we finally learn that the various kings *will make war on the Lamb* (17:14), it becomes clear that the image is intended to be a universal embodiment of the principle of evil.

What, then, is represented by the woman, who is also said to be *the great city* (17:18)? She is the human race in community in rebellion against God. In the Old Testament era one form of such evil was Babylon. In John's day, it was Rome. It has taken many forms since then, and it will assume an ultimate form at the end of history.

The entire eighteenth chapter announces the coming doom of Babylon. It belongs to a familiar type of satire found in Old Testament prophecy, the doom song. The lament of the world over Babylon (18:9–19) describes her as a worldwide commercial empire. The references to contemporary Rome are unmistakable in the description, but the picture is also as up to date as our own daily newspaper. While the evil world laments the collapse of its system, heaven rejoices over the fall of Babylon (18:20), reminding us of the great conflict that will rage to the very end of Revelation.

The effect of the two chapters devoted to Babylon is suffocating. With relief we turn to the second of the last signs, the marriage supper of the Lamb (19:1–10). The virginal bride of Christ, dressed in *fine linen, bright and pure* (v. 8), is the great opposite of the whore of Babylon clad in red. In place of the lament of the nations in the preceding vision, the singing of four songs of praise punctuates the brief account of the marriage supper. The triumphal archetype that dominates the conclusion of Revelation—the marriage of a conquering hero to a bride—is now firmly established in our imaginations.

The next three visions are built around the motif of warfare and conquest. They are a vision of Christ as a conquering warrior, defeating the beast and false prophet (19:11–21), the binding of Satan for a thousand years, accompanied by the millennial reign of Christ (20:1–6), and a final battle between the forces of good and evil, ending with defeat of Satan (20:7–10). These are epic events, large and mysterious and awe-inspiring, mingling clarity and mystery.

With the defeat of evil complete, the sequence moves to the final judgment (20:11–15). The picture is filled out with familiar biblical archetypes of judgment—God seated on a great white throne, the disappearance of the earth and sky, multitudes of the dead resurrected and standing before the throne, the opening of the books of deeds and the book of life, and the lake of fire.

The final climax, culminating many earlier and foreshortened climaxes in Revelation, is the description of the new heaven and new earth (chaps. 21 and 22). These pages are uniquely powerful and moving. There is nothing like the effect anywhere else. These paragraphs are a veritable repository of ideal archetypes, including the water of life, the dazzling brightness of light, the secure city, and paradisal plants along a flowing river. There is a wealth of enamelled images to suggest the preciousness and permanence of the place: jasper, crystal, sapphire, and many others. Complementing these positive archetypes are the moving negations of fallen experience: no more tears, death, pain, darkness, or falsehood.

Quite apart from the specific details, the sheer abundance takes on a symbolic value. The detailed account of the heavenly city is an implied rejoinder to the descriptions of Babylon that darkened two earlier chapters. The foursquare measurements of the city (21:16) symbolize its completeness, as does the emphasis on twelve—twelve gates, twelve angels, twelve tribes, twelve foundations, twelve apostles (21:12–14). Overriding all else is the symbolic richness—of dimension, of design, of decoration, of detail.

The Grand Finale to the Bible

The last two chapters of Revelation are the grand climax not only of the Book of Revelation but of the Bible as a whole. At the end of a work of literature we look for a sense of the resolution of the issues that have been introduced. This feeling of closure is exactly what we get at the end of Revelation, and it consists of two motifs—the sense of an ending and the sense of a beginning. After all those biblical stories and poems and visions that portray the havoc that evil brought into human experience, we are assured that the forces of evil have been destroyed. But there is also a sense of new beginnings. The language is reminiscent of Genesis 1 and 2, the archetype of new beginnings. Here at the end of the Bible we are surrounded by the atmosphere of a new heaven and a new earth.

A second ingredient of literary conclusions is a reminder or echo of the beginning—something that leads us to recall where the story began. At the end of a story, it is natural to remember where it all started. This strategy is especially crucial in the Bible, which begins with a perfect world and where any true resolution of the conflict between good and evil must be in some sense a return to the beginning. The first two chapters of the Bible and the last two are like frames around the history of fallen history. Satan enters the story in the third chapter and exits in the third chapter from the end. We end the Bible with a recreation of the world that was created in early Genesis. The paradisal imagery of the opening verses of Revelation 22 takes us back to the first paradise: "then he showed me the river of the water of life . . .; also, on either side of the river, the tree of life with its twelve kinds of fruit, yielding its fruit each month."

Finally, great and momentous stories leave things where they did not begin. At the end, we are aware of the progress that has occurred. In this connection we should contrast the garden that stands at the beginning of the Bible and the city with numberless hosts that stands at the end. There is a sense of completeness with the city whose gates are always open that is not present in the picture of the first two humans living in an enclosed garden. The one is a beginning, the other an ending. The garden is a memory, the city a hope.

Here at the end of the Bible we can see its overall structure, which stretches from creation to apocalypse. The Bible truly begins at the beginning and concludes with the end. It is a complete whole, the story of all things.

Epilogue
The Poetics of Biblical Literature

To conclude this literary introduction to the Bible, and to bring my survey of biblical literature into a unified focus here at the end, I can do no better than to conduct a brief excursion into the poetics of biblical literature. By *poetics* I mean the theory of writing with which biblical writers approach their work. This, in turn, provides a framework of interpretive assumptions within which we can profitably read the Bible.

I begin with the most explicit statement by a biblical writer about how he approached his work as a writer:

> Besides being wise, the Preacher also taught the people knowledge, weighing and studying and arranging proverbs with great care. The preacher sought to find pleasing words, and uprightly he wrote words of truth. [Eccles. 12:9–10]

The writer of Ecclesiastes here speaks for biblical writers more generally.

He obviously espouses a didactic view of literature, meaning that he writes with an intention to teach. No work in the Bible exists only or primarily for the sake of artistic pleasure or enjoyment. The latter are definitely present, but they come as by-products of more practical and serious aims.

507

Those aims are specifically religious. The Bible is a continuously religious book. It is always ready to sacrifice literary concerns for didactic ones, and even when it does not do so, its literary dimension is permeated with religious and moral preoccupations. C. S. Lewis has captured the spirit of biblical writers very well on this point when he comments that the Bible is

> through and through a sacred book. Most of its component parts were written, and all of them were brought together, for a purely religious purpose. . . . It demands incessantly to be taken on its own terms: it will not continue to give literary delight very long except to those who go to it for something quite different.[1]

The writer of Ecclesiastes also affirms his commitment to tell the truth, and this, too, is an important part of the poetics of biblical writers. The voice of conviction is strong in the pages of the Bible. Reading the Bible has a strong element of encounter to it. Erich Auerbach contrasts the Bible to Homer on this point: "The Bible's claim to truth is not only far more urgent than Homer's, it is tyrannical—it excludes all other claims. The world of the Scripture stories is not satisfied with claiming to be a historically true reality—it insists that it is the only real world."[2]

We should, of course, differentiate levels or types of truth that the Bible gives us. It gives us propositional or expository truth in the form of direct religious and moral statements and commands. It also frequently aims to record historical truth. But its truth cannot be limited to propositional and historical assertions.

The truth conveyed by biblical writers often consists of truthfulness to human experience, and at such points the Bible shows itself to be literary in nature. As we have seen throughout this study, the writers of the Bible frequently image the truth about God, people, and the world. They do so in such concrete and experiential forms as stories, characters, settings, and poetic images. The writers of the Bible repeatedly let us "know" by means of our imagination. Nearly everywhere we turn in the Bible we find ourselves in touch with actual human experience, not simply with abstract ideas.

The writer of Ecclesiastes calls our attention to a whole further dimension of biblical literature when he speaks of "weighing and studying and arranging proverbs with great care" and of seeking to find "pleasing

---

1. C. S. Lewis, *The Literary Impact of the Authorized Version* (Philadelphia: Fortress, 1963), pp. 32–33. Lewis puts the same insight into his usual aphoristic form when he comments that "those who read the Bible as literature do not read the Bible" (p. 30).

2. Erich Auerbach, *Mimesis: The Representation of Reality in Western Literature*, trans. Willard R. Trask (Princeton: Princeton University Press, 1953), pp. 14–15.

words." Here is the writer as craftsman and self-conscious artist. It is impossible to read the Bible without sensing that aesthetic considerations were important to its writers. They knew how to tell well-made stories and handle poetic language. The Bible is an aesthetically accomplished book and consistently invites us to view it from that dimension as well as others. A famous skeptic did not hesitate to call the Bible "unquestionably the most beautiful book in the world."[3]

The writer of Ecclesiastes also hints at a further feature of the writing that we find in the Bible when he identifies his work as belonging to the specific genre of the proverb. There can be no doubt that biblical writers often wrote with an awareness of literary genres and conventions. They knew that a lament psalm had five main parts and that a praise psalm began with a formal call to praise. Biblical writers often use technical generic terms when referring to their writing. Examples include song, saying, complaint or lament, parable, hymn, and so forth. As this book has demonstrated, a literary approach to the Bible is based at every turn on an awareness of literary genres.

All that I have said thus far of course sets an agenda of expectations and interpretive activities for readers of the Bible. We should read the Bible expecting to encounter religious and moral truth. More often than not, that truth will come to us in a literary form—in stories, poems, proverbs, and visions, for example. To understand the Bible, therefore, we need to know how these literary genres work. Our enjoyment of the Bible will be enhanced if we have developed the capacity to perceive its artistry and beauty. In short, the Bible is not an occasionally literary book—it is *mainly* a work of literature.

It should go without saying that we are free to discuss the religious truth, the history, and literature of the Bible with the best analytic tools at our disposal. One of the most frivolous interpretive restrictions that I have seen suggested for the Bible is that we should use only the literary (and by implication other) terms that the writers of the Bible themselves used. This is not a restriction that we place on other writing, nor can I imagine anything that would produce a more impoverished reading of the Bible than to refuse to use the best descriptive and interpretive tools that we possess. Even a good translation of the Bible depends on the use of modern linguistic insights. For that matter, how can someone today master biblical Hebrew or Greek without using modern grammatical terms? By the same token, we should use the best tools of current literary criticism when discussing the literature of the Bible.

3. H. L. Mencken, *Treatise on the Gods* (New York: Knopf, 1946), p. 286.

We can infer further strands in the poetics of biblical writers from the actual writing that we find in the Bible. I trust that these principles have been evident in the book that I have written.

The poetics of biblical writers, for example, is based on a principle of realism. Biblical writers tend overwhelmingly to write about ordinary characters and events, and they place these firmly in historical circumstances. They show no interest in avoiding what is unideal in character and action. This bias toward realism sets the Bible apart from most other literature of the ancient world. It also makes the Bible eminently accessible and believable. Jewish novelist Chaim Potok has the following tribute to the realism of biblical characters:

> The people of the Hebrew Bible. . . were my early heroes, all of them mortals with smoldering passions, jealousies, many of them experiencing moments of grandeur as well as pitiful lowliness and defeat. . . . Above all, there was always for me a sense of the real when I read about those people— a feeling that the Bible did not conceal from me the truth about the less pleasant side of man.[4]

The realism of the Bible makes it a universal and elemental book. It portrays what has been true for all people in all times and places. The very vocabulary of the Bible, writes one scholar, "is compact of the primal stuff of our common humanity—of its universal, sensory experiences."[5] The chief corollary of this for the reader is that the Bible is a mirror in which we see ourselves and our own experiences. Despite the remoteness of its world and customs, the Bible gives us recognizable human experience. It tells us not only what happened but also what happens. Knowing that this is so, as readers of the Bible we need to answer two interpretive questions: What did it mean? What does it mean now? Bridging the gap between the biblical text and our own experiences is not only possible but also necessary if the Bible is to be a living book.

Another important part of the poetics of biblical literature is that much of the Bible originally existed in oral form, and even when it was written down it circulated within its community in oral form. Oral speech forms permeate the Bible, from the high incidence of quoted speeches and dialogue in its stories to the fact that its lyric poetry tends to consist of songs and hymns sung in group worship. The very style of the Bible, strongly aphoristic and memorable, is an oral style.

Once we realize that the Bible is a very oral book, other features fall

4. Chaim Potok, "Heroes for an Ordinary World," in *The Great Ideas Today*, ed. Robert M. Hutchins and Mortimer J. Adler (Chicago: Encyclopaedia Britannica, 1973), p. 75.

5. John Livingston Lowes, "The Noblest Monument of English Prose," in *Literary Style of the Old Bible and the New*, ed. D. G. Kehl (Indianapolis: Bobbs-Merrill, 1970), p. 9.

naturally into place. One of these is the preference of biblical writers for the brief unit. The writers of the Bible overwhelmingly work with short units that are relatively self-contained. Even the genres show this bias: lyric, proverb, parable, prophetic oracle or vision, and letter. The individual episodes in the stories of the Bible, moreover, are rarely elaborated. We catch only momentary glimpses of the characters.

The oral nature of the Bible helps to make it a book for common people. It is folk literature, intended for the entire community from which it arose. It appeals to the whole range of people in its original society and ours, all the way from children to scholars.

Oral literature has to be simple enough on the surface to be understandable, and this is a further characteristic of the Bible. It is hard to miss the simple, obvious point of a biblical passage. In this sense it confirms a principle that one scholar calls foolproof composition. Of course the simplicity of the Bible is not drab or unartistic. In the words of Northrop Frye, "The simplicity of the Bible is the simplicity of majesty. . . ; its simplicity expresses the voice of authority."[6]

Along with the surface simplicity of the Bible, there is sophistication of technique and subtlety of content. The Bible is a multilayered book in which we can find as much complexity and profundity as our experience of life and literature equips us to see. Scholars have shown the immense complexity that lies below the surface, but there is no requirement that we read the Bible at these levels in order to understand and enjoy it. The Bible is the most flexible of all books.

The simultaneous simplicity and complexity of the Bible are evident in its style. That style is spare, unembellished, and concrete. Its surface meaning is therefore obvious. Even poetic or prophetic passages that are difficult to interpret convey an initial affective meaning. But the very spareness of this style means that biblical literature calls for interpretation. It tells what happened but does not explain it. It is fraught with background, but we receive no extensive help in constructing that background.

The writers of the Bible continually return to a list of master images as their basic vocabulary. In modern literary terms, they speak a language of archetypes—recurrent images, plot motifs, and character types. God is rock and light and shepherd throughout the Bible. Life is a pilgrimage or journey. The language of images that we find in the Bible is a shared storehouse. There is little to distinguish one author from another. The most helpful principle of classification is by genre, not by author.

6. Northrop Frye, *The Great Code: The Bible and Literature* (New York: Harcourt Brace Jovanovich, 1981), p. 211.

The poetics or philosophy of writing that underlies the Bible includes the agenda of topics that the writers presuppose are most worthy of their readers' attention. Heading the list is the character of God and the question of how people relate to him. Biblical writers likewise assume that we need to know what people are like. The issues of evil and suffering are a preoccupation. So are questions of values, morality, and virtue or human conduct. I earlier spoke of the realistic grasp of human failing that pervades the Bible, but equally characteristic is a prevailing idealism: everywhere the effect of reading the Bible is that we feel called to something higher and better.

To sum up, the literature of the Bible is the product of a set of assumptions with which biblical writers wrote. Those assumptions included a religious view of life, the ability to write in an accomplished artistic style, a grasp of literary genres and their conventions, sensitivity to oral forms of literature, and a commitment to life as we find it in the real world.

Glossary

The following glossary provides definitions of the literary terms that appear in the text. Parenthetical page numbers that accompany some of the definitions refer to the pages in the text where a more complete discussion appears.

Acrostic. A poem in which the successive units begin with the consecutive letters of the Hebrew alphabet (p. 197).

Allegory. A work of literature in which some or all of the details have a corresponding other meaning and refer to either a concept or historical particular.

Allusion. A reference to past history or literature.

Antagonist. The force(s) or character(s) with which the protagonist of a story is in conflict.

Anti-hero. A literary protagonist who exhibits an absence of the character traits that are conventionally associated with literary heroes.

Anti-romance. A work of literature, or part of a work of literature, that presents unideal experience; a literary world of total bondage and the absence of the ideal.

Antithetic parallelism. A two-line poetic unit in which the second line states the truth of the first in the opposite way or introduces a contrast.

Aphorism. A short, memorable statement of truth (p. 445).

Apocalyptic literature. A type of Hebrew visionary literature (pp. 480–81).

Apostrophe. A figure of speech in which the writer addresses someone absent or something nonhuman as if it were present or human and could respond to the address.

Archetype. An image, plot motif, or character type that recurs throughout literature and is part of a reader's total literary experience.

Blazon. A love poem that praises the attractive features and/or virtues of the beloved by means of a catalogue or listing technique (p. 275).

Calling stories. In the Gospels, stories in which Jesus calls a person to follow him or to respond to a command (pp. 378–79). Also called *vocation stories.*

513

Climactic parallelism. A form of parallelism in which the first line is left incomplete until the second line repeats part of it and then makes it a whole statement by adding to it.

Comedy. A story with a U-shaped plot in which the action begins in prosperity, descends into potentially tragic events, and rises to a happy ending.

Conflict stories. Gospel stories that narrate Jesus' controversies with an opposing person or group (pp. 380–81). Also called *controversy stories.*

Denouement. The last phase of a story, following the climax; literally the "tying up of loose ends."

Didactic. Having the intention or impulse to teach.

Discourse. An address to an audience.

Dramatic irony. A situation where the reader knows something of which some or all the characters in a story are ignorant.

Dramatic monologue. A literary work in which a single speaker addresses an implied but silent listener and in which various details keep this dramatic situation alive in the reader's consciousness.

Emblem. A symbolic and sometimes pictorial image to which a person or thing is compared.

Emblematic blazon. A love poem that lists the features of the beloved and compares them to objects or emblems in nature or human experience (pp. 283–84).

Encomium. A work of literature that praises an abstract quality or a generalized character type (pp. 293–94).

Encounter stories. Gospel stories in which a person is confronted with the claims of Jesus, which that person must either accept or reject (p. 380).

Epic. A long narrative having a number of conventional characteristics (pp. 127–29, 481–83).

Epiphany. A moment of heightened insight in a literary work.

Epistle. A letter that attains literary status by virtue of the literary techniques used in it (pp. 435–39).

Epithalamion. A lyric poem that celebrates a wedding (p. 273). (Also spelled *epithalamium.*)

Epithet. An exalted title for a person or thing; a feature of the high style, especially as found in epic.

Explication. The literary term for close reading of a text. It implies not only careful analysis of a text but also putting one's analysis into organized form for written or oral presentation to an audience.

Exposition. The opening phase of a story in which the writer presents the background information that the reader needs in order to understand the plot that will subsequently unfold.

Expository writing. Writing whose main purpose is to convey information (p. 12).

Foil. Something within a work of literature that heightens or sets off a main element in the work. A foil is usually a contrast (either a character, event, or image), but sometimes it is a parallel.

Folk literature. Literature couched in the language of everyday speech and appealing to the common person (pp. 404–5). Also called *popular literature.*

Genre. A literary type or kind.

Hero. A protagonist who is exemplary and representative of a whole community.

Hero story, heroic narrative. A story built around the character and exploits of a protagonist who is exemplary and representative of a whole community (pp. 107–9).

Hybrid forms. Gospel stories that combine elements of one or more genres.

Hyperbole. A figure of speech in which a writer uses conscious exaggeration for the sake of effect, usually emotional effect.

Image. Any concrete picture of reality or human experience, including any sensory experience, a setting, a character, or an event.

Imagination. The human capacity for image-making and image-perceiving.

Intertext, intertextual reading. A situation in which the full meaning of a text depends on its interaction with another text.

Irony. An incongruity or discrepancy. There are three main types of literary irony. Dramatic irony occurs when a reader knows more about what is happening than characters in a story do. Verbal irony occurs when a writer states something but means exactly the opposite. Irony of situation occurs when a situation is the opposite of what is expected or appropriate.

Lyric. A short poem containing the thoughts or feelings of a speaker (pp. 197–98, 227–30). The emotional quality, even more than the reflective, is usually considered the differentia of lyric.

Metaphor. A figure of speech in which the writer makes an implied comparison between two phenomena (pp. 166–67).

Miracle stories. Gospel narratives that focus on miracles that Jesus performed (pp. 381–82).

Monomyth. The generalized, composite story that encompasses the whole body of literature in a single circular story (pp. 48–50).

Motif. A discernible pattern composed of individual units, either in a single work or in literature generally. Roughly synonymous with *pattern.*

Narrative. A story; a series of events.

Narrator. The character or "voice" of the writer as it exists in a work of literature.

Normative character. A character in a story who expresses or embodies what the storyteller wishes us to understand is correct.

Occasional literature. A work of literature that takes its origin from a particular historical event or a particular situation in the writer's life.

Ode. An exalted lyric poem that celebrates a dignified subject in a lofty style.

Parable. A brief narrative that explicitly embodies one or more themes (pp. 404–9).

Paradox. An apparent contradiction that upon reflection is seen to express a genuine truth; the contradiction must be resolved or explained before we see its truth.

Parallelism. The verse form in which all biblical poetry is written. The general definition that will cover the various types of parallelism is as follows: two or more lines that form a pattern based on repetition or balance of thought or grammar. The phrase *thought couplet* is a good working synonym (pp. 180–85).

Parody. A work of literature that parallels but inverts the usual meaning of a literary genre or a specific earlier work of literature.

Passion stories. Gospel stories that narrate the events surrounding the trial, death, and resurrection of Jesus (p. 382).

Pastoral. Literature in which the setting, characters, and events are those of the shepherd's world.

Personification. A figure of speech in which human attributes are given to something nonhuman, such as animals, objects, or abstract qualities (pp. 178–79).

Plot. The sequence of events in a story, usually based on a central conflict and having a beginning, middle, and end (pp. 62–71).

Poetic justice. The feature of stories by which good characters are rewarded and evil characters are punished.

Poetic license. Figurative language that is not literally true or factual.

Pronouncement stories. A brief Gospel story in which an event in Jesus' life is linked with one of his memorable sayings (p. 381).

Protagonist. The leading character in a story, whether sympathetic or unsympathetic.

Proverb. A concise, memorable expression of truth (pp. 313–17, 445–49).

Pun. A play on words, often using a word that sounds like another word but that has a different meaning.

Quest stories. Stories built around progress toward a goal.

Rhetorical question. A figure of speech in which the writer asks a question whose answer is so obvious that it is left unstated; a question asked, not to elicit information, but for the sake of effect, usually an emotional effect.

Romance. A work of literature, or part of a work of literature, that presents ideal experience; a phase of the monomyth. Also, a narrative genre that includes a high incidence of the marvelous (pp. 37–39).

Satire. The exposure, through ridicule or rebuke, of human vice or folly (pp. 329–31).

Satiric norm. The standard by which the object of attack is criticized in a satire.

Saying. A proverb or aphorism.

Simile. A figure of speech in which the writer compares two phenomena, using the explicit formula *like* or *as.*

Stairstep parallelism. A type of parallelism in which the last key word of a line becomes the first main word in the next line.

Symbol. Any detail in a work of literature that in addition to its literal meaning stands for something else.

Synonymous parallelism. A type of parallelism in which two or more lines state the same idea in different words but in similar grammatical form; the second line repeats the content of all or part of the first line.

Synthetic parallelism. A type of parallelism in which the second line completes the thought of the first line, but without repeating anything from the first line. Also called *growing parallelism.*

Theme. A generalization about life that a work of literature as a whole embodies or implies.

Tragedy. A narrative form built around an exceptional calamity stemming from the protagonist's wrong choice (pp. 145–48).

Type scene. A situation or set of conventions that recurs throughout a work of literature or body of literature and that therefore produces a set of expectations in the readers when they encounter that situation in a literary text.

Well-made plot. A plot that unfolds according to the following pattern: exposition (background information), inciting moment (or inciting force), rising action, turning point (the point from which, at least in retrospect, the reader can begin to see how the plot conflict will be resolved), further complication, climax, and denouement.

Wisdom literature. A branch of biblical literature in which the writer depends heavily on the proverb as the basic unit.

Witness stories. Gospel stories in which either Jesus or another character testifies about Jesus or his works (pp. 379–80). Also called *testimony stories.*

Index of Subjects

Index of Authors

Index of Scripture